COMPREHENSIVE

DOS
5.0/6.0/6.2

WITH WINDOWS™ 3.1

1BB
Bill Henderod.

COMPREHENSIVE

DOS
5.0/6.0/6.2

WITH WINDOWS™ 3.1

HARRY L. PHILLIPS
Santa Rosa Junior College

Course Technology, Inc. One Main Street, Cambridge, MA 02142

Comprehensive DOS 5.0/6.0/6.2 with Windows 3.1 is published by Course Technology, Inc.

Vice President, Publisher	Joseph B. Dougherty
Product Manager	Darlene Bordwell
Director of Production	Myrna D'Addario
Senior Production Editor	Kathryn Dinovo
Composition	Gex, Inc.
Production Assistant	Christine Spillett
Copyeditor	Joan Wilcox
Proofreader	Joyce Churchill
Indexer	Sherri Dietrich
Product Testing and Support Supervisor	Jeff Goding
Student Testers	Chris Greacen
	Rich Gorham
	Kevan Schultz
Photo Researcher	Elyse Rieder
Prepress Production	Gex, Inc.
Manufacturing Manager	Elizabeth Martinez
Senior Design Specialist, Text Designer	Kim Munsell
Cover Designer	John Gamache

Trademarks

Course Technology and the open book logo are registered trademarks of Course Technology, Inc.

Windows is a trademark of Microsoft Corporation.

Some of the product names used in this book have been used for identification purposes only and may be trademarks or registered trademarks of their respective manufacturers and sellers.

Disclaimer

Course Technology, Inc. reserves the right to revise this publication and make changes in its content from time to time without notice.

ISBN 1-56527-150-5

Printed in the United States of America

10 9 8 7 6

From the Publisher

At Course Technology, Inc., we believe that technology will transform the way that people teach and learn. We are excited about bringing you, college professors and students, the most practical and affordable technology-related products available.

The Course Technology Development Process

Our development process is unparalleled in the higher education publishing industry. Every product we create goes through an exacting process of design, development, review, and testing.

Reviewers give us direction and insight that shape our manuscripts and bring them up to the latest standards. Every manuscript is quality tested. Students whose backgrounds match the intended audience work through every keystroke, carefully checking for clarity and pointing out errors in logic and sequence. Together with our own technical reviewers, these testers help us ensure that everything that carries our name is error-free and easy to use.

Course Technology Products

We show both *how* and *why* technology is critical to solving problems in college and in whatever field you choose to teach or pursue. Our time-tested, step-by-step instructions provide unparalleled clarity. Examples and applications are chosen and crafted to motivate students.

The Course Technology Team

This book will suit your needs because it was delivered quickly, efficiently, and affordably. Every employee contributes to this process. The names of all our employees are listed below:

Tim Ashe, David Backer, Stephen M. Bayle, Josh Bernoff, Erin Bridgeford, Ann Marie Buconjic, Jody Buttafoco, Kerry Cannell, Jim Chrysikos, Susan Collins, John M. Connolly, David Crocco, Kim Crowley, Myrna D'Addario, Lisa D'Alessandro, Howard S. Diamond, Kathryn Dinovo, Katie Donovan, Joseph B. Dougherty, MaryJane Dwyer, Chris Elkhill, Don Fabricant, Kate Gallagher, Laura Ganson, Jeff Goding, Laurie Gomes, Eileen Gorham, Andrea Greitzer, Cathie Griffin, Tim Hale, Roslyn Hooley, Nicole Jones, Matt Kenslea, Kim Mai, Susannah Lean, Suzanne Licht, Laurie Lindgren, Elizabeth Martinez, Debbie Masi, Dan Mayo, Kathleen McCann, Jay McNamara, Mac Mendelsohn, Laurie Michelangelo, Kim Munsell, Amy Oliver, Kristine Otto, Debbie Parlee, Kristin Patrick, Charlie Patsios, Jodi Paulus, Darren Perl, Kevin Phaneuf, George J. Pilla, Cathy Prindle, Nancy Ray, Marjorie Schlaikjer, Christine Spillett, Susan Stroud, Michelle Tucker, David Upton, Mark Valentine, Renee Walkup, Donna Whiting, Lisa Yameen.

Preface

Course Technology, Inc. is proud to present *Comprehensive DOS 5.0/6.0/6.2 with Windows 3.1*, designed for a first course on today's most popular operating system, DOS. This text, targeted at beginning students, clearly describes concepts related to DOS, the DOS Shell, and Windows operating environments. It is designed for use in a first one-semester course in DOS. The text assumes the student has no knowledge of DOS.

Organization and Coverage

Comprehensive DOS 5.0/6.0/6.2 with Windows 3.1 contains an "Essential Computer Concepts" chapter, six introductory DOS tutorials, five advanced DOS tutorials, and two Windows tutorials. "Essential Computer Concepts" presents an up-to-date overview of computers and covers basic hardware and software concepts. The 11 DOS tutorials provide hands-on instruction. In these tutorials students learn how to use DOS and the DOS Shell for disk, directory, and file management on computer systems with hard drives and one or more diskette drives. Students perform operations from both the DOS prompt and the DOS Shell so that they know how to complete tasks in both environments. Special icons in the margin of the text call students' and instructors' attention to differences among DOS 5.0, 6.0, and 6.2, the three DOS versions covered in the book. Mouse icons also call out special steps for mouse users, where appropriate. The two Windows tutorials, again with hands-on instruction, introduce students to basic Windows features, emphasize the use of the mouse, and describe how to use File Manager for disk, directory, and file management operations.

Approach

All of the components of this text—"Essentials Computer Concepts," the DOS tutorials, and the Windows tutorials—are unique in their approach. They motivate students by demonstrating why they need to learn the concepts and skills described in the tutorials. This text teaches DOS using a task-driven rather than a feature-driven approach. By working through the tutorials—each motivated by a realistic case scenario—students learn how to use DOS in situations they are likely to encounter in the workplace, rather than learn a list of commands one by one, out of context. Each discussion motivates students by explaining *why* they will perform a given task.

Features

Comprehensive DOS 5.0/6.0/6.2 with Windows 3.1 includes the following features:

- **"Read This Before You Begin" Page** This page is consistent with Course Technology's unequaled commitment to helping instructors introduce technology into the classroom. Technical considerations and assumptions about hardware, software, and default settings are listed in one place at the front of the book to help instructors save time and eliminate unnecessary aggravation.
- **Objectives** A list of objectives at the beginning of each tutorial orients students to the goals of that tutorial.
- **Tutorial Scenario** Each tutorial begins with a short problem that students could reasonably encounter in business so that the process of solving the problem will be meaningful to students.

◆ **Step-by-Step Methodology** The unique Course Technology, Inc. methodology keeps students on track. They click or press keys, always within the context of solving the problem posed in the case. The text constantly guides students, letting them know *why* they are pressing the keys and describing the results. The numerous screen shots include labels that direct students' attention to what they should look at on the screen.

◆ **Page Design** Each page is designed to help students easily differentiate between what they are expected to *do* and what they are expected to *read*. The steps are easily identified by the typeface and numbered bullets.

◆ **Chapter Summary** Each tutorial concludes with a concise overview of the features and topics covered in the tutorial.

◆ **Command Summary/Features Summary** The Command Summary at the end of each DOS tutorial and the Features Summary at the end of each Windows tutorial provide important reference tools for students prior to examinations.

◆ **Questions** Each tutorial contains meaningful, conceptual questions that test students' understanding of what they learned in the tutorial.

◆ **Tutorial Assignments** These assignments provide students with additional practice on the skills they learned in the tutorial. Students practice by modifying the problems they solved in the tutorial and by applying what they learned to solve new problems.

◆ **DOS and Windows Reference Cards** Removable command and features summaries at the end of the text provide a handy, quick reference for all DOS commands and Windows features covered in the book.

Supplements

◆ **Instructor's Manual** The Instructor's Manual is written by the author and is quality-assurance tested. It includes:
  - Answers and solutions to all the Questions and Tutorial Assignments
  - A disk containing solutions to all the Tutorial Assignments
  - Tutorial Notes, which contain background information from the author about the tutorial scenario and the instructional progression of each tutorial
  - Technical Notes, which include troubleshooting tips as well as information on how to customize the student's screens to closely emulate the screen shots in the book
  - Transparency Masters of key concepts, selected by the author
  - Sample course syllabi

◆ **Test Bank** The Test Bank contains more than 50 questions per tutorial in true/false, matching, and short-answer formats. Each question has been quality-assurance tested by students to achieve clarity and accuracy.

Acknowledgments

I want to thank John Connolly, President of Course Technology, Inc., for his initial and ongoing commitment to the production of high-quality textbooks. I also want to thank the dedicated staff members of Course Technology for their invaluable professional contributions to this textbook. In particular, I thank Joe Dougherty, Publisher, for initiating this project and for his ideas, interest, and ongoing support. I especially thank Darlene Bordwell, Product Manager, for her insight, support, cooperation, and successful management of this project. As my primary contact on a day-by-day basis, Darlene facilitated and guided this project with grace and ease.

In addition, I thank Jeff Goding, Product Testing and Support Supervisor, for his supervision of the quality assurance process. The student testers, Richard Gorham, Kevan Schultz, and Chris Greacen, thoroughly tested the text and offered valuable suggestions for improving the quality of the presentation. I thank Kathryn Dinovo, Senior Production Editor, for carefully supervising the final assembly of the book; Kim Munsell, Senior Design Specialist, for her contributions to the book's design; Joan Wilcox, Copyeditor, for her editing and for her suggestions, which improved the flow and comprehension of the text; and Joyce Churchill, Proofreader, for verifying the accuracy of the final text.

The reviewers of this textbook—Susan Isermann, Illinois Valley Community College; Charles Fromme, Queensborough Community College; Lloyd E. Stallkamp, Northern Montana College; Kathy Medved, Pierce College; Stephanie J. Snyder, Lake Tahoe Community College; and Patrick Chan, Porterville College—all offered constructive comments on the direction and coverage, as well as the presentation of concepts and features, and deserve special thanks for their efforts.

Finally, I thank my many friends, coworkers, colleagues, family, and parents for their unqualified support while I worked on this project.

Harry L. Phillips

Brief Contents

Table of Contents

Essential Computer Concepts

♦

Essential Computer Concepts

OBJECTIVES

In this chapter you will learn to:

◆ Define and describe a computer and its major functions

◆ Distinguish among a microcomputer, a minicomputer, a mainframe, and a supercomputer

◆ Describe the major hardware components of a computer

◆ Describe the functions of common input and output devices

◆ Understand the function of processing hardware

◆ Measure storage capacities of memory and disks

◆ List the sizes and capacities of common storage media

◆ Describe the major types of computer software, including systems software and applications software

◆ Understand the importance and use of computer networks

WHAT IS A COMPUTER?

A **computer** is an electronic tool that automates tasks by performing operations at remarkably fast speeds. These operations include mathematical calculations, comparisons of numbers and characters, restructuring of text, and the display of graphic images. Computers therefore organize and process **data**—facts, figures, and images—to produce useful information.

To accomplish these operations, computer systems must include specific types of hardware that operate under the control of software. The **hardware** includes the physical components that enable the computer system to access, process, display, and print data. The **software** consists of **programs**, or sets of instructions, for accomplishing a task. One important and indispensable software component is the **operating system**, which manages the operation of the computer system and the use of other software.

Businesses use computers to manage financial information, produce business projections, develop business strategies, enhance the preparation and presentation of important business documents, design graphics, transmit information nearly instantaneously from one business office to another around the world, handle business transactions, and perform many other essential business tasks. Computers improve the productivity and efficiency of employees, and enable businesses to meet timelines critical to their success in the marketplace. Computers also play an important role in agriculture, industry, engineering, aeronautics, astronomy, space exploration, oceanography, the biological sciences, physics, mathematics, medicine, the judicial system, politics, environmental studies, music, and the arts.

TYPES OF COMPUTERS

Computers often are classified by their size, speed, and cost. **Microcomputers**, or **personal computers** (**PCs**), are priced from $500 to $15,000 for individual and business use. Microcomputers are designed for use by a single person and easily fit on a desktop (Figure 1). **Laptop computers** are smaller microcomputers that fit comfortably on your lap (Figure 2). **Notebook computers** are even smaller microcomputers that can easily fit into a briefcase (Figure 3). Laptop

Figure 1
Microcomputers in an office environment

and notebook computers are compatible with other, larger microcomputers. They use the same operating system and can share software and data. Microcomputers of all sizes are used extensively in businesses of all sizes as well as for personal use.

Figure 2
A laptop computer

Figure 3
A notebook computer

Large businesses, government agencies, colleges and universities, and other institutions also use larger and faster types of computers called **minicomputers** (Figure 4). Minicomputers require more office space than microcomputers, operate 3 to 25 times faster than microcomputers, store and

Figure 4
A minicomputer

process much larger quantities of data, and are priced from $15,000 to $500,000. Minicomputers can support multiple users working on **workstations**, or computer **terminals**, in remote offices.

A still larger and more powerful type of computer is the **mainframe computer** (Figure 5). Mainframes have even larger capacities for storing and processing data, run 10 to 100 times faster than microcomputers, require a specially controlled environment, and are priced from $100,000 to $2,000,000. Mainframes also support a much larger number of multiple users than minicomputers.

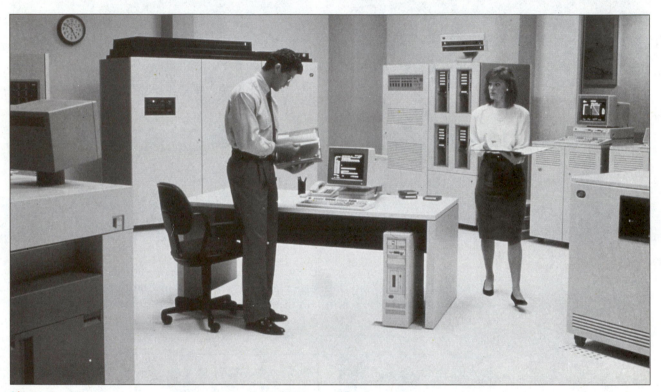

Figure 5
A mainframe computer

Supercomputers, the largest and fastest computers, expend so much energy that they require their own internal cooling systems to dissipate the heat generated during their operation (Figure 6). Supercomputers are expensive, often costing hundreds of millions of dollars. Only the largest corporations, government agencies, and universities can afford supercomputers. Typically, supercomputers run 50 to 10,000 times faster than microcomputers and handle such complex problems as weather forecasting, earthquake prediction, and petroleum surveying.

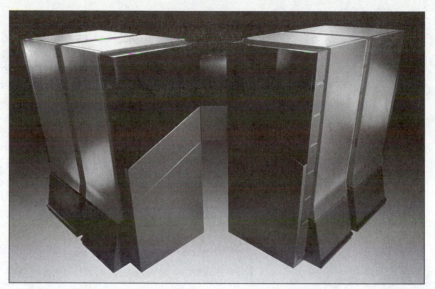

Figure 6
A Cray supercomputer

As a result of the rapid changes in technology, the criteria used to distinguish these types of computers is also changing. For example, newer and more sophisticated types of microcomputers outperform some minicomputers.

TYPES OF MICRO-COMPUTERS

Most microcomputers use one of two similar operating systems to manage the internal operation of the computer system: PC-DOS (Personal Computer Disk Operating System) or MS-DOS (Microsoft Disk Operating System). IBM Corporation assembles IBM PCs that use PC-DOS. Other manufacturers, such as Compaq and Dell, assemble IBM-compatible microcomputers that use MS-DOS. Both IBM PCs and most compatibles contain Intel microprocessors. The **microprocessor** is a special computer chip that processes data using program instructions. Over the years, Intel Corporation has produced new and more powerful microprocessors for use in IBM PCs and compatibles.

In contrast, microcomputers produced by Apple Computer, such as the Macintosh, use microprocessors produced by Motorola and use a different operating system. These microcomputers are noted for their high-quality display and graphics and ease of use as well as desktop publishing capabilities.

MAJOR FUNCTIONS OF A COMPUTER

Computers perform four basic functions: input, processing, output, and storage (Figure 7). **Input** refers to the process of providing data and instructions to a computer system so that it can accomplish some type of useful task with that data. **Processing** refers to the ways in which the computer uses input to produce meaningful information. Processing includes operations such as arithmetic computations, logical comparisons, rearrangement of data, and the production of images or pictures. **Output** refers to the transmission of the results of computer processing to you, the user. For example, the computer might display or print the results of processing, thus producing output. **Storage** refers to the process of recording data and information to some type of permanent storage medium, such as a disk or magnetic tape, for later use. To perform these basic operations, a computer system must include both hardware and software.

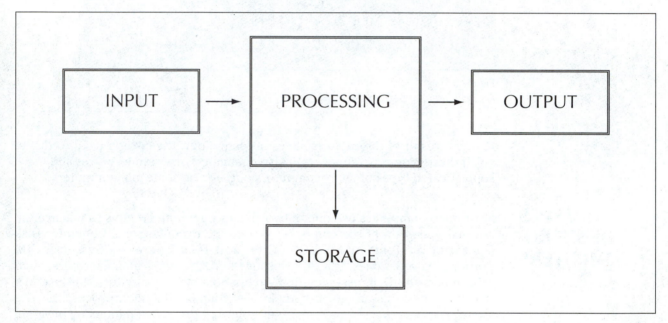

Figure 7
Major functions of a computer

COMPUTER HARDWARE

Computer hardware is typically divided into four categories to reflect the types of activities that the hardware performs: input devices, processing hardware, output devices, and storage media (Figure 8). The term **device** refers to a component within a computer system. The standard hardware components in a microcomputer system include a keyboard, a system unit, a monitor (or video display unit), disk drives, and a printer.

Input Devices

You use **input devices** to provide data and **commands** (instructions) to the computer. The two primary microcomputer input devices are the keyboard and the mouse.

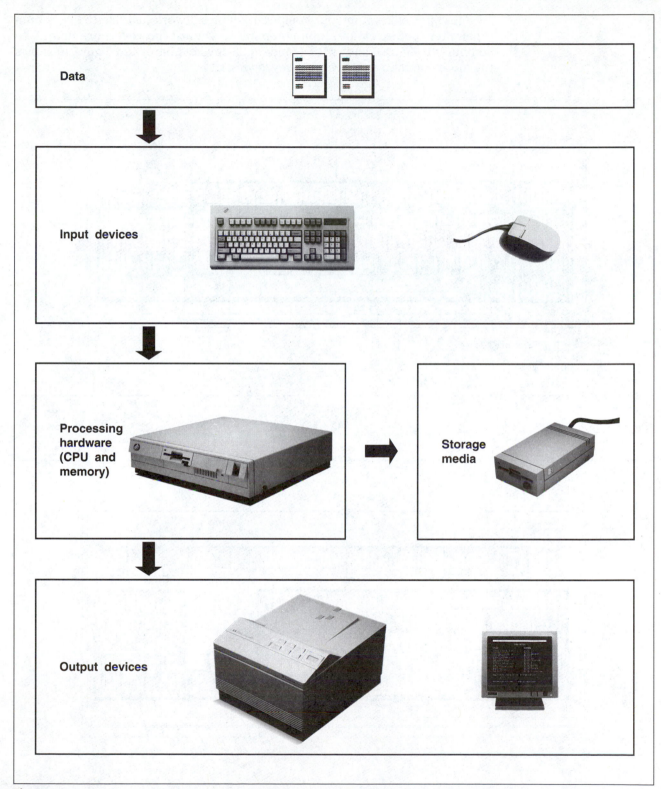

Figure 8
The relationship among input devices, processing hardware, output devices, and storage media

Most of the keys on your computer keyboard work just like the keys on a typewriter. Some features of a computer keyboard, however, are unique to computers. Figure 9 shows the standard 83-key keyboard, and Figure 10 shows the more common enhanced 101-key keyboard.

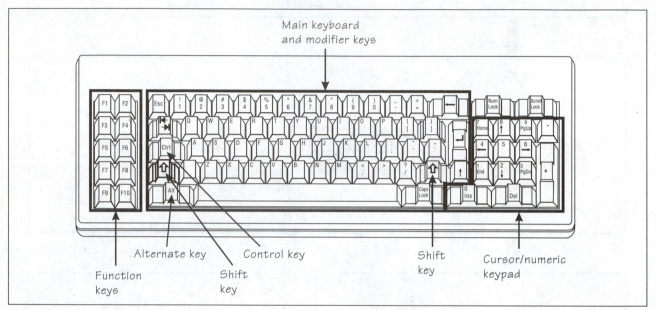

Figure 9
The standard 83-key keyboard

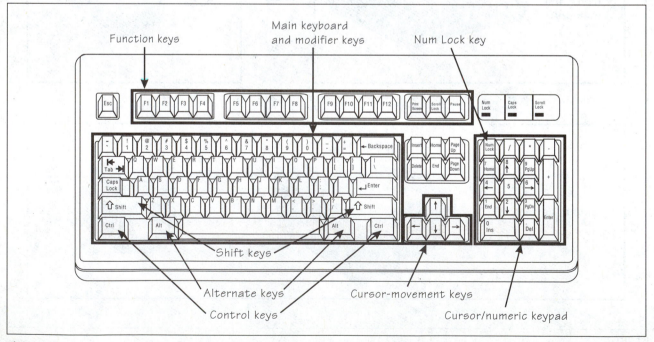

Figure 10
The enhanced 101-key keyboard

These computer keyboards include groups of keys that form the main keyboard, numeric keypad, cursor movement keys, editing keys, and function keys. The keys on the main keyboard work like the keys on a typewriter. To type text, you just press the keys. Sometimes you press more than one key. A **modifier key** is a key that is pressed in conjunction with another key to change the keyboard output. For instance, to type uppercase letters or symbols, such as the colon (:), you press the Shift key (a modifier key) and, while holding it down, press the desired keyboard letter or symbol key, and then release both keys. In addition, you can combine modifier keys, such as the Shift key, the Alt (alternate) key, and the Ctrl (control) key, with other keystrokes to accomplish special tasks, such as saving or printing data, within particular programs. It is important to remember that these key combinations vary with the type of program you use.

The **numeric keypad** on both the standard and the enhanced keyboards is located to the right of the main keyboard. You can use the keys on the numeric keypad in two ways: to enter numbers or to move the cursor. The **cursor** is either a blinking underscore character (_) or a small solid rectangle that marks where the next character that you type will appear on the screen. The Num Lock key permits you to alternate between entering numbers and moving the cursor with the numeric keypad. When you turn [Num Lock] on, you can use keys in the numeric keypad to type numbers and other special symbols, such as the decimal point, the plus sign, and the minus sign. When you turn [Num Lock] off, you can use keys in the keypad to move the cursor. This key is an example of a **toggle key**, a kind of on/off key that alternates between two uses each time you press the key.

Enhanced keyboards contain a separate set of cursor-movement keys between the main keyboard and the numeric keypad. Thus, you can leave [Num Lock] on, use the numeric keypad to enter numbers, and use the separate set of cursor-movement keys to move the cursor.

The **editing keys** allow you to change, or modify, what you type. The editing keys include [←] (Backspace), [Del] or [Delete], [Ins] (Insert), and [Esc] (Escape). The Backspace key deletes the character to the left of the cursor, and the Del and Delete keys delete the character at the cursor position. The Ins key is a toggle key that alternates between insert mode and typeover or overtype modes. In **insert mode**, what you type is inserted at the position of the cursor and characters to the right of the cursor are shifted to the right. In **typeover** or **overtype mode**, what you type replaces existing text on a character-by-character basis. Depending on the program you use, the Esc key clears or cancels editing changes.

The **function keys** are the keys labeled **F1** through **F10** or **F1** through **F12**. The function keys are located to the left of the main keyboard on a standard keyboard and above the main keyboard on an enhanced keyboard. You use the function keys alone or with the modifier keys [Shift], [Alt], and [Ctrl] to perform specific tasks, such as saving or printing. Programs that you use will assign specific operations to these keys, and these operations might differ among programs. For example, if you press the F1 function key, many programs, but not all, will display **help information**, which assists you with the task you are performing in the program.

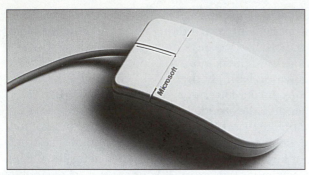

Figure 11
A mouse

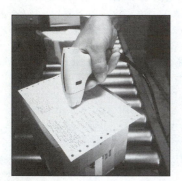

Figure 12
A hand-held scanner

Your computer system might also be equipped with a mouse (Figure 11). A **mouse** allows you to position a mouse pointer anywhere on the screen so that you can select options and perform specific operations. As you move the mouse over your desk with your hand, you also move the mouse pointer on the screen in the same relative direction. The **mouse pointer** usually appears in the shape of an arrow or a rectangle; however, its shape may change to reflect the type of activity you are performing in a program. Sometimes you can accomplish tasks more efficiently by using a mouse than by using a keyboard.

Another increasingly important input device is a scanner (Figure 12). A **scanner** is a device that you move over an image on paper to copy that image into the computer system and store it so that you can later enhance and print it. Although some graphics scanners are similar to copier machines, small hand-held scanners are a popular and less expensive alternative.

Memory

One important hardware component used for processing is memory. The computer's **memory** consists of a set of storage locations where instructions and data are stored while you use a microcomputer. Computers store these program instructions and data with the use of electronic switches, which can be either *on* or *off*. By associating an *on* switch with the number 1 and an *off* switch with the number 0, we can represent computer data in the binary numbering system with the value 0 or 1. The values 0 and 1 are referred to as **bits**, or **b**inary dig**its**. Computers generally store data in groups of eight bits, called a **byte**. A byte with all eight bits set to 0 (i.e., 00000000) represents the whole number, or **integer**, 0. The integer 1 is represented by 00000001. The integer 2 is represented by 00000010. Figure 13 shows the binary representation of some of the integers from 0 through 255. Each byte can also represent a character, such as the letter A or the @ symbol. For example, in IBM compatibles, the letter A is represented by 01000001, B by 01000010, and C by 01000011. The exclamation point (!) is represented by 00100001, a period (.) by 00101110, and a plus sign (+) by 00101011. All instructions and data used by a computer must be encoded as bytes. As a computer user, you do not have to know the binary representation of numbers, characters, and instructions to use a computer, because the computer handles all the necessary conversions internally.

Number	Binary representation
0	00000000
1	00000001
2	00000010
3	00000011
4	00000100
5	00000101
6	00000110
7	00000111
8	00001000
⋮	⋮
14	00001110
15	00001111
16	00010000
17	00010001
⋮	⋮
253	11111101
254	11111110
255	11111111

Figure 13
Binary representation of some numbers between 0 and 255

In addition to bits and bytes, storage capacities are also measured and expressed as kilobytes, megabytes, and gigabytes. A **kilobyte** is 1,024 bytes, or approximately 1,000 bytes. The abbreviations K and KB are also used to indicate kilobytes. A **megabyte** is 1,024 kilobytes, or approximately one million bytes. The abbreviations M, MB, and meg are also used to indicate megabytes. A **gigabyte** is 1,024 megabytes, or approximately one billion bytes. The abbreviations G and GB are also used to indicate gigabytes.

A microcomputer contains two basic types of memory: Read-Only Memory and Random-Access Memory. **Read-Only Memory**, or **ROM**, is that part of memory reserved for special instructions and data that are required for the internal operation of the computer. The manufacturer places these instructions and data in ROM at the time it produces the computer. ROM includes instructions for starting the computer system, for testing the system components at start-up (the POST, or Power-On Self-Test), for locating drive A and C, and for transferring the operating system software from the disk in drive A or C to Random-Access Memory. The microprocessor can retrieve, or **read**, the instructions and data stored in ROM, but it cannot erase or change the data. When you turn off your computer, the instructions and data in ROM remain intact, ready for use when you turn the computer back on.

Random-Access Memory, or **RAM**, also stores program instructions as well as input you provide the computer and the data it processes. RAM is your workspace, or working memory. A computer's microprocessor can retrieve, or **read**, data from and store, or **write**, data to any location in RAM at any time. For example, when you create or modify a document, such as a letter, memo, or report, the document is stored in RAM as you work on it. Because this memory is **volatile**, that is, it is temporary and dependent on the availability of power, you must save your work on some type of permanent storage medium. If you turn the power off, or if the power fails, then any instructions or data stored in RAM will be lost.

The amount of RAM in a computer system can vary. When you purchase a computer system, you can specify how much RAM you want. Most computers today have 2, 4, 8, or 16 megabytes of RAM to meet the demands of software.

Processing Hardware

Another important and essential processing hardware component is the **microprocessor**, a specialized computer chip. The microprocessor constitutes the **central processing unit** (or **CPU**) of a computer system and is responsible for processing input to produce output. Figure 14 lists microprocessors used in IBM and IBM-compatible microcomputers from 1981 to 1993. Intel Corporation produced these microprocessors and assigned a number as the name for each one. Although these microprocessors differ in a variety of ways, including the design of the chip itself, the capabilities of microprocessors are generally described in terms of the amount of data they can process, the amount of data they can transmit or receive, their operating speeds, and the amount of memory they can access.

Microprocessor	8088	8086	80286	80386DX	80386SX	80486DX	80486SX	80486DX2	Pentium
Used in	IBM PC & IBM PC/XT	XT Compatibles	ATs (IBM PC/ AT & 286s)	386DX	386SX	486DX	486SX	486DX2	Pentium PC
Introduced	1981	1983–84	1984	1985	1988	1989	1991	1992	1993
Amount of data processed	16 Bits	16 Bits	16 Bits	32 Bits	32 Bits	32 Bits	32 Bits	32 Bits	32 Bits
Number of data lines	8	16	16	32	16	32	32	32	64
Amount of data transmitted	8 Bits	16 Bits	16 Bits	32 Bits	16 Bits	32 Bits	32 Bits	32 Bits	64 Bits
Number of address lines	20	20	24	32	24	32	32	32	128
Type of address bus	20-Bit	20-Bit	24-Bit	32-Bit	24-Bit	32-Bit	32-Bit	32-Bit	128-Bit
Maximum amount of memory addressed	1MB	1MB	16MB	4GB	16MB	4GB	4GB	4GB	Almost unlimited
Operating speed (clock rate)	5–8MHz	5–10MHz	8–12MHz	16–33MHz	16–20MHz	25–50MHz	16–25MHz	50–66MHz	60–100MHz
Math coprocessor	Not included	Not included	Not included	Not included	Not included	Included	Disabled	Included	Included

Figure 14
Microprocessors used in IBMs and IBM compatibles

A microprocessor uses **data lines** to transmit and receive data from other hardware components. The microprocessor can transmit one bit on each data line. The data lines as a group are called a **data bus**, which consists of the electronic circuitry that connects the CPU with internal and external hardware components. A microprocessor also uses **address lines**, which together constitute an **address bus**, to access memory. The number of address lines determine the maximum amount of memory that the microprocessor can access and use.

The speed of a microprocessor is determined by its **clock rate**, or **clock speed**. The computer clock is part of a group of electronic circuits associated with the microprocessor. You can think of the clock rate as the "heartbeat" or "pulse" of the computer; it controls the timing of operations within the computer. The higher the clock rate, the faster the computer. The clock rate is measured in millions of cycles per second, or **megahertz** (**MHz**).

The history of microprocessor development is one of rapid technological improvements. In 1981 Intel developed the 8088 microprocessor for the IBM PC and PC/XT (XT stands for Extended Technology). This microprocessor processed 16 bits (two bytes) of data at a time, received and transmitted 8 bits (one byte), accessed 1MB of RAM, and operated at 5 to 8 MHz. This microprocessor, however, was soon updated by the 8086, which was developed for XT compatibles. It had 16 data lines, so it could transmit and receive twice as much information as the 8088. Next came the 80286 microprocessor in the AT (Advanced Technology), which accessed up to 16MB and doubled the operating speed of the 8088. Although some 286s are still in use today, the 8088 and 8086 are both outdated and are rarely used.

The next generation of microprocessors was the 80386DX. Introduced in 1985, this chip doubled the speed of the 286 in terms of data processing and transmittal, and has a clock speed two to four times faster. It can address up to 4096MB—or 4GB—of memory. The 80386DX was a popular but fairly expensive microprocessor; Intel introduced a slightly less powerful but cheaper version, called the 80386SX. Both microprocessors are in wide use today, although they are rapidly being replaced by the newer 80486 chip.

The first 80486 microprocessor, the 80486DX, was marketed in 1989, and has a clock rate of 25 to 50 MHz. It operates 50 times faster than the original 8088. The 486DX system includes a **math coprocessor**, which works in conjunction with the microprocessor to dramatically increase the speed of mathematical calculations and graphics processing. The math coprocessor enhances the overall performance of the computer. An even faster 486 microprocessor, the 80486DX2, operates at twice the speed of the 486DX. Again, because of the 486's popularity, Intel also offers a slightly less powerful system, the 80486SX, at a price that individuals can more easily afford. The 80486 series of microprocessors are in widespread use in homes and offices.

In 1993, Intel introduced its newest and most powerful microprocessor—the Pentium. This microprocessor operates twice as fast as the 80386DX2 and 200 times faster than the 8088. It has a clock rate of 60 to 100 MHz and can access a nearly unlimited amount of memory. The microprocessor has some unique features—such as the ability to process two instructions per clock cycle instead of one—that open up new possibilities for designing and using the newest types of software.

Understanding the features and capabilities of microprocessors is important when you purchase a computer system, evaluate new hardware and software for your computer, configure your system, and optimize its memory.

The System Unit

The microprocessor and the memory chips used for RAM and ROM are housed in the computer case, or **system unit**, on a system board. This **system board**, or **motherboard**, is a fiberglass board with electronic circuits etched, or printed, onto it. The **system bus** consists of the network of electronic circuitry that is responsible for transmitting data and signals between the microprocessor and various components as well as for storing information on the location of instructions and data in memory. The data and address lines, along with **control lines** for synchronizing operations, constitute the system bus.

The system unit also contains other circuit boards, called **adapter cards** or **add-in cards**, that enable the computer system to work with various types of hardware components included in the computer system (Figure 15 on the following page). These adapter cards are added into available **expansion slots** and attach to the main system board. For example, an adapter card might be added to a computer system so that you can use a mouse. The system unit also contains a power supply that provides power to all of the components in the computer system.

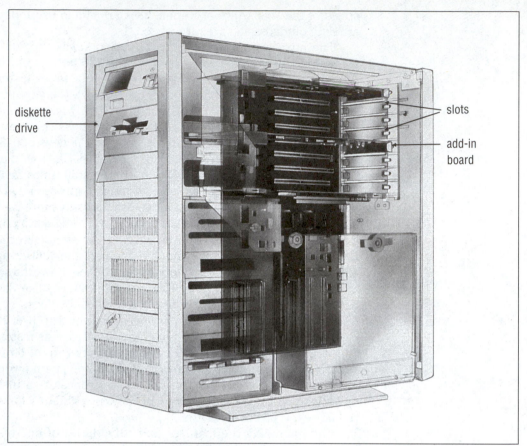

Figure 15
Slots in a vertically-configured microcomputer

The system unit uses **ports** as electronic pathways to pass data between the computer's microprocessor and its **peripherals**, the hardware components, such as printers and monitors, that are connected to the system unit. Microcomputers have two types of ports and use one of two types of techniques for transmitting data: serial and parallel (Figure 16). **Serial ports** send information between the microprocessor and other components one bit at a time. In contrast, **parallel ports** usually transmit eight bits, or one byte, at a time. For example, computer printers are often designated as serial or parallel to indicate the type of port to which they connect. Serial printers are usually connected to the port called COM1 or COM2 (for COMmunications port 1 or 2), and parallel printers are usually connected to the port called LPT1 or LPT2 (for Line PrinTer port 1 or 2). The port for the first system printer is designated PRN (for PRiNter) and usually corresponds to LPT1.

When you buy a printer or any other peripheral, be sure your computer has a port that matches the peripheral. For example, if a new laser printer requires a serial port, be sure your computer has an available serial port to which you can connect the printer. If not, you can buy and install a board, or add-in card, that contains one or more additional ports.

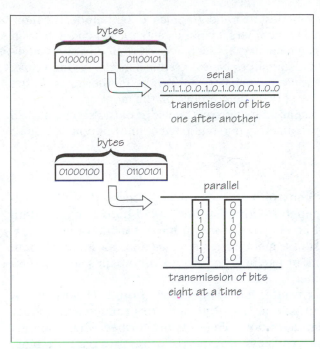

Figure 16
A comparison of data transmission using serial and parallel ports

Figure 17
A color monitor

Output Devices

The microprocessor uses **output devices** to display, print, or store information that results from processing data. The most commonly used output devices are monitors, printers, and disk drives.

Monitors

A **monitor** is a TV-like video screen that displays text and graphics (Figure 17). Most microcomputers use a **cathode ray tube**, or **CRT**, for displaying an image. Most laptop computers use a flat-panel display, such as a **liquid crystal display**, or **LCD**.

The text and graphics displayed on computer monitors are created with little dots of light called **pixels**—short for "picture elements" (Figure 18). Each pixel on a monochrome monitor has only one color—green, amber, or white—when the pixel is illuminated and no color (black) when the pixel is not illuminated. Each pixel on a color monitor, on the other hand, can appear in any of several colors.

The entire monitor screen is a grid of pixels that combine to create the illusion of a continuous image. For example, a **video graphics array**, or **VGA**, monitor has a 640 × 480 grid. There are 640 pixels across the width of the screen and 480 pixels down the length of the screen. If you multiply 640 × 480, you have a total of 307,200 pixels available for creating and displaying an image on a VGA monitor. **SuperVGA** (**SVGA**) monitors, with a resolution of 1024 × 768 pixels, have a total of 786,432 pixels and can display even more impressive graphics. The higher the number of pixels on a monitor, the greater the **resolution** and the clearer and sharper the graphics images it can display.

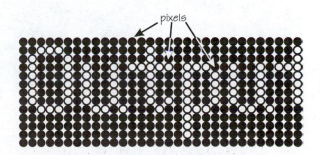

Figure 18
Illumination of pixels to produce a text image

Monitors have two display modes: text and graphics. In **text mode**, the monitor can display only text—letters, numbers, symbols, and special characters. In **graphics mode**, the monitor can display graphic images as well as text. All monitors have a text mode, but not all monitors have a graphics mode. A **video card**, or **graphics adapter**, mounted in an expansion slot on the motherboard in the system unit controls the display of text and graphics on the monitor.

Most monitors display 80 characters across the width of the screen and 25 lines down the screen, or approximately one-half page of information at a time.

Printers

A **printer** produces a paper copy of text or graphics processed by the computer. The paper copy of computer output is often called **hard copy**. Printers are classified as impact and non-impact printers. **Impact printers** produce a character on paper by striking a metallic element against an inked ribbon. **Non-impact printers** spray ink or use heat to fuse ink onto paper and thereby produce an image of a character.

The most popular impact printer is the dot-matrix printer (Figure 19). A **dot-matrix printer** uses small pins in the print head to produce a character composed of an array, or matrix, of dots. The dots are formed when the pins strike an inked ribbon. Less expensive dot-matrix printers have nine pins, whereas more expensive models have 24 pins and produce higher-quality output. These printers can operate in draft mode or near-letter-quality mode. In **draft mode**, the printer prints faster but produces lower-quality output. In **near-letter-quality (NLQ) mode**, the printer prints more slowly but produces higher-quality output. Figure 20 shows the text output from a 24-pin dot-matrix printer in draft mode and also in NLQ mode. Dot-matrix printers can also print graphics as well as text.

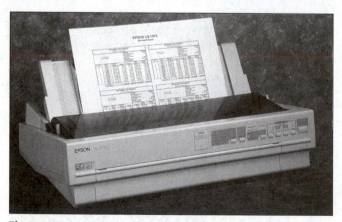

Figure 19
A dot-matrix printer

```
This is sample output from a
 24-pin dot-matrix printer
        in DRAFT mode


This is sample output from a
24-pin dot-matrix printer
        in NLQ mode
```

Figure 20
Samples of draft-quality and near-letter-quality output from a dot-matrix printer

Figure 21
An ink-jet printer

The most popular types of non-impact printers are ink-jet printers and laser printers. **Ink-jet printers** spray tiny dots of ink onto the paper to form text or graphics (Figure 21). Most ink-jet printers are faster than dot-matrix printers. They produce graphics of reasonable quality and text of high quality.

Laser printers use a laser beam to form an electrostatic, or electrically-charged, image on a rotating photosensitive drum. These electrostatic areas on the drum then attract a black, powdery substance called a **toner**. Subsequent heating bonds the toner to the paper—similar to the process in a photocopying machine. The laser printer produces the highest-quality text and graphics of any type of printer (Figures 22 and 23). Moreover, laser printers are faster and quieter than dot-matrix and ink-jet printers. As a result of these features, laser printers are becoming the standard printer in the business world.

Figure 22
A laser printer

This is Courier.

This is Times Roman.

This is Helvetica.

This is Bookman.

Figure 23
Sample output from a laser printer showing four fonts (different typefaces in different sizes)

Disk Drives and Storage Media

A **disk drive** is actually classified as both an input and an output device because the microprocessor can record data onto, or retrieve data from, secondary storage media in the disk drive (Figure 24 on the following page). A disk drive stores data in much the same way that a VCR stores images and sound, except that instead of advancing a tape, the disk drive spins a disk or diskette.

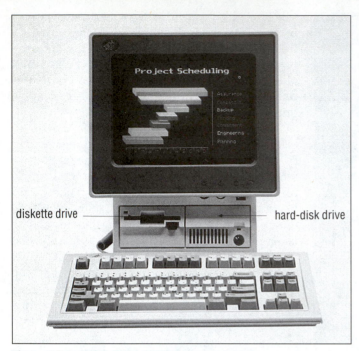

Figure 24
Disk drives in a computer

The most common storage media for microcomputers are diskettes and hard disks. Sometimes called a **floppy disk**, a **diskette** is a flat, circular plastic disk with a magnetic coating enclosed in a square case called a **disk jacket**. The most common sizes of diskettes for microcomputers are 3½ inches and 5¼ inches (Figure 25). The 5¼-inch diskettes have soft, flexible disk jackets and are usually stored in paper sleeves for protection. The 3½-inch diskettes have hard plastic cases and do not require sleeves. The most common types of diskettes are double-sided, double-density (DS/DD) and double-sided, high-density (DS/HD). On **double-sided** disks, information is recorded on both sides of the diskette. The terms **double-density** and **high-density** refer to the amount of information that is stored within a unit area on the diskette. High-density diskettes can store two to four times as much data as double-density diskettes.

The 5¼-inch double-density diskettes have a capacity of 360 kilobytes (abbreviated K), and the 3½-inch double-density diskettes have a capacity of 720K. The 5¼-inch high-density diskettes have a capacity of 1.2MB. The 3½-inch high-density diskettes have a capacity of 1.44MB.

Figure 25
A 3½-inch diskette *(left)* and a 5¼-inch diskette *(right)*

Diskette drives are also available in double-density and high-density types. A high-density diskette drive can read from and record on both high-density and double-density diskettes. A double-density diskette drive, on the other hand, can read from and record on only double-density diskettes. Before you purchase diskettes, be sure they match your type of diskette drive. For example, if you have a 3½-inch high-density diskette drive, you should buy and use

3½-inch DS/HD diskettes. To distinguish between the two types of disks, note that the 3½-inch high-density diskettes have a hole in the lower-right corner, directly opposite the square hole with the write-protect tab (described below), whereas the 3½-inch double-density diskettes have only the square hole with the write-protect tab. In addition, high-density diskettes sometimes have "HD" written on their cases. Usually, however, you have to rely on the information printed on the packaging.

After you store information on a diskette, you might want to be sure that no one records more information on the diskette or erases the information from the diskette. For this purpose, diskettes provide **write protection**, which serves as a safeguard against losing valuable information. To write-protect a 5¼-inch diskette, you place a write-protect tab over the write-protect notch; to write-protect a 3½-inch diskette, you open the write-protect window by pressing a small square tab down so that you can see through a square hole in the diskette (Figure 26).

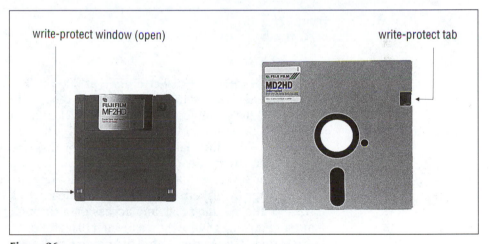

write-protect window (open)   write-protect tab

Figure 26
A write-protected 3½-inch diskette *(left)* and a 5¼-inch diskette *(right)*

Hard disks, also called **fixed disks**, consist of two or more unremovable metallic disks, or **platters**, with a magnetic coating on both sides of each platter (Figure 27 on the following page). The hard disk is mounted permanently within the system unit. Hard disks have two advantages over diskettes: speed and capacity. The speed of a hard disk is measured by its **access time**, that is, the time required to read or write a byte of data. A typical hard disk has access times one-third to one-tenth those of a diskette; therefore, a hard disk is 3 to 10 times faster at accessing data.

The capacity of hard disks is commonly measured in megabytes (MB). A hard disk with a capacity of 200MB can store the equivalent of about 80,000 pages of text, compared to only about 600 pages of text on a 1.2MB 5¼-inch diskette. Most microcomputer hard disks have capacities in the range of 20MB to 600MB. These high capacities are more than just a convenience; much of the work currently performed by businesses using microcomputers requires these higher-capacity hard disks.

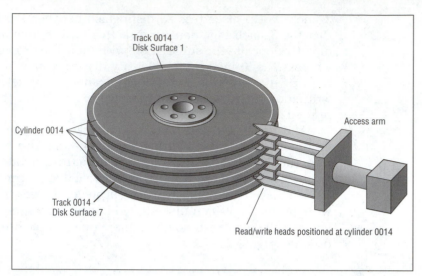

Figure 27
Read/write heads and platters in a hard disk drive

Diskettes spin in a diskette drive at 300 or 360 revolutions per minute, or rpm, whereas platters in a hard disk drive spin at 3,600 rpm—10 to 12 times faster. Hard disks spin continuously, but diskettes spin only when the computer reads from or writes to the diskette. As a hard disk or diskette spins, the computer reads or writes data onto a platter or diskette with the use of read/write heads. A **read/write head** consists of an arm that moves across the surface of a hard disk or diskette to locate and read data or to record data onto the surface of the platter or diskette. The read/write heads in a diskette drive rest on the surface of the spinning disk and access data through the **head slot** (or the oval-shaped recording window) on a 5¼-inch diskette or through the **access hole** on a 3½-inch diskette. A metal **shutter** covers the access hole when the 3½-inch diskette is not in the drive. Once inserted in the drive, the shutter opens to expose the access hole for the read/write heads.

In the case of a hard disk, the read/write heads fly on a cushion of air a few millionths of an inch above the surface of each disk platter (Figure 27). As a result, hard disks must be sealed within a unit that protects the hard disk from contaminants, such as dust, hair, and other minute particles. If a contaminant comes between the read/write head and the hard disk platter, the hard disk will suffer a **head crash** and the read/write head might gouge the surface of the platter. The hard disk is then unusable, and all the data on the hard disk is lost. A head crash can also occur as the result of a jolt to the system unit.

To reduce the likelihood of damage to one or more of the platters in a hard disk drive, newer computer systems have an **auto-park feature** that automatically moves and **parks**, or rests, the read/write heads in a **landing zone** on the innermost surface of the hard disk when you turn off the computer's power. The read/write heads then rest on a surface of the disk where no data is stored.

CD-ROMs and Optical Disks

CD-ROMs (Compact Disc Read-Only Memory) and optical disks are also popular storage devices. The CD-ROM disk is similar to an audio compact disc and requires a CD-ROM disk drive that is similar to an audio compact disc player (Figure 28). You connect the CD-ROM drive to your computer system via an existing port or through the use of an expansion card inserted inside the system unit. In a CD-ROM drive, a laser beam reads data stored on the CD-ROM disk. A CD-ROM disk can store up to 700MB of data; however, you can only read data from the drive. You cannot record data onto the CD-ROM diskette. You also need special software to operate the CD-ROM drive. CD-ROMs are commonly used to store reference information, such as legal precedents, medical information, encyclopedias, and catalogs, as well as graphic images and font files, which require an enormous amount of disk storage space.

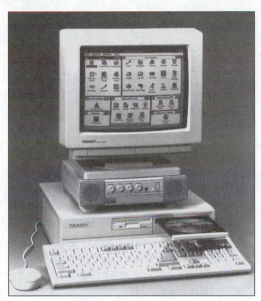

Figure 28
A CD-ROM disk and CD-ROM drive

The **optical disk** is similar to a CD-ROM, but the primary difference is that you can record information on the optical disk using a magneto-optical drive. You can also use optical disks that require a **WORM** (Write Once, Read Many) drive. You can write to this type of optical disk, but only once.

Modems

Another common input and output device is a modem. A **modem** is a hardware device that enables you to transmit and receive data between your computer system and a computer in another office or location. The term modem is an abbreviation for **mo**dulator/**dem**odulator. When transmitting data, the modem modulates, or converts, digital electronic *on* and *off* signals inside the computer to analog wave signals in a telephone line. **Digital** refers to data stored in discrete units, such as 0s and 1s, whereas **analog** refers to data that varies continuously over a range, such as the amplitude of a sound wave signal. When receiving data from another source over the telephone line, the modem demodulates, or reverts, the analog wave signals in the telephone line to digital electronic *on* and *off* signals for use in the computer.

An **internal modem** is mounted on a card that is inserted into one of the expansion slots inside the computer, while an **external modem** consists of a separate hardware unit that connects to one of the serial ports on the computer system. Both types of modems also connect to your telephone or directly to the telephone jack.

COMPUTER SOFTWARE

Just as a tape recorder or a compact disc player would be worthless without tapes or compact discs, computer hardware would be worthless without computer software. As you've learned, software, also referred to as computer programs, consists of detailed step-by-step instructions that tell the computer what to do. Figure 29 on the following page illustrates an example of a computer program that prompts the user for a number, then computes and prints the square and the square root of that number.

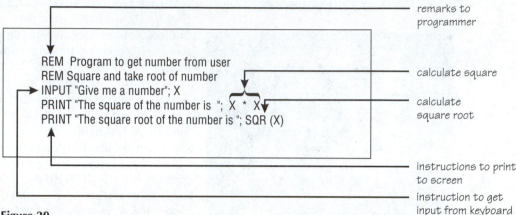

Figure 29
A computer program written in the BASIC programming language

The types of software that you use determine what you can do with your computer. For example, word processing software lets you use a computer to prepare documents, and graphics software lets you use a computer to create graphs and illustrations. Software can be divided into two general categories: systems software and applications software.

Systems Software

Systems software includes the programs that run the fundamental operations within your computer, such as starting the computer, **loading** or copying programs and data into memory, **executing** or carrying out the instructions in programs, saving data to a disk, displaying information on the monitor, and sending information through a port to a peripheral. Systems software includes three similar types of software: operating system software, system utility software, and programming language software.

Operating system software coordinates the activities within a computer, including all the input and output operations to and from the peripherals. The most popular operating system for IBM and IBM-compatible microcomputers is **DOS** (rhymes with "boss"), an abbreviation for **Disk Operating System**. There are two types of DOS: PC-DOS and MS-DOS. Microsoft Corporation developed both operating systems in conjunction with IBM and, as a result, PC-DOS and MS-DOS operate in a similar manner. (More about that in a moment.) This text focuses on the use of MS-DOS. Many operating system concepts and features that you will learn about in the following DOS tutorials apply equally well to PC-DOS and to larger, more powerful operating systems on minicomputers, mainframes, and supercomputers.

Another systems software program developed by Microsoft Corporation is **Windows**, a graphics-based operating environment designed to make your computer easier to use. An **operating environment** interfaces between the operating system (DOS) and an application or utility. The current version, Windows 3.1, offers an alternate approach to managing your computer system and its resources with a graphical user interface. A **graphical user interface** provides a more visual method for interacting with the operating system through the use of icons, menus, and multiple windows. **Icons** are images or pictures displayed on the screen that represent commonly used objects, such as a drive, disk, program, or file. **Menus** display a list of command choices. **Windows** consist of outlined areas of the screen, through which you use programs, view information, and display the contents of files.

Three other operating systems—OS/2, Unix, and Windows NT—require higher-performance computer systems with additional memory and disk space. Microsoft and IBM developed OS/2 (Operating System 2) for use on IBM microcomputers. OS/2 supports **multitasking**, the ability to use several different programs at the same time. Unix (Uniplexed Information and Computing System) not only supports multitasking but also **multiusers**; that is, several people, each with their own keyboard and monitor, can use the same computer at the same time. Microsoft Corporation's new Windows NT operating system supports multitasking and maintains compatibility with DOS and programs designed for use with DOS. Because OS/2 and Windows NT require a 32-bit internal data bus, these operating systems require computer systems with an 80386, an 80486, or a Pentium microprocessor.

All three of these operating systems also manage memory more efficiently than DOS. DOS has more widespread use because more programs operate under DOS, and DOS requires less memory and disk space.

System utility software includes special programs provided with operating system software to enhance the performance of your computer system, such as optimizing the use of memory, maximizing the use of storage space on a hard disk, correcting errors on a hard disk, obtaining technical or diagnostic information about your computer system, or preparing diskettes for use on a computer system.

Programming language software includes programs that enable you to design and write your own application software for use on a computer system. One popular programming language is BASIC (Beginners All-purpose Symbolic Instruction Code), an example of which you saw in Figure 29. On IBMs and compatibles, a version of BASIC is automatically provided with the operating system software. Microsoft supplies QBASIC (Quick BASIC) with MS-DOS 6.0. Other important and popular programming languages include C, COBOL (short for COmmon Business-Oriented Language), FORTRAN (FORmula TRANslator), and Pascal (named for mathematician Blaise Pascal).

The Development of DOS

Before the introduction of DOS, most microcomputers used another operating system called CP/M (Control Program/Microcomputers). When IBM decided to introduce its own microcomputer into the marketplace in 1981, one of its subcontractors, a small company named Microsoft, offered to provide the operating system software for the IBM PC. Microsoft then contracted with another company to complete work on an operating system named 86-DOS, which was similar to CP/M. DOS 1.0 resulted from this joint venture, and eventually Microsoft bought complete rights to the software. Since 1981, DOS has become the predominant operating system used on microcomputers around the world.

Microsoft and IBM have released different versions of DOS to meet the rapid changes in microcomputer technology. Many of the DOS versions extended support for new hardware components, added new features to extend the capabilities of DOS, provided new system utilities, and corrected problems in earlier releases. Figure 30 lists the DOS versions and some of their important features. You will examine many of these features in later tutorials.

Version	Date	Features
1.0	1981	The first version of DOS included basic functions required of an operating system: • Ability to use single-sided diskettes • Reading, writing, and managing files stored on disk • Loading and executing applications and utilities • Communicating with standard hardware components • Interpreting user commands • Programs for performing system-related operations
1.1	1982	Supported the use of double-sided diskettes
2.0	1983	Supported the use of hard disk drives and subdirectories
2.1	1983–84	Provided support for IBM's PCjr microcomputer
3.0	1984	Supported the use of larger hard disk drives and high-density 5¼-inch diskette drives
3.1	1984	Supported the use of computer networks
3.2	1985–86	Supported the use of 3½-inch double-density diskette drives
3.3	1987	Supported the use of 3½-inch high-density diskette drives, increased hard disk support, and improved support for languages outside the United States
4.0	1988	Supported the use of hard disk drives over 32MB, introduced the DOS Shell graphical user interface, and increased memory support
5.0	1991	Supported the use of extra-high-density diskette drives, introduced new disk and file management utilities, enhanced the DOS Shell graphical user interface, provided extensive on-line help, introduced the MS-DOS text editor, and improved memory management
6.0	1993	Supported compression of hard disk drives to increase storage space; multiple start-up configurations; increased Windows support as well as new utilities for optimizing memory, optimizing disk storage space, backing up and restoring data to a hard disk drive, checking for computer viruses, undeleting files, and unformatting disks
6.2	1993	Enhanced the disk compression (DoubleSpace) utility

Figure 30
Versions of DOS and their features

When DOS undergoes a major change, the number before the decimal point changes. For example, the change from DOS 5.0 to DOS 6.0 is a **major upgrade**. When DOS undergoes a minor change, the number after the period changes. For example, the change from DOS 6.0 to DOS 6.2 is a **minor upgrade**.

The PC-DOS and MS-DOS versions of 1.0 through 5.0 offer the same features. Starting with DOS 6.0, PC-DOS and MS-DOS differ in the types of utilities included with each software product.

Applications Software

A wide variety of software exists to help you accomplish specific tasks on your computer. This type of software is called **applications software**, because it allows you to apply your computer to accomplish a particular goal. The major types of applications software are word processing, electronic spreadsheets, database management, graphics, communications, and desktop publishing.

Word processing software allows you to create, edit, enhance, and print documents electronically (Figure 31). With a word processing system, you can produce many more types of documents and perform many more editing tasks than you can on a typewriter. For example, you can move text within and between documents, check spelling, create tables and columns, center titles, adjust margins, draw lines, change the appearance of text (to boldface or underlined, for example), and view how a document will appear before you print it. Word processing software simplifies the process of creating and printing headers, footers, page numbers, footnotes, and line numbers. Many word processing applications include advanced features for assembling and printing complex documents.

Electronic spreadsheets allow you to perform calculations on numbers arranged in a table of

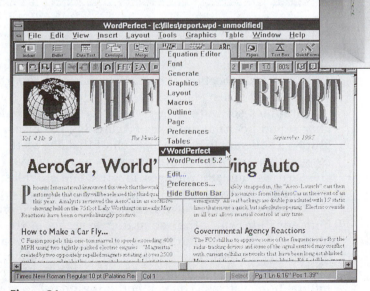

Figure 31
Example of a report produced with WordPerfect software and its pull-down menus

columns and rows on the computer screen (Figure 32). You can enter numbers, formulas, text, dates, and other kinds of data into the spreadsheet and automatically perform computations. By using the appropriate data and formulas, you can use an electronic spreadsheet to prepare financial reports and statements, analyze investment portfolios, calculate amortization tables, project income and expenses, and prepare a payroll.

Database software helps you manage information that is stored in the form of **records**; for example, information about employees, clients, schedules, supplies, equipment, inventories, or catalog entries (Figure 33). Database software

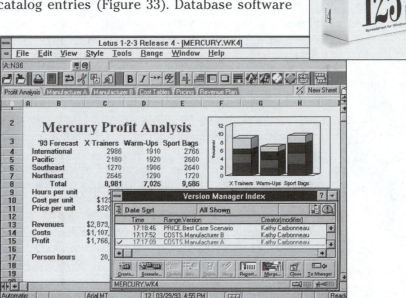

Figure 32
Example of a spreadsheet model created with Lotus 1-2-3 software

allows you to easily retrieve, search, sort, select, delete, organize, compare, and update a collection of data. You can print reports after selecting data, or you can print mailing labels.

Graphics software allows you to create illustrations, diagrams, graphics, charts, and freehand drawings (Figure 34). For example, you can use business graphics software to create a pie chart that shows the change in yearly income for your company. Most graphics software allows you to draw lines, boxes, circles, arrows, and other images; mix text and graphics; and enter data to create charts and graphs for your business presentations, reports, and newsletters.

Communications software enables you to use your computer system to communicate with other computer systems in the same office or in other offices around the country or world. With the use of a modem and a telephone line connection, you can transmit and receive data via electronic mail, participate in computer conferences and forums, and access on-line database and information systems. You can add a **fax board** to your computer so that you can send and receive facsimiles, or faxes. These faxes can include text as well as graphics.

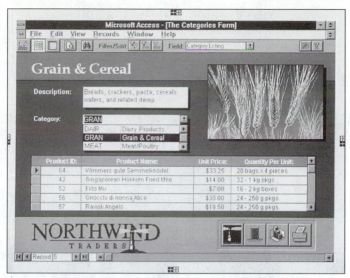

Figure 33
Example of a database created with Microsoft Access software

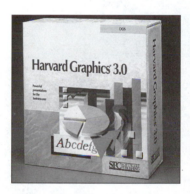

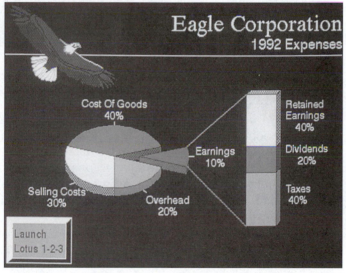

Figure 34
Example of a graphic design created with Harvard Graphics from Software Publishing Corporation

With **desktop publishing software**, you can produce high-quality, professional-looking documents for presentation or reproduction (Figure 35). You can combine text, graphics, and tables from other software applications into one final document. You can enhance the appearance of the final document so that it takes on a typeset appearance when printed.

Figure 35
Example of brochures produced with Pagemaker desktop publishing software

Yet another category of software, called **integrated software**, combines two or more applications into one product. Lotus 1-2-3, for example, combines an electronic spreadsheet application with a graphics application and a database application. Once you enter data into an electronic spreadsheet, you can use the same data to produce graphs and perform database operations. Lotus 1-2-3 also contains its own programming languages so that you can automate routine, repetitive operations with macros. A **macro** is a set of keystrokes or commands that executes an operation or set of operations.

Microsoft Works is another example of a popular integrated software package. Microsoft Works contains word processor, electronic spreadsheet, and database tools. You can produce charts or graphs using data in a spreadsheet. You can also place a spreadsheet or graph in a word-processed document or convert a spreadsheet to a database. You can even combine, or **merge**, a list of names and addresses stored in a database with a form letter created with the word processor to print personalized letters.

NETWORKS

In the business world you usually do not work alone but rather as part of a team. As a team member, you will probably use a computer **network**, a collection of interconnected computers and peripherals. A network allows you to share software, hardware, and data with other members of your team.

Typically, one of the computers on a network is equipped with a high-capacity hard drive and is designated as a **server**; that is, it "serves" the data to the other computers and peripherals on the network. The most common type of network involving microcomputers is a local-area network. In a **local-area network** (**LAN**), computers are joined by direct cable links and are located relatively close to each other, usually in the same building (Figure 36). Each computer in the LAN has a special **network board** inserted into one of its expansion slots, and each board is joined by an electrical cable to the server. Other computer equipment, such as laser printers and modems, may also be included in the LAN. Networks provide a standardized and predictable working environment for employees in a business and maximize the use of software and hardware resources.

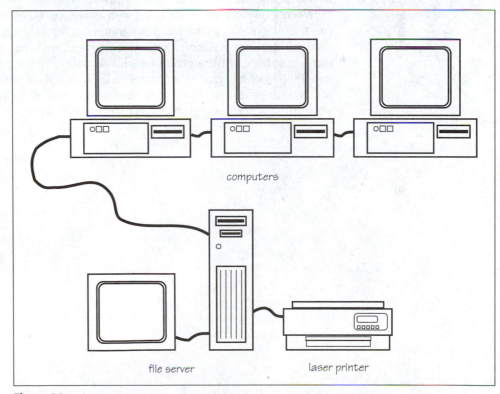

computers

file server   laser printer

Figure 36
A local-area network, or LAN

SUMMARY

In this chapter, you learned that a computer is an electronic tool that uses software and hardware to perform many types of business tasks. Microcomputers, minicomputers, mainframe computers, and supercomputers differ in size, speed, processing capacity, and cost. You reviewed the four basic functions of a computer system: input, processing, output, and storage. You examined the major types of input devices: keyboard, mouse, and scanner. Processing hardware consists of the microprocessor, memory, and supporting electronic circuitry known as the system bus. You learned how Read-Only Memory (ROM) and Random-Access Memory (RAM) differ. You familiarized yourself with the units of measurement—bits, bytes, kilobytes, megabytes, and gigabytes—for describing the storage capacity of memory, diskettes, and hard disks. You examined the use of common types of output devices—monitors, printers, disk drives, CD-ROMs, and optical disks.

You examined the two major categories of software—systems software and applications software. You learned the importance of operating system software in managing the operation of a computer system. You examined the difference between PC-DOS and MS-DOS, as well as the versions of DOS. You learned about the use of system utilities and programming language software. You explored the uses of applications software—word processing, electronic spreadsheet, database, graphics, communications, and desktop publishing. You also examined the capabilities of integrated software.You learned that networks allow you to share software resources, hardware resources, and data with other individuals in your local workgroup or located in a remote office.

QUESTIONS

1. Define or describe the following terms:
   a. Computer
   b. Hardware
   c. Software
   d. Memory

2. List and describe the four major functions of a computer system.

3. Describe each of the following hardware components:
   a. Keyboard
   b. Mouse
   c. System Unit
   d. Microprocessor
   e. Monitor

4. Identify the major groups of keys on a computer keyboard.

5. Describe the two types of memory used by microcomputers and how they differ.

6. Define or describe the following terms for measuring storage capacity on a microcomputer:
   a. Bit
   b. Byte
   c. Kilobyte
   d. Megabyte
   e. Gigabyte

7. Fill in the empty boxes in the following table with the storage capacities in kilobytes (K or KB) or megabytes (M or MB) of each type of diskette:

	3½-Inch Diskettes	5¼-Inch Diskettes
Double-sided, double-density		
Double-sided, high-density		

8. List the two major advantages of using a hard disk over a diskette.

9. What is a modem and how can you use it?

10. What is the difference between a serial and a parallel port?

11. What is the difference between text mode and graphics mode?

12. What is systems software, and why is it important?

13. List and briefly describe the six major types of applications software.

14. What is integrated software? What advantage does it offer over applications that focus on a single use?

15. What is a network? What is the advantage of using computer networks in business?

Photography Credits for *Essential Computer Concepts*

Figure	Credit	Page
1	Courtesy of International Business Machines	EC 4
2	Courtesy of Toshiba America Information Systems, Inc.	EC 5
3	Courtesy of Dell Computer Corporation	EC 5
4	Courtesy of International Business Machines	EC 5
5	Courtesy of International Business Machines	EC 6
6	Photo by Paul Shambroom, courtesy of Cray Research, Inc.	EC 7
8 keyboard	Courtesy of International Business Machines	EC 9
mouse	Courtesy of Microsoft Corporation	EC 9
CPU	Courtesy of International Business Machines	EC 9
disk drive	Courtesy of International Business Machines	EC 9
printer	Photo courtesy of Hewlett-Packard Company	EC 9
monitor	Courtesy of I-O Corporation	EC 9
11	Courtesy of Microsoft Corporation	EC 12
12	Courtesy OptoWand, Inc.	EC 12
15	Courtesy of International Business Machines	EC 16
17	Courtesy of NEC Technologies, Inc.	EC 17
19	Courtesy of Epson America, Inc.	EC 18
21	Photo courtesy of Hewlett-Packard Company	EC 19
22	Photo courtesy of Hewlett-Packard Company	EC 19
24	Courtesy of International Business Machines	EC 20
25	Richard Morgenstein	EC 20
26	Richard Morgenstein	EC 21
28	Courtesy of Radio Shack/Tandy Corporation	EC 23
31	Courtesy of WordPerfect. WordPerfect is a registered trademark of WordPerfect Corporation.	EC 27
32	Courtesy of Lotus Development Corporation	EC 28
33	Courtesy of Microsoft Access	EC 29
34	The Harvard Graphics package photo is used with the permission of Software Publishing Corporation, which owns the copyright to such product. Harvard Graphics is a registered trademark of Software Publishing Corporation. Harvard Graphics is a product of Software Publishing Corporation and has no connection with Harvard University.	EC 29
35	Courtesy of Aldus Corporation	EC 30

Essential Computer Concepts Index

A

access hole, EC 22
access time, EC 21
adapter cards, EC 15
add-in cards, EC 15
address bus, EC 14
address lines, EC 14
analog, EC 23
Apple Computer, EC 7
application software, EC 27-30
    communications, EC 28
    database, EC 28
    desktop publishing, EC 30
    electronic spreadsheet, EC 27-28
    graphics, EC 28-29
    integrated, EC 30
    word processing, EC 27
auto-park feature, EC 22

B

binary digits. *See* bits
bits, EC 12
bytes, EC 12

C

cathode ray tube (CRT), EC 17
CD-ROM (Compact Disc Read-Only Memory), EC 23
central processing unit (CPU). *See* microprocessor
chips, EC 13
circuit boards, EC 15
clock rate, EC 14
clock speed. *See* clock rate
COM1-COM2, EC 16
commands, EC 8
communications software, EC 28
compact disc read-only memory (CD-ROM), EC 23
computers
    definition of, EC 4
    functions of, EC 8
    hardware for. *See* hardware
    software for. *See* software
    types of, EC 4-7

CPU (central processing unit). *See* microprocessor
CRT (cathode ray tube), EC 17
cursor, EC 11

D

data, EC 4, EC 14
    telecommunication, EC 23, EC 28
    transmission, EC 16-17
database software, EC 28
data bus, EC 14
data lines, EC 14
desktop publishing, EC 7
    software, EC 30
digital, EC 23
disk drive, EC 19
disk jacket, EC 20
diskettes, EC 20
    drives, EC 20-22
    sizes, EC 20
    types, EC 20
    write protecting, EC 21
disk operating system (DOS), EC 24-27
display modes, EC 18
DOS (disk operating system), EC 24-27
    development of, EC 25
    types of, EC 24
    versions of, EC 26-27
dot-matrix printers, EC 18
double-sided, double-density (DS/DD), EC 20
double-sided, high-density (DS/HD), EC 20
draft mode, EC 18
DS/DD (double-sided, double-density) diskettes, EC 20
DS/HD (double-sided, high-density) diskettes, EC 20

E

editing keys, EC 11
electronic spreadsheets, EC 27-28
enhanced keyboard, EC 10-11
executing, EC 24
expansion slots, EC 15

INTRODUCTORY DOS
5.0 / 6.0 / 6.2

Tutorials

◆

Read This Before You Begin

To the Student

To use this book, you must have a Data Disk and a Windows Data Disk. Your instructor will provide you with a copy of the Data Disk and you will make your own copy of it by following the instructions in Tutorial 1. Later, your instructor will give you the Windows Data Disk, which you will copy for one of the Windows tutorials. See your instructor for further information. If you are going to work through this book using your own computer, you need a computer system running DOS 5.0, 6.0, or 6.2, Microsoft Windows 3.1, and a Data Disk. You will not be able to complete the tutorials and exercises in this book using your own computer until you have a Data Disk.

To the Instructor

Making the Data Disks To complete the first five tutorials in this book, your students must have a copy of a Data Disk. Later, you will need to provide your students with a copy of a Windows Data Disk for Tutorial 8. You can prepare these data disks from your Instructor Resource Disk. If some of your students will use their own computers to complete the tutorials and exercises in this book, they must first make a copy of the Data Disk for Tutorial 1 and the Windows Data Disk for Tutorial 8.

Installing the CTI Data Directories The Instructor Resource Disk contains a CTI Setup program that installs CTI data directories on drive C so that you can reproduce the Data Disk and the Windows Data Disk. The CTI Setup program also creates a subdirectory named AceForms for hard-disk backups performed by students in Tutorial 6. To use the CTI Setup program, follow the instructions provided in the Instructor's Manual that accompanies this text.

README File A README.TXT file located on the Instructor Resource Disk provides additional technical notes, troubleshooting advice, and tips for using the CTI Setup program in your school's computer lab. You can view the README.TXT file using any word processor you choose.

System Requirements

The minimum software and hardware requirements for your computer system are as follows:
- DOS 5.0, 6.0, OR 6.2 on a local hard drive or network drive.
- A 386 or higher processor with a minimum of 4MB of RAM (6MB or more is strongly recommended) for the Windows tutorials. The DOS tutorials can be completed on any computer system that supports DOS 5.0, 6.0, or 6.2 and that has the standard 640K of conventional memory.
- A mouse supported by Windows 3.1.
- A VGA 640 × 480 16-color display is recommended; an 800 × 600 or 1024 × 768 SVGA, VGA monochrome, or EGA display is also acceptable. The DOS tutorials can be completed with a monochrome monitor.
- 2 MB of free hard-disk space
- Student workstations with at least 1 high-density disk drive, preferably a 3½-inch disk drive. A 5¼-inch Data Disk can be prepared from the Instructors Resource Disk if you have a computer system with a 5¼-inch and a 3½-inch disk drive.
- If you want to install the CTI Data Directories with the CTI Setup Disk on a network drive, your network must support Microsoft Windows.

Understanding DOS

OBJECTIVES

In this tutorial you will learn to:

- Describe the basic functions of operating system software
- Select filenames
- Use drive and directory names
- Follow the numbered steps in the DOS tutorials
- Start a computer system
- Enter commands at the DOS prompt
- Identify the DOS version installed on a computer
- Clear the screen
- Set the date and time
- Use [F3] and DOSKEY to recall commands
- Use the Help switch
- Print a screen
- Format a diskette
- Make a copy of a diskette
- Turn off the computer system

Imagine you have just purchased your first computer system. From extensive research and careful evaluation of the capabilities of microcomputers, you discovered that you can use your new computer to prepare presentation-quality documents, develop a personal budget, keep business and personal records, and build valuable computer skills. You can streamline time-consuming tasks that you once did by hand so you can "work smarter."

The salesperson emphasized that you will need to invest some time up front to train yourself. You must understand the capabilities of the hardware and software included within your computer system. This initial investment in time will pay off in increased productivity in the future. Furthermore, with these skills, you will be able to troubleshoot many problems that might arise and install new software on your system.

After arriving home with your new computer system, you follow the instructions for getting started and set up your new computer system within half an hour. You examine the manual and other reference materials provided with the computer and learn that one of the most important types of software you will use is operating system software.

◆

WHAT IS THE ROLE OF OPERATING SYSTEM SOFTWARE?

Operating system software manages the basic processes required of a computer system and, in the process, coordinates the interaction of hardware and software. For example, the operating system handles all input and output operations. As you type, the operating system interprets the keys that you press on the keyboard and then displays the corresponding characters on the monitor. The operating system also interprets instructions, or **commands**, that you enter from the keyboard. If you enter a command to use a software application or utility, the operating system locates the program instructions on disk. Then, it copies, or **loads**, those program instructions into the computer's memory so you can use that software. When you issue a command to save a document, the program you are using relays this request to the operating system, which then stores a permanent copy of the document on a hard disk or a diskette. If you want to print a copy of the document, the operating system handles the transfer of data from the software application to the printer. When you are ready to work with another document, the request is again relayed to the operating system from the program you are using. The operating system locates the document on disk, retrieves a copy of the document, and displays that copy on the monitor. If a hardware or software problem occurs while you are using the computer system, the operating system attempts to resolve the problem or notifies you so that you can solve the problem.

USING MS-DOS AND PC-DOS

As you learned in the "Essential Computer Concepts" chapter, the most popular operating system on IBM and IBM-compatible microcomputers is the Disk Operating System, known as DOS. *Disk* refers to one of the important hardware resources—hard disks and diskettes—managed by the operating system. DOS is actually a generic term for two related operating systems: PC-DOS and MS-DOS. PC-DOS is designed specifically for the hardware in IBM microcomputers, whereas MS-DOS is designed for the hardware in IBM compatibles. Although there are differences between PC-DOS and MS-DOS, both manage the hardware and software resources within computer systems in similar ways. If you are familiar with either PC-DOS or MS-DOS, then you will know enough about DOS to operate the other version.

This text covers the use of MS-DOS on IBM compatibles and focuses on three popular versions: MS-DOS 5.0, 6.0, and 6.2. Features of these versions of DOS are comparable to features included in PC-DOS used on IBMs. PC-DOS 5.0 is similar to MS-DOS 5.0, and PC-DOS 6.1 is similar to MS-DOS 6.0.

5.0

6.0

6.2

This text will use icons to identify features unique to a particular version of DOS. For example, if a feature is implemented differently in DOS 5.0, a DOS 5.0 icon will appear next to the text where the difference is discussed. Unless you see an icon denoting a specific version of DOS, you should assume that the concepts and steps under discussion apply to each of the three versions of DOS and that features operate the same way in each of these versions.

USING FILES AND FILENAMES

While you are working on a computer system, the computer's memory contains part of the operating system software. If you are using a word processing application to produce a document, the computer's memory also contains a copy of that software application and the document. If you turn off the power to the computer system, or if the power fails, you lose your working copy of DOS, the application software that you are using, and, more important, the document that you are creating or modifying. You can always retrieve another copy of DOS and the application software from your original disks. However, you must periodically save your work onto a diskette or hard disk to guarantee that you have a permanent copy of your document.

When you save your work, your document is stored in a file. A **file** consists of a certain amount of storage space on a diskette or hard disk that is set aside for the contents of a document. You must give each file a unique name to identify its location on a diskette or hard disk and also to identify its contents. A **filename** is one to eight characters in length. The characters can include letters of the alphabet and the numbers 0 through 9. For example, if you prepare a résumé, you might store the document in a file with the filename RESUME. If you produce two versions of your résumé, you might store the first version in a file named RESUME1 and the second in a file named RESUME2. You *cannot* use the same filename for two different files stored in the same location on disk, even if the files contain the same or similar information. If you attempt to use the same name as an existing file, you might replace the contents of the existing file with the contents of the new document.

You can also use certain types of symbols, such as a dash or underline, as part of a filename. For example, you might save a copy of your most recent tax records under the filename TAX-RECS or TAX_RECS. Since a filename *cannot* contain any blank spaces, the dash or underscore is commonly used to separate two parts of the same filename. You cannot use other symbols, such as a slash or asterisk, as part of a filename because these symbols are commonly used with DOS commands. To simplify the process of naming files, it is a good idea to limit the use of symbols in filenames.

You cannot use a filename that is the same as a reserved device name. A **device name** is a name DOS assigns to one of the devices, or hardware components, in a computer system. For example, DOS reserves PRN as the device name for the first printer port, so you cannot use it as a filename. Figure 1-1 lists the device names used by DOS. The NUL device is a special device used to store discarded bits of data.

Device Name	Meaning	Assigned To
LPT1	Line printer 1	First parallel port
LPT2	Line printer 2	Second parallel port
LPT3	Line printer 3	Third parallel port
PRN	Printer	First printer port
COM1	Communications port 1	First serial port
COM2	Communications port 2	Second serial port
COM3	Communications port 3	Third serial port
COM4	Communications port 4	Fourth serial port
AUX	Auxiliary device	First serial port
CON	Console unit	Monitor and keyboard
CLOCK$	System clock	System clock
A:	Drive A	First diskette drive
B:	Drive B	Second diskette drive
C:	Drive C	First hard disk drive
NUL	Null device	"Bit Bucket"

Figure 1-1
Reserved device names

Using File Extensions

If you need a filename that is longer than eight characters, you can include a **file extension** that contains an additional one to three characters. When you add a file extension, you use a period to separate the main, or **root**, part of the filename from the file extension. The file extension follows the same guidelines and rules as the main part of the filename. For example, you might use the filename RESUME.LTR for a file that contains a cover letter for your résumé. File extensions are usually optional, but some applications require a file extension.

File extensions usually identify the type of information stored in a file. For example, files with the file extension EXE (for executable) and COM (for command) are **program files** that contain program instructions for a software application or utility. Other types of files have file extensions that indicate they contain program code or settings used by programs. For example, files with the OVL extension are **overlay files**—files that contain a module of program code (such as a spelling checker) that is only loaded into memory when needed. Files with the INI extension are **initialization files** that contain settings used by programs. Figure 1-2 is a list of some of the important types of file extensions used for program files and auxiliary files included with a software product. These auxiliary files contain additional program code or data required by the application program you use.

File Extension	Abbreviation For	Example	Contents of Example
BAT	Batch file (User-Defined or User-Created Program File)	AUTOEXEC.BAT	DOS commands and other program commands that are executed when starting a computer
CNF	Configuration file	123.CNF	Configuration settings for Lotus 1-2-3 application software
COM	Command file	MOUSE.COM	Software for operating a mouse
EXE	Executable file	WP.EXE	WordPerfect application program
HLP	Application or utility Help file	WORKS.HLP	Help information for Microsoft Works application software
INI	Initialization file	WIN.INI	Initial settings used by Windows 3.1 operating environment software
OVL	Overlay file	SPELL.OVL	Spelling checker software used with Microsoft Works application software
SYS	System configuration file	CONFIG.SYS	Commands for configuring DOS when starting a computer

Figure 1-2
Important file extensions used for program and program-related files

Data files are files that contain documents or data. You usually produce these files with a software application or perhaps utility software. The software application or utility might assign a specific file extension to the file. For example, Microsoft Word, a word processing software package, assigns the file extension DOC to document files produced by that program. Figure 1-3 on the following page shows a list of file extensions assigned to data files by popular software applications packages.

File Extension	Meaning	Example	Example's Application Package
BAK	Backup file	5YRPLAN.BAK	Lotus 1-2-3
BK!	Backup file	RESUME.BK!	WordPerfect
DBF	Database file	CLIENT.DBF	dBASE
DOC	Document file	RESUME.DOC	Microsoft Word
PCX	Graphics file	FIGURE1.PCX	Collage Plus (screen capture software)
WK1	Worksheet file	5YRPLAN.WK1	Lotus 1-2-3

Figure 1-3
Some common file extensions assigned to document or data files by applications software

In many cases, you can choose your own file extensions to reflect the type of information a document contains. For example, you might use the file extension RPT for a document file that contains a report, such as CLIENT.RPT. Figure 1-4 shows a list of file extensions you might choose to use for data files. This figure also illustrates another valuable use of file extensions: If you have a set of documents that are related to each other (for example, budget documents), you can use the same word for the main part of the filename, but vary the file extension. All of the sample files in Figure 1-4 contain budget information for the 1994 fiscal year.

File Extension	Meaning	Example
DAT	Data	94BUDGET.DAT
DOC	Document	94BUDGET.DOC
FRM	Form	94BUDGET.FRM
LST	List	94BUDGET.LST
LTR	Letter	94BUDGET.LTR
MEM	Memo	94BUDGET.MEM
RPT	Report	94BUDGET.RPT
TBL	Table	94BUDGET.TBL

Figure 1-4
Some common file extensions for document files

Whenever you select a filename, use one that closely describes the contents of the file, so you will be able to find that file easily and distinguish it from other files.

USING DRIVE, DIRECTORY, AND PATH NAMES

In addition to providing a name for a file, you might also need to tell DOS which disk drive to use when it stores or retrieves a file. DOS uses **drive names** to distinguish the disk drives in your computer system. These drive names are device names for the disk drives. The drive names **A:** and **B:** are used for the first and second diskette drives. If you only have one diskette drive, you can refer to that drive as either drive A or drive B. The drive name **C:** is used for the first drive on your hard disk.

Your hard disk might be **partitioned**, or divided, into additional drives, with drive names such as D:, E:, and so on. On a computer network, you might work with network drives that have drive names such as F:, G:, or H:. Whenever you specify a drive name, you must always include the colon immediately after the letter of the alphabet that identifies the drive.

On a hard disk drive, program and document files are typically stored in separate storage compartments called **directories** or **subdirectories**. A good way to think of directories is to compare them to hanging files in a file cabinet. The hanging file is the directory. The individual file folders contained in the hanging file are subdirectories of that directory. In Tutorial 4, you will examine the concept and use of directories and subdirectories in more detail.

Directories have names similar to filenames. For example, you might have a directory named DOS that contains the program files that are included with MS-DOS 6.2, and another one named RESUMES that contains different versions of your résumé. When saving a file to a directory on the hard disk, you must specify the name of the directory. When you indicate the drive name, directory name, and filename for DOS to use when it stores or retrieves a file, you are identifying a **full path** for that file. For example, Figure 1-5 shows the full path for a program file named FORMAT.COM that is stored in a directory named DOS on drive C. Note that a Backslash (\) separates the drive name from the directory name, and the directory name from the filename. The full path identifies a specific location for your file. In Tutorial 4 you will examine more closely the importance and use of directories and paths.

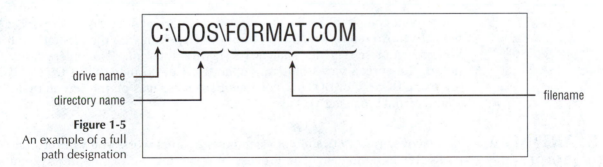

Figure 1-5
An example of a full path designation

As you work with DOS, you will find that there are some instances where you must specify the full path—drive name, directory name, and filename. In other instances, you may need to specify only part of the path because DOS makes an assumption about the remainder of the path. For example, if you do not specify a drive name, DOS assumes you want to use the **default**, or **current**, **drive**. The default drive is the current drive you are using. For example, the default drive might be drive A, B, or C. If you do not specify the proper path, then DOS might not be able to find the program or data file that you need to use.

HOW TO FOLLOW THE NUMBERED STEPS IN THE DOS TUTORIALS

Before you start your computer and learn more about DOS, you need to know how to follow the step-by-step instructions in this text. The steps are displayed as numbered items, as shown in Figure 1-6. *Do not attempt to follow these steps now.* They are only examples to demonstrate the way you use the tutorials in this book.

To access the DOS 6.0 and 6.2 Help system:

1. Type **HELP** and press **[Enter]**.
2. Press **[Tab]** and then **[↓]** (Down Arrow) until you highlight <Format>.
3. Press **[Enter]** to display a Help screen on formatting a disk.
4. Press **[PgDn]** to view subsequent Help screens.
5. Press **[PgUp]** to return to the first Help screen. On some computers, you can also use **[Ctrl][Home]**.

Figure 1-6
An example of step-by-step tutorial instructions

In Figure 1-6 notice that:

◆ The numbers, letters, and special characters that you will type are printed in a distinct bold typeface: Type **HELP**.

◆ The keys that you will press are printed in a distinct bold typeface: Press **[Enter]** means "Press the Enter key."

◆ Keys that you will press in *succession* are shown as follows: Press **[Tab]** and then **[↓]** (Down Arrow). This indicates that you press the first key and release it, then press the second key and release it.

◆ Keys that you will press *simultaneously* are shown as follows: On some computers, you can also use **[Ctrl][Home]**. While pressing and holding the first key, you press the second key, then you release both keys.

As you complete the steps, you will compare screen views on your monitor with those reproduced in the tutorials. Depending on the type of hardware you use, your screen views might be slightly different. Also, unless otherwise noted, the screen views illustrate operations performed with DOS 6.0. If you are using DOS 5.0 or DOS 6.2, you might see messages on the screen that differ slightly from those in DOS 6.0.

STARTING A COMPUTER SYSTEM

To discover how DOS and your computer system work, you will turn on your computer in a moment. The process of powering on a computer system and loading DOS into memory is called **booting** a computer system. When you power on a computer system, you are performing a **cold boot**. During a cold boot, the microprocessor locates and executes program instructions for a Power-On Self Test (called a POST), which checks for hardware errors. The instructions for the POST are stored on a ROM chip. Then, the microprocessor uses additional program instructions stored on this same chip to check drive A for the operating system software. If the operating system software is not on the diskette in drive A or if drive A does not contain a diskette, it checks drive C for DOS. After it locates DOS on either drive A or drive C, it loads DOS into memory. Because DOS manages the computer, the system must be able to locate DOS and copy it into memory before you can use the computer. It is important to note that older PCs might require you to load the operating system from a disk in drive A; otherwise, you see an error message.

If you are using a computer and need to restart it for some reason, you can perform a **warm boot** by holding down [Ctrl] and [Alt] while you press [Del], then releasing all three keys. (You can also press the Reset button on your computer if your computer system has this button.) A warm boot clears memory of any programs and data. The microprocessor then loads DOS into memory, but skips the POST. This operation is also called a **system reset**.

Whether you perform a cold or a warm boot, the microprocessor loads the three DOS system files into RAM. The DOS **system files** contain the operating system software that manages the computer. On an IBM-compatible that uses MS-DOS, these files are named IO.SYS, MSDOS.SYS, and COMMAND.COM. On an IBM microcomputer that uses PC-DOS, the operating system files are named IBMBIO.COM, IBMDOS.COM, and COMMAND.COM. IO.SYS in MS-DOS and IBMBIO.COM in PC-DOS handle the basic input and output operations required of DOS. MSDOS.SYS in MS-DOS and IBMDOS.COM in PC-DOS manage the use of drives, directories, and files and constitute the majority of what you think of as DOS. COMMAND.COM in both MS-DOS and PC-DOS is the **command interpreter** or **command processor**. One of its primary functions is to interpret, or process, commands that you issue to DOS.

During the booting process, you will see additional information displayed on the monitor. This information may include technical specifications about your computer system and the amount of available memory, as well as information displayed by programs that are automatically executed when you boot. When you **execute** a program, DOS loads the program into memory and the microprocessor carries out, or processes, the program instructions.

You must know whether your computer system boots from the hard drive or from a diskette drive. This text assumes you have a hard drive. If this is not the case, your instructor will provide you with additional instructions for getting started and for completing the tutorials.

To perform a warm boot of your computer system:

1. If drive A contains a diskette, remove the diskette from drive A.

2. Turn the power switch on. You may also need to turn on the monitor. If the computer is already on, ask your instructor or technical support person for permission to turn it off and then on again. The computer system will perform a self-test and then load DOS into memory.

6.2

3. The easiest way to perform a warm boot is to simultaneously press and hold down **[Ctrl]** and **[Alt]** with your left hand, and then press **[Del]** with your right hand. Then release [Del], [Ctrl], and [Alt]. The screen will clear. During the booting process, you will see technical information about the computer displayed on your monitor. If you are using DOS 6.2, you might also see other information as it examines your system. DOS will eventually display the DOS prompt, which you'll learn more about in a moment. See Figure 1-7. In some cases, DOS might ask you for the current date and time before it displays the DOS prompt. If you do not see the DOS prompt on the screen, your computer system might be **customized**, or specifically configured, for your needs. For example, if a menu appears with a list of options for using your computer, ask your instructor or technical support person to show you how to exit to the DOS prompt.

6.2

If you are using DOS 6.2, you will see other information displayed on the screen. Just ignore these messages for the moment.

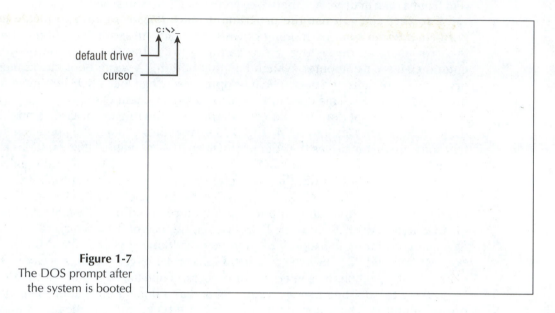

default drive ——

cursor ——

`c:\>_`

Figure 1-7
The DOS prompt after
the system is booted

4. If DOS prompts you for the date, press **[Enter]** to accept the currently set date

5. If DOS prompts you for the time, press **[Enter]** again to accept the currently set time. DOS then displays the DOS prompt.

WORKING AT THE DOS PROMPT

The **DOS prompt** identifies the name of the drive from which the system booted or, in some cases, the drive that DOS automatically uses after the booting process is complete. If you prefer, you can change from this drive to another drive. The drive name shown in the DOS prompt identifies the default drive—the drive DOS uses at any given point in time to find files or execute commands. As you work, DOS keeps track of the current drive so that it can locate program and data files.

To the right of the DOS prompt, you will see a small blinking underscore called a **cursor**. The cursor identifies your current working position on the screen. If you type a character, that character is displayed on the screen where the cursor was positioned. The cursor then appears after the character you typed.

When you see the DOS prompt, you are working at the **operating system level**. You can enter internal and external commands to execute programs included with DOS. An **internal command** is a command for which the program instructions are stored in the computer's memory as part of DOS. In fact, the program code for internal commands is stored in the command interpreter, COMMAND.COM. DOS can quickly locate and execute program instructions for internal commands because they are stored in RAM and are easily accessed.

An **external command** is a command for which the program instructions are stored in a file on a hard disk or diskette. DOS must first locate the file with the program instructions. Then it must copy those program instructions into RAM so that you can use the program. It takes longer for DOS to locate and load an external command than an internal command because accessing disks is slower than accessing memory. External commands allow you to use the system utilities included with DOS.

IDENTIFYING THE VERSION OF DOS

After you boot the computer system, you may want to check which version of DOS is installed on your computer. Identifying your version of DOS is useful for several reasons. First, each version of DOS has slightly different capabilities. If you attempt to perform a certain operation with DOS and you experience difficulties, checking the version of DOS you are using will tell you if it is the one that contains this feature. The VER command—described below—is one of the first tools a computer specialist will use to troubleshoot a problem on a computer.

Second, if you are experiencing difficulties in using a software package on your computer system, you can contact the company that produces that software. One of the first questions a technical support representative is likely to ask you is what version of DOS you are using. The company representative uses that information as a starting point for finding the solution to the problem you are experiencing.

Finally, when you purchase a new software package, the instructions for that new software product may indicate that you need a specific version of DOS. Before you install the software, you should check the DOS version used on that computer system.

To identify the version of DOS on your computer, you can use the VER command, which is an internal command. Each command has its own **syntax**, which is the order in which you must enter a command. The syntax for the VER command is very simple:

VER

To use this command, you type VER at the DOS prompt and then press the Enter key.

Let's check your version of DOS.

To check the DOS version:

1. Be sure you see the DOS prompt. Then, type **VER**. It is important to enter DOS commands exactly as they are written, with the correct punctuation and spacing. However, case does not matter. You can use uppercase or lowercase. If you make a typing mistake, use the Backspace key to correct the error before you press the Enter key. If DOS displays the message "Bad command or file name," then you mistyped the command *or* DOS is unable to locate the program file for an external command. No harm is done. DOS returns you to the DOS prompt so that you can try again.

2. Press **[Enter]**. DOS displays your computer's DOS version number, and then redisplays the DOS prompt (Figure 1-8). When you press the Enter key after entering a command at the DOS prompt, DOS executes the instructions for the command. If you type a command and do not press the Enter key, nothing will happen.

VER command →
command output →

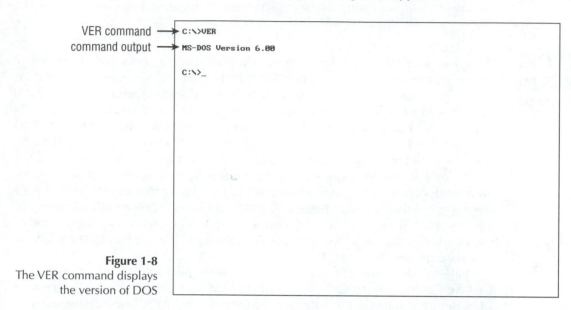

```
C:\>VER

MS-DOS Version 6.00

C:\>_
```

Figure 1-8
The VER command displays
the version of DOS

CHANGING THE DATE

Next, you want to verify that the date and time are set correctly on your computer system. The correct date and time are important because DOS records the date and time with the filename when you save a file. Then, for example, if you have two versions of your résumé stored in two different files, you can check the date and time that each file was saved to determine which file contains the most recent version of your résumé.

You want your computer system to use the correct date and time, because you want to ensure that any files you create and save have the correct **date stamp** and **time stamp**. If you notice that the date is incorrect on your computer, you can use the DATE command to change it. The DATE command is another internal command, and its syntax is as follows:

DATE [*mm-dd-yy*]

To use this command, you can type DATE and press the Enter key, or you can type DATE followed by a specific date in the format shown and then press the Enter key. The information enclosed within square brackets is an optional **parameter**, or item of information. To indicate a specific date using the format shown in brackets, you type one or two digits for the month, a dash, one or two digits for the day, a dash, and the last two digits of the year.

Newer computer systems have a battery-powered "clock" that stores the date and time when you turn off the power to the computer. Earlier computer systems did not have this battery feature, and the date and time is not stored when you turn off the power to the computer. On these older systems, you have to enter and, in some cases, change the date.

To check the current date:

1. Type **DATE** and press **[Enter]**. On the next available line, DOS displays the current date, with the day of the week. On the line after the one with the current date, DOS displays a prompt for you to enter a new date (Figure 1-9). This type of *prompt* is an example of a request for information from a program. DOS also shows you the proper format for entering a date—mm-dd-yy.

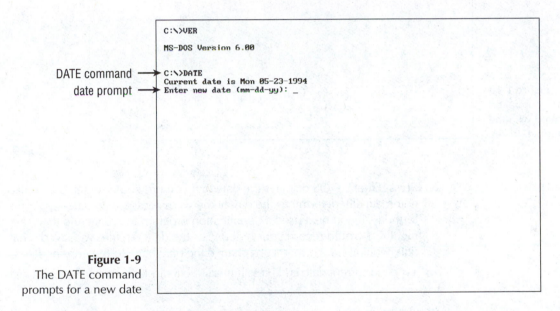

DATE command ——→

date prompt ——→

```
C:\>VER

MS-DOS Version 6.00

C:\>DATE
Current date is Mon 05-23-1994
Enter new date (mm-dd-yy): _
```

Figure 1-9
The DATE command prompts for a new date

2. Type the date of your next birthday. For example, if your next birthday is September 22, 1994, type **9-22-94**. Then press **[Enter]**. DOS displays the DOS prompt again. You do not type the day of the week. The operating system has a calendar that determines the day of the week from the date (e.g., that September 22, 1994 is a Thursday). If you enter the date in the incorrect format, DOS will prompt you for the date again.

Using the Repeat Key

To verify the new date, you can enter the DATE command again, or you can use the Repeat key, F3, to recall the last DOS command you entered.

To verify the date change:

1. Press **[F3]** (Repeat). DOS displays the previous DATE command that you entered (Figure 1-10). If [F3] (Repeat) does not work, you might have pressed [Enter] twice after the last command you entered. In that case, you will have to type the DATE command again.

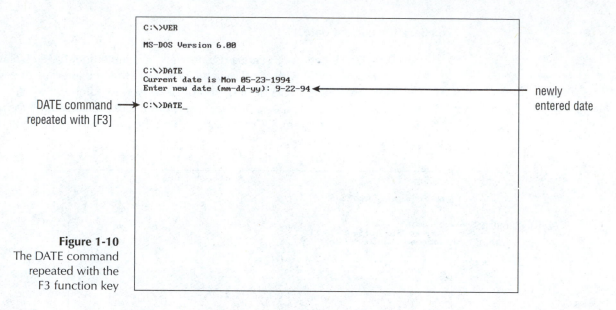

DATE command repeated with [F3] →

newly entered date

```
C:\>VER

MS-DOS Version 6.00

C:\>DATE
Current date is Mon 05-23-1994
Enter new date (mm-dd-yy): 9-22-94

C:\>DATE_
```

Figure 1-10
The DATE command repeated with the F3 function key

2. Press **[Enter]**. DOS displays the date that you previously entered and also automatically determines the day of the week for the new date—your next birthday. If you next used an application program to create and then save a file, DOS would record your birthday as the date the file was saved. That date would be incorrect. Let's change the date back to the current date.

3. Type the current date and press **[Enter]**. DOS displays the DOS prompt again.

If you know in advance what date you want to use, you can type the DATE command followed by the date. For example, if you want to change the date to July 9, 1994, you can enter DATE 7-9-94. DOS will not prompt you for the date and will not show you the date change.

USING DOSKEY

Although [F3] (Repeat) is useful, it allows you to recall only the last DOS command you entered. You can use a system utility called **DOSKEY** to keep track of the last 20 or so commands you enter at the DOS prompt, so that you can recall them rather than enter them again. To use this feature, you enter the command DOSKEY at the DOS prompt. Then you recall a command using the [↑] (Up Arrow) and [↓] (Down Arrow) keys.

DOSKEY is an external command with a complicated syntax and a variety of options. After you enter this command, DOS looks for a file on disk with a file-name identical to the command that you type and with one of three file extensions—COM (for command file), EXE (for executable file), and BAT (for batch file). In this case, DOS will find a file named DOSKEY.COM and then load the program instructions stored in this file into RAM so that you can use the program.

DOSKEY is an example of a **Terminate-and-Stay-Resident (TSR) utility**. After DOS loads a utility such as DOSKEY, the TSR program remains in memory and active while you use other programs. In contrast, if you instruct DOS to load a software application and then exit that program, the program code for that application no longer remains in memory. That memory becomes available for other programs. If you use certain other utilities, the program code for that utility no longer remains in memory after the utility completes its operations.

To activate DOSKEY:

5.0   6.0

6.2

1. Type **DOSKEY** and press **[Enter]**. If you are using DOS 5.0 or 6.0, DOS will display the message "DOSKey installed" if DOSKEY is not already installed on your computer. If you do not see this message with DOS 5.0 or 6.0, DOSKEY is already installed. DOS 6.2 will not display a message.

DOSKEY keeps track of the commands you enter at the DOS prompt in a small area of memory known as the **command stack**. When the command stack fills up, DOSKEY eliminates the oldest commands so that it has room for new commands that you enter. After you enter a few commands, you will use DOSKEY to recall a specific command.

SETTING THE TIME

Next, you want to check the current time on your computer system to verify that it is correct. You use another internal command, TIME, with the following syntax:

TIME [*time*]

You can type TIME and press the Enter key, or you can type TIME followed by the time change you want to make and then press the Enter key.

To check the time:

1. Type **TIME** and press **[Enter]**. DOS displays the current time in hours, minutes, seconds, and either "a" for a.m. or "p" for p.m. For example, 1:54:31.12p means 1:54 p.m. and 31.12 seconds. On the next line, DOS prompts you to enter a new time. See Figure 1-11.

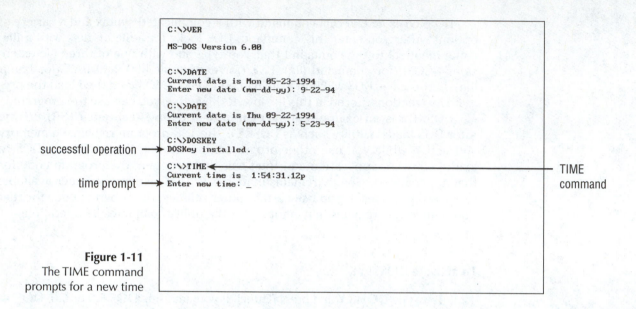

successful operation →

time prompt →

TIME command

Figure 1-11
The TIME command
prompts for a new time

2. Type a new time that is one hour later than the current time and press
    [Enter]. For example, if the current time is 10:30 a.m., you type **11:30a**
    and press **[Enter]**. If the current time is 3:30 p.m., you type **4:30p** and
    press **[Enter]**. If you do not type "a" or "p" with the new time, DOS
    assumes that the time is an a.m. time. If you enter the time in the incor-
    rect format, DOS will prompt you for the time again, or it might change
    the time to an incorrect time.

3. Press **[↑]** (Up Arrow). DOSKEY displays the previous TIME command.
    You can use this feature to recall previously entered commands at any
    time while you are working at the DOS prompt. Each time you press [↑],
    DOSKEY displays the last command you typed. To use a command you
    recall, you press the Enter key.

4. Press **[Enter]**. DOS displays the current time and prompts for a new time.
    If you now use an applications program to create and then save a file,
    DOS will record the incorrect time with the filename. Let's change the
    time to the current time.

5. Type the correct time in the proper format and press **[Enter]**.

Like the DATE command, if you know in advance the time you want reflected
in your time stamp, you can enter the new time with the TIME command. For
example, if you type "TIME 5:00p" and press [Enter], DOS will make the change
and display the DOS prompt again, without asking you for any other information.

CLEARING THE SCREEN

Notice that the screen is cluttered with commands, messages, prompts, and
your responses to the prompts, and you are now entering commands at the
bottom of the screen. To clear the screen so that you can work more easily, you
use another internal command, the CLS command, with the following syntax:

CLS

Clearing the screen before issuing commands is a good habit to develop
because you can focus on one command operation at a time.

Let's clear the screen.

To clear the screen:

1. Type **CLS** and press **[Enter]**. DOS clears the screen and displays the DOS prompt and cursor in the upper left corner of the screen.

Now that you understand how to work with DOS commands, this is a good opportunity to stop for a few minutes and take a break.

FORMATTING DISKETTES

When you acquired your computer, it is likely that you also bought a word processing software package. Now you want to use this software package to design a new résumé. Until you learn more about how to use a hard disk, you decide to store the final copy of your résumé in a file on a diskette. One advantage of using a diskette is that it provides you with portability. You can carry the diskette with you and print copies of your files from any computer that has the same word processing software you have.

DOS requires that you use a formatted diskette in a disk drive. A **formatted diskette** is a diskette prepared by DOS so that DOS can store data on it. You can purchase **unformatted**, or blank, diskettes as well as **preformatted** diskettes. Some manufacturers of diskettes format the diskettes before selling them. These preformatted diskettes cost more, but you do not need to spend time formatting them before you can use them. You must format an unformatted diskette before DOS can record data on the diskette.

During the formatting process, DOS magnetically creates concentric recording bands, or **tracks**, on the diskette (Figure 1-12). DOS then subdivides the tracks into sectors. A **sector** is the basic unit of storage space on a diskette or hard drive. Each sector on a diskette can store 512 bytes of data. That means that you can store 512 characters, or approximately 10 lines of text, in a sector.

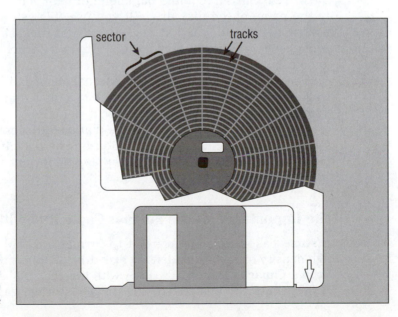

Figure 1-12
Tracks and sectors on a formatted 3½-inch diskette

Diskette Storage Capacities

Diskettes are sold in three common storage capacities: double-density, high-density, and extra-high-density. A high-density diskette stores two to four times as much data as a double-density diskette. An extra-high-density diskette stores twice as much data as a high-density diskette. Because diskettes are available in two sizes (5¼" and 3½") and three storage capacities, you want to be sure that you purchase the proper type for use in your computer (Figure 1-13). The difference in storage capacities depends on the number of tracks and sectors formatted on each side of a diskette. (For a review of the differences between 3½-inch and 5¼-inch diskettes, see the "Essential Computer Concepts" chapter at the beginning of this book.)

Size	Density	Storage Capacity	Sides	Tracks	Sectors	Bytes per Sector	Sectors per Allocation Unit
5¼"	Double	360K	2	40	9	512	2
5¼"	High	1.2M	2	80	15	512	1
3½"	Double	720K	2	80	9	512	2
3½"	High	1.44M	2	80	18	512	1
3½"	Extra-high	2.88M	2	80	36	512	1

Figure 1-13
Characteristics
of diskettes

Using the FORMAT Command

To format a diskette to the maximum capacity of the disk drive, you use the FORMAT command, which has the following syntax:

FORMAT *drive name*:

The drive name is a required parameter or item of information. You must specify the name of the disk drive. If you use this syntax, you must also use a diskette that has the same storage capacity as the disk drive you are using. For example, if you want to format a diskette in a 3½-inch high-density disk drive, you must use a 3½-inch high-density diskette.

The FORMAT command is an external command, so DOS must locate the program instructions for this command in a file on disk and then load the program into memory so that you can use it.

You can also reformat a diskette that already contains information. If you do, you will erase all the information on the diskette. Before you format a diskette, be sure it does not contain any important information or software that you need.

The Importance of the Format Capacity Switch

In some cases, you might need to format a double-density diskette in a high-density or extra-high-density disk drive. If this is the case, you can use the **Format Capacity switch**, /F:*<size>*, with the FORMAT command to ensure that DOS formats the diskette to the proper storage capacity. (A **switch** is an optional parameter that modifies the way in which a command operates. A switch starts with a Slash (/) and is followed by one or more additional codes.)

When you use the Format Capacity switch, you type the FORMAT command and then type /F, followed by a colon and the size, or storage capacity, of the diskette. DOS uses the word *size* to indicate capacity. When you specify the size, you list the storage capacity in kilobytes or megabytes. For example, if you want to format a double-density diskette in a high-density drive A to a storage capacity of 720K, you use the following command:

FORMAT A: /F:720

When you type a switch with a DOS command, you do not need a space before the switch. However, a space before the switch makes the DOS command easier to read.

If you forget to use the Format Capacity switch and format a double-density diskette as a high-density diskette, DOS might report a large number of defective sectors.

Preparing Your Diskettes

Your instructor or technical support person will assist you in the preparation of data diskettes that contain the files you will use to complete the tutorials as well as the end-of-chapter Questions and Tutorial Assignments in this book. Because this text assumes you will use a computer system with a 3½-inch double-density or high-density disk drive, you will need two 3½-inch, double-density diskettes. You will use one diskette to work through the tutorial steps in each chapter; you will use the other diskette for the end-of-chapter Questions and Tutorial Assignments. Initially, both diskettes will contain the same data. However, as you complete the tutorials and the end-of-chapter Questions and Tutorial Assignments, the contents of the two diskettes will change. As you proceed with the tutorials and end-of-chapter Tutorial Assignments, you might need additional diskettes to practice DOS commands.

First, you should label each diskette to identify which diskette you will use for the tutorials and which diskette you will use for the end-of-chapter Tutorial Assignments. You can use the blank adhesive labels provided with the diskettes when you purchased them. Before you place labels on the newly formatted diskettes, you should write a short description on each label to identify the diskette's intended use and contents. If you have already placed the blank labels on the diskettes, you can use a felt-tip pen to gently write the description on the label. Do *not* use a ballpoint pen or pencil to write on the label. You might damage the surface of the diskette.

On one label, write "Tutorial Disk," and on the other label, write "Exercise Disk." Then place the labels on the diskettes. Figure 1-14 shows how to place a label on a 3½-inch diskette.

Identifying Storage Capacities of Diskettes and Drives

Before you can format a diskette, you must know the capacity of the diskette you want to format and find out whether your computer system has a double-density, high-density, or extra-high-density disk drive. You might need to use the Format Capacity switch to format the diskette to the proper capacity. Check the labeling on the diskettes and your disk drive unit for the storage capacities of the diskettes and drive.

Double-density diskettes might be labeled "DD" or "DS/DD" (for Double-Sided, Double-Density), high-density diskettes "HD" or "DS/HD" (for Double-Sided, High-Density), and extra-high-density diskettes "ED." Also, double-density diskettes have one square hole for the write-protect tab; high-density diskettes have two square holes, one directly opposite the other on the sides of the diskette. Extra-high-density diskettes have two square holes, each at positions opposite each other on the two sides of the diskette. Double-density diskettes might be labeled "360K" or "720K," high-density diskettes "1.2 M" or "1.44M," and extra-high-density diskettes "2.88M." Double-density diskettes might also be labeled "1M," high-density diskettes "2M," and extra-high-density diskettes "4M"; however, these diskettes are not formatted to these capacities. You might also find that the disk drives or disk drive ejector buttons are labeled with the proper storage capacity of the disk drive. If you are unsure, ask your instructor or technical support person for assistance.

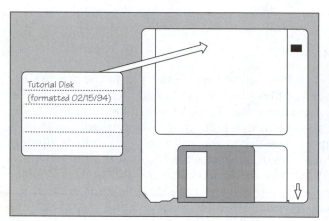
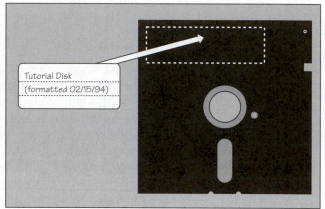

Figure 1-14
Applying an adhesive label to a
3½-inch and a 5¼-inch diskette

Formatting a Diskette —Backup disk

Now you are ready to format the diskettes that you will use for the tutorials and the end-of-chapter Tutorial Assignments.

To format a diskette:

1. Insert an unformatted 3½-inch double-density or high-density diskette into drive A or B and, if necessary, close the drive door. See Figure 1-15, which illustrates how to insert a 3½-inch diskette into a disk drive.

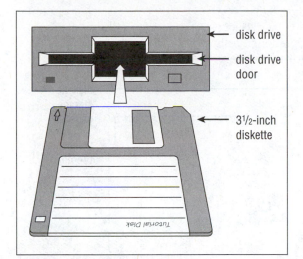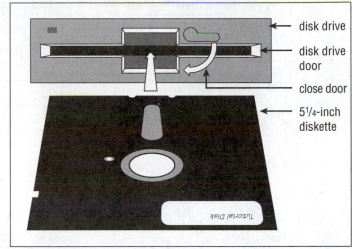

Figure 1-15
Inserting a 3½-inch and a 5¼-inch
diskette into a disk drive

2. Format the diskette to the proper storage capacity using one of the following options. If you are using drive B instead of drive A, use B: instead of A: for the drive name in the commands.

◆ If you are formatting a 3½-inch double-density diskette in a double-density drive, a 3½-inch high-density diskette in a high-density drive, or a 3½-inch extra-high-density diskette in an extra-high-density drive, type **FORMAT A:** and press **[Enter]**. You do not need to use the Format Capacity switch because DOS will automatically format the diskette to the maximum capacity of the drive.

◆ If you are formatting a 3½-inch double-density diskette in a high-density or extra-high-density drive, type **FORMAT A: /F:720** and press **[Enter].**

◆ If you are formatting a 3½-inch high-density diskette in an extra-high-density drive, type **FORMAT A: /F:1.44** and press **[Enter].**

DOS then prompts you to insert a new diskette into drive A or B, which you did in Step 1.

3. Press **[Enter]**. You will know DOS is formatting the diskette when you see the first message, "Checking existing disk format." See Figure 1-16. If the diskette is already formatted, you will see the message "Saving UNFORMAT information" as DOS saves information that allows you to unformat the diskette later. Then DOS informs you that it is formatting the diskette to a specific storage capacity. DOS then displays a percentage to show you how much of the formatting process is complete. When this percentage reaches 100%, DOS informs you that the formatting is complete. If DOS displays an error message at any time, try another diskette or ask your instructor or technical support person for assistance. If you experience difficulty formatting two diskettes in a row and if you are using the proper value for the Format Capacity switch, the disk drive might be malfunctioning.

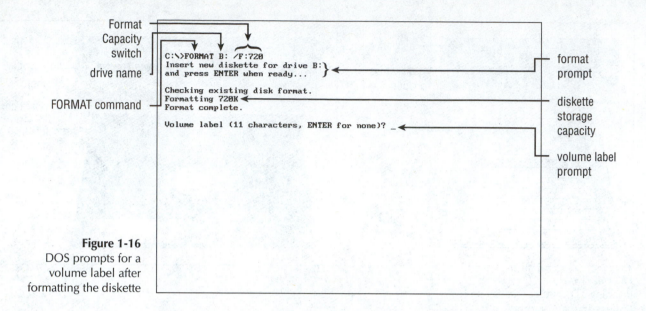

Figure 1-16
DOS prompts for a
volume label after
formatting the diskette

During the formatting operation, the diskette spins in the disk drive unit at approximately 300 to 360 rpm (revolutions per minute) and the drive light is on. You should *not* remove a diskette from, or insert a diskette into, a disk drive when the drive light is on. When the drive light is off, you can safely remove a diskette and insert another diskette.

Assigning a Volume Label

After DOS completes the formatting, it prompts for a volume label (Figure 1-16). A **volume label** is a name for the diskette, that usually identifies the type of information you will store on the diskette. For example, if you intend to store copies of your résumés and cover letters on a diskette, you could use the volume label JOB SEARCH. The volume label, or name, is one to 11 characters in length and can include spaces. Certain types of symbols, such as a period, are not allowed. If you attempt to use an invalid or unacceptable character, DOS will inform you of this problem and will prompt you again for the volume label.

You will need to choose a volume label that will be appropriate for both diskettes you will use as you work through this book. Because both diskettes will be duplicate copies of the data disk provided to your instructor and will contain files used in a business environment, you decide to use BUSINESS as the volume label.

To enter a volume label for your diskette during formatting:

1. Type **BUSINESS** and press **[Enter]**. DOS assigns the volume label to the diskette, displays information on how it formatted the diskette, assigns a volume name and serial number, and asks if you want to format another diskette (Figure 1-17).

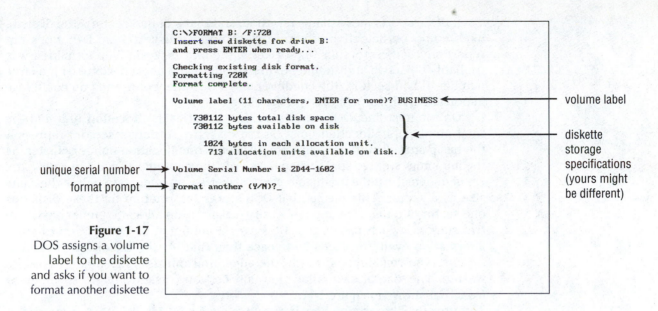

unique serial number →

format prompt →

Figure 1-17
DOS assigns a volume label to the diskette and asks if you want to format another diskette

Now format your second data diskette.

2. Type **Y** for "Yes" and press **[Enter]**. DOS prompts you to insert a new diskette into the drive. *If you already have two blank, formatted diskettes with the volume label BUSINESS, type **N** for No, then press **[Enter]**. You have finished formatting your diskettes and do not need to perform Steps 3 through 5.*

3. Insert another unformatted, 3½-inch double-density diskette, and press **[Enter]**. DOS repeats the formatting process.

4. When DOS prompts you for the volume label for this diskette, type **BUSINESS** and press **[Enter].**

5. When DOS asks if you want to format another diskette, type **N** for "No" and press **[Enter]**. DOS returns you to the DOS prompt.

Evaluating the Disk Storage Space Report

After formatting a diskette, DOS displays information on the storage capacity of the newly formatted diskette (Figure 1-17). Your storage capacities might be different. The first number shows the total amount of storage space on the diskette in bytes. The second number shows how much of this storage space is available for use, again in bytes. Usually, these two numbers are identical and indicate that you can use all of the formatted storage space available on the diskette. If these numbers are different, you will also see a message that indicates the diskette contains a certain number of bytes in bad sectors. When DOS formats a diskette, it checks the surface of the disk for defects. **Bad sectors** are defective areas on the diskette that DOS marks as unusable. You can still use the rest of the diskette. When DOS records information onto the diskette, it does not use sectors marked as defective or bad.

If DOS reports more than a few thousand bytes of bad sectors, the diskette itself could be defective. If you format another diskette and DOS does not report any bad sectors for that diskette, the first disk that you formatted was probably defective and should be thrown out. If you use a diskette with a large number of bad sectors, the condition might become worse and you could lose important information stored on the diskette.

On the next line, DOS reports on the size of each **allocation unit** and the total number of allocation units on the diskette. Although sectors represent the basic storage unit on a diskette, DOS uses an allocation unit, or **cluster**, as the minimum storage space when it records the contents of a file on a diskette. On high-density and extra-high-density diskettes, an allocation unit is the same size as a sector. This means that DOS stores information on these diskettes one sector at a time. On double-density diskettes, an allocation unit consists of two sectors, which means that DOS uses a minimum of two sectors to store information even if it needs less space than that for the file or for the end of the file. The remaining space in the allocation unit is unused and therefore wasted. The size of each allocation unit on your diskette might be different from that shown in Figure 1-17.

After DOS reports on how the storage space on the diskette is allocated, it identifies the serial number assigned to the diskette. The **serial number** is a unique ID number produced by DOS from the date and time on the computer system. The serial number represents another way to identify a diskette. Your serial number will be different from the one shown in Figure 1-17. Finally, DOS asks you if you want to format another diskette.

Caring for Diskettes

It is also important to protect your work by taking good care of your diskettes. Figure 1-18 summarizes guidelines you should follow.

- ◆ Store your diskettes in a safe, dry place—away from dust and other contaminants.
- ◆ Keep diskettes away from magnets and equipment that contains magnets, such as a telephone, stereo speaker, and color TV tube, as well as walk-through X-ray machines at airports, department stores, and libraries.
- ◆ Do not expose diskettes to extreme heat or extreme cold; for example, do not leave diskettes exposed to the hot sun in a car.
- ◆ Keep diskettes away from water, coffee, tea, and other liquids.
- ◆ Keep diskettes away from solvents.
- ◆ Place 5¼-inch diskettes in their sleeves when you are not using them.
- ◆ Hold 5¼-inch diskettes so that you do not touch any of the exposed surfaces of the diskette with your fingers.
- ◆ Do not bend 5¼-inch diskettes.
- ◆ Do not place paper clips on 5¼-inch diskettes.
- ◆ Use a felt-tip pen to record information on a 5¼-inch diskette's label; do not use a sharp pen or pencil.

Figure 1-18
Guidelines for the proper care of diskettes

CHANGING THE DEFAULT DRIVE

Now that you have formatted your diskettes, you are ready to make a duplicate copy of the data diskette provided to your instructor. You can perform this operation from drive C or from a diskette drive. You will find that many DOS operations are simpler if you change drives, because you do not need to specify the drive name in each DOS command that requires the drive name. If you omit the drive name, DOS assumes you want to use the drive from which you are currently working.

To change from one drive to another at the DOS prompt, you type the name of the drive followed by a colon (:) and press the Enter key. You *must* include the colon after the letter of the alphabet that identifies the drive. Otherwise, DOS will assume that you have entered a command. It will then look for the program instructions and inform you that you entered a "Bad command or file name" when it cannot find the program instructions. Also, do not confuse the semicolon (;) with the colon (:).

To change to the drive that contains your data diskette:

1. Be sure drive A or B contains one of the two diskettes you just formatted.
2. If your diskette is in drive A, type **A:** and press **[Enter]**. If your diskette is in drive B, type **B:** and press **[Enter]**. DOS updates the DOS prompt to show the new default drive. See Figure 1-19.

previous default drive →

current default drive →

drive name command

Figure 1-19
Changing the default drive from C to A

USING THE HELP SWITCH

Now you are ready to make copies of the diskette provided to your instructor. You can use the DISKCOPY command to duplicate a diskette. First, you decide to use the DOS Help switch to provide you with help information on how to properly use the DISKCOPY command. The **Help switch**, /?, displays a help screen with information on a specific DOS command. The syntax for this switch is as follows:

[*command*] **/?**

To access help information, you type a DOS command followed by /?. For example, to obtain help information on the DISKCOPY command, you type DISKCOPY /? and press the Enter key. The Help switch works with any DOS command.

To obtain help information on the DISKCOPY command:

1. Type **DISKCOPY /?** and press **[Enter]**. DOS displays a help screen that summarizes the features of the DISKCOPY command (Figure 1-20). *Be sure you type a Slash rather than a Backslash.* A Slash (/) leans to the right; a Backslash (\ ) leans to the left. If you type a Backslash, DOS displays the error message "Too many parameters," and then displays the DOS prompt again.

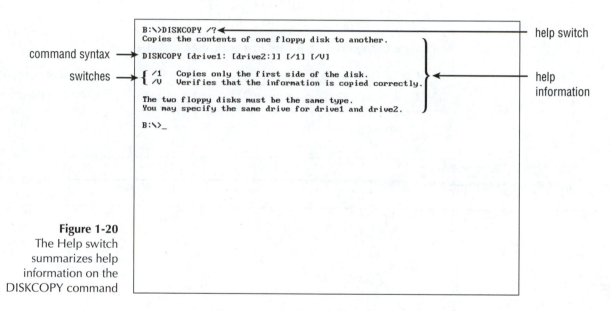

command syntax →

switches →

help switch

help information

Figure 1-20
The Help switch
summarizes help
information on the
DISKCOPY command

6.2

If you are using DOS 6.2, one additional switch—the /M switch—will appear on your screen.

Printing the Help Screen

You want to print a copy of this Help screen to use later for reference. Before you follow the next set of steps, ask your instructor or technical support person if the type of computer system you are using will permit you to print a screen. If not, skip these steps.

To print the Help screen:

1. Be sure the printer is operational. If necessary, ask your instructor or technical support person to show you how to use the printer.

2. Press **[Print Screen].** This key is located in the upper-right corner of the keyboard. If your keyboard has a key labeled PrtSc or [PrtScrn] rather than Print Screen, press **[Shift][PrtSc]** or **[Shift][PrtScrn]** (Print Screen).

3. If the printer does not automatically eject a sheet of paper, press the **Form Feed (FF) button** on the printer to advance the paper in the printer (Figure 1-21). If nothing happens when you press Form Feed, press the **On Line button**, press **Form Feed** again, and then press **On Line** a final time.

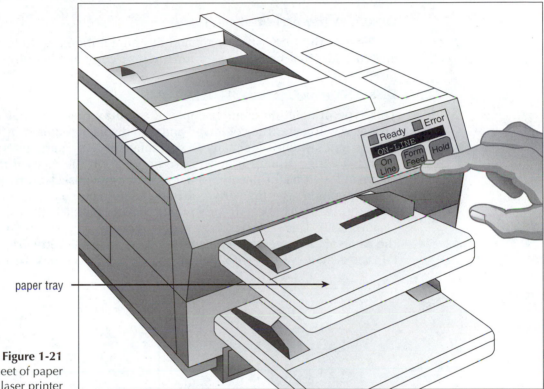

paper tray

Figure 1-21
Ejecting a sheet of paper
from a laser printer

4. Remove your printed copy of the Help screen from the printer.

MAKING A COPY OF A DISKETTE

It is important to copy the contents of diskettes that contain critical information, such as documents you create and software you use, onto other diskettes. You can keep the extra copies of your data diskettes and the original copies of software in reserve as **backup** copies. That way, if your working copy of a diskette fails, you can immediately make a duplicate of your backup copy. Then, you use the new copy as your working diskette.

If you examine your printed copy of the Help screen for the DISKCOPY command, you will note that this command copies the contents of one diskette to another. The notes for this command inform you that the two diskettes must be of the same type. That means the diskettes *must* be the same size *and* have the same storage capacity. For example, if you want to make a copy of a 3½-inch double-density diskette, you must use another 3½-inch double-density diskette for the new copy. You cannot perform a disk copy from a double-density diskette to a high-density diskette or vice versa. You cannot perform a disk copy from a 5¼-inch diskette to a 3½-inch diskette or vice versa.

You cannot use this command to make a copy of the contents of your hard disk drive. This command works only with diskettes.

Understanding the Syntax of the DISKCOPY Command

The help information tells you that the syntax for this external command is as follows:

DISKCOPY [*drive1:* [*drive2:*]] [/1] [/V]

6.2

In DOS 6.2, the DISKCOPY command has an additional switch, the **Multipass switch** (/M), that uses memory for the disk copy and requires you to swap diskettes.

DISKCOPY [*drive 1:*[*drive 2:*]] [/1] [/V] [/M]

This type of notation is an example of a **syntax diagram** that describes the proper way to enter the command and also displays required or optional parameters and switches for many DOS commands. Any parameters or switches included within square brackets are optional. In the case of the DISKCOPY command, you might need to specify one or two diskette drives for the disk copy operation. The first drive, **drive1**, is the name of the source drive. The **source drive** is the diskette drive that contains the diskette you want to copy (Figure 1-22). This diskette is the **source diskette**. The second drive, **drive2**, is the name of the target drive. The **target drive** is the diskette drive that will contain the diskette you copy to. This diskette is the **target diskette** (Figure 1-22).

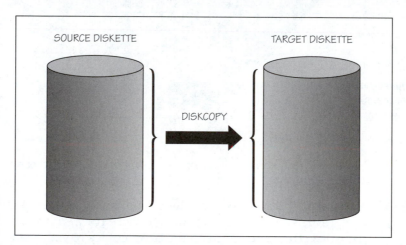

SOURCE DISKETTE   TARGET DISKETTE

DISKCOPY

Figure 1-22
Copying an entire diskette
to another diskette

If you specify only drive1, the DISKCOPY command assumes you want to use the same drive for the source and target disks. Because the DISKCOPY command requires that both diskettes be the same size and the same storage capacity, you often use the same drive for both the source and target disks. If you use the same drive for the source and target disks, you *must* switch diskettes during the disk copy operation. If you have two drives that are the same size *and* the same storage capacity, you can perform the disk copy using both drives. You insert your source diskette in one drive and your target diskette in the other drive.

5.0 **6.0**

6.2

In DOS 5.0 and 6.0, the DISKCOPY command has two optional switches. The /1 switch copies only the one side of a diskette. This switch is included for use with single-sided drives that were used on earlier computer systems. The Verify switch, /V, verifies that the information on the diskette is copied correctly. This switch is rarely used because the disk copy process is quite reliable and verification slows it down. In DOS 6.2, the DISKCOPY command has an additional switch, /M, which forces a multipass copy using memory only.

DOS 5.0 and 6.0 copy part of the contents of the source diskette into RAM, then copy that data from RAM to the destination diskette. As a result, you usually need to insert the source and destination diskettes more than once to complete the disk copy. DOS 6.2 can copy the contents of the source diskette to the hard disk and then to the destination diskette so that you do not need to swap diskettes repeatedly.

Using the DISKCOPY Command

You want to make two copies of the data diskette. Because this data diskette is a double-density diskette, you must use another double-density diskette for the target diskette. However, you can perform the disk copy in either a double-density or high-density disk drive.

Before you make copies of the data diskette, you should **write-protect** the diskette so that you do not inadvertently record over its contents. That way, the files are protected from accidental deletion. To write-protect a 3½-inch diskette, hold the diskette so that the label on the diskette faces away from you with the metal shutter at the bottom. On the upper-left side of the diskette, you will see a rectangular notch in the diskette. The rectangular notch contains a square plastic tab. With your fingernail, press on the square tab until it slides up and exposes an open, square hole in the diskette (Figure 1-23). The diskette is now write-protected.

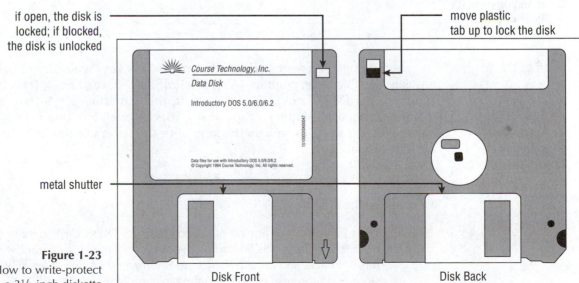

if open, the disk is locked; if blocked, the disk is unlocked

move plastic tab up to lock the disk

Course Technology, Inc.

Data Disk

Introductory DOS 5.0/6.0/6.2

Data files for use with Introductory DOS 5.0/6.0/6.2
© Copyright 1994 Course Technology, Inc. All rights reserved.

metal shutter

Disk Front

Disk Back

Figure 1-23
How to write-protect a 3½-inch diskette

Now you are ready to make two copies of the data diskette.

steps for disk copy:

To copy the data diskette:

1. Insert the data diskette provided by your instructor or technical support person.

2. Type **DISKCOPY** and press **[Enter]**. DOS prompts you to insert the **source diskette**, the diskette that you want to copy, and prompts you to press any key to continue. See Figure 1-24. The source diskette is the data diskette that you just inserted in the disk drive. *Because you did not specify a source drive and a target drive, DOS assumes that this disk drive will be used for both the source diskette and the target diskette.* You could also use the command DISKCOPY A: or DISKCOPY A: A: to copy the data diskette. If DOS displays the message "Bad command or file name," DOS cannot locate the program file for the DISKCOPY command on drive C. Ask your instructor or technical support person for assistance.

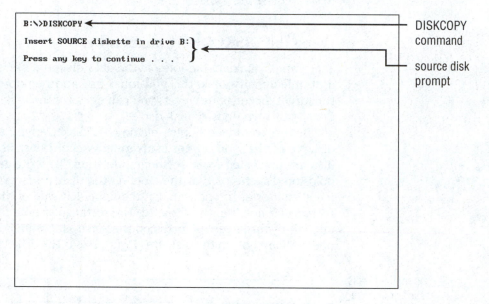

```
B:\>DISKCOPY

Insert SOURCE diskette in drive B:

Press any key to continue . . .
```

DISKCOPY command

source disk prompt

Figure 1-24
The DISKCOPY command prompts for the source diskette

Even though you were prompted to press "any key," you cannot press just any key. Certain keys, such as [Alt], [Ctrl], [Shift], [Caps Lock], [Scroll Lock], [Pause], and [Num Lock], do not work in this situation. Keys that do work include [Spacebar], [Enter], [Tab], [Esc], [Backspace], function keys, and cursor movement keys, as well as the keys with the letters of the alphabet, numbers, and symbols.

To continue the disk copy:

1. Press **[Spacebar]** or any other key to continue. DISKCOPY identifies the diskette specifications, including the number of tracks, the number of sectors per track, and the number of sides formatted on this diskette. It then stops and prompts you to insert the target diskette. See Figure 1-25.

```
B:\>DISKCOPY

Insert SOURCE diskette in drive B:

Press any key to continue . . .

Copying 80 tracks
9 sectors per track, 2 side(s)

Insert TARGET diskette in drive B:

Press any key to continue . . .
```

source
diskette
specifications

target
diskette
prompt

Figure 1-25
The DISKCOPY
command prompts
for the target diskette

2. When you are prompted for the target diskette, wait for the drive light to go off. Then remove the data diskette from the drive, insert your formatted diskette labeled "Tutorial Disk," and press **[Spacebar]** or any other key to continue. DISKCOPY copies data onto this new diskette. When the copying process is complete, DOS might prompt you to reinsert the source diskette. See Figure 1-26. If this occurs, the DISKCOPY program is ready to copy another part of the original data diskette. If you are using DOS 6.2, DISKCOPY might perform the copy in one pass, then ask if you want to create another copy of the same diskette. If this occurs in DOS 6.2, type **Y** for Yes, press **[Enter]**, skip Steps 4 and 5, and continue with Step 6.

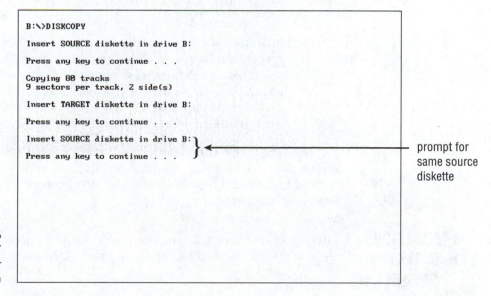

```
B:\>DISKCOPY

Insert SOURCE diskette in drive B:

Press any key to continue . . .

Copying 80 tracks
9 sectors per track, 2 side(s)

Insert TARGET diskette in drive B:

Press any key to continue . . .

Insert SOURCE diskette in drive B:

Press any key to continue . . .
```

prompt for
same source
diskette

Figure 1-26
The DISKCOPY
command prompts for
the source diskette again

3. If prompted to insert the source diskette, wait for the drive light to go off. Then remove the target diskette from the diskette drive, reinsert the data diskette, and press **[Spacebar]** or any other key to continue. DISKCOPY continues the copy process. When it stops, you will be prompted to insert the target diskette again. See Figure 1-27.

```
B:\>DISKCOPY

Insert SOURCE diskette in drive B:

Press any key to continue . . .

Copying 80 tracks
9 sectors per track, 2 side(s)

Insert TARGET diskette in drive B:

Press any key to continue . . .

Insert SOURCE diskette in drive B:

Press any key to continue . . .

Insert TARGET diskette in drive B:

Press any key to continue . . .
```

Figure 1-27
The DISKCOPY command prompts for the target diskette again

4. When prompted to insert the target diskette, wait for the drive light to go off. Then remove the data diskette from the drive, reinsert the Tutorial Disk, and press **[Spacebar]** or any other key to continue. The DISKCOPY program copies the remainder of the data diskette from memory onto the target diskette. Then it asks if you want to copy another diskette.

5. Remove the newly prepared disk copy.

6. Insert the original source diskette (the data diskette), type **Y** for "Yes" and press **[Spacebar]** or any other key to continue. The DISKCOPY command will repeat the same process. However, this time the target diskette is your other diskette, the one labeled "Exercise Disk." After you make both copies of the data diskette, type **N** for "No" when asked whether you want to make another copy. DOS then returns you to the DOS prompt.

The DISKCOPY command performs a sector-by-sector copy of a diskette, so the new diskette that results from the disk copy operation is an identical copy of the original diskette, except for one feature. The new diskette has a different serial number.

FINISHING YOUR WORK SESSION

After you finish using a computer, you should remove any diskettes from the diskette drives. You might also need to shut off the power to the computer system.

To end your work session:

1. Be sure the DOS prompt is displayed on the screen.

2. Be sure the drive lights are off. Then remove any diskettes from the diskette drives. If you experience any difficulty, ask your instructor or technical support person to show you how to remove the diskettes.

3. If you are working in a computer lab, ask your instructor or technical support person if it is necessary to turn off the computer. If so, locate the power switch and turn it to the "off" position. Also locate the power switch for the monitor and turn it off.

◆

SUMMARY

In this tutorial, you learned that operating system software plays an important role in the management and use of a computer system. DOS is the predominant operating system software used on IBM microcomputers and IBM compatibles.

The primary storage media used on microcomputer systems are the hard disk and the diskette. Diskettes differ in their storage capacities and sizes and must be used in disk drive units that support them. Documents and programs are stored in files on a diskette or on a hard disk. Each file has a filename that you provide. The filename identifies the file's location on the disk and its contents. When you save a file to disk, you might also need to provide a drive name so that a document is stored on the correct drive.

After you boot a computer system, DOS displays the DOS prompt unless your computer system is customized. You can enter internal or external commands at the DOS prompt. In this tutorial, you used the VER command to display the version of DOS installed on your computer system. You also used the DATE and TIME commands to set, or verify, the date and time used by your computer system. You cleared the screen with the CLS command. You used the DOSKEY command to load a Terminate-and-Stay Resident program to keep track of commands that you entered at the DOS prompt. You recalled those commands with the Up and Down Arrow keys.

You formatted a diskette with the FORMAT command so that you can use the diskette in the computer system. The Format Capacity switch allows you to format double-density diskettes in high-density or extra-high-density disk drives and high-density diskettes in extra-high-density drives.

You changed the default drive by specifying the name of the drive you wanted to use as the new default drive. You used the Help switch to obtain help information on the DISKCOPY command, and you used the DISKCOPY command to make duplicate copies of a diskette.

Command Reference	
Syntax	**Use**
[*drive name*:]	Changes the current, or default, drive; for example, A: changes from the current drive to drive A, and drive A becomes the current drive
CLS	An internal command that clears the screen and displays the DOS prompt and cursor in the upper-left corner of the screen
DATE	An internal command that displays the date used on the computer system, prompts for a new date, and keeps or changes the date
DATE [*mm-dd-yy*]	An internal command that sets the date on the computer; for example, DATE 5-21-94 sets the date to May 21, 1994
DISKCOPY [*source*] [*target*]	An external command that makes a copy of a diskette
[DOS command] /?	Displays a screen with help information on the specified DOS command; for example, DATE /? displays help information on the DATE command
DOSKEY	An external command that keeps track of commands entered at the DOS prompt and that allows you to recall the commands with [↑] and [↓]
FORMAT *drive name*:	An external command that prepares a diskette for use on a computer system by formatting the diskette to the highest storage capacity of the disk drive; for example, FORMAT A: formats the diskette in drive A
FORMAT *drive name*: /F:*size*	An external command that prepares a diskette for use on a computer system by formatting the diskette to the specified storage capacity; for example, FORMAT A: /F:720 formats a 3½-inch double-density diskette to 720K

TIME	An internal command that displays the time used on a computer system, prompts for a new time, and keeps or changes the time
TIME [*hh:mm:ss*]	An internal command that sets the time on a computer system to a specific time; for example, TIME 10:30a sets the time to 10:30 a.m.
VER	An internal command that displays the version of DOS used on a computer system

QUESTIONS

1. Identify two important types of operations performed by operating system software.
2. On what types of systems do you use MS-DOS and PC-DOS?
3. What is a filename, and why is it important?
4. What is a drive name, and why is it important?
5. What is the current, or default, drive?
6. What is the difference between a cold and a warm boot?
7. What is the difference between an internal and an external command? Give an example of each type of command.
8. What information does the DOS prompt provide?
9. Name one reason it is useful to know the version of DOS installed on your computer system. How do you find out what that version is?
10. After you type a command at the DOS prompt, what must you do for DOS to execute the command?
11. If DOS displays the message "Bad command or file name" when you enter a command, what is the likely cause of the error?
12. How would you change the date on a computer system from March 20, 1994, to March 21, 1994?
13. What function key can you use at the DOS prompt to repeat the last DOS command that you entered?
14. What does DOSKEY do, and how do you use it?
15. When you check the time on your computer system, you find that the time is set at 7:15 a.m., but the time is actually 7:25 p.m. What command can you enter to correct this setting, and how would you enter it?
16. What does DOS do when it formats a diskette? What is a track? What is a sector?
17. What are the two common storage capacities for double-density and high-density diskettes?

Ello!

18. What is an allocation unit?

19. What features account for the different storage capacities of double-density, high-density and extra-high-density diskettes?

20. What must you specify when you use the FORMAT command?

21. What command would you use to format a double-density diskette with a storage capacity of 720K in a high-density disk drive with a storage capacity of 1.44M?

22. What command would you use to format a high-density diskette with a storage capacity of 1.4M in an extra-high-density disk drive with a storage capacity of 2.88M?

23. What happens if you format a double-density diskette in a high-density drive and do not specify the storage capacity of the double-density diskette?

24. What is a volume label?

25. What is a switch? How are switches used? Give one example of a switch.

26. How do you change the default drive?

27. What is the Help switch and how do you use it?

28. What command can you use to make a copy of a diskette? How does it work?

29. What command would you enter to perform a disk copy if the DOS prompt is C:\ but the source and target diskettes are in drive A?

30. When you perform a disk copy, what two features must the diskettes have in common?

TUTORIAL ASSIGNMENTS

1. **Issuing DOS Commands**: After you boot your computer system and access the DOS prompt, use DOS commands to answer the following questions. List the full command that you use for each step, and answer the questions.
   a. What version of DOS is installed on your computer system? *6.20*
   b. Clear the screen. *DONE*
   c. Insert a formatted diskette into drive A or B and change to that drive. *DONE*
   d. Clear the screen. *DONE*
   e. After DOS executes a command, does DOS always return to the same drive? How can you tell? *YES, displayed on screen*

2. **Setting the Time**: Assume that the time on your computer system is incorrect. Adjust the time in each of the following steps, list the full command or commands that you use, and answer the questions.
   a. What is the current setting for the time on your computer system?
   b. If the time is an a.m. time, change it to a p.m. time. If the time is a p.m. time, change it to an a.m. time. How did you verify this change?
   c. Change the time to 7:30 without specifying an a.m. or p.m. time. Then, check the time. Is DOS using an a.m. or a p.m. time? What does this feature tell you about DOS?
   d. Change the time to 7:30 p.m.
   e. Set the time back to the correct time.

3. **Using the Help Switch**: As you perform the following steps, list the command that you use, and answer any questions.

Pg 20

   a. Use the Help switch to display help information on the FORMAT command.
   b. What parameter does DOS require for the FORMAT command?
   c. What format capacities can you specify for the Format Capacity switch?
   d. Print a copy of this Help screen.

4. **Formatting Diskettes**: Format a new diskette using drive A or drive B. As you format the diskette, answer the following questions. *Be sure you use a new diskette for this exercise. If you format your Tutorial Disk or Exercise Disk, you will erase all the information on the diskette.*

Pg 25-26

   a. When DOS starts to format the diskette, what storage capacity does it use for the diskette?
   b. After the diskette is formatted, how many total bytes are available? Are there any bad, or defective, sectors? What is the size of an allocation unit on the diskette?
   c. You should be able to tell from the size of the allocation unit whether you are using a double-density or a high-density diskette. Which type of diskette are you using?
   d. Did you assign a volume label to the diskette? If so, what volume label did you use?
   e. Print a copy of the information DOS displays on the screen about the formatting process.

5. **Copying a Diskette**: Use the DISKCOPY command to make a copy of your Tutorial Disk from drive C. Since you have not made any changes to your Tutorial Disk or Exercise Disk, you can use the Exercise Disk as the target diskette. If you completed Tutorial Assignment 4 and formatted a new diskette, you can use that new diskette as your target disk. As you copy the Tutorial Disk, answer the following questions:
   a. The Tutorial Disk is a double-density diskette. What type of diskette must you use to perform the disk copy?
   b. What is the density of the diskette drive you are using?
   c. What command did you enter to perform a disk copy from drive C?
   d. Does the DISKCOPY command warn you that it is replacing the contents of the target diskette?

TUTORIAL **2**

Displaying Directories

OBJECTIVES

In this tutorial you will learn to:

- Display a directory of filenames
- Use switches with the DIR command
- Display filenames one screen at a time
- Produce a wide directory
- Display files by name, extension, size, and date and time
- Use wildcards to select groups of files
- Combine wildcards and switches
- Specify default settings for the DIR command
- View the contents of the DOS environment
- Use a graphical user interface
- Start the DOS Shell
- Use a mouse
- Customize the DOS Shell for graphics mode
- Change the directory display in the DOS Shell
- Use wildcards in the DOS Shell
- Exit the DOS Shell

Imagine you are starting a small company with a business acquaintance. This company will prepare high-quality business documents for clients, such as résumés, cover letters, flyers, brochures, and newsletters. Your business partner has already created computer files for anticipating start-up costs, projecting income, and preparing checklists for equipment and insurance as well as templates for preparing client business documents. **Templates** are files that contain the general format or layout of a document but little or no data.

Your business partner provides you with a copy of this diskette. Before you meet with your partner to discuss the next phase in opening this business, you want to check the contents of the diskette to verify that it contains all the templates and start-up files that your new business needs.

◆

DISPLAYING A DIRECTORY

Your first step is to view the names assigned to the files on this diskette. You can use the DIR command to display a list, or **directory**, of the files stored on a diskette or a hard disk. When you use the DIR command, you must specify the name of the disk drive if it is different from the current drive. The format of the DIR command is

DIR [*drive name*:]

The DIR command is an internal command.

Before you start working with DOS, it is a good idea to install DOSKEY so that you can recall commands you previously entered at the DOS prompt. After you install this utility, DOSKEY stores a list of the commands that you enter at the DOS prompt in an area of memory called the **command stack**. You can then press [↑] (Up Arrow) or [↓] (Down Arrow) to step backward or forward through the list of commands in the command stack. Instead of repeatedly typing a command, you can use these arrow keys to find a copy of the command you need.

To activate DOSKEY:

1. Power on your computer system, and be sure you see the C:\> prompt displayed on the screen. If you see a prompt for some other drive, type **C:** and press **[Enter]** to change to drive C.

2. Type **DOSKEY** and press **[Enter]**. If you are using DOS 5.0 or 6.0, DOS will display the message "DOSKey installed" if DOSKEY is not already installed on your computer. If you do not see this message with DOS 5.0 or 6.0, DOSKEY is already installed. DOS 6.2 will not display a message.

Now you are ready to view a directory of the filenames stored on the diskette provided by your business partner.

To display a directory of filenames:

1. Insert the Tutorial Disk into drive A or B.

2. Type **DIR**, press **[Spacebar]**, type the name of the drive (**A:** or **B:**), and press **[Enter]**. Be sure you leave a space between the DIR command and

the drive name. Also, remember to type the colon (:) after the drive letter. DOS displays a directory of your diskette (Figure 2-1).

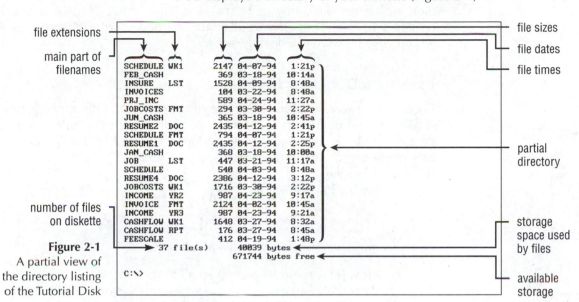

file extensions

main part of filenames

number of files on diskette

Figure 2-1
A partial view of the directory listing of the Tutorial Disk

file sizes

file dates

file times

partial directory

storage space used by files

available storage

```
SCHEDULE WK1      2147 04-07-94   1:21p
FEB_CASH           369 03-18-94  10:14a
INSURE   LST      1528 04-09-94   8:48a
INVOICES           104 03-22-94   8:48a
PRJ_INC            589 04-24-94  11:27a
JOBCOSTS FMT       294 03-30-94   2:22p
JUN_CASH           365 03-18-94  10:45a
RESUME2  DOC      2435 04-12-94   2:41p
SCHEDULE FMT       794 04-07-94   1:21p
RESUME1  DOC      2435 04-12-94   2:25p
JAN_CASH           368 03-18-94  10:00a
JOB      LST       447 03-21-94  11:17a
SCHEDULE           540 04-03-94   8:48a
RESUME4  DOC      2386 04-12-94   3:12p
JOBCOSTS WK1      1716 03-30-94   2:22p
INCOME   YR2       987 04-23-94   9:17a
INVOICE  FMT      2124 04-02-94  10:45a
INCOME   YR3       987 04-23-94   9:21a
CASHFLOW WK1      1648 03-27-94   8:32a
CASHFLOW RPT       176 03-27-94   8:45a
FEESCALE           412 04-19-94   1:48p
        37 file(s)      40039 bytes
                      671744 bytes free

c:\>
```

Through a process called **scrolling**, DOS adjusts the screen view because the monitor can display only 25 lines at one time. Once DOS scrolls through the first part of the directory list, a partial directory remains on the screen. DOS lists the files in **disk order**—the order in which DOS keeps track of the files on the diskette. If your directory is listed in a different order from the one shown in Figure 2-1, ask your instructor or technical support person to restore the DOS default settings so that DOS displays the filenames in disk order.

The directory contains five columns of information:

◆ The first column shows the main part of the filename. As you learned in Tutorial 1, a filename can have two parts—the main part of the filename and an optional file extension. The main part of the filename is one to eight characters in length. For example, the last file on the list in Figure 2-1 is named FEESCALE.

◆ The second column shows the file extension for those files that have one. The file extension is one to three additional characters in length. The last file, FEESCALE, does not have a file extension. The file listed before it, CASHFLOW.RPT, has the file extension RPT, an abbreviation for "report." Because the main part of the filename and the file extension are listed in two separate columns on the directory listing for ease of use, you do not see a period separating the two parts of the filename, although you would always use one as a separator.

◆ The third column lists the size of each file in bytes (or characters). For example, FEESCALE is 412 bytes in size. When it displays file sizes, DOS 6.2 uses commas to offset every three places to the left of the decimal point.

◆ The fourth column shows the date that each file was either created or last modified. For example, FEESCALE was created or last saved on April 19, 1994. Each time you save a file to disk, DOS records the current date with the filename.

◆ The fifth column shows the time that each file was created or last modified. For example, FEESCALE was created or last saved at 1:48 p.m. DOS also records the time with the filename when you save a file to disk.

Below the directory listing, DOS shows the total number of files and the total disk storage space used by those files. The Tutorial Disk has a total of 37 files, which use 40,039 bytes of space. A total of 671,744 free bytes of space remain on the diskette. If your diskette has bad sectors, then the total space left on your diskette will be different.

Pausing a Directory Listing

Because you were unable to see the first part of this directory listing due to scrolling, you decide to try the Pause switch with the DIR command. The **Pause switch**, /P, modifies the DIR command so that DOS displays a directory listing one screen at a time, pausing to give you a chance to read the information on the screen.

Let's try the Pause switch.

To view a directory listing one screen at a time:

1. Press [↑] (Up Arrow) once to recall the command DIR A: or DIR B:. Press **[Spacebar]** and type **/P**. The command should now read "DIR A: /P." Press **[Enter]**. DOS displays the first screen, which contains part of the directory. See Figure 2-2. At the top of the screen, the DIR command displays the volume label. If you did not assign a volume name to the diskette when you formatted it, DOS will tell you that the volume in the drive has no label. In this figure, DOS also shows the diskette's serial number. On the third line, DOS informs you that you are seeing a directory for a specific disk drive. In Figure 2-2, the listing is for drive A. If your current drive is drive B, this line will read "Directory of B:\." At the bottom of this screen, DOS displays a prompt to press any key to continue. As noted in the previous tutorial, certain keys do not work.

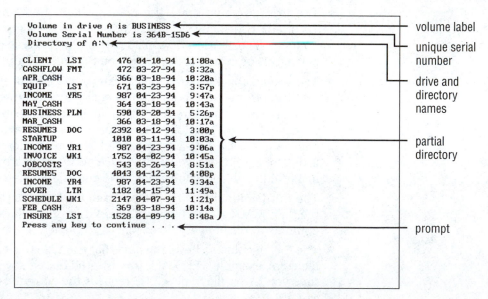

Figure 2-2
DOS pauses after displaying the first screen of the directory

2. Press **[Spacebar]** or any other key to continue. DOS displays the second, and last, screen with the remainder of the directory. See Figure 2-3. At the top of the directory listing on this screen, DOS displays the message "(continuing A:\)" to remind you that you are viewing a directory listing of the files stored in the root directory of drive A (or drive B).

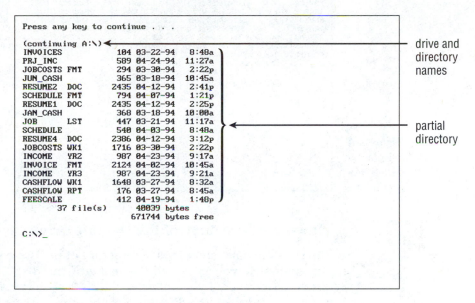

```
Press any key to continue . . .

(continuing A:\)◀──────────────────────── drive and
INVOICES          104 03-22-94   8:48a ╲      directory
PRJ_INC           589 04-24-94  11:27a         names
JOBCOSTS FMT      294 03-30-94   2:22p
JUN_CASH          365 03-18-94  10:45a
RESUME2  DOC     2435 04-12-94   2:41p
SCHEDULE FMT      794 04-07-94   1:21p
RESUME1  DOC     2435 04-12-94   2:25p
JAN_CASH          368 03-18-94  10:00a
JOB      LST      447 03-21-94  11:17a ◀──────── partial
SCHEDULE          540 04-03-94   8:48a         directory
RESUME4  DOC     2386 04-12-94   3:12p
JOBCOSTS WK1     1716 03-30-94   2:22p
INCOME   YR2      987 04-23-94   9:17a
INVOICE  FMT     2124 04-02-94  10:45a
INCOME   YR3      987 04-23-94   9:21a
CASHFLOW WK1     1648 03-27-94   8:32a
CASHFLOW RPT      176 03-27-94   8:45a
FEESCALE          412 04-19-94   1:48p ╱
        37 file(s)      40039 bytes
                       671744 bytes free

C:\>_
```

Figure 2-3
DOS displays the next, and last, screen of the directory

Viewing a Wide Directory Listing

Another approach for viewing directory listings with many files is to use the Wide switch. The **Wide switch**, /W, displays filenames in five columns across the width of the screen and thus enables you to view more filenames at once. Although this switch displays the full filename, with a period separating the main part of the filename from the file extension, it does not show the file size, date, and time.

Let's view a directory listing using the Wide switch. Remember that you can use DOSKEY to recall the last command that you entered. Then you can modify, or **edit**, the command so it uses a different switch.

To view a wide directory listing:

1. Type **CLS** and press **[Enter]**. DOS clears the screen of the last directory listing.

2. Press **[↑]** (Up Arrow) twice to recall the last DIR command. Press **[Backspace]** until you delete the "P." Then type **W**. The command should read "DIR A:/W." Now press **[Enter]**. DOS produces a directory listing that includes all the files on the Tutorial Disk on one screen. See Figure 2-4 on the following page.

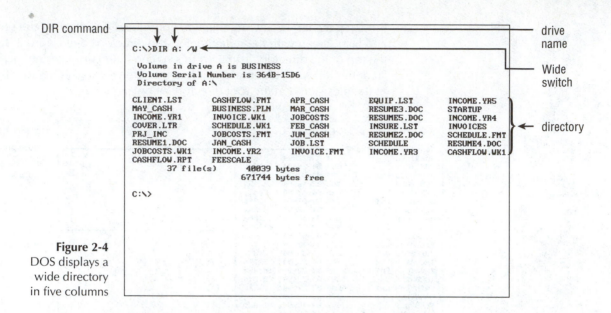

DIR command

drive
name

Wide
switch

directory

Figure 2-4
DOS displays a
wide directory
in five columns

Viewing a Directory of the Default Drive

The DIR command shows you a directory of the drive you specify. In the previous examples, you specified the name of the disk drive that contains your diskette. However, if you do not specify a drive name, DOS will look to the DOS prompt and display the directory for that drive. Many DOS commands operate in the same way.

To view a directory of a diskette drive without specifying the drive name:

1. Type **A:** or the drive name that contains your Tutorial Disk and press **[Enter]**. DOS updates the DOS prompt to show you the current drive.

2. Type **DIR /P** and press **[Enter]**. The DIR command displays a directory of your diskette one screen at a time, but you did not specify the drive name this time. Instead, DOS uses the current drive specified in the DOS prompt.

3. Press **[Spacebar]** or any other key to view the next screen and return to the DOS prompt.

Specifying a Sort Order for Directory Listings

Next, you want to verify that your business partner included the file that contains the business plan. Because DOS does not display the directory in an order that makes it easy to find a file, you decide to use the **Order switch**, /O, which displays filenames in alphabetical order. You can also combine this switch with the Pause switch to view one screen at a time. Let's try it.

To display the directory one screen at a time in alphabetical order by filename:

1. Press [↑] once to recall the last DOS command, DIR /P. Press **[Spacebar]** and type **/O**. *Be sure you type the letter "O" and not a zero for the Order switch.* The command should read "DIR /P /O." Now press **[Enter]**. DOS displays the first screen of filenames in alphabetical order. See Figure 2-5. The second file, BUSINESS.PLN, is the one that you want to locate.

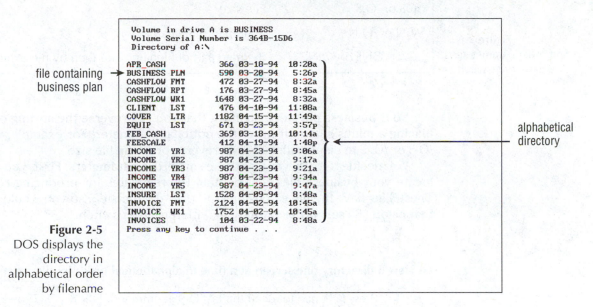

file containing business plan

alphabetical directory

Figure 2-5
DOS displays the directory in alphabetical order by filename

```
Volume in drive A is BUSINESS
Volume Serial Number is 364B-15D6
Directory of A:\

APR_CASH          366 03-18-94   10:20a
BUSINESS PLN      590 03-20-94    5:26p
CASHFLOW FMT      472 03-27-94    8:32a
CASHFLOW RPT      176 03-27-94    8:45a
CASHFLOW WK1     1648 03-27-94    8:32a
CLIENT   LST      476 04-10-94   11:08a
COVER    LTR     1182 04-15-94   11:49a
EQUIP    LST      671 03-23-94    3:57p
FEB_CASH          369 03-18-94   10:14a
FEESCALE          412 04-19-94    1:48p
INCOME   YR1      987 04-23-94    9:06a
INCOME   YR2      987 04-23-94    9:17a
INCOME   YR3      987 04-23-94    9:21a
INCOME   YR4      987 04-23-94    9:34a
INCOME   YR5      987 04-23-94    9:47a
INSURE   LST     1528 04-09-94    8:48a
INVOICE  FMT     2124 04-02-94   10:45a
INVOICE  WK1     1752 04-02-94   10:45a
INVOICES          104 03-22-94    8:48a
Press any key to continue . . .
```

2. Press **[Spacebar]** or any other key. DOS displays the filenames in the next, and last, screen in alphabetical order. DOS also returns to the DOS prompt.

Using Sort Order Parameters

The ability to display an alphabetical list of filenames is important for the daily operation of your business. However, you and your business partner want to quickly locate files with similar types of information by their file extensions, as well as recently created files by using the file date. Furthermore, you want to check file dates and file sizes periodically to determine how efficiently you are using disk space. When your disk begins to fill, you might need to store, or **archive**, large and less frequently used client files on other diskettes.

Your business partner informs you that you can use **sort order parameters** with the Order switch to view a directory in order by file extension, size, and date and time. These sort order parameters are codes added to the Order switch (Figure 2-6 on the following page).

Sort Order Parameters	Displays Filenames in Order By
/OE or /O:E	File extension only
/OEN or /O:EN	File extension, then by main part of filename
/OD or /O:D	File date and time
/OS or /O:S	File size
/ON or /O:N	Main part of filename only
/O or /ONE or /O:NE	By main part of filename and then by file extension

Figure 2-6
Sort order parameters
for the Order switch

Your business partner also notes that you can reverse the sorting order by placing a minus sign in front of the optional parameter. For example, you use /O-S or /O:-S to display filenames in reverse order by file size.

You decide to try several of these sort order parameters. First, you want to locate your business files that contain the templates for producing résumés. These files have the file extension DOC (for "document"), so you would use the **Extension** (E) **sort order parameter** with the Order switch.

To view a directory one screen at a time in alphabetical order by file extension:

1. Press [↑] once to recall the last DOS command, DIR /P /O. Type **E**. *Be sure you do not include a space between the /O and E.* The command should read "DIR /P /OE." Then press **[Enter]**. DOS displays a directory and stops after the first screen of filenames. DOS first lists files without extensions, and then lists the files in alphabetical order by file extension. See Figure 2-7. The résumé template files are listed together by file extension. However, the main part of the filename is not listed in order.

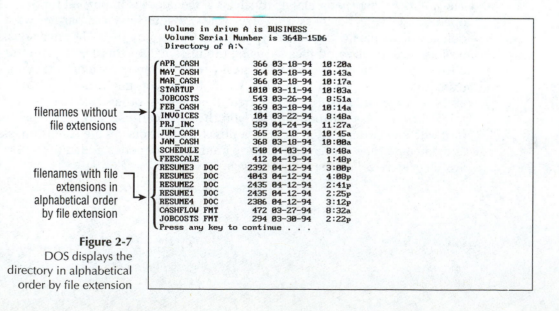

filenames without
file extensions →

filenames with file
extensions in
alphabetical order
by file extension

```
Volume in drive A is BUSINESS
Volume Serial Number is 364B-15D6
Directory of A:\

APR_CASH          366 03-18-94   10:20a
MAY_CASH          364 03-18-94   10:43a
MAR_CASH          366 03-18-94   10:17a
STARTUP          1010 03-11-94   10:03a
JOBCOSTS          543 03-26-94    8:51a
FEB_CASH          369 03-18-94   10:14a
INVOICES          104 03-22-94    8:48a
PRJ_INC           589 04-24-94   11:27a
JUN_CASH          365 03-18-94   10:45a
JAN_CASH          368 03-18-94   10:00a
SCHEDULE          540 04-03-94    8:48a
FEESCALE          412 04-19-94    1:48p
RESUME3  DOC     2392 04-12-94    3:00p
RESUME5  DOC     4043 04-12-94    4:00p
RESUME2  DOC     2435 04-12-94    2:41p
RESUME1  DOC     2435 04-12-94    2:25p
RESUME4  DOC     2386 04-12-94    3:12p
CASHFLOW FMT      472 03-27-94    8:32a
JOBCOSTS FMT      294 03-30-94    2:22p
Press any key to continue . . .
```

Figure 2-7
DOS displays the
directory in alphabetical
order by file extension

2. Press **[Spacebar]** or any other key to continue. DOS displays the remainder of the sorted directory and the DOS prompt.

In a rush on a busy day, you might need to quickly locate important client files that you created or modified that day. You can display a directory in order by date by using the **Date** (D) **sort order parameter** with the Order switch. When you use this switch, DOS lists the files in order by date, from the file with the oldest date to the most recently created file. However, because you need to locate newly created files quickly, you can reverse this order by placing a minus sign in front of the Date sort order parameter. DOS lists the files in reverse order by date, with the most recently created files listed first.

To view a directory by file date from the most recent date:

1. Press **[↑]** once to recall the last DOS command, DIR /P /OE. Press **[Backspace]** until you delete the "E." Then type **-D**. *Be sure you do not include a blank space between the /O and -D.* The command should read "DIR /P /O-D." Then press **[Enter]**. DOS displays filenames in order from the most recent file dates to the oldest file date. See Figure 2-8.

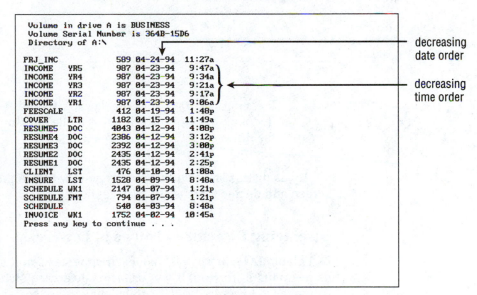

```
Volume in drive A is BUSINESS
Volume Serial Number is 364B-15D6
Directory of A:\
PRJ_INC              589 04-24-94  11:27a
INCOME   YR5         987 04-23-94   9:47a
INCOME   YR4         987 04-23-94   9:34a
INCOME   YR3         987 04-23-94   9:21a
INCOME   YR2         987 04-23-94   9:17a
INCOME   YR1         987 04-23-94   9:06a
FEESCALE             412 04-19-94   1:48p
COVER    LTR        1182 04-15-94  11:49a
RESUME5  DOC        4043 04-12-94   4:08p
RESUME4  DOC        2386 04-12-94   3:12p
RESUME3  DOC        2392 04-12-94   3:00p
RESUME2  DOC        2435 04-12-94   2:41p
RESUME1  DOC        2435 04-12-94   2:25p
CLIENT   LST         476 04-10-94  11:08a
INSURE   LST        1528 04-09-94   8:48a
SCHEDULE WK1        2147 04-07-94   1:21p
SCHEDULE FMT         794 04-07-94   1:21p
SCHEDULE             540 04-03-94   8:48a
INVOICE  WK1        1752 04-02-94  10:45a
Press any key to continue . . .
```

decreasing date order

decreasing time order

Figure 2-8
DOS displays the directory in reverse order by file date and time

2. Press **[Spacebar]** or any other key to continue. DOS displays the remainder of the directory. Files with the oldest file dates are listed last in the directory.

Finally, you want to check file sizes periodically to determine how efficiently you are using storage space on your diskette. You can use the **Size** (S) **sort order parameter** of the Order switch to list files from the smallest to the largest, or in reverse order from the largest to the smallest. Because large files have the greatest impact on the availability of disk space, let's list file sizes in reverse order.

To view a directory in reverse order by file size:

1. Press [↑] to recall the last DOS command, DIR /P /O-D. Press **[Backspace]** until you delete the "D." Then type **S**. The command should read "DIR /P /O-S." Then press **[Enter]**. DOS displays the first screen of directory information. The files are listed in reverse order by file size, starting with the largest file on the diskette. See Figure 2-9.

```
Volume in drive A is BUSINESS
Volume Serial Number is 364B-15D6
Directory of A:\
                                            ──────────   decreasing
RESUME5  DOC     4043 04-12-94   4:08p                   order by file
RESUME2  DOC     2435 04-12-94   2:41p                   size
RESUME1  DOC     2435 04-12-94   2:25p
RESUME3  DOC     2392 04-12-94   3:00p
RESUME4  DOC     2386 04-12-94   3:12p
SCHEDULE WK1     2147 04-07-94   1:21p
INVOICE  FMT     2124 04-02-94  10:45a
INVOICE  WK1     1752 04-02-94  10:45a
JOBCOSTS WK1     1716 03-30-94   2:22p
CASHFLOW WK1     1648 03-27-94   8:32a
INSURE   LST     1528 04-09-94   8:48a
COVER    LTR     1182 04-15-94  11:49a
STARTUP          1010 03-11-94  10:03a
INCOME   YR5      987 04-23-94   9:47a
INCOME   YR1      987 04-23-94   9:06a
INCOME   YR4      987 04-23-94   9:34a
INCOME   YR2      987 04-23-94   9:17a
INCOME   YR3      987 04-23-94   9:21a
SCHEDULE FMT      794 04-07-94   1:21p
Press any key to continue . . .
```

Figure 2-9
DOS displays the directory in reverse order by file size

2. Press **[Spacebar]** or any other key to continue. DOS displays the remainder of the directory. The last files in the directory are the smallest files on the diskette.

By using this last option, you can quickly locate the largest files on the first screen and decide whether to archive these files.

Displaying Directory Listings in Lowercase

By default, DOS displays filenames in uppercase, and many people find the filenames difficult to read. If you use the **Lowercase switch**, /L, DOS displays the filenames in lowercase so that the filenames are easier to read. Let's try it.

To display an alphabetical directory in lowercase:

1. Press [↑] until you recall the command, DIR /P /O-S. Press **[Backspace]** until you delete the "-S." Next, press **[Spacebar]** and type **/L**. The command should read "DIR /P /O /L." Then press **[Enter]**. DOS displays the first screen of directory information. The filenames are listed in alphabetical order and in lowercase. See Figure 2-10.

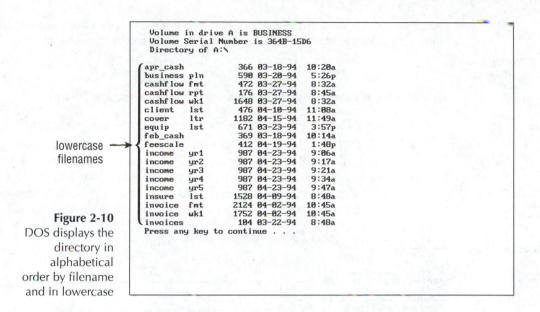

```
Volume in drive A is BUSINESS
Volume Serial Number is 364B-15D6
Directory of A:\

apr_cash          366  03-18-94   10:20a
business  pln     590  03-20-94    5:26p
cashflow  fmt     472  03-27-94    8:32a
cashflow  rpt     176  03-27-94    8:45a
cashflow  wk1    1648  03-27-94    8:32a
client    lst     476  04-10-94   11:08a
cover     ltr    1182  04-15-94   11:49a
equip     lst     671  03-23-94    3:57p
feb_cash          369  03-18-94   10:14a
feescale          412  04-19-94    1:48p
income    yr1     987  04-23-94    9:06a
income    yr2     987  04-23-94    9:17a
income    yr3     987  04-23-94    9:21a
income    yr4     987  04-23-94    9:34a
income    yr5     987  04-23-94    9:47a
insure    lst    1528  04-09-94    8:48a
invoice   fmt    2124  04-02-94   10:45a
invoice   wk1    1752  04-02-94   10:45a
invoices          104  03-22-94    8:48a
Press any key to continue . . .
```

lowercase filenames

Figure 2-10
DOS displays the directory in alphabetical order by filename and in lowercase

2. Press **[Spacebar]** or any other key to continue. DOS displays the remainder of the directory in lowercase and the DOS prompt.

The DIR command and its wide assortment of switches are invaluable for identifying which files are stored on a diskette or for locating information on files. If you forget which diskette contains a client file that you need, you can quickly check a diskette's contents with this command. The DIR command is also useful when you are looking for a specific copy of a file. You can check the dates and times of each version of that file to find the one you need.

USING WILDCARDS

The diskette provided by your business partner contains 37 files. You expect the number to increase as your business gets under way. When you need to use a group of files, such as the résumé templates, you want to select them without having to view the names of all the other files on the diskette. To simplify the process of selecting files with similar filenames, you can use **wildcards** to substitute for part or all of a filename when executing the DIR command and other DOS commands that operate on files.

There are two wildcard characters—the question mark and the asterisk. The **question mark** (?) substitutes for a single character in a filename, whereas the **asterisk** (*) substitutes for one or more characters. You can also combine wildcards with switches to improve the results of your selections.

Using the Question Mark Wildcard

One common use of the question mark wildcard is to select a group of files that have filenames that are identical except for one character. For example, the résumé template files on your diskette are named RESUME1.DOC, RESUME2.DOC, RESUME3.DOC, RESUME4.DOC, and RESUME5.DOC. The only difference in the names of these files is the character in the seventh position of the main part of the filename. To view a directory of just these files, you can substitute the question mark wildcard for the seventh character. Let's select these files.

To select the résumé template files using the question mark wildcard:

1. Type **CLS** and press **[Enter]**. DOS clears the screen of the last directory.

2. Type **DIR RESUME?.DOC   /O** and press **[Enter]**. DOS displays an alphabetical directory with the five résumé template files. See Figure 2-11. You can also omit the file extension by typing DIR RESUME? /O, and DOS will produce the same selection. If you do not specify a file extension, DOS automatically selects filenames with or without a file extension.

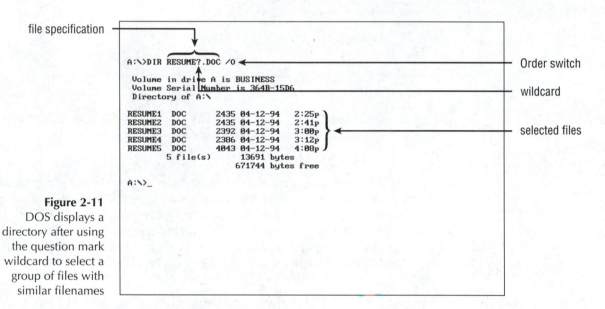

file specification

Order switch

wildcard

selected files

Figure 2-11
DOS displays a directory after using the question mark wildcard to select a group of files with similar filenames

The filename included with a DIR command, with or without wildcards, is called a **file specification**. DOS uses the file specification to select a single file with a specific filename or a group of files with similar filenames.

Next, you want to display a directory of your business files that track cash flow on a monthly basis. The files are named JAN_CASH, FEB_CASH, MAR_CASH, APR_CASH, MAY_CASH, and JUN_CASH. The first three characters in these filenames are different. To select these files as a group, you decide to use a question mark wildcard for each of the first three characters.

To view a directory of your monthly cashflow files in date order:

1. Press **[↑]** until you recall the CLS command and press **[Enter]**.

2. Type **DIR ???_CASH /OD** and press **[Enter]**. To type the underscore (_), press [Shift] and the key with the underscore and dash symbols. DOS displays your six monthly cashflow files. The Date (D) sort order parameter lists the files in month order by using the file date *and* time. See Figure 2-12.

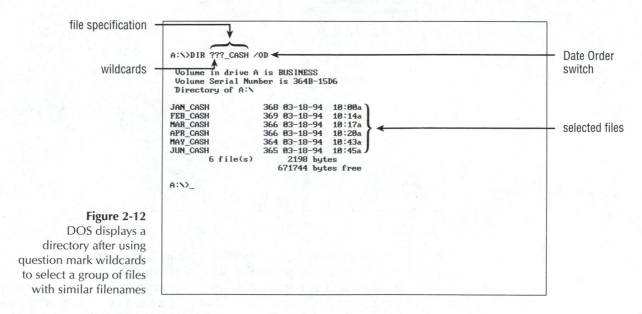

file specification

wildcards

Date Order switch

selected files

Figure 2-12
DOS displays a directory after using question mark wildcards to select a group of files with similar filenames

It is important to note that you cannot use an asterisk in place of the three question mark wildcards. If you do, DOS ignores anything after the asterisk and selects all the files.

Using the Asterisk Wildcard

You next want to display a directory of the files that contain your business checklists for insurance, equipment, jobs, and clients. Each of these files has the file extension LST. Because the filename represents more than one character, you use the asterisk wildcard to substitute for the main part of the filename.

To select your business checklist files with the asterisk wildcard:

1. Press [↑] until you recall the CLS command and press **[Enter]**. DOS clears the screen.

2. Type **DIR *.LST /O** and press **[Enter]**. DOS displays the names of all files with the LST file extension. See Figure 2-13 on the following page. The asterisk substitutes for any combination of characters in the main part of the filename.

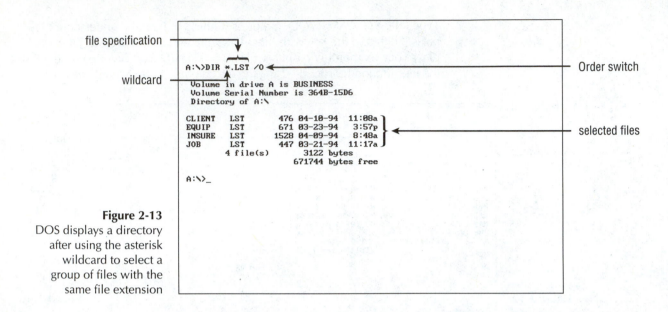

file specification

wildcard

Order switch

selected files

Figure 2-13
DOS displays a directory
after using the asterisk
wildcard to select a
group of files with the
same file extension

Another common use of the asterisk wildcard is to select all filenames that begin with a certain character or combination of characters. For example, suppose you want to locate the business file that contains your projected income for the first six months of your business, but you do not remember its exact name or even whether it has a file extension. All you remember is that "P" is the first character of the filename.

To locate this file:

1. Press [↑] until you recall the CLS command and press **[Enter]**. DOS clears the screen.

2. Type **DIR P*.*** and press **[Enter]**. DOS locates one file that meets this condition, and its filename is PRJ_INC. See Figure 2-14. You can obtain the same result by just typing "DIR P*" and pressing the Enter key. If you do not use an asterisk for the file extension, DOS assumes you want filenames with or without a file extension.

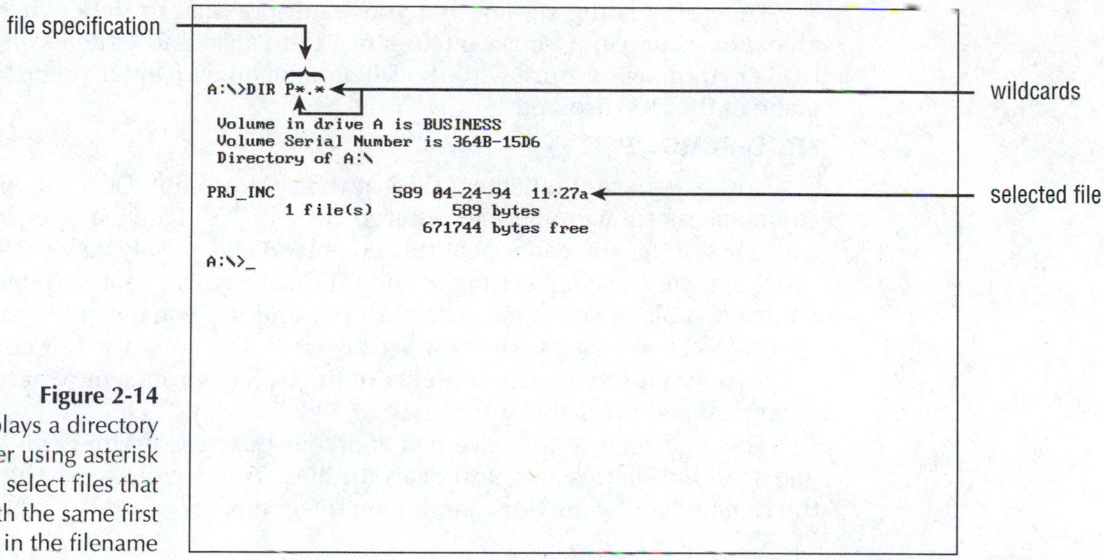

file specification

```
A:\>DIR P*.*

 Volume in drive A is BUSINESS
 Volume Serial Number is 364B-15D6
 Directory of A:\

PRJ_INC          589 04-24-94  11:27a
        1 file(s)          589 bytes
                        671744 bytes free

A:\>_
```

wildcards

selected file

Figure 2-14
DOS displays a directory
after using asterisk
wildcards to select files that
start with the same first
character in the filename

In your business, you can use wildcards with switches as one more tool for quickly locating and selecting files.

SPECIFYING DEFAULT SWITCHES

After examining the use of various switches for the DIR command, you realize that you and your business partner will commonly use the Order and Pause switches for directory listings. Rather than enter these switches manually each time you need them and rather than recall them with DOSKEY, you can specify default switches for the DIR command. DOS will automatically use these switches each time you enter the DIR command.

DOS stores important settings in a small area of memory called the **DOS environment**. As you work on your computer, DOS checks the DOS environment if it needs a specific setting. DOS assigns each setting in the DOS environment to an **environment variable**. For example, DOS uses the DIRCMD environment variable for default switches for the DIR command.

The SET command is an internal command that assigns a setting to an environment variable. Its syntax is as follows:

SET *environment variable = string*

The **string** is the setting that you want to assign to the environment variable. For example, if you want to store the Pause and Order switches in the DOS environment for use with the DIR command, you enter the following command at the DOS prompt:

SET DIRCMD=/P /O

Now, whenever you enter "DIR" at the DOS prompt, DOS will execute your command as though you had entered "DIR /P /O." Later, if you prefer to use another setting, you can repeat this command and specify new switches.

When you assign a setting to the DIRCMD environment variable, you must *not* leave a blank space between DIRCMD and the equal sign. If you include a space, DOS does not use the new setting when you enter the DIR command.

If you want to view the contents of the DOS environment, you type the SET command and press the Enter key.

This DOS feature will save you and your business partner valuable time as you search diskettes and hard disks for files. You decide to use this feature for the remainder of your work session on the computer.

To specify default switches for the DIR command:

1. Type **SET DIRCMD=/P /O** and press **[Enter]**. DOS displays the DOS prompt. If DOS displays an error message indicating that you are out of environment space, the DOS environment does not contain any additional room to store new settings. Ask your instructor or technical support person to adjust the size of the DOS environment, and then try again.

   Now verify that this setting is stored in the DOS environment.

2. Type **SET** and press **[Enter]**. DOS displays settings in the DOS environment. See Figure 2-15. Your settings will be different. The variable DIRCMD and the Pause and Order switches are listed as the last setting in the DOS environment. Later, you will examine the use of some of these other settings.

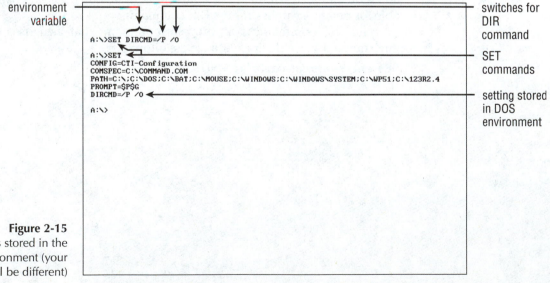

Figure 2-15
Settings stored in the DOS environment (your settings will be different)

Now display a directory of your business files.

3. Type **DIR** and press **[Enter]**. *Do not type any switches*. Because you have set the /P and /O switches as defaults, DOS automatically pauses after each screen and displays an alphabetical directory. See Figure 2-16.

```
Volume in drive A is BUSINESS
Volume Serial Number is 364B-15D6
Directory of A:\

APR_CASH          366 03-18-94  10:20a
BUSINESS PLN      590 03-20-94   5:26p
CASHFLOW FMT      472 03-27-94   8:32a
CASHFLOW RPT      176 03-27-94   8:45a
CASHFLOW WK1     1648 03-27-94   8:32a
CLIENT   LST      476 04-10-94  11:08a
COVER    LTR     1182 04-15-94  11:49a
EQUIP    LST      671 03-23-94   3:57p
FEB_CASH          369 03-18-94  10:14a
FEESCALE          412 04-19-94   1:48p
INCOME   YR1      987 04-23-94   9:06a
INCOME   YR2      987 04-23-94   9:17a
INCOME   YR3      987 04-23-94   9:21a
INCOME   YR4      987 04-23-94   9:34a
INCOME   YR5      987 04-23-94   9:47a
INSURE   LST     1528 04-09-94   8:48a
INVOICE  FMT     2124 04-02-94  10:45a
INVOICE  WK1     1752 04-02-94  10:45a
INVOICES          104 03-22-94   8:48a
Press any key to continue . . .
```

Figure 2-16
The DIR command uses switches stored in the DOS environment to display a directory in alphabetical order and to pause after each screen

4. Press **[Spacebar]** or any other key to continue. DOS redisplays the DOS prompt.

This setting stays in the DOS environment and remains in effect until you specify a new setting, remove this setting, or turn off your computer. To specify a new setting, you enter "SET DIRCMD=" with a list of the new switches you now want to use. To remove this setting from the DOS environment, you type "SET DIRCMD=" without any settings and press the Enter key. Each time you start your computer, you can use this command to specify default switches for the DIR command.

You also can temporarily override these settings by entering the DIR command with the new switch that you want to use. For example, you might want to locate the file that your business partner most recently worked on today. Let's try this feature.

To display filenames in order by date:

1. Press **[↑]** once to recall the last command, DIR. Press **[Spacebar]** and type **/O-D**. The command should read "DIR /O-D." Then, press **[Enter]**. DOS displays the filenames in reverse order by date and time. See Figure 2-17 on the following page. Because you changed the parameter associated with the /O switch, DOS overrides the default setting for the Order switch in the DOS environment. However, DOS still uses the Pause switch.

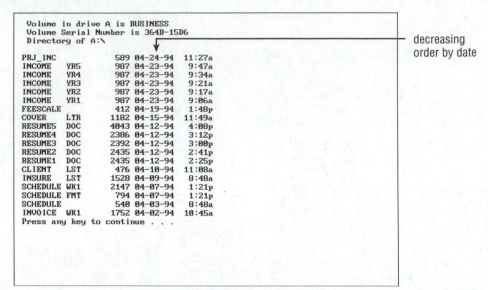

```
Volume in drive A is BUSINESS
Volume Serial Number is 364B-15D6
Directory of A:\

PRJ_INC           589 04-24-94  11:27a
INCOME    YR5     987 04-23-94   9:47a
INCOME    YR4     987 04-23-94   9:34a
INCOME    YR3     987 04-23-94   9:21a
INCOME    YR2     987 04-23-94   9:17a
INCOME    YR1     987 04-23-94   9:06a
FEESCALE          412 04-19-94   1:48p
COVER     LTR    1182 04-15-94  11:49a
RESUME5   DOC    4043 04-12-94   4:00p
RESUME4   DOC    2386 04-12-94   3:12p
RESUME3   DOC    2392 04-12-94   3:00p
RESUME2   DOC    2435 04-12-94   2:41p
RESUME1   DOC    2435 04-12-94   2:25p
CLIENT    LST     476 04-10-94  11:08a
INSURE    LST    1528 04-09-94   8:48a
SCHEDULE  WK1    2147 04-07-94   1:21p
SCHEDULE  FMT     794 04-07-94   1:21p
SCHEDULE          540 04-03-94   8:48a
INVOICE   WK1    1752 04-02-94  10:45a
Press any key to continue . . .
```

decreasing order by date

Figure 2-17
DOS displays a directory in reverse date order, overriding one of the switches in the DOS environment

2. Press **[Spacebar]** or any other key to continue. DOS redisplays the DOS prompt.

This time-saving tool not only simplifies directory operations, but can also streamline your daily business operations and improve efficiency and productivity.

This is a good opportunity to stop for a few minutes and take a break.

USING COMMAND LINE AND GRAPHICAL USER INTERFACES

Now that you are familiar with entering DOS commands at the DOS prompt, you are ready to learn a more visual approach for interacting with DOS. Your business partner tells you about the DOS Shell and explains that it simplifies command operations and saves time and effort.

When you enter a DOS command at the DOS prompt, you are using a **command line interface,** also called a **text user interface** (abbreviated **TUI,** pronounced "tooey"). An **interface** refers to the way in which you interact with the computer system. When you use DOS, your interface is the DOS prompt. When you use a command line interface, you enter commands on a line-by-line basis and wait for the results of each command operation. The only information displayed on the screen is the DOS prompt with the name of the drive and directory. This is the type of interface you have been using so far in these tutorials.

All versions of DOS allow you to interact with DOS using the command line interface. However, starting with DOS 4.0, you can also use a **graphical user interface** (abbreviated **GUI**, pronounced "gooey"), which provides a more visual frame of reference and additional on-screen information for interacting with the operating system. The DOS GUI is the DOS Shell. In the DOS Shell, you work with menus, windows, and **icons** (graphical images or pictures) that represent objects in a computer system, such as a disk drive, directory, program, or file. The DOS Shell contains all the tools you need to work with DOS and your computer system.

The DOS Shells in DOS 4.0 and 4.01 are different from the ones in DOS 5.0, 6.0, and 6.2. However, the DOS Shells in DOS 5.0, 6.0, and 6.2 are almost identical to each other.

Because a picture is worth a thousand words, let's view the DOS Shell so that you have a better idea of what constitutes a graphical user interface.

USING THE DOS SHELL

You decide to compare the use of the DOS Shell with the use of commands at the DOS prompt so that you and your business partner can choose the most effective and efficient way to work on your computer systems to complete business contracts. As an afterthought, you realize that you might complete some of your contract work in client offices. You must know how to work from the DOS Shell *and* from the DOS prompt in the event that the DOS Shell is not available on your clients' computers.

In order to view the DOS Shell, DOS must be able to locate the program that displays this graphical user interface. If you are using a computer system with a hard disk or if you are working on a network, this program must be installed on the hard disk or network in order to be available for your use. Check with your instructor or technical support person to be sure the DOS Shell program is installed on your computer or network.

To access the DOS Shell:

1. If necessary, insert your Tutorial Disk in a diskette drive and change to that drive.

2. Type **DOSSHELL** (as one word with no spaces) and press **[Enter]**. After DOS loads the DOS Shell program into the computer's memory from drive C or the network drive, you will see the DOS Shell screen. See Figure 2-18 on the following page. Because there are different ways to customize the screen view of the DOS Shell, your view might be different from the one in the figure. If you are unable to access the DOS Shell, or if your screen looks different from the screen in Figure 2-18, check with your instructor or technical support person.

title bar →

menu bar →

current drive →

drive window ←

directory tree window →

file list window ←

current directory →

status bar →

program list window ←

Figure 2-18
The MS-DOS Shell displayed in text mode

command key →

mouse pointer

```
                              MS-DOS Shell
 File  Options  View  Tree  Help
 A:\
 [A:]  [B:]  [C:]
┌──────── Directory Tree ────────┐┌──────── A:\*.*  ─────────────┐
 [ ] A:\                          ▶ APR_CASH       366  03-18-94
                                    BUSINESS.PLN    590  03-20-94
                                    CASHFLOW.FMT    472  03-27-94
                                    CASHFLOW.RPT    176  03-27-94
                                    CASHFLOW.WK1  1,648  03-27-94
                                    CLIENT  .LST    476  04-10-94
                                    COVER   .LTR  1,182  04-15-94
                                    EQUIP   .LST    671  03-23-94
┌──────────────────── Main ─────────────────────┐
 Command Prompt
 Editor
 MS-DOS QBasic
 [Disk Utilities]
└────────────────────────────────────────────────┘
 F10=Actions  Shift+F9=Command Prompt              8:12p
```

The view of the DOS Shell as shown in Figure 2-18 is referred to as text mode. In **text mode**, DOS uses standard keyboard characters and symbols to represent drives, directories, programs, and files. When you install DOS, the DOS Shell is automatically installed in text mode. On your system, the DOS Shell might be configured for graphics mode. See Figure 2-19. In **graphics mode**, the DOS Shell uses icons to represent drives, directories, programs, and files. These icons provide a more user-friendly and informative interface. If your screen view looks different from Figure 2-18 or Figure 2-19, see your instructor or technical support person for help in returning it to the default setting or to the setting initially installed with DOS.

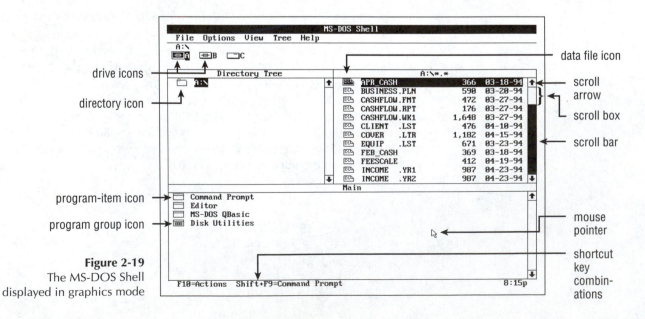

data file icon

drive icons

directory icon

scroll arrow

scroll box

scroll bar

program-item icon

program group icon

mouse pointer

shortcut key combinations

Figure 2-19
The MS-DOS Shell displayed in graphics mode

The DOS Shell screen is divided into areas, or **windows**, which you can customize. At the top of the screen is a **title bar** with the title "MS-DOS Shell." The **menu bar** on the next line contains the following menu names: File, Options, View, Tree, and Help. When you select one of these menu names, a list of options appears. You can select and execute commands from these menus.

The **drive window**, located immediately below the menu bar, shows the current directory and the drives available on your computer system. If your computer system contains a hard drive and two diskette drives, the DOS Shell will list drives A, B, and C. If you are using a network, the DOS Shell will also list network drives, such as drive F, G, or H. The DOS Shell highlights the icon for the current drive. One of the advantages of using the DOS Shell is that you know immediately which drives are included on your computer system.

The DOS Shell uses the **directory tree window** to represent the organization of files on a hard disk or diskette. Currently, all the files on your Tutorial Disk are stored in the root directory of the diskette. The **root directory** is the first and most important directory on a hard disk or diskette. The FORMAT command creates the root directory when it formats a hard disk or diskette. To the right of the directory tree window, the **file list window** shows the files contained in the root directory of your diskette.

The window at the bottom of the screen, with the title "Main," is called the **program list window**, which displays the list of program groups or programs that you can access from the DOS Shell. The **Command Prompt** option allows you to temporarily exit to the DOS prompt. The **Editor** option allows you to use the MS-DOS Editor, a simple text editing utility, from the DOS Shell. The **MS-DOS QBasic** option allows you to use the Quick BASIC programming language included with DOS. The **Disk Utilities** option contains a group of options for using DOS utilities, such as the one for formatting diskettes. You can add software applications, such as WordPerfect or Lotus 1-2-3, to this list so that you can use them directly from the DOS Shell. This feature allows you to organize and access all of the programs you commonly use on your computer system.

Below the Main window is the status bar. The **status bar** displays the shortcut key "F10=Actions" for accessing the menu bar and "Shift+F9=Command Prompt" for temporarily exiting the DOS Shell to display the DOS prompt. Although it is not shown on the status bar, you can also use the Alt (Alternate) key to access the menu bar. The status bar also displays the current time on the far right.

As you work in a window, your reference point is a **selection cursor**, a special type of cursor used in the DOS Shell to highlight a drive, directory name, filename, or program name. When you load the DOS Shell, the selection cursor highlights the current drive in the drive window. You move the selection cursor from window to window by pressing the Tab key or by using a mouse. A **mouse** is a hand-held device that moves a mouse pointer around the screen in the direction that you move the mouse. Once you load the DOS Shell, the **mouse pointer** becomes active and appears as a rectangle in text mode or as an arrow in outline in graphics mode. You use the mouse pointer to select an option displayed on the screen.

You can use the mouse in the DOS Shell, but you cannot use the mouse at the DOS prompt. If you have a mouse connected to your computer system and want to learn how to use it, read the next section. If you are not using a mouse, skip the next section.

USING THE MOUSE

You can perform the following types of operations with the mouse:

◆ When you **point** with the mouse, you move the mouse pointer to a specific area of the screen so that it highlights a menu, command, drive name, file-name, icon, or another object displayed on the screen.

◆ To **click** the left mouse button, you quickly press and release it. Clicking permits you to select a command, drive name, filename, icon, or object on the screen or a specific area of the screen. Note that your mouse might include a right mouse button. When working in the DOS Shell, you use only the *left* mouse button.

◆ When you **double-click** the left mouse button, you quickly press it twice. You double-click to execute a command.

◆ When you **drag** the mouse, you hold down the left mouse button, move the mouse to highlight the area you want to select, and then release the mouse button. You would use this feature, for example, to select a group of file-names or to select and move an object on the screen.

In some cases, you can perform operations more easily with the mouse than with the keyboard; in other instances, the keyboard is easier to use. In these tutorials, you will be given instructions for using both the keyboard and the mouse to complete particular steps. The mouse instructions are indicated by a small mouse icon to the left of the steps.

CUSTOMIZING THE DOS SHELL

You prefer to switch the DOS Shell from text mode to graphics mode on the computer system in your business office so that you and your business part-ner can work with, and benefit from, a graphical user interface. Before you can use graphics mode, however, you must have a graphics adapter (or card) and a monitor that supports graphics mode.

If you are working in a computer lab, you must have permission to change the display mode of the DOS Shell. If you are using the DOS Shell on a network, your network might not permit changes to the configuration of programs such as the DOS Shell. Ask your instructor or technical support person if you can change from the default text mode to graphics mode. If you do not have per-mission to change the display mode of the DOS Shell, read but do not execute the following steps so that you understand the general process for making this change. You might need to customize the DOS Shell on another computer sys-tem in the future.

To customize the DOS Shell so that it uses graphics mode:

1. Press **[F10]** (Actions) to access the menu bar, press **[→]** (Right Arrow) to highlight the Options menu, and press **[Enter]**.

   If you are using the mouse, click on the menu name **Options**.

The DOS Shell displays the Options drop-down menu. See Figure 2-20. Notice that the commands on the Options drop-down menu are listed in two ways: with or without an ellipsis. Those commands that are followed by an *ellipsis* (...) are commands that display dialog boxes. Many *dialog boxes* display options from which you can select so that the DOS Shell can complete a command. Some dialog boxes display information, such as warnings. Commands without an ellipsis are those that the DOS Shell executes immediately. To select a command using the keyboard, you move the selection cursor with [↓] (Down Arrow) and press the Enter key, or you can type the underlined, boldface, or otherwise highlighted character in the menu or command name. For example, to choose the Colors option, you could type "o." If you are using the mouse, you can click the menu name or command.

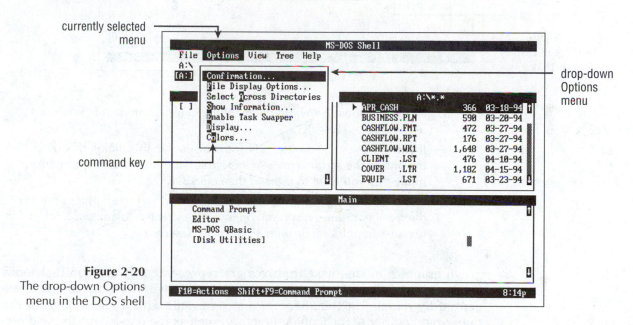

Figure 2-20
The drop-down Options menu in the DOS shell

2. Press [↓] (Down Arrow) until you highlight the Display command. Press [**Enter**]. If you are using the mouse, click **Display**.

The DOS Shell displays the Screen Display Mode dialog box. See Figure 2-21 on the following page. The Screen Display Mode dialog box is a *list box*, which lists options for using text and graphics mode, depending on the capabilities of your video display adapter and monitor. As shown in Figure 2-21, you can customize the DOS Shell to work in text mode with 25, 43, or 50 lines per screen, or in graphics mode with 25 lines per screen. To view the remaining options for graphics mode—30, 34, 43, and 60 lines per screen—you first have to adjust the view of the list box with the selection cursor or the *scroll arrows* on the *scroll bars* at the right side of the dialog box. When you use the mouse to click a scroll arrow, the DOS Shell adjusts your view in the dialog box's window. The more lines you display per screen, the smaller the characters appear on the screen and the higher the resolution. A setting of 30 or 34 lines per screen works well in graphics mode.

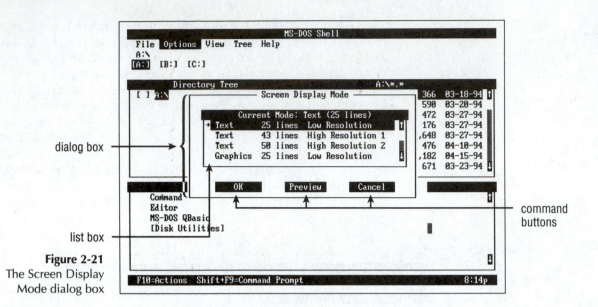

dialog box ⟶

list box ⟶

Figure 2-21
The Screen Display
Mode dialog box

⟵ command
buttons

3. Press **[↓]** (Down Arrow) to highlight the graphics mode that you want to use and press **[Enter]**.

If you are using the mouse, adjust the display in this dialog box by clicking **one of the scroll arrows** in the scroll bar. Next, click the **graphics mode** that you want to use and then click **OK**.

The DOS Shell updates the display mode from text to graphics and sets the number of lines displayed on the screen. The remaining figures in this text use graphics mode with 30 lines per screen.

In graphics mode, diskette drives are represented by an icon that looks similar to the outward appearance of a diskette drive. Hard drives are represented by an icon in the shape of a system unit with a small dash in the upper-right corner of the icon. A directory, such as the one for A:\ in the directory tree window, is represented by a file folder icon. Data files in the file list window are represented by an icon of a sheet of paper with writing on it and with its upper-right corner folded down. Programs and program files are represented by a rectangular icon with a bar across the top; program groups have similar icons with a rectangular grid in the icon.

Because graphical user interfaces are common on most computer systems in use today, the figures of the DOS Shell in this textbook will use graphics mode to illustrate the advantages and features of working with a full graphical user interface.

DISPLAYING DIRECTORIES IN THE DOS SHELL

One advantage of using the DOS Shell is that it automatically displays file-names in alphabetical order. However, you can change the sort order, and you can select groups of files with the Options menu. In your business, an alphabetical list or a list in order by date are the best options for locating important business files quickly. To compare how you control the directory display within the DOS Shell to that at the DOS prompt, you decide to list files in order by date using the DOS Shell.

To view your business files in order by date using the DOS Shell:

1. Press **[F10]** (Actions) to access the menu bar, press **[→]** to highlight the Options menu, and press **[Enter]**.

    If you are using the mouse, click **Options**.

    The DOS Shell displays the drop-down Options menu.

2. Press **[↓]** to highlight File Display Options and press **[Enter]**.

    If you are using the mouse, click **File Display Options**.

    The DOS Shell displays the File Display Options dialog box. See Figure 2-22.

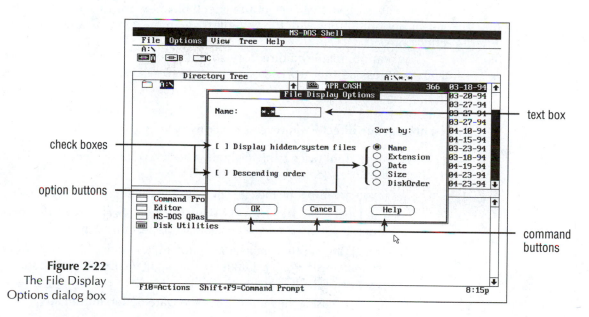

Figure 2-22
The File Display Options dialog box

In a dialog box, you may see one or more **text boxes**, in which you can change the entry. For example, in Figure 2-22, the Name text box shows the current type of file selection—***.*** (pronounced "star-dot-star"). This notation indicates that the DOS Shell is selecting all files. It uses the first asterisk wildcard to select any combination of characters in the main part of the filename and the second asterisk wildcard to select any combination of characters in the file extension.

This dialog box provides options for displaying hidden files and system files. **Hidden files** are files that are not displayed in a directory in order to protect them from inadvertently being deleted. **System files** are the program files that constitute DOS. System files are also hidden to protect them. If you select the **check box** next to "Display hidden/system files" by placing a check mark (an "X") in this box, the DOS Shell will display any hidden or system files included in a directory. If you are using the keyboard, you can use the Tab key to move the cursor to the check box and press the Spacebar to change the setting. If you are using the mouse, you can change the setting by clicking the check box.

The **option buttons** listed under "Sort by" allow you to display a directory in order by name, extension, date and time, size, and disk order. You can select only one of these options, and the files are automatically displayed in ascending order (from A to Z or 0 to 9). If you want to reverse the order (from Z to A or 9 to 0), you can select the check box next to "Descending order." You select option buttons with the keyboard and mouse in the same way you select check boxes.

You want to display a directory so that you can view the files that you and your business partner worked on in the last two days.

To arrange the directory in reverse order by date:

1. Press **[Tab]** twice to highlight the check box for descending order, and then press **[Spacebar]** to check this box.

   If you are using the mouse, click the **Descending order check box**.

   The DOS Shell displays a check mark in the check box for descending order. If you do not see a check mark, repeat this step.

2. Press **[Tab]** to select the Name option button under "Sort by." You cannot see the cursor. Press **[↓]** until you highlight the Date option button. As you press **[↓]**, DOS Shell moves the dot to the next option.

   If you are using the mouse, click the **Date option button box**.

   The DOS Shell displays a dot in the option button for the Name. If you do not see a dot next to this option, repeat this step.

3. Press [**Enter**] to select OK.

   If you are using the mouse, click **OK**.

   DOS Shell saves the new settings, closes the dialog box, and updates the directory display. See Figure 2-23. You can now see the business files that you and your partner worked on in the last two days. These settings remain in effect until you change them.

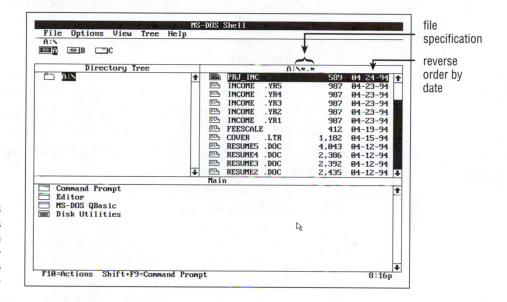

Figure 2-23
The DOS Shell displays a directory of files in descending order by date and time in the file list window

Using Wildcards in the DOS Shell

Next, you want to check the diskette for your yearly income projection template files. You and your partner agreed to name these files INCOME and use a file extension with YR and a single digit representing the year. You can select these files by specifying wildcards on the File Display Options dialog box.

To view a directory of the yearly income projections in order by file extension:

1. Press [**F10**] (Actions) to access the menu bar, press [→] (Right Arrow) to highlight the Options menu, and press [**Enter**].

   If you are using the mouse, click **Options**.

   The DOS Shell displays the drop-down Options menu.

2. Press [↓] to highlight File Display Options and press [**Enter**].

If you are using the mouse, click **File Display Options**.

The DOS Shell displays the File Display Options dialog box, and the Name text box is highlighted. To replace the default file selection criteria, you must type a new condition over it.

3. Type ***.YR?** to replace *.* in the Name text box. Press [**Tab**] twice to select the Descending Order check box. Then press [**Spacebar**] to remove the check mark.

If you are using the mouse, type ***.YR?** and click the **Descending order check box**.

In this operation, you are combining the use of the asterisk and question mark wildcards to select a group of files with similar file extensions.

4. Press [**Tab**] to select the Date option button under Sort by. Press [↑] to select Extension.

If you are using the mouse, click the **Extension option button**.

5. Press [**Enter**].

If you are using the mouse, click **OK**.

The DOS Shell closes this dialog box with the new settings. DOS updates the file list window and shows that there are five template files for income projections for the first five years of your new business. See Figure 2-24. When you and your business partner meet, you can work on the first year's projection.

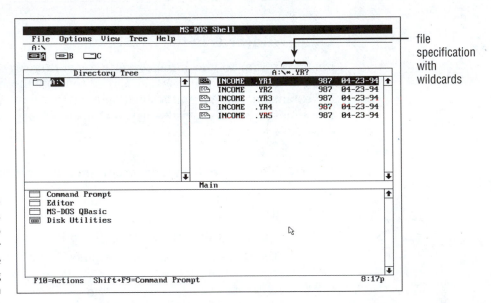

Figure 2-24
The DOS Shell uses wildcards to select a group of files with similar filenames and displays the filenames in ascending order by file extension

As you work with the DOS Shell, you and your business partner will usua_
want files displayed alphabetically by filename, so you decide to change the
file display options back to the DOS Shell's default settings.

To specify the default settings for the filename display:

1. Press **[F10]** (Actions) to access the Menu Bar, press **[→]** to highlight
   Options, and press **[Enter]**.

   If you are using the mouse, click **Options**.

   The DOS Shell displays the drop-down Options menu.

2. Press **[↓]** to highlight File Display Options and then press **[Enter]**.

   If you are using the mouse, click **File Display Options**.

   The DOS Shell displays the File Display Options dialog box.

3. Type ***.*** in the Name text box, press **[Tab]** three times to select the
   Extension option button, and press **[↑]** to select the Name option button.

   If you are using the mouse, type ***.*** in the Name text box and click the
   Name option button.

4. Press **[Enter]**.

   If you are using the mouse, click **OK**.

   The DOS Shell stores the new settings and updates the Files window.

EXITING THE DOS SHELL

Your workday is almost over. Now that you know how to select sort orders
and groups of files with the DOS Shell, you are ready to exit the DOS Shell. You
can exit the DOS Shell with the Exit command on the File menu, or you can
bypass the menu and use the shortcut key for this command, "Alt+F4." You
can also use the shortcut key [F3] (Exit), even though the DOS Shell does not
show this shortcut key on the status bar.

To exit the DOS Shell:

1. Press **[F10]** (Actions) to access the menu bar and press **[Enter]** to select
   the File menu.

   If you are using the mouse, click **File**.

   The DOS Shell displays the drop-down File menu. See Figure 2-25 on the
   following page. You can use some, but not all, of the commands on this
   menu. In this figure, the DOS Shell underlines and highlights those com-
   mands that you can use. For example, you can use the Open, Run, and
   Exit commands. You cannot use other commands, such as Move, Copy,
   Delete, and Rename, because you cannot use these commands on drives.
   However, if you move the selection cursor to the file list window, then
   the DOS Shell will highlight these commands when you next access the
   File menu because you can use these commands on files. Note that the
   DOS Shell displays shortcut key combinations for certain commands. You
   can bypass this menu by using those shortcut keys.

Because the appearance of commands on this menu depends on the capabilities of your graphics adapter and the screen colors you choose to use, your view of the File menu might be different from that in Figure 2-25. The DOS Shell might display those commands that you cannot use in gray, it might dim them, or it might not show those commands at all.

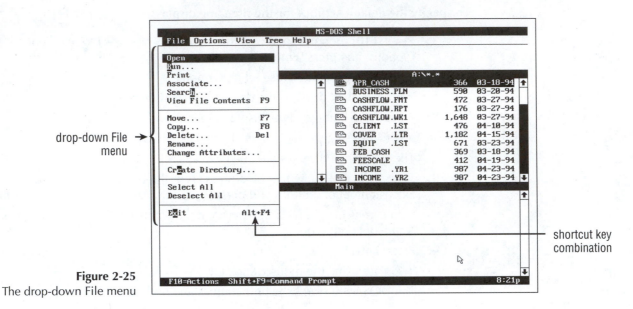

drop-down File menu →

shortcut key combination

Figure 2-25
The drop-down File menu

2. Type **X** to select the Exit command. You can type the highlighted or underlined character shown in a menu option to select that command.

If you are using the mouse, click **Exit**.

DOS displays the DOS prompt for the current drive.

◆

SUMMARY

In this tutorial, you learned how to use the Directory (DIR) command to display a list of the names of files stored on a diskette. You used the Pause switch to display filenames one screen at a time and the Wide switch to display filenames in five columns across the screen. You used the Order switch and its optional sort order parameters to display filenames in order by name, extension, size, date, and time. You also reversed this order by placing a minus sign in front of the sort order parameter. You used the Lowercase switch to display filenames in lowercase rather than uppercase. As you worked with various switches for the DIR command, you used DOSKEY to recall and edit previously entered commands.

You substituted the question mark and asterisk wildcards for part or all of a filename to select groups of files with similar filenames. You also combined these two wildcards with each other and with switches to control the directory display.

You used the SET command to specify default switches for the DIR command and to view the contents of the DOS environment. You displayed a directory with these default switches, and you overrode a switch in the DOS environment.

You worked with the DOS command line interface at the DOS prompt and with the DOS Shell graphical user interface. After loading the DOS Shell, you explored its screen features and its windows. You switched the DOS Shell screen display from text to graphics mode to take full advantage of the graphical user interface.

You used the File Display Options command on the Options menu to change the sort order for displaying files and to select groups of files with wildcards. You returned these settings to the default settings used by the DOS Shell and then you exited the DOS Shell with the Exit command on the File menu.

Command Reference	
DOS Commands	
DIR [*drive name:*]	An internal command that displays a directory listing of the diskette in the current drive, another drive, or a hard drive
DIR [*file specification*]	An internal command that displays a directory listing of a file or group of files on the diskette in the current drive, another drive, or a hard drive
DIR /L	An internal command that displays a directory listing in lowercase
DIR /O	An internal command that displays a directory listing in alphabetical order by filename and file extension
DIR /O<*sort order*> or DIR /O:<*sort order*>	An internal command that displays a directory listing in order by using a sort order parameter. The sort order parameters include: D File date and time E File extension N Main part of filename S File size
DIR /O-<*sort order*> or DIR /O:-<*sort order*>	An internal command that displays a directory listing in reverse order by using a sort order parameter. The sort order parameters include: D File date and time E File extension N Main part of filename S File size

DIR /P	An internal command that displays a directory listing and pauses after each screen
DIR /W	An internal command that displays a directory listing in five columns across the width of the screen, without specifying file sizes, dates, or times
DOSSHELL	An external command that loads the DOS Shell graphical user interface
SET	An internal command that displays settings stored in the DOS environment
SET DIRCMD=	An internal command that removes the default settings assigned to the DIRCMD environment variable from the DOS environment
SET DIRCMD=[*switches*]	An internal command that assigns default switches to the DIRCMD environment variable in the DOS environment for use with the Directory (DIR) command
DOS Shell Commands	
File/Exit	Exits the DOS Shell
Options/Display	Changes the screen display mode for the DOS Shell from text to graphics mode, or vice versa
Options/File Display Options	Displays a file selection in the file list window

QUESTIONS

Use your DOS Exercise diskette to assist you with these questions.

1. What types of information does the DIR command provide on files stored on a diskette or hard disk?
2. What does DOS do if you enter the DIR command and do not specify a disk drive?
3. What does the Pause switch do? Give an example of how you would enter a DIR command with this switch.
4. What does the Wide switch do? Give an example of how you would enter a DIR command with this switch.

5. What does the Order switch do? Give an example of how you would enter a DIR command with this switch.

6. List four sort order parameters that you can use with the Order switch.

7. How can you reverse a sort order parameter when you use the Order switch?

8. What command would you enter at the DOS prompt to display filenames in alphabetical order by file extension only?

9. What command would you enter at the DOS prompt to display filenames in order by file size, from the smallest to the largest file?

10. What command would you enter at the DOS prompt to display filenames in order by file size, from the largest to the smallest file?

11. What command would you enter at the DOS prompt to display filenames in order by date and time, starting with the oldest date and time?

12. What command would you enter at the DOS prompt to display filenames in order by date and time, starting with the most recent date and time?

13. What command would you enter at the DOS prompt to display filenames first in order by file extension, then by the main part of the filename?

14. What does the Lowercase switch do? Give an example of how you would enter a DIR command with this switch.

15. What is a wildcard? What wildcards can you use with DOS? Give an example of how you can use each wildcard.

16. What is the DOS environment, and what does DOS store in the DOS environment?

17. How can you view the contents of the DOS environment?

18. What command would you enter to store in the DOS environment switches for displaying filenames in order by date, one screen at a time, and using lowercase?

19. What command would you enter to remove default switches or settings stored in the DOS environment for the Directory command (DIR)?

20. What command would you enter to display an alphabetical list of all files that have WP for a file extension?

21. What is a command line interface?

22. What is a graphical user interface?

23. What is the DOS Shell? How does it differ from the DOS prompt?

24. What two operating modes can you specify in the DOS Shell?

25. What is the default order used by the DOS Shell to display filenames in the file list window?

26. What DOS Shell command controls the display of filenames in the file list window?

27. How do you use wildcards in the DOS Shell to select groups of filenames to display in the file list window?

28. Name three ways to exit the DOS Shell.

29. What is an icon, and how does the DOS Shell use icons?

30. What is the difference between text mode and graphics mode in the DOS Shell?

TUTORIAL ASSIGNMENTS

Use your Exercise Disk for the following Tutorial Assignments.

1. **Displaying a Directory:** Insert your Exercise Disk into drive A or drive B. Then, perform the following operations from the DOS prompt on drive C. List the command that you use to accomplish each step.
   a. Display a directory of all files on the diskette in drive A or drive B from drive C.
   b. Change to drive A or drive B.
   c. Display a directory of drive A without specifying the drive name.
   d. Display a directory of drive C.

2. **Using Switches**: Perform the following operations from the DOS prompt on drive C. List the command that you use to accomplish each step.
   a. Display a directory of all files on the diskette in drive A in alphabetical order by filename and file extension.
   b. Display a directory of all files on the diskette in drive A in reverse order by file size.
   c. Display a directory of all files on the diskette in drive A in reverse order by date and in lowercase.
   d. Print the directory, or partial directory, displayed on the screen.

3. **Using Wildcards**: Perform the following operations from the DOS prompt on drive A. List the command that you use to accomplish each step.
   a. Display an alphabetical directory of all files with "I" as the first character in the filename.
   b. Display an alphabetical directory of all files with "DOC" for the file extension.
   c. Display an alphabetical directory of all files with "WK" as the first two characters of the file extension and any character after "WK".
   d. Print the directory displayed on the screen.
   e. Display an alphabetical directory of all files with "JOB" as the first three characters of the filename.
   f. Display a directory of all files with "LST" as the file extension, in date order.

4. **Specifying Default Settings for the Directory Command in the DOS Environment**: Perform the following operations from the DOS prompt. List the command that you use to accomplish each step.
   a. Display the settings in the DOS environment.
   b. Print the DOS environment settings displayed on the screen.

    c. Assign switches to an environment variable so that DOS automatically displays filenames one screen at a time in alphabetical order by filename and in wide mode.

    d. Check the newly entered setting in the DOS environment.

    e. Display a directory using the switches in the DOS environment.

    f. Override the Order switch in the DOS environment and display a directory in file size order.

    g. Restore the original settings for the DIRCMD variable in the DOS environment. If the DOS environment did not contain a setting for this variable, remove the switches that you assigned to this variable.

5. **Using the DOS Shell**: Perform the following operations from the DOS Shell. Assume that you are currently using drive A and that DOS Shell is configured to operate in text mode. List the commands and steps for each of these operations.

    a. Load the DOS Shell.

    b. Change the operating mode from text mode to graphics mode.

    c. Specify that DOS Shell display filenames in disk order.

    d. Select all filenames that start with "S" and display them in date order.

    e. Select all filenames with the "WK1" file extension and display them in descending date order.

    f. Return the file specification to the default setting of all files (*.*) and the default sort order to name so that the DOS Shell shows all the filenames in the File List window in alphabetical order by name.

TUTORIAL **3**

Working with Files

OBJECTIVES

In this tutorial you will learn to:

◆ Understand the importance and features of ASCII files

◆ View the contents of a text file

◆ Redirect the output of a DOS command

◆ Use the MORE filter

◆ Print text files

◆ Copy files

◆ Rename files

◆ Delete files

◆ Compare file operations from the DOS prompt and the DOS Shell

After carefully evaluating two job offers, you accept a position with a small business that produces business documents for clients. On your first day at your new job, your supervisor takes you on a short tour of the office and its facilities and introduces you to the other staff members. Your supervisor also provides you with an overview of how the company meets the business needs of its clients.

You are assigned a job for a specific client for whom you will produce the appropriate business documents from existing template files, each of which contains a general format for a specific type of document. As you recall, **templates** are files that contain the general format or layout of a document but little or no data. When you start a client job, you first check the contents of files that you intend to use to verify that you are starting with the correct files. Then you copy the template files to produce new files as your working copies. After you modify the new files for your client, you print either drafts or final copies of the documents. When you complete a client job, you make duplicate, or backup, copies of the files you produced in the event you encounter a problem with the original copies of those files. You also may be required to move files from one disk to another. Once a week, you reserve some time to check the files on your diskette and you archive or delete files that you no longer need.

Your supervisor emphasizes that many client jobs require you to meet tight deadlines, so you must know how to perform these operations quickly and efficiently. Although the office staff uses the DOS Shell to simplify and automate routine file operations like the ones described, you must also know how to work from the DOS prompt. Some clients request that you complete these jobs in their offices, and because they might not have the DOS Shell on their systems, you must be prepared to work under conditions different from those at your office. Your supervisor asks that you compare and contrast file operations from the DOS prompt and the DOS Shell as you work so that you are familiar with both approaches.

◆

GETTING STARTED

Your first client needs a résumé prepared in two different formats. Before you start, you decide to specify default settings for displaying directories, activate DOSKEY, and check the files on the template diskette provided you by your supervisor. The tutorial assumes you will use the CLS command to clear the screen before issuing a command, except in certain cases where it is necessary to show two or more steps in one figure.

To activate DOSKEY:

5.0

6.0

6.2

1. Power on your computer system, and be sure you see the C:\> prompt displayed on the screen. If you see a prompt for some other drive, type **C:** and press **[Enter]** to change to drive C.

2. Type **DOSKEY** and press **[Enter]**. If you are using DOS 5.0 or 6.0, DOS will display the message "DOSKey installed" if DOSKEY is not already installed on your computer. If you do not see this message with DOS 5.0 or 6.0, DOSKEY is already installed. DOS 6.2 will not display a message.

Now specify default switches for the Directory command.

3. Type **SET DIRCMD=/P /O** and press **[Enter]**. DOS displays the DOS prompt. If DOS displays an error message indicating that you are out of environment space, ask your instructor or technical support person to adjust the size of the DOS environment, and then try again.

Next, verify that this setting is stored in the DOS environment.

4. Type **SET** and press **[Enter]**. DOS displays all the settings currently stored in the DOS environment. See Figure 3-1. The variable DIRCMD and the Pause and Order switches are listed as the last setting entered in the DOS environment.

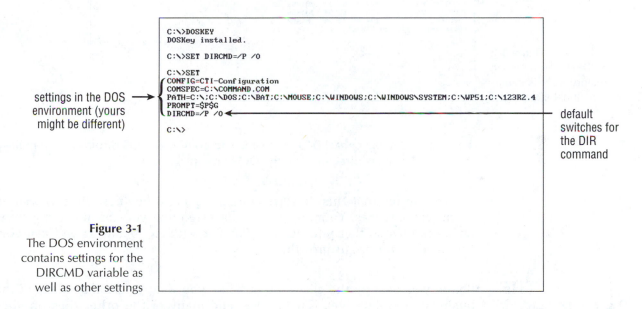

settings in the DOS environment (yours might be different) →

default switches for the DIR command

```
C:\>DOSKEY
DOSKey installed.

C:\>SET DIRCMD=/P /O

C:\>SET
CONFIG=CTI-Configuration
COMSPEC=C:\COMMAND.COM
PATH=C:\;C:\DOS;C:\BAT;C:\MOUSE;C:\WINDOWS;C:\WINDOWS\SYSTEM;C:\WP51;C:\123R2.4
PROMPT=$P$G
DIRCMD=/P /O ◄

C:\>
```

Figure 3-1
The DOS environment contains settings for the DIRCMD variable as well as other settings

Now you are ready to view a directory of the template files on the diskette provided by your supervisor.

To display a directory of your working diskette:

1. Insert your Tutorial Disk into drive A (or drive B).

2. Type **A:** (or **B:**) to change to drive A (or drive B).

3. Type **DIR** and press **[Enter]**. *Do not type any switches.* DOS displays an alphabetical directory and pauses after each screen. See Figure 3-2.

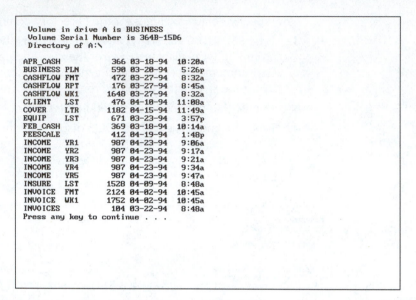

```
Volume in drive A is BUSINESS
Volume Serial Number is 364B-15D6
Directory of A:\

APR_CASH          366 03-18-94   10:20a
BUSINESS PLN      590 03-20-94    5:26p
CASHFLOW FMT      472 03-27-94    8:32a
CASHFLOW RPT      176 03-27-94    8:45a
CASHFLOW WK1     1648 03-27-94    8:32a
CLIENT   LST      476 04-10-94   11:08a
COVER    LTR     1182 04-15-94   11:49a
EQUIP    LST      671 03-23-94    3:57p
FEB_CASH          369 03-18-94   10:14a
FEESCALE          412 04-19-94    1:48p
INCOME   YR1      987 04-23-94    9:06a
INCOME   YR2      987 04-23-94    9:17a
INCOME   YR3      987 04-23-94    9:21a
INCOME   YR4      987 04-23-94    9:34a
INCOME   YR5      987 04-23-94    9:47a
INSURE   LST     1528 04-09-94    8:48a
INVOICE  FMT     2124 04-02-94   10:45a
INVOICE  WK1     1752 04-02-94   10:45a
INVOICES          104 03-22-94    8:48a
Press any key to continue . . .
```

Figure 3-2
The first screen of a directory with filenames in alphabetical order

4.   Press **[Spacebar]** or any other key to continue. DOS displays the remainder of the directory and the DOS prompt.

You notice that this diskette contains general business files as well as client template files. Your supervisor suggested that you examine the general business files so that you become familiar with the business and can contribute ideas toward its growth.

THE IMPORTANCE OF ASCII FILES

Before you start on the client job at hand, you want to examine some of the business template files. These files, and many of the other files on your diskette, are ASCII (pronounced "ask key") files. An **ASCII file** is a simple file format in which data is stored as text. The name ASCII stands for **A**merican **S**tandard **C**ode for **I**nformation **I**nterchange. Computer companies recognize this standard coding format for storing information in a file and adapt their software packages to use, or **support**, this file format. The primary feature of an ASCII file is that users can read and decipher the contents of the file if it is displayed on the screen. In other words, the information is stored in a readable format.

In contrast, files produced by word processing software store formatting codes for special features, such as boldface and underlining, and you must use that software when you work on the file. However, most types of word processing software work with ASCII files. Furthermore, many of these word processing packages can automatically convert ASCII files into the file format typically used by that software. One advantage of storing general-use business template files as ASCII text files is that you can use them with whatever word processing application is available. In your business, this provides you with flexibility when working off-site at client offices.

The terms **DOS files**, **DOS text files**, **text files**, and **print files** also refer to ASCII files. Although you can store documents as ASCII files, many of the important configuration and initialization files on your computer system are

ASCII files. Therefore, it is important to become familiar with this file format and the DOS commands that operate on ASCII files.

The original ASCII character set contains codes for 128 characters, such as letters of the alphabet, numbers, and symbols as well as control codes. **Control codes** are codes for the use of the Ctrl (Control) key with another key. For example, when you press the Tab key to indent a line while creating an ASCII file, you insert a tab code, [Ctrl][I]. At the end of each line in an ASCII file, there is an ASCII code for a carriage return, [Ctrl][M]; a line feed, [Ctrl][J]; or both. Some ASCII files contain a form feed code, [Ctrl][L], to indicate a page break and the start of a new page. The last character in an ASCII file is a special type of code—an **end-of-file (EOF) code**, [Ctrl][Z].

Each ASCII character is assigned a numerical code, called the **ASCII code** or **ASCII value**. In the original ASCII character set, these values range from 0 (zero) to 127, for a total of 128 codes. The extended ASCII code has values that range from 0 (zero) to 255. The 128 additional codes include values for European characters, graphics characters, and scientific characters. You can produce an ASCII control code or character by pressing and holding [Alt] while you type the ASCII value *on the numeric keypad*. In some cases, applications programs redefine these codes. Figure 3-3 contains examples of ASCII characters and codes for both the original and extended ASCII character sets.

ASCII Character	Type of Character	ASCII Value
^I	Control code for a tab	009
Esc	Escape key	027
9	Number	057
A	Uppercase letter	065
a	Lowercase letter	097
£	British pound	156
┌	Graphics line	201
σ	Sigma symbol	229
÷	Division symbol	246

Figure 3-3
Examples of ASCII characters and codes

Viewing the Contents of an ASCII File

Because an ASCII file contains information stored as text, you can use the TYPE command, an internal DOS command, to display the contents of an ASCII file on the screen. The syntax of the TYPE command is as follows:

**TYPE [*drive:*][*path*]*filename*

If you use the TYPE command, you do not need to start a program and then retrieve a file to view its contents. However, you cannot use the TYPE command to view the contents of a program file or a file produced by an application such as Lotus 1-2-3. If you do, DOS attempts to interpret the file's contents as ASCII characters and displays unintelligible symbols on the screen or no symbols at all. Also, you can use the TYPE command to view the contents of only one file at a time.

In your job, you want to become familiar with the client fee scale and with the two résumé template files that you need to use for your first client. You decide to use the TYPE command to examine the file with the fee scale and the first résumé template file.

To view the contents of the file with your company's fee scale:

1. Type **TYPE FEESCALE** and press **[Enter]**. The file named FEESCALE does not have a file extension. DOS displays the contents of this ASCII file on the screen, and then displays the DOS prompt. See Figure 3-4. The fee scale reflects the current rates for work in your region.

TYPE command

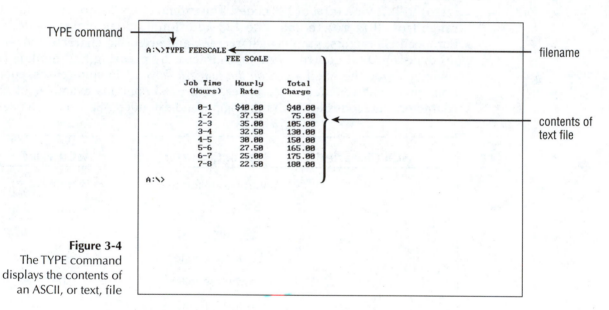

filename

contents of text file

Figure 3-4
The TYPE command
displays the contents of
an ASCII, or text, file

Now view the contents of the file with the first résumé template.

2. Type **TYPE RESUME1.DOC** and press **[Enter]**. Unlike FEESCALE, the file named RESUME1.DOC does have a file extension. DOS displays the contents of this ASCII file on the screen, followed by the DOS prompt. Because the file contains more than 25 lines, DOS scrolls to adjust the screen view. The last half-page of the file remains displayed on the monitor. See Figure 3-5. This template identifies the type of information required to complete this résumé for a client.

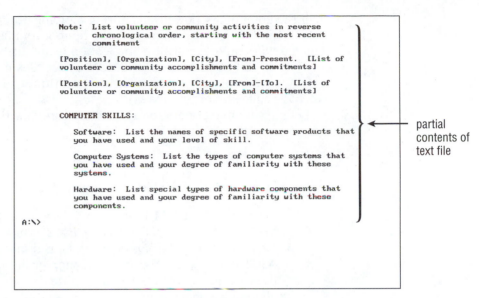

```
      Note:  List volunteer or community activities in reverse
             chronological order, starting with the most recent
             commitment

      [Position], [Organization], [City], [From]-Present.  [List of
      volunteer or community accomplishments and commitments]

      [Position], [Organization], [City], [From]-[To].  [List of
      volunteer or community accomplishments and commitments]


      COMPUTER SKILLS:

         Software:  List the names of specific software products that
         you have used and your level of skill.

         Computer Systems:  List the types of computer systems that
         you have used and your degree of familiarity with these
         systems.

         Hardware:  List special types of hardware components that
         you have used and your degree of familiarity with these
         components.

 A:\>
```

partial
contents of
text file

Figure 3-5
A partial view of the
contents of an ASCII file

The scrolling was so quick that you were unable to view the entire contents of the file. To control the scrolling, you must use two other DOS features with the TYPE command: the MORE filter and the pipe operator.

PIPING OUTPUT TO THE MORE FILTER

The TYPE command does not have a Pause switch, and it is not uncommon for ASCII files to contain more than 25 lines of text. To display only one screen at a time and avoid automatic scrolling, you must send the output of the TYPE command to the MORE filter. A **filter** is a DOS command that can modify the output of another DOS command. The MORE filter, or command, displays a screen of output, pauses, and displays a More prompt, which permits you to continue when you are ready.

To combine the MORE filter with another DOS command, you use the pipe redirection operator. The **pipe operator** (|) redirects the output of one DOS command operation so that it then becomes the input for another DOS command. For example, the following command will display the output of an ASCII file one screen at a time:

TYPE RESUME1.DOC | MORE

The first command, TYPE, produces the output, and DOS stores this output in a temporary file on disk. After the TYPE command completes its operation, DOS uses the contents of the temporary file on disk as the input for the MORE filter. The MORE command displays the contents of the temporary file one screen at a time. After MORE displays the entire contents of the temporary file, DOS deletes the temporary file from disk. This transfer of data from one DOS command to another is called **piping**.

In order to complete this operation without error, DOS must be able to create a temporary, or **intermediate**, file. If the default disk drive is write-protected or if it does not contain enough space for the temporary file, DOS displays the error message "Intermediate file error during pipe."

If the computer's power fails during a piping operation, the temporary file remains on disk. You can recognize the temporary file because it is assigned a filename that you or a software application is not likely to use—names such as ACAPCPGB, AKCEDKAO, or APBNCMGA. These files might contain information or, if you interrupt a DOS command operation, these files might be empty (i.e., have a file size of zero bytes).

Let's try a piping operation so that we can view the entire contents of the résumé template file.

To display the contents of the résumé template file one screen at a time:

1. Type **TYPE RESUME1.DOC | MORE** and press **[Enter]**. *Be sure you press the key with a vertical bar (the one that contains a space in the middle of the character) for the pipe operator.* DOS displays the first part of this ASCII file. See Figure 3-6. Your monitor might show a different number of lines. In this part of the résumé template file, you enter the client's name, address, telephone number, professional goals, and areas of expertise.

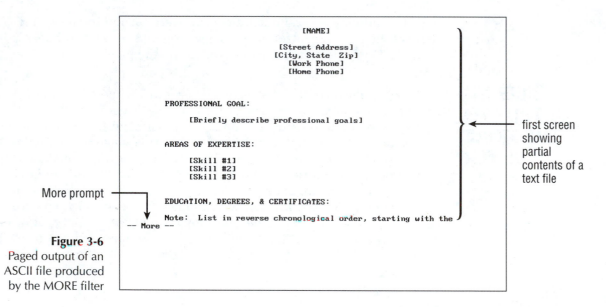

Figure 3-6
Paged output of an ASCII file produced by the MORE filter

2. Press **[Spacebar]** or any other key to continue. DOS displays the next part of this ASCII file, where you enter the client's educational background and degrees as well as professional experience.

3. Press **[Spacebar]** or any other key to continue. DOS displays the next part of this ASCII file, where you enter the client's volunteer experience and computer skills.

4. Press **[Spacebar]** or any other key to continue. DOS displays the remainder of this ASCII file, and then displays the DOS prompt.

You can use the TYPE command, the pipe operator, and the MORE filter to view the contents of "read me" files included with software packages. When software manufacturers release a software package, they include files with the latest information on the use of the product. These files are ASCII files with names such as README, READ.ME, or README.DOC, and they are copied to your hard disk when you install the software. You can then examine these files for important information that you might need to configure the software application so that it works well with the hardware components of your computer system.

You can also use the pipe operator and the MORE filter with any other DOS command that produces more than a full screen of output so that you can view all the information.

VIEWING ASCII FILES IN THE DOS SHELL

Next you want to use the DOS Shell to examine the other résumé template file. As you have discovered, the DOS Shell allows you to work with DOS in a menu-driven and more visually pleasing way than is possible when you work at the DOS prompt. In the file list window, the DOS Shell displays the names of files in the current drive and directory. From this window, you can select commands on the File menu that operate on one or more files. Let's use the DOS Shell to view the contents of an ASCII file.

To access the DOS Shell:

1. Be sure the current drive contains your Tutorial Disk. If necessary, change your current drive.

2. Type **DOSSHELL** and press **[Enter]**. The DOS Shell shows the names of the files in the root directory of drive A (or drive B). The files are listed in alphabetical order—the default order used by the DOS Shell. See Figure 3-7. If the DOS Shell does not list files in alphabetical order on your system, the DOS Shell is using some other order, such as disk order. Also, you might notice other differences if the DOS Shell is customized on your computer.

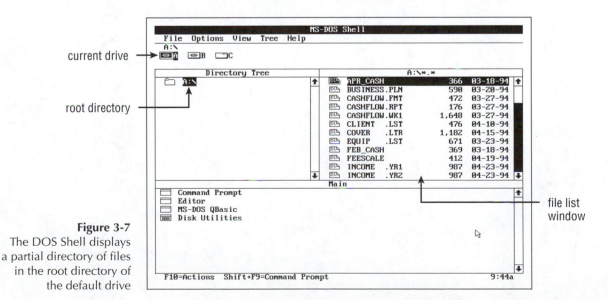

Figure 3-7
The DOS Shell displays a partial directory of files in the root directory of the default drive

3. If the filenames in the file list window are not in alphabetical order, press **[F10]** (Actions), type **O** for the Options menu, and type **F** for File Display Options. The DOS Shell displays the File Display Options dialog box. If necessary, type ***.*** in the Name text box to select all files. If the Descending Order check box has an X, press **[Tab]** until you select this check box, then press **[Spacebar]** to remove the X so that you can use Ascending Order. Press **[Tab]** until you select the Sort By option buttons, point to the Name sort option, and press **[Enter].**

If the filenames in the file list window are not in alphabetical order and if you are using the mouse, click **Options**, and then click **File Display Options**. The DOS Shell displays the File Display Options dialog box. If necessary, type ***.*** in the Name text box to select all files. If the Descending Order check box has an X, click this **check box** to remove the X so that you can use Ascending Order. Click the **Name option**, then click **OK**.

The DOS Shell now displays the filenames in the file list window in alphabetical order.

Now let's select the file list window.

4. Press **[Tab]** twice to move the selection cursor to the file list window.

If you are using the mouse, click the **file list window title bar**.

The DOS Shell then highlights the title bar for the file list window.

Next, let's select the résumé template file.

5. Type **R** to quickly move the selection cursor to the first file that starts with the letter "R." Then press **[↓]** (Down Arrow) until you highlight the file named RESUME5.DOC.

If you are using the mouse, click **[↓]** (Down Scroll Arrow) on the vertical scroll bar to the right of the filenames until you see the filename RESUME5.DOC. Then click the filename **RESUME5.DOC**.

6. Press **[F10]** (Actions) to access the menu bar. Press **[Enter]** to select the File menu.

If you are using the mouse, click the **File menu**.

The DOS Shell displays the drop-down File menu. See Figure 3-8.

currently selected menu →

View option →

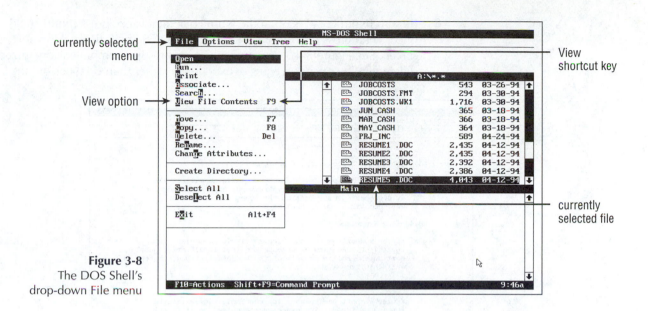

View shortcut key

currently selected file

Figure 3-8
The DOS Shell's
drop-down File menu

7. Press **[↓]** (Down Arrow) until you highlight the View File Contents command. Then press **[Enter]**. (Note that you can also use the shortcut View key [F9] to issue the command and bypass the menu.)

If you are using the mouse, click the **View File Contents** command.

The DOS Shell displays part of the file. See Figure 3-9. Your screen view might be different. Note that this screen has its own title bar, menu bar, and status bar. Below the menu bar, the DOS Shell provides information on how to use scrolling keys to view the rest of the file. By using [PgDn] (Page Down) and [PgUp] (Page Up), you can scroll forward and backward one screen at a time. You can also use [↓] (Down Arrow) and [↑] (Up Arrow) to adjust your screen view onto the file.

title bar with filename →

menu bar →

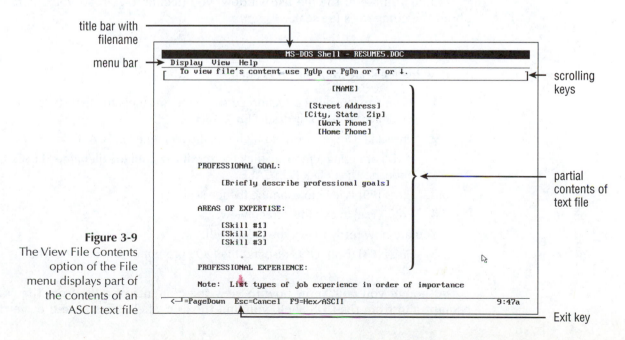

scrolling keys

partial contents of text file

Figure 3-9
The View File Contents
option of the File
menu displays part of
the contents of an
ASCII text file

Exit key

8. Be sure [Num Lock] is off. If the Num Lock light is on, press **[Num Lock]** once. Then press **[PgDn]** (Page Down). The DOS Shell displays the next screen. See Figure 3-10. As you can see, this résumé template is organized differently. It focuses on types of experience rather than on types of jobs.

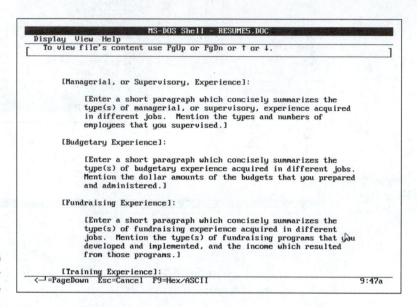

```
┌──────────────────────────────────────────────────────────────────────────┐
│                   MS-DOS Shell - RESUME5.DOC                               │
│ Display  View  Help                                                        │
│ ┌────────────────────────────────────────────────────────────────────────┐│
│ │  To view file's content use PgUp or PgDn or ↑ or ↓.                     ││
│                                                                            │
│                                                                            │
│     [Managerial, or Supervisory, Experience]:                             │
│                                                                            │
│         [Enter a short paragraph which concisely summarizes the            │
│         type(s) of managerial, or supervisory, experience acquired         │
│         in different jobs.  Mention the types and numbers of               │
│         employees that you supervised.]                                    │
│                                                                            │
│     [Budgetary Experience]:                                                │
│                                                                            │
│         [Enter a short paragraph which concisely summarizes the            │
│         type(s) of budgetary experience acquired in different jobs.        │
│         Mention the dollar amounts of the budgets that you prepared        │
│         and administered.]                                                 │
│                                                                            │
│     [Fundraising Experience]:                                              │
│                                                                            │
│         [Enter a short paragraph which concisely summarizes the            │
│         type(s) of fundraising experience acquired in different            │
│         jobs.  Mention the type(s) of fundraising programs that you        │
│         developed and implemented, and the income which resulted           │
│         from those programs.]                                              │
│                                                                            │
│     [Training Experience]:                                                 │
│ ←┘=PageDown  Esc=Cancel  F9=Hex/ASCII                            9:47a     │
└──────────────────────────────────────────────────────────────────────────┘
```

Figure 3-10
Scrolling to the next view of the résumé template file

9. Press **[PgDn]** repeatedly until you view the entire file. The DOS Shell will beep when there are no more screens to view.

Now let's exit this screen view of the file.

10. Press **[Esc]**. You return to the file list window.

While you are in the file list window, you decide to refresh your memory about the company's fee scale.

To view the fee scale from the DOS Shell:

1. Type **F** to move the selection cursor to the first filename that starts with the letter "F"—in this case, FEB_CASH.

2. Press **[↓]** (Down Arrow) to highlight the filename FEESCALE.

   If you are using a mouse, click the **scroll bar** until the filename FEESCALE appears. Then click **FEESCALE**.

3. Press **[F9]** (View) to examine the fee scale.

4. Press **[Esc]** to exit this screen view.

You are now ready to exit the DOS Shell.

5. Press **[F3]** (Exit). DOS displays the DOS prompt for the current drive.

Although you now know how to view the contents of a file from the DOS prompt and from the DOS Shell, you find the DOS Shell is faster and easier to use for your business needs. The DOS Shell automatically organizes filenames so that you can locate a file more quickly. When you view the contents of a file, it automatically pauses and displays the first screen. You can then adjust the view one screen at a time, or you can adjust that screen view in smaller increments than is possible at the DOS prompt. Furthermore, you can scroll backward through the document, which is not possible at the DOS prompt.

PRINTING AN ASCII FILE FROM THE DOS PROMPT

Next, you want to print copies of the two résumé template files that you will modify for your first client. Then, you can work with those printed copies until you become more familiar with all the files that you will use as an employee.

You can use the PRINT command to print a copy of an ASCII file. The PRINT command has a more complex syntax, with a variety of switches. However, if you want to print a file using the default settings for the PRINT command, you use the following syntax:

PRINT [[*drive:*][*path*]*filename*[...]]

The ellipsis option ([...]) after the filename indicates that you can specify more than one file. If you want to print a series of files, you list each filename separately and include a space between each filename. You might also need to specify the drive and path for each file. If you type "PRINT" without specifying a filename, PRINT displays a list of the files in the print queue. A **print queue** is a list of files that are waiting to be printed.

When you issue this command for the first time from the DOS prompt using the above syntax, DOS prompts you for the name of your printer port. As you may remember, a **port** is a connection between your computer system and another hardware component, such as a printer. Just as DOS assigns names to each of the disk drives, DOS assigns names to each of the ports in your computer system. Because it is possible to connect more than one printer to a computer system, DOS assigns the name PRN to the first printer port on your computer system. The other port names are LPT1, LPT2, and LPT3 for the first through third line printer, or parallel, ports; and COM1, COM2, COM3, and COM4 for the first through fourth communications, or serial, ports. In most cases, you can specify PRN or LPT1 as the printer port, and DOS will know which port to use.

To print a copy of the résumé template file:

1. Be sure the printer is on. If the printer is off, turn on the power switch.

2. Be sure the printer has paper and that the paper is properly aligned.

3. Be sure the printer is on-line and capable of receiving output from the computer. If the printer is off-line, press the **On Line button** once.

4. At the DOS prompt, type **PRINT RESUME1.DOC** and press **[Enter]**. DOS might prompt you for the name of the list device. A *list device* is a printer port—the name of the port DOS uses to list the contents of the file. If DOS does not prompt for the list device, the PRINT program is already loaded into memory.

5. If necessary, press **[Enter]** to accept the default list device, PRN, or if your printer port is different, type in the name of your printer port. DOS loads

the PRINT program into memory and informs you that the file is currently being printed. See Figure 3-11. If the printer does not print the file or if DOS displays an error message, check with your instructor or technical support person. You may need to specify the name of another printer port or check the status of the printer.

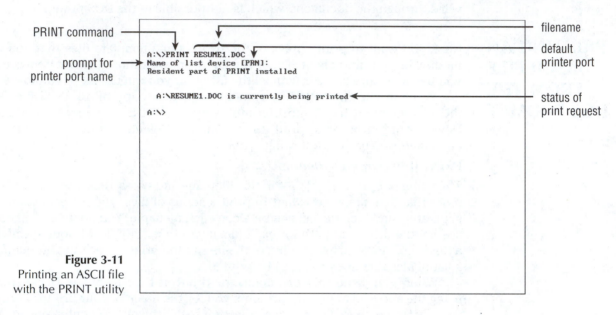

PRINT command → filename

prompt for printer port name → default printer port

```
A:\>PRINT RESUME1.DOC
Name of list device [PRN]:
Resident part of PRINT installed

    A:\RESUME1.DOC is currently being printed

A:\>
```

status of print request

Figure 3-11
Printing an ASCII file
with the PRINT utility

6. Remove your printed copy of the résumé template file from the printer.

The PRINT utility is another example of a Terminate-and-Stay-Resident (TSR) program. After DOS loads a TSR into memory, the TSR stays in memory as you work with other utilities or with software applications so that you can continue to use the TSR. The memory allocated to a TSR is not available for use by other programs. In contrast, if you load a software application or a utility that is not a TSR, the memory occupied by that program becomes available when you exit the software application or when the utility completes its intended function. You can access and remove, or unload, some TSRs from memory with the use of a **hot key**—a combination of keys that the TSR recognizes. To remove other TSRs, such as the PRINT utility, from memory, you must reboot your computer system; however, *do not* reboot your computer now.

PRINTING AN ASCII FILE FROM THE DOS SHELL

Next, you want to use the DOS Shell to print a copy of the other résumé template file. Before you can print from the DOS Shell, the PRINT program must be loaded into memory. You can load the PRINT utility before you load the DOS Shell, or you can use the Run option on the File menu in the DOS Shell to load the PRINT utility. Since you have already performed this step, the PRINT program is stored in RAM and ready for use with the DOS Shell.

To print the file with the other résumé template from the DOS Shell:

1. Type **DOSSHELL** and press **[Enter]**.

2. Press **[Tab]** twice to move the selection cursor to the file list window.

   If you are using the mouse, click the **file list window title bar**.

   Now let's select the résumé template file.

3. Type **R** to quickly move the selection cursor to the first file that starts with the letter "R." Then, press **[↓]** (Down Arrow) until you highlight the file named RESUME5.DOC.

   If you are using the mouse, click the **down scroll arrow** on the vertical scroll bar to the right of the filenames until you see the filename RESUME5.DOC. Then, click the filename **RESUME5.DOC**.

4. Press **[F10]** (Actions), and then press **[Enter]** to select the File menu. Press **[↓]** (Down Arrow) twice to highlight the Print option, then press **[Enter]**.

   If you are using the mouse, click the **File menu** and then the **Print command**.

   The DOS Shell relays a request to the PRINT program to print a copy of the selected file.

5. Remove your printed copy of the résumé template file from the printer.

6. Press **[F3]** (Exit) to exit the DOS Shell.

You have completed the job for your first client, so you decide to take a short break before you start on your next task.

COPYING FILES

Your supervisor asks you to make a copy of one of the résumé template files and to revise it so that you have a new version of that résumé format. These résumé templates are invaluable in your job because they enable you to provide fast turnaround times for clients and to produce a variety of résumés in popular formats.

You can use the COPY command to copy the contents of an existing file into a new file on the same diskette (Figure 3-12). The COPY command is an internal command that you can use in a variety of ways. If you want to copy a file to another location, without specifying any switches, the syntax is as follows:

COPY [*source*] [*destination*]

The file that you copy is the **source file**—in this case, RESUME5.DOC. The new file that you produce from the copy operation is the **destination file**, or **target file**—in this case, RESUME6.DOC. You might need to specify all or part of the path for each file so that DOS can locate the source file and create a destination file where you need it. Recall that the full path includes the disk drive name, the directory name, and the filename. Because your current drive is the drive that contains your Tutorial Disk, all you need to specify are the source and target filenames.

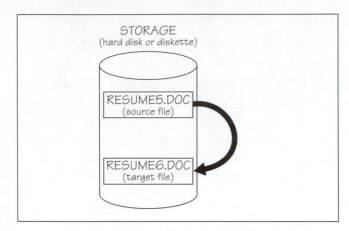

Figure 3-12
Copying a file to the
same diskette with
a new filename

Before you make a copy of a file, you should use the DIR command to verify that the destination disk or directory does not already contain a file with the same name as the one you intend to use for the new file if you are using DOS 5.0 or 6.0. If you inadvertently use an existing filename, DOS 5.0 and 6.0 will copy over that file without warning you, and you will lose that file's contents. By default, DOS 6.2 automatically asks for verification before it overwrites a file. After you make a copy of a file, you should verify that the copy operation worked.

5.0

6.0

6.2

To copy the file containing the format for preparing a résumé:

1. If necessary, power on your computer system, install DOSKEY, and specify default switches for the DIR command using the instructions on pages 55 through 58.

2. Be sure the current drive is the one with your Tutorial Disk. If this is not the case, you *must* specify the drive name for the source and target files in the next three steps.

3. Type **DIR RESUME?** and press **[Enter]** to check that the Tutorial Disk does not already contain a file named RESUME6.DOC. DOS assumes you want to use the current drive and that you want to include any file extensions. Also, filenames are displayed in alphabetical order because earlier you specified default switches in the DOS environment. You do not need to repeat those switches with the DIR command. Because your diskette does not contain a file named RESUME6.DOC, you are ready to perform the copy operation.

4. Type **COPY RESUME5.DOC RESUME6.DOC** and press **[Enter]**. DOS displays the message "1 file(s) copied" and then displays the DOS prompt again.

Now verify that the new file exists.

5. Press **[↑]** (Up Arrow) until you recall the command DIR RESUME? and then press **[Enter]**. The file RESUME6.DOC is shown in the directory. See Figure 3-13. Note that the new file contains the same number of bytes and date and time of creation as RESUME5.DOC. Because you have not yet made any changes to RESUME6.DOC, it is identical to RESUME5.DOC.

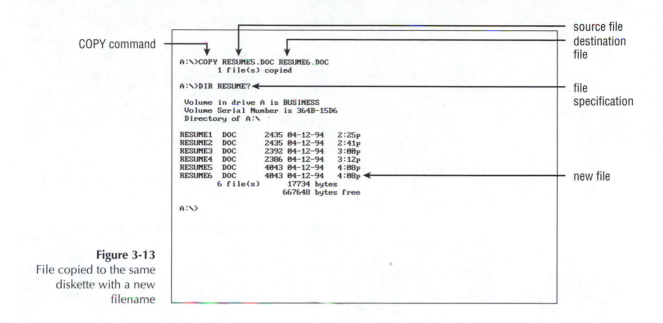

Figure 3-13
File copied to the same diskette with a new filename

The computer systems in your office have different types of disk drives to accommodate different types of diskettes. For example, your computer has a 3½-inch and a 5¼-inch high-density drive. Other computers have only one high-density drive for either a 3½-inch or a 5¼-inch diskette. Because you might work on one of the other computers, you will need to know how to copy from one disk drive to another as well as to and from a hard disk drive.

The next three sections describe how to copy files from one drive to another from the DOS prompt. Complete the section or sections that apply to the number of disk drives of the computer you are using.

Copying a File Using One Disk Drive

You want to copy the file RESUME6.DOC from your Tutorial Disk to your Exercises Disk so that you have a backup copy of this new file.

If you have a single disk drive, you can copy from one diskette to another diskette using the same drive. DOS treats this disk drive as drive A *and* drive B. If your computer has two diskette drives, skip this section because you *cannot* perform this operation.

To copy a file to another diskette using a computer *with only one diskette drive*:

1. Be sure drive A is the current drive.
2. Remove your Tutorial Disk, and insert your Exercise Disk into the diskette drive.
3. Type **DIR RESUME**? and press **[Enter]** to verify that you do not have a file named RESUME6.DOC on your Exercise Disk.
4. Remove your Exercise Disk, and insert your Tutorial Disk into the diskette drive.

5. Type **COPY RESUME6.DOC B:** and press **[Enter]**. After DOS copies the file, it prompts you to insert the diskette for drive B (the target diskette) and to press any key when you are ready.

6. Remove the Tutorial Disk, and insert your Exercise Disk. After the drive light goes off, press **[Spacebar]** or any other key. DOS displays the message "1 file(s) copied." See Figure 3-14. DOS copies the file to the target diskette and prompts you to insert the diskette for drive A (the source diskette) and to press any key when you are ready.

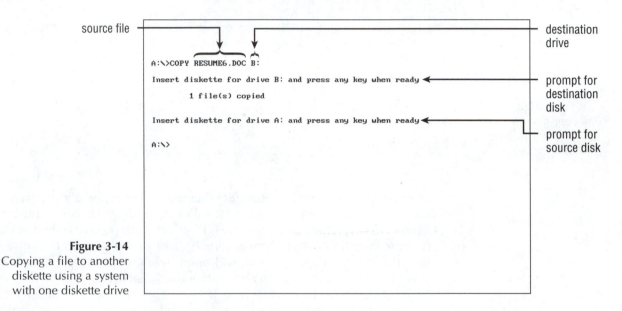

Figure 3-14
Copying a file to another diskette using a system with one diskette drive

7. Remove the Exercise Disk, and insert your Tutorial Disk. After the drive light goes out, press **[Spacebar]** or any other key. DOS displays the DOS prompt for drive A.

8. Remove your Tutorial Disk, and insert your Exercise Disk.

Now verify that the copy operation worked.

9. Press **[↑]** (Up Arrow) to recall the command DIR RESUME? and press **[Enter]**. You should see the filename RESUME6.DOC in the directory listing.

10. Remove the Exercise Disk, and insert your Tutorial Disk into the diskette drive.

Copying a File Using Two Disk Drives

A coworker has asked you to copy RESUME6.DOC from your diskette to his diskette, so that he can use it to prepare a résumé for one of his clients.

If your computer has two disk drives, you can copy a file from a diskette in one drive to a diskette in another drive, even if the diskettes are different sizes and have different storage capacities (Figure 3-15). You can copy a file from a 5¼-inch disk drive to another 5¼-inch disk drive, from a 3½-inch disk drive to another 3½-inch disk drive, from a 5¼-inch disk drive to a 3½-inch disk drive, and from a 3½-inch disk drive to a 5¼-inch disk drive.

To complete this section, you will copy a file from your Tutorial Disk to the diskette in the other disk drive. Therefore, you will need an additional formatted diskette that matches the size of your other disk drive. *See pages 19 through 27 for instructions on how to format a diskette.*

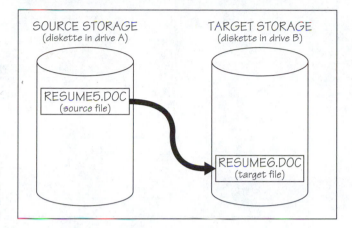

Figure 3-15
Copying a file from a diskette in drive A to a diskette in drive B

To copy a file from drive A to B, or from drive B to A:

1. If necessary, format an additional diskette for use in your other diskette drive as a destination diskette. *Do not format your Tutorial Disk or your Exercise Disk.*

2. Insert your Tutorial Disk (the source diskette) into one of the diskette drives.

3. Be sure you insert the newly formatted diskette (the destination diskette) that matches the size of the other diskette drive in the computer.

4. If you are copying from drive A to B, type **COPY A:\RESUME6.DOC B:** and press **[Enter]**. If you are copying from drive B to A, type **COPY B:\RESUME6.DOC A:** and press **[Enter]**. DOS copies this file from one diskette drive to another. If you specify the location of the source drive, you can copy from either drive. If you perform the copy operation from drive C, as shown in Figure 3-16, you must specify the drive name of both the source and target files. If you do not specify the name of the target file, DOS assumes you want to use the same name.

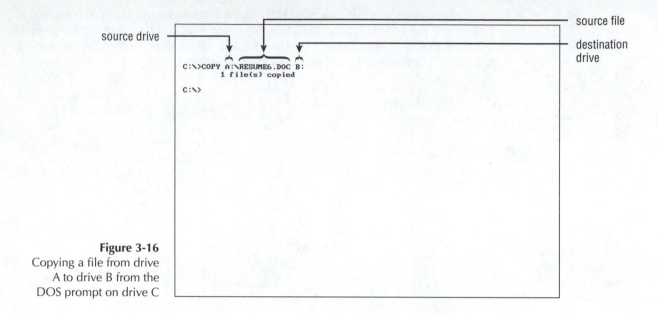

source file

source drive

destination drive

```
C:\>COPY A:\RESUME6.DOC B:
        1 file(s) copied

C:\>
```

Figure 3-16
Copying a file from drive
A to drive B from the
DOS prompt on drive C

Next, you want to verify the copy operation.

5. If drive B contains your target diskette, type **DIR B:** and press **[Enter]**. If drive A contains your target diskette, type **DIR A:** and press **[Enter]**. You should see the filename RESUME6.DOC in the directory listing.

Copying a File or Files from a Diskette to a Hard Disk, and from a Hard Disk to a Diskette

You want to copy your résumé template file, RESUME6.DOC, from your diskette onto your hard disk drive so that you can prepare a résumé for one of your clients. You can copy files from a diskette to a hard drive, or vice versa (Figure 3-17). If you are completing the copy procedure in a computer lab, ask your instructor or technical support person for permission to copy to the root directory of the hard disk.

Figure 3-17
Copying a file from
a diskette in drive
A to a hard disk

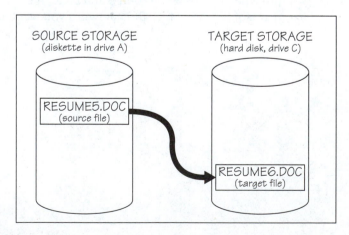

To copy a file on your Tutorial Disk to the hard disk:

1. Be sure the current drive contains your Tutorial Disk.

2. Type **DIR C:\RESUME6.DOC** and press **[Enter]** to verify that the hard disk does not contain a file with the name RESUME6.DOC in the root directory. If you see the message "File not found," as shown near the top of Figure 3-18, you can complete the next two steps. If DOS informs you there is a file named RESUME6.DOC, ask your instructor or technical support person if you can copy over that file. Another student might have already copied that file to the hard disk drive. The volume label, serial number, and number of bytes free on your drive C will be different.

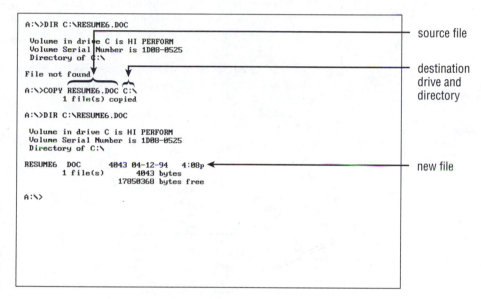

```
A:\>DIR C:\RESUME6.DOC                                    ──── source file

 Volume in drive C is HI PERFORM
 Volume Serial Number is 1D08-0525
 Directory of C:\                                         ──── destination
                                                               drive and
File not found                                                 directory

A:\>COPY RESUME6.DOC C:\
        1 file(s) copied

A:\>DIR C:\RESUME6.DOC

 Volume in drive C is HI PERFORM
 Volume Serial Number is 1D08-0525
 Directory of C:\

RESUME6  DOC      4043 04-12-94   4:08p  ◄───              ──── new file
        1 file(s)          4043 bytes
                       17850368 bytes free

A:\>
```

Figure 3-18
Copying a file from a
diskette to the hard drive

3. Type **COPY RESUME6.DOC C:** and press **[Enter]**. The Backslash (\) in C:\ instructs DOS to copy the file to the root directory of drive C. If you do not specify a filename for the target file, DOS uses the same name as that of the source file.

4. Press **[↑]** (Up Arrow) until you recall the command DIR C:\RESUME6.DOC. Press **[Enter]** to verify the copy operation. DOS displays the name of the copied file. See Figure 3-18.

Later, after you prepare the client résumé, you will want to copy your client file from the hard drive to a diskette so that you have a backup, or duplicate copy, of that file. To copy from the hard disk to a diskette, you just reverse the process described above: You specify the source drive as drive C and the target drive as either drive A or drive B.

After copying RESUME6.DOC to the hard disk, you decide it might be a good idea to copy all the résumé template files to the hard disk so that you can quickly find the one you need for a client.

To copy the résumé template files on your Tutorial Disk to the hard disk:

1. Type **CLS** and press **[Enter]** to clear the screen.

2. Type **DIR C:\RESUME*.*** and press **[Enter]** to verify that the hard disk does not contain files in the root directory that start with the name RESUME, other than RESUME6.DOC, which you just copied to the hard disk. If DOS informs you there are other files that start with the name "RESUME," ask your instructor or technical support person if you can copy over those files. Another student may have already copied those files to the hard disk.

3. Type **COPY RESUME*.* C:** and press **[Enter]**. DOS copies the files to the root directory of the hard disk. See Figure 3-19. If you do not specify filenames for the target files, DOS uses the source filenames. If you are using DOS 5.0 or 6.0, DOS copies RESUME6.DOC to the hard disk again and overwrites the copy already stored there. If you are using DOS 6.2, DOS might ask if you want to overwrite the existing file on drive C. If this occurs, type **Y** for Yes and press **[Enter]**.

5.0

6.0

6.2

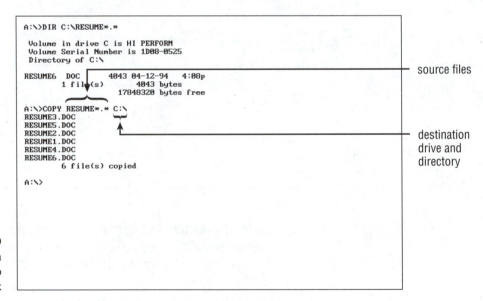

```
A:\>DIR C:\RESUME*.*

 Volume in drive C is HI PERFORM
 Volume Serial Number is 1D08-0525
 Directory of C:\

RESUME6  DOC      4043 04-12-94   4:08p
         1 file(s)        4043 bytes
                      17048320 bytes free

A:\>COPY RESUME*.* C:\
RESUME3.DOC
RESUME5.DOC
RESUME2.DOC
RESUME1.DOC
RESUME4.DOC
RESUME6.DOC
         6 file(s) copied

A:\>
```

source files

destination
drive and
directory

Figure 3-19
Copying files from a
diskette in drive A to
the hard disk

4. Press **[↑]** (Up Arrow) until you recall the command DIR C:\RESUME*.* and then press **[Enter]**. DOS displays the copied files and uses the default switches in the DOS environment to control the file display. See Figure 3-20.

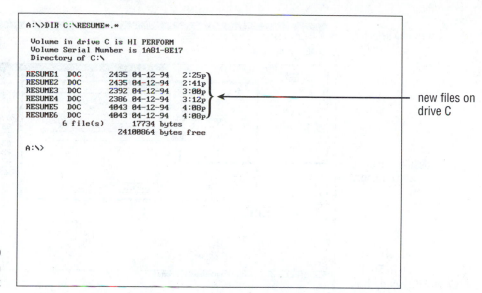

```
A:\>DIR C:\RESUME*.*

 Volume in drive C is HI PERFORM
 Volume Serial Number is 1A81-8E17
 Directory of C:\

RESUME1  DOC      2435 04-12-94   2:25p
RESUME2  DOC      2435 04-12-94   2:41p
RESUME3  DOC      2392 04-12-94   3:00p
RESUME4  DOC      2386 04-12-94   3:12p
RESUME5  DOC      4043 04-12-94   4:08p
RESUME6  DOC      4043 04-12-94   4:08p
         6 file(s)        17734 bytes
                       24100864 bytes free

A:\>
```

new files on
drive C

Figure 3-20
Verifying a copy operation
to the hard disk

COPYING A FILE IN THE DOS SHELL

Next, you want to copy the template for projecting business income on a yearly basis so that you can produce a new template for projecting income on a quarterly basis. For each job, staff members will develop new files from this template and other templates. To work more efficiently, you want to learn how to use the DOS Shell to copy files.

To copy this template file using the DOS Shell:

1. Be sure the current drive contains your Tutorial Disk.

2. Type **DOSSHELL** and press **[Enter]**.

3. Press **[Tab]** twice to move the selection cursor to the file list window.

    If you are using the mouse, click the **file list window's title bar**.

4. Type **P** to select the first, and only, file that has the letter "P" at the beginning of its filename.

    If you are using a mouse, click in the **scroll bar** to the right of the filenames until the filename PRJ_INC comes into view; then, click **PRJ_INC**.

5. Press **[F10]** (Actions), press **[Enter]** to select the File menu, and type **C** to select the Copy command.

    If you are using the mouse, click **File**, then click **Copy**.

    Note that you can also use the shortcut Copy key, [F8]. The DOS Shell displays the Copy File dialog box. See Figure 3-21. Next to the From prompt is the name of the currently highlighted file, which is the source file. The DOS Shell will copy this file. Next to the To prompt, the DOS Shell displays the current drive and directory, which is also the target drive and directory. If you want to use another drive, you can type a new drive name. You can also specify a different filename for the copied file. Because this is the correct source file and target drive and directory, you do not need to make any changes.

currently selected menu →

destination drive and directory ——

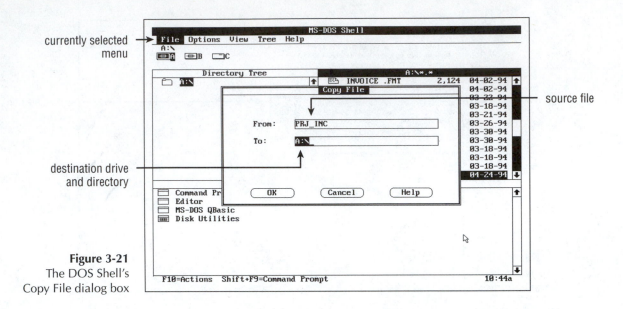

source file

Figure 3-21
The DOS Shell's
Copy File dialog box

6. Be sure [Num Lock] is off. Then press **[End]** to position the cursor so that you can enter a filename after the drive name.

    If you are using the mouse, click **after the drive name**.

    If you do not press [End] or click after the drive name, the filename that you type will write over the drive name. If this happens, you might need to retype the drive name before typing the filename.

7. Type **QTR_INC**. Then press **[Enter]**. *Remember to include the underline character in the filename.*

    If you are using the mouse, type **QTR_INC**, then click **OK**.

    The DOS Shell copies the file. If a file exists with this same filename, the DOS Shell will ask you to verify that you want to copy over that file.

8. Press **[↓]** (Down Arrow) to view the next filename. The next filename is RESUME1.DOC.

If your version of DOS does not display QTR_INC as the next filename, you must instruct the DOS Shell to reread your diskette and update the list of file-names in the file list window.

To reread your Tutorial Disk and update the file listing:

1. Press **[F10]** (Actions), press **[→]** (Right Arrow) twice to highlight View, and press **[Enter]** to select View. The DOS Shell displays the View menu. See Figure 3-22.

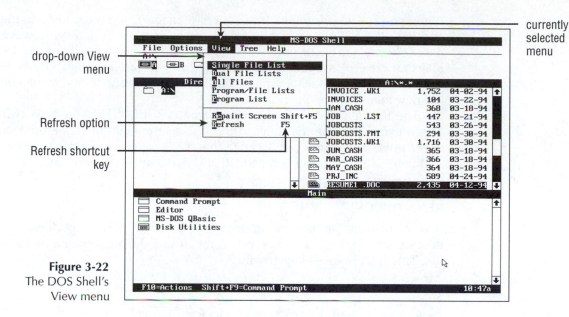

drop-down View menu

currently selected menu

Refresh option

Refresh shortcut key

Figure 3-22
The DOS Shell's
View menu

2. Press [↓] (Down Arrow) until you highlight Refresh and press **[Enter]**.

If you are using the mouse, click the **View** menu, then click the **Refresh command**.

You can also use [F5] (Refresh) to update the screen. The selection cursor returns to the drive window.

3. Press **[Tab]** twice to return to the file list window.

If you are using the mouse, click the **file list window title bar**.

4. Type **Q** to highlight the new file QTR_INC. Note that this file currently has the same size and date as PRJ_INC. Because you have not yet made any changes to QTR_INC, it is identical to PRJ_INC.

5. Press **[F3]** (Exit) to exit the DOS Shell.

In your business, you can quickly make copies of your template files with the DOS Shell, as you have seen. You can then modify them to produce final copies of documents for clients.

RENAMING FILES

You want to rename some of the files on your diskette so that the filenames more clearly identify the contents of the files. Later, when you are facing deadlines, you will not need to spend valuable time checking to make sure you have the correct file. Again, you want to compare this type of file operation at the DOS prompt with the use of the DOS Shell.

You can use the RENAME command, or its abbreviated version, REN, to change the name of a file. If you use wildcards with these commands, you can change the names of a group of files. The general syntax for these internal commands is as follows:

RENAME [*drive:*][*path*]*filename1 filename2*

REN [*drive:*][*path*]*filename1 filename2*

When you specify *filename1* (the source filename), you must include the drive and path if the file is on another drive or in another directory. However, you *never* specify a drive or path with the destination filename. If you do, DOS displays an error message because it thinks you are attempting to move the file, and this command does not move files. The destination filename, *filename2*, is the new name for the file.

The first file that you want to rename is JOBCOSTS. You have two other files on your diskette that have JOBCOSTS as the main filename but that have descriptive file extensions. Because this file is a report, you want to rename it JOBCOSTS.RPT. You can enter the RENAME command in two ways:

REN JOBCOSTS JOBCOSTS.RPT

REN JOBCOSTS *.RPT

If you substitute an asterisk wildcard for the main part of the filename in the destination file, DOS assumes you want to use the same name as the source file. This feature saves keystroking.

To rename the JOBCOSTS file from the DOS prompt:

1. Be sure the current drive contains your Tutorial Disk.

2. Type **DIR JOBCOSTS** and press **[Enter]** to verify the file exists. DOS lists files with and without file extensions. See Figure 3-23.

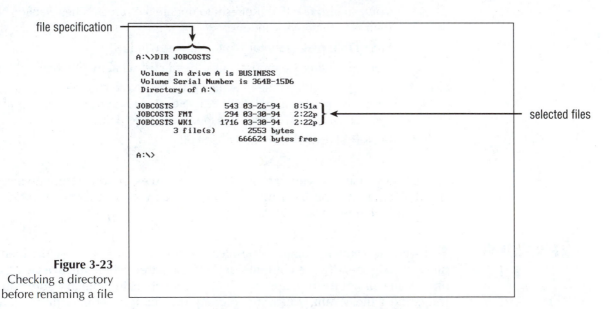

file specification

```
A:\>DIR JOBCOSTS

 Volume in drive A is BUSINESS
 Volume Serial Number is 364B-15D6
 Directory of A:\

JOBCOSTS          543 03-26-94    8:51a
JOBCOSTS FMT      294 03-30-94    2:22p
JOBCOSTS WK1     1716 03-30-94    2:22p
        3 file(s)         2553 bytes
                        666624 bytes free

A:\>
```

selected files

Figure 3-23
Checking a directory
before renaming a file

3. Type **REN JOBCOSTS *.RPT** and press **[Enter]**. DOS assumes that you want to rename the file on the current drive and that the main part of the new filename is the same. DOS will not let you rename a file if there is already a file by the name that you want to use. *You can also use RENAME instead of REN.*

4. Press [↑] (Up Arrow) until you recall the command DIR JOBCOSTS, and press **[Enter]** to verify the change. DOS added a file extension when it renamed the file. See Figure 3-24.

current filename

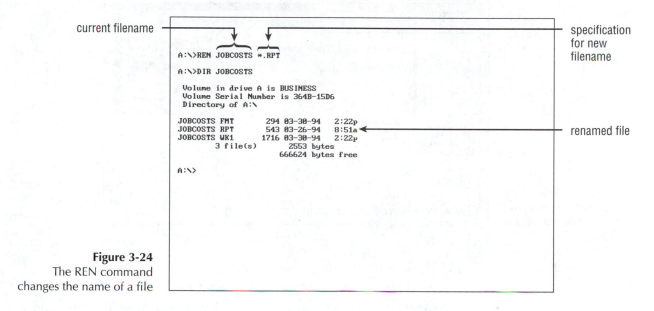

```
A:\>REN JOBCOSTS *.RPT

A:\>DIR JOBCOSTS

 Volume in drive A is BUSINESS
 Volume Serial Number is 364B-15D6
 Directory of A:\

JOBCOSTS FMT       294 03-30-94   2:22p
JOBCOSTS RPT       543 03-26-94   8:51a
JOBCOSTS WK1      1716 03-30-94   2:22p
        3 file(s)        2553 bytes
                       666624 bytes free

A:\>
```

specification for new filename

renamed file

Figure 3-24
The REN command changes the name of a file

RENAMING FILES IN THE DOS SHELL

The next file that you want to rename is COVER.LTR. Because it is the letter sent with a client's résumé, you want to rename it RESUME.LTR. This time you want to use the DOS Shell to rename the file.

To rename the COVER.LTR file from the DOS Shell:

1. Be sure the current drive contains your Tutorial Disk. Then type **DOSSHELL** and press **[Enter]**.

2. Press **[Tab]** until the selection cursor moves to the file list window.

   If you are using the mouse, click the **file list window title bar**.

3. Press [↓] (Down Arrow) to highlight the filename COVER.LTR.

   If you are using the mouse, click the filename **COVER.LTR**.

4. Press **[F10]** (Actions), press **[Enter]** to select the File menu, and type **N** to select the Rename option.

   If you are using the mouse, click **File**, then click **Rename**.

   The DOS Shell displays the Rename File dialog box. See Figure 3-25. The Current name field shows the file's current name. Next to the New name prompt, you type the name you want to use.

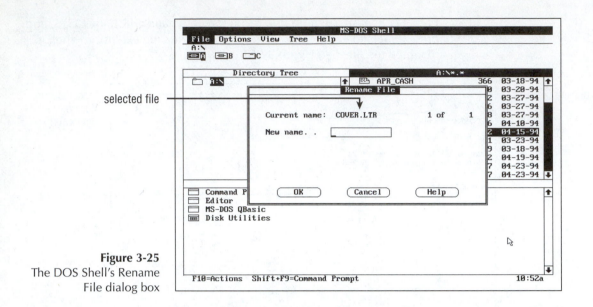

selected file ────

Figure 3-25
The DOS Shell's Rename
File dialog box

5. Type **RESUME.LTR** and press [**Enter**].

    If you are using the mouse, type **RESUME.LTR** and then click **OK**.

    After the DOS Shell renames the file, it places the new filename in the file list in alphabetical order. The original filename, COVER.LTR, is no longer displayed because you changed the filename.

6. Type **R** to display the filenames that start with the letter "R." The selection cursor moves to the filename RESUME.LTR. You successfully renamed the file with the cover letter for résumés.

7. Press [**F3**] (Exit) to exit the DOS Shell.

When you name a file, the name you select may be logical at the time, but later, you may realize that there is a better name for that file. You can rename it from the DOS prompt or the DOS Shell. The DOS Shell has the added advantage of updating the list of filenames quickly.

DELETING FILES

You realize that there are a couple of files you do not need and you want to remove them from your diskette so that they do not take up valuable space. You can delete files from the DOS prompt with the DEL or ERASE commands. The general syntax is as follows:

DEL [*drive:*][*path*]*filename*

ERASE [*drive:*][*path*]*filename*

Both commands are internal commands, and both produce the same results.

Deleting files from the DOS prompt is risky. If you use wildcards, you can inadvertently delete important files. DOS does not ask you if you are sure you want to delete a file or a group of files, except in one case. If you enter DEL *.* at the DOS prompt, DOS will automatically ask you if you want to delete all the files in the directory. As a precautionary measure, you should first test your file specification with the DIR command. If the DIR command selects the files you expect, then you can use the DEL or ERASE command with the same file specification.

You can also use the **Prompt for Verification switch**, /P. When you use this switch, DOS displays a prompt and asks you to verify whether or not you want to delete the file.

You no longer need the JOB.LST file, so you decide to delete it.

To delete the file named JOB.LST at the DOS prompt:

1. Be sure the current drive contains your Tutorial Disk.

2. Type **DIR JOB.LST** and press **[Enter]** to verify that the file exists. If you specify the exact name of a file, the directory listing will include only that file.

3. Type **DEL JOB.LST /P** and press **[Enter]**. DOS prompts for verification, displaying the message, "Delete (Y/N)?". *You can also use the ERASE command to achieve the same result.*

4. Type **Y**. You do not need to press the Enter key. DOS displays the DOS prompt after deleting the file.

Now you want to verify the deletion.

5. Press **[↑]** (Up Arrow) until you recall the command DIR JOB.LST, and then press **[Enter]**. The file JOB.LST is no longer on your diskette. See Figure 3-26.

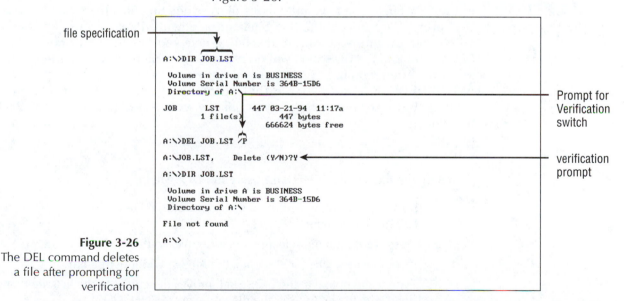

file specification

Prompt for Verification switch

verification prompt

Figure 3-26
The DEL command deletes a file after prompting for verification

```
A:\>DIR JOB.LST

 Volume in drive A is BUSINESS
 Volume Serial Number is 364B-15D6
 Directory of A:\

JOB      LST      447 03-21-94  11:17a
        1 file(s)          447 bytes
                        666624 bytes free

A:\>DEL JOB.LST /P

A:\JOB.LST,    Delete (Y/N)?Y

A:\>DIR JOB.LST

 Volume in drive A is BUSINESS
 Volume Serial Number is 364B-15D6
 Directory of A:\

File not found

A:\>
```

Deleting a File from Another Drive

While you are thinking of it, you decide to delete this same file from the duplicate copy of your Tutorial Disk. You decide to perform this operation from drive C so that you know how to delete a file from another drive. When you delete a file on another drive, you must specify the drive name and in some cases, the filename's path.

To delete a file from another drive:

1. Type **C:** and press **[Enter]**. DOS displays the prompt for drive C.
2. Remove the Tutorial Disk from the diskette drive and insert your Exercise Disk.
3. Type **DIR A:\JOB.LST** (or **DIR B:\JOB.LST**) and press **[Enter]** to verify that the file exists on the diskette in the diskette drive. The Backslash (\) tells DOS to check the root directory of the drive you specify for the filename.
4. Type **DEL A:\JOB.LST /P** (or **DEL B:\JOB.LST /P**) and press **[Enter]**. DOS prompts for verification. Again, you are specifying the file's exact location using the drive name and path (the Backslash).
5. Type **Y**. You do not need to press the Enter key. DOS displays the DOS prompt after deleting the file.

Now you want to verify the deletion.

6. Press **[↑]** (Up Arrow) until you recall the command DIR A:\JOB.LST or DIR B:\JOB.LST. Then press **[Enter]**. The file JOB.LST is no longer on your diskette.
7. Remove the Exercise Disk, and insert your Tutorial Disk into the diskette drive.
8. Type **A:** (or **B:**) to change to the disk drive that contains your Tutorial Disk.

DELETING FILES IN THE DOS SHELL

In the DOS Shell, you have more control over deleting files than you do at the DOS prompt. By default, the DOS Shell automatically displays a prompt asking you if you are sure you want to delete the selected file. Unlike working at the DOS prompt, in the DOS Shell you do not have to remember to use the Prompt for Verification switch.

SCHEDULE is another file that is taking up valuable space on your diskette. Because you have a copy of this file, you decide to use the DOS Shell to delete it.

To delete the file named SCHEDULE using the DOS Shell:

1. Be sure the current drive contains your Tutorial Disk. Then type **DOSSHELL** and press **[Enter]**.
2. Press **[Tab]** until the selection cursor moves to the file list window.

    If you are using the mouse, click the **file list window title bar**.
3. Type **S** and note that the DOS Shell moves the cursor to the first file that starts with the letter "S"—the file you want, SCHEDULE.

   If you are using the mouse, click in the **scroll bar** to the right of the file-names until the DOS Shell displays the filename SCHEDULE. Then click the filename **SCHEDULE**.

4. Press the shortcut key **[Del]** or **[Delete]**. The DOS Shell displays the Delete File Confirmation dialog box. See Figure 3-27. The cursor is positioned on the Yes button. (*You can also use the Delete command on the File menu to delete files.*)

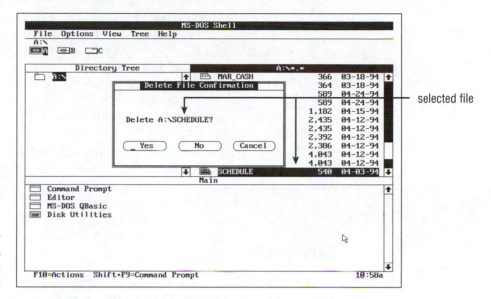

selected file

Figure 3-27
The DOS Shell's Delete File Confirmation dialog box

5. Press **[Enter]** to delete the file.

   If you are using the mouse, click the **Yes button**.

   The DOS Shell displays a dialog box that verifies it is deleting the filename you specified. Then the DOS Shell updates the file list.

6. Press **[↓]** (Down Arrow) twice. The filename SCHEDULE is no longer in the file list.

7. Press **[F3]** (Exit) to exit the DOS Shell.

   When combined with the DIR command, the COPY, RENAME, and DEL commands assist you in one of the most important tasks you face when you use a computer system—managing your files. You can more easily and efficiently perform file operations from the DOS Shell, with less chance of inadvertently losing files.

FINISHING UP   If you completed the section of this tutorial where you copied the résumé template files from your Tutorial Disk to drive C, you will need to remove those files from your computer system's hard disk.

To remove the résumé template files from drive C:

1. Type **C:** and press **[Enter]** to change to drive C.

2. Remove your Tutorial Disk from drive A so that you do not inadvertently delete the résumé template files from that diskette.

3. Type **DIR C:\RESUME*.*** and press **[Enter]** to verify that these files are in the root directory of drive C. If the directory listing contains the filenames RESUME1.DOC, RESUME2.DOC, RESUME3.DOC, RESUME4.DOC, RESUME5.DOC, and RESUME6.DOC, complete the next step. If DOS displays other files in the directory listing, check with your instructor or technical support person before you attempt to delete files in the next step. If you do not see any files that start with the name "RESUME," you do not need to perform the next step.

4. Type **DEL C:\RESUME*.*** and press **[Enter]**. DOS deletes these files from the root directory of drive C.

◆

SUMMARY

In this tutorial, you learned the importance of ASCII files and studied many of their features. You viewed the contents of an ASCII file with the TYPE command at the DOS prompt and with the View File Contents option on the File menu in the DOS Shell. You used the pipe redirection operator and the MORE filter with the TYPE command at the DOS prompt to display the contents of an ASCII file one screen at a time. You printed an ASCII file with the PRINT command at the DOS prompt and with the Print option on the File menu in the DOS Shell.

You copied files with the COPY command at the DOS prompt and the Copy option on the File menu in the DOS Shell. You copied files to the same diskette, a different diskette, and a hard drive using a different or the same filename. You renamed files with the REN command at the DOS prompt and the Rename option on the File menu in the DOS Shell. You deleted files with the DEL command at the DOS prompt and with the Delete key in the DOS Shell.

You worked with filenames in the file list window in the DOS Shell, and you updated the directory with the Refresh option on the View menu.

Command Reference

DOS Commands

COPY [*source*] [*destination*]	An internal command that copies the contents of a file (called the source file) and produces a new file (called the destination, or target, file)
DEL [*drive*:] [*path*] *filename* [/P]	An internal command that deletes a file or a group of files; the Prompt for Verification switch (/P) asks you if you want to delete the file(s)
ERASE [*drive*:] [*path*] *filename* [/P]	An internal command that deletes a file or a group of files; the Prompt for Verification switch (/P) asks you if you want to delete the file(s)
[*command-name*] ¦ MORE	A DOS filter, or external command, that modifies output of a DOS command and displays it one screen at a time
PRINT [[*drive*:] [*path*] *filename*[...]]	An external command that prints a text file
RENAME [*drive*:] [*path*] *filename1* *filename2* REN [*drive*:] [*path*] *filename1* *filename2*	An internal command that renames a file or a group of files
TYPE [drive:] [path] filename	An internal command that displays the contents of a text file on the screen

DOS Shell Commands

File/Copy or [F8]	Copies one or more files
File/Delete, [Del], or [Delete]	Deletes a file
File/Print	Prints a text file from the DOS Shell after the PRINT program is loaded from the DOS prompt or from the DOS Shell
File/Rename	Renames one or more files
File/Run	Executes a DOS command from the DOS Shell
File/View File Contents or [F9]	Displays the contents of a text file
View/Refresh or [F5]	Updates the directory listing in the file list window after the DOS Shell rereads a diskette or hard disk

QUESTIONS

1. What is an ASCII file?

2. What control codes can an ASCII file contain?

3. What DOS command displays the contents of an ASCII file from the DOS prompt? Give an example of how to use this command.

4. How can you view the contents of a long ASCII file one screen at a time?

5. What is a DOS filter and how do you use it?

6. What is the pipe operator and how do you use it?

7. What does the MORE command do?

8. What are "read me" files, and why are they important?

9. How do you view an ASCII file from the DOS Shell?

10. What DOS command prints an ASCII file from the DOS prompt? What information does this command require?

11. What is a TSR?

12. How do you print an ASCII file from the DOS Shell?

13. Before you use the Print option on the File menu in the DOS Shell to print an ASCII file, what program must you first load into memory?

14. What does the COPY command do? What is the difference between a source file and a destination, or target, file?

15. What does DOS do when you copy a file but do not specify a drive name for the source file?

16. What does DOS do when you copy a file but do not specify a drive name for the target file?

17. What does DOS do when you copy a file to another disk but do not specify a filename for the new file?

18. What precaution should you take before you copy a file?

19. How do you copy a file in the DOS Shell?

20. What must you do in the DOS Shell to update the file list window?

21. What two commands can you use at the DOS prompt to change a filename?

22. What does DOS do if you rename a file and specify a drive for the destination file?

23. How do you rename a file in the DOS Shell?

24. What two commands can you use at the DOS prompt to delete a file?

25. Before you delete a file, what check should you perform?

26. What switch can you use when deleting a file from the DOS prompt to ensure you are deleting the correct file?

27. How do you delete a file from the DOS Shell?

28. How would you use the question mark wildcard to rename PROJBID1, PROJBID2, and PROJBID3 to PROJBID1.WP, PROJBID2.WP, and PROJBID3.WP in one step?

29. Assume drive A is the current drive. What command would you enter to copy the file named 94SALES from drive A to drive C?

30. Assume drive C is the current drive. What command would you enter to delete the file named MTGNOTES on drive B?

TUTORIAL ASSIGNMENTS

1. **Viewing and Printing the Contents of a Text File**: *Use your Tutorial Disk to perform the following operations from the DOS prompt.* List the command that you use to accomplish each step.
   a. Display the contents of the file named EQUIP.LST.
   b. Display the contents of the file named STARTUP.
   c. Print a copy of the file named RESUME2.DOC.

2. **Using the MORE Filter**: *Use your Tutorial Disk to perform the following operations from the DOS prompt.* List the command that you use to accomplish each step.
   a. Display the contents of the file named BUSINESS.PLN one screen at a time.
   b. Display the contents of the file named RESUME4.DOC one screen at a time.

3. **Copying Files**: *Use your Exercise Disk to perform the following operations from the DOS prompt.* List the command that you use to accomplish each step.
   a. Copy the file named SCHEDULE to produce a new file with the name WORKLOG. *copy schedule worklog*
   b. Copy the file named CASHFLOW.RPT to produce a new file with the name SUMMARY.
   c. Use question mark wildcards to copy JAN_CASH, FEB_CASH, MAR_CASH, APR_CASH, MAY_CASH, and JUN_CASH to produce files named JAN_CASH.RPT, FEB_CASH.RPT, MAR_CASH.RPT, APR_CASH.RPT, MAY_CASH.RPT, and JUN_CASH.RPT in one copy operation.

3-5 write command you use for each answer

4. **Renaming Files**: *Use your Exercise Disk to perform the following operations from the DOS prompt.* List the command that you use to accomplish each step.
   a. Rename the file FEESCALE to FEES.
   b. Rename the file PRJ_INC to PRJ_INC.RPT.
   c. Use question mark wildcards to rename the files JAN_CASH, FEB_CASH, MAR_CASH, APR_CASH, MAY_CASH, and JUN_CASH to JAN-CASH, FEB-CASH, MAR-CASH, APR-CASH, MAY-CASH, and JUN-CASH in one operation.

5. **Managing Files in the DOS Shell**: *Use your Exercise Disk to perform the following operations from the DOS Shell.* List the steps for each of these operations, including the steps required to select a file.
   a. Copy the file CLIENT.LST to produce a new file named CUSTOMER.LST.
   b. Rename the file INVOICE.WK1 to INVOICES.WK1.
   c. Change the filename STARTUP to STARTUP.EST.
   d. View the contents of the file RESUME3.DOC.
   e. Print a copy of the file RESUME3.DOC.

Using Subdirectories

OBJECTIVES

In this tutorial you will learn to:

◆ Create and change subdirectories

◆ Move files to subdirectories

◆ List and copy files in subdirectories

◆ Delete files in subdirectories

◆ Expand a directory structure

◆ View and print a directory tree

Your new business venture is growing rapidly! Your client files are increasing daily, and you want to more efficiently organize your client and business files on your hard disk and diskettes so that you can quickly locate important documents.

Most of the hard disks in your office have 120MB to 240MB of storage space and a variety of installed software packages and utilities, including Windows, WordPerfect, Lotus 1-2-3, and dBASE. Each software application includes hundreds of files and requires from 5MB to 15MB of hard disk storage space. Already, the majority of each hard disk's storage capacity is dedicated to these software applications and utilities that you use on a daily basis. Not only must you manage the use of the data files that you create with these software packages, but you must also manage the program files included with the software.

◆

MANAGING FILES

File management is one of the major tasks faced by any user of a computer system. This task is more complicated on a hard disk because of the enormous storage capacity of the drives and the number of files stored on them. To assist you in this task, DOS allows you to group related files together on a hard disk or diskette. You can then work with those grouped files as a separate unit, independent of all other files.

When you format a diskette or hard disk, DOS creates a special file, called a **directory file**, to keep track of information on files. When you use the DIR command, DOS shows you some of the information stored in this special directory file—the name, extension, size, date, and time of each file. The first directory created by the FORMAT command is called the **root directory**, or **main directory**.

After you format a diskette or hard disk, you can create other directories called subdirectories. A **subdirectory** is a directory that is *subordinate* to the root directory or to another subdirectory. Because each subdirectory is nothing other than a special file that tracks information about a group of files, a subdirectory is also a directory. (The term *directory* also describes the output produced by the DIR command.)

You can compare the use of drives, directories, subdirectories, and files to a filing cabinet's drawers, dividers, folders, and printed documents, respectively (Figures 4-1 and 4-2). Each drawer in a file cabinet is comparable to a disk drive. Within each drawer, each hanging folder corresponds to a DOS subdirectory. For example, you might have a file drawer labeled REPORTS, which contains different types of organizational reports, such as sales and budget reports. Within each hanging folder in the drawer, you might have folders that organize the reports by category, such as SALES and BUDGET. These folders correspond to subdirectories below the directory named REPORTS on your disk drive. Within each folder, the individual reports, such as SALES93.RPT and 95BUDGET, correspond to single files on your disk.

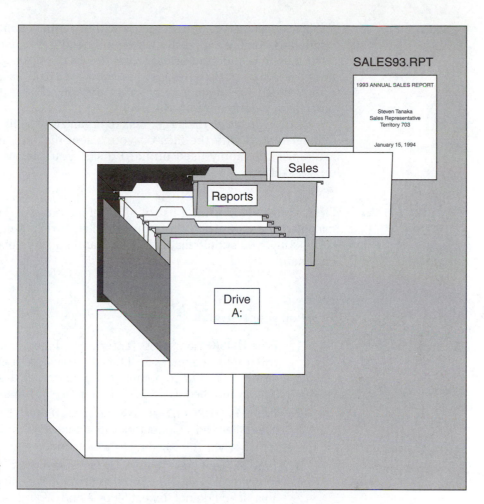

Figure 4-1
Organization of
files in a filing cabinet

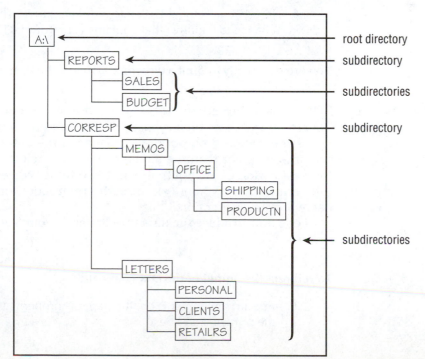

Figure 4-2
Organization of
directories and
subdirectories on a
diskette or hard disk

The organization of documents within a filing cabinet enables you to find a document quickly and easily when you need it. Similarly, if you organize your hard disk into subdirectories, store files in the appropriate subdirectory, and maintain the subdirectories, you can locate files easily and quickly. By approaching file management in an organized way, you and your business partner can work more productively.

Before you tackle the larger task of organizing the files on your hard disk, you decide to start with the files on your client diskette. Although subdirectories are more commonly used on hard disks, you can also create subdirectories on a diskette.

GETTING STARTED

First, you want to print a list of all the files on your Tutorial Disk so that you can plan the organization of your subdirectories. Before you print this directory listing, you should install DOSKEY and specify default switches for the DIR command.

To set up your system:

5.0
6.0
6.2

1. Type **DOSKEY** and press **[Enter]**. If you are using DOS 5.0 or 6.0, DOS will display the message "DOSKey installed" if DOSKEY is not already installed on your computer. If you do not see this message, DOSKEY is already installed. DOS 6.2 will not display a message.

2. Type **SET DIRCMD=/P /O** and press **[Enter]**. DOS will now display your client files and subdirectories in alphabetical order and pause after each screen when you use the DIR command.

3. Type **SET** and press **[Enter]**. DOS displays the contents of the DOS environment. You should see the setting you specified for the DIRCMD variable. If you do not, repeat Steps 2 and 3.

4. Insert your Tutorial Disk into a diskette drive. Then, type **A:** or **B:** to change to the drive that contains your Tutorial Disk.

You are now ready to print a directory listing of the filenames on your diskette.

PRINTING A DIRECTORY

DOS expects input from the keyboard and directs output to the monitor. Therefore, DOS uses the keyboard as the **standard input device** and the monitor as the **standard output device**. To send the output of a DOS command to the printer rather than the monitor, you must tell DOS to **redirect**, or change the destination of, that output with the **output redirection operator**, which is the greater-than symbol (>). After the redirection operator, you specify the name of your printer port.

Let's now produce the directory listing of your Tutorial Disk.

To redirect the output of the DIR command:

1. Be sure the printer is on, the paper is properly aligned in the printer, and the printer is on-line.

2. Type **DIR /-P > PRN** and press **[Enter]**. *Be sure you type a minus sign before the "P" in the /P switch.* /-P overrides the Pause switch setting in the DOS environment so that DOS does not pause after each screen. DOS still uses the Order switch in the DOS environment to print an alphabetical directory. Figure 4-3 shows a sample printout of the directory of the Tutorial Disk. Your volume serial number will be different. If you are using DOS 6.2, you will see commas every three places to the left of the decimal.

6.2

```
Volume in drive A is BUSINESS
Volume Serial Number is 142E-14F9
Directory of A:\

APR_CASH           366 03-18-94   10:20a
BUSINESS PLN       590 03-20-94    5:26p
CASHFLOW FMT       472 03-27-94    8:32a
CASHFLOW RPT       176 03-27-94    8:45a
CASHFLOW WK1      1648 03-27-94    8:32a
CLIENT   LST       476 04-10-94   11:08a
EQUIP    LST       671 03-23-94    3:57p
FEB_CASH           369 03-18-94   10:14a
FEESCALE           412 04-19-94    1:48p
INCOME   YR1       987 04-23-94    9:06a
INCOME   YR2       987 04-23-94    9:17a
INCOME   YR3       987 04-23-94    9:21a
INCOME   YR4       987 04-23-94    9:34a
INCOME   YR5       987 04-23-94    9:47a
INSURE   LST      1528 04-09-94    8:48a
INVOICE  FMT      2124 04-02-94   10:45a
INVOICE  WK1      1752 04-02-94   10:45a
INVOICES           104 03-22-94    8:48a
JAN_CASH           368 03-18-94   10:00a
JOBCOSTS FMT       294 03-30-94    2:22p
JOBCOSTS RPT       543 03-26-94    8:51a
JOBCOSTS WK1      1716 03-30-94    2:22p
JUN_CASH           365 03-18-94   10:45a
MAR_CASH           366 03-18-94   10:17a
MAY_CASH           364 03-18-94   10:43a
PRJ_INC            589 04-24-94   11:27a
QTR_INC            589 04-24-94   11:27a
RESUME   LTR      1182 04-15-94   11:49a
RESUME1  DOC      2435 04-12-94    2:25p
RESUME2  DOC      2435 04-12-94    2:41p
RESUME3  DOC      2392 04-12-94    3:00p
RESUME4  DOC      2386 04-12-94    3:12p
RESUME5  DOC      4043 04-12-94    4:08p
RESUME6  DOC      4043 04-12-94    4:08p
SCHEDULE FMT       794 04-07-94    1:21p
SCHEDULE WK1      2147 04-07-94    1:21p
STARTUP           1010 03-11-94   10:03a
       37 file(s)      43684 bytes
                     668672 bytes free
```

Figure 4-3
A printed copy of the directory listing for your Tutorial Disk

3. If you need to eject the paper from the printer, press the **Form Feed button** on the printer. If the printer does not respond, press the **On Line button** to place the printer off-line. Then press the **Form Feed button**. After the printer ejects the page, press the **On Line button** to place the printer back on-line.

4. Remove your hardcopy from the printer.

CREATING SUB-DIRECTORIES

After examining the types of files on your Tutorial Disk, you prepare a sketch of the subdirectory structure that you want to use to organize your files (Figure 4-4).

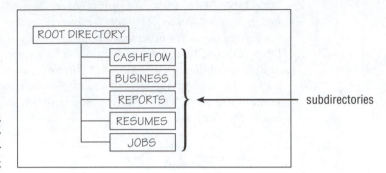

Figure 4-4
The planned directory
structure for your
Tutorial Disk

The DOS commands for creating a subdirectory are MD and MKDIR (both abbreviations for Make Directory). These internal commands have the following syntax:

MD [*drive:*] *path*
MKDIR [*drive:*] *path*

You must specify the drive name if you want to create the subdirectory on another drive. You also must specify the directory's path. In other words, you must identify its name and location relative to another directory, such as the root directory.

The rules for naming a subdirectory are the same as those for naming a file. Just as a filename identifies the type of document stored in the file, a subdirectory's name describes the types of files that you will store in the subdirectory.

Before you create a subdirectory, you should check the DOS prompt to be sure you create the subdirectory in the right place—just as you would read the label on a file cabinet drawer before placing a folder in it. You have learned that the prompt shows the current drive. It also tells you the current directory. For example, if you see A:\ or B:\ in the DOS prompt, the letters A and B indicate the drive name and the \ (Backslash) indicates that you are in the root directory. The \ (Backslash) is the notation DOS assigns to the root directory. If your DOS prompt looks like one of these examples, you are ready to create a subdirectory.

If DOS displays your prompt as A> or B>, you must use the PROMPT command to change the appearance of the DOS prompt. The syntax for this internal command is

PROMPT [*text*]

The text can consist of characters that you want to display as part of the prompt. You can also include special codes that customize the appearance of the DOS prompt. For example, if you enter PROMPT PG, the $P code instructs DOS to construct the prompt so that it shows the full path—the drive name and path for the current directory. The $G tells DOS to include the greater-than symbol (>) after the full path. This separates the path in the DOS prompt from commands that you enter at the DOS prompt.

Check your prompt to make sure it shows the path.

To change the prompt to display the current directory:

1. If your DOS prompt does not appear as A:\> or B:\>, type
   PROMPT PG and press **[Enter]**. DOS updates the DOS prompt
   to show the full path.

You are now ready to create a subdirectory. The first subdirectory that
you create below the root directory will store files for tracking the cashflow in
your business. You decide to name it CASHFLOW.

To create the CASHFLOW subdirectory:

1. Type **MD CASHFLOW** and press **[Enter]**. DOS creates the subdirectory
   below the root directory of the disk drive containing your diskette and
   displays the DOS prompt. If you perform this operation from another
   drive, such as drive C, you would include the drive name before the subdirectory name. Also, if the disk contains a file with the same name as the
   one you want to use as the subdirectory name, DOS will display an error
   message that tells you it is unable to create the directory.

   Now verify that this new subdirectory exists.

2. Type **DIR C*** and press **[Enter]**. DOS displays a screen with an alphabetical list of the files in the root directory that begin with the letter "C,"
   regardless of whether they have a file extension. See Figure 4-5. The first
   file in the directory listing is the name of your newly created subdirectory.
   DOS displays <DIR> next to each subdirectory name in a directory listing.

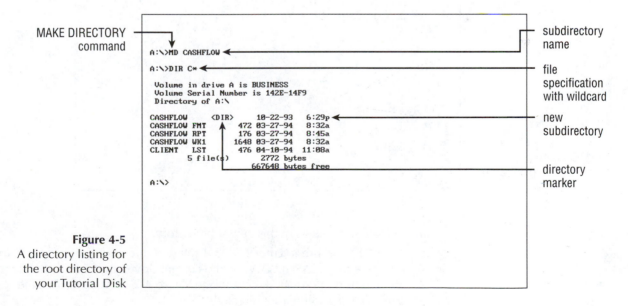

MAKE DIRECTORY command

subdirectory name

file specification with wildcard

new subdirectory

directory marker

Figure 4-5
A directory listing for
the root directory of
your Tutorial Disk

CHANGING DIRECTORIES

Once you create a subdirectory, you can switch to that subdirectory by typing CD or CHDIR (both abbreviations for Change Directory) at the DOS prompt. These internal commands have the following syntax:

CD [*drive:*] *path*
CHDIR [*drive:*] *path*

If you specify a drive name, you change from one directory to another on that disk drive, even if you are working on another disk drive. When you specify the path, you are telling DOS the name of the directory that you want to change to and its location relative to another directory, such as the root directory.

After you change to a subdirectory, you can work more easily with the files stored in the subdirectory. Let's change to the CASHFLOW directory and examine its contents.

To change to the CASHFLOW subdirectory:

1. Type **CD CASHFLOW** and press **[Enter]**. DOS updates the DOS prompt to show the full path of the subdirectory. See Figure 4-6. The DOS prompt A:\CASHFLOW (or B:\CASHFLOW) tells you that CASHFLOW is a subdirectory below the root directory of the diskette in the current drive.

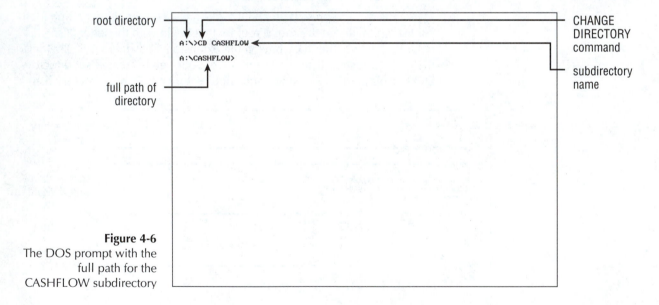

root directory

A:\>CD CASHFLOW

A:\CASHFLOW>

full path of
directory

CHANGE
DIRECTORY
command

subdirectory
name

Figure 4-6
The DOS prompt with the
full path for the
CASHFLOW subdirectory

Now view the contents of this new subdirectory.

2. Type **DIR** and press **[Enter]**. DOS displays a directory listing for the current directory, CASHFLOW, on the current drive, and reports that there are two files in this subdirectory. See Figure 4-7. You do not see the names of files in the root directory.

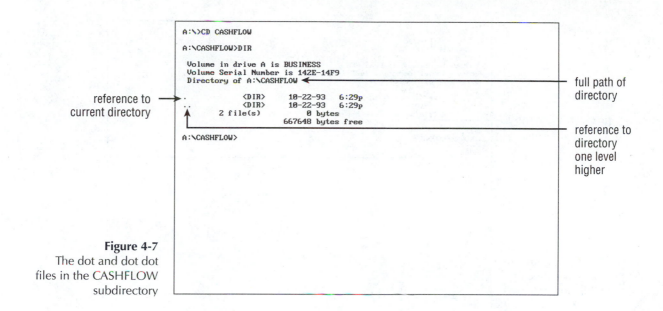

reference to
current directory →

full path of
directory

reference to
directory
one level
higher

```
A:\>CD CASHFLOW

A:\CASHFLOW>DIR

 Volume in drive A is BUSINESS
 Volume Serial Number is 142E-14F9
 Directory of A:\CASHFLOW ◄

 .              <DIR>      10-22-93    6:29p
 ..             <DIR>      10-22-93    6:29p
       2 file(s)              0 bytes
                        667648 bytes free

A:\CASHFLOW>
```

Figure 4-7
The dot and dot dot
files in the CASHFLOW
subdirectory

Whenever DOS creates a subdirectory, it always creates these two files. The first file, named . (pronounced "dot"), is a notation that refers to the current directory. The second file, named .. (pronounced "dot dot"), is a notation that refers to the directory one level higher than the current directory. The directory one level higher is also called the **parent directory**. In this case, the parent directory of CASHFLOW is the root directory. Every subdirectory has a parent directory. DOS uses the . and .. files to keep track of the current directory and the parent directory as you move from one directory to another.

Now that you have created one of the subdirectories planned for this diskette, you want to move the appropriate files to this subdirectory. To simplify this operation, you decide to return to the root directory where these files are currently stored. Again, you use the CD or CHDIR commands. For the root directory's name, you use the Backslash (\) symbol—the notation that identifies the root directory.

To return to the root directory from any subdirectory:

1. Type **CD ** and press **[Enter]**. DOS updates the DOS prompt and shows the root directory as the current directory. See Figure 4-8. If you type a Slash (/) instead of a Backslash (\), DOS will tell you that you have entered an invalid switch, because switches start with a Slash symbol. If you type CD and do not specify a directory name, DOS will display the name of the current directory.

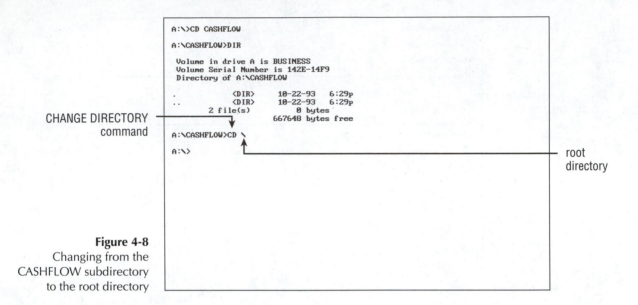

CHANGE DIRECTORY
command

root
directory

Figure 4-8
Changing from the
CASHFLOW subdirectory
to the root directory

```
A:\>CD CASHFLOW

A:\CASHFLOW>DIR

 Volume in drive A is BUSINESS
 Volume Serial Number is 142E-14F9
 Directory of A:\CASHFLOW

 .              <DIR>      10-22-93    6:29p
 ..             <DIR>      10-22-93    6:29p
        2 file(s)              0 bytes
                         667648 bytes free

A:\CASHFLOW>CD \

A:\>
```

MOVING FILES TO A SUB-DIRECTORY

Next you check the printed copy of files on your diskette and highlight the files that you want to move to the CASHFLOW subdirectory (Figure 4-9).

Figure 4-9
Shading indicates the files
you want to move to the
CASHFLOW subdirectory

```
 Volume in drive A is BUSINESS
 Volume Serial Number is 364B-15D6
 Directory of A:\

APR_CASH           366 03-18-94   10:20a
BUSINESS PLN       590 03-20-94    5:26p
CASHFLOW FMT       472 03-27-94    8:32a
CASHFLOW RPT       176 03-27-94    8:45a
CASHFLOW WK1      1648 03-27-94    8:32a
CLIENT   LST       476 04-10-94   11:08a
EQUIP    LST       671 03-23-94    3:57p
FEB_CASH           369 03-18-94   10:14a
FEESCALE           412 04-19-94    1:48p
INCOME   YR1       987 04-23-94    9:06a
INCOME   YR2       987 04-23-94    9:17a
INCOME   YR3       987 04-23-94    9:21a
INCOME   YR4       987 04-23-94    9:34a
INCOME   YR5       987 04-23-94    9:47a
INSURE   LST      1528 04-09-94    8:48a
INVOICE  FMT      2124 04-02-94   10:45a
INVOICE  WK1      1752 04-02-94   10:45a
INVOICES           104 03-22-94    8:48a
JAN_CASH           368 03-18-94   10:00a
JOBCOSTS FMT       294 03-30-94    2:22p
JOBCOSTS RPT       543 03-26-94    8:51a
JOBCOSTS WK1      1716 03-30-94    2:22p
JUN_CASH           365 03-18-94   10:45a
MAR_CASH           366 03-18-94   10:17a
MAY_CASH           364 03-18-94   10:43a
PRJ_INC            589 04-24-94   11:27a
QTR_INC            589 04-24-94   11:27a
RESUME   LTR      1182 04-15-94   11:49a
RESUME1  DOC      2435 04-12-94    2:25p
RESUME2  DOC      2435 04-12-94    2:41p
RESUME3  DOC      2392 04-12-94    3:00p
RESUME4  DOC      2386 04-12-94    3:12p
RESUME5  DOC      4043 04-12-94    4:08p
RESUME6  DOC      4043 04-12-94    4:08p
SCHEDULE FMT       792 04-07-94    1:21p
SCHEDULE WK1      2147 04-07-94    1:21P
STARTUP           1010 03-11094   10:03a
       37 file(s)        43684 bytes
                        668672 bytes free
```

_6.0_ _6.2_   If you are using DOS 6.0 or 6.2, you can use the MOVE command, an external command, to move these files in one step. If you want to move one or more files from one directory to another with the MOVE command, you use the following syntax:

MOVE [_drive:_][_path_]_filename_ _destination_

The drive name, path, and filename are those of the source file or files you want to move to another location. You must specify the drive name for the source file or files if they are located on another drive. You must also specify the path if it is different from that of the current directory. The destination includes the path and name of the directory in which you want DOS to store the moved files. The destination might also include a drive name. If you are moving one file, you can also specify a new filename for that file. If you are moving a group of files, the destination must be a directory name.

For example, to move the file CLIENT.LST from the root directory of drive A to the BUSINESS subdirectory on drive A, you would enter this command:

MOVE CLIENT.LST BUSINESS

To move all the files with the file extension LST from the root directory of drive A to the BUSINESS subdirectory on drive A, you would enter this command:

MOVE *.LST BUSINESS

To move a file named BUSINESS.PLN from the current directory on drive C to drive A, you would enter this command:

MOVE BUSINESS.PLN A:

Be careful when moving files in DOS 6.0. If there is a file in the destination directory with the same filename as a source file you are moving, DOS 6.0 will overwrite the file in the destination directory. DOS 6.2 will automatically prompt you first.

_5.0_   If you are using DOS 5.0, you must move the files in two steps, because DOS 5.0 does not have a MOVE command. First, you use the COPY command to copy the files to the new subdirectory from the directory in which they are currently stored. You then use the DEL or ERASE command to delete the files from the original directory. It is always a good idea to verify these operations by using the DIR command.

Now you are ready to move your cashflow files to the CASHFLOW directory. Because these files have similar names, you can use wildcards to move the files as a group rather than moving one file at a time. Even though you work with DOS 6.0 and 6.2, you decide to use the COPY and DEL commands before you try the MOVE command. A number of your clients use DOS 5.0, so you should know how to move files in DOS 5.0.

To copy the cashflow files to the CASHFLOW subdirectory:

1. Type **DIR CASH*** and press **[Enter]**. DOS displays the names of the cashflow files you want to move. See Figure 4-10. You also see the CASHFLOW directory name with a directory marker, <DIR>, next to its name.

file specification

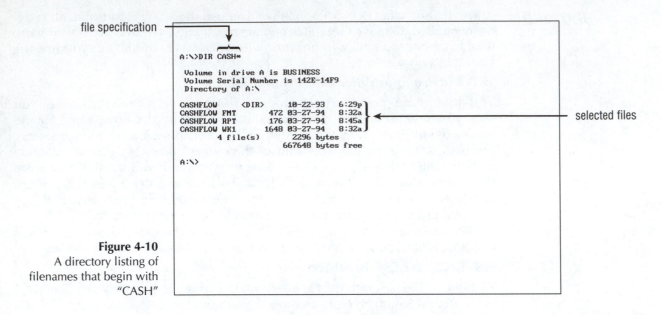

selected files

Figure 4-10
A directory listing of
filenames that begin with
"CASH"

2. Type **COPY CASH*.* CASHFLOW** and press **[Enter]**. As DOS copies these three files, it displays their filenames on the screen and tells you it copied three files. See Figure 4-11.

source files

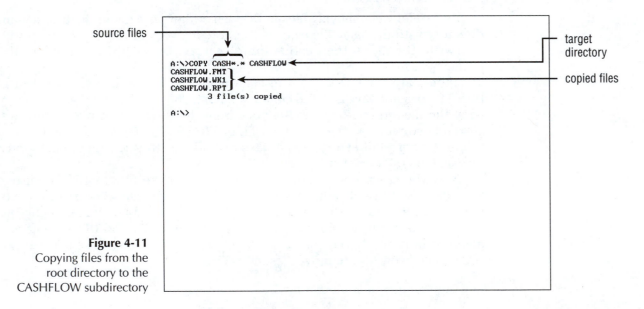

target directory

copied files

Figure 4-11
Copying files from the
root directory to the
CASHFLOW subdirectory

How does DOS know in this last command that CASHFLOW refers to the name of a subdirectory? The directory file for the root directory contains a list of all the files in the root directory of your diskette as well as all the names of subdirectories located below the root directory. During this copy operation, DOS examines this directory file and locates a subdirectory named CASHFLOW. It then copies the files you specified to that subdirectory. If the root directory did not contain a subdirectory named CASHFLOW, DOS would copy *and combine* all the files you specified into one larger file named CASHFLOW and store this new file in the root directory.

When you enter the COPY command, you can also use \CASHFLOW for the directory name, to indicate it is a subdirectory below the root directory. If you do not specify the Backslash (\) for the root directory and if the current directory is the root directory (as is the case here), DOS assumes the CASHFLOW subdirectory is located in the root directory.

Now you are ready to verify the copy operation.

To check the contents of the CASHFLOW directory:

1. Type **DIR CASHFLOW** and press **[Enter]**. The three copied files are now stored in the CASHFLOW subdirectory. See Figure 4-12.

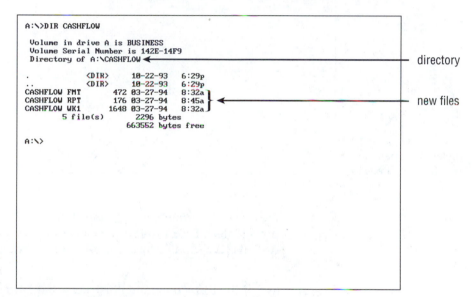

```
A:\>DIR CASHFLOW

 Volume in drive A is BUSINESS
 Volume Serial Number is 142E-14F9
 Directory of A:\CASHFLOW ◄──────────────────── directory

 .            <DIR>      10-22-93    6:29p
 ..           <DIR>      10-22-93    6:29p
CASHFLOW FMT       472 03-27-94    8:32a ⎫
CASHFLOW RPT       176 03-27-94    8:45a ⎬ ◄───── new files
CASHFLOW WK1      1648 03-27-94    8:32a ⎭
        5 file(s)        2296 bytes
                       663552 bytes free

A:\>
```

Figure 4-12
The files copied to the CASHFLOW subdirectory

2. Press **[↑]** (Up Arrow) until you recall the command DIR CASH* and press **[Enter]**. The original versions of the three files copied to the CASHFLOW directory are still in the root directory.

You now have two copies of these files. One copy is in the CASHFLOW subdirectory and one copy is in the root directory. You do not need or want two copies of these files in two different directories, because you would not be using available disk space efficiently. You want to delete the original versions of the files in the root directory.

To delete the original files in the root directory:

1. Type **DEL CASH*.*** and press **[Enter]**. DOS deletes all files that match this file specification.

2. Press [↑] (Up Arrow) until you recall the command DIR CASH* and then press **[Enter]**. DOS displays an updated list of file and directory names in the root directory. See Figure 4-13. The DEL command deleted the original set of files that you copied to the CASHFLOW subdirectory, but it did not delete the CASHFLOW subdirectory.

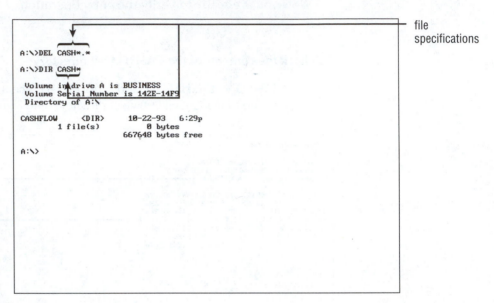

file specifications

```
A:\>DEL CASH*.*

A:\>DIR CASH*

 Volume in drive A is BUSINESS
 Volume Serial Number is 142E-14F9
 Directory of A:\

CASHFLOW    <DIR>      10-22-93   6:29p
        1 file(s)           0 bytes
                       667648 bytes free

A:\>
```

Figure 4-13
Verifying the deletion of
files from the root directory

3. Press [↑] (Up Arrow) until you recall the command DIR CASHFLOW and press **[Enter]**. DOS displays the names of the files currently stored in the CASHFLOW subdirectory. The DEL command did not delete these files.

This use of the DEL command illustrates that DOS can treat a subdirectory as if it were a separate disk drive. The DEL command deleted files in the root directory without affecting the files in the CASHFLOW subdirectory. Furthermore, the DEL command did not delete, or remove, this subdirectory. The DEL command deletes only files; it cannot delete, or remove, a reference to a disk drive, and it cannot remove a subdirectory.

Moving Files with the Yearly Income Projections

Now, you are ready to move the files with the yearly income projections.

If you are using DOS 6.0 or 6.2, you will use the MOVE command. If you are using DOS 5.0, you will use the COPY and DEL commands.

Follow the steps in the section that describes how to perform these operations using the version of DOS on your system.

6.0 6.2   **To move the files with the yearly income projections** *using DOS 6.0 or 6.2*:

1. Be sure the current drive contains your Tutorial Disk and that you are at the root directory of that diskette drive.

2. Type **MOVE INCOME.* CASHFLOW** and press **[Enter]**. As DOS moves each file, it verifies the operation. See Figure 4-14. The files are moved in disk order—the order in which the files were placed on the diskette.

```
A:\>MOVE INCOME.* CASHFLOW
a:\income.yr5 => a:\cashflow\income.yr5 [ok]
a:\income.yr1 => a:\cashflow\income.yr1 [ok]
a:\income.yr4 => a:\cashflow\income.yr4 [ok]
a:\income.yr2 => a:\cashflow\income.yr2 [ok]
a:\income.yr3 => a:\cashflow\income.yr3 [ok]

A:\>
```

Figure 4-14
DOS verifies a move operation of a selected group of files

3. Type **DIR CASHFLOW** and press **[Enter]**. DOS displays an updated listing of the CASHFLOW subdirectory. See Figure 4-15. This list includes the five moved files.

```
A:\>DIR CASHFLOW

 Volume in drive A is BUSINESS
 Volume Serial Number is 142E-14F9
 Directory of A:\CASHFLOW

.            <DIR>       10-22-93   6:29p
..           <DIR>       10-22-93   6:29p
CASHFLOW FMT       472 03-27-94   8:32a
CASHFLOW RPT       176 03-27-94   8:45a
CASHFLOW WK1      1648 03-27-94   8:32a
INCOME   YR1       987 04-23-94   9:06a
INCOME   YR2       987 04-23-94   9:17a
INCOME   YR3       987 04-23-94   9:21a
INCOME   YR4       987 04-23-94   9:34a
INCOME   YR5       987 04-23-94   9:47a
       10 file(s)       7231 bytes
                      667648 bytes free

A:\>
```

Figure 4-15
The current contents of the CASHFLOW subdirectory

4. Type **DIR INCOME.*** and press **[Enter]**. DOS finds no files with this file specification in the root directory, verifying that they have been moved.

If you are using DOS 6.0 or 6.2, skip to the section entitled "Moving the Monthly Income Report Files."

5.0   **To move the files with the yearly income projections *using DOS 5.0*:**

1. Type **COPY INCOME.* CASHFLOW** and press **[Enter]**. As DOS copies these files, it displays their filenames and tells you it copied five files. See Figure 4-16.

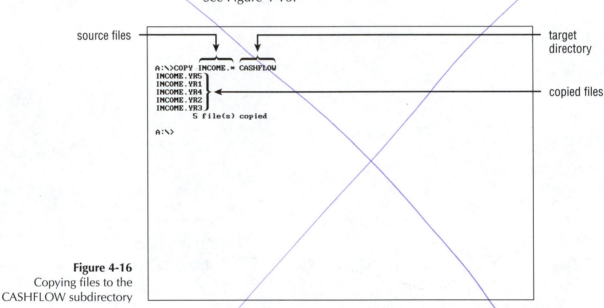

source files

target directory

copied files

```
A:\>COPY INCOME.* CASHFLOW
INCOME.YR5
INCOME.YR1
INCOME.YR4
INCOME.YR2
INCOME.YR3
        5 file(s) copied

A:\>
```

Figure 4-16
Copying files to the
CASHFLOW subdirectory

2. Type **DIR CASHFLOW** and press **[Enter]**. The CASHFLOW directory contains the five files with names that begin with INCOME.

Now remove these files from the root directory.

3. Type **DEL INCOME.*** and press **[Enter]**. DOS deletes files that match this file specification.

Moving the Monthly Income Report Files

Now you are ready to move the monthly income report files to the CASHFLOW subdirectory. Again, follow the steps in the section below that describe how to perform these operations using the version of DOS on your system.

6.0 6.2   **To move the files with the monthly income reports *using DOS 6.0 or 6.2*:**

1. Type **MOVE ???_INC CASHFLOW** and press **[Enter]**. As DOS moves each file that meets the file specification ???_INC, it verifies the operation.

2. Type **DIR CASHFLOW** and press **[Enter]**. The CASHFLOW directory contains two copied files, PRJ_INC and QTR_INC, that meet the file specification.

Now change to the CASHFLOW directory.

3. Type **CD CASHFLOW** and press **[Enter]**. DOS updates the DOS prompt to show that the current directory is CASHFLOW.

If you are using DOS 6.0 or 6.2, skip to the section entitled "Moving the Invoice Files."

5.0 **To move the files with the monthly income reports *using DOS 5.0*:**

1. Type **COPY ???_INC CASHFLOW** and press **[Enter]**. As DOS copies the two files that match this file specification, it displays their filenames.

2. Type **DIR CASHFLOW** and press **[Enter]**. The CASHFLOW directory contains the two copied files, PRJ_INC and QTR_INC.

3. Type **DEL ???_INC** and press **[Enter]**. DOS deletes files in the root directory that match this file specification.

Now change to the CASHFLOW directory.

4. Type **CD CASHFLOW** and press **[Enter]**. DOS updates the DOS prompt to show that the current directory is CASHFLOW.

Moving the Invoice Files

After examining the CASHFLOW directory, you realize that three other files belong in this subdirectory. You decide to move them from the root directory to the current directory. The source files are the files in the root directory that you want to copy, and the target file is the current subdirectory, CASHFLOW. Follow the steps in the section below that describe how to perform these operations using the version of DOS on your system.

6.0 6.2 **To move the invoice files from the root directory to the current subdirectory *using DOS 6.0 or 6.2*:**

1. Type **MOVE \INVOICE*.*** and press **[Spacebar]**. Type **.** (a period) and press **[Enter]**. As DOS moves each file that meets the specification INVOICE*.*, it verifies the operation. The Backslash (\) in the source specification tells DOS to look to the root directory for these files. Because you did not specify the source drive, DOS uses the current drive. The . (a period) after \INVOICE*.* is the target specification. It tells DOS that the target is the current directory. Remember, DOS uses a single dot to represent the current directory.

2. Type **DIR** and press **[Enter]** to verify the move operation. The CASHFLOW directory contains three filenames that begin with INVOICE. See Figure 4-17.

```
A:\CASHFLOW>DIR

 Volume in drive A is BUSINESS
 Volume Serial Number is 142E-14F9
 Directory of A:\CASHFLOW

.            <DIR>      10-22-93   6:29p
..           <DIR>      10-22-93   6:29p
CASHFLOW FMT      472 03-27-94   8:32a
CASHFLOW RPT      176 03-27-94   8:45a
CASHFLOW WK1     1648 03-27-94   8:32a
INCOME   YR1      987 04-23-94   9:06a
INCOME   YR2      987 04-23-94   9:17a
INCOME   YR3      987 04-23-94   9:21a
INCOME   YR4      987 04-23-94   9:34a
INCOME   YR5      987 04-23-94   9:47a
INVOICE  FMT     2124 04-02-94  10:45a
INVOICE  WK1     1752 04-02-94  10:45a
INVOICES         104 03-22-94   8:48a
PRJ_INC          589 04-24-94  11:27a
QTR_INC          589 04-24-94  11:27a
       15 file(s)       12389 bytes
                       667648 bytes free


A:\CASHFLOW>
```

Figure 4-17
A directory of the
CASHFLOW subdirectory
after a move operation

If you are using DOS 6.0 or 6.2, skip to the section entitled "Copying Files Within a Subdirectory."

5.0   To move the invoice files from the root directory to the current directory *using DOS 5.0*:

1. Type **COPY \INVOICE*.*** and press **[Spacebar]**. Type **.** (a period) and press **[Enter]**. DOS copies three files. See Figure 4-18. The Backslash (\) in the source specification tells DOS to look to the root directory for these files. Because you did not specify the source drive, DOS uses the current drive. The . (period) after \INVOICE*.* is the target specification. It tells DOS that the target is the current directory. Remember, DOS uses a single dot to represent the current directory.

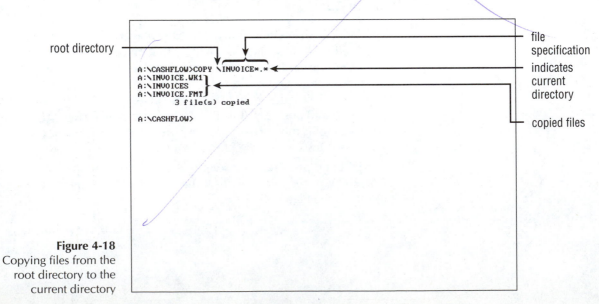

root directory

```
A:\CASHFLOW>COPY \INVOICE*.*
A:\INVOICE.WK1
A:\INVOICES
A:\INVOICE.FMT
        3 file(s) copied

A:\CASHFLOW>
```

file
specification

indicates
current
directory

copied files

Figure 4-18
Copying files from the
root directory to the
current directory

2. Type **DIR** and press **[Enter]** to verify the move operation. The CASHFLOW directory contains the three files you copied to this subdirectory.

You can now remove these files from the root directory.

3. Type **DEL \INVOICE*.*** and press **[Enter]**. *Be sure you type the Backslash (\) before INVOICE*.*. If you forget the Backslash, you will delete the files that you just copied to the current directory.* DOS deletes files that match this file specification in the root directory.

4. Type **DIR** and press **[Enter]**. You should still see three filenames that begin with INVOICE. If you do not, you will need to repeat these steps.

COPYING FILES WITHIN A SUBDIRECTORY

To anticipate cash needs for your business venture, you want to project expected income and expenses. You also want to keep a record of your actual income and expenses so that you can later compare this information with your initial projections and improve your future projections.

Your new directory already contains files that you will use to project income and expenses. To save time and effort, you decide to copy these files so that you can modify them later to track actual income and expenses. Because you will use these two groups of files in conjunction with each other, you want to keep them in the same subdirectory.

To copy the cashflow files within the CASHFLOW subdirectory:

1. Be sure you are in the CASHFLOW subdirectory. The DOS prompt should contain the name of this directory.

2. Type **COPY CASHFLOW.* CASH.*** and press **[Enter]**. DOS copies three files and produces three new files with new filenames.

3. Type **DIR CASH*** and press **[Enter]** to view the new files. See Figure 4-19. Now there are six files that begin with CASH in the CASHFLOW subdirectory. At the end of the month, you can modify the three new files to track actual income and expense.

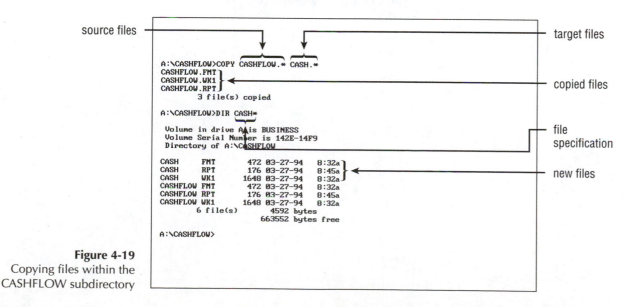

Figure 4-19
Copying files within the CASHFLOW subdirectory

Now you want to return to the root directory before you create other subdirectories.

4. Type **CD ** and press **[Enter]**.

EXPANDING A DIRECTORY STRUCTURE

Next you want to create a subdirectory named BUSINESS for your general business files. These files include the ones with your business plan, estimated start-up costs, and checklists for starting and maintaining this business.

To create the BUSINESS subdirectory:

1. Type **MD BUSINESS** and press **[Enter]**. DOS creates the subdirectory and displays the DOS prompt.

2. Type **DIR** and press **[Enter]**. From the directory listing, you can verify that you have created a new subdirectory. DOS first lists subdirectories in alphabetical order, then lists filenames in alphabetical order. Press **[Spacebar]** or any other key until you return to the DOS prompt.

You are now ready to move files to this new subdirectory. Follow the steps in the section below that describes how to perform these operations using the version of DOS on your system.

6.0 *6.2*

To move the general business files to this new subdirectory *using DOS 6.0 or 6.2*:

1. Type **MOVE BUSINESS.PLN BUSINESS** and press **[Enter]**. DOS moves one file to this subdirectory.

2. Type **MOVE STARTUP BUSINESS** and press **[Enter]**. DOS moves another file to the same subdirectory.

3. Type **MOVE *.LST BUSINESS** and press **[Enter]**. DOS moves three files with the LST file extension to this subdirectory.

4. Type **CD BUSINESS** and press **[Enter]**. DOS changes to the BUSINESS subdirectory.

5. Type **DIR** and press **[Enter]**. DOS displays a directory listing with the names of the five moved files. See Figure 4-20.

```
A:\>CD BUSINESS

A:\BUSINESS>DIR

 Volume in drive A is BUSINESS
 Volume Serial Number is 142E-14F9
 Directory of A:\BUSINESS

 .            <DIR>     10-23-93   10:20a
 ..           <DIR>     10-23-93   10:20a
 BUSINESS PLN      590 03-20-94    5:26p
 CLIENT   LST      476 04-10-94   11:08a
 EQUIP    LST      671 03-23-94    3:57p
 INSURE   LST     1528 04-09-94    8:48a
 STARTUP          1010 03-11-94   10:03a
        7 file(s)        4275 bytes
                       662528 bytes free

A:\BUSINESS>
```

Figure 4-20
The files moved to the
BUSINESS subdirectory

If you are using DOS 6.0 or 6.2, skip to the section entitled "Creating a Directory for Reports."

5.0 **To move the general business files to this new subdirectory *using DOS 5.0*:**

1. Type **COPY BUSINESS.PLN BUSINESS** and press **[Enter]**. DOS copies one file to this subdirectory.

2. Type **COPY STARTUP BUSINESS** and press **[Enter]**. DOS copies another file to the same subdirectory.

3. Type **COPY *.LST BUSINESS** and press **[Enter]**. DOS copies three files that have the LST file extension to this subdirectory. See Figure 4-21.

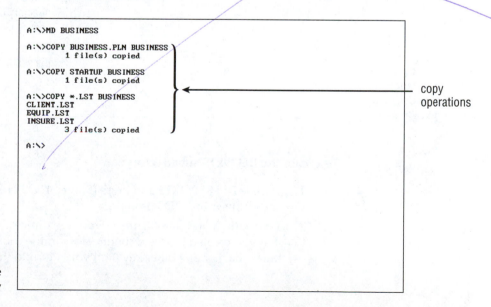

```
A:\>MD BUSINESS

A:\>COPY BUSINESS.PLN BUSINESS
        1 file(s) copied

A:\>COPY STARTUP BUSINESS
        1 file(s) copied

A:\>COPY *.LST BUSINESS
CLIENT.LST
EQUIP.LST
INSURE.LST
        3 file(s) copied

A:\>
```

copy
operations

Figure 4-21
The files copied to the
BUSINESS subdirectory

4. Type **DIR BUSINESS** and press **[Enter]** to verify the move operation. This subdirectory contains the five files that you copied to it.

You can now delete these files from the root directory.

5. Type **DEL BUSINESS.PLN** and press **[Enter]**. Next, type **DEL STARTUP** and press **[Enter]**. DOS deletes these two files.

6. Type **DEL *.LST** and press **[Enter]**. DOS deletes the three files with the LST file extension.

Next, change to the BUSINESS directory.

7. Type **CD BUSINESS** and press **[Enter]**. DOS changes to the BUSINESS subdirectory.

8. Type **DIR** and press **[Enter]**. DOS displays the contents of the BUSINESS directory. The DEL command did not affect the files in this directory.

Creating a Directory for Reports

You also want to create a subdirectory for your monthly business cashflow reports. You want to name this directory REPORTS and create it below the root directory. Although you are still working in the BUSINESS subdirectory, you can create this new subdirectory if you provide DOS with enough of its path. You must specify the name of the root directory before the directory name—as \REPORTS—so that DOS creates this new subdirectory below the root directory (Figure 4-22). If you specify only the directory name REPORTS, DOS will create the new subdirectory below the current directory—the BUSINESS subdirectory (Figure 4-22). It is important to specify enough of the path so that DOS places the subdirectory in the correct location in the directory structure.

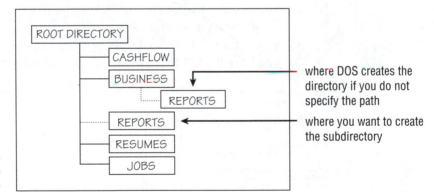

Figure 4-22
The importance of the path in specifying the location of a directory

To create the REPORTS subdirectory:

1. Type **MD \REPORTS** and press **[Enter]**. DOS creates this subdirectory and displays the DOS prompt.

2. Type **DIR ** and press **[Enter]**. From the directory listing, you can verify that you created this new subdirectory in the root directory. Press **[Spacebar]** or any other key until you return to the DOS prompt.

Now you can move files from the root directory to this new subdirectory. Follow the steps in the section below that describe how to perform these operations using the version of DOS on your system.

6.0 6.2 **To move the monthly cashflow reports to the REPORTS subdirectory** *using DOS 6.0 or 6.2:*

?? = CASH (Hyphen not underscore)

1. Type **MOVE \???_CASH** and press **[Spacebar]**. Type **\REPORTS** and press **[Enter]**. DOS moves six files that meet the file specification ???_CASH from the root directory to the REPORTS directory. You must specify the name of the root directory for the source files so that DOS knows where the files are located. You must also inform DOS that the target subdirectory is below the root directory; otherwise, DOS will assume it is below the current subdirectory. If there is a subdirectory by this same name below the current directory, DOS will move the files to a directory other than the one you want. If there is no subdirectory by this name, DOS will move and combine all the files into one larger file named REPORTS in the current directory.

2. Type **DIR \REPORTS** and press **[Enter]**. This operation verifies that the files are stored in the correct directory. See Figure 4-23.

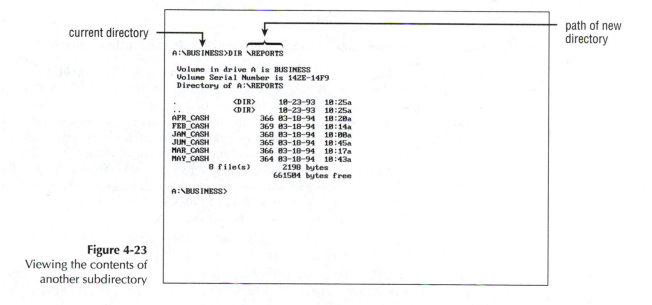

current directory ——

path of new directory

```
A:\BUSINESS>DIR \REPORTS

 Volume in drive A is BUSINESS
 Volume Serial Number is 142E-14F9
 Directory of A:\REPORTS

.              <DIR>       10-23-93   10:25a
..             <DIR>       10-23-93   10:25a
APR_CASH         366  03-18-94   10:20a
FEB_CASH         369  03-18-94   10:14a
JAN_CASH         368  03-18-94   10:00a
JUN_CASH         365  03-18-94   10:45a
MAR_CASH         366  03-18-94   10:17a
MAY_CASH         364  03-18-94   10:43a
        8 file(s)        2198 bytes
                       661504 bytes free

A:\BUSINESS>
```

Figure 4-23
Viewing the contents of another subdirectory

3. Type **CD ** and press **[Enter]**. DOS returns to the root directory.

4. Type **DIR** and press **[Enter]**. DOS displays the names of the subdirectories and of the remaining files in the root directory of your Tutorial Disk. See Figure 4-24.

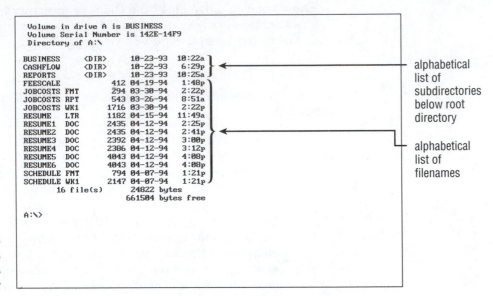

```
Volume in drive A is BUSINESS
Volume Serial Number is 142E-14F9
Directory of A:\

BUSINESS     <DIR>      10-23-93   10:22a  ⎤
CASHFLOW     <DIR>      10-22-93    6:29p  ⎬
REPORTS      <DIR>      10-23-93   10:25a  ⎦
FEESCALE             412 04-19-94    1:48p  ⎤
JOBCOSTS FMT         294 03-30-94    2:22p
JOBCOSTS RPT         543 03-26-94    8:51a
JOBCOSTS WK1        1716 03-30-94    2:22p
RESUME   LTR        1182 04-15-94   11:49a
RESUME1  DOC        2435 04-12-94    2:25p
RESUME2  DOC        2435 04-12-94    2:41p  ⎬
RESUME3  DOC        2392 04-12-94    3:00p
RESUME4  DOC        2386 04-12-94    3:12p
RESUME5  DOC        4043 04-12-94    4:08p
RESUME6  DOC        4043 04-12-94    4:08p
SCHEDULE FMT         794 04-07-94    1:21p
SCHEDULE WK1        2147 04-07-94    1:21p  ⎦
        16 file(s)        24822 bytes
                         661504 bytes free

A:\>
```

alphabetical
list of
subdirectories
below root
directory

alphabetical
list of
filenames

Figure 4-24
The subdirectories
and remaining files
in the root directory

DOS 6.0 and 6.2 users: This is a good opportunity to take a break. Afterward, continue with the next section, entitled "Viewing the Directory Structure."

5.0

To move the monthly cashflow reports to the REPORTS subdirectory *using DOS 5.0*:

1. Type **COPY \???_CASH** and press **[Spacebar]**. Then type **\REPORTS** and press **[Enter]**. DOS copies six files from the root directory to the REPORTS directory. You must specify the name of the root directory for the source files so that DOS knows where the files are located. You must also inform DOS that the target subdirectory is below the root directory; otherwise, DOS will assume it is below the current subdirectory. If there is a subdirectory by the same name below the current directory, DOS will copy the files to a directory other than the one you want. If there is no subdirectory by this name, DOS will copy and combine all the files into one larger file named REPORTS in the current directory.

2. Type **DIR \REPORTS** and press **[Enter]**. This operation verifies that the files are stored in the correct directory. See Figure 4-23.

3. Type **DEL \???_CASH** and press **[Enter]**. *Be sure you type a Slash (\) before the file specification.* DOS deletes these files from the root directory.

4. Type **CD ** and press **[Enter]**. DOS returns to the root directory.

5. Type **DIR** and press **[Enter]**. DOS displays the names of your subdirectories and the names of the remaining files in the root directory of your Tutorial Disk. See Figure 4-24.

DOS 5.0 users: This is a good opportunity to take a break.

VIEWING THE DIRECTORY STRUCTURE

You want to view a graphical representation of the partially completed directory structure of your diskette. You can use the TREE command to display a directory tree from the DOS prompt. A **directory tree** is a diagrammatic representation of the directory structure of a hard disk or diskette. It shows the current directory and all subdirectories below the current directory. The TREE command is an external command with the following syntax:

TREE [*drive:*][*path*]

If you want to view a directory of another drive, you must specify its drive name. If you want to start with a specific subdirectory in the directory structure of a hard disk or diskette, you specify that directory's path. If you do not specify a drive or path, DOS assumes you want to view the directory structure of the current drive, starting with the current directory. If you want this directory tree to include the root directory and all subdirectories, you must start at the root directory or specify the root directory as the path.

To view a directory tree of your Tutorial Disk:

1. If necessary, power on your computer system, install DOSKEY, and specify default switches for the DIR command using the instructions on pages 56 through 58.

2. Be sure the current drive contains your Tutorial Disk. Also be sure the current directory is the root directory.

3. Type **CLS** and press [**Enter**] to clear the screen.

4. Type **TREE** and press [**Enter**]. DOS displays a diagrammatic representation of the directory structure of your diskette. See Figure 4-25. Next to the name of the drive, DOS displays a dot (.) to indicate that the directory tree starts at the current directory. The directory tree shows the three subdirectories you created earlier at the DOS prompt.

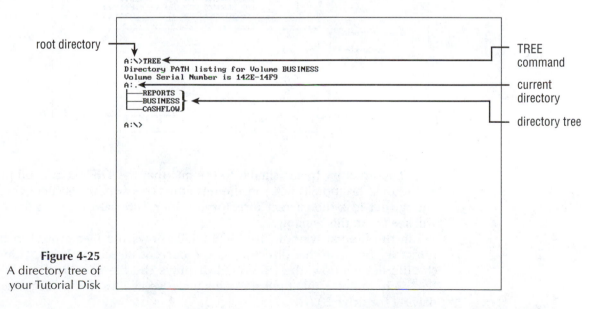

Figure 4-25
A directory tree of your Tutorial Disk

In this directory tree, you see the relationship of the subdirectories to the root directory. As you construct or revise the directory structure of your hard disk or diskettes from the DOS prompt to meet the changing needs of your business, you can quickly view the directory structure to verify directory operations and to refresh your memory of the disk's directory structure.

CREATING A SUBDIRECTORY IN THE DOS SHELL

You decide to create the additional subdirectories from the DOS Shell. As you have discovered, the DOS Shell provides a visual interface with menus and icons, automatically displays filenames, and simplifies DOS command operations. You will find that you can use the DOS Shell to move files from one subdirectory to another and to quickly verify these operations.

To load the DOS Shell:

1. Type **DOSSHELL** and press **[Enter]**. After DOS loads the DOS Shell, note that the directory tree window contains a diagrammatic representation of the directory structure of the diskette. See Figure 4-26.

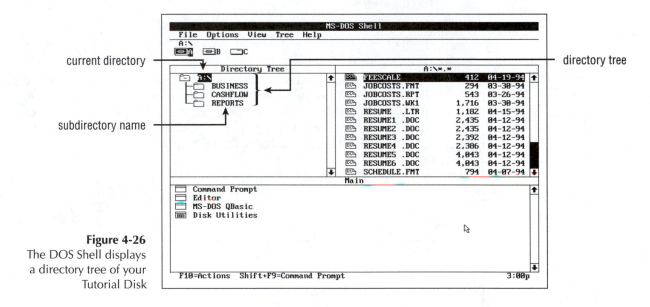

Figure 4-26
The DOS Shell displays a directory tree of your Tutorial Disk

This directory tree is similar to the one that the TREE command produces at the DOS prompt. The A:\ in the directory tree window is highlighted, indicating that it is the current directory. If your Tutorial Disk is in drive B, you will see B:\ in this window.

In the file list window, the DOS Shell shows the files stored in the root directory because that directory is the current directory. In the title bar for the file list window, the DOS Shell displays the file specification A:*.* (or B:*.*) to indicate that the list of files includes all files in the root directory of drive A (or drive B).

You need to create two more directories according to your original plan—RESUMES and JOBS.

To create the RESUMES subdirectory with the DOS Shell:

1. Press **[Tab]** to move the selection cursor to the directory tree window.

   If you are using the mouse, click the **directory tree window title bar**.

2. Press **[F10]** (Actions) to access the menu bar, press **[Enter]** to select the File menu, and then type **E** to select the Create Directory option.

   If you are using the mouse, click **File**, then click **Create Directory**.

   The DOS Shell displays the Create Directory dialog box. See Figure 4-27. The dialog box shows the parent directory name, which in this case is A:\, and prompts for the new directory name.

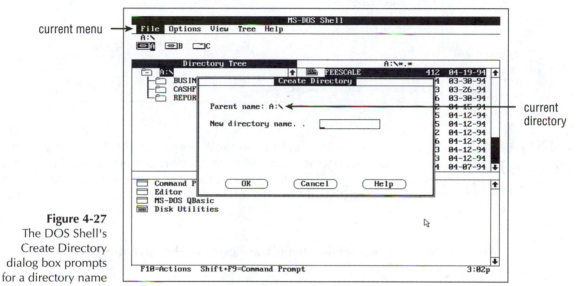

Figure 4-27
The DOS Shell's Create Directory dialog box prompts for a directory name

3. Type **RESUMES** and press **[Enter]**.

   If you are using a mouse, type **RESUMES** and click **OK**.

   The DOS Shell creates the RESUMES subdirectory on the current drive and updates the directory tree. See Figure 4-28.

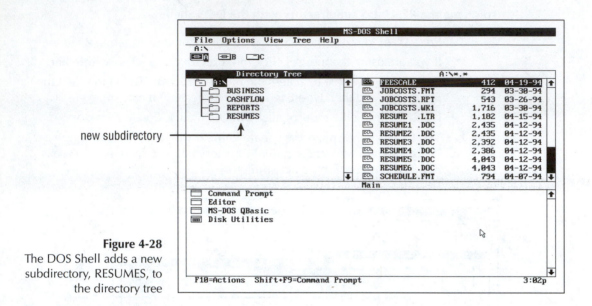

new subdirectory ——————→

Figure 4-28
The DOS Shell adds a new
subdirectory, RESUMES, to
the directory tree

MOVING FILES IN THE DOS SHELL

You must now select the files to move to the RESUMES directory. Instead of moving the files one at a time, you can move them as a group in one step. Even if you use DOS 5.0, you do not need to copy the files to a new directory and then delete them from the original directory.

To move the résumé template files from the root directory to the RESUMES subdirectory:

1. Press **[Tab]** to move the selection cursor to the file list window.

    If you are using the mouse, click in the **file list window's title bar**.

2. Type **R** to move the selection cursor to the first file that starts with the letter "R"—RESUME.LTR.

    If you are using the mouse, click the filename **RESUME.LTR**.

    The DOS Shell highlights the filename RESUME.LTR.

3. Press and hold down **[Shift]** while you press **[↓]** (Down Arrow) to highlight all the files that have RESUME as the first six characters of the filename. The last filename in this group is RESUME6.DOC. Then release [Shift].

    If you are using the mouse, press and hold down **[Shift]** while you click **RESUME6.DOC**, the last filename you want to include in this selection. Then release [Shift].

    Figure 4-29 shows the selected files.

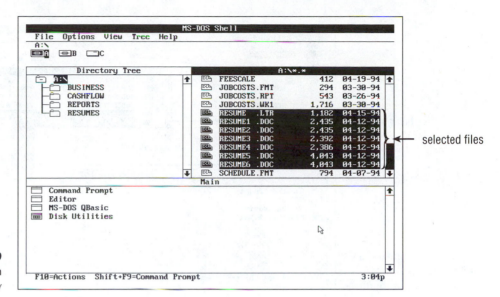

Figure 4-29
A group of selected files in the file list window

4. Press **[F10]** (Actions) and press **[Enter]** to select the File menu. Type **M** to select the Move option. (You can also use the shortcut Move key, **[F7]**.) The DOS Shell displays the Move File dialog box. See Figure 4-30. The selected files are listed in the first text box, next to the From prompt. The DOS Shell shows only a partial list of files in this text box. Your view might be different from that shown in Figure 4-30. The cursor is in the next text box, to the right of the To prompt. The DOS Shell assumes you want to move the files to the current directory. Press **[End]** to move the cursor past the path of the current directory. Then type **RESUMES** to specify the remainder of the path for the new subdirectory, and press **[Enter]**. *Be sure the target directory is A:\RESUMES (or B:\RESUMES)*. The DOS Shell displays a "Moving file" dialog box as it moves the seven files to the RESUMES subdirectory. See Figure 4-31.

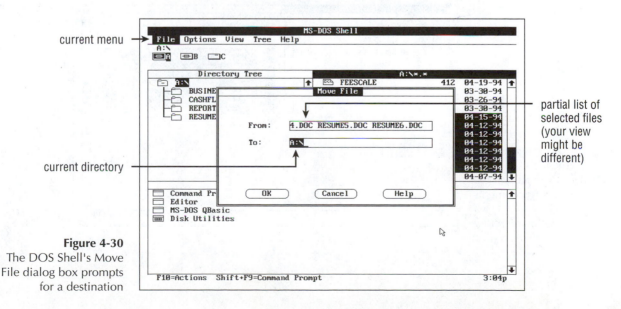

Figure 4-30
The DOS Shell's Move File dialog box prompts for a destination

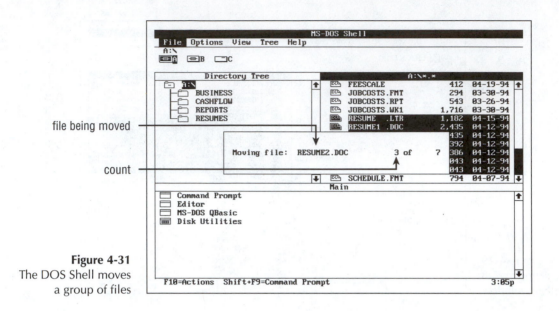

file being moved

count

Figure 4-31
The DOS Shell moves
a group of files

If you are using the mouse, click **one of the selected files**, hold down the left mouse button, and drag the pointer to the folder icon adjacent to the subdirectory name RESUMES in the directory tree window. As you point to this subdirectory, the pointer changes to an arrow if you are in text mode or a stack of documents or files if you are in graphics mode. See Figure 4-32. Release the mouse button. The DOS Shell displays the Confirm Mouse Operation dialog box and asks if you want to move the selected files to A:\RESUMES (or B:\RESUMES). See Figure 4-33. Click **Yes**. The DOS Shell moves the files to the RESUMES subdirectory.

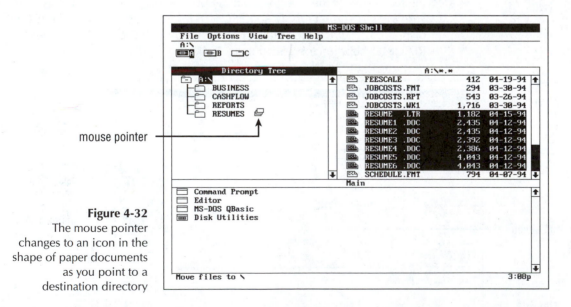

mouse pointer

Figure 4-32
The mouse pointer
changes to an icon in the
shape of paper documents
as you point to a
destination directory

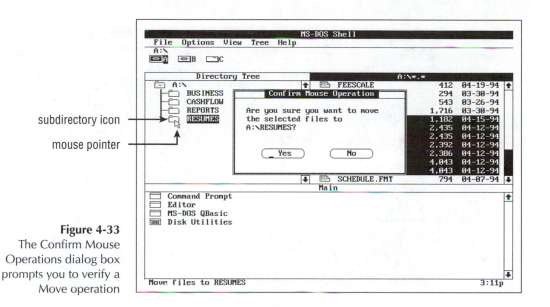

subdirectory icon →

mouse pointer →

Figure 4-33
The Confirm Mouse
Operations dialog box
prompts you to verify a
Move operation

REFRESHING THE DOS SHELL

You next want to verify these operations and be sure your business files are stored in the correct directory. If you now select the RESUMES subdirectory, you will not see any filenames listed in the file list window if you are using DOS 5.0 or 6.0. You must first use [F5] (Refresh) in DOS 5.0 and 6.0 so that the DOS Shell rereads your Tutorial Disk. DOS 6.2 automatically updates the file list.

To refresh the display of the files on your Tutorial Disk:

1. Press **[F5]** (Refresh).

    If you are using the mouse, click **View**, then click **Refresh**.

    The DOS Shell rereads your Tutorial Disk.

2. Press **[Tab]** to move the selection cursor to the directory tree window. Then press **[↓]** (Down Arrow) until you highlight the name of the RESUMES subdirectory.

    If you are using the mouse, click **RESUMES** in the directory tree window.

    The DOS Shell updates the file list window to show the files in the selected subdirectory. RESUMES contains the seven files that you just moved. See Figure 4-34.

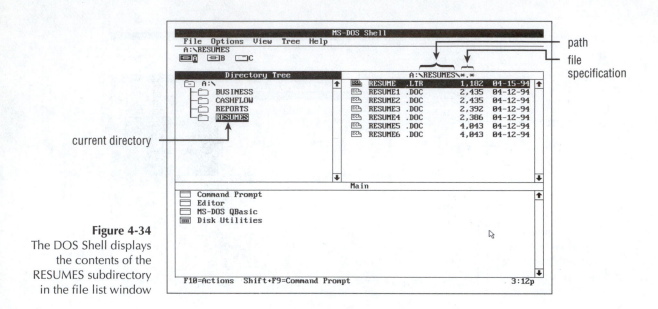

path
file specification

current directory

Figure 4-34
The DOS Shell displays
the contents of the
RESUMES subdirectory
in the file list window

3. Press **[Home]** to move the selection cursor to the root directory.

    If you are using the mouse, click the **root directory icon**.

COMPLETING A DIRECTORY STRUCTURE WITH THE DOS SHELL

According to your organizational plan, you have one more subdirectory to create. This subdirectory, named JOBS, will contain the files that store information on each job that you do for a client.

To complete the directory structure:

1. Create the JOBS subdirectory according to your original plan for organizing subdirectories and files on your Tutorial Disk.

2. After you create the JOBS subdirectory, move the remaining files in the root directory to this subdirectory. You can select the file list window, and then use the Select All option on the File menu to select all the files at once.

3. Reread your Tutorial Disk.

4. Select the JOBS subdirectory. The DOS Shell updates the file list window to show the files in the JOBS subdirectory. See Figure 4-35.

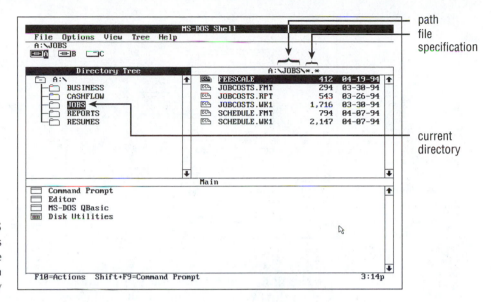

path
file
specification

current
directory

Figure 4-35
The DOS Shell displays
the contents of the
JOBS subdirectory in
the file list window

5. Return to the root directory.

You have created five subdirectories and moved groups of files to those subdirectories using commands at the DOS prompt and in the DOS Shell. Because your Tutorial Disk has changed significantly, you might want to make a backup copy of it now. If you would like to make a backup copy, use the DISKCOPY command and refer to page 29 for help.

EXPANDING THE SUBDIRECTORY STRUCTURE

After reorganizing the files on your diskette into subdirectories, you realize that you could create several subdirectories below the CASHFLOW subdirectory and organize the files into smaller groups, which would allow you to work more easily with these files. You can also add more files to each subdirectory as the need arises. Figure 4-36 shows your updated plan for organizing the CASHFLOW subdirectory into three subdirectories—one called PRJCASH for storing cashflow projections for your business, one called INVOICES for storing files used to track the status of outstanding invoices, and one called SUMMARY for files with summary reports on your business.

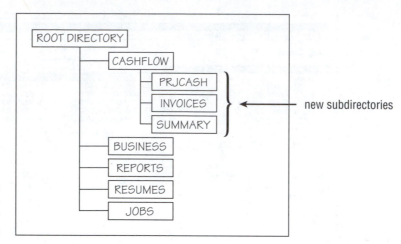

Figure 4-36
The revised directory structure of your Tutorial Disk

The first subdirectory you will create is PRJCASH. This subdirectory will contain the five files that begin with the word INCOME (but which have different file extensions), as well as the files PRJ_INC and QTR_INC. You decide to use the DOS Shell to create the subdirectory.

To create the PRJCASH subdirectory below the CASHFLOW subdirectory:

1. Be sure the current drive contains your Tutorial Disk.

2. Be sure the selection cursor is on the root directory in the directory tree window.

3. Press [↓] (Down Arrow) twice to highlight the subdirectory named CASHFLOW.

   If you are using the mouse, click the subdirectory name **CASHFLOW** in the directory tree window.

   The DOS Shell selects this subdirectory and updates the file list window.

4. Press [**F10**] (Actions) to access the menu bar, press [**Enter**] to select the File menu, and then type **E** to select the Create Directory option.

   If you are using the mouse, click **File**, then click **Create Directory**.

   The DOS Shell displays the Create Directory dialog box. The parent directory's name is A:\CASHFLOW (or B:\CASHFLOW).

5. Type **PRJCASH** and press [**Enter**].

   If you are using the mouse, type **PRJCASH** and click **OK**.

   The DOS Shell creates the PRJCASH subdirectory below the current directory. See Figure 4-37.

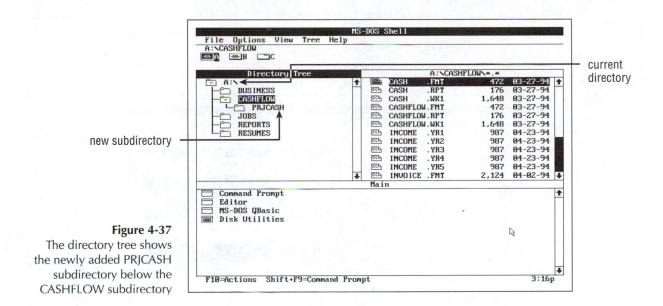

Figure 4-37
The directory tree shows the newly added PRJCASH subdirectory below the CASHFLOW subdirectory

6. Press [**Tab**] to move to the file list window.

   If you are using the mouse, click the **file list window title bar**.

   Now you are ready to select the files to move.

7. Type **I** to move the selection cursor to the filename INCOME.YR1.

   If you are using the mouse, click the filename **INCOME.YR1**.

8. Press and hold down [**Shift**] while you press [↓] (Down Arrow) and select INCOME.YR1, INCOME.YR2, INCOME.YR3, INCOME.YR4, and INCOME.YR5.

   If you are using the mouse, press and hold down [**Shift**], click the filename **INCOME.YR5**, and release [Shift].

Extending a File Selection

You need to add two more files to your selection, but they do not follow the files you just highlighted on the file list. If you are using the keyboard, you can use [Shift][F8] (Add) to add more files to the selection. You point to each additional file and press [Spacebar]. If you are using a mouse, you can hold [Ctrl] while you click on each file you want to add to the selection.

To add the files PRJ_INC and QTR_INC:

1. Press and hold down [**Shift**] while you press [**F8**] (Add). Then release both [F8] and [Shift]. The ADD indicator appears in the lower-right corner of the status bar. Type **P** to move the selection cursor to the file PRJ_INC. Press [**Spacebar**] to add this file to the selection. Press [↓] (Down Arrow) to highlight QTR_INC. Finally, press [**Spacebar**] to add this file to the selection.

If you are using the mouse, click the **scroll bar** until you see the filename QTR_INC. Press and hold **[Ctrl]** while you click **PRJ_INC** and then **QTR_INC**. Release [Ctrl].

Figure 4-38 shows the selected files.

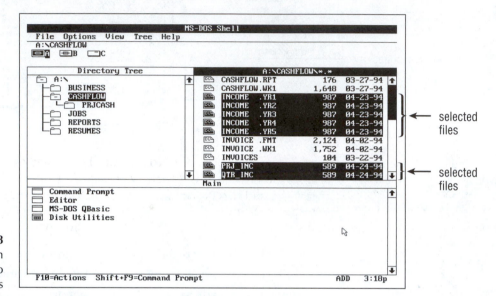

Figure 4-38
Extending a selection in the file list window to include two groups of files

Now move the selected files.

2. Press **[F7]** (Move). The DOS Shell displays the Move File dialog box with the directory name A:\CASHFLOW (or B:\CASHFLOW). Press **[End]** and type **\PRJCASH**. You *must* type the Backslash (\) before PRJCASH to separate the name of this subdirectory from its parent directory name. See Figure 4-39 to be sure you enter the path correctly. Then press **[Enter]**.

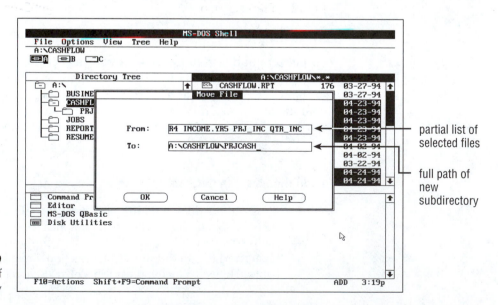

Figure 4-39
Specifying the full path of the target subdirectory

If you are using the mouse, click **one of the selected files**, hold down the mouse button, and drag the pointer to the folder icon next to the subdirectory name PRJCASH in the directory tree window. Then release the left mouse button. The DOS Shell displays the Confirm Mouse Operation dialog box and asks you if you want to move the files to A:\CASHFLOW\PRJCASH (or B:\CASHFLOW\PRJCASH). Click **Yes**.

The DOS Shell moves the files to the PRJCASH subdirectory.

You want to verify these operations before your make any more subdirectories.

3. Press **[F5]** (Refresh) to refresh the display of files on your diskette.

If you are using the mouse, click **View**, then click **Refresh**.

EXPANDING THE DIRECTORY TREE

After you tell the DOS Shell to refresh the display of files on a diskette, it automatically collapses the directory tree so that you see only the subdirectories below the root directory. However, the DOS Shell places a plus sign (+) next to the subdirectory name CASHFLOW to indicate that there are subdirectories below it. You can use the Expand All option on the Tree menu to display the entire directory tree.

To expand the directory tree and include these subdirectories as part of the directory tree:

1. Press **[F10]** (Actions), press **[→]** (Right Arrow) three times to highlight the Tree menu, and press **[Enter]** to select Tree.

If you are using the mouse, click **Tree**.

The drop-down Tree menu appears with options for controlling the display of the directory tree.

2. Press **[↓]** (Down Arrow) *twice* to highlight Expand All and press **[Enter]** to select this option.

If you are using the mouse, click **Expand All**.

The DOS Shell expands the directory tree, so you can view the files in each of the subdirectories below the CASHFLOW subdirectory.

3. Press **[Tab]** to move the selection cursor to the directory tree window. Press **[↓]** (Down Arrow) until you highlight the subdirectory name PRJCASH.

If you are using the mouse, click the subdirectory name **PRJCASH**.

The file list window displays the files that you moved to the PRJCASH subdirectory. See Figure 4-40. Note the full path in the title bar of the file list window.

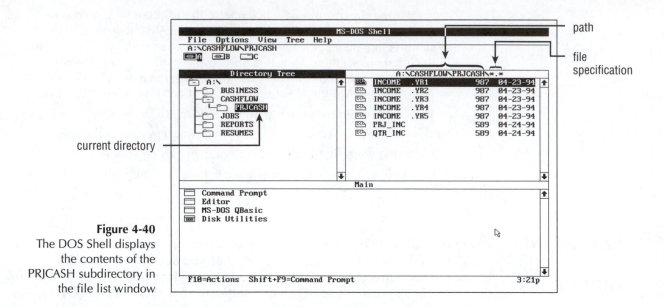

path

file
specification

current directory

Figure 4-40
The DOS Shell displays
the contents of the
PRJCASH subdirectory in
the file list window

Creating a Directory for Invoice Files

Because a new business must stay on top of its cash flow, you want to be able to quickly examine the status of outstanding invoices. You decide to create another new subdirectory below the CASHFLOW directory and move the invoice-tracking files to that subdirectory.

To create the INVOICES subdirectory:

1. Press **[↑]** (Up Arrow) to select the CASHFLOW subdirectory.

   If you are using the mouse, click the subdirectory name **CASHFLOW**.

2. Press **[F10]** (Actions) to access the menu bar, press **[Enter]** to select the File menu, and type **E** to select the Create Directory option.

   If you are using the mouse, click **File**, then click **Create Directory**.

3. Type **INVOICES** and then press **[Enter]**.

   If you are using the mouse, type **INVOICES** and click **OK**.

   The DOS Shell displays the Create Directory dialog box and displays the message "Access denied." See Figure 4-41. An error has occurred. The subdirectory name that you specified is also the name of an existing file. The dialog box asks you to verify whether you want to continue or not. You have two options—rename the file or select another name for the new subdirectory. You decide to rename the file.

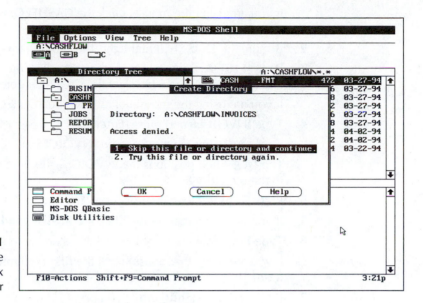

Figure 4-41
The DOS Shell's Create
Directory dialog box
warns of an error

4. Press **[Enter]**.

If you are using the mouse, click **OK**.

The DOS Shell skips this directory and lets you continue.

5. Press **[Tab]** to move the selection cursor to the file list window.

If you are using the mouse, click the **file list window title bar**.

6. Type **I** to select the first filename that starts with the letter "I." Then press **[↓]** (Down Arrow) twice to highlight the filename INVOICES.

If you are using the mouse, click the **scroll arrow** until you see the file-name INVOICES. Then click **INVOICES**.

7. Press **[F10]** (Actions), press **[Enter]** to select File, and type **N** for the Rename command.

If you are using the mouse, click **File**, then click **Rename**.

The DOS Shell displays the Rename File dialog box.

8. Type **INVOICE.RPT** and press **[Enter]**.

If you are using the mouse, type **INVOICE.RPT** and click **OK**.

The DOS Shell renames the file and updates the file list window.

Now that you have renamed the INVOICES file, you can create a subdirectory with the name INVOICES.

To create the INVOICES subdirectory:

1. Press **[Shift][Tab]** (Backtab). This returns you to the directory tree window. This key combination is called the **Backtab key** because it allows you to move back to the previous window.

If you are using the mouse, click the **CASHFLOW** subdirectory in the directory tree window.

2. Be sure the DOS Shell highlights the subdirectory name CASHFLOW.

3. Press **[F10]** (Actions) to access the menu bar, press **[Enter]** to select the File menu, and type **E** to select the Create Directory option.

    If you are using the mouse, click **File**, then click **Create Directory**.

4. Type **INVOICES** and press **[Enter]**.

    If you are using the mouse, type **INVOICES** and click **OK**.

    The DOS Shell positions the INVOICES subdirectory below CASHFLOW in the directory tree.

5. Press **[Tab]** to move the selection cursor to the file list window.

    If you are using the mouse, click the **file list window title bar**.

6. Type **I** to select the first filename that starts with the letter "I."

    If you are using the mouse, click the **first filename that starts with the letter "I."**

7. Press and hold **[Shift]** while you press **[↓]** (Down Arrow) twice to select the three invoice files. Then release **[Shift]**.

    If you are using the mouse, press **[Shift]** and then click the filename **INVOICE.WK1** to select the three invoice files.

8. Press **[F7]** (Move). The DOS Shell displays the Move File dialog box. Press **[End]**, type **\INVOICES** and press **[Enter]**.

    If you are using the mouse, click **File**, then click **Move**. When the DOS Shell displays the Move File dialog box, click **after the path**. Then type **\INVOICES** and click **OK**.

    The DOS Shell moves the files to the INVOICES subdirectory.

You are now ready to reread the Tutorial Disk.

To update the file list window:

1. Press **[F5]** (Refresh).

    If you are using the mouse, click **View**, then click **Refresh**.

    The DOS Shell rereads your Tutorial Disk.

2. Press **[F10]** (Actions) and type **T** to select the Tree menu.

    If you are using the mouse, click **Tree** to select the Tree menu.

3. Type **A** to select Expand All.

    If you are using the mouse, click **Expand All**.

    The DOS Shell expands the directory tree.

Now verify the move operation.

4. Press **[Tab]** to move the selection cursor to the directory tree window.

    If you are using a mouse, click the **directory tree window title bar**.

5. Press **[↓]** (Down Arrow) until you highlight the directory name INVOICES.

If you are using a mouse, click the directory name **INVOICES**.

DOS displays the newly moved files in the file list window.

6. Press [↑] (Up Arrow) to select the CASHFLOW subdirectory.

Creating a Directory for Summary Files

You have one more subdirectory to create according to your revised plan. This subdirectory, which you want to call SUMMARY, will store the files that contain the cashflow summaries.

To create the SUMMARY subdirectory:

1. Create the SUMMARY subdirectory under the CASHFLOW directory, according to your revised plan for organizing subdirectories and files on your Tutorial Disk.

2. After you create the SUMMARY subdirectory, move the remaining files in the CASHFLOW directory to this subdirectory.

3. Reread your Tutorial Disk, then expand the directory tree.

4. Move to the directory tree window and select the SUMMARY subdirectory. The DOS Shell shows the files that you moved to the SUMMARY subdirectory. See Figure 4-42.

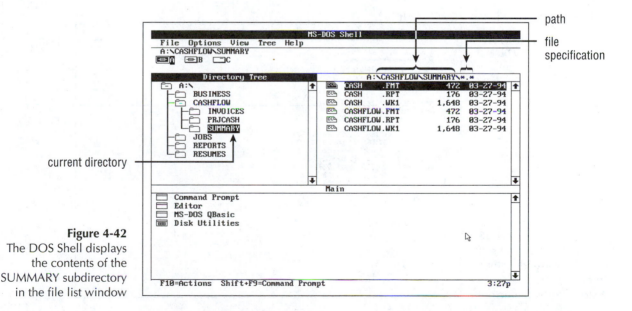

Figure 4-42
The DOS Shell displays the contents of the SUMMARY subdirectory in the file list window

5. Select the root directory before you exit the DOS Shell.

6. Exit the DOS Shell.

Navigating the Directory Tree at the DOS Prompt

In the DOS Shell, you selected and viewed the contents of directories below the CASHFLOW subdirectory by moving the selection cursor in the directory tree window. Now you want to learn how to navigate within the directory tree at the DOS prompt so that you can use both approaches in the daily operations of your business and when you work in client offices.

There are two techniques you can use: You can change to a subdirectory in one step by specifying its full path or you can traverse the directory tree one subdirectory at a time by specifying the directory's name. However, in some cases you might also need to specify part of the path.

You want to examine each of the subdirectories of CASHFLOW and return to the root directory. First, let's change to the INVOICES directory by specifying its full path.

To change to the INVOICES subdirectory in one step:

1. Be sure you are at the root directory of the drive that contains your Tutorial Disk.

2. Type **CD CASHFLOW\INVOICES** and press **[Enter]**. The DOS prompt shows that the current directory is the INVOICES subdirectory.

3. Type **DIR** and press **[Enter]** to view the files in this subdirectory. See Figure 4-43.

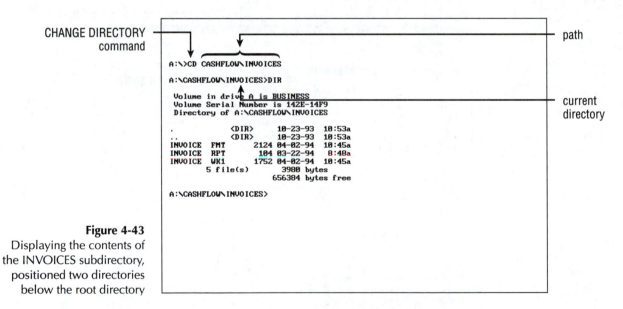

CHANGE DIRECTORY command — path — current directory

Figure 4-43
Displaying the contents of the INVOICES subdirectory, positioned two directories below the root directory

4. Type **CD ** and press **[Enter]**. As you can tell from the DOS prompt, DOS moved up two directories to the root directory.

Stepping Down the Directory Tree

You next want to examine the CASHFLOW and the PRJCASH subdirectories. You can step down the directory tree one directory at a time.

To change to the CASHFLOW subdirectory and then the PRJCASH subdirectory:

1. Type **CD CASHFLOW** and press **[Enter]**. The DOS prompt shows that the current directory is the CASHFLOW subdirectory.

2. Type **DIR** and press **[Enter]**. DOS displays a list of the subdirectories below CASHFLOW. See Figure 4-44.

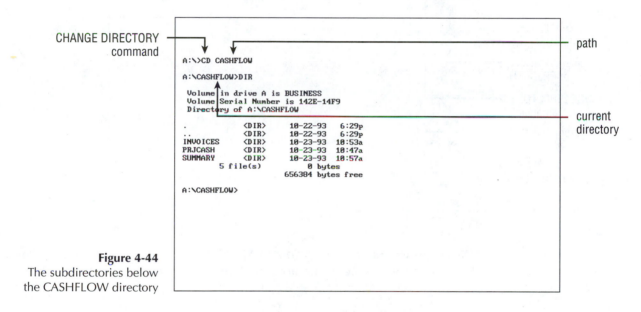

CHANGE DIRECTORY command

path

current directory

```
A:\>CD CASHFLOW

A:\CASHFLOW>DIR

 Volume in drive A is BUSINESS
 Volume Serial Number is 142E-14F9
 Directory of A:\CASHFLOW

.            <DIR>      10-22-93    6:29p
..           <DIR>      10-22-93    6:29p
INVOICES     <DIR>      10-23-93   10:53a
PRJCASH      <DIR>      10-23-93   10:47a
SUMMARY      <DIR>      10-23-93   10:57a
       5 file(s)              0 bytes
                         656384 bytes free

A:\CASHFLOW>
```

Figure 4-44
The subdirectories below the CASHFLOW directory

3. Type **CD PRJCASH** and press **[Enter]**. The DOS prompt shows that the current directory is the PRJCASH subdirectory, which is positioned below the CASHFLOW subdirectory.

4. Type **DIR** and press **[Enter]** to view the files in this subdirectory.

Stepping Up the Directory

You first want to return to the CASHFLOW directory and then to the root directory. If you change to a subdirectory and then want to move one level higher in the directory tree to its parent directory, you can use one of these variations of the Change Directory commands:

CD ..

CHDIR ..

Because .. (dot dot) refers to the parent directory of the current directory, you can change to a parent directory without specifying its full path.

Let's return to the root directory, one directory level at a time.

To change to the parent directory of PRJCASH:

1. Type **CD ..** and press **[Enter]**. Remember, the DOS prompt shows that the current directory is the CASHFLOW subdirectory. You can now use this same command to move to the parent directory of CASHFLOW.

2. Type **CD ..** and press **[Enter]**. The DOS prompt shows that you are at the root directory. See Figure 4-45.

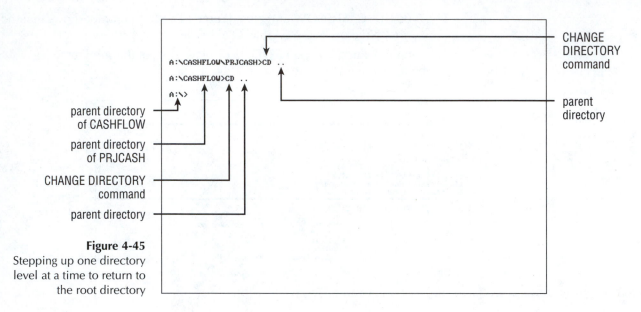

parent directory of CASHFLOW

parent directory of PRJCASH

CHANGE DIRECTORY command

parent directory

CHANGE DIRECTORY command

parent directory

```
A:\CASHFLOW\PRJCASH>CD ..
A:\CASHFLOW>CD ..
A:\>
```

Figure 4-45
Stepping up one directory level at a time to return to the root directory

Next you want to change to the SUMMARY subdirectory, examine its files, and switch to the INVOICES subdirectory before returning to the root directory.

To traverse the subdirectories of CASHFLOW:

1. Type **CD CASHFLOW\SUMMARY** and press **[Enter]**. The DOS prompt shows that the current directory is SUMMARY.

2. Type **DIR** and press **[Enter]** to view the files in this subdirectory.

3. Type **CD ..\INVOICES** and press **[Enter]**. This command tells DOS to change to the INVOICES subdirectory, which is below the parent directory of SUMMARY. The DOS prompt shows that the current directory is INVOICES. See Figure 4-46. You could also enter CD \CASHFLOW\INVOICES to achieve the same result.

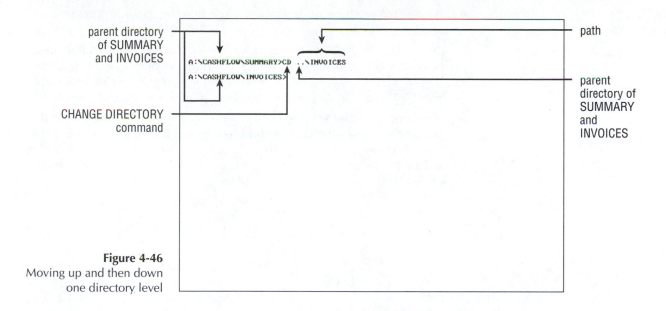

parent directory
of SUMMARY
and INVOICES

path

```
A:\CASHFLOW\SUMMARY>CD ..\INVOICES
A:\CASHFLOW\INVOICES>
```

parent
directory of
SUMMARY
and
INVOICES

CHANGE DIRECTORY
command

Figure 4-46
Moving up and then down
one directory level

4. Type **CD** \ and press **[Enter]** to return to the root directory.

You can use the same techniques to navigate the more complex directory structure of your hard disk in order to locate client or business files.

PRINTING A DIRECTORY TREE FROM THE DOS PROMPT

You want to print a copy of your directory tree and the files contained in each of the subdirectories. If the diskette fails or becomes damaged, you can quickly reconstruct the subdirectory structure and restore your business files to the proper subdirectories.

Earlier you used the TREE command to view a directory tree at the DOS prompt. You can use a variation of the same command to view filenames by directory. You can then redirect that output to print a copy of the directory tree. The **Filename switch** (/F) displays the directory tree and lists the filenames in each directory. When you print this information, you can also include the **ASCII switch** (/A) if your printer cannot print the graphics lines in the directory tree. If you use the ASCII switch, DOS substitutes other symbols for the graphics lines. Let's try it.

To display a directory tree of your Tutorial Disk:

1. Be sure the current disk drive contains your Tutorial Disk.
2. Be sure you are at the root directory. If not, type **CD** \ and press **[Enter]**.
3. Type **TREE** **/F** and press **[Enter]**. The TREE command displays the directory tree and lists the filenames in each subdirectory. The first part of this directory tree scrolls off the screen.

4. Be sure the printer is on and on-line, and that the paper is properly aligned in the printer.

5. Type **TREE /F /A > PRN** and press **[Enter]**. You can redirect the output of any DOS command to the printer by using the output redirection operator (>) and the name of your printer port. If your printer can print graphics characters, you can perform this operation without the /A switch.

6. If necessary, press the **Form Feed button** on the printer. If the printer does not respond, press the **On Line button** to place the printer off-line. Then press **Form Feed** again. After the printer ejects the page, press the **On Line button** to place the printer back on-line. Figure 4-47 shows the printed copy of the directory tree with filenames.

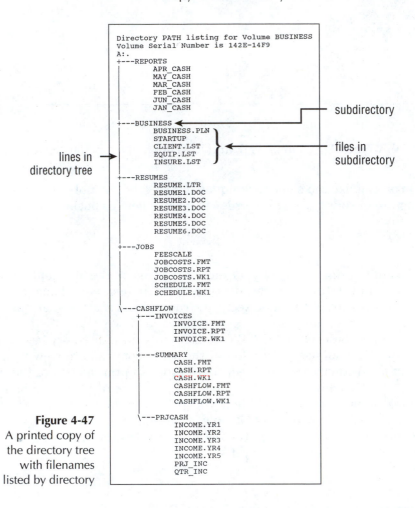

lines in
directory tree →

subdirectory

files in
subdirectory

Figure 4-47
A printed copy of
the directory tree
with filenames
listed by directory

For a quick overview of the subdirectory structure of a hard disk or diskette, use the TREE command at the DOS prompt or view the directory tree from the DOS Shell. You can then locate specific subdirectories and periodically evaluate the organization of subdirectories on diskettes or hard disks.

SUMMARY

In this tutorial, you learned how to work with subdirectories from the DOS prompt and from the DOS Shell. You created subdirectories with the MD, or Make Subdirectory, command at the DOS prompt and with the Create Directory option on the File menu in the DOS Shell. You learned how to navigate from one subdirectory to another with the use of the CD, or Change Subdirectory, command at the DOS prompt and by selecting subdirectories from the DOS Shell. You also learned how to change to a parent directory and to return to the root directory.

You used the DIR command and the DOS Shell to display the contents of subdirectories. You used the COPY command at the DOS prompt and the Copy option on the File menu in the DOS Shell to copy files from one subdirectory to another. In DOS 6.0 and 6.2, you moved files from one directory to another with the MOVE command at the DOS prompt. In DOS 5.0, you moved files with the COPY and DEL commands. You also used the Move option on the File menu in the DOS Shell to move files. You deleted files from a directory with the DEL command.

You viewed the directory tree of your Tutorial Disk with the TREE command at the DOS prompt and in the directory tree window in the DOS Shell. You also printed a directory tree from the DOS prompt with the TREE command and included filenames by directory.

Command Reference

DOS Commands

CD [*drive:*]*path* CHDIR [*drive:*]*path*	Internal commands that change from one directory to another
CD .. CHDIR ..	Internal commands that change to the directory above the current directory
CD \ CHDIR \	Internal commands that change from the current directory to the root directory
MD [*drive:*]*path* MKDIR [*drive:*]*path*	Internal commands that create, or make, a subdirectory
MOVE [*drive:*][*path*]*filename destination*	*DOS 6.0 and 6.2*: An external command that moves one or more files to another drive, directory, or drive and directory
PROMPT [*text*]	An internal command that customizes the appearance of the DOS command; for example, PROMPT PG displays the full path in the DOS prompt
TREE [*drive:*][*path*] [/F] [/A]	An external command that displays a diagram of the directory tree; the /F switch includes filenames with the directory tree, and the /A switch displays the lines in the directory tree with ASCII characters

DOS Shell Commands

File/Create Directory	Creates a subdirectory
File/Move	Moves one or more files to another directory
Tree/Expand All	Expands the directory tree to show all subdirectories

QUESTIONS

1. What command would you enter to create a subdirectory named TOOLS below the root directory of the current drive? Assume the current directory is the root directory.

2. What command would you enter to create a subdirectory named WP51 (for WordPerfect 5.1) below a directory named \TOOLS? Assume the current directory is \TOOLS, and assume \TOOLS is a subdirectory below the root directory.

3. What command would you enter to change from the root directory to a subdirectory named TOOLS on the current drive?

4. What command would you enter to change to a subdirectory named WP51 below a directory named TOOLS? Assume the current directory is TOOLS.

5. What command would you enter to change from a subdirectory named \TOOLS\WP51 to the root directory?

6. List two commands that you could use to change from a subdirectory named \TOOLS\WP51 to the subdirectory named \TOOLS.

7. How do you move files from one subdirectory to another at the DOS prompt in DOS 5.0?

8. How do you move files from one subdirectory to another at the DOS prompt in DOS 6.0 and 6.2?

9. What command would you enter to display a directory tree from the root directory? Assume the current directory is the root directory.

10. What command would you enter to display a directory tree from the root directory? Assume the current directory is the TOOLS directory (below the root directory).

11. How would you create a subdirectory named CREDIT below the root directory in the DOS Shell?

12. How would you change from the root directory to another subdirectory named \CREDIT\CARDS in the DOS Shell?

13. How would you move files from a subdirectory named CARDLIST to another named CREDIT\CARDS in the DOS Shell?

14. How can you control the display of the directory tree in the DOS Shell?

15. After you move files in the DOS Shell, how can you update the file lists for each directory?

16. Suppose you have a subdirectory named \MARKETS on drive C. If this subdirectory is below the root directory of drive C, what command would you enter at the DOS prompt to change to this subdirectory? Assume the current directory is the root directory of drive C.

17. If there is a subdirectory named FUTURE below \MARKETS on drive C, what command would you enter to change to that subdirectory from the root directory? Assume the current directory is the root directory of drive C. What command would you enter to return to the root directory of drive C in one step?

18. Suppose you have a subdirectory named BENEFITS on drive C. This subdirectory is below the root directory of drive C. What command would you enter at the DOS prompt to display a list of the files in this subdirectory from the root directory of drive C?

19. Suppose you have a subdirectory named BIDS below the root directory and another subdirectory named 1994 below the one named BIDS. Assume these subdirectories are located on drive C. What is the full path of the subdirectory BIDS? Of the subdirectory 1994? Assume the current directory is the root directory of drive C. What command would you enter at the DOS prompt to change from the root directory to the 1994 subdirectory in one step? What command would you enter to change to its parent directory?

20. Suppose you have just created a new subdirectory named C:\WPFILES. You want to move all the files from the root directory with the file extension DOC to this new subdirectory. What command or commands would you enter at the DOS prompt to perform this operation? Assume the current directory is the root directory of drive C.

21. You keep all your work files in a subdirectory named C:\WORK. The number of files in this subdirectory now exceeds 50. You want to create a new subdirectory named C:\MEMOS and copy all the files with the file extension MEM from the subdirectory C:\WORK to C:\MEMOS. Then you want to delete those files from C:\WORK. List the steps and commands that you would use to accomplish this operation. Assume you are working at the DOS prompt and assume the current directory is the root directory of drive C.

22. You are working in the file list window of the DOS Shell. The DOS Shell is displaying the files in the root directory of drive C. You want to move all of the files with a file extension LTR to a subdirectory named LETTERS positioned immediately below the root directory of drive C. List the steps that you would follow to perform this operation.

23. You are working in the file list window of the DOS Shell. You want to select another subdirectory named \PAYROLL so that you can view the files in that subdirectory. List the steps that you would follow to change to this subdirectory.

24. After you power on your computer system, the DOS prompt appears as **C>**. You want to change the prompt so that you can see the full path of each subdirectory as you change from one subdirectory to another. What command can you enter at the DOS prompt so that the DOS prompt shows the full path? Assume you are working at the root directory of drive C. After you enter this command, what does the DOS prompt look like?

25. When you view a directory listing of a subdirectory, you see two files—one named . (dot) and the other named .. (dot dot). What do these two files represent?

26. What is a parent directory?

27. How can you display a directory tree from the DOS prompt so that it includes filenames for all directories? Assume you are working at the root directory of drive C.

28. How can you redirect a copy of a directory tree, with filenames by subdirectory, to the printer?

29. How does DOS designate a subdirectory in a directory listing produced with the DIR command so that you can distinguish the subdirectory from files?

30. How do you expand the directory tree in the DOS Shell?

TUTORIAL ASSIGNMENTS

1. **Displaying a Directory Listing**: *Use your Tutorial Disk to perform the following operations from the DOS prompt.* List the command that you use to accomplish each step.
   a. Display an alphabetical list of all files in the subdirectory named BUSINESS one screen at a time from the root directory.
   b. Display an alphabetical list of all files in the root directory from the subdirectory named BUSINESS.
   c. Display an alphabetical list of all files in the JOBS subdirectory while working in the CASHFLOW subdirectory.
   d. Display an alphabetical list of all files in the CASHFLOW\INVOICES subdirectory from the root directory.
   e. Change to the CASHFLOW subdirectory, and display a directory tree with filenames for the CASHFLOW directory and its subdirectories.

2. **Creating Subdirectories at the DOS Prompt**: *Use your Exercise Disk to perform the following operations from the DOS prompt.* Start at the root directory, and list the command that you use to accomplish each step.
   a. Create a subdirectory named CLIENTS below the root directory.
   b. Change to the CLIENTS subdirectory.
   c. Create a subdirectory named REPORTS below the CLIENTS directory.
   d. Create a subdirectory named PROJECTS below the CLIENTS directory.
   e. Create a subdirectory named BIDS below the root directory.
   f. Change to the root directory.
   g. Display a directory tree.
   h. Print a directory tree.

3. **Creating Subdirectories and Moving Files at the DOS Prompt**: *Use your Exercise Disk to perform the following operations from the DOS prompt.* List the command that you use to accomplish each step.
   a. From the root directory, create a subdirectory named DOCUMENT below the root directory.
   b. Change to the DOCUMENT subdirectory.
   c. Create a subdirectory named RESUMES below the DOCUMENT directory.
   d. Move all files in the root directory with a file extension of DOC to the RESUMES subdirectory.
   e. Change to the root directory.
   f. First display, then print, a directory tree with filenames.

4. **Creating Subdirectories from the DOS Shell**: *Use the Exercise Disk to perform the following operations from the DOS Shell*. List the step or steps for each of these operations.
   a. Create a subdirectory named 123FILES below the root directory.
   b. Move all the files in the root directory with the file extension WK1 and FMT to the subdirectory named 123FILES.
   c. Create another subdirectory named FINANCES below the root directory.
   d. Change to the subdirectory FINANCES and create a subdirectory named CASHFLOW below FINANCES.
   e. Move all the files in the root directory that have CASH as the last four characters of an eight-character filename and any file extension to the subdirectory named CASHFLOW.
   f. Exit the DOS Shell.
   g. First display, then print, a directory tree with filenames.

5. **Navigating Directories at the DOS prompt and in the DOS Shell**: *Use your Tutorial Disk to perform the following operations*. Be sure you start at the root directory of drive A or drive B. List the step or steps for each of these operations.
   a. Change to the REPORTS subdirectory.
   b. Change to the SUMMARY subdirectory below the CASHFLOW directory.
   c. Change to the JOBS subdirectory.
   d. Change to the root directory.
   e. Load the DOS Shell.
   f. Expand the directory tree.
   g. Change to the BUSINESS subdirectory.
   h. Change to the PRJCASH subdirectory below the CASHFLOW directory.
   i. Change to the root directory.
   j. Exit the DOS Shell.

Managing a Hard Disk

OBJECTIVES

In this tutorial you will learn to:

◆ Evaluate a hard disk's directory structure

◆ Reorganize a directory structure

◆ Rename a subdirectory

◆ Remove a subdirectory

◆ Locate files within a directory structure

◆ Eliminate file fragmentation and optimize a disk

◆ Check for computer viruses

Imagine that your supervisor asks you to evaluate the organization of subdirectories and files on the hard disks of your office computer systems and to recommend more efficient approaches for storing and accessing business and client records. Once you complete your evaluation, he wants to hold a general staff meeting to discuss your recommendations and develop a consensus for improving the performance of the computer systems. Ultimately, your goal is to standardize the computer systems so that staff members can work efficiently and easily on any of the computers.

◆

GETTING STARTED

To simplify the task of examining the organization of files in subdirectories, you decide to install DOSKEY and specify default switches for the DIR command.

To set up your system:

5.0 6.0

6.2

1. After you power on your computer system, access drive C.

2. Type **DOSKEY** and press **[Enter]**. If you are using DOS 5.0 or 6.0, DOS will display the message "DOSKey installed" if DOSKEY is not already installed on your computer. If you do not see this message with DOS 5.0 or 6.0, DOSKEY is already loaded. DOS 6.2 will not display a message.

3. Type **SET DIRCMD=/P /O** and press **[Enter]**. DOS will now display your client files and subdirectories in alphabetical order and will pause after each screen.

4. Type **SET** and press **[Enter]** to verify that you correctly entered the switches for the DIRCMD environment variable. If not, repeat Step 3.

VIEWING THE DIRECTORY STRUCTURE OF A HARD DISK DRIVE

You want to display and then print the directory structure of the hard drive on one of the office computer systems. Because most hard disk drives have a complex, multi-tiered directory tree, you can pipe the output of the TREE command to the MORE filter so that you can view the directory tree one screen at a time.

To display a directory tree of a hard disk drive:

1. Type **TREE ¦ MORE** and press **[Enter]**. DOS displays the first part of the directory tree, displays the More prompt, and pauses. Figure 5-1 shows the first page of a directory tree of a hard disk drive. Your directory will be different.

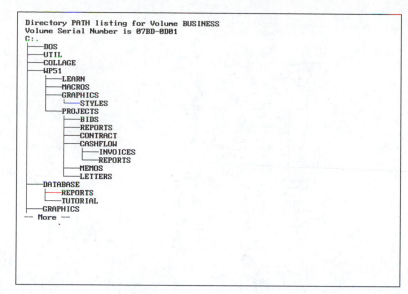

```
Directory PATH listing for Volume BUSINESS
Volume Serial Number is 07BD-0D01
C:.
├───DOS
├───UTIL
├───COLLAGE
├───WP51
│   ├───LEARN
│   ├───MACROS
│   ├───GRAPHICS
│   │   └───STYLES
│   ├───PROJECTS
│   │   ├───BIDS
│   │   ├───REPORTS
│   │   ├───CONTRACT
│   │   ├───CASHFLOW
│   │   │   ├───INVOICES
│   │   │   └───REPORTS
│   │   ├───MEMOS
│   │   └───LETTERS
├───DATABASE
│   ├───REPORTS
│   └───TUTORIAL
├───GRAPHICS
-- More --
```

Figure 5-1
A paged view of a
directory tree for a hard
disk drive

2. Press **[Spacebar]** or any other key to continue. Repeat this process until you view the entire directory tree.

PRINTING THE DIRECTORY STRUCTURE OF A HARD DISK

Now you want to print a copy of the directory tree so that you can evaluate the directory structure of this hard disk. You will redirect the output of the TREE command to the printer port.

To print the directory tree:

1. Be sure the printer is on and on-line, and that the paper is properly aligned in the printer.

2. Type **TREE > PRN** and press **[Enter]**. DOS redirects the output and prints the directory tree. See Figure 5-2. If you experience difficulty, ask your instructor or technical support person for assistance. DOS must be able to locate the printer port.

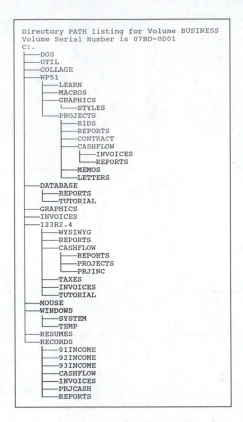

```
Directory PATH listing for Volume BUSINESS
Volume Serial Number is 07BD-0D01
C:.
├───DOS
├───UTIL
├───COLLAGE
├───WP51
│   ├───LEARN
│   ├───MACROS
│   ├───GRAPHICS
│   │   └───STYLES
│   ├───PROJECTS
│   │   ├───BIDS
│   │   ├───REPORTS
│   │   ├───CONTRACT
│   │   ├───CASHFLOW
│   │   │   ├───INVOICES
│   │   │   └───REPORTS
│   ├───MEMOS
│   └───LETTERS
├───DATABASE
│   ├───REPORTS
│   └───TUTORIAL
├───GRAPHICS
├───INVOICES
├───123R2.4
│   ├───WYSIWYG
│   ├───REPORTS
│   ├───CASHFLOW
│   │   ├───REPORTS
│   │   ├───PROJECTS
│   │   └───PRJINC
│   ├───TAXES
│   ├───INVOICES
│   └───TUTORIAL
├───MOUSE
├───WINDOWS
│   ├───SYSTEM
│   └───TEMP
├───RESUMES
└───RECORDS
    ├───91INCOME
    ├───92INCOME
    ├───93INCOME
    ├───CASHFLOW
    ├───INVOICES
    ├───PRJCASH
    └───REPORTS
```

Figure 5-2
A printed copy of
a directory tree
for a hard disk

3. If necessary, press the **Form Feed button** on the printer. If the printer does not respond, press the **On Line button** to place the printer off-line. Then press **Form Feed** again. After the printer ejects the page, press the **On Line button** to place the printer back on-line.

EVALUATING THE ORGANIZATION OF DIRECTORIES ON A HARD DISK

As you examine the printed copy of the directory structure shown in Figure 5-2, you notice that the hard disk contains subdirectories, positioned below the root directory, for software applications, utilities, DOS, and Windows. The DOS subdirectory contains the DOS system utilities. The DOS 5.0, 6.0, and 6.2 installation programs automatically create this subdirectory. The MOUSE subdirectory contains the software for operating the mouse. The UTIL subdirectory contains other utility software. The WINDOWS subdirectory contains program files for the Windows operating environment.

The WP51 and 123R2.4 subdirectories contain the software for the WordPerfect 5.1 and Lotus 1-2-3 Release 2.4 applications, respectively. The 123R2.4 subdirectory illustrates that subdirectories, like filenames, can have file extensions. Positioned below these two subdirectories are other subdirectories, such as a tutorial subdirectory, that contain additional files provided with the software application. You assume the DATABASE and GRAPHICS subdirectories contain software for these types of applications, document files, or perhaps both program and data files. Other subdirectories contain specialized software.

Some client and business files are stored in the INVOICES, RESUMES, and RECORDS subdirectories, which are located below the root directory. Other client and business files are stored in subdirectories that already contain applications software or in subdirectories subordinate to the applications software directory. For example, the WP51 and 123R2.4 directories contain subdirectories for client files.

After examining this directory tree, you realize that you can improve the directory structure of this hard disk. First, you can consolidate subdirectories and files into one directory. For example, you can consolidate the four INVOICE subdirectories into one so that invoice files are easier to locate. This consolidation will also reduce the chances of saving different versions of the same file in different subdirectories.

Second, you can separate files produced by software applications from the program files for those applications. For example, you can separate the WordPerfect software in the WP51 directory from the subdirectories that contain client files produced by WordPerfect, and staff members would no longer need to look for a client file among hundreds of program files.

Third, you can move files currently stored in the root directory to the appropriate subdirectory so that only important system files would remain in the root directory.

Finally, you can reduce the complexity of the directory structure by limiting the number of subdirectory levels. For example, rather than having a MEMOS subdirectory three levels below the root directory, you can place it directly beneath the root directory. When you use the DIR command to display the contents of the root directory, the directory listing will look like a table of contents. Then you and other staff members can quickly distinguish software directories from client directories. Furthermore, DOS works faster and more efficiently with a directory structure that contains fewer directory levels.

RECOMMEND-ING A NEW DIRECTORY STRUCTURE

You prepare and submit to your supervisor a summary of your findings and a diagram that illustrates the proposed directory structure for the office computers (see Figure 5-3). In this report, you emphasize the importance of organizing information by project, client, business records, and software use, and the importance of using a consistent approach when adding new directories. You also recommend that software and client subdirectories be positioned directly below the root directory, and that the directory structure contain no more than two or three levels of subdirectories.

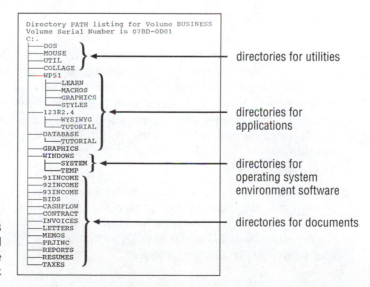

Figure 5-3
A proposed
directory structure
for a hard disk

After your supervisor reviews this report, he calls a general staff meeting to discuss the recommendations and to adopt a course of action. The general staff consensus is to proceed with your recommendations. Your supervisor asks that you first test your proposal on a copy of your client diskette before you actually revamp the directory structure of the hard drives in the office.

Before you can start the test, you need a printed copy of the directory tree on your client diskette. You can then prepare a sketch of a new directory structure for this disk.

To print the directory tree:

1. Insert your Tutorial Disk into drive A or drive B, and change to that drive.

2. Be sure the printer is on and on-line, and that the paper is properly aligned in the printer.

3. Type **TREE > PRN** and press **[Enter]**. DOS redirects the output and prints the directory tree. See Figure 5-4. The order of subdirectories in your tree might be different.

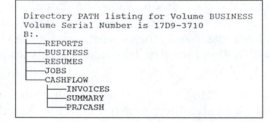

Figure 5-4
A directory tree of the Tutorial Disk

```
Directory PATH listing for Volume BUSINESS
Volume Serial Number is 17D9-3710
B:.
├───REPORTS
├───BUSINESS
├───RESUMES
├───JOBS
└───CASHFLOW
    ├───INVOICES
    ├───SUMMARY
    └───PRJCASH
```

4. If necessary, press the **Form Feed button** on the printer. If the printer does not respond, press the **On Line button** to place the printer off-line. Then press **Form Feed** again. After the printer ejects the page, press the **On Line button** to place the printer back on-line.

DEVELOPING A STRATEGY FOR REORGANIZING A DIRECTORY STRUCTURE

The CASHFLOW directory has three subdirectories: INVOICES, PRJCASH, and SUMMARY. You decide to position these subdirectories below the root directory. To make these changes from the DOS prompt, you must create a new subdirectory, move all the files from the original subdirectory to the new subdirectory, and remove the original subdirectory.

To create a new subdirectory, you use the MD (Make Directory) command as follows:

MD [*drive:*]*path*

You specify the path and name of the subdirectory. You must also specify the drive if you are creating the subdirectory on another disk drive. The directory name cannot be the same as a filename.

6.0 6.2

If you are using DOS 6.0 or 6.2, you can use the MOVE command to move files from one directory to another:

MOVE [*drive*:][*path*]*filename destination*

You specify the name of the file or files you want to move and the destination. If the file or files you want to move are located in another directory, you also must specify the name of that directory. If the file or files you want to move are located on another drive, you must specify the drive name for the file(s). The destination is the name of the directory where you want to move the file or files.

5.0

If you are using DOS 5.0, you must use the COPY command to copy all the files in the original subdirectory to the new subdirectory. After you verify the copy operation, you can use the DEL command to erase the files from the original subdirectory.

To remove a subdirectory, you use the RD or RMDIR (Remove Directory) command. The subdirectory that you remove *must* be empty. The subdirectory *cannot* contain any files *or* subdirectories. Also, you *cannot* remove the root directory with this command. The syntax for this internal command is as follows:

RD [*drive*:]*path*

You specify the path and name of the subdirectory. If the subdirectory is located on another drive, you also must specify the drive name.

MODIFYING THE DIRECTORY STRUCTURE

Now you are ready to reorganize the directory structure of your diskette. You decide to position the INVOICES subdirectory below the root directory. First, you need to create a new INVOICES subdirectory.

To create a new INVOICES subdirectory:

1. Be sure you are at the root directory of drive A or drive B.

2. Type **MD \INVOICES** and press **[Enter]**. DOS creates this subdirectory below the root directory of the disk drive containing your diskette and displays the DOS prompt.

   Now verify that this new subdirectory exists:

3. Type **TREE** and press **[Enter]**. DOS displays an updated directory tree. See Figure 5-5. The order of subdirectories in your tree might be different.

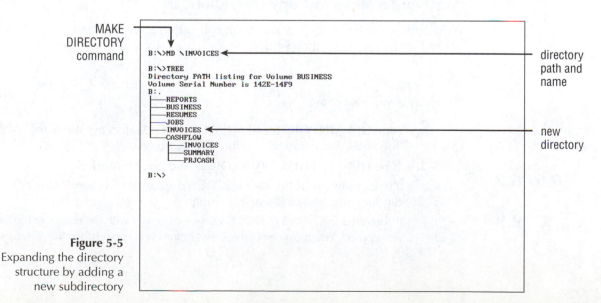

MAKE DIRECTORY command

directory path and name

new directory

```
B:\>MD \INVOICES

B:\>TREE
Directory PATH listing for Volume BUSINESS
Volume Serial Number is 142E-14F9
B:.
    ├───REPORTS
    ├───BUSINESS
    ├───RESUMES
    ├───JOBS
    ├───INVOICES
    └───CASHFLOW
        ├───INVOICES
        ├───SUMMARY
        └───PRJCASH

B:\>
```

Figure 5-5
Expanding the directory structure by adding a new subdirectory

Moving Files from Directory to Directory

Now you are ready to move the files from the original INVOICES directory to the new INVOICES directory. Follow the steps in the section below for the version of DOS that you are using on your computer.

6.0 *6.2* **To move these files** *using DOS 6.0 or 6.2*:

1. Type **MOVE \CASHFLOW\INVOICES*.* \INVOICES** and press **[Enter]**. The source files are the files in the INVOICES subdirectory located below the CASHFLOW directory. The destination directory is the INVOICES subdirectory located below the root directory. The backslash before \CASHFLOW\INVOICES and \INVOICES completes the path for these subdirectories and emphasizes that CASHFLOW and INVOICES are located below the root directory of the current drive. DOS displays a list of the files that it moves.

DOS 6.0 and 6.2 users should skip the next step list and proceed directly to the section entitled "Verifying a Move or Copy Operation."

5.0 **To move these files** *using DOS 5.0*:

1. Type **COPY \CASHFLOW\INVOICES \INVOICES** and press **[Enter]**. The source files are the files in the INVOICES subdirectory located below the CASHFLOW directory. The destination, or target, directory is the INVOICES subdirectory located below the root directory. The backslash before \CASHFLOW\INVOICES and \INVOICES completes the path for these subdirectories and emphasizes that CASHFLOW and INVOICES are located below the root directory of the current drive. DOS displays a list of the files that it copies.

Verifying a Move or Copy Operation

You now want to verify the move or copy operation to ensure the files are stored in the correct subdirectory.

To verify a move or copy:

1. Type **DIR \INVOICES** and press **[Enter]**. DOS displays the names of the three files that it moved into this new directory.

2. Type **DIR \CASHFLOW\INVOICES** and press **[Enter]**.

6.0 *6.2* If you are using DOS 6.0 or 6.2, DOS displays a directory listing of this subdirectory, showing that it is empty.

5.0 If you are using DOS 5.0, DOS displays a directory with the names of the files you copied. You must delete these files before you can remove the directory.

5.0   3. *If you are using DOS 5.0,* type **DEL \CASHFLOW\INVOICES** and press **[Enter]**. DOS asks you to verify this operation. Type **Y** and press **[Enter]**.

Removing an Empty Directory

Now you are ready to remove the \CASHFLOW\INVOICES directory, which is empty.

To remove a directory:

1. Type **RD \CASHFLOW\INVOICES** and press **[Enter]**. DOS displays the DOS prompt.
2. Type **DIR \CASHFLOW** and press **[Enter]**. The CASHFLOW directory no longer has a subdirectory named INVOICES. See Figure 5-6.

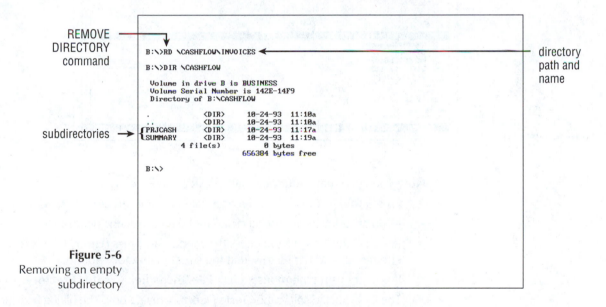

REMOVE
DIRECTORY
command

directory
path and
name

```
B:\>RD \CASHFLOW\INVOICES

B:\>DIR \CASHFLOW

 Volume in drive B is BUSINESS
 Volume Serial Number is 142E-14F9
 Directory of B:\CASHFLOW

.            <DIR>      10-24-93   11:10a
..           <DIR>      10-24-93   11:10a
PRJCASH      <DIR>      10-24-93   11:17a
SUMMARY      <DIR>      10-24-93   11:19a
       4 file(s)            0 bytes
                       656384 bytes free

B:\>
```

subdirectories →

Figure 5-6
Removing an empty
subdirectory

REORGANIZING A DIRECTORY STRUCTURE WITH THE DOS SHELL

You decide to move the other two subdirectories in the DOS Shell. Like working at the DOS prompt, you create a new subdirectory, move all the files from the original subdirectory to the new subdirectory, and delete the original subdirectory. Based on your previous experience, you anticipate that it will be easier working in the DOS Shell than it is working at the DOS prompt.

To start the DOS Shell:

1. Type **DOSSHELL** and press **[Enter]**. DOS loads the DOS Shell and displays the directory structure of the Tutorial Disk in the directory tree window.

Next, expand the directory tree.

2. Press **[F10]** (Actions) to access the menu bar, type **T** for the Tree menu, and type **A** for the Expand All option.

If you are using the mouse, click **Tree**, then click **Expand All**.

The DOS Shell expands the directory tree to show all subdirectories. See Figure 5-7. Your view of the directory tree and file list windows will be different if you are using text mode. You can switch to graphics mode by using the Display option on the Options menu.

current drive

current directory

expanded directory tree

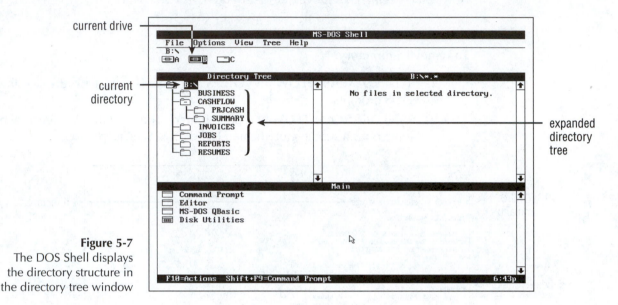

Figure 5-7
The DOS Shell displays the directory structure in the directory tree window

Now you can create your new SUMMARY subdirectory.

3. Press **[Tab]** to move the selection cursor to the directory tree window.

   If you are using the mouse, click the **root directory** in the directory tree window.

4. Press **[F10]** (Actions) to access the menu bar, press **[Enter]** to select the File menu, and type **E** to select the Create Directory option.

   If you are using the mouse, click **File**, then click **Create Directory**.

   The DOS Shell displays the Create Directory dialog box. The dialog box shows the parent name, in this case B:\, and prompts for the new directory name.

5. Type **SUMMARY** and press **[Enter]**.

   If you are using the mouse, type **SUMMARY** and click **OK**.

   The DOS Shell creates the SUMMARY subdirectory on the current drive below the root directory, and then updates the directory tree. See Figure 5-8.

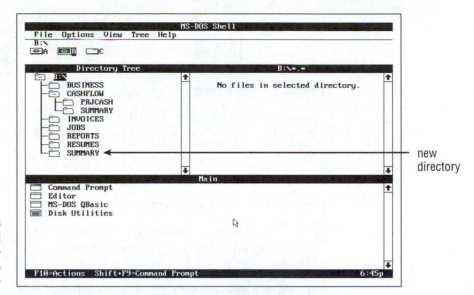

Figure 5-8
The newly created
SUMMARY directory
added to the directory tree
below the root directory

Moving Files from Directory to Directory

You are now ready to move the files from the \CASHFLOW\SUMMARY directory to the \SUMMARY directory. Because both directories have the same name, SUMMARY, you must distinguish between the directories by specifying their paths.

To move the files to the new directory:

1. Press [↓] (Down Arrow) until you highlight the SUMMARY subdirectory *located below the \CASHFLOW directory. Do not select the \SUMMARY subdirectory.*

    If you are using the mouse, click the **folder icon** next to the \CASHFLOW\ SUMMARY directory.

2. Press **[Tab]**. The DOS Shell moves the selection cursor to the file list window.

    If you are using the mouse, click the **file list window title bar**.

3. Press **[F10]** (Actions) and press **[Enter]** to select the File menu. Type **S** for the Select All option.

    If you are using the mouse, click **File**, then click **Select All**.

    DOS selects all the files in the file list window.

4. Press **[F7]** (Move). The DOS Shell displays the Move File dialog box with a partial view of the selected files in the From text box. Type **\SUMMARY** to specify the name for the target directory, and press **[Enter]**. *You must type the Backslash before the directory name so that the DOS Shell knows exactly where you want to move the files.* The DOS Shell moves the files to the \SUMMARY subdirectory.

    If you are using the mouse, move the mouse pointer next to the selected files. Hold down the left mouse button and drag the pointer to the folder icon adjacent to the subdirectory name SUMMARY in the directory tree window. Be sure you select the SUMMARY directory that is located below the root directory. Then release the mouse button. The DOS Shell displays the Confirm Mouse Operation dialog box and asks if you want to move the selected files to A:\SUMMARY or B:\SUMMARY. Click **Yes**. The DOS Shell moves the files to this subdirectory.

Removing an Empty Directory

You can now remove the \CASHFLOW\SUMMARY directory, which is empty. To remove a directory in the DOS Shell, you select the directory and press the Delete key.

To remove this empty subdirectory:

1. Press **[Del]** or **[Delete]**. The DOS Shell displays the Delete Directory Confirmation dialog box. See Figure 5-9.

currently selected directory

prompt for verification

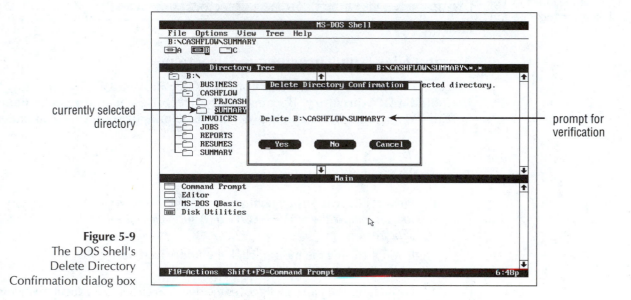

Figure 5-9
The DOS Shell's Delete Directory Confirmation dialog box

2. Press **[Enter]** to select the Yes button.

   If you are using the mouse, click **Yes**.

   The DOS Shell removes the SUMMARY subdirectory that is located below the CASHFLOW directory.

You next want to verify these operations to be sure your business files are stored in the correct subdirectory. But first you might need to reread your Tutorial Disk and refresh the display of files in the file list window.

To refresh the display of the files on your Tutorial Disk:

1. Press **[F5]** (Refresh). The DOS Shell rereads your Tutorial Disk.

Next, expand the directory tree.

2. Press **[F10]** (Actions) to access the menu bar, type **T** for the Tree menu, and type **A** for the Expand All option.

   If you are using the mouse, click **Tree**, then click **Expand All**.

   The DOS Shell expands the directory tree to show all subdirectories.

3. Press **[Tab]** to move the selection cursor to the directory tree window. Type **S** to move the selection cursor to the \SUMMARY subdirectory.

   If you are using the mouse, click the **\SUMMARY** subdirectory that is located below the root directory in the directory tree window.

   The DOS Shell shows that the files are now in this subdirectory.

4. Press **[Home]** to select the root directory.

   If you are using a mouse, click the **root directory** in the directory tree window.

Completing the Reorganization of the Directory Structure

According to your plan, you also want to create a subdirectory named \PRJCASH, which will be located below the root directory, to move the files from \CASHFLOW\PRJCASH to \PRJCASH, and to remove \CASHFLOW\PRJCASH.

To complete the reorganization of the directory structure of your Tutorial Disk:

1. Create the \PRJCASH subdirectory according to your plan for reorganizing subdirectories on your Tutorial Disk.

2. After you create this subdirectory, move the files in the \CASHFLOW\PRJCASH subdirectory to \PRJCASH.

3. If necessary, reread your Tutorial Disk and expand the directory tree.

4. Select the \PRJCASH subdirectory and verify that this subdirectory contains the moved files.

5. Remove the \CASHFLOW\PRJCASH subdirectory, and then remove the \CASHFLOW subdirectory.

6. Select the root directory. Your directory tree should look like the one shown in Figure 5-10.

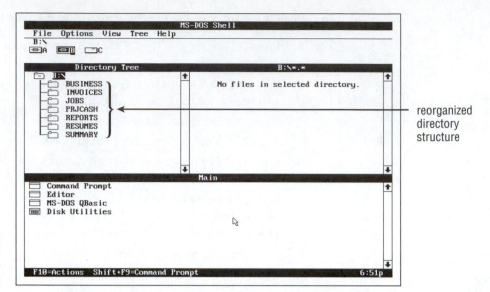

Figure 5-10
The reorganized
directory structure for
the Tutorial Disk

Because you have successfully restructured the directories on your client diskette, you have the necessary skills and correct plan to actually reorganize the directory structure of the hard disk drives in your office.

RENAMING DIRECTORIES

You decide to change the name of the SUMMARY subdirectory to CASHFLOW because this directory contains files with the company's cashflow reports. If you work at the DOS prompt in DOS 5.0, you must create a directory, move files, and then delete the original directory. If you work at the DOS prompt in DOS 6.0 or 6.2, you can use the MOVE utility to rename directories. If you work in the DOS Shell in DOS 5.0 or 6.0, you can use the Rename option on the File menu to rename files and subdirectories in one step. In a business workplace, features such as this one save you and your business time and money.

To rename the SUMMARY subdirectory:

1. Type **S** to move the selection cursor to the SUMMARY subdirectory.

    If you are using the mouse, click the **SUMMARY** subdirectory below the root directory in the directory tree window.

2. Press **[F10]** (Actions) and press **[Enter]** to select the File menu. Type **N** to select the Rename option.

    If you are using the mouse, click **File**, then click **Rename**.

    The DOS Shell displays the Rename Directory dialog box. See Figure 5-11.

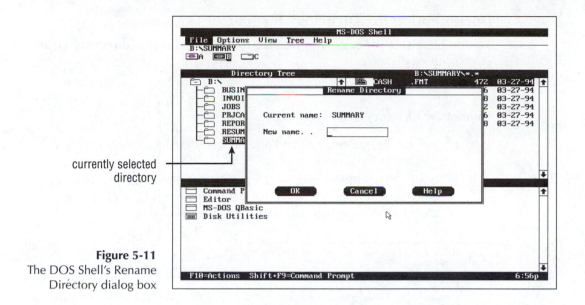

currently selected
directory

Figure 5-11
The DOS Shell's Rename
Directory dialog box

3. Type **CASHFLOW** and press **[Enter]**.

   If you are using the mouse, type **CASHFLOW**, then click **OK**.

   The DOS Shell renames this subdirectory and updates the directory tree. You can now exit the DOS Shell.

4. Press **[F3]** (Exit) to exit the DOS Shell and return to the DOS prompt.

5. Be sure you are at the root directory. If not, type **CD ** and press **[Enter]**.

6. Type **DIR** and press **[Enter]**. DOS displays a directory listing of the contents of the root directory of the Tutorial Disk. The directory structure reads like a table of contents in alphabetical order. See Figure 5-12.

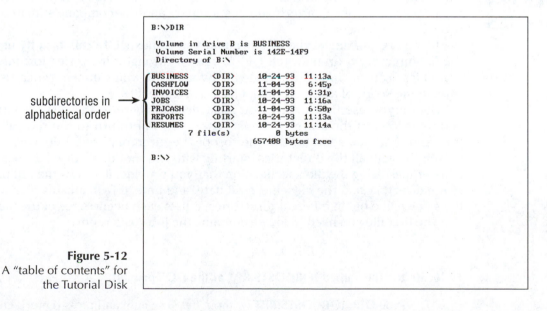

subdirectories in
alphabetical order

Figure 5-12
A "table of contents" for
the Tutorial Disk

Documenting the Directory Structure

To complete this process, you want to document the new directory structure of your client diskette.

To print the directory tree:

1. Be sure the printer is on and on-line, and that the paper is properly aligned in the printer.

2. Type **TREE > PRN** and press **[Enter]**. DOS redirects the output and prints the directory tree. See Figure 5-13. The order of subdirectories in your directory tree might be different.

Figure 5-13
A printed copy of the reorganized directory tree

```
Directory PATH listing for Volume BUSINESS
Volume Serial Number is 142E-14F9
B:.
├───REPORTS
├───BUSINESS
├───RESUMES
├───JOBS
├───INVOICES
├───CASHFLOW
└───PRJCASH
```

3. If necessary, press the **Form Feed button** on the printer. If the printer does not respond, press the **On Line button** to place the printer off-line. Then press **Form Feed** again. After the printer ejects the page, press the **On Line button** to place the printer back on-line.

LOCATING FILES IN DIRECTORIES

Your supervisor asks you to update some important business files on your client diskette before you leave for a two-week vacation. He gives you a list of the changes for your quarterly job costs report and the company's insurance and client check lists.

If you are working at the DOS prompt, you can expedite this task by using the Subdirectory Search switch (/S) to search through directories for one or more files. You can look for a single file by name, or you can use wildcards to expand the scope of a search and look for a group of files.

Before you use this switch, you must decide where in the directory tree you want to start the search. In most cases, you will return to the root directory and start the search from the top of the directory tree. DOS will then search through all the directories, starting with the root directory. If it locates a file or files using the file specification that you provide, it shows the full path of the directory and the filename, size, date, and time. If DOS locates files with the same name but in different directories, it lists each occurrence of the file.

The first file you need to locate contains the job costs report.

To locate the file named JOBCOSTS.RPT at the DOS prompt:

1. Type **DIR JOBCOSTS.RPT** (without the /S switch) and press **[Enter]**. DOS reports that it found no file by that name. Because you did not include the /S switch, DOS limited its search to the root directory. It did not search the directories below the root directory.

2. Press **[↑]** (Up Arrow) to recall the DIR JOBCOSTS.RPT command. Then press **[Spacebar]**. Type **/S** and press **[Enter]**. DOS locates the file in the directory JOBS. See Figure 5-14.

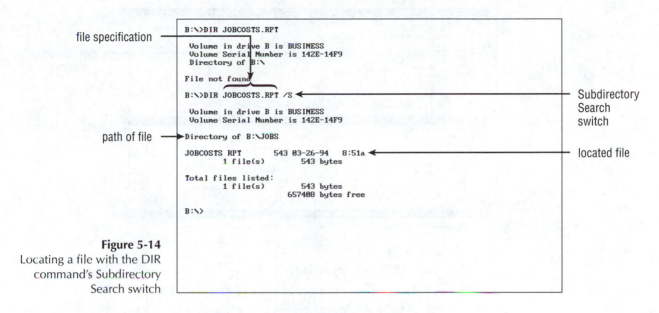

file specification

path of file

Subdirectory
Search
switch

located file

Figure 5-14
Locating a file with the DIR
command's Subdirectory
Search switch

Searching for Files in the DOS Shell

To locate the files with the insurance and client lists, you decide to use the DOS Shell. The Search option on the File menu will search an entire disk for one or more files, based on a file specification that you provide.

Let's start the DOS Shell and locate these files.

To locate a group of files in the DOS Shell:

1. Type **DOSSHELL** and press **[Enter]**. DOS loads the DOS Shell.

2. Press **[F10]** (Actions), press **[Enter]** to select the File menu, and type **H** for the Search option.

If you are using the mouse, click **File**, then click **Search**.

The DOS Shell displays a Search File dialog box. See Figure 5-15. The DOS Shell shows the default file specification for searches. The check in the check box shows that the DOS Shell will search the entire disk.

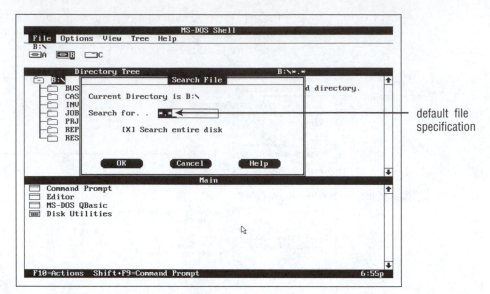

default file
specification

Figure 5-15
The DOS Shell's Search
File dialog box

3. Type ***.LST** and press **[Enter]**.

If you are using a mouse, type ***.LST** and click **OK**.

DOSSHELL displays a screen labeled "Search Results for: *.LST" that alphabetically lists the files that meet this specification. See Figure 5-16. The two
files that you want to locate, INSURE.LST and CLIENT.LST, are included in
this selection. The DOS Shell also shows the full path of each file so that
you know exactly where the files are stored. In the DOS Shell, you do not
need to specify an Order switch or a Subdirectory Search switch.

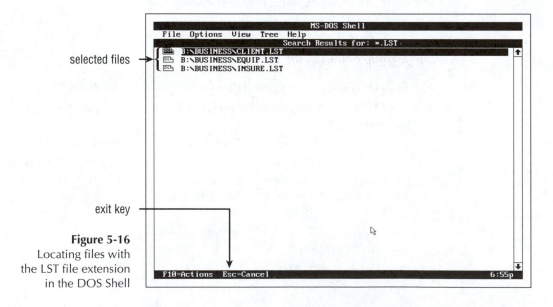

selected files

exit key

Figure 5-16
Locating files with
the LST file extension
in the DOS Shell

4. Press **[Esc]** to exit this screen view.
5. Press **[F3]** to exit the DOS Shell.

Now you have two useful tools for locating files quickly, either from the DOS prompt or from the DOS Shell. You also can use this feature to quickly locate duplicate copies of files stored in various directories or to locate different versions of the same file stored in different directories.

This is a good opportunity to stop for a few minutes and take a break.

DEFRAGMENT- ING HARD DISKS AND DISKETTES

Your company purchased your computer system approximately a year ago. Over the last several months, you have noticed that its performance is not optimal. DOS takes longer to display directories, load software applications, and load document files from the hard disk drive than it used to. Your supervisor suggests that you run the Microsoft defragmenting utility that was introduced with DOS 6.0. A **defragmenting utility** is a program that rearranges files on a hard disk or a diskette so that all sectors of each file are stored in consecutive sectors. If you are using DOS 5.0, you do not have the Microsoft defragmenting utility and cannot complete the steps in this section of the tutorial. However, you can read the introductory material so that you are familiar with the use of a defragmenting utility.

How Does File Fragmentation Occur?

As you create, modify, and save files to a hard disk or diskette, DOS attempts to store the different parts of a file in **contiguous**, or adjacent, sectors on the hard disk or diskette. However, over time, as you add, delete, and modify files, DOS may not be able to store all parts of a file in consecutive sectors. Instead, DOS must store different parts of a file in **noncontiguous**, or nonadjacent, sectors that are scattered across the surface of a diskette. The file is then called a **fragmented** file.

Each time you issue a command to retrieve a file from a hard disk or diskette, DOS must locate each of the file sectors and reassemble those sectors so that the program you are using can work with the entire file or with a portion of a large file. Likewise, when you issue a command to save a new or modified file to a hard disk or diskette, DOS must locate available sectors for that file. If a file is stored in noncontiguous sectors, it takes DOS longer to read the file from the hard disk or diskette and to write the file to the hard disk or diskette. The problem is compounded if all or a majority of the files on a hard disk or diskette are fragmented.

Let's examine a simple example of how file fragmentation occurs. (As you follow this example, remember that it applies to both hard disks and diskettes.) Assume you have used a client diskette heavily over the last year. You have added files to the diskette, and you have deleted and modified files on the diskette. As a result of these changes, DOS has used all of the clusters on the diskette at one time or another. Let's also assume that part of this diskette contains three files (Figure 5-17). You have a file with a client résumé that occupies three clusters, a file with a brief letter that occupies the next available cluster, a file with a client report that occupies the next four clusters, and two previously used clusters that are now available for use again. You decide you no longer need the letter, so you delete the file with the letter from the diskette. By removing this file, you have created an available cluster (Figure 5-18). Now you prepare a bid for a client and save it to the same diskette. DOS uses the cluster that was previously occupied by the letter and the next two available clusters—which happen to be located after the clusters containing the client report (Figure 5-19). Thus, the file with the client bid becomes a fragmented file because it is stored in noncontiguous sectors. From this example, you can see that if you reduce the size of files or delete files from a diskette, you free up clusters that DOS might use later for part of a file. If you increase the size of files or add new files to a diskette, DOS will store the files in noncontiguous clusters if the diskette does not contain enough consecutive clusters to hold the entire file.

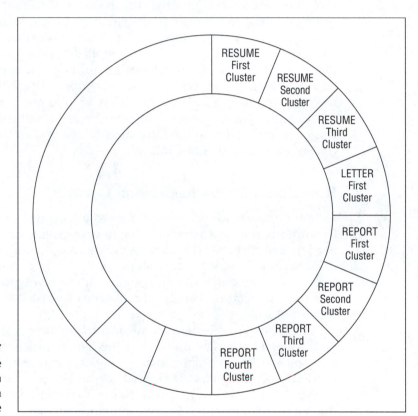

Figure 5-17
An example of the arrangement of files in contiguous clusters on a hard disk or diskette

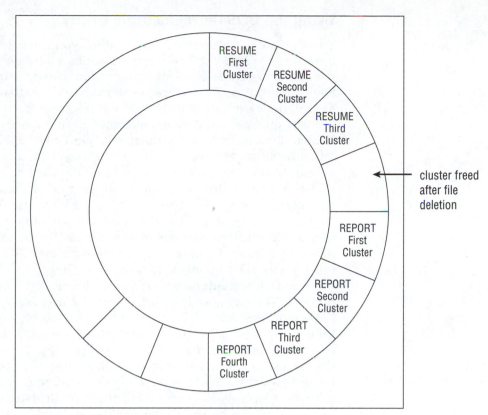

Figure 5-18
DOS frees a cluster
after a file deletion

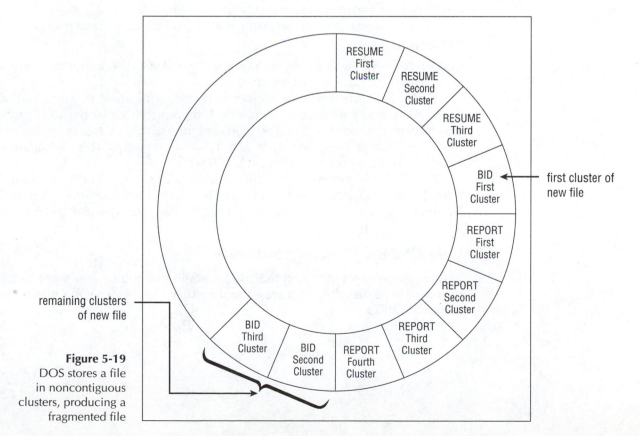

remaining clusters
of new file

Figure 5-19
DOS stores a file
in noncontiguous
clusters, producing a
fragmented file

Using the DOS Defragmenting Utility

To eliminate or reduce file fragmentation, you can use the Defragmenter utility introduced in DOS 6.0. This utility examines a hard disk or diskette and recommends one of three types of optimization: None, Unfragment Files Only, and Full Optimization. If the Defragmenter informs you that no optimization is necessary, the hard disk or diskette is not fragmented, or the amount of fragmentation is minimal and does not affect the performance of the computer system. If the utility recommends "Unfragment Files Only," it will eliminate file fragmentation by storing each part of a file in adjacent sectors. This option may result in unused storage space between files on the hard disk or diskette, a condition that can later contribute to file fragmentation. If the utility recommends Full Optimization, it will not only eliminate file fragmentation but also the unused storage space between files. If you select this option and fully optimize a hard disk or diskette that contains subdirectories, the Defragmenter moves the subdirectory files to the outer edge of the hard disk or diskette so that DOS can quickly access information stored in these files.

The Defragmenter also arranges files in order during the optimization process. You can specify a sort criterion: Unsorted, Name, Extension, Size, or Date and Time. You also can specify a sort order: Ascending or Descending. When you specify **ascending sort order**, files are arranged in alphabetical order by filename or file extension, in order by file size from the smallest to the largest file, or in order by date and time from the oldest file to the most recently used file. When you specify **descending sort order**, files are arranged in reverse alphabetical order by filename or file extension, in reverse order by file size from the largest to the smallest file, and in reverse order by date and time from the most recently used file to the oldest file.

DEFRAG is an external command, with the following general syntax:

DEFRAG [*drive:***]**

The drive is optional. If you do not specify a drive, the utility assumes you want to defragment the current drive.

You cannot use the Defragmenter to optimize files on a network hard disk drive. Also, you cannot load Windows, temporarily exit to the DOS prompt, and then run this utility. If you do, you may lose data. You must run this utility from the DOS prompt. Windows has its own version of this Defragmenter, which you can use while working in Windows.

5.0

If DOS 5.0 is installed on your computer system, you do not have the Defragmenter. However, you can purchase other utility software, such as The Norton Utilities, and use its defragmenter to optimize your hard disk and diskettes.

Checking the Directory Structure

Before you use this utility on the computers in your office, you want to test it on your client diskette. Let's view the directory tree before you optimize your client diskette.

To display the directory tree:

1. Be sure the current drive is the one with your Tutorial Disk. If necessary, switch to drive A or drive B.

2. Type **TREE** and press **[Enter]**. DOS displays the directory tree. The subdirectories are not listed in alphabetical order in the directory tree. See Figure 5-20.

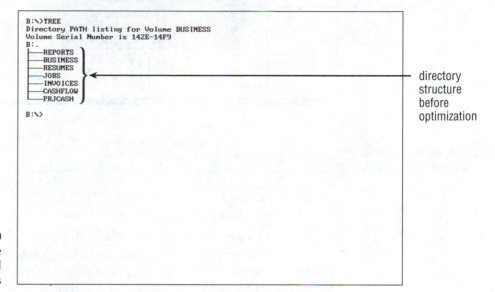

```
B:\>TREE
Directory PATH listing for Volume BUSINESS
Volume Serial Number is 142E-14F9
B:.
    ┌──────REPORTS
    ├──────BUSINESS
    ├──────RESUMES
    ├──────JOBS
    ├──────INVOICES
    ├──────CASHFLOW
    └──────PRJCASH

B:\>
```

directory structure before optimization

Figure 5-20
The directory tree before optimizing the Tutorial Disk's directories and files

Loading the Defragmenter

5.0

If you are using DOS 6.0 or 6.2, you can now load the Defragmenter.

If you are using DOS 5.0, skip the remainder of this section and start with the section entitled "Checking for Computer Viruses," or you can read this section and examine the figures so that you are familiar with the use of a defragmenter.

6.0 6.2

To load the Defragmenter *using DOS 6.0 or 6.2*:

1. Type **DEFRAG** and press **[Enter]**. DOS loads the utility, and the Defragmenter prompts you to select the drive to be optimized. See Figure 5-21. In this instance, the current drive is drive B and it is automatically highlighted. Your screen view will be different if you are using graphics mode.

   If your monitor displays unusual graphics characters for borders, outlines, or symbols, press **[ESC]** to display the Optimize menu. Then type **X** for Exit to return to the DOS prompt. Type **DEFRAG /G0** (the letter "G" followed by the number "0") and press **[ENTER]**. The *No Graphics Characters* switch (/G0) disables the graphics mouse and graphic character set so you should be able to view the Defragmenter screens properly.

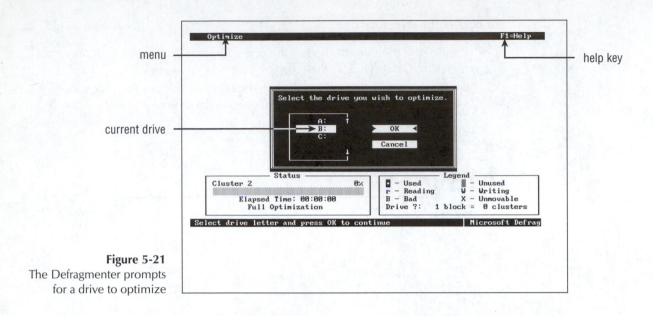

Figure 5-21
The Defragmenter prompts
for a drive to optimize

2. Press **[Enter]** to select the current drive.

If you are using the mouse, click **OK**.

The Defragmenter reads and analyzes information from the diskette and recommends the type of optimization. See Figure 5-22. In this example, the Defragmenter states that the diskette in drive B is not fragmented and recommends no optimization. The Defragmenter might display a different recommendation for your diskette and the organization of clusters with data might differ from that shown in Figure 5-22.

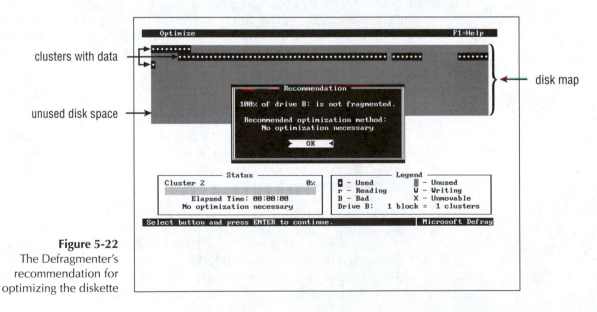

Figure 5-22
The Defragmenter's
recommendation for
optimizing the diskette

Understanding the Map of Disk Space Usage

In the background of the screen display, the Defragmenter maps the usage of storage space on the diskette: A rectangle with a dot represents a cluster with data; a rectangle without a dot is an empty cluster (Figure 5-22). A **cluster** is the minimum amount of storage space that DOS allocates to a file. If you use the Defragmenter on a hard disk drive, each rectangle represents a number of clusters.

The map also shows that there is empty space between files on this diskette. Although the Defragmenter recommends no optimization for this diskette, you can still optimize the diskette so that you are familiar with the use of this utility. Let's examine the Optimize menu and its options.

To display the Optimize menu:

1. If the Defragmenter recommends "No Optimization," press **[Enter]**. If the Defragmenter recommends "Full Optimization" or "Unfragment Files Only," press **[Esc]**.

   If you are using the mouse and if the Defragmenter recommends "No Optimization," click OK. If the Defragmenter recommends "Full Optimization" or "Unfragment Files Only," press **[Esc]**.

   The Defragmenter displays the Optimize menu. See Figure 5-23.

Optimize menu →

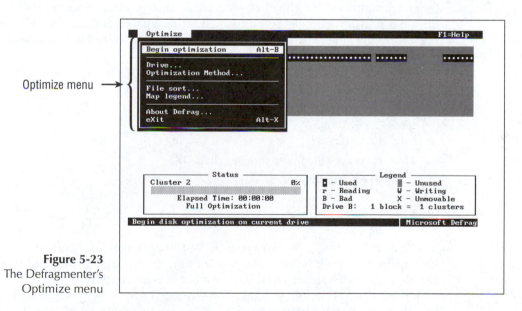

Figure 5-23
The Defragmenter's
Optimize menu

Now view an explanation of disk space usage.

2. Press **[↓]** until you highlight the Map legend option. Then press **[Enter]**.

   If you are using the mouse, click **Map legend**.

   The Defragmenter displays a Disk Map Legend window with information on the notations used to describe disk space usage. See Figure 5-24.

```
■ Optimize ━━━━━━━━━━━━━━━━━━━━━━━━━━━━━━━━━━━━━━━━━━━━━━━━━━━━  F1=Help

  ••••••••
 ▪••••••••••••••••••••••••••••••••••••••••••••••••••  ••••••  ••••••••
 ▪
        ┌─────────────────────────────────────────────────────┐
        │                    Disk Map Legend                  │
        │  ─────────────────────────────────────────────────  │
        │    ▪  - Disk space used by files                    │
        │    •  - Disk space optimized already                │
        │    ▪  - Unused disk space                           │
        │    X  - Disk space used by files that will not be moved │
        │    B  - Bad disk space (untouched by DEFRAG)        │
        │    r  - Disk space that is being read               │
        │    W  - Disk space that is being written            │
        │                                                     │
        │              ►│        OK        │◄                 │
        └─────────────────────────────────────────────────────┘

  ┌────────────────────────────────┐ ┌──────────────────────────────┐
  │ Cluster 2              0%       │ │▪ - Used      ▒ - Unused      │
  │ ▒▒▒▒▒▒▒▒▒▒▒▒▒▒▒▒▒▒▒▒▒▒▒▒        │ │r - Reading   W - Writing     │
  │    Elapsed Time: 00:00:00       │ │B - Bad       X - Unmovable   │
  │       Full Optimization         │ │Drive B:   1 block = 1 clusters│
  └────────────────────────────────┘ └──────────────────────────────┘
 ▪ Show the map symbols definitions                    │ Microsoft Defrag
```

Figure 5-24
The Defragmenter's Disk Map Legend informational dialog box

On the map, a rectangle with a dot represents disk space currently in use by a file. If a rectangle is highlighted, that disk space is already optimized. A small rectangle with shading and no dot indicates unused disk space. If a rectangle contains an "X," the clusters contain an operating system file that cannot be moved. If a rectangle contains a "B," the cluster contains a defective, and therefore unusable, sector. These options are summarized in the Legend box.

Let's return to the Optimize menu.

To exit the Disk Map Legend window:

1. Press [**Enter**].

   If you are using the mouse, click **OK**.

   The Optimize Menu reappears.

Selecting an Optimization Method

You can choose one of two types of optimization from the Optimize menu: Unfragment Files Only or Full Optimization. If you use Unfragment Files Only, the Defragmenter stores each part of a file in consecutive sectors on a diskette or a hard disk. However, it might leave unused space between files. If you use Full Optimization, the Defragmenter will arrange each part of a file in consecutive sectors and will eliminate any unused storage space between files. Also, it can sort the files and directories during the process.

You can select an optimization method that is different from the one recommended by the Defragmenter. If you do not want to optimize a diskette or hard disk, you can exit the Defragmenter without making any changes. If you want to optimize your diskette or hard disk, you select the Optimization Method menu option from the Optimize menu and choose either "Unfragment Files Only" or "Full Optimization."

Let's use full optimization so that you can see the full process for optimizing a disk.

To select full optimization:

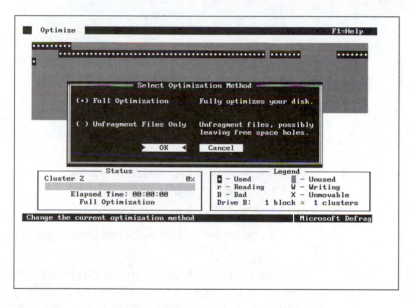

1. Press [↑] (Up Arrow) until you highlight the Optimization Method option. Then press **[Enter]**.

    If you are using the mouse, click **Optimization Method**.

    The Select Optimization Method dialog box appears. See Figure 5-25. In this figure, the Defragmenter automatically highlights the first option, Full Optimization. (The Defragmenter might highlight the other option for your Tutorial Disk.) The Unfragment Files Only option eliminates file fragmentation but not unused space between files. If necessary, press [↑] (Up Arrow) to select Full Optimization, then press **[Spacebar]**.

Figure 5-25
The Defragmenter's Select Optimization Method dialog box

2. Press **[Enter]** to select Full Optimization.

    If you are using the mouse, click **Full Optimization**, then click **OK**.

    The Optimize Menu appears.

3. Press [↓] (Down Arrow) once to highlight the File sort option. Then press **[Enter]**.

    If you are using the mouse, click **File sort**.

    The File Sort dialog box appears. See Figure 5-26. You can specify the Sort Criterion and the Sort Order. The Sort Criterion options box shows that the default is Unsorted. If you use this option, files are stored on the diskette in the order in which DOS placed them on the diskette.

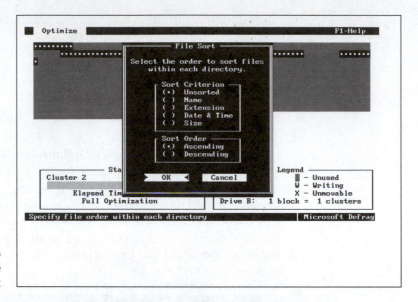

Figure 5-26
The Defragmenter's File
Sort dialog box

4. Press [↓] to highlight the check box for the next option, Name, and press **[Spacebar]** to select this option.

    If you are using a mouse, click **Name**.

    A dot appears in the check box. The Defragmenter will now arrange files and directories in order by filename. The default Sort Order is Ascending.

5. Press **[Enter]**.

    If you are using the mouse, click **OK**.

    The Optimize menu reappears.

6. Press **[Home]** to highlight Begin Optimization and press **[Enter]**.

    If you are using a mouse, click **Begin Optimization**.

The Defragmenter first optimizes directories and places directory files in order at the outer edge of the diskette (Figure 5-27). It then optimizes files within each directory. As the Defragmenter reads data from the diskette and writes it back onto the diskette, you can see it rearrange the small rectangles that represent storage space used by files on the diskette. The Defragmenter will label clusters that it is reading from the diskette with an "r," and clusters that it is writing to the diskette with a "W." After the optimization, which may take only seconds, the Defragmenter displays a dialog box that tells you it has finished condensing (Figure 5-28). (In the Status box, the last processed cluster and the elapsed time on your computer might be different.) If you examine the disk storage map, you can see that the files are now arranged in order from the outer edge of the diskette and that there is no unused storage space between files.

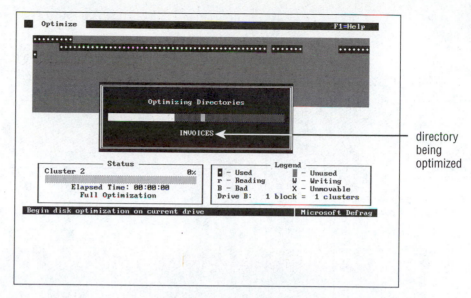

directory
being
optimized

Figure 5-27
The Defragmenter
optimizes directories
on the diskette

rearranged
and sorted
data clusters

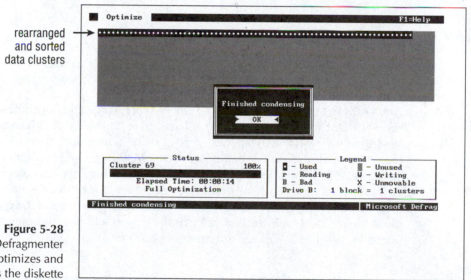

Figure 5-28
The Defragmenter
optimizes and
condenses the diskette

Now that the optimization is complete, let's exit the Defragmenter.

To exit the Defragmenter:

1. Press **[Enter]**.

   If you are using the mouse, click **OK**.

   A dialog box appears with three options: Another Drive, Configure, or Exit DEFRAG. The Configure option allows you to perform another optimization.

2. Press **[→]** until you highlight Exit DEFRAG, then press **[Enter]**.

If you are using a mouse, click **Exit DEFRAG**.

You return to the DOS prompt.

3. Type **TREE** and press **[Enter]**. DOS displays a directory tree. The subdirectories are now listed in alphabetical order. See Figure 5-29.

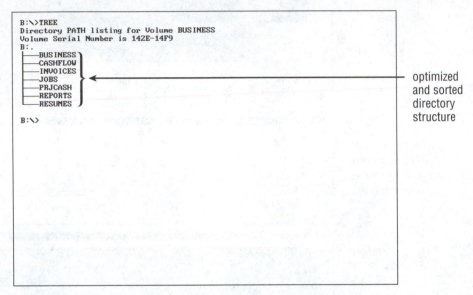

```
B:\>TREE
Directory PATH listing for Volume BUSINESS
Volume Serial Number is 142E-14F9
B:.
    ├──BUSINESS
    ├──CASHFLOW
    ├──INVOICES
    ├──JOBS          ◄───────────────    optimized
    ├──PRJCASH                           and sorted
    ├──REPORTS                           directory
    └──RESUMES                           structure

B:\>
```

Figure 5-29
The optimized directory structure

Optimizing a hard disk drive takes more time than optimizing a diskette. The amount of storage space on a hard drive, the degree of fragmentation, and the type of optimization that you choose will affect the time required to optimize a hard disk. For example, in one instance, the Defragmenter fully optimized a 116M hard disk in 7 minutes 58 seconds. This hard disk was 1% fragmented and had 93MB of data, 362 directories, and 5,423 files. It optimized 47,921 clusters of data. Larger hard disks with greater file fragmentation will take longer. After a hard disk is optimized, you will see an immediate improvement in the speed and performance of your computer system.

CHECKING FOR COMPUTER VIRUSES

A coworker just informed you that she discovered a computer virus on one of her client diskettes. She recommends that you check your hard disk and your client diskettes immediately before you lose valuable client documents.

Computer viruses are programs that adversely affect the performance of a computer system. These programs might even damage the hard drive or some other hardware component. For example, the Michelangelo virus activates on the artist Michelangelo's birthday (March 6) each year, and can destroy all the information on a hard disk and render the hard disk unusable. The media coverage of the Michelangelo virus, first identified in 1992, increased the general public's awareness of the dangers of computer viruses.

Currently, more than 2,000 computer viruses have been identified, and two or three new ones are discovered every week. These viruses affect computer systems in many different ways. Like the Michelangelo virus, most computer viruses are transferred from one computer system to another by users sharing or trading diskettes. Because computer viruses can rapidly spread from one computer system to another via infected diskettes, you must frequently check your diskettes and hard disk for the appearance of computer viruses. Many computer systems and networks are set up so that a special program, called an **antiviral program**, automatically checks for the presence of viruses when the computer systems are turned on and when a diskette is inserted into a disk drive.

Sites of Infection

The majority of computer viruses infect one of three areas on a computer system: the boot sector of a hard disk or diskette, the hard disk partition table, and program files with certain types of file extensions. When you format a diskette, DOS creates a boot sector in the first sector on the first track of the first side of the diskette. The **boot sector**, or **boot record**, is a hidden file that contains information about the version of DOS used to format the diskette and the physical characteristics of the diskette, such as the number of bytes per sector, sectors per cluster, maximum number of files per disk, total number of sectors, and sectors per track. If the diskette is a boot, or system, disk, the boot sector also contains a **bootstrap loader program**, which locates and loads DOS from the diskette. If the diskette is not a boot disk, then the boot sector does not contain this program, but instead contains common error messages, such as the "Non-System disk or disk error" message that appears if you attempt to boot from a diskette that is not a boot disk. The hard drive from which DOS boots a computer system also contains a boot record. The boot sector, or record, is very important because DOS uses the information in this file to work with a hard disk or diskette.

The **hard disk partition table** is another important file. It contains information that identifies where each drive starts and which drive on the hard disk is the boot drive. If a computer virus affects the boot sector of a diskette or hard drive or the hard disk partition table, DOS is unable to work with the diskette or hard disk.

Computer viruses also commonly attach to program files with the file extensions COM or EXE and, in some cases, to **overlay files** (modules of program code) with the file extension OVL and **device drivers** (program code for managing hardware) with the file extension SYS. When the virus attaches itself, the program files increase in size and may not function properly. Some computer viruses even keep re-infecting and increasing the size of program files.

Computer Virus Activity

When certain types of computer viruses gain access to a computer system, they immediately affect the performance of that system. Other computer viruses can remain dormant until they are triggered by an event, such as a specific date or time. Once activated, that computer virus might destroy or overwrite the boot sector or hard disk partition table, destroy file linkages so that DOS cannot recognize what parts of a file belong to a given file, destroy data files, modify program files so that they do not operate properly or at all, disable ports such as LPT1 and COM1, disable diskette drives, and reformat the hard disk.

The two computer viruses most frequently found are the Stoned and Michelangelo viruses. They account for approximately one-half of all current infections on computer systems. The Stoned virus destroys or overwrites the boot sector and destroys file linkages. The Michelangelo virus infects diskettes inserted into a computer and, once it gains access to the hard disk, damages file linkages, damages or overwrites the boot sector, and reformats the hard drive. As is typical of many computer viruses, the Stoned and Michelangelo viruses are small—only 512 bytes in size.

Anti-Viral Software

Software manufacturers have developed a class of software, called **anti-viral software**, to protect computer systems from viruses. This software usually includes a program for scanning a diskette or hard drive for the presence of computer viruses, a program for cleaning or eliminating computer viruses from a diskette or hard drive, and a program that monitors for the presence of computer viruses on the computer system and on diskettes inserted into disk drives.

Anti-viral software locates computer viruses in three ways. First, it checks for computer virus signatures. A **signature** is a sequence of program code unique to a specific virus or a family of viruses that affect a computer system in similar ways. Second, it checks for suspicious activity, such as attempts to modify the operating system files. And, finally, this software checks locations where computer viruses hide, such as memory, the boot sector, the hard disk partition table, and program files.

Microsoft Corporation introduced the Microsoft Anti-Virus utility in DOS 6.0 to check for the presence of computer viruses. If Microsoft Anti-Virus locates a virus that it recognizes, it can eliminate the virus from a diskette or hard disk. If it does not recognize a virus, either the program is not able to detect it or it is a newly introduced virus. As with other types of software, you must periodically purchase updates of anti-viral software so that it can check for new computer viruses.

5.0

DOS 5.0 does not have the Microsoft Anti-Virus utility. However, you can purchase an anti-viral software product similar to Microsoft Anti-Virus and use it to check your computer for viruses.

Starting Microsoft Anti-Virus

To ensure the integrity of your client diskette, you want to check it for the presence of computer viruses and remove any viruses that are found. To start the Microsoft Anti-Virus from the DOS prompt, you use the following external command:

MSAV [*drive:*]

"MSAV" is an abbreviation for Microsoft Anti-Virus. If you do not specify a drive, MSAV assumes you want to check for computer viruses on the current drive.

5.0

If you are using DOS 5.0, you cannot complete the steps in this section because DOS 5.0 does not include the Microsoft Anti-Virus utility. Skip to the Summary section, or you can read the steps and examine the figures in this section to familiarize yourself with the process of checking for the presence of computer viruses with an anti-viral utility like Microsoft Anti-Virus.

6.0 6.2

To start the Microsoft Anti-Virus *using DOS 6.0 or 6.2*:

1. Be sure the current drive contains your Tutorial Disk.

2. At the DOS prompt, type **MSAV** and press **[Enter]**. The Microsoft Anti-Virus Main Menu appears. See Figure 5-30. The Main Menu contains five options. The status bar shows the options that are available through the function keys. For example, [F1] accesses Help. Your screen view will look different if you are using graphics mode.

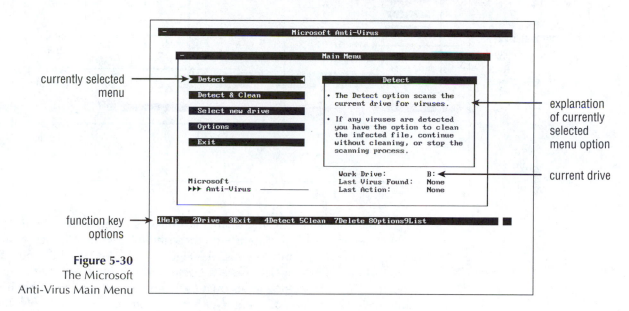

Figure 5-30
The Microsoft
Anti-Virus Main Menu

If your monitor displays strange or unusual graphics characters for borders, outlines, or symbols, type **X** for Exit and then press **[Enter]** for OK to return to the DOS prompt. Then type **MSAV /BF** and press **[Enter]**. Microsoft recommends that you use the *BIOS Font switch* (/BF) to disable the graphics mouse and graphics character set if the graphics characters do not display properly. If this switch does not work, type **X** (for Exit), press **[Enter]** for OK to return to the DOS prompt again, then type **MSAV /NF** and press **[Enter]**. The *No Fonts switch* (/NF) does not use graphics characters.

Displaying Information on Computer Viruses

The Microsoft Anti-Virus utility contains information on over 1,000 computer viruses. You can display information on a specific virus with [F9] (List). Let's examine information on the two most common computer viruses.

To display information on the Michelangelo and Stoned viruses:

1. Press **[F9]** (List). Microsoft Anti-Virus displays the Virus List. See Figure 5-31. Your Virus List might be different because Microsoft provides an option for periodic upgrades to this utility. The computer viruses are

listed in alphabetical order. Aliases are listed beneath the name of the more common virus in the family. For example, Red State is an alias of AirCop.

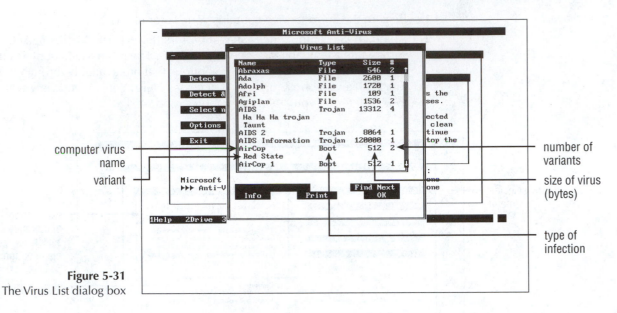

computer virus name
variant
number of variants
size of virus (bytes)
type of infection

Figure 5-31
The Virus List dialog box

2. Type **Mic** (for Michelangelo). Microsoft Anti-Virus searches for the first computer virus name that starts with these three letters, and it locates the listing for the Michelangelo virus. See Figure 5-32. The Type column tells you that the Michelangelo virus is a *boot sector virus*, a type of virus that replaces the boot sector with its own program code to guarantee that it is automatically loaded into memory when the computer system boots. The last column shows that there are five variants of this computer virus.

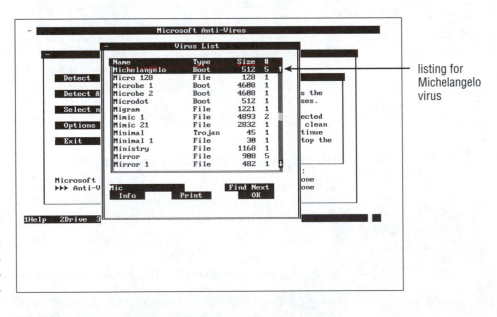

listing for Michelangelo virus

Figure 5-32
The listing for the Michelangelo computer virus

3. Press **[Enter]**. Microsoft Anti-Virus displays a Virus Characteristics window with information on the Michelangelo virus. See Figure 5-33. From this information, you can tell that it infects the boot sector of diskettes and the hard disk partition table. It stays, or remains *resident*, in memory after a computer system boots and continues to infect the computer system and any diskettes inserted into disk drives. Microsoft Anti-Virus also lists its side effects, i.e., how it affects the computer system.

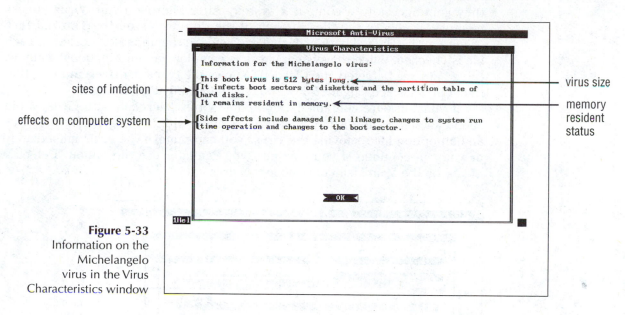

Figure 5-33
Information on the
Michelangelo
virus in the Virus
Characteristics window

4. Press **[Enter]**.

   If you are using the mouse, click **OK**.

   Microsoft Anti-Virus displays the Virus List screen.

5. Press **[Backspace]** three times to delete the characters "Mic" (for Michelangelo).

6. Type **Sto** (for Stoned). Microsoft Anti-Virus locates the listing for the Stoned virus, another boot sector virus.

7. Press **[Enter]**. Microsoft Anti-Virus displays the Virus Characteristics window for this virus. Like the Michelangelo virus, it infects the boot sector of diskettes as well as the hard disk partition table, and it remains resident in memory.

8. Press **[Enter]**.

   If you are using the mouse, click **OK**.

   Microsoft Anti-Virus displays the Virus List.

9. Press **[Esc]** to exit the Virus List.

Scanning a Disk

You are now ready to scan your client diskette for computer viruses. The scanning process only checks for the presence of computer viruses; it does not remove them from the diskette or hard disk.

To scan the Tutorial Disk:

1. Be sure the first option, Detect, is highlighted or selected. Press **[Enter]**. Microsoft Anti-Virus scans the disk.

Microsoft Anti-Virus first checks the computer's memory (RAM) for viruses (Figure 5-34). Computer viruses load themselves into memory once they gain access to a computer system. After Microsoft Anti-Virus checks memory, it checks the files in each of the directories on the Tutorial Disk (Figure 5-35). The full path of each file is listed in the upper-left corner as each file is checked. When the system check is complete, an informational window, titled "Viruses Detected and Cleaned," shows the types of drives and files that the utility checked (Figure 5-36). Your scan time might be different.

If your diskette contained a computer virus, Microsoft Anti-Virus would sound an alarm and display a message window with information on the virus and an option for removing the virus. You can remove the virus immediately or you can continue. If you continue, you can later use the option "Detect & Clean" on the Main Menu to remove the virus.

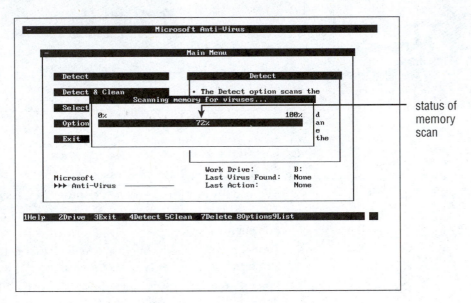

Figure 5-34
The memory scan for computer viruses

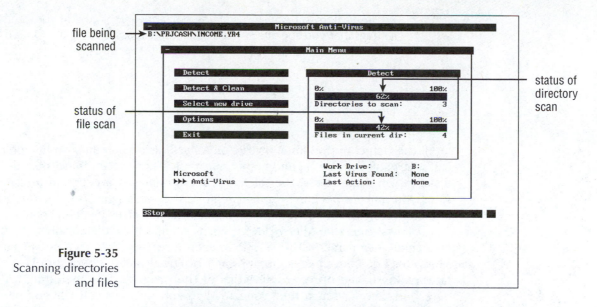

file being scanned

status of file scan

status of directory scan

Figure 5-35
Scanning directories and files

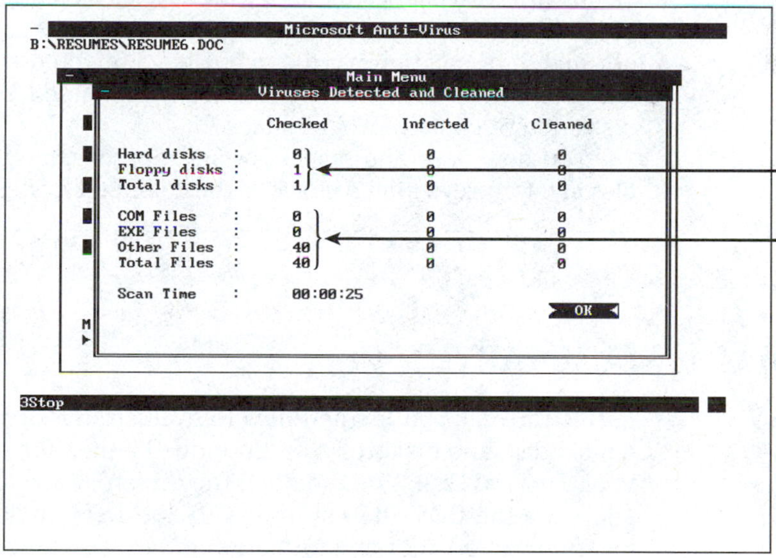

drives checked

files checked

Figure 5-36
The Viruses Detected and Cleaned informational window

Let's return to the Main Menu and exit Microsoft Anti-Virus.

To return to the Main Menu:

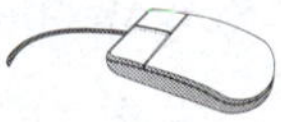

1. Press [**Enter**].

   If you are using the mouse, click **OK**.

   The Main Menu appears.

2. Press [↓] until you highlight Exit, and press [**Enter**].

   If you are using a mouse, click **Exit**.

A Close Microsoft Anti-Virus dialog box appears. Note that you can save settings that you specify in Microsoft Anti-Virus. By using the Options menu option, you can customize Microsoft Anti-Virus.

3. Press [**Enter**].

If you are using the mouse, click **OK**.

DOS displays the DOS prompt.

If the Detect option finds a virus on a hard disk, you can stop immediately, exit Microsoft Anti-Virus, and copy important files from the hard disk drive to diskettes. In some cases, the "clean" process damages a program or data file. After you make a backup, you can remove the virus from the hard disk with Microsoft Anti-Virus. You should also check the diskettes used for the backup.

The first time that Microsoft Anti-Virus scans a hard disk or diskette, it creates small files named CHKLIST.MS in each directory that contains programs. These files contain checksums for each program file. A **checksum** is a calculated value based on characteristics of the program file, including its size, date, and time. The next time you use Microsoft Anti-Virus, it will compare the values in these checksum files with newly calculated values for the same program files to determine if the program files have changed. If the checksums do not match, a computer virus might have infected the program. Your Tutorial and Exercises Disks will not contain a file named CHKLIST.MS because these disks do not contain program files.

You now have another important tool for maintaining the integrity of your files and for preventing damage to the computer systems and disks in your office.

◆

SUMMARY

In this tutorial, you learned how to evaluate the organization of directories on a hard disk and diskette. You developed a plan for reorganizing directories on your Tutorial Disk. You modified the directory structure from the DOS prompt and with the DOS Shell so that you and DOS could more easily and quickly locate files and access information on a diskette. You used commands at the DOS prompt and the DOS Shell to move subdirectories and their files, as well as to rename and remove subdirectories. You used the Subdirectory Search switch with the DIR command at the DOS prompt and the Search option on the File menu in the DOS Shell to locate a single file or a group of files within the directory structure of your diskette.

You used the Defragmenter utility in DOS 6.0 and 6.2 to optimize the directory structure, the organization of files, and storage space usage on your diskette. You used the Microsoft Anti-Virus utility in DOS 6.0 and 6.2 to scan your Tutorial Disk for the presence of computer viruses. You also learned how to locate information about specific viruses.

Command Reference

DOS Commands

DEFRAG [*drive:*]	An external command for a DOS utility that optimizes directories and eliminates or reduces file fragmentation
DIR [*file specification*] /S	An internal command that searches through subdirectories for filenames that match the file specification and then displays the full path of matching filenames
MSAV [*drive:*]	An external command for a DOS utility that checks for the presence of computer viruses and, if necessary, cleans or removes computer viruses from a diskette or hard drive
RD [*drive:*]*path*	An internal command that removes an empty subdirectory from the directory structure of a diskette or hard drive

DOS Shell Commands

File/Search	Locates all filenames in all directories that match a file specification and then displays the full path of the filenames

QUESTIONS

1. What command would you use to view the directory structure of a hard disk drive one screen at a time from the DOS prompt?

2. What command would you use to print the directory structure of a hard disk drive from the DOS prompt?

3. List four factors that you can use to evaluate the organization of subdirectories on a hard disk?

4. What command removes a subdirectory at the DOS prompt? List three conditions under which this command will not work?

5. Describe the three basic steps required to move a subdirectory from one level to another level in the directory tree at the DOS prompt.

6. Describe the three basic steps required to move a subdirectory from one level to another in the directory tree in the DOS Shell.

7. How do you rename a subdirectory in the DOS Shell?

8. What switch can you use with the DIR command to locate files with similar file specifications stored in different directories on a hard disk drive? Give an example.

9. How do you locate a file, or set of files, in the DOS Shell?

10. What is file fragmentation, and why is it a problem?

11. List two ways that you can optimize a hard disk or diskette with the Defragmenter utility.

12. What sort criteria can the Defragmenter use to arrange files on a diskette or hard disk?

13. What sort orders can the Defragmenter use to arrange files on a diskette or hard disk?

14. When you view the usage of disk space with the Defragmenter, how does this utility identify disk space occupied by files versus unused disk space?

15. What is a computer virus?

16. Name one computer virus commonly found on computer systems and describe how it affects the computer system?

17. List the three sites on a computer system commonly infected by viruses.

18. What is a boot sector, or boot record? What information does it contain? Why is it important to DOS?

19. What is a hard disk partition table? What information does it contain?

20. List three types of program operations commonly performed by anti-viral software?

21. What is a computer virus signature?

22. How does a boot sector virus affect a computer system?

23. What is a checksum? How does Microsoft Anti-Virus use checksums to check for computer viruses?

24. What is the most common vehicle for the transmission of computer viruses?

25. You have a directory named OLDFORMS on drive C that is below the root directory, and you want to remove this directory. Assume this directory has files that you no longer need. What command(s) would you use to remove this directory?

26. You want to locate a file named 93TAXES.REC. What command would you enter from the root directory to check all subdirectories so that you could find this file?

27. You keep all your work files in a directory named C:\WORK. The number of files in this directory now exceeds 50. You want to create a new directory named C:\MEMOS so that you can copy all the files with the file extension MEM (for "Memo") from the directory C:\WORK to C:\MEMOS. Then you want to delete those files from C:\WORK. List the steps and commands you would use to accomplish these operations. Assume you are working at the DOS prompt.

28. What command would you enter at the DOS prompt to locate a file named 93BUDGET.DOC on drive C? Assume that you are working on drive D in a subdirectory named \BUDGET and that the file could be stored in any of the directories on drive C.

29. What command would you enter at the DOS prompt to locate all the budget document files on drive C for the last three years? Assume that the files begin with two digits for the year—91, 92, and 93—and that you are working in a subdirectory named \CASHFLOW on drive C. Also, the files might contain any combination of characters after the year and any file extension.

30. What command would you enter at the DOS prompt to locate all the tax records on drive C for the last three years? Assume that all the files have the file extension REC and that you are working in the directory named C:\EARNINGS.

TUTORIAL ASSIGNMENTS

1. **Evaluating the Directory Structure of a Hard Disk**: After examining the directory structure of a hard disk, you make the following observations:

   ◆ DOS utilities, such as the programs for formatting and making copies of diskettes, are stored in the root directory along with programs for other software utilities.

   ◆ The WordPerfect directory, WP51, contains several hundred program files included with this software application and several hundred document files produced over a several-year period.

   ◆ The same version of Lotus 1-2-3 is installed twice in two separate directories at different levels in the directory tree.

   ◆ The hard disk contains seven levels of subdirectories.

   Describe how you would reorganize and improve the directory structure of the hard disk and resolve the problems described above.

2. **Reorganizing the Directory Tree**: *Use your Exercise Disk for this Tutorial Assignment.* Complete the following steps from the DOS prompt.
   a. Print a copy of the directory tree for the Exercise Disk.
   b. Print a copy of the directory of all the files in all the directories on the Exercise Disk.
   Evaluate the organization of directories and files on the Exercise Disk. Then prepare a diagram of a new directory structure for the diskette.
   c. Create the new directory structure based on your diagram. After you create each new directory, move files from the root directory or from any existing directories to their new directories. Use your best judgment in determining where to place files. Be sure no files remain in the root directory.
   d. Print a copy of the new directory structure of the Exercise Disk.

3. **Locating Files**: *Use your Tutorial Disk to perform the following operations from both the DOS prompt and the DOS Shell.* List the command that you use to accomplish each step.
   Using the DOS Prompt:
   a. Display an alphabetical list, one screen at a time, of all files in all directories that have filenames with the file extension "RPT."
   b. Display an alphabetical list, one screen at a time, of all files in all directories that have "WK" as the first two characters of the file extension.

Using the DOS Shell:

c. Display an alphabetical list of all files in all directories that have a "DOC" file extension.

d. Display an alphabetical list of all files in all directories that have "CASH" as the last four characters of an eight-character filename.

6.0 6.2

4. **Optimizing a Diskette**: *Use your Exercise Disk to complete this Tutorial Assignment.* As you perform the following steps, answer the questions.

a. Load the Defragmenter.
   (1) What drive does the Defragmenter select?
   (2) Is this drive your current drive?

b. Select the current drive.
   (1) What percentage of the disk is not fragmented?
   (2) What is the recommended optimization method?
   (3) How many clusters are in a block?

c. Select Full Optimization.

d. Specify a Sort Criterion that arranges files in order of file size.

e. Specify a Sort Order that arranges files from the largest size to the smallest size in each directory.

f. Optimize the diskette. After optimization, describe the arrangement of used and unused storage space on the diskette.

g. Exit the Defragmenter.

6.0 6.2

5. **Scanning for Computer Viruses**: *Use your Exercise Disk to complete this Tutorial Assignment.* As you perform the following steps, answer the questions.

a. Load Microsoft Anti-Virus.
   (1) What drive does the Microsoft Anti-Virus select?
   (2) Is this drive your current drive?

b. Scan the Exercises Disk for computer viruses.
   (1) How many viruses did Microsoft Anti-Virus find?
   (2) How many files did it check on the diskette?

c. If necessary, remove any computer viruses from the diskette.

d. Display information on the Dark Avenger computer virus, another common and destructive virus.
   (1) What type of virus is it?
   (2) How many variants are there?
   (3) What is the size of the Dark Avenger virus?
   (4) What site or sites does the Dark Avenger infect?
   (5) Does it remain resident in memory?
   (6) What side effects does the Dark Avenger produce?

e. Exit Microsoft Anti-Virus.

Backing Up a Hard Disk

OBJECTIVES

In this tutorial you will learn to:

- Distinguish between types of backups
- Back up a hard disk
- Perform a system compatibility test for backups
- Create setup files for backups
- Restore backed-up files
- Perform extended copies
- Develop a backup strategy

The end of the month is rapidly approaching and it is time for the monthly backup of computer files. When you perform this backup, you start a new **backup cycle** and back up all your client and business files for the last month onto diskettes. After you finish the backup, you will have a complete set of all the important files that you use on a daily basis in your business. If you should inadvertently delete a file during your daily work, you can restore a copy of that file from your **backup set**. If your hard disk fails, you can repair or replace the hard disk and restore all your client and business files from your backup diskettes.

If you do not back up a hard disk and if that disk fails, you will have to reconstruct all your client and business files. Microsoft Corporation estimates that it would take an average of 2,000 hours to replace lost files on a typical hard disk. If you are operating a business, you cannot afford to lose important files, nor can you afford the time and cost required to reconstruct them. A regular backup of your hard disk is like an insurance policy because it protects your investment in your business.

◆

BACKING UP FILES, DISKETTES, AND HARD DISKS

DOS provides several commands for backing up files and disks. You can use the COPY command to make a duplicate copy of a single file or, with the use of wildcards, duplicate copies of a group of files. For example, after you create an important business file and save it to your hard disk, you can take a few seconds and immediately copy that file to a diskette so that you have a **backup**, or duplicate copy, of the file. If you should inadvertently delete, overwrite, or damage that business file, you can immediately copy the duplicate copy of the file from the diskette to the hard disk and continue your work.

However, the COPY command has limitations. For example, although you can copy one or more files in a directory, you cannot copy more than one directory at a time. Therefore, you cannot use this command to back up an entire hard disk. Also, if you are copying files to a diskette and the space on that diskette fills up before you are able to copy all the files you want, the COPY command stops and tells you that the diskette is full. You can continue the copy operation on another diskette, but you must specify a new COPY command with a new file specification so that you do not copy the same set of files again. This command does not automatically start where it left off, and it cannot split a file between diskettes. The COPY command, therefore, is most useful for quick backups of a single file or a set of files.

You also can use the DISKCOPY command to make a backup copy of a diskette. For example, if you store important client files on a diskette and work from that diskette, you can take a few minutes and make a backup copy of the client diskette. If your original working diskette fails, you can make a duplicate copy of the backup diskette and use the duplicate copy as your new working diskette. If you inadvertently delete an important client file, you can copy that file from your backup diskette.

Like the COPY command, the DISKCOPY command has its limitations. You cannot use the DISKCOPY command to back up the contents of a hard disk. Use of DISKCOPY is limited to copying diskettes. However, if you store most of your work on a diskette, you will find the DISKCOPY command useful.

In all versions of DOS except DOS 6.2, you can use the BACKUP utility to back up all or part of a hard disk. The BACKUP utility can copy one directory after another to a series of diskettes. You can copy part of the directory tree or the entire directory tree and each directory's files. During the backup operation, the BACKUP utility uses all of the storage space available on a diskette and can split a file between two diskettes. When a diskette is full, the BACKUP utility stops and prompts you to insert another diskette.

To recover a file or group of files from backup copies produced with the BACKUP utility, you must use the RESTORE command because the backed-up files are stored in a special format on the backup diskettes. You should use the RESTORE command that comes with the version of DOS that you used to create the backup copies. Otherwise, you might not be able to restore files from your backup diskettes. A BACKUP utility in another version of DOS might store the backed-up files in a different format than does the version of DOS you used.

DOS 6.0 and DOS 6.2 contain a new backup utility called MSBACKUP. You can use MSBACKUP like the BACKUP utility to back up all or part of a hard disk onto diskettes. You can also use this utility to restore files to a hard disk from backup diskettes. MSBACKUP is intended as a replacement for the BACKUP and RESTORE utilities in DOS 6.0 and later versions of DOS. Not only does it improve the speed, efficiency, and reliability of backups, but it offers a variety of options for performing backups. If you are using DOS 5.0 or an earlier version of DOS, you must use the separate BACKUP and RESTORE utilities. If you are using DOS 6.2, you must use the MSBACKUP utility to back up your hard disk, because the DOS 6.2 installation program removes the BACKUP utility from your DOS subdirectory.

You want to back up the directory on your hard disk that contains your client and business records. This directory has the same name as your business, AceForms. Before you can back up this directory and its subdirectories, however, you must perform some preliminary operations.

GETTING STARTED

Your instructor or technical support person will have created a directory named AceForms on your hard disk drive for this tutorial. *Before you make changes to that hard drive, be sure you have permission from your instructor or the technical support person in your computer laboratory. If you are using a network without a hard disk drive C, ask your instructor for directions on how to complete this tutorial.*

You will begin by installing DOSKEY and specifying switches for the DIR command in the DOS environment. Then you will format your Tutorial Disk and Exercise Disk so that you can use them as backup diskettes for this tutorial. *Because the formatting will eliminate all files and directories on the Tutorial Disk and Exercise Disk, be sure you have completed all previous tutorials.*

To set up your system:

1. After you power on your computer system, access the DOS prompt for your hard drive.

5.0   **6.0**

2. Type **DOSKEY** and press **[Enter]**. If you are using DOS 5.0 or 6.0, DOS will display the message "DOSKey installed" if DOSKEY is not already installed on your computer. If you do not see this message with DOS 5.0 or 6.0, DOSKEY is already loaded. DOS 6.2 will not display a message.

6.2

3. Type **SET DIRCMD=/P /O** and press **[Enter]**. DOS will now display your client files and subdirectories in alphabetical order and pause after each screen.

4. Type **SET** and press **[Enter]** to verify that you correctly entered the switches for the DIRCMD environment variable. If not, repeat Step 3.

Formatting Diskettes for a Backup

Next you need to format the Tutorial Disk and Exercise Disk before you can perform the backup operation. As noted earlier, be sure you do not need any of the information on these diskettes. When you reformat a diskette, you can use the **Unconditional Switch** (/U) with the FORMAT command to erase all information from the diskette.

To format a diskette:

1. Insert your Tutorial Disk into drive A or drive B and, if necessary, close the drive door.

2. Format the diskette to the proper storage capacity using one of the following options:

 ◆ If you are formatting a double-density diskette in a double-density drive, a high-density diskette in a high-density drive, or an extra-high-density diskette in an extra-high-density drive, type **FORMAT A: /U** (or **FORMAT B: /U**) and press **[Enter]**. You do not need to use the Format Capacity switch because DOS will automatically format the diskette to the maximum capacity of the drive.

 ◆ If you are formatting a double-density diskette in a high-density or extra-high-density drive, type **FORMAT A: /F:720 /U** (or **FORMAT B: /F:720 /U**) and press **[Enter]**.

 ◆ If you are formatting a high-density diskette in an extra-high-density drive, type **FORMAT A: /F:1.44 /U** (or **FORMAT B: /F:1.44 /U**) and press **[Enter]**.

DOS then prompts you to insert a diskette into drive A or drive B.

3. Press **[Enter]**. After DOS completes the formatting, it prompts for a volume label.

4. Press **[Enter]** to indicate that you do not want a volume label assigned to this diskette. DOS asks you whether you want to format another diskette.

5. Type **Y** and press **[Enter]**. DOS prompts you to insert a diskette into the diskette drive.

6. Remove your Tutorial Disk from the drive, and insert your Exercise Disk or an unformatted diskette *with the same storage capacity* as the one you just formatted. Press **[Enter]**. DOS formats this diskette to the same storage capacity and prompts for a volume label.

7. Press **[Enter]** to indicate that you do not want a volume label assigned to this diskette. DOS asks you whether you want to format another diskette.

8. Type **N** and press **[Enter]**. DOS displays the DOS prompt.

USING THE BACKUP UTILITY

You can use the BACKUP command in DOS 5.0 and 6.0 to back up all or part of a hard disk onto diskettes. Although the setup program for DOS 6.2 removes this utility from the DOS subdirectory when you install DOS 6.2, DOS 6.2 users should read this discussion to become familiar with the BACKUP utility's use and syntax. You might need to use this utility on a computer that has DOS 5.0 or 6.0 installed. The general syntax for this external command is:

BACKUP *source destination-drive*:

The source might be an entire hard drive, part of the directory structure of a hard drive, a group of files in a subdirectory, or even a single file. The destination drive is the name of the diskette drive to which BACKUP will copy files. The source and destination drives are required parameters.

If you back up an entire hard drive or part of the directory structure, you should use the **Subdirectory switch** (/S) so that DOS backs up all subdirectories and files below the directory or drive that you specify. For example, to back up an entire hard disk (drive C) to drive A, you use the following command:

BACKUP C:*.* A: /S

This command instructs DOS to start at the root directory of drive C and back up all files in the root directory and in all subdirectories below the root directory to drive A.

If you want to start at a specific directory, you specify the path and directory name. For example, to back up a directory named BIDS on drive C and all subdirectories and files below this directory to drive A, you would enter the following command:

BACKUP C:\BIDS A: /S

Another useful switch is the **Log File switch** (/L). When you use this switch, the BACKUP command creates a file that contains a list of the full path and filename of all the backed-up files. For example, to back up a BIDS directory on drive C and create a log file named 070994.LOG (for July 9, 1994) in a directory named LOGS on drive C, you would enter the following command:

BACKUP C:\BIDS A: /S /L:C:\LOGS\070994.LOG

After the /L in the Log File switch, you type a colon, followed by the drive name and path (C:), directory name (\LOGS), and filename of the log file (070994.LOG). During the backup operation, you will see a message that BACKUP is logging to this file.

Viewing the Contents of the AceForms Directory

Before you back up your data directory, you want to view its contents.

To view the contents of the AceForms directory:

1. Be sure you are at the root directory of the hard drive you are using. The remainder of these steps will assume drive C for the source drive and drive A for the destination drive. If you are using different drive names for the source and destination drives, substitute your drive names whenever you enter commands that require them.

2. Type **DIR \ACEFORMS /S** and press **[Enter]**. DOS displays the contents of the AceForms directory, directory by directory. It lists the directory names and filenames in alphabetical order and pauses after each screen. See Figure 6-1. *If DOS reports "File not found," ask your instructor or technical support person to create this directory and its files before you continue.*

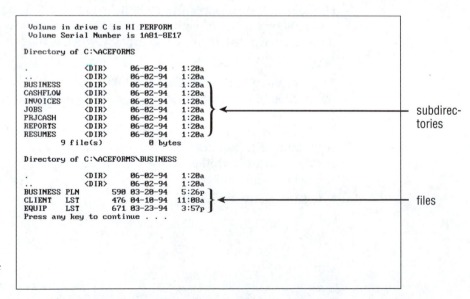

Figure 6-1
A partial directory listing of the AceForms subdirectory

3. Keep pressing **[Spacebar]** or any other key until you view the entire directory listing and return to the DOS prompt.

Next, because you are responsible for preparing, updating, and maintaining these documents for your company, you want to verify the contents of one of the AceForms subdirectories, the one named REPORTS.

To view the contents of a subdirectory below AceForms:

1. Type **DIR \ACEFORMS\REPORTS** and press **[Enter]**. DOS displays the contents of this subdirectory. See Figure 6-2. *If DOS reports "File not found" or if you do not see the same filenames as shown in Figure 6-2, ask your instructor or technical support person to create this directory and its files before you continue.*

6.2

If you are using DOS 6.2, you cannot complete the sections of this tutorial that illustrate the use of the BACKUP and RESTORE utilities. Instead, skip these sections and continue with the section entitled "Using MSBACKUP."

5.0 6.0

If you are using DOS 5.0 or 6.0, continue with the next section, entitled "Backing Up the AceForms Directory."

```
C:\>DIR \ACEFORMS\REPORTS  ◄──────────────      directory
                                                 path and
  Volume in drive C is HI PERFORM                name
  Volume Serial Number is 1A81-8E17
  Directory of C:\ACEFORMS\REPORTS

  .            <DIR>      06-02-94    1:20a
  ..           <DIR>      06-02-94    1:20a
  APR_CASH          366 03-18-94   10:20a
  FEB_CASH          369 03-18-94   10:14a
  JAN_CASH          368 03-18-94   10:00a
  JUN_CASH          365 03-18-94   10:45a
  MAR_CASH          366 03-18-94   10:17a
  MAY_CASH          364 03-18-94   10:43a
          8 file(s)        2198 bytes
                       27471872 bytes free

  C:\>
```

Figure 6-2
A directory listing of the \ACEFORMS\REPORTS subdirectory

Backing Up the AceForms Directory

Now you are ready to back up the AceForms directory and all its subdirectories and files.

To back up the AceForms directory:

1. Be sure you are at the root directory of drive C.

2. Type **BACKUP C:\ACEFORMS A: /S /L:C:\DOS\LOGFILE1**
   (or **BACKUP C:\ACEFORMS B: /S /L:C:\DOS\LOGFILE1**) and press
   [Enter]. *If your DOS subdirectory has another name, use that name with
   the Log File switch.* BACKUP prompts you to insert backup diskette 01
   into the diskette drive you specified, warns you that all files in the root
   directory will be erased, and prompts you to press any key when you are
   ready to continue. See Figure 6-3.

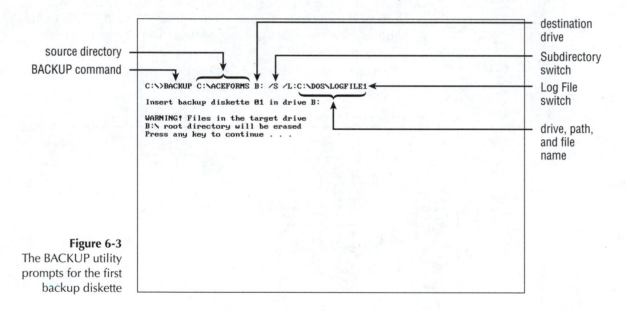

source directory
BACKUP command

destination
drive

Subdirectory
switch

Log File
switch

drive, path,
and file
name

```
C:\>BACKUP C:\ACEFORMS B: /S /L:C:\DOS\LOGFILE1

Insert backup diskette 01 in drive B:

WARNING! Files in the target drive
B:\ root directory will be erased
Press any key to continue . . .
```

Figure 6-3
The BACKUP utility
prompts for the first
backup diskette

3. Insert your Tutorial Disk in the appropriate disk drive, then press **[Enter]**.
   BACKUP informs you that it is backing up to drive A and logging to a file
   named C:\DOS\LOGFILE.001. It displays the full path and filename of
   each file as it backs up each file to the diskette drive. See Figure 6-4. After
   the backup is complete, DOS displays the DOS prompt. If BACKUP fills
   the first diskette, it will prompt you for another diskette.

prompt for first
diskette

logging backup message

warning

path and
filenames of
backed-up
files

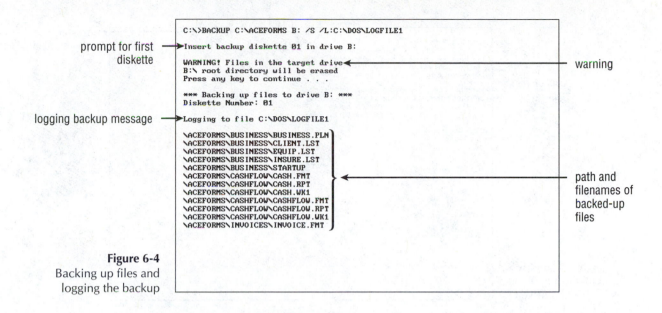

Figure 6-4
Backing up files and
logging the backup

Checking the Backup Process

Now you want to view a directory of the backup diskette so that you can see which files the BACKUP utility stored on your Tutorial Disk. You also want to examine the log file.

You should not automatically assume a backup worked. You should always check the backup diskette to verify the backup. If there are no files on the backup diskette or if the files are zero bytes in size, the backup did not work. You should then repeat the backup.

To view the contents of the Tutorial Disk:

1. Type **DIR A:** (or **DIR B:**) and press **[Enter]**. DOS shows you that the BACKUP command assigned the volume name BACKUP.001 to the diskette and that it created two files. See Figure 6-5. The BACKUP.001 file contains all the files that the BACKUP command backed up to this diskette. These files are stored together to maximize the use of disk space on the backup diskette. The CONTROL.001 file contains information about the backed-up files, including the path names. In both cases, the file extension identifies the diskette number. In this example, these files use 47,969 bytes of storage space.

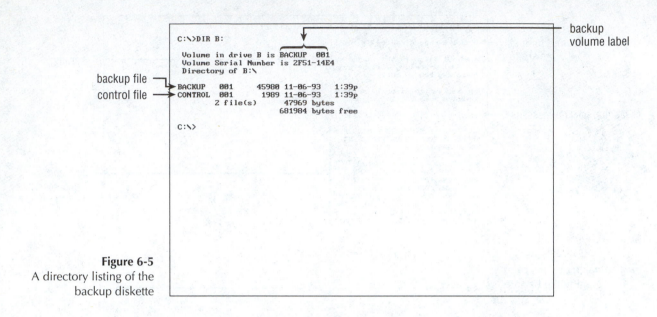

```
C:\>DIR B:

 Volume in drive B is BACKUP  001
 Volume Serial Number is 2F51-14E4
 Directory of B:\

BACKUP   001     45980 11-06-93   1:39p
CONTROL  001      1989 11-06-93   1:39p
         2 file(s)      47969 bytes
                       681984 bytes free


C:\>
```

backup volume label

backup file

control file

Figure 6-5
A directory listing of the backup diskette

Now view the contents of the log file.

6.0

2. Type **TYPE C:\DOS\LOGFILE1 | MORE** and press **[Enter]**. DOS pages the output and displays the first part of the information stored in the log file. See Figure 6-6. The log file contains the disk number, the full path, and filename of each file. In DOS 6.0, you see the date and time of the backup at the beginning of the log file.

```
11-06-1993  13:38:30
001  \ACEFORMS\BUSINESS\BUSINESS.PLN
001  \ACEFORMS\BUSINESS\CLIENT.LST
001  \ACEFORMS\BUSINESS\EQUIP.LST
001  \ACEFORMS\BUSINESS\INSURE.LST
001  \ACEFORMS\BUSINESS\STARTUP
001  \ACEFORMS\CASHFLOW\CASH.FMT
001  \ACEFORMS\CASHFLOW\CASH.RPT
001  \ACEFORMS\CASHFLOW\CASH.WK1
001  \ACEFORMS\CASHFLOW\CASHFLOW.FMT
001  \ACEFORMS\CASHFLOW\CASHFLOW.RPT
001  \ACEFORMS\CASHFLOW\CASHFLOW.WK1
001  \ACEFORMS\INVOICES\INVOICE.FMT
001  \ACEFORMS\INVOICES\INVOICE.RPT
001  \ACEFORMS\INVOICES\INVOICE.WK1
001  \ACEFORMS\JOBS\FEESCALE
001  \ACEFORMS\JOBS\JOBCOSTS.FMT
001  \ACEFORMS\JOBS\JOBCOSTS.RPT
001  \ACEFORMS\JOBS\JOBCOSTS.WK1
001  \ACEFORMS\JOBS\SCHEDULE.FMT
001  \ACEFORMS\JOBS\SCHEDULE.WK1
001  \ACEFORMS\PRJCASH\INCOME.YR1
001  \ACEFORMS\PRJCASH\INCOME.YR2
-- More --
```

backup diskette number

date and time of backup

path and filenames of backed-up files

Figure 6-6
Viewing the contents of the backup log file

3. Press **[Spacebar]** or any other key to continue. DOS displays the next screen with names of the backed-up files. If necessary, press **[Spacebar]** or any other key to view the next and last screen, then return to the DOS prompt.

REMOVING A DIRECTORY

Your supervisor informs you that a coworker will now be responsible for the monthly cashflow reports. He asks you to copy those files to the hard disk in your coworker's computer. Because you have already backed up your files, you can remove the directory that contains the monthly cashflow reports.

You will use the DEL command to remove the files from this directory and the RD (Remove Directory) command to remove the directory itself.

To remove the REPORTS directory:

1. Type **CD \ACEFORMS** and press **[Enter]**. DOS changes from the root directory to the ACEFORMS subdirectory.
2. Type **DEL REPORTS** and press **[Enter]**. DOS asks you to verify that you want to delete the entire directory.
3. Type **Y** for Yes and press **[Enter]**.
4. Type **RD REPORTS** and press **[Enter]**. DOS removes the directory.
5. Type **DIR** and press **[Enter]**. The directory listing does not contain the name of the REPORTS subdirectory, so you know DOS has removed the directory.

Soon after you remove this directory, the Finance Manager asks you for a copy of one of the monthly cashflow reports. You decide to quickly restore this directory to your hard disk from your backup set so that you can print a copy of the report for her.

RESTORING FILES FROM A BACKUP SET

The RESTORE command restores all or part of the files from a backup set to your hard disk. The general syntax of this external command is

RESTORE *source-drive: target-drive:[path[filename]]*

The source drive is the diskette drive that you will use for the backup diskettes. The target drive is the name of a drive, directory, group of files, or a single file that you want to restore to the hard disk. The source and target drives are required parameters. You can also use the Subdirectory switch (/S) to restore all subdirectories and their files below the drive or directory that you specify for the target drive.

If you want to view the contents of a backup set without restoring to the hard disk, you can use the **Display switch** (/D). This switch is useful if you want to verify that you have the right backup set or if you want to verify that the files you need to restore are on a particular backup set.

Before you restore the files to the REPORTS directory, you want to view the contents of the backup diskette using the Display switch.

To view the contents of the backup set:

1. Type **RESTORE A: C:\ACEFORMS\REPORTS*.* /D /S** (or **RESTORE B: C:\ACEFORMS\REPORTS*.* /D /S**) and press **[Enter]**.
   RESTORE prompts you to insert the first backup diskette into the specified drive.

2. Press **[Enter]**. DOS displays the full paths and filenames of the backed-up files for the \ACEFORMS\REPORTS directory on the backup diskette. See Figure 6-7.

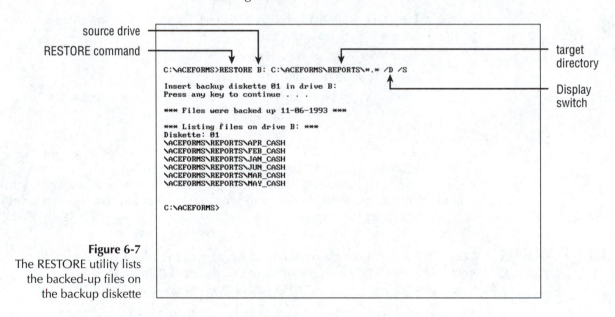

source drive
RESTORE command

target
directory

Display
switch

```
C:\ACEFORMS>RESTORE B: C:\ACEFORMS\REPORTS\*.* /D /S

Insert backup diskette 01 in drive B:
Press any key to continue . . .

*** Files were backed up 11-06-1993 ***

*** Listing files on drive B: ***
Diskette: 01
\ACEFORMS\REPORTS\APR_CASH
\ACEFORMS\REPORTS\FEB_CASH
\ACEFORMS\REPORTS\JAN_CASH
\ACEFORMS\REPORTS\JUN_CASH
\ACEFORMS\REPORTS\MAR_CASH
\ACEFORMS\REPORTS\MAY_CASH


C:\ACEFORMS>
```

Figure 6-7
The RESTORE utility lists
the backed-up files on
the backup diskette

Now restore the REPORTS directory.

3. Type **RESTORE A: C:\ACEFORMS\REPORTS*.***
   (or **RESTORE B: C:\ACEFORMS\REPORTS*.***) and press **[Enter]**.
   RESTORE prompts for diskette 01.

4. Press **[Enter]**. RESTORE displays the paths and names of the files it restores to the hard disk. See Figure 6-8. It restores only the REPORTS directory and its files.

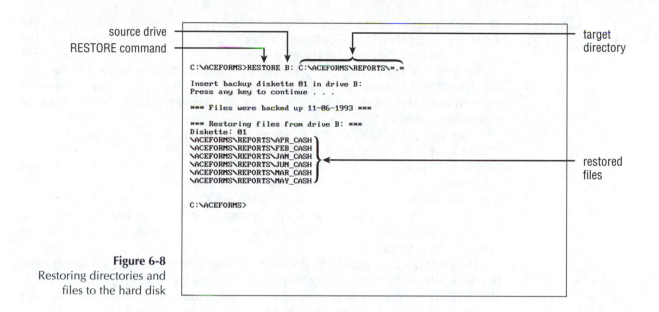

Figure 6-8
Restoring directories and
files to the hard disk

Now verify the restore operation.

5. Type **DIR REPORTS** and press **[Enter]**. DOS displays the names of files in the
    REPORTS directory. DOS recreated the directory before it restored the files.

6. Type **CD** \ to return to the root directory.

You have successfully backed up part of the directory tree of a hard disk,
removed a directory, and restored a directory from a backup set.

Performing a Backup and Restore from the DOS Shell

You can execute the BACKUP and RESTORE utilities in one of three ways:

◆ You can use the Run option on the File menu to load and execute the
   BACKUP and RESTORE utilities. If you use this approach, you temporarily
   leave the DOS Shell and work with the BACKUP and RESTORE utilities. After
   the operation is complete, you return to the DOS Shell.

◆ You can temporarily exit the DOS Shell with the key combination [Shift][F9]
   (Command Prompt). Then, at the DOS prompt, you execute the BACKUP and
   RESTORE utilities. When you are ready to return to the DOS Shell, you type
   "EXIT" and press the Enter key.

◆ You can use the DOS Utilities program-group icon in the Main window in the
   DOS Shell. After you select this icon, the DOS Shell displays options for common DOS operations, including "Backup Fixed Disk" and "Restore Fixed
   Disk." The DOS Shell displays dialog boxes that prompt you for the parameters of each command.

In each case, you temporarily exit the DOS Shell and use the BACKUP and
RESTORE utilities just as you would at the DOS prompt.

This is a good opportunity to stop for a few minutes and take a break.

USING MSBACKUP

The **MSBACKUP utility** in DOS 6.0 and 6.2 is a menu-driven utility that provides you with a variety of options for backing up and restoring files. You also can run compatibility tests and verify backups.

If you are using DOS 5.0, you will not be able to complete this section because DOS 5.0 does not contain the MSBACKUP utility. You may, however, want to read this information so that you are familiar with the capabilities of this backup utility.

When you use MSBACKUP, you specify a variety of settings for a backup. These settings are stored in a special type of file called a **setup file**. MSBACKUP provides you with an initial setup file, named DEFAULT.SET. You can specify any additional settings or modify any existing settings you need, then save all the settings in a new setup file with a different name. You can create and save up to 50 setup files with settings for different types of backups. Whenever you need to perform the same type of backup again, you recall the setup file that you need.

During a backup, MSBACKUP also creates a backup catalog. A **backup catalog** is a file that contains information about the files you backed up. MSBACKUP assigns a name to the file using the following guidelines: The first two characters of the filename are the letters of the drives you backed up. If you back up only one drive, the same drive letter is used twice. The third character is the last digit of the current year. The fourth and fifth characters are digits for the current month. The sixth and seventh characters are digits for the current day. The eighth, and last, character is a letter of the alphabet that distinguishes one backup from another performed the same day. One of three file extensions is assigned to identify the type of backup. For example, the backup catalog name CC40709A.FUL indicates that drive C was backed up on July 9, 1994. It was the first backup performed that day (indicated by the letter "A") and it was a full backup (the default). A **full backup** indicates the start of a new backup cycle.

Later, when you examine backup strategies, you will learn about the types of backups, the value of each type of backup, and how you can combine them into an effective backup strategy.

The syntax for the MSBACKUP external command is

MSBACKUP

6.0 6.2

If you are using DOS 6.0 or 6.2, you are ready to configure and perform backup and restore operations with MSBACKUP.

If you are using DOS 6.0, you must format your Tutorial Disk again to remove the backup files produced with the BACKUP utility, following the steps below. If you are using DOS 6.2, you do not need to format your Tutorial Disk.

5.0

If you are using DOS 5.0, you will not be able to complete this section because DOS 5.0 does not contain the MSBACKUP utility. If you are using DOS 5.0, skip to the section entitled "Using XCOPY for Backups."

6.0 **6.2** **To prepare your Tutorial Disk** *in DOS 6.0 and 6.2:*

1. Format your Tutorial Disk using the instructions on pages 56 through 58.

2. Be sure you are at the root directory of your hard disk drive.

Now start MSBACKUP.

3. Type **MSBACKUP** and press **[Enter]**.

   After you load the MSBACKUP utility, MSBACKUP will display one of two screens:

   ◆ MSBACKUP will display an Alert dialog box that informs you that you must configure MSBACKUP for your computer system before you can perform any backups. See Figure 6-9. If the Alert dialog box is displayed, follow the instructions in the following section, "Running a Compatibility Test."

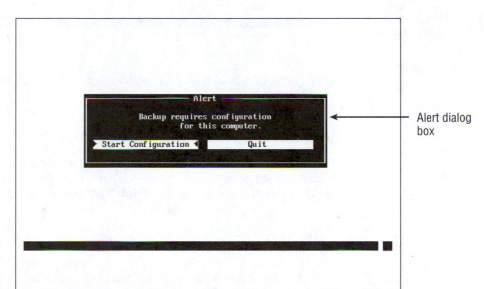

Alert dialog box

Figure 6-9
The MSBACKUP utility displays a configuration Alert dialog box

6.0 **6.2**

◆ If you are using DOS 6.0, MSBACKUP will read information from your hard disk and then display the Microsoft Backup 6.0 menu. If you are using DOS 6.2, it will immediately display the Microsoft Backup 6.0 menu. See Figure 6-10. MSBACKUP is already configured for use on your computer system. *If your system is already configured, do not run the compatibility test to reconfigure the system.* Skip the next section, entitled "Running a Compatibility Test," and continue this tutorial at the section entitled "Backing Up a Directory."

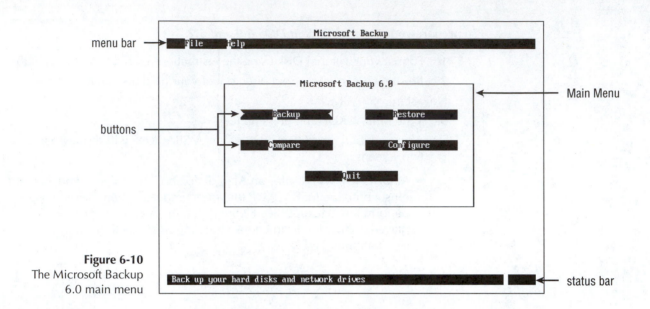

menu bar

buttons

Main Menu

status bar

Figure 6-10
The Microsoft Backup
6.0 main menu

Your view of the MSBACKUP may differ from those in Figures 6-9 and 6-10 if you are using graphics mode.

Running a Compatibility Test

During the compatibility test, MSBACKUP automatically configures itself, performs a test backup, and checks for errors in the backup process. *Complete the steps in this section only if the MSBACKUP utility requires configuration.*

To configure MSBACKUP:

1. Press **[Enter]** to select the Start Configuration menu option.

   If you are using the mouse, click **Start Configuration**.

   MSBACKUP displays a Video and Mouse Configuration dialog box and instructs you to accept the configuration as shown. See Figure 6-11. MSBACKUP has already determined the characteristics of the video display and mouse.

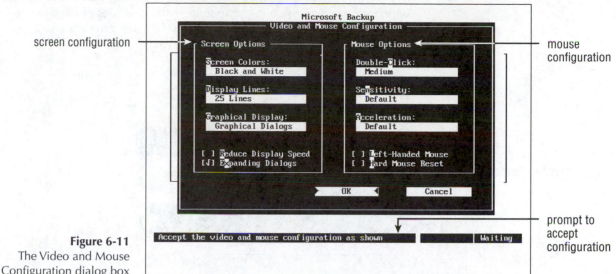

Figure 6-11
The Video and Mouse
Configuration dialog box

screen configuration

mouse configuration

prompt to accept configuration

2. Press **[Enter]** to accept the configuration.

If you are using the mouse, click **OK** to accept the configuration.

MSBACKUP displays a Floppy Drive Change Line Test dialog box. See Figure 6-12. MSBACKUP explains that this test will determine whether it can detect when a disk is changed in the diskette drive. It also asks you to remove any diskettes from the diskette drives.

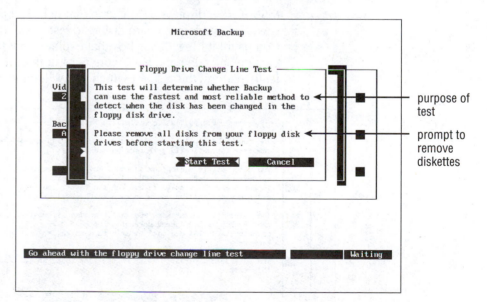

Figure 6-12
The Floppy Drive Change
Line Test dialog box

purpose of test

prompt to remove diskettes

3. If necessary, remove any diskettes from drive A and drive B.

4. Press **[Enter]** to select Start Test.

If you are using the mouse, click **Start Test**.

MSBACKUP tests your system and displays a Backup Devices dialog box, which shows the size, storage capacities, and densities of the diskette drives in your computer system. MSBACKUP again prompts you to accept the configuration as shown. See Figure 6-13.

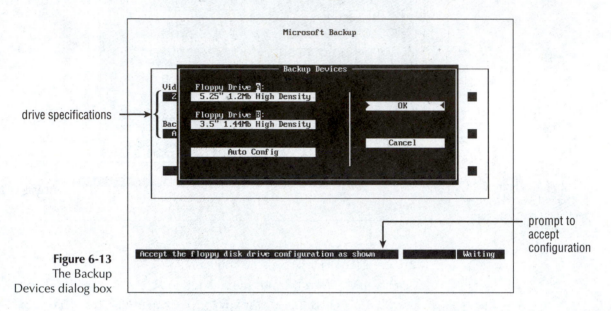

drive specifications ───►

prompt to accept configuration

Figure 6-13
The Backup
Devices dialog box

5. Press **[Enter]** to accept the configuration.

If you are using the mouse, click **OK** to accept the configuration.

MSBACKUP displays a Configure dialog box. It then tests the processor speed and performs a hard disk read test. Next, it displays a Floppy Disk Compatibility Test dialog box that explains that it intends to do a small backup and compare. See Figure 6-14. It informs you that it will automatically perform this test, for which you will need two diskettes.

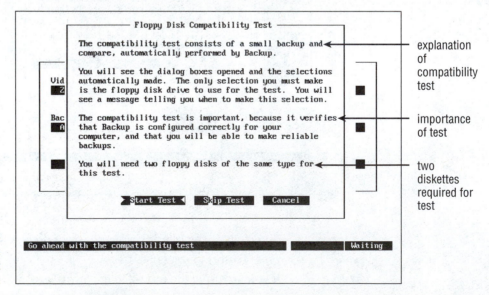

explanation of compatibility test

importance of test

two diskettes required for test

Figure 6-14
The Floppy Disk
Compatibility Test
dialog box

6. Press **[Enter]** to select Start Test.

   If you are using the mouse, click **Start Test**.

   MSBACKUP reads information and examines all files on the hard disk, and automatically selects files from the DOS subdirectory to back up. It displays an Alert dialog box, which tells you that it will pause to let you select a drive for the backup test.

7. Press **[Enter]** to select Continue.

   If you are using the mouse, click **Continue**.

   MSBACKUP displays a Backup To dialog box so that you can select a drive. See Figure 6-15. If your computer system has one or more high-density drives, you will see options for using those drives to perform a backup on either high-density or double-density diskettes. Your drive options might be different.

drive options ⟶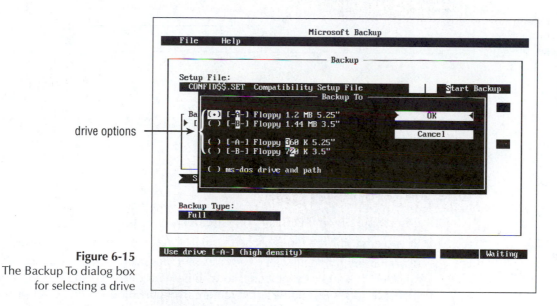

Figure 6-15
The Backup To dialog box
for selecting a drive

8. Highlight the option for the drive you intend to use for a backup. You can use the [↓] (Down Arrow) and [↑] (Up Arrow) keys to select the drive. Then press **[Spacebar]** to select the backup drive. *Be sure you select the right capacity for the backup.*

   If you are using the mouse, click on the **option for the drive you intend to use** as the backup drive. *Be sure you select the correct capacity for the backup.*

9. Press **[Enter]** to save the drive setting.

   If you are using the mouse, click **OK** to save the drive setting.

   MSBACKUP displays an Alert dialog box and prompts you to insert diskette #1 in the drive you selected for the backup. See Figure 6-16.

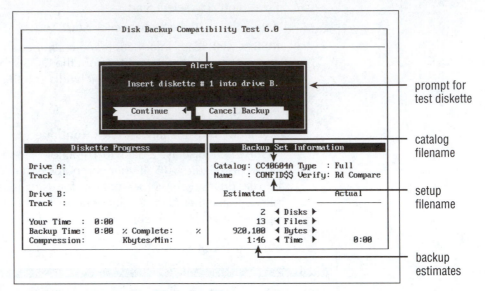

Figure 6-16
An Alert box prompts for
a backup test diskette

Performing the Test Backup

Now you will perform a test backup with MSBACKUP as part of the Compatibility Test.

To perform the test backup:

1. Insert your Tutorial Disk and press **[Enter]**.

    If you are using the mouse, insert your Tutorial Disk and click **Continue**.

    If you insert a diskette with directories and files, MSBACKUP will display an Alert box and prompt you as to whether you want to overwrite the disk. If this occurs, press **[Enter]** or if you are using the mouse, click **Overwrite**. MSBACKUP displays a Disk Backup Compatibility Test 6.0 dialog box and records selected DOS files on the diskette. The Diskette Progress dialog box shows the drive, track number, and percentage of the backup that is complete. After this operation is done, MSBACKUP displays the message "Insert Diskette # 2." Wait until MSBACKUP displays an Alert dialog box that prompts you to insert the next diskette in the same drive.

2. Remove your Tutorial Disk, and insert your Exercise Disk. Then press **[Enter]**.

    If you are using the mouse, click **Continue**.

    MSBACKUP backs up files to the second diskette. After the backup is complete, MSBACKUP displays a Backup Complete dialog box, which includes information on how many files were backed up, how many backup diskettes were used, the total number of bytes required for the backup, the total time required for the backup, and the number of kilobytes backed up per minute. See Figure 6-17.

6.2

    DOS 6.2 backs up more files then DOS 6.0. If you are using DOS 6.2, your summary information might be different, and you might not see part of the directory tree for the hard disk.

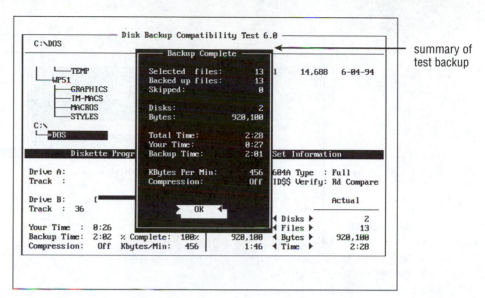

summary of
test backup

Figure 6-17
The Backup Complete
dialog box

Verifying the Backup Process

Now you will check to be sure the backup process worked.

To verify the backup process:

1. Press **[Enter]** to continue.

   If you are using the mouse, click **OK** to continue.

   MSBACKUP then proceeds to the second part of the compatibility test, where it compares the backed up files on the diskette with the original files on the hard disk to check for errors in the backup process. After a series of operations, MSBACKUP prompts you to insert diskette #1 into the backup drive. See Figure 6-18. In this figure, note that the catalog file's name is CC40604A.FUL. The name of your catalog file will be different.

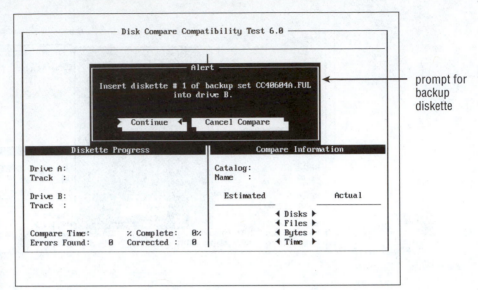

Figure 6-18
An Alert box prompts for the first diskette in a backup set (your catalog filename will be different)

2. Remove your Exercise Disk, and insert your Tutorial Disk in the diskette drive used for the backup.

3. Press **[Enter]** to continue.

   If you are using the mouse, click **Continue**.

   MSBACKUP checks the backup files for errors, then prompts for the next diskette.

4. Remove your Tutorial Disk, and insert your Exercise Disk in the same diskette drive.

5. Press **[Enter]** to continue.

   If you are using the mouse, click **Continue**.

   6.2

   MSBACKUP checks the backup files on the second diskette for errors. When the operation is complete, MSBACKUP displays a Compare Complete dialog box. See Figure 6-19. DOS 6.2 compares more files than DOS 6.0. This summary reports that MSBACKUP found no errors. If MSBACKUP reported errors, backups you make with this utility might be unreliable. You should perform another backup and compare the results. If MSBACKUP still reports problems, you might need to reconfigure MSBACKUP or service your diskette drive.

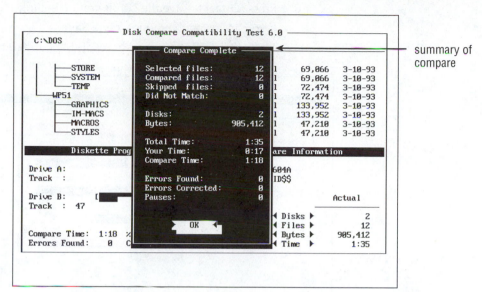

summary of compare

Figure 6-19
The Compare
Complete dialog box

6. Press **[Enter]** to continue.

   If you are using the mouse, click **OK** to continue.

   MSBACKUP should display a Compatibility Test dialog box that tells you the compatibility test was successful and that you can perform backups reliably on your computer system. If MSBACKUP reports problems with the Compatibility Test, check with your instructor or technical support person.

7. Press **[Enter]** to continue.

   If you are using the mouse, click **OK** to continue.

   MSBACKUP displays the Configure Menu so that you can save configuration changes. See Figure 6-20.

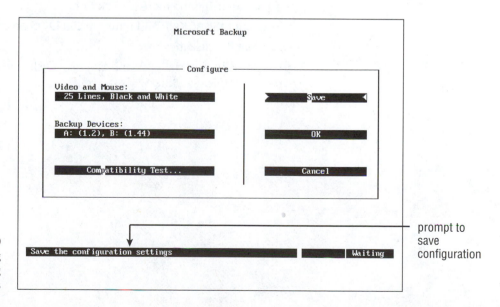

prompt to save configuration

Figure 6-20
A Configure dialog box for saving configuration settings

8. Press **[Enter]** to save the configuration settings.

   If you are using the mouse, click **Save**.

   MSBACKUP displays the Microsoft Backup 6.0 menu. See Figure 6-21.

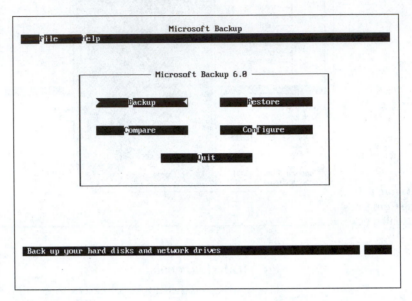

Figure 6-21
The Microsoft Backup
6.0 main menu

You must now temporarily exit MSBACKUP so that you can format the diskettes for the next part of the tutorial.

To exit MSBACKUP 6.0 or 6.2:

1. Type **Q** to select Quit.

   If you are using the mouse, click **Quit**.

   You exit MSBACKUP and return to the DOS prompt.

   Now format the diskettes.

2. Format your Tutorial Disk and Exercise Disk using the instructions on pages 56 through 58.

Backing Up a Directory

You want to back up the AceForms directory on your hard disk. MSBACKUP will not only back up the files in each of the subdirectories, but it will also record the directory structure so that you can restore the entire directory later to the same hard disk or another hard disk.

To load MSBACKUP and select the Backup option:

1. Type **MSBACKUP** and press **[Enter]**. If you are using DOS 6.0, MSBACKUP will read the information from your hard disk, including the name and path of every file, then will display the MSBACKUP 6.0 menu. If you are using DOS 6.2, it will immediately display the Microsoft Backup 6.0 menu.

2. Type **B** (or press **[Enter]**) to select Backup.

   If you are using the mouse, click **Backup**.

   MSBACKUP displays the Backup screen. See Figure 6-22. The Backup From box shows drive C as the default drive from which to back up files. The Backup To box might show drive A (or drive B) as the default drive for the backup. The Backup Type box shows the default type as Full. The Setup File box shows the name of the default setup file, DEFAULT.SET. MSBACKUP uses the last settings that were in effect.

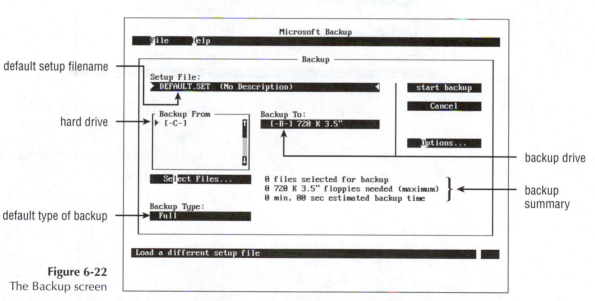

Figure 6-22
The Backup screen

Creating a Setup File

Now you want to save the default setup file under a new name so that it will store the settings you use to back up the AceForms directory, and then you'll select the files to back up.

To assign a new name to the default setup file:

1. Press and hold **[Alt]** while you press **F** to access the File menu.

   If you are using the mouse, click **File**.

   MSBACKUP displays its File menu. See Figure 6-23.

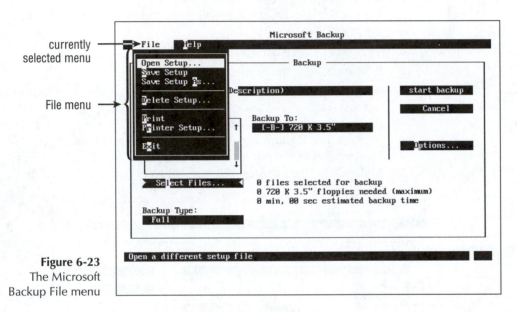

Figure 6-23
The Microsoft
Backup File menu

2. Press **[↓]** (Down Arrow) until you highlight Save Setup As, then press **[Enter]**.

   If you are using the mouse, click **Save Setup As**.

   MSBACKUP displays a Save Setup File dialog box. See Figure 6-24.

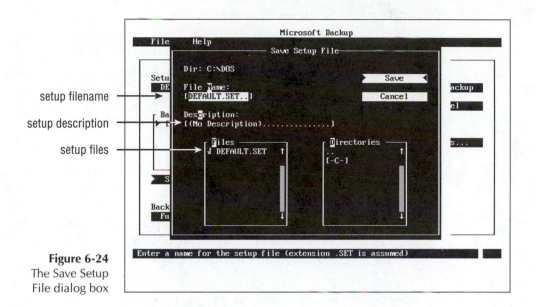

Figure 6-24
The Save Setup
File dialog box

3. Type **ACEFORMS** in the File Name text box, then press **[Tab]** to select the Description text box.

    If you are using the mouse, type **ACEFORMS** and click the **Description** text box.

4. Type **(Client Files)** *including the parentheses* and press **[Enter]**.

    If you are using the mouse, type **(Client Files)** *including the parentheses* and click **OK**. MSBACKUP returns to the Backup screen. The new name of the setup file is ACEFORMS.SET. See Figure 6-25.

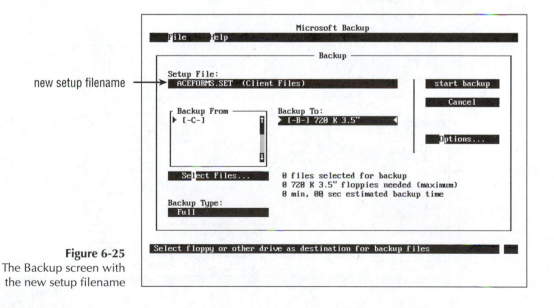

Figure 6-25
The Backup screen with
the new setup filename

Changing the Settings in a Setup File

Next you will modify the default settings from the DEFAULT.SET setup file and save them under the new setup filename, ACEFORMS.SET.

If the drive setting in the Backup To list box is not the one you want to use, you can change the setting for the backup drive.

To specify the drive you want to use:

1. Type **A** for Backup To. Use [↓] (Down Arrow) to highlight the backup drive name with the proper storage capacity. Press **[Spacebar]** to select this drive. Press **[Enter]** to save this setting.

   If you are using the mouse, click **Backup To**, click the **backup drive name** with the proper storage capacity, and click **OK**.

   MSBACKUP returns to the Backup screen.

Now you're ready to select the directories and files for the backup.

To select the directories and files for the backup:

1. Type **L** for Select Files.

   If you are using the mouse, click **Select Files**.

   MSBACKUP reads disk information and displays the Select Backup Files screen. See Figure 6-26. On this screen, you see the current drive (in this case, C:), the specification for selecting files (in this case, C:*.*), a window with a partial view of the directory tree for the current drive, and a window with filenames and other file information.

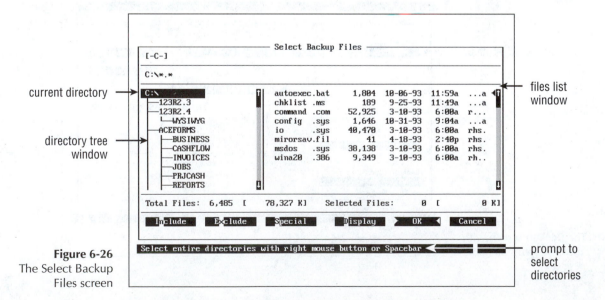

Figure 6-26
The Select Backup
Files screen

2. Press [↓] (Down Arrow) until you highlight the ACEFORMS directory in the directory tree window. Press [↓] (Down Arrow) to highlight the BUSINESS subdirectory. Then press **[Spacebar]** to select this directory.

   If you are using the mouse, click **ACEFORMS** in the directory tree window with the right mouse button, then double-click the **BUSINESS** subdirectory.

   MSBACKUP selects this subdirectory for the backup; an arrow in the directory tree points to this subdirectory.

3. Select each of the remaining subdirectories under the ACEFORMS directory: CASHFLOW, INVOICES, JOBS, PRJCASH, REPORTS, and RESUMES.

4. Press [↑] (Up Arrow) to highlight the ACEFORMS directory name. Figure 6-27 shows the selected subdirectories.

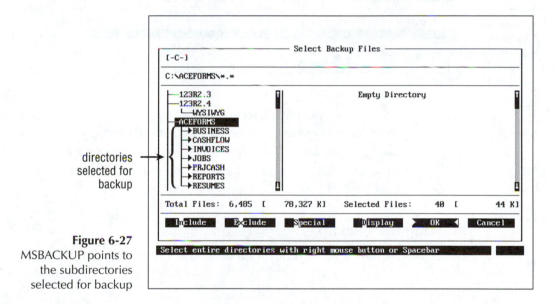

directories
selected for
backup

Figure 6-27
MSBACKUP points to
the subdirectories
selected for backup

5. Press **[Enter]** to save these settings.

   If you are using the mouse, click **OK** to save these settings.

   MSBACKUP displays the Backup screen and shows you that 41 files are selected for the backup, including the catalog file. See Figure 6-28. In this case, MSBACKUP indicates that one 720K 3.5-inch diskette is needed for the backup and indicates an estimated backup time of 15 seconds. (MSBACKUP's recommendation on your computer might be different.)

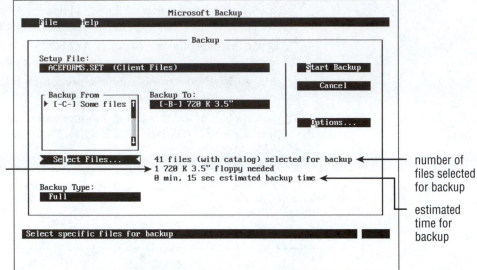

recommended number
of backup diskettes

Figure 6-28
The Backup screen's
recommendations for the
backup (your screen
might be different)

number of
files selected
for backup

estimated
time for
backup

6. Press and hold **[Alt]** while you press **F** to access the File menu. Press **[↓]** (Down Arrow) to select Save Setup, then press **[Enter]**.

   If you are using the mouse, click **File,** then click **Save Setup**.

   MSBACKUP saves your new settings under the setup file named ACEFORMS.SET.

Starting the Backup

Now that you have specified the settings, you are ready to start the backup.

To back up the AceForms directory:

1. Type **S** to select Start Backup.

   If you are using the mouse, click **Start Backup**.

   MSBACKUP creates a catalog for the backup, loads the Backup program, and displays an Alert dialog box, which prompts you to insert the first diskette. See Figure 6-29.

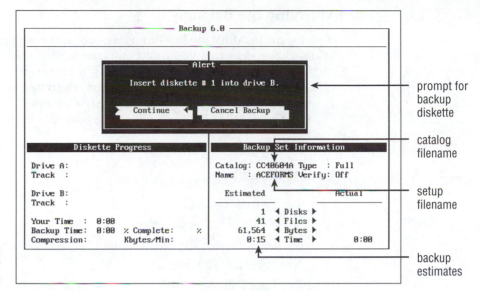

Figure 6-29
An Alert box prompts for the first backup diskette

2. Insert your Tutorial Disk in the diskette drive and press **[Enter]**.

   If you are using the mouse, insert your Tutorial Disk in the diskette drive and click **Continue**.

   MSBACKUP displays a Backup Complete dialog box. See Figure 6-30. In this example, MSBACKUP backed up 41 files occupying 61,564 bytes of storage space at a compression ratio of 1.9 to 1. It reduced the storage space required for these files by almost one-half. MSBACKUP might report different results on your computer.

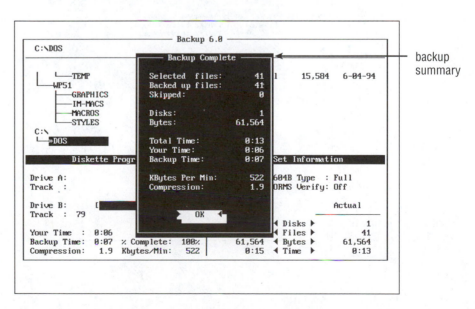

Figure 6-30
The Backup Complete dialog box

3. Press **[Enter]** to continue.

   If you are using the mouse, click **OK** to continue.

   The Microsoft Backup 6.0 menu appears.

Verifying the Backup

If you want to verify the backup operation, you could perform a Compare operation. However, when you first configure MSBACKUP, it verifies the reliability of the backup process by performing a compare on a test backup. If you change or reconfigure hardware in your computer system, you should reconfigure MSBACKUP to guarantee reliable backups.

Let's exit MSBACKUP and check the contents of the backup diskette.

To exit MSBACKUP:

1. Type **Q** for Quit.

    If you are using the mouse, click **Quit**.

    DOS displays the DOS prompt.

    Now check the backup disk.

2. Type **DIR A:** (or **DIR B:**) and press **[Enter]**. DOS displays the contents of the backup diskette. See Figure 6-31. In this example, the volume name is ACEFORMSFUL, and the backup file is named CC40604A.001. This file contains all of the files backed up to this disk, and all the files are stored together in one file to maximize the use of disk space. This backup file-name indicates that drive C was backed up on June 4, 1994, was the first backup (A) performed that day, and that the file was stored on the first diskette (001) in the backup set.

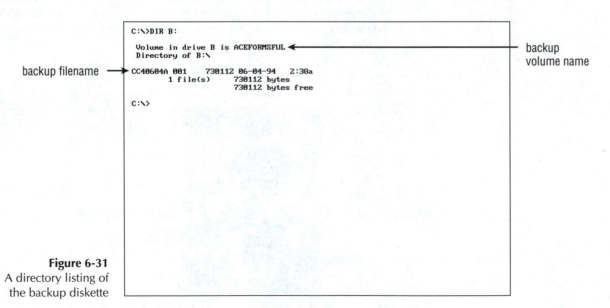

Figure 6-31
A directory listing of
the backup diskette

Removing Part of the Directory Tree

Your supervisor informs you that your new computer system has arrived. He asks you to remove your client and business files from your old computer because an employee in another department will use it. Fortunately, you have just backed up your hard disk's files onto diskettes, so you can remove your data directory.

In DOS 6.0 and 6.2, you can use the DELTREE command to delete part of the directory tree. The syntax is

DELTREE [*drive:*]*path*

You specify the path and directory name of the subdirectory you want to delete. The DELTREE command starts at the subdirectory you specify and removes all files and all subdirectories positioned below that directory. You specify the drive if the directory is on another disk drive. Be careful when you use this command, because you can quickly delete a large amount of information from a disk.

_**5.0**_

DOS 5.0 does not contain the DELTREE command. If you want to delete a subdirectory and all its subordinate directories in DOS 5.0, you must first delete all the files in the subdirectory and its subordinate directories with the DEL or ERASE command. Next, you use the RD or RMDIR (Remove Directory) command to remove each subdirectory, starting from the innermost directory and working your way to the parent directory.

_**6.0 6.2**_

To remove the AceForms directory *using DOS 6.0 and 6.2*:

1. Type **DELTREE ACEFORMS** and press **[Enter]**. DOS asks if you are sure you want to remove this directory and all its subdirectories.

2. Type **Y** for Yes, then press **[Enter]**. DELTREE informs you that it is "Deleting aceforms..."

Now verify this operation.

3. Type **DIR ACEFORMS** and press **[Enter]**. DOS tells you that it found no such file. See Figure 6-32. You have successfully deleted the directory, its subdirectories, and all the files in each of the subdirectories.

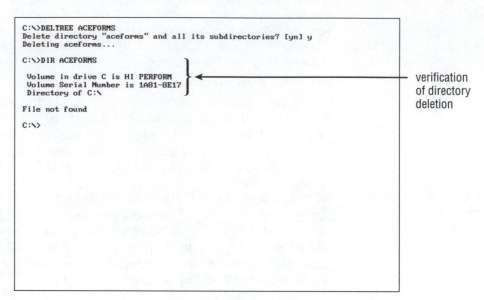

C:\>DELTREE ACEFORMS
Delete directory "aceforms" and all its subdirectories? [yn] y
Deleting aceforms...

C:\>DIR ACEFORMS

 Volume in drive C is HI PERFORM   } ←——————— verification
 Volume Serial Number is 1A81-8E17   }   of directory
 Directory of C:\   }   deletion

File not found

C:\>

Figure 6-32
Verifying removal of
part of a directory tree

Restoring Directories and Files

After unpacking and setting up your new computer system, you install the software applications you need. You are now ready to restore the client and business files from your backup set so that you can return to work.

To restore files from a backup set:

6.0

6.2

1. Type **MSBACKUP** and press **[Enter]**. If you are using DOS 6.0, MSBACKUP will read information from your hard disk, including the full path and name of all files, then will display the Microsoft Backup 6.0 menu. If you are using DOS 6.2, it will immediately display the Microsoft Backup 6.0 menu.

2. Type **R** to select Restore.

   If you are using a mouse, click **Restore**.

   MSBACKUP displays a Restore screen with the current settings for the last backup. See Figure 6-33. If you had actually switched to a new computer system, you would have had to copy the setup files from your old computer or create new setup files on your new computer system. By default, MSBACKUP saves setup files in your DOS subdirectory.

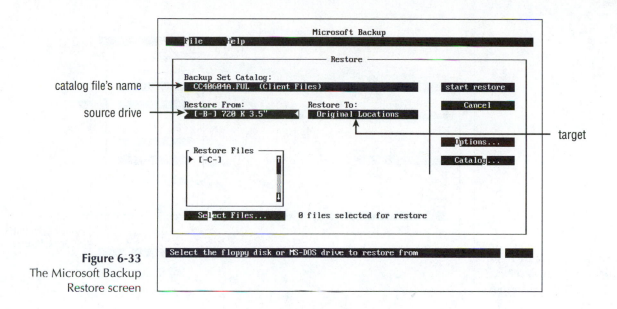

catalog file's name

source drive

target

Figure 6-33
The Microsoft Backup
Restore screen

3. If MSBACKUP does not display the name of your setup file, type **K** to select Backup Set Catalog. Select the catalog file's name in the Catalog Files box, then press **[Enter]** to select the Load button.

   If you are using the mouse, click the **list box** for Backup Set Catalog. Click the **catalog file's name** in the Catalog Files list box, then click **Load**.

4. If MSBACKUP does not display the name of your backup drive or if you need to specify a different storage capacity for that drive, type **E** to select Restore From. Highlight the backup drive option you want to use and press **[Spacebar]** to select that option. Press **[Enter]** to return to the Restore screen.

   If you are using the mouse, click **Restore From**, click the **backup drive option** you want to use, and click **OK** to return to the Restore screen.

5. Type **I** to select Restore Files. Highlight the drive name of the hard disk you want to use, then press **[Spacebar]**.

   If you are using the mouse, click the name of the hard drive.

   MSBACKUP displays "All Files" next to [-C-] (or your hard drive name) and automatically selects 40 files. See Figure 6-34.

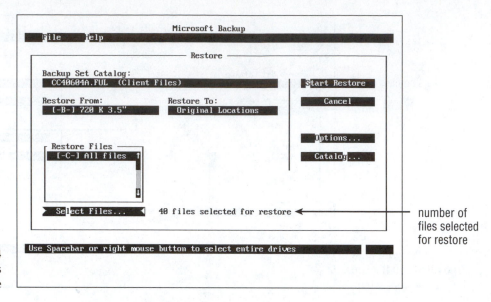

Figure 6-34
Microsoft Backup selects
40 files to restore

To start the restore:

1. Press and hold **[Alt]** while you press **S** to select Start Restore. If MSBACKUP does not respond, press and hold **[Alt]** while you press **S**.

   If you are using the mouse, click **Start Restore**.

   MSBACKUP displays an Alert dialog box prompting for diskette #1 for a specific backup set. See Figure 6-35.

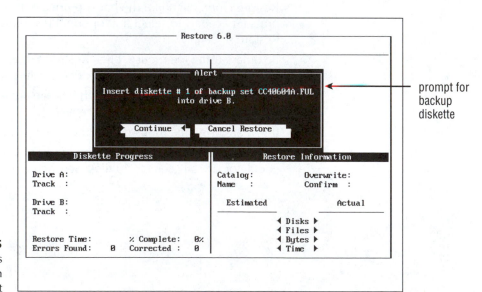

Figure 6-35
An Alert box prompts
for the first diskette in
a backup set

2. Press **[Enter]** to continue.

   If you are using the mouse, click **Continue**.

   MSBACKUP restores files directory by directory and displays a Restore Complete dialog box with information on the restore process. See Figure 6-36.

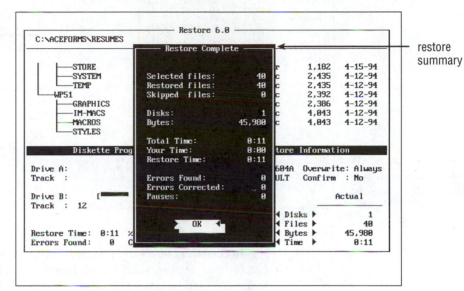

Figure 6-36
The Restore
Complete dialog box

3. Press **[Enter]**.

   If you are using the mouse, click **OK**.

   If you are using DOS 6.0, MSBACKUP will read information from your hard disk and then display the Microsoft Backup 6.0 menu. If you are using DOS 6.2, it will immediately display the Microsoft Backup 6.0 menu.

Verifying the Restore

Now you want to exit MSBACKUP and verify the restore operation.

To exit MSBACKUP:

1. Type **Q** for Quit.

   If you are using the mouse, click **Quit**.

   You exit MSBACKUP and return to the DOS prompt.

   Now verify the restore.

2. Type **DIR ACEFORMS** and press **[Enter]**. DOS displays the subdirectories in the AceForms directory. See Figure 6-37. MSBACKUP recreated the entire directory tree.

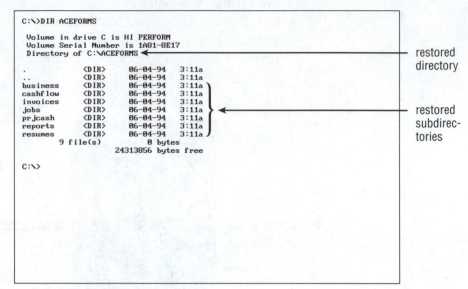

```
C:\>DIR ACEFORMS

 Volume in drive C is HI PERFORM
 Volume Serial Number is 1A81-8E17
 Directory of C:\ACEFORMS

.            <DIR>      06-04-94    3:11a
..           <DIR>      06-04-94    3:11a
business     <DIR>      06-04-94    3:11a
cashflow     <DIR>      06-04-94    3:11a
invoices     <DIR>      06-04-94    3:11a
jobs         <DIR>      06-04-94    3:11a
prjcash      <DIR>      06-04-94    3:11a
reports      <DIR>      06-04-94    3:11a
resumes      <DIR>      06-04-94    3:11a
        9 file(s)              0 bytes
                       24313856 bytes free

C:\>
```

— restored directory

— restored subdirectories

Figure 6-37
A directory listing of subdirectories restored by MSBACKUP

3. Type **TREE ACEFORMS /F ¦ MORE** and press **[Enter]**. DOS displays a directory tree, starting with the AceForms directory, lists the files in each subdirectory, and pauses after displaying the first screen of information. See Figure 6-38.

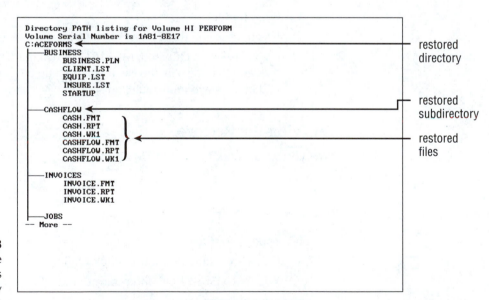

```
Directory PATH listing for Volume HI PERFORM
Volume Serial Number is 1A81-8E17
C:ACEFORMS
├───BUSINESS
│       BUSINESS.PLN
│       CLIENT.LST
│       EQUIP.LST
│       INSURE.LST
│       STARTUP
│
├───CASHFLOW
│       CASH.FMT
│       CASH.RPT
│       CASH.WK1
│       CASHFLOW.FMT
│       CASHFLOW.RPT
│       CASHFLOW.WK1
│
├───INVOICES
│       INVOICE.FMT
│       INVOICE.RPT
│       INVOICE.WK1
│
├───JOBS
-- More --
```

— restored directory

— restored subdirectory

— restored files

Figure 6-38
A partial directory tree with restored files listed by subdirectory

4. Press **[Spacebar]** or any other key to continue. Repeat this process until you view the entire directory tree and return to the DOS prompt.

You have successfully backed up part of the directory tree of a hard disk, removed part of the directory tree, and restored the same directory tree from a backup set.

USING XCOPY FOR BACKUPS

Occasionally, you need to work on client and business files on your home computer. You decide to copy your data directory from your hard drive in the office to a diskette you can use on your home computer system.

In DOS 5.0, 6.0, and 6.2, you can use the XCOPY command to make backups. The XCOPY is similar to the COPY command, except it can copy more than one directory. The "X" in XCOPY stands for "Extended" to indicate that the XCOPY command is a more extensive command than COPY. The general syntax of this external command is

XCOPY *source* [*destination*]

The *source* is a directory, a group of files, or a single file and is a required parameter. The *destination* is the name of the drive *or* directory to which you want to copy the files. You can omit the destination if you want to copy to the current drive or directory. If you want to include all the subdirectories located below a directory, you can include the Subdirectory switch (/S).

Like the COPY command, XCOPY has some limitations. You cannot use it to make a backup copy of the contents of an entire hard disk. Like COPY, XCOPY automatically stops when it fills a diskette. It does not automatically prompt for another diskette as the MSBACKUP and Backup utilities do. However, like COPY, you can use the files produced with XCOPY because the files are not combined into one larger file on the backup diskette.

Before you use XCOPY, you need to format your Tutorial Disk.

To prepare a diskette:

1. Format your Tutorial Disk using the instructions on pages 56 through 58.

Now copy a directory with XCOPY.

2. Type **XCOPY C:\ACEFORMS*.* A: /S**
    (or **XCOPY C:\ACEFORMS*.* B: /S**)
    and press **[Enter]**. XCOPY copies the directories
    and files to your data diskette. See Figure 6-39.

source directory ── source files

source drive ──────────────────────── destination drive

xcopy command ────────────── Subdirectory switch

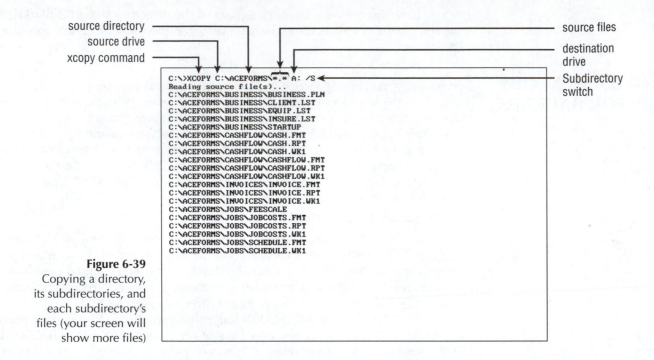

```
C:\>XCOPY C:\ACEFORMS\*.* A: /S
Reading source file(s)...
C:\ACEFORMS\BUSINESS\BUSINESS.PLN
C:\ACEFORMS\BUSINESS\CLIENT.LST
C:\ACEFORMS\BUSINESS\EQUIP.LST
C:\ACEFORMS\BUSINESS\INSURE.LST
C:\ACEFORMS\BUSINESS\STARTUP
C:\ACEFORMS\CASHFLOW\CASH.FMT
C:\ACEFORMS\CASHFLOW\CASH.RPT
C:\ACEFORMS\CASHFLOW\CASH.WK1
C:\ACEFORMS\CASHFLOW\CASHFLOW.FMT
C:\ACEFORMS\CASHFLOW\CASHFLOW.RPT
C:\ACEFORMS\CASHFLOW\CASHFLOW.WK1
C:\ACEFORMS\INVOICES\INVOICE.FMT
C:\ACEFORMS\INVOICES\INVOICE.RPT
C:\ACEFORMS\INVOICES\INVOICE.WK1
C:\ACEFORMS\JOBS\FEESCALE
C:\ACEFORMS\JOBS\JOBCOSTS.FMT
C:\ACEFORMS\JOBS\JOBCOSTS.RPT
C:\ACEFORMS\JOBS\JOBCOSTS.WK1
C:\ACEFORMS\JOBS\SCHEDULE.FMT
C:\ACEFORMS\JOBS\SCHEDULE.WK1
```

Figure 6-39
Copying a directory, its subdirectories, and each subdirectory's files (your screen will show more files)

Now verify the copy operation.

3. Type **TREE A:** (or **TREE B:**) and press **[Enter]**. DOS shows you the directory tree of the diskette in drive A (or drive B). See Figure 6-40. XCOPY reproduced the directory structure exactly.

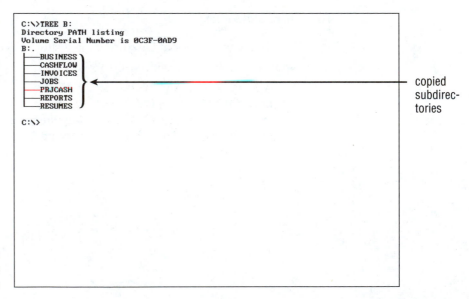

```
C:\>TREE B:
Directory PATH listing
Volume Serial Number is 0C3F-0AD9
B:.
    ├──BUSINESS
    ├──CASHFLOW
    ├──INVOICES
    ├──JOBS
    ├──PRJCASH
    ├──REPORTS
    └──RESUMES

C:\>
```

copied subdirectories

Figure 6-40
A directory tree of the diskette

4. Type **TREE A: /F | MORE** (or **TREE B: /F | MORE**) and press **[Enter]**. Figure 6-41 shows a partial directory tree with filenames. XCOPY copied files to the correct directories on this disk.

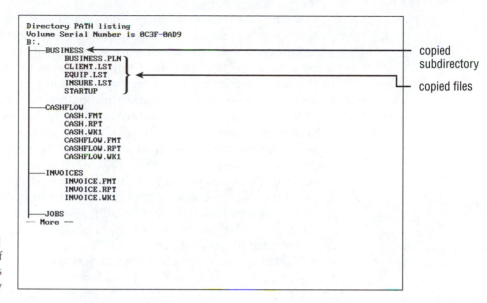

```
Directory PATH listing
Volume Serial Number is 0C3F-0AD9
B:.
├──BUSINESS ◄──────────────────────────────  copied
│       BUSINESS.PLN ┐                          subdirectory
│       CLIENT.LST   │
│       EQUIP.LST    ├ ◄────────────────────── copied files
│       INSURE.LST   │
│       STARTUP      ┘
│
├──CASHFLOW
│       CASH.FMT
│       CASH.RPT
│       CASH.WK1
│       CASHFLOW.FMT
│       CASHFLOW.RPT
│       CASHFLOW.WK1
│
├──INVOICES
│       INVOICE.FMT
│       INVOICE.RPT
│       INVOICE.WK1
│
├──JOBS
── More ──
```

Figure 6-41
A partial directory tree of the diskette, with files listed by subdirectory

You can reverse this operation and copy a directory structure to a hard disk with the versatile XCOPY command.

FINISHING UP

If you completed this tutorial in a computer lab, you should remove files produced by MSBACKUP from the computer system.

To remove backup files from the hard disk:

6.0 6.2

1. If you are using DOS 6.0 or 6.2, type **DEL \DOS\ACEFORMS.*** and press **[Enter]**. DOS deletes the catalog and setup files produced by MSBACKUP.

2. If you are using DOS 6.0 or 6.2, type **DEL \DOS*.BAK** and press **[Enter]**. DOS deletes files with the BAK (Backup) file extension produced by MSBACKUP.

5.0 6.0

3. If you are using DOS 5.0 or 6.0, type **DEL \DOS\LOGFILE1** and press **[Enter]**. DOS deletes the BACKUP log file.

DEVELOPING A BACKUP STRATEGY

To protect your time and investment in the files that you produce on your computer system, you should develop a backup strategy that will enable you to restore files to your computer system if you inadvertently delete those files or if your hard disk fails.

As part of a backup strategy, you should perform a full backup at regular intervals, such as every month or quarter. A **full backup** represents the start of a **backup cycle** and can include the entire contents of your hard disk. Or, in the interest of saving time and effort, you might want to limit your full backups just to the document or data files on your computer system. These files are obviously quite important because you are constantly changing and updating them.

You do not need to repeatedly back up directories that contain installed software, because software settings change infrequently or not at all. After you install and configure a software application on your computer system, you might want to back it up once so that you can install a new copy later if the need arises. It is quicker to restore software from a backup copy than it is to reinstall the original software application and respecify its default settings.

If you perform a full backup monthly, you can perform either an incremental or a differential backup on a weekly or daily basis. An **incremental backup** includes only those files that have *changed* since your last full or last incremental backup. You can combine full and incremental backups to guarantee that you can restore all the files you have worked on during a backup cycle. For example, after you perform a full backup, you can perform your first incremental backup at the end of the first week. This backup will include all files that changed during the first week. At the end of the second week, you perform your second incremental backup. This backup includes all files that changed during the second week. At the end of the third week, you perform your third and last incremental backup. This backup includes all files changed during the third week. At the end of the month, you perform a new full backup and start a new backup cycle. Although you could reuse the same diskettes, it is a good habit to keep two or three of the most recent backup sets and alternate them. When you are ready to perform another full backup, you use your oldest backup set. If you need to restore files to a hard disk, you can restore your last full backup and then each of the incremental backups in the order in which you produced them.

One advantage of incremental backups is that you have different versions of the same file stored in different backup sets, and you therefore can locate a specific version of a file. To perform an incremental backup with BACKUP in DOS 5.0 and 6.0, you use the **Modified switch** (/M) to select all files that were *created* or *modified* since the last backup, whether it was a full or an incremental backup. You can also include the **Add switch** (/A) to add the next set of backup files to the existing set of backup diskettes. To perform an incremental backup with MSBACKUP in DOS 6.0 and 6.2, you specify Incremental as the Backup Type on the Backup screen.

A **differential backup** includes all files altered since your last full backup. This type of backup takes longer than an incremental backup and keeps only the most recent version of files. For example, after you perform a full backup, you can perform your first differential backup at the end of the first week. This backup will include all files that were created or modified during the first week since the full backup. At the end of the second week, you perform your second differential backup. This backup will include all files that were created or modified during the first and second weeks, again since the full backup. At the end of the third week, you perform your third and last differential backup. This backup will include all files created and modified during the first, second and third weeks since the full backup. At the end of the month, you perform a new full backup and start a new backup cycle. Just as with an incremental backup, it is a good habit to keep two or three of the most recent backup sets and alternate them rather than reuse the same set of diskettes for each differential backup. When you are ready to perform another full backup, you use your oldest backup set. If you need to restore files to a hard disk, you can restore files from your last full backup and your last differential backup in that backup cycle.

To perform a differential backup with BACKUP in DOS 5.0 and 6.0, you use the **Date switch** (/D) to select all files since the date of the last full backup. If you performed a full backup on June 30, 1994, you would perform each differential backup (of the entire hard drive) in July with the following command:

BACKUP C:*.* A: /S /D:7-1-94

BACKUP would then backup all files created or modified on or after July 1, 1994. Again, you should rotate backup sets of both the full and the differential backups.

To perform a differential backup with MSBACKUP in DOS 6.0 and 6.2, you specify Differential for the Backup Type on the Backup screen.

When you use MSBACKUP in DOS 6.0 and 6.2, it creates a backup catalog file that tracks information for each backup. It uses the file extension FUL for full backups, INC for incremental backups, and DIF for differential backups. It also creates a **master catalog** file that keeps track of all backups performed during a backup cycle. You can use the master catalog to restore a complete backup cycle.

No matter what type of backup strategy you choose to implement, you should have at least two and maybe three backup sets of a full backup and an incremental or differential backup. If one of the backup sets fails, then you can use one of the other backup sets. It is also common practice to save full backups done at one-year intervals and to store one set of backups off-site.

Like insurance, these backups are invaluable when you need them. You may find yourself in a situation where you need to reconstruct all your company's business records after a major disaster, like an earthquake or fire, or some other incident, like a theft. A couple of years ago, the news media reported that thieves stole a computer system that belonged to a small business. The owner of the company claimed that the only thing that she wanted the thieves to return was her backups.

◆

SUMMARY

In this tutorial, DOS 5.0 and 6.0 users learned how to use BACKUP to backup files from a hard disk to diskettes and how to use RESTORE to restore files from diskettes to a hard disk. You learned how to use the Subdirectory and Log File switches with BACKUP and the Subdirectory and Display switches with RESTORE. You also learned of the importance of the Modified and Date switches when performing incremental and differential backups.

DOS 6.0 and 6.2 users learned how to use MSBACKUP to backup files from a hard disk to diskettes and to restore files from diskettes to a hard disk. You also learned how to perform a compatibility test and to configure MSBACKUP for the hardware in your computer system. DOS 6.0 and 6.2 users also deleted a part of the directory tree of a hard disk with the DELTREE command.

You learned how to use XCOPY and its Subdirectory switch to copy a directory, its subdirectories, and each subdirectory's files from a hard disk to a diskette.

You learned about the importance of developing a backup strategy. You learned about the use of full, incremental, and differential backups as well as their advantages and disadvantages. You learned how to integrate these backups in an overall backup strategy.

Command Reference	
DOS Commands	
BACKUP *source destination-drive:*	*DOS 5.0 and 6.0*: An external command that backs up an entire hard drive, a directory, a group of files, or a single file onto a set of backup diskettes. Common switches include:
	/S Subdirectory switch for backing up all subdirectories located below the specified drive or directory
	/L Log File switch for specifying the name of a file that stores information on backed-up files
	/M Modified switch for backing up only those files that changed since the last backup
	/A Add switch for adding another backup set to an existing set of backup diskettes
	/D Date switch for performing a backup of all files created or modified on or after a certain date

DELTREE [*drive:*]*path*	*DOS 6.0 and 6.2* : An external command that deletes a directory tree, all its subdirectories, and all files in the specified directories
MSBACKUP	*DOS 6.0 and 6.2* : An external command that backs up an entire hard drive, a directory or combination of directories, a group of files, or a single file from a hard disk to a set of backup diskettes; restores selected directories or files from a set of backup diskettes to a hard disk; and performs a compatibility test to verify the backup process
RESTORE *source-drive:* *target-drive:*[*path*[*filename*]]	*DOS 5.0, 6.0, and 6.2* : An external command that restores an entire hard disk, a directory, a group of files, or a single file from a set of backup diskettes. Common switches include: /S Subdirectory switch for restoring all subdirectories located below the specified drive or directory /D Display switch for displaying a list of path names and filenames of files stored on a set of backup diskettes
XCOPY *source* [*destination*]	*DOS 5.0, 6.0, and 6.2* : An external command that copies a directory and its subdirectories and files, a group of files, or a single file to another disk. Common switches include: /S Subdirectory switch for copying all subdirectories located below the specified directory

QUESTIONS

1. List the advantages and disadvantages of using the COPY command for backups.

2. List the advantages and disadvantages of using the DISKCOPY command for backups.

3. What happens when you use the Subdirectory switch with BACKUP?

4. What is the Log File switch, how do you use it with BACKUP, and what advantage does it provide?

5. After you back up a directory that contains several hundred files, you check your backup disk's directory and find that there are only two files—BACKUP.001 and CONTROL.001. Where did BACKUP store all the files? What is the difference between these two files? What is the significance, if any, of the file extension?

6. What types of information does BACKUP store in a log file?

7. What command can you use to restore files backed up with the BACKUP command?

8. How can you display the contents of a backup disk produced with BACKUP without actually restoring the files?

9. When using BACKUP, how can you select only those files that have changed since the last backup?

10. When using BACKUP, how can you add new backup files to an existing backup set?

11. When using BACKUP, how can you select only those files created or modified since the last backup?

12. What is a setup file, and how do you use it?

13. Explain the conventions used to name backup catalog files.

14. What is the purpose of MSBACKUP's compatibility test?

15. How do you save settings for a setup file in MSBACKUP?

16. Name one way in which you can select an entire directory from the MSBACKUP Select Backup Files screen.

17. Name two options that MSBACKUP automatically uses during a backup.

18. After you back up a directory that contains several hundred files, you check your backup diskette and find that there is one file named CC40709A.FUL. What drive did MSBACKUP back up? What type of backup did it perform? What is the date of the backup?

19. What command can you use in DOS 6.0 and 6.2 to remove an entire directory and all its subordinate directories and files?

20. One of your backup sets contains the backup file CC40922A.FUL. What drive did MSBACKUP back up? What type of backup did it perform? What is the date of the backup?

21. Name three advantages of using MSBACKUP over BACKUP?

22. How does XCOPY differ from COPY? What advantage, if any, does it have over the COPY command?

23. What is a full backup, and what phase does it represent in a backup cycle?

24. What is an incremental backup?

25. How can you use a full and an incremental backup in a backup cycle?

26. What is a differential backup?

27. How can you use a full and a differential backup in a backup cycle?

28. What is a master catalog file?

29. How many backup sets should you have of a hard disk drive, and where should you store those backup sets, if at all possible?

30. Assume you use MSBACKUP to perform a full backup of drives C and D on October 31, 1994. What name would MSBACKUP assign to the backup file?

TUTORIAL ASSIGNMENTS

1. **Developing a Backup Strategy**: Suppose you want to develop a backup strategy for your hard disk. What backup strategy would you choose based on the following factors, and how would you implement this backup strategy?
   Use the following factors in choosing a backup strategy:

   ◆ You create and modify many different files each work day.
   ◆ You want to keep different versions of the same file in the event you need to restore a specific version of a file.
   ◆ You store all your work files in one branch of the directory tree on your hard disk.

   Explain how you would implement these backups with either MSBACKUP (in DOS 6.0 or 6.2) or BACKUP (in DOS 5.0 or 6.0).

2. **Backing Up Directories with BACKUP in DOS 5.0 and 6.0**: This Tutorial Assignment assumes that the AceForms directory you used in this tutorial is stored on the hard disk you are using. Perform the following operations, and describe the commands or selections you make for each step.
   a. Unconditionally format a diskette to use for the backup.
   b. Back up the BUSINESS directory, and create a log file in the DOS directory.
   c. Back up the RESUMES directory to the same backup diskette, and log the backup process to the same log file. Note: BACKUP automatically adds to the existing file.
   d. Display the contents of the log file.
   e. Display a list of the backed-up files on the backup diskette.
   f. Remove the RESUMES directory from the hard disk.
   g. Restore the RESUMES directory to the hard disk.
   h. Verify the restore operation.

3. **Backing Up Directories with MSBACKUP in DOS 6.0 and 6.2**: This Tutorial Assignment assumes that the AceForms directory you used in this tutorial is stored on the hard disk you are using. Perform the following operations, and describe the commands or selections you make for each step.
   a. Unconditionally format a diskette to use for the backup.
   b. Load the MSBACKUP utility.
   c. Create a setup file from DEFAULT.SET to store settings that you specify for a backup.
   d. Select the CASHFLOW and PRJCASH directories for the backup.
   e. Perform the backup.
   f. Exit MSBACKUP and remove the CASHFLOW directory.
   g. Load MSBACKUP and restore the CASHFLOW directory.
   h. Exit MSBACKUP and verify the restore operation.

4. **Using XCOPY to Back Up a Directory**: This Tutorial Assignment assumes that the AceForms directory you used in this tutorial is stored on the hard disk you are using. Perform the following operations, and describe the commands or selections you make for each step.
   a. Unconditionally format a diskette to use for the backup.
   b. Back up the INVOICES directory with the XCOPY command.
   c. Display a directory tree of the backup diskette to verify its directory structure.
   d. Back up the REPORTS directory with the XCOPY command.
   e. Display a directory tree of the backup diskette to verify its directory structure.
   f. Remove the INVOICES directory from the hard disk.
   g. Restore the INVOICES directory to the hard disk.
   h. Verify the restore operation.

5. **Comparison of BACKUP and MSBACKUP in DOS 6.0**: One of the important considerations people face when backing up their computer system is the amount of time required for the backup. In DOS 6.0, you can use either BACKUP or MSBACKUP to back up your hard disk. In this exercise, you will compare the differences between these two backup utilities by calculating the time required for each of these utilities to back up a directory and its subdirectories and files.

This Tutorial Assignment assumes that the AceForms directory that you used in this tutorial is stored on the hard disk that you are using. Perform the following operations.

Using BACKUP:

a. Unconditionally format a diskette to use for the first backup.

b. Record the time in minutes and seconds when you start the first backup.

c. Use BACKUP to back up the entire AceForms directory to the backup diskette, and create a log file in the DOS directory.

d. Record the time in minutes and seconds when the backup ends. Calculate the amount of time required for the backup.

Using MSBACKUP:

e. Unconditionally format the diskette so that you can use it for the second backup.

f. Record the time in minutes and seconds when you start the second backup.

g. Load MSBACKUP, create a new setup file, specify backup settings, select the AceForms directory and its subdirectories, save the settings in the setup file, and perform a full backup of the AceForms directory.

h. After the backup is complete, exit MSBACKUP and record the time in minutes and seconds when you end the backup process. Calculate the amount of time required for the backup.

Although this backup is on a smaller scale than one you would normally perform on a computer system, compare the differences in time required for the two types of backups. Based only on this time difference, which backup utility would you choose to use? What other factors might affect your decision to use one of the two backup utilities?

ADVANCED DOS
5.0 / 6.0 / 6.2

Tutorials

◆

Using Troubleshooting Tools

OBJECTIVES

In this tutorial you will learn to:

◆ Prepare a boot disk

◆ Examine and set file attributes

◆ Check the status of a hard disk or diskette

◆ Track deleted files

◆ Undelete erased files

◆ Unformat a reformatted diskette

◆ Use a diagnostic utility

Imagine you have a new position as a microcomputer specialist in a large firm. The job requires you to develop a set of troubleshooting tools and skills to resolve common problems encountered by other staff members with their computer systems. Your list of initial duties calls for you to prepare a boot disk for each computer system, set file attributes for important system files, install a utility that keeps track of deleted files, and print a diagnostic report for each computer system. You also must show staff members how to check the status of their hard disks and diskettes, how to recover erased files, and how to unformat diskettes. Staff members will then be able to reduce the likelihood of disk errors on their hard disks and client diskettes. They will also be able to recover client files that they inadvertently delete and client diskettes that they might inadvertently format.

◆

THE IMPORTANCE OF A BOOT DISK

Your first task is to prepare a boot disk for each computer to help avoid problems if one of two situations arises: (1) if drive C fails on a computer system, you cannot boot the computer from that hard disk; or (2) if DOS experiences difficulties reading drive C, you might not be able to access important files stored on the hard disk. If either of these situations occurs, you can use a specially prepared diskette, called a boot disk, to start your computer from drive A. A **boot disk**, or **system disk**, is a diskette that contains the DOS operating system files and, in some cases, other files you might need to configure your computer. Once you start a computer with a boot disk, you can attempt to locate the source of a problem and resolve it. You might need to reformat the hard disk, reinstall software applications and utilities, and restore your document or data files from a backup set. If you keep a backup copy of software installed on your computer system, then instead of reinstalling the software from scratch, you can simply restore the software from the backup copy.

If your computer system becomes infected with a computer virus, you can start your computer system from drive A with a write-protected boot disk that also contains anti-viral software. The write-protection prevents the computer virus from gaining access to the boot disk. After you boot the computer, you can scan the system for computer viruses and attempt to remove any you find.

Using the System Switch

One way to prepare a boot disk is to format the diskette with the **System switch** (/S). After DOS formats the diskette, it copies the operating system files from your hard drive to the diskette. If you are using MS-DOS 6.0 or 6.2, the operating system files are named IO.SYS, MSDOS.SYS, DBLSPACE.BIN, and COMMAND.COM. If you are using PC-DOS on an IBM microcomputer, the operating system files are named IBMBIO.COM, IBMDOS.COM, and COMMAND.COM. DOS 5.0 contains the same operating system files as 6.0 and 6.2, except for DBLSPACE.BIN.

The Operating System Files

IO.SYS in MS-DOS and IBMBIO.COM in PC-DOS contain the operating system program code for handling basic input and output (I/O) operations. This part of DOS communicates with the peripherals connected to the computer system. MSDOS.SYS in MS-DOS and IBMDOS.COM in PC-DOS contain the operating system program code for managing drives, directories, and files. This part of DOS, which constitutes its core, works in conjunction with IO.SYS (or IBMBIO.COM) to control the transfer of data to and from the peripherals. DBLSPACE.BIN in DOS 6.0 and 6.2 allows DOS to access compressed drives. In these DOS versions, you can increase the storage capacity of your hard disk by compressing program and data files by 60% to 100%.

COMMAND.COM is the **command interpreter**, also called the **command processor**. One of the primary functions of this program is to interpret the commands that you enter at the DOS prompt. It is also responsible for displaying the DOS prompt, for locating and loading the program code for external commands and software applications, and for redirecting input and output.

Preparing a Boot Disk

Now you are ready to prepare a boot disk for your computer. Usually you use drive A to prepare a boot disk, but if drive B is the same size and supports the same disk storage capacities as drive A, you can use drive B. However, to actually boot your computer, you must be able to use a boot disk in drive A.

Because you will later use the boot disk from drive A to start your system, you will prepare the boot disk in drive A. You can use your Tutorial Disk, but if your Tutorial Disk is a different size than drive A, you will have to use a diskette that fits that drive. Because the formatting process will erase all information on the boot disk that you prepare, be sure you no longer need the information on the diskette. After you prepare the boot disk, you will reboot your computer, so you do not need to install DOSKEY and specify default switches for the DIR command.

To prepare a boot disk:

1. Insert your Tutorial Disk, or another diskette, into drive A.
2. Format the diskette with the appropriate formatting option:
   - ◆ To format a high-density diskette in a high-density drive, a double-density diskette in a double-density drive, or an extra-high-density diskette in an extra-high-density drive, type **FORMAT A: /U /S** and press **[Enter]**.
   - ◆ To format a 3½-inch double-density diskette in a high-density or extra-high-density drive, type **FORMAT A: /F:720 /U /S** and press **[Enter]**.
   - ◆ To format a 5¼-inch double-density diskette in a high-density drive, type **FORMAT A: /F:360 /U /S** and press **[Enter]**.

   If you are using your Tutorial Disk or reformatting another diskette, the *Unconditional switch* (/U) will erase any information already on the diskette. If you are using a new diskette, DOS automatically performs an *Unconditional format* on the diskette. The *System switch* (/S) copies the operating system files to the diskette after DOS formats it.

   FORMAT prompts you to insert a diskette into drive A. If you have not yet inserted a diskette, do so now.

3. Press [**Enter**]. After the formatting process is complete, DOS copies the operating system files to the diskette and then prompts for a volume label. See Figure 7-1.

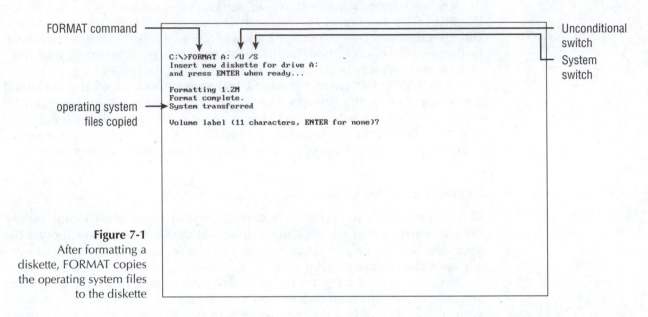

FORMAT command

Unconditional switch

System switch

operating system files copied

```
C:\>FORMAT A: /U /S
Insert new diskette for drive A:
and press ENTER when ready...

Formatting 1.2M
Format complete.
System transferred

Volume label (11 characters, ENTER for none)?
```

Figure 7-1
After formatting a diskette, FORMAT copies the operating system files to the diskette

4. Type **BOOT DISK** and press [**Enter**]. DOS displays information on the total disk space, the amount of storage space used by the operating system, the remaining available disk space, the size of each allocation unit, and the number of allocation units. See Figure 7-2. Your disk usage information might be different. The information reported on your system will depend on the diskette size, the diskette storage capacity, and the DOS version.

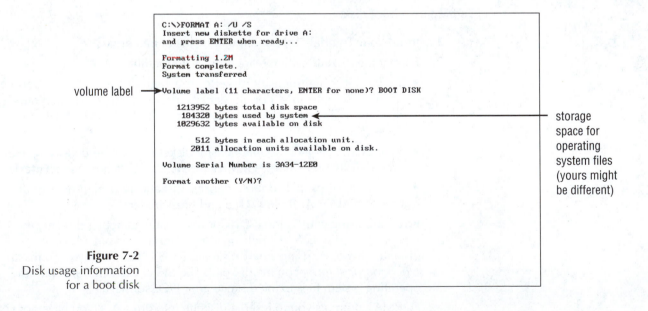

volume label

```
C:\>FORMAT A: /U /S
Insert new diskette for drive A:
and press ENTER when ready...

Formatting 1.2M
Format complete.
System transferred

Volume label (11 characters, ENTER for none)? BOOT DISK

  1213952 bytes total disk space
   184320 bytes used by system
  1029632 bytes available on disk

      512 bytes in each allocation unit.
     2011 allocation units available on disk.

Volume Serial Number is 3A34-12E0

Format another (Y/N)?
```

storage space for operating system files (yours might be different)

Figure 7-2
Disk usage information for a boot disk

5. When FORMAT asks if you to want to format another diskette, type **N** and press **[Enter]**. DOS then displays the DOS prompt.

6. Type **DIR A:** and press **[Enter]**. DOS displays a directory with one filename, COMMAND.COM. See Figure 7-3. Your serial number will be different, and your directory information might be different. The file size, date, and time for COMMAND.COM depends on the DOS version you use. The free storage space depends on the diskette size and storage capacity.

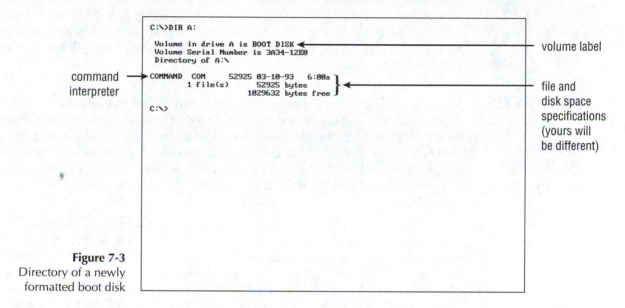

command
interpreter →

← volume label

file and
disk space
specifications
(yours will
be different)

```
C:\>DIR A:

     Volume in drive A is BOOT DISK
     Volume Serial Number is 3A34-12E0
     Directory of A:\

COMMAND  COM       52925 03-10-93    6:00a
          1 file(s)       52925 bytes
                        1029632 bytes free

C:\>
```

Figure 7-3
Directory of a newly
formatted boot disk

DOS does not show you the other operating system files because they are **hidden files** or **system files**. DOS does not display hidden files in a directory listing to protect them from deletion or modification. In MS-DOS 6.0 and 6.2, the hidden system files are IO.SYS, MSDOS.SYS, and DBLSPACE.BIN. In MS-DOS 5.0, the hidden files are IO.SYS and MSDOS.SYS. Only COMMAND.COM is displayed in directory listings. Even though COMMAND.COM is an important part of DOS, it is not considered a system file because you can purchase and use another command processor if you prefer.

Testing a Boot Disk

Next you want to test the boot disk to ensure that it is reliable.

To test the newly prepared boot disk:

1. Be sure your boot disk is in drive A.

2. Press **[Ctrl][Alt][Del]** or press your computer's **Reset button**. After the computer reboots, DOS prompts for the date and the time. Press **[Enter]** twice to accept the current settings. You will then see the DOS prompt for drive A, which indicates that you have successfully booted your computer.

During a reboot, you will notice the screen clear when the contents of RAM are erased. Then a program stored on a ROM chip checks drive A for a boot disk containing operating system files. If drive A contains a boot disk, then the computer boots from drive A and displays the A prompt. If there is no boot disk in drive A, this program will check drive C. If the operating system files are found on drive C, the computer boots from that drive and displays the C prompt.

If you reboot your computer system with a diskette in drive A that is not a boot disk, you will see a "Non-System disk or disk error" message. If you see this message, either remove the diskette from drive A and press any key to continue or insert a boot disk into drive A and press any key to continue. If you press a key with a non-system diskette in drive A, you will see the same error message again.

USING THE SYSTEM COMMAND TO PREPARE A BOOT DISK

You can also use the System (SYS) command to prepare a boot disk. If you have formatted a diskette and then realize that you want to use that diskette as a boot disk, you can use this external command to copy the operating system files to the diskette. This command is also useful if you need to update the system files on a boot disk or on a hard disk, because this command will copy over the existing system files. The syntax for this external command is:

SYS *drive:*

The drive is the one that will receive a copy of the operating system files.

It is a good idea to prepare more than one boot disk. If drive C fails and if your first boot disk does not work for some reason, you have another boot disk on which to rely. So you decide to prepare a second boot disk with the SYS command. You also realize that you must reboot your computer system from drive C or the network drive because your boot disk does not contain all the files necessary for the proper configuration of your computer system.

To reconfigure your computer system:

1. Remove your first boot disk from drive A.

2. Press **[Ctrl][Alt][Del]** or press your computer's **Reset button**. The computer reboots.

3. If necessary, display the DOS prompt for the root directory of drive C.

4. Insert the Exercise Disk or another diskette in drive A.

5. Format the diskette with the appropriate formatting option:
   ◆ To format a high-density diskette in a high-density drive, a double-density diskette in a double-density drive, or an extra-high-density diskette in an extra-high-density drive, type **FORMAT A: /U** and press **[Enter]**.
   ◆ To format a 3½-inch double-density diskette in a high-density or extra-high-density drive, type **FORMAT A: /F:720 /U** and press **[Enter]**.
   ◆ To format a 5¼-inch double-density diskette in a high-density drive, type **FORMAT A: /F:360 /U** and press **[Enter]**.

If you are using your Exercise Disk or reformatting another diskette, the Unconditional switch (/U) will erase any information already on the diskette. If you are using a new diskette, DOS automatically performs an Unconditional format on the diskette.

FORMAT prompts you to insert a diskette into drive A. If you have not yet inserted a diskette, do so now.

6. Press [Enter]. After the formatting process is complete, DOS prompts for a volume label.

7. Type **BOOT DISK** and press [Enter]. DOS displays information on the total disk space, the available disk space, the size of each allocation unit, and the number of allocation units.

8. When FORMAT asks if you to want to format another diskette, type **N** and press [Enter]. DOS then displays the DOS prompt.

Using the System Command

You are now ready to copy the operating system files from drive C onto your newly formatted diskette using the SYS command.

To copy the system files to your second boot disk:

1. Type **SYS A:** and press [Enter]. After the operation is complete, SYS displays the message "System transferred." If SYS displays an error message indicating that it cannot copy COMMAND.COM, ask your instructor or technical support person for assistance. COMMAND.COM might be a hidden file.

2. Type **DIR A:** and press [Enter]. DOS displays one filename, COMMAND.COM. See Figure 7-4. The other system files are hidden, and their filenames are not displayed in the directory. Your directory information might be different. Again, the file size, date, and time for COMMAND.COM depend on the DOS version, and the free storage space depends on the diskette size and storage capacity.

SYS command ⟶   target drive

command interpreter ⟶

file and disk specifications (yours might be different)

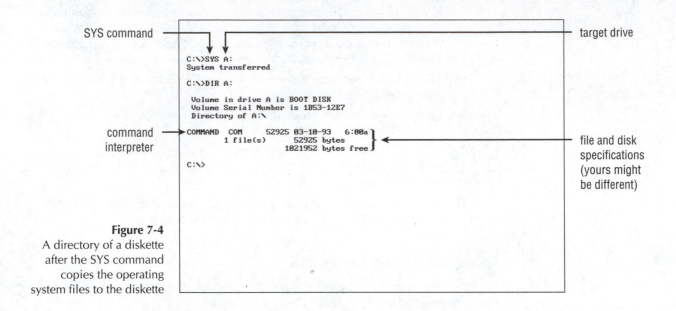

```
C:\>SYS A:
System transferred

C:\>DIR A:

 Volume in drive A is BOOT DISK
 Volume Serial Number is 1B53-12E7
 Directory of A:\

COMMAND  COM      52925 03-10-93   6:00a
        1 file(s)         52925 bytes
                        1021952 bytes free

C:\>
```

Figure 7-4
A directory of a diskette after the SYS command copies the operating system files to the diskette

Now test this boot disk.

3. Press **[Ctrl][Alt][Del]** or press your computer's **Reset button**. After the system reboots, DOS prompts for the date and time. Press **[Enter]** twice to accept the current settings. DOS displays the prompt for drive A, indicating your second boot disk worked.

Now reconfigure your computer system again.

4. Remove your boot disk from drive A.

5. Press **[Ctrl][Alt][Del]** or press your computer's **Reset button**. The computer system reboots.

6. If necessary, display the DOS prompt for drive C.

Next, load DOSKEY and specify switches for the DIR command.

5.0 6.0

6.2

7. Type **DOSKEY** and press **[Enter]**. If you are using DOS 5.0 or 6.0, DOS displays the message "DOSKey installed" if DOSKEY is not already installed on your computer. If you do not see this message with DOS 5.0 or 6.0, DOSKEY is already loaded. DOS 6.2 will not display a message.

8. Type **SET DIRCMD=/P /O** and press **[Enter]**. When viewing directory listing, DOS will display subdirectories and files in alphabetical order and will pause after each screen.

9. Type **SET** and press **[Enter]** to verify that you correctly entered the switches for the DIRCMD environment variable. If not, repeat Step 8.

Whenever you prepare a boot disk, test it to be sure it is working properly. Do not prepare a boot disk and leave it untested, assuming it will work when you most need it. As an additional precautionary measure, you may want to prepare a second or even third boot disk. You might also want to include other DOS utilities, such as the SYS utility, and other important configuration

IDENTIFYING SYSTEM, HIDDEN, AND READ-ONLY FILES

You can view the names of the hidden operating system files stored on your boot disk by using the DIR command and its **Attribute switch** (/A). In addition to keeping track of filenames, extensions, sizes, dates, and times, DOS also keeps track of file attributes. An **attribute** is a special characteristic assigned to a file. Attributes include the System, Hidden, Read-Only, and Archive attributes. The **System attribute**, represented by the code "S," identifies a file as a system file. The **Hidden attribute**, represented by the code "H," indicates that the file is not displayed in a directory listing. The **Read-Only attribute**, represented by the code "R," indicates that you can read from, but not write to, a file. This attribute protects a file from inadvertent deletion or modification. DOS assigns the **Archive attribute**, represented by the code "A," to a file that is either a new or modified file to indicate that it has not been backed up. DOS uses the Archive attribute when you perform an incremental backup to identify which files have been created or modified since the last backup.

To use the Attribute switch (/A) to locate a file with one of these attributes, you include a one-letter code for the type of attribute with the Attribute switch. Figure 7-5 lists these options.

Command	Effect
DIR /AA	Displays a list of files with the Archive attribute (A)
DIR /AH	Displays a list of files with the Hidden attribute (H)
DIR /AR	Displays a list of files with the Read-Only attribute (R)
DIR /AS	Displays a list of files with the System attribute (S)

Figure 7-5
Options for displaying attributes with the Attribute switch

If you want to view all files in all directories on a hard disk or diskette that have a specific attribute, you can specify the Attribute switch in combination with the **Subdirectory switch** (/S). For example, to display a list of all system files in all directories on drive C, you would enter this command from the root directory:

DIR /AS /S

The first switch, /AS, is the Attribute switch, with an option for selecting System (S) files. The second switch, /S, is the Subdirectory switch, which examines all subordinate directories below the current directory (or the directory you specify).

These switches are useful when you are troubleshooting problems with a computer system or when you need to reconfigure a computer system. You can quickly identify System, Hidden, and Read-Only files that are important to the operation of the computer system.

Now let's check for system files on your boot disk.

To view the system files:

   1. If necessary, insert one of your boot disks into drive A, then change from drive C to drive A. Drive A is now the default drive.

6.0 6.2

5.0

2. Type **DIR /AS** and press **[Enter]**. DOS displays files on your boot disk with the System attribute. See Figure 7-6. The operating system files with the System attribute in MS-DOS 6.0 and 6.2 are IO.SYS, MSDOS.SYS, and DBLSPACE.BIN. Your directory information might be different. If you are using MS-DOS 5.0, you will see IO.SYS and MSDOS.SYS, but not DBLSPACE.BIN. If you are using PC-DOS, the operating system files are IBMBIO.COM and IBMDOS.COM. DOS does not include COMMAND.COM because it is not assigned the System attribute.

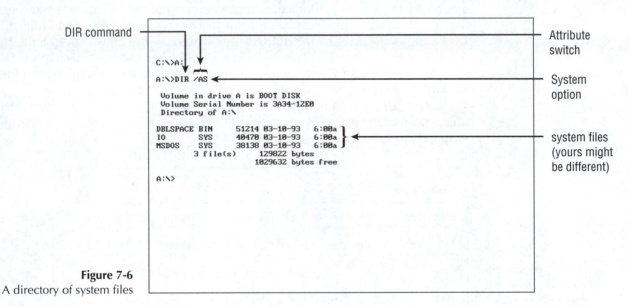

DIR command

Attribute switch

System option

system files (yours might be different)

```
C:\>A:

A:\>DIR /AS

 Volume in drive A is BOOT DISK
 Volume Serial Number is 3A34-12E0
 Directory of A:\

DBLSPACE BIN      51214 03-10-93   6:00a
IO       SYS      40470 03-10-93   6:00a
MSDOS    SYS      38138 03-10-93   6:00a
         3 file(s)      129822 bytes
                       1029632 bytes free

A:\>
```

Figure 7-6
A directory of system files

System files are also assigned the Hidden and Read-Only attributes to protect them from inadvertent deletion or modification. You can use the Attribute switch to identify which files DOS treats as Hidden and Read-Only.

To view Hidden files in a directory:

6.0 6.2

5.0

1. Press **[↑]** (Up Arrow) until you recall the command "DIR /AS." Press **[Backspace]** to delete the "S," then type **H** (for the Hidden attribute). The command should read "DIR /AH." Press **[Enter]**. DOS displays files assigned the Hidden attribute on your boot disk. See Figure 7-7. The operating system files with the Hidden attribute in MS-DOS 6.0 and 6.2 are IO.SYS, MSDOS.SYS, and DBLSPACE.BIN. Your directory information might be different. If you are using MS-DOS 5.0, you will see IO.SYS and MSDOS.SYS, but not DBLSPACE.BIN. If you are using PC-DOS, the operating system files are IBMBIO.COM and IBMDOS.COM. DOS does not include COMMAND.COM because it is not assigned the Hidden attribute.

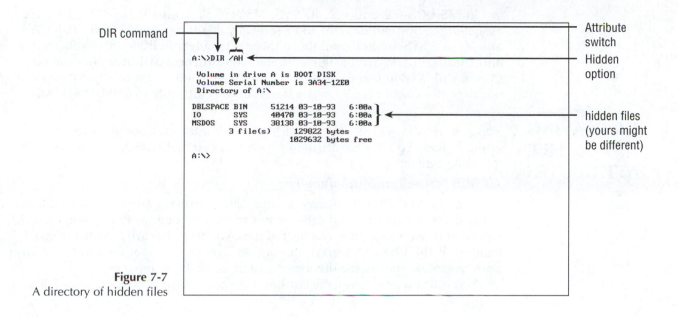

DIR command

Attribute switch

Hidden option

hidden files (yours might be different)

```
A:\>DIR /AH

Volume in drive A is BOOT DISK
Volume Serial Number is 3A34-12E0
Directory of A:\

DBLSPACE BIN     51214 03-10-93    6:00a
IO       SYS     40470 03-10-93    6:00a
MSDOS    SYS     38138 03-10-93    6:00a
         3 file(s)      129822 bytes
                       1029632 bytes free

A:\>
```

Figure 7-7
A directory of hidden files

Now view Read-Only files in a directory.

2. Press **[↑]** (Up Arrow) until you recall the command "DIR /AH." Press **[Backspace]** to delete the "H," then type **R** (for the Read-Only attribute). The command should read "DIR /AR." Press **[Enter]**. DOS displays the Read-Only files on your boot disk. See Figure 7-8. This figure shows the operating system files in MS-DOS 6.0 with the Read-Only attribute. MS-DOS 6.2 also assigns the Read-Only attribute to COMMAND.COM. If you are using MS-DOS 5.0, IO.SYS and MSDOS.SYS are assigned the Read-Only attribute. If you are using PC-DOS, the operating system files are IBMBIO.COM and IBMDOS.COM. Your directory information will therefore depend on the DOS version.

6.0 6.2

5.0

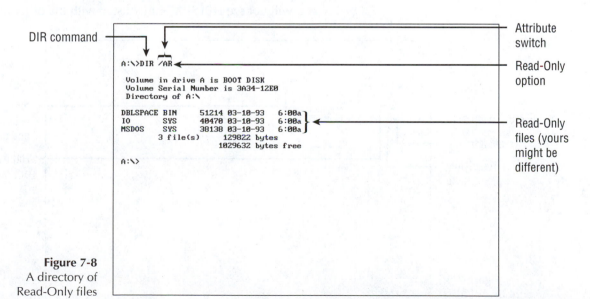

DIR command

Attribute switch

Read-Only option

Read-Only files (yours might be different)

```
A:\>DIR /AR

Volume in drive A is BOOT DISK
Volume Serial Number is 3A34-12E0
Directory of A:\

DBLSPACE BIN     51214 03-10-93    6:00a
IO       SYS     40470 03-10-93    6:00a
MSDOS    SYS     38138 03-10-93    6:00a
         3 file(s)      129822 bytes
                       1029632 bytes free

A:\>
```

Figure 7-8
A directory of
Read-Only files

In MS-DOS 6.0 and 6.2, IO.SYS, MSDOS.SYS, and DBLSPACE.BIN are assigned the System, Hidden, and Read-Only attributes. In MS-DOS 5.0, IO.SYS and MSDOS.SYS are assigned these three attributes. In PC-DOS, IBMBIO.COM and IBMDOS.COM are assigned these same three attributes. In contrast, COMMAND.COM in these versions is not assigned any of these attributes, with one exception. MS-DOS 6.2 assigns the Read-Only attribute to COMMAND.COM.

DISPLAYING FILE ATTRIBUTES

You can use the ATTRIB command to view all attributes assigned to a file or group of files. To view file attributes with this external command, you use the following syntax:

ATTRIB [*drive:*][*path*][*filename*]

If you enter ATTRIB without any parameters, it displays attributes for all files in the current directory and drive. You can specify a single file by name or, if you want to view attributes of selected files, you use wildcards in the file specification. If the files are stored on another drive or in another directory, or both, you must specify the drive name, path, or both parameters.

You will now examine all the attributes assigned to the files on your boot disk.

To view the attributes of files on your boot disk:

1. Be sure one of your boot disks is in drive A, and be sure drive A is the current drive.

2. Type **ATTRIB** and press **[Enter]**. DOS displays a list of all files on your boot disk by name and lists their attributes. See Figure 7-9. ATTRIB displays the attributes before the drive, path, and filename of each file. An "A" indicates a file with an Archive attribute, "H" indicates a Hidden file, "R" indicates a Read-Only file, and "S" indicates a System file. In this example, IO.SYS, MSDOS.SYS, and DBLSPACE.BIN are assigned all three attributes. COMMAND.COM is assigned only the Archive attribute. Your attribute information and directory order might differ. If you are using DOS 5.0, you will not see DBLSPACE.BIN listed with the other filenames.

5.0

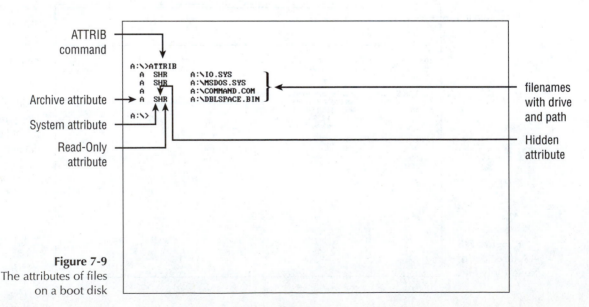

Figure 7-9
The attributes of files on a boot disk

CHANGING FILE ATTRIBUTES

You can also use the ATTRIB command to assign or remove file attributes. For example, if you want to protect a file, such as COMMAND.COM, from deletion, you can assign it the Read-Only attribute. To assign or remove an attribute for a file or group of files, you use the following general syntax:

ATTRIB [*filename*] ±[*attribute*]

To assign an attribute, you use the plus sign followed by a one-letter code for the attribute. For example, to assign the Read-Only attribute to COMMAND.COM, you would use this command:

ATTRIB COMMAND.COM +R

To remove an attribute, you use the minus sign before the code for the attribute. For example, to remove a Read-Only attribute assigned to COMMAND.COM, you would enter this command:

ATTRIB COMMAND.COM –R

You can assign and remove several attributes by listing each attribute switch. Figure 7-10 shows the switches for assigning and removing the Archive, Hidden, and Read-Only attributes.

Switch	Used
+A	To assign the Archive attribute to a file or group of files
–A	To remove the Archive attribute from a file or group of files
+H	To assign the Hidden attribute to a file or group of files
–H	To remove the Hidden attribute from a file or group of files
+R	To assign the Read-Only attribute to a file or group of files
–R	To remove the Read-Only attribute from a file or group of files

Figure 7-10
Common switches for the ATTRIB command

You can also assign attributes to a subdirectory and clear subdirectory attributes by specifying the subdirectory's name when you use the ATTRIB command. For example, you might want to assign the Hidden attribute to a subdirectory to limit access to that subdirectory and its files.

On your boot disk, you want to assign the Read-Only and Hidden attributes to COMMAND.COM so that you or someone else cannot inadvertently delete this important file. Since the Read-Only attribute is already assigned to COMMAND.COM in DOS 6.2, you can skip Steps 2 and 3 and continue with Step 4 if you are using DOS 6.2.

To assign the Read-Only attribute:

1. Be sure one of your boot disks is in drive A, and be sure drive A is the current drive.

5.0 6.0
6.2

2. If you are using DOS 5.0 or 6.0, type **ATTRIB COMMAND.COM** and press **[Spacebar]** once, then type **+R** and press **[Enter]**. DOS displays the DOS prompt. If you are using DOS 6.2, skip this step and Step 3 and continue with Step 4.

Now view its file attributes.

3. If you are using DOS 5.0 or 6.0, press **[↑]** (Up Arrow) until you recall the command "ATTRIB." Then press **[Enter]**. ATTRIB shows attributes for files on your boot disk in drive A. COMMAND.COM now has the Read-Only attribute. See Figure 7-11. Your attribute information might be different. If you are using DOS 5.0, DBLSPACE.BIN will not appear in your directory listing.

5.0

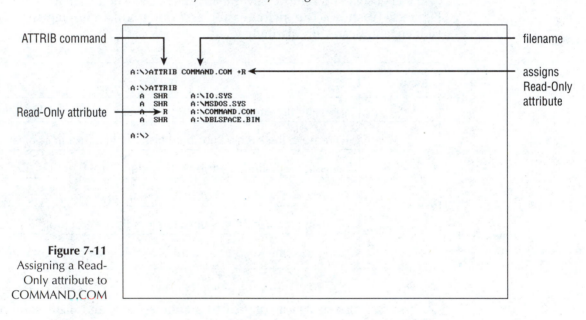

Figure 7-11
Assigning a Read-Only attribute to COMMAND.COM

Now test the Read-Only attribute.

4. *Be sure COMMAND.COM is assigned the Read-Only attribute.* Then type **DEL COMMAND.COM** and press **[Enter]**. DOS displays the message "Access denied." See Figure 7-12. DOS will not let you delete or modify this file.

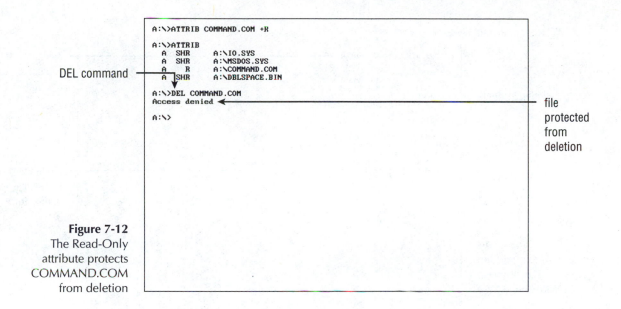

DEL command

```
A:\>ATTRIB COMMAND.COM +R

A:\>ATTRIB
  A   SHR      A:\IO.SYS
  A   SHR      A:\MSDOS.SYS
  A    R       A:\COMMAND.COM
  A   SHR      A:\DBLSPACE.BIN

A:\>DEL COMMAND.COM
Access denied

A:\>
```

file
protected
from
deletion

Figure 7-12
The Read-Only
attribute protects
COMMAND.COM
from deletion

Now you want to make COMMAND.COM a hidden file.

To assign the Hidden attribute to COMMAND.COM:

1. Press [↑] (Up Arrow) until you recall the command "ATTRIB COMMAND.COM +R." Press **[Backspace]** to delete the "R" and type **H**. The command should read "ATTRIB COMMAND.COM +H." Then press **[Enter]**. DOS displays the DOS prompt.

2. Press [↑] (Up Arrow) until you recall the command "ATTRIB." Then press **[Enter]**. ATTRIB shows attributes for files on your boot disk in drive A. COMMAND.COM now has the Hidden attribute. Your attribute information might differ. If you are using DOS 5.0, DBLSPACE.BIN will not appear in your directory listing.

5.0

Now test this attribute.

3. Type **DIR** and press **[Enter]**. DOS displays the message "File not found." See Figure 7-13. Although this command usually indicates that a diskette has no files, DOS is actually telling you that there are no files *without* the Hidden attribute.

ATTRIB command

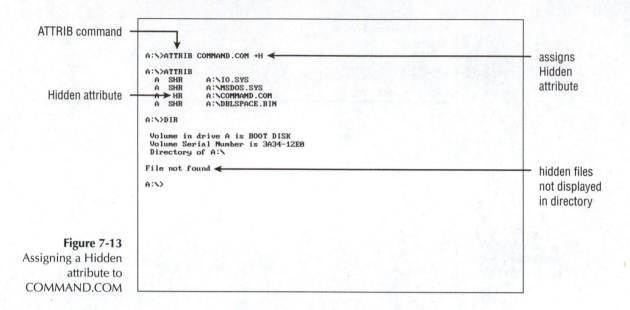

```
A:\>ATTRIB COMMAND.COM +H          ◄────────────── assigns
                                                   Hidden
A:\>ATTRIB                                         attribute
  A   SHR     A:\IO.SYS
  A   SHR     A:\MSDOS.SYS
  A   HR      A:\COMMAND.COM
  A   SHR     A:\DBLSPACE.BIN

A:\>DIR

  Volume in drive A is BOOT DISK
  Volume Serial Number is 3A34-12E0
  Directory of A:\

  File not found  ◄────────────────────────────── hidden files
                                                   not displayed
A:\>                                               in directory
```

Hidden attribute

Figure 7-13
Assigning a Hidden
attribute to
COMMAND.COM

REMOVING FILE ATTRIBUTES

You decide that the Read-Only attribute is the only one you need to protect COMMAND.COM on your boot disk, so you want to remove the Hidden attribute.

To remove the Hidden attribute:

1. Press [↑] (Up Arrow) until you recall the command "ATTRIB COMMAND.COM +H." Press [←] (Left Arrow) until the cursor is on the plus sign. Type – (a minus sign). The command should read "ATTRIB COMMAND.COM –H." Then press **[Enter]**. DOS displays the DOS prompt.

2. Press [↑] (Up Arrow) until you recall the command "ATTRIB." Then press **[Enter]**. ATTRIB shows attributes for files on your boot disk in drive A. COMMAND.COM no longer has the Hidden attribute.

3. Type **DIR** and press **[Enter]**. DOS displays COMMAND.COM in the directory listing. See Figure 7-14.

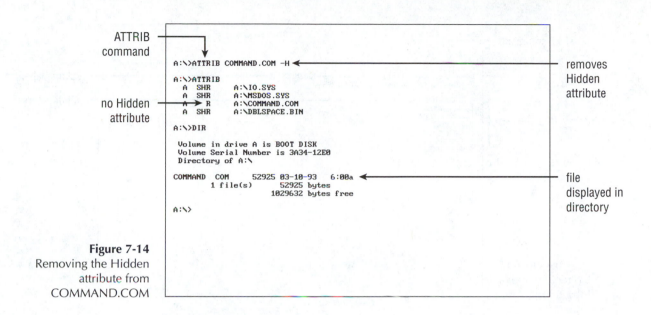

ATTRIB command → `A:\>ATTRIB COMMAND.COM -H` ← removes Hidden attribute

```
A:\>ATTRIB
  A   SHR      A:\IO.SYS
  A   SHR      A:\MSDOS.SYS
  A     R      A:\COMMAND.COM
  A   SHR      A:\DBLSPACE.BIN

A:\>DIR

 Volume in drive A is BOOT DISK
 Volume Serial Number is 3A34-12E0
 Directory of A:\

COMMAND  COM      52925 03-10-93   6:00a
         1 file(s)        52925 bytes
                        1029632 bytes free

A:\>
```

no Hidden attribute → (pointing to `A:\COMMAND.COM` line)

file displayed in directory ← (pointing to `COMMAND COM` line)

Figure 7-14
Removing the Hidden
attribute from
COMMAND.COM

Now that you are able to control file attributes, you can protect important files on your hard disk drive from accidental deletion or modification, you can view currently assigned file attributes to determine if any changes are warranted, and you can examine your hard disk for important hidden or system files before you reconfigure or reformat the hard disk.

PREPARING NEW TUTORIAL AND EXERCISE DISKS

You will need to prepare a new Tutorial Disk and Exercise Disk to complete the remainder of this tutorial. Ask your instructor or technical support person for a copy of the DOS Tools Disk.

To make copies of the DOS Tools Disk:

1. Insert the DOS Tools Disk into drive A (or drive B), and change to the drive with the DOS Tools Disk.

2. Follow the instructions on pages 29 through 31 of Tutorial 1 for using the DISKCOPY command to make a copy of a diskette. During this disk copy operation, your source diskette is the DOS Tools Disk and your destination diskette is your Tutorial Disk.

3. Repeat Step 2 and copy the contents of the DOS Tools Disk onto your Exercise Disk. This time your source diskette is the DOS Tools Disk and your destination diskette is the Exercise Disk.

Now view a directory tree of the new Tutorial Disk.

4. If necessary, remove the Exercise Disk and insert the Tutorial Disk in drive A (or drive B).

5. Type **TREE** and press **[Enter]**. TREE displays a directory tree of the diskette. See Figure 7-15.

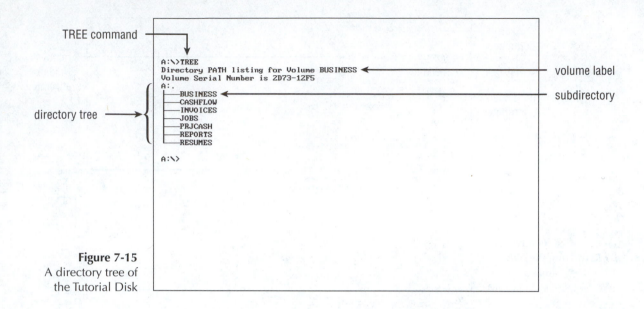

TREE command

volume label

subdirectory

directory tree

Figure 7-15
A directory tree of
the Tutorial Disk

6. Type **TREE /F ¦ MORE** and press **[Enter]**. DOS displays a partial directory tree with filenames by subdirectory and pauses. Press **[Spacebar]** or any other key until you view the remaining directory structure and return to the DOS prompt.

7. Return the Tools Disk to your instructor or technical support person.

This is a good opportunity to take a break.

CHECKING THE STATUS OF DISKS

One of the important responsibilities assigned to you by your supervisor is to check the hard disks on your company's computers for errors. If errors are found, you must attempt to remove them from the hard disks.

You can use the Check Disk (CHKDSK) command to check for potential problems in the logical structure of a hard disk. When DOS checks the **logical structure** of a disk, it examines the File Allocation Tables, the directory file, and the subdirectory files to determine if there are any errors in the allocation or usage of space on a hard disk or diskette.

The **File Allocation Table** contains a list of each allocation unit or cluster on a disk as well as information on whether each allocation unit or cluster is available, in use, or defective (i.e., contains a bad sector). For example, when you save a large file to a hard disk or diskette, DOS records the number of the starting cluster in the **directory file** (or a subdirectory file), along with the filename, extension, size, date, and time of the file. From the directory or subdirectory file, DOS knows where the first cluster of the file is stored on disk. Next to that cluster number, in the File Allocation Table, DOS records the number of the cluster where the next part of the file is stored, and so on. Each cluster, therefore, *points* to the next cluster of the file. The last cluster is identified by a special end-of-file (EOF) code.

When you issue a command to retrieve a file from a hard disk or diskette, DOS uses the directory file and File Allocation Table to locate each cluster on the disk or diskette, and reassembles the file so that you can use it.

Lost Clusters

Errors can develop in the File Allocation Table. For example, some of the clusters that belong to a file may become lost clusters. A **lost cluster** is a cluster on a hard disk or diskette that does not belong to any file. The lost cluster contains program code or data, but there is no record in the File Allocation Table to indicate which file the cluster belongs to. Lost clusters may develop when a power failure occurs, when you reboot a computer system after it locks up, or when brownouts or power surges occur. In these cases, DOS may not be able to record information on the location of all clusters of a file in the File Allocation Table or the starting cluster in the directory file. Over time, lost clusters may increase in number, waste valuable disk space, and lead to further disk errors. Lost cluster errors are the most common type of problem encountered on hard disks.

Using Diagnostic and Fixup Modes

By default, the CHKDSK command operates in **diagnostic mode**, that is, if CHKDSK encounters certain types of errors on a disk, it reports the presence of these errors and asks if you want to correct them. You can safely indicate "Yes" because the CHKDSK command will only *simulate* how it will correct the problem. After you see how CHKDSK corrects the problem, you can decide whether you need to make backups of the hard disk or diskette before you attempt to correct the problem with the CHKDSK command's **Fixup switch** (/F).

For example, if CHKDSK reports the presence of lost clusters, you might want to first back up or copy important document files on your hard disk or diskette. Then you use the CHKDSK command in combination with the Fixup switch. CHKDSK operates in **Fixup mode**, and converts each **chain**, or sequence of lost clusters that once belonged to a file, into a file and stores the new file in the root directory. CHKDSK assigns a name to each new file it creates from a chain of lost clusters. The first file is named FILE0000.CHK, the second FILE0001.CHK, the third FILE0002.CHK, and so on. After CHKDSK converts each chain of lost clusters to a new file, you use the TYPE command to view the contents of each of these files. In some cases, you may recognize parts of a text file and you may be able to combine the contents of this file with the original file. In other cases, you will see only extraneous characters or symbols and may not be able to identify whether the file is a program file or a data file. In these cases, you can just delete the files. If a program fails to operate properly or at all, you can reinstall that program on your hard disk or restore it from a backup set. If you are missing part of a data file, you can restore it from a backup set.

Cross-Linked Clusters

Another common type of error in the logical structure of a disk is cross-linked clusters. A **cross-linked cluster** is a cluster that belongs to or is shared by two files. In the File Allocation Table, DOS has recorded the cross-linked cluster as the next available cluster for two different files. When you retrieve and change one of these files, the other file is automatically updated. To correct this problem, you copy both files to another disk or diskette or to another directory. Then you delete the two original files. Next, if the files are data files, you examine each of the files with the original software application that produced them. One file may be intact and the other may contain extraneous characters, which you can delete, or both files might contain extraneous characters. You might need to reconstruct all or part of each file.

The Importance of the File Allocation Table

The File Allocation Table is so important to DOS that it keeps two copies of the file. The files are referred to as FAT1 (for File Allocation Table 1) and FAT2 (for File Allocation Table 2). If DOS is unable to read information stored in FAT1, DOS will attempt to read FAT2, and it will display a message to this effect. If this condition occurs, you should make several backup copies of your document files on the hard disk and a backup copy of the installed software, reformat the hard disk, and restore your installed software and document files to the hard disk.

Checking for Allocation Errors

The CHKDSK command also can locate and automatically correct small errors in the logical structure of a hard disk or diskette. For example, if there is a discrepancy between the file size in the directory file and the file size calculated from the clusters in use by that file, CHKDSK will automatically adjust the file size in the directory table. This type of error is called an **allocation error**.

Checking the Directory Structure

In addition to checking discrepancies in the allocation of space in the directory file and the File Allocation Table, the CHKDSK command examines the entire directory structure of a hard disk or diskette to ensure that the directory structure is functional and intact. CHKDSK also provides a summary report on the use of memory and disk space.

Monitoring the Status of a Disk

To prevent the accumulation of errors in the allocation of disk and file space, you should use the CHKDSK command on your hard disk at least once a month. You can also use the command more frequently to catch errors early, before they develop into more serious errors. This command is one of your most important tools, because it can extend the longevity and integrity of your hard disk by eliminating disk errors that might result in more serious problems.

Syntax of the Check Disk Command

Although the CHKDSK command is more commonly used on hard disks, you can also use it to check diskettes. The syntax for using CHKDSK in diagnostic mode is:

CHKDSK [*drive:*]

If you do not specify a drive name, CHKDSK uses the current drive. You do not need to be at the root directory to use CHKDSK. You cannot use CHKDSK to check a network drive.

Checking the Status of a Hard Disk

You are now ready to check the status of both your hard disk and your Tutorial Disk.

To check the status of the hard disk:

1. If necessary, change to drive C.

2. Type **CHKDSK** and press **[Enter]**. After checking the hard disk, CHKDSK will display a report on disk and memory usage or it might first report on disk errors, such as lost clusters. If CHKDSK finds a problem, it might ask you if you want to correct the problem, it might inform you that it will not write corrections to the disk, or it might automatically correct a small problem and inform you of the result. If CHKDSK asks you if you want to correct a problem, type **Y** for "Yes" so that you can see what this utility will do if you later use the Fixup switch. *Before you use the Fixup switch, obtain permission from your instructor or technical support person.* Figure 7-16 shows a report on the status of a hard disk. If you are using DOS 6.2, it will recommend that you try another utility called ScanDisk, which you will examine later.

6.2

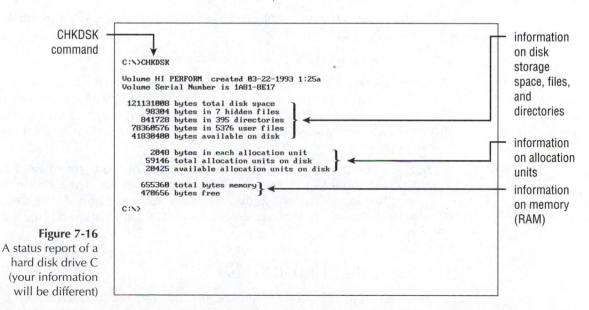

CHKDSK command

```
C:\>CHKDSK

Volume HI PERFORM   created 03-22-1993 1:25a
Volume Serial Number is 1A81-8E17

121131008 bytes total disk space
    98304 bytes in 7 hidden files
   841728 bytes in 395 directories
 78360576 bytes in 5376 user files
 41830400 bytes available on disk

     2048 bytes in each allocation unit
    59146 total allocation units on disk
    20425 available allocation units on disk

   655360 total bytes memory
   470656 bytes free

C:\>
```

information on disk storage space, files, and directories

information on allocation units

information on memory (RAM)

Figure 7-16
A status report of a hard disk drive C (your information will be different)

In Figure 7-16, CHKDSK shows the volume name of the hard disk and the date and time the volume name was assigned, as well as its serial number. Your screen information will be different.

The next part of the report shows:

◆ The total disk space in bytes (in this case, 121,131,008). If you divide this value by 1,024 twice, then you will find that this hard disk has approximately 116MB of storage space. You use 1,024 rather than 1,000 because one kilobyte equals 1,024 bytes and one megabyte equals 1,024 kilobytes. Make the same calculation with the information for your hard disk.

◆ The number of hidden files (in this case, seven) and the storage space used by those files (98,304 bytes).

◆ The number of directories (in this case, 395) and the storage space used by those directories (841,728 bytes).

◆ The number of user files (in this case, 5,376), including program and data files, and the storage space used by those files (78,360,576 bytes).

◆ The amount of available space on the disk (in this case, 41,830,400 bytes).

If a disk contains defective sectors, CHKDSK will display how many bytes of storage space are used for those sectors.

The next part of the report explains how disk space is allocated:

◆ The size of each allocation unit, or cluster, in bytes. In this example, each allocation unit on the hard disk uses 2,048 bytes. This is the minimum amount of space DOS allocates when a file is saved to this hard disk. If you divide this value by 512 bytes, you will find that each allocation unit, or cluster, on this hard disk includes four sectors. You use 512 because one sector stores 512 bytes of data. Make this same calculation with the information for your hard disk.

◆ The total number of allocation units, or clusters, on the disk (in this case, 59,146).

◆ The available number of allocation units, or clusters, on the disk (in this case, 20,425).

The last part of the report shows memory usage:

◆ The total number of bytes of memory, or RAM (in this case, 655,360). If you divide this value by 1,024 bytes, you will know how many kilobytes of RAM this system contains. In this example, the computer has the standard 640K of RAM. Make this same calculation with the information on total memory in your system.

◆ The amount of RAM available. In this case 470,656 bytes of RAM are available for application software, utilities, and data files. If you divide this value by 1,024 bytes, you will know how many kilobytes of RAM are free on your system. Make this same calculation with the information on free memory in your system.

Printing the CHKDSK Report

You want a printed copy of this report for your records. To obtain a printed copy, you can redirect the output of the CHKDSK command to your printer.

To print the CHKDSK report:

1. Be sure your printer is on and on-line, and that the paper is properly aligned.

2. Press [↑] (Up Arrow) to recall the command "CHKDSK." Press **[Spacebar]** and type **> PRN** to redirect the output to the first printer port. The command should read "CHKDSK > PRN." *If your printer port is different, be sure you use the correct port name.* Press **[Enter]**. DOS prints a copy of the output normally sent to the monitor.

3. If necessary, press the **Form Feed button** on the printer. If the printer does not respond, press the **On Line button** to place the printer off-line. Then press **Form Feed** again. After the printer ejects the page, press the **On Line button** to place the printer back on-line.

Checking the Status of a Diskette

You next want to check your client diskette for errors.

To check the status of this diskette:

1. Insert your Tutorial Disk into drive A (or drive B).

2. Type **CHKDSK A:** (or **CHKDSK B:**) and press **[Enter]**. After checking the diskette, CHKDSK will display a report on disk and memory usage or it might first report on disk errors. If CHKDSK finds a problem, it might ask you if you want to correct the problem, it might inform you that it will not write corrections to the disk, or it might automatically correct a small problem and inform you of the result. If CHKDSK asks you if you want to correct a problem, type **Y** for "Yes" so that you can see what this utility will do if you later use the Fixup switch. Figure 7-17 shows a sample report on the status of the Tutorial Disk. This report shows that DOS allocates space differently on your Tutorial Disk than on your hard disk. In this example, each allocation unit, or cluster, is 512 bytes and consists of one sector (512 bytes divided by 512 bytes/sector = one sector). Your report might be different. If you are using a double-density diskette, each allocation unit, or cluster, consists of 1,024 bytes (or two sectors). As noted earlier, if you are using DOS 6.2, it will recommend that you try another utility called ScanDisk, discussed in the following section.

6.2

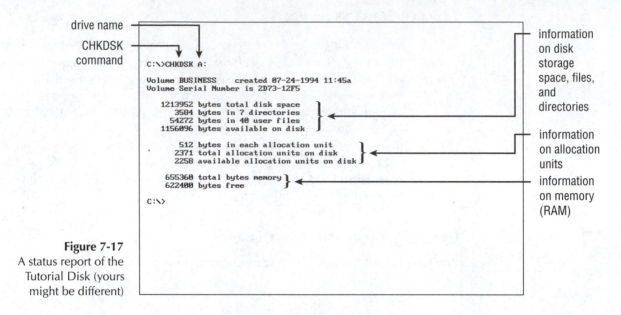

drive name
CHKDSK command

```
C:\>CHKDSK A:

Volume BUSINESS     created 07-24-1994 11:45a
Volume Serial Number is 2D73-12F5

 1213952 bytes total disk space
    3584 bytes in 7 directories
   54272 bytes in 40 user files
 1156096 bytes available on disk

     512 bytes in each allocation unit
    2371 total allocation units on disk
    2258 available allocation units on disk

  655360 total bytes memory
  622400 bytes free

C:\>
```

information on disk storage space, files, and directories

information on allocation units

information on memory (RAM)

Figure 7-17
A status report of the Tutorial Disk (yours might be different)

USING SCANDISK IN DOS 6.2

If you perform a CHKDSK in DOS 6.2, it will recommend that you try ScanDisk. ScanDisk is a new utility available in DOS 6.2 for diagnosing and repairing disk problems. ScanDisk performs the same functions as CHKDSK but has additional capabilities for repairing disk errors.

After you load ScanDisk, it verifies the media descriptor byte, verifies that the two copies of the File Allocation Table match, examines the integrity of the directory structure, and checks the allocation of storage space for files to ensure that each cluster belongs to only one file. The **media descriptor** is a byte stored in the boot sector that identifies the disk drive as one that will work with MS-DOS or PC-DOS. If ScanDisk encounters a problem, it identifies the problem. You can correct the problem, or you can continue without correcting it. In either case, ScanDisk then performs a surface scan, checking for the presence of bad sectors. If it finds a bad sector, it moves data stored in that sector to another part of the disk and marks the sector as unusable.

During ScanDisk's check of a disk, you can pause the process, display information on the current operation using the "More Info" button, or exit the utility.

If you are using DOS 6.2, you will use ScanDisk to check your Tutorial Disk. Because the ScanDisk utility is not available in DOS 5.0 or 6.0, you will not be able to perform the following tutorial steps with DOS 5.0 or 6.0. If you are using DOS 5.0 or 6.0, skip to the next section, entitled "Tracking Deleted Files."

_6.2_

To use the ScanDisk utility _in DOS 6.2_:

1. Type **A:** and press **[Enter]** to change to drive A.
2. Type **SCANDISK** and press **[Enter]** DOS 6.2 loads the ScanDisk utility. As it checks the media descriptor, File Allocation Tables, directory structure, and file system, it places a check mark next to the item it examined. See Figure 7-18. Then ScanDisk displays a dialog box that informs you this utility tested the file structure of the disk, and that it is ready to perform a surface scan, and asks you if you want to continue. See Figure 7-19.

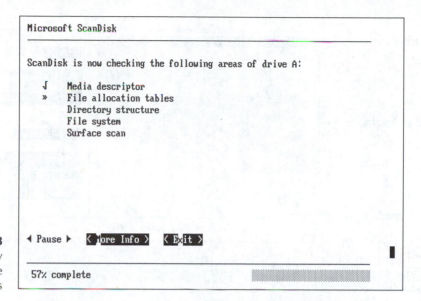

Figure 7-18
The ScanDisk utility examines a diskette for errors

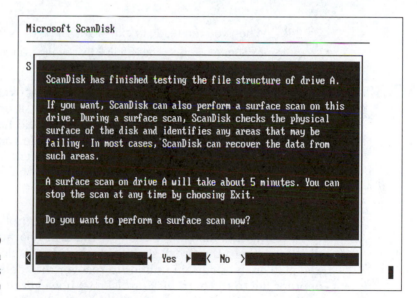

Figure 7-19
ScanDisk displays a dialog box that explains the surface scan

3. Press **[Enter]** for Yes.

   If you are using a mouse, click **Yes**.

   ScanDisk displays a map of the drive that identifies areas of the disk with unused clusters, used clusters and any bad clusters. See Figure 7-20. It also shows the number of clusters on the disk. As it examines each group of clusters, it highlights the area of the disk checked and shows the percentage complete. During the surface scan, ScanDisk may identify specific problems and ask you whether you want to fix the problem or continue. If the disk has no errors, ScanDisk will report no problems at the end of the surface scan.

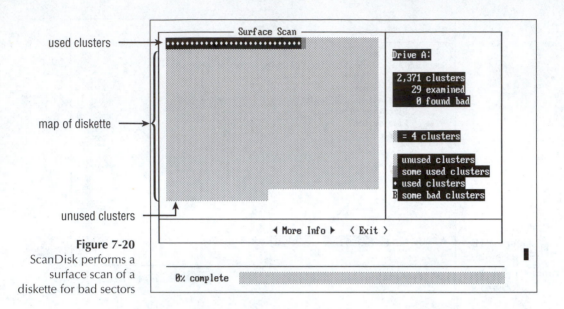

used clusters

map of diskette

unused clusters

Figure 7-20
ScanDisk performs a
surface scan of a
diskette for bad sectors

4. When you are ready to exit ScanDisk, type **X** for Exit.

If you are using a mouse, click **Exit** when you are ready to exit ScanDisk.

TRACKING DELETED FILES

As you and other staff members may have discovered, it is easy to inadvertently erase an important file from the hard disk or a diskette. If you do not have a backup of a file that was deleted, you will have to reconstruct the file from scratch. In the process, you lose valuable time. Even if you do have a backup, that backup may not be the most recent version of the file. In that case, you will have to reconstruct the changes that you made to the file since you last worked on it. Therefore, it is important for you to know how to recover deleted files.

When DOS deletes a file from disk, it does not physically erase the contents of the file. Instead, it changes the first character of the filename in the directory file to the Greek sigma character (σ), which marks a file for deletion and also enables certain utilities to recover the "deleted" file. When DOS saves another file to the hard disk or diskette, however, it might use the space occupied by a "deleted" file to store the new file. If this occurs, the file is physically erased and you cannot recover it.

Thus, if you delete an important client or business file, you *might* be able to recover the file with the UNDELETE command. The general syntax for this external command is:

UNDELETE [*drive:*][*path*][*filename*]

If you use UNDELETE without any parameters, UNDELETE assumes you want to recover all deleted files in the current directory. You can specify a filename to recover a file or use wildcards to select and restore a group of files. If the files are stored on another drive or in another directory, or both, you must specify the drive name, the path, or both parameters.

For this command to effectively restore a deleted file, you must act immediately after you delete a file. The longer you wait before you use the

UNDELETE command, the less your chances for recovering the deleted file, because DOS might have already recorded the contents of another file over it.

DOS 6.0 and 6.2 provide three levels of protection for deleted files: Standard, Delete Tracker, and Delete Sentry. DOS 5.0 provides two levels of protection: Standard and Delete Tracker. Let's take a closer look at each of these levels.

Using the Standard Level of Protection

The **Standard level** of protection is the default, and it provides the least amount of protection. UNDELETE can recover the file only if DOS has not recorded the contents of another file over the storage space occupied by the deleted file. UNDELETE will display the filename of the deleted file, with a question mark for the first character in the filename, and ask you if you want to recover the file. If you respond "Yes," UNDELETE prompts you for the first character of the filename and then restores the file. If you use wildcards in the file specification, UNDELETE displays a list of all deleted files, one at a time, and prompts you if you want to restore each file.

Using the Delete Tracker Level of Protection

When you use **Delete Tracker**, a small Undelete TSR utility is loaded into memory to monitor file deletions. This utility creates a hidden system file named PCTRACKR.DEL in the root directory of drive C. When you delete a file, the Undelete TSR stores the location of that deleted file in PCTRACKR.DEL. If you issue a command to undelete a deleted file, DOS checks the contents of PCTRACKR.DEL to ascertain where the deleted file is located on disk. It then restores the entire file as long as DOS has not saved the contents of another file in the same location. The primary advantages of the Delete Tracker over the Standard level of protection is that it keeps a record of the full filename, including the first character, and you have a better chance of recovering at least a part of a deleted file.

To install Delete Tracker *in DOS 6.0 and 6.2*, you use the **Tracker switch** (/T) with the UNDELETE command, as follows:

UNDELETE /T[*drive*]

You must specify a drive by listing the drive name (without a colon) after the Tracker switch. For example, if you enter UNDELETE /TC, you enable Delete Tracker for drive C. If you want to specify several drives, you use a Tracker switch for each drive.

To install Delete Tracker *in DOS 5.0*, you use the MIRROR command and its **Tracker switch** (/T):

MIRROR /T[*drive*]

You must specify a drive by listing the drive name (without a colon) after the Tracker switch.

Using the Delete Sentry Level of Protection

The Delete Sentry level of protection is available in DOS 6.0 and 6.2, but not DOS 5.0. When you use **Delete Sentry**, a small Undelete TSR is loaded into memory to monitor file deletions. This TSR creates a hidden directory named

SENTRY on drive C. When you delete a file, the TSR moves the contents of the deleted file to this hidden directory. It preserves the reference to the starting cluster in the directory file and to each of the clusters in the File Allocation Table that the file originally used. However, when you display a directory, you do not see the name of the file listed. If you issue a command to restore a deleted file with Delete Sentry, DOS checks the SENTRY subdirectory and automatically restores the file to its original location.

To activate Delete Sentry in DOS 6.0 and 6.2, you use the **Sentry switch** (/S) with UNDELETE, as follows:

UNDELETE /S[*drive*]

If you do not specify a drive, Delete Sentry is enabled for the current drive. You can specify a drive by including the drive name (without a colon) immediately after the Sentry switch.

Delete Sentry provides a greater level of protection than either the Delete Tracker or Standard level of protection, but it also requires more hard disk space because it actually stores copies of the deleted files. Delete Tracker provides a greater level of protection than the Standard level, but it requires hard disk space to track filenames and storage locations of deleted files. Both Delete Sentry and Delete Tracker require memory for the Undelete TSR utility.

The Importance of the UNDELETE.INI File

UNDELETE uses settings stored in a file named UNDELETE.INI, "INI" for initialization file. Figure 7-21 shows the contents of a sample UNDELETE.INI file for DOS 6.0. The "days" setting specifies how long UNDELETE will keep deleted files in the SENTRY subdirectory. By default, UNDELETE keeps deleted files for seven days. The "percentage" setting specifies how much hard-disk storage space to use for the hidden subdirectory. By default, UNDELETE uses 20% of the hard-disk storage space. You might want to reduce this setting, because UNDELETE would, for example, set aside 20MB of a 100MB hard disk, leaving only 80MB for your applications and files.

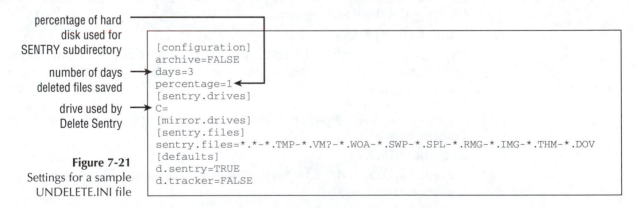

percentage of hard disk used for SENTRY subdirectory

number of days deleted files saved

drive used by Delete Sentry

```
[configuration]
archive=FALSE
days=3
percentage=1
[sentry.drives]
C=
[mirror.drives]
[sentry.files]
sentry.files=*.*-*.TMP-*.VM?-*.WOA-*.SWP-*.SPL-*.RMG-*.IMG-*.THM-*.DOV
[defaults]
d.sentry=TRUE
d.tracker=FALSE
```

Figure 7-21
Settings for a sample UNDELETE.INI file

The setting for "sentry drives" shows which drives Delete Sentry will monitor for file deletions when you load UNDELETE with the Sentry switch (/S). Even if you specify other drives on the command line when you load UNDELETE, it will use the drives specified in UNDELETE.INI. You might need to occasionally delete drive references from UNDELETE.INI.

Before you open this ASCII file with the MS-DOS Editor and change the settings, be sure you make a duplicate copy of this file.

Restoring Deleted Files with the Standard Level of Protection

You want to test the default level of protection and Delete Sentry so that you can train and assist other staff members in recovering deleted files. First, you need to delete one of the files from your client diskette.

To delete a file from your Tutorial Disk:

1. Be sure the current drive contains your Tutorial Disk. Change to drive A (or drive B), and be sure you are at the root directory of that drive.

2. Type **CD BUSINESS** and press **[Enter]**. DOS changes to the BUSINESS directory and updates the DOS prompt to show the full path.

3. Type **DIR** and press **[Enter]**. DOS displays the files in the BUSINESS directory.

4. Type **DEL BUSINESS.PLN** and press **[Enter]**. You just "inadvertently" deleted the file with your company's business plan—a situation that could actually happen in your daily work, especially if you are working quickly or under the pressure of a deadline.

5. Type **DIR** and press **[Enter]**. DOS displays the files in the BUSINESS directory. The file with your company's business plan is no longer listed in the directory.

Now you will use the Standard level of protection to recover the deleted file. If Delete Tracker (in DOS 5.0, 6.0, and 6.2) and Delete Sentry (in DOS 6.0 and 6.2) are not activated, then you can enter the following command to use the Standard level of protection to undelete the file:

UNDELETE [*filename*]

If UNDELETE is monitoring file deletions with Delete Sentry or Delete Tracker, UNDELETE will automatically use Delete Sentry or Delete Tracker to recover the deleted file. If Delete Sentry and Delete Tracker are not installed, you can recover the deleted file with the **DOS switch** (/DOS):

UNDELETE [*filename*] /DOS

The DOS switch (/DOS) instructs UNDELETE to check the directory file for any files that are marked for deletion and that have filenames similar to the one you specified.

Let's use the Standard level of protection to recover the deleted file.

To recover a deleted file:

6.0 *6.2*

5.0

1. Type **UNDELETE BUSINESS.PLN /DOS** and press **[Enter]**. In Figure 7-22, UNDELETE displays a message that there is no Delete Sentry file (in DOS 6.0 or 6.2) or no Delete Tracker file (in DOS 5.0, 6.0, or 6.2). It also displays a message that it is using the MS-DOS directory method. UNDELETE indicates that one file matches the filename you specified. The first character in the filename is a question mark. UNDELETE also shows information on the file size, date, time, and file attributes for the file in question. Finally, it asks if you want to undelete the file.

UNDELETE command → 〔 deleted file

DOS switch

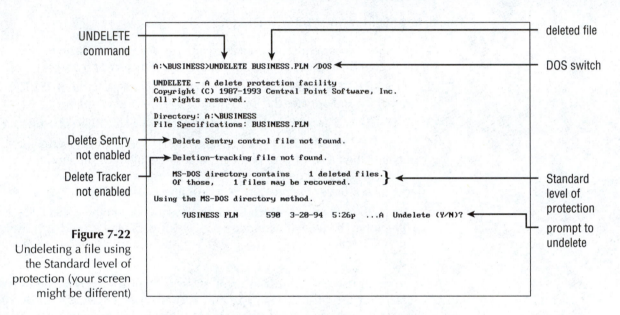

Delete Sentry not enabled →

Delete Tracker not enabled →

Standard level of protection

prompt to undelete

Figure 7-22
Undeleting a file using the Standard level of protection (your screen might be different)

2. Type **Y** for "Yes." UNDELETE prompts for the first character of the filename. See Figure 7-23.

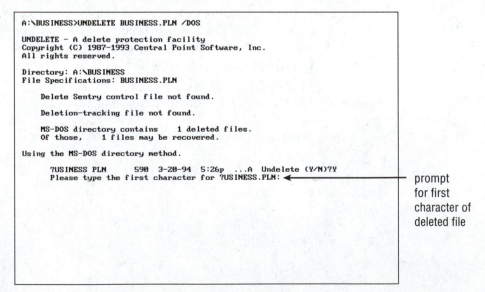

prompt for first character of deleted file

Figure 7-23
UNDELETE prompts for the first character of the filename

3. Type **B** for "BUSINESS." UNDELETE successfully restores the file. See Figure 7-24.

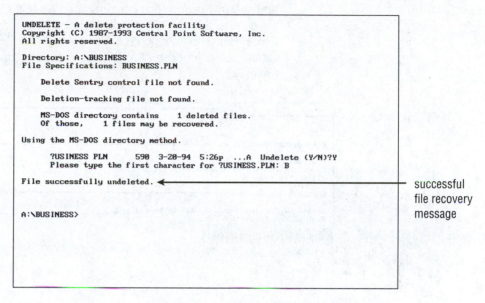

```
UNDELETE - A delete protection facility
Copyright (C) 1987-1993 Central Point Software, Inc.
All rights reserved.

Directory: A:\BUSINESS
File Specifications: BUSINESS.PLN

    Delete Sentry control file not found.

    Deletion-tracking file not found.

    MS-DOS directory contains     1 deleted files.
    Of those,     1 files may be recovered.

Using the MS-DOS directory method.

    ?USINESS PLN      590  3-20-94  5:26p  ...A  Undelete (Y/N)?Y
    Please type the first character for ?USINESS.PLN: B

File successfully undeleted. ◄──────────────────────────────    successful
                                                                 file recovery
                                                                 message

A:\BUSINESS>
```

Figure 7-24
A successful recovery of a deleted file

4. Type **DIR** and press **[Enter]**. DOS lists the BUSINESS.PLN file in the directory. You have successfully restored a deleted file using the default Standard level of protection.

5. Type **CD** \ and press **[Enter]**. DOS returns to the root directory.

Restoring Deleted Files with Delete Sentry

Next you want to recover a file with Delete Sentry. Again, you want to delete one of the files from your client diskette so that you can recover it with Delete Sentry. First, you must install Delete Sentry. *Because Delete Sentry creates a hidden directory on drive C, be sure to ask your instructor or technical support person for permission to use this feature.* Although Delete Sentry and Delete Tracker function differently and provide different levels of protection, UNDELETE will display similar information on the screen for both utilities.

If you are using DOS 5.0, you can skip to the next section, entitled "Unformatting Diskettes," because DOS 5.0 does not have the Delete Sentry level of protection.

If you experience difficulty with these tutorial steps, ask your instructor or technical support person for assistance. Your instructor or technical support person might need to rename the UNDELETE.INI file so that UNDELETE does not use settings already stored in this file.

6.0 6.2 **To install Delete Sentry** *using DOS 6.0 or 6.2*:

1. Type **UNDELETE /SA** for drive A (or **UNDELETE /SB** for drive B). *Be sure you specify the drive that contains your Tutorial Disk after the /S switch.* Then press **[Enter]**. DOS installs Delete Sentry and informs you that the Delete Protection Method is Delete Sentry. See Figure 7-25. It enables Delete Sentry for drive A (or drive B). Your system might report additional drives.

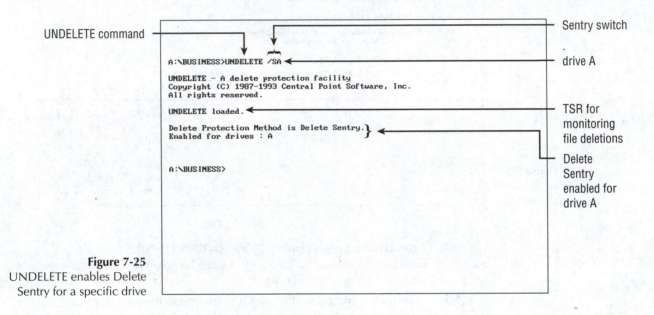

UNDELETE command

Sentry switch

drive A

TSR for monitoring file deletions

Delete Sentry enabled for drive A

```
A:\BUSINESS>UNDELETE /SA

UNDELETE - A delete protection facility
Copyright (C) 1987-1993 Central Point Software, Inc.
All rights reserved.

UNDELETE loaded.

Delete Protection Method is Delete Sentry.
Enabled for drives : A


A:\BUSINESS>
```

Figure 7-25
UNDELETE enables Delete Sentry for a specific drive

Now delete the business plan.

2. Type **DEL BUSINESS.PLN** and press **[Enter]**. Then type **DIR** and press **[Enter]** to verify that this file is deleted.

Now recover this deleted file using Delete Sentry.

3. Type **UNDELETE BUSINESS.PLN** and press **[Enter]**. By default, UNDELETE automatically uses Delete Sentry if it is available. UNDELETE informs you that it has located one deleted file. See Figure 7-26. It also indicates if you can use the Delete Tracker or Standard level of protection to recover the deleted file. It displays information on the file, including the filename, and informs you the file can be 100% undeleted. Finally, it asks if you want to undelete the file.

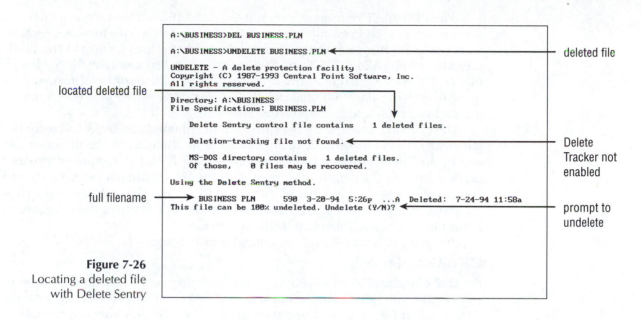

located deleted file

full filename

deleted file

Delete Tracker not enabled

prompt to undelete

Figure 7-26
Locating a deleted file
with Delete Sentry

4. Type **Y** for "Yes." Delete Sentry successfully restores the deleted file. See Figure 7-27.

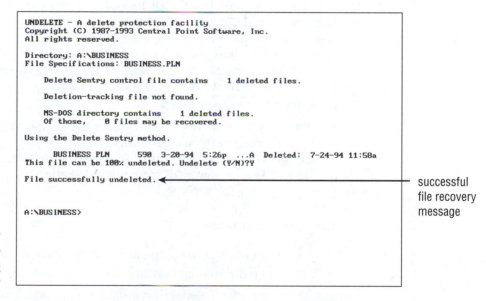

successful file recovery message

Figure 7-27
A successful recovery
of a deleted file using
Delete Sentry

5. Type **DIR** and press **[Enter]**. DOS lists the BUSINESS.PLN file in the directory. You have successfully restored a deleted file using the Delete Sentry level of protection provided in DOS 6.0 and 6.2.

UNFORMATTING DISKETTES

Another important skill you need to teach other staff members is how to unformat diskettes. Every so often, someone inserts a diskette containing valuable files into a disk drive and inadvertently formats the diskette. Then staff members must know how to unformat the diskette and recover the information.

When FORMAT reformats a diskette, it performs a Safe format as long as you do not use the Unconditional switch (/U). During a **Safe format**, FORMAT does not erase the data on the diskette. Instead, it stores a copy of the directory file and File Allocation Table in a special file called a **mirror file**, or **image file**, on the reformatted diskette. If you perform an **Unconditional format** on a diskette with the Unconditional switch (/U), FORMAT does not create a mirror file, and you cannot unformat the diskette.

The FORMAT command uses the external command MIRROR to create the mirror file on the diskette. It then erases the information in the directory file and in the File Allocation Table. Not only is the FORMAT command process quicker than an Unconditional format with the Unconditional switch (/U), but you can also use the UNFORMAT command to restore the diskette to its original state. When you unformat a diskette, UNFORMAT restores the information in the File Allocation Table and the directory file.

The general syntax for this command is as follows:

UNFORMAT [*drive:*]

For this command to be effective, you must unformat the diskette *as soon as you realize you have made a mistake and before you store new files on the diskette*. If you store new information on the diskette, you may not be able to recover all the original information and you may also lose the new information you have added to the diskette.

You can also reformat a diskette by performing a Quick format with the **Quick switch** (/Q). The **Quick format** is faster than the standard Safe format because FORMAT does not check the surface of the diskette for defective areas. As with the Safe format, FORMAT creates a mirror file when you use the Quick format so that you can unformat the diskette.

You can also use the UNFORMAT command to restore a hard-disk drive that you have formatted. The syntax is as follows:

UNFORMAT [*drive:*] /PARTN

The **Partition switch** (/PARTN) restores the hard-disk partition table. You cannot use this command on a network drive.

Before you show other staff members how to unformat a diskette, you decide to test it on a copy of your client diskette.

To reformat a diskette:

1. If necessary, change to the root directory of drive C.
2. Insert the Tutorial Disk into drive A (or drive B).
3. Format the Tutorial Disk using the appropriate formatting option:

    ◆ To format a high-density diskette in a high-density drive or a double-density diskette in a double-density drive, type **FORMAT A:** (or **FORMAT B:**). Then press **[Enter]**.
    ◆ To format a 3½-inch double-density diskette in a high-density drive, type **FORMAT A: /F:720** (or **FORMAT B: /F:720**). Then press **[Enter]**.
    ◆ To format a 5¼-inch double-density diskette in a high-density drive, type **FORMAT A: /F:360** (or **FORMAT B: /F:360**). Then press **[Enter]**.

    FORMAT prompts you to insert a diskette into drive A (or drive B). If you have not yet inserted a diskette, do so now.

4. Press **[Enter]**. DOS displays the message "Checking existing disk format" and informs you that it is saving unformat information. See Figure 7-28. The *unformat information* is the copy of the File Allocation Table and directory file that is stored in the mirror file. FORMAT then clears the directory file and File Allocation Table.

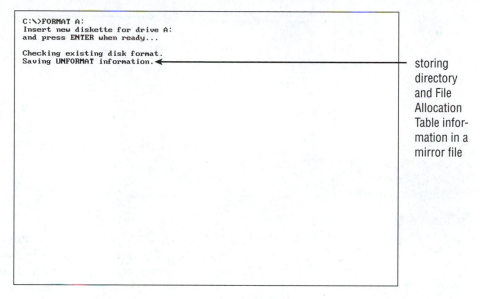

```
C:\>FORMAT A:
Insert new diskette for drive A:
and press ENTER when ready...

Checking existing disk format.
Saving UNFORMAT information.◄──────────
```
storing
directory
and File
Allocation
Table infor-
mation in a
mirror file

Figure 7-28
Creating a mirror image file during reformatting of a diskette

5. When prompted for a volume label, press **[Enter]** for "none." When FORMAT asks you if you want to format another diskette, type **N** for "No" and press **[Enter]**.

6. Type **DIR A:** (or **DIR B:**) and press **[Enter]**. DOS informs you that it found no file. The diskette was successfully reformatted.

Rebuilding a Formatted Diskette

Now you are ready to restore the Tutorial Disk to its original condition using the UNFORMAT utility.

To rebuild your Tutorial Disk:

1. Be sure the reformatted copy of the Tutorial Disk is in drive A (or drive B).

2. Type **UNFORMAT A:** (or **UNFORMAT B:**) and press **[Enter]**. UNFORMAT prompts you to insert the disk that is to be rebuilt in the specified drive. See Figure 7-29.

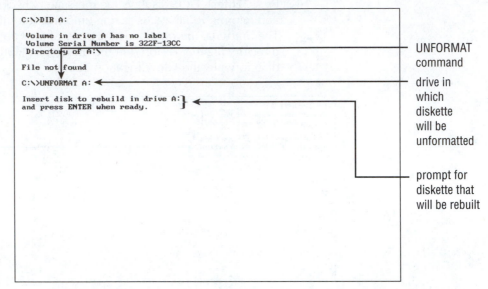

Figure 7-29
UNFORMAT prompts for
the diskette to rebuild

3. Press **[Enter]**. UNFORMAT informs you that it will restore the system
area on the diskette by using the image file created by MIRROR. See
Figure 7-30. The **system area** is the area that contains the boot sector,
File Allocation Tables, and directory file. Next, it displays warnings on
the use of this command and indicates that it has validated the mirror
image file. Finally, it asks you if you are sure you want to update the
system area.

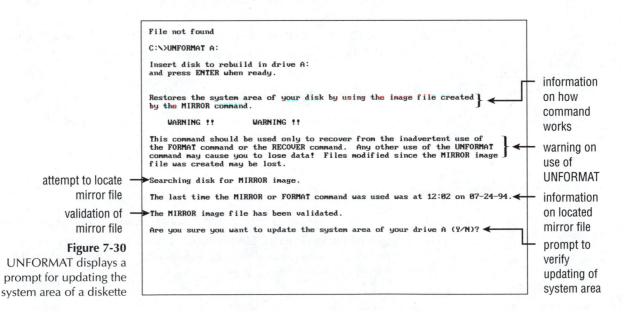

Figure 7-30
UNFORMAT displays a
prompt for updating the
system area of a diskette

4. Type **Y** for "Yes." UNFORMAT rebuilds the system area on the diskette.
See Figure 7-31.

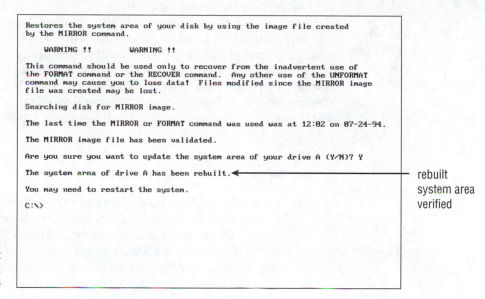

```
Restores the system area of your disk by using the image file created
by the MIRROR command.

     WARNING !!          WARNING !!

This command should be used only to recover from the inadvertent use of
the FORMAT command or the RECOVER command.  Any other use of the UNFORMAT
command may cause you to lose data!  Files modified since the MIRROR image
file was created may be lost.

Searching disk for MIRROR image.

The last time the MIRROR or FORMAT command was used was at 12:02 on 07-24-94.

The MIRROR image file has been validated.

Are you sure you want to update the system area of your drive A (Y/N)? Y

The system area of drive A has been rebuilt.◄─────
                                                        rebuilt
You may need to restart the system.                     system area
                                                        verified
C:\>
```

Figure 7-31
UNFORMAT verifies that it rebuilt the system area of the diskette

Now verify the unformat operation.

5. Type **TREE A: /F │ MORE** and press **[Enter]**. DOS displays a partial directory tree with filenames by subdirectory. See Figure 7-32. UNFORMAT restored the original volume label, serial number, subdirectories, and files. Press **[Enter]** to view each of the next screens and to return to the DOS prompt.

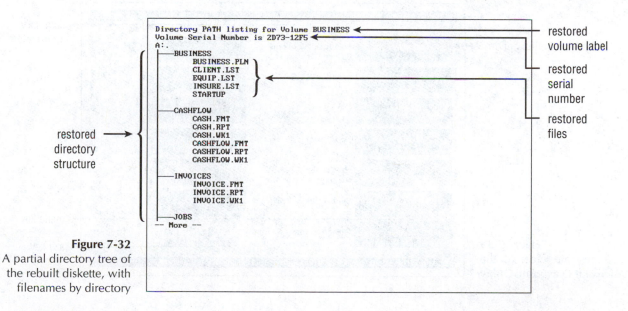

```
Directory PATH listing for Volume BUSINESS ◄─────      restored
Volume Serial Number is 2D73-12F5 ◄─────               volume label
A:.
    ┌──BUSINESS
    │      BUSINESS.PLN ┐                               restored
    │      CLIENT.LST   │                               serial
    │      EQUIP.LST    ├─◄─────                        number
    │      INSURE.LST   │
    │      STARTUP      ┘                               restored
    │                                                   files
    ├──CASHFLOW
    │      CASH.FMT
    │      CASH.RPT
    │      CASH.WK1
    │      CASHFLOW.FMT
    │      CASHFLOW.RPT
    │      CASHFLOW.WK1
    │
    ├──INVOICES
    │      INVOICE.FMT
    │      INVOICE.RPT
    │      INVOICE.WK1
    │
    └──JOBS
-- More --
```

Figure 7-32
A partial directory tree of the rebuilt diskette, with filenames by directory

USING THE MICROSOFT DIAGNOSTIC UTILITY

Your supervisor has asked you to prepare a technical report on each of the company's computer systems using the Microsoft Diagnostic Utility. If a problem develops with one of the computer systems, you and other members of the technical support staff can attempt to troubleshoot the problem using the information included on the diagnostic report for the computer system in question.

The **Microsoft Diagnostic Utility** in DOS 6.0 and 6.2 provides you with technical information on your computer system. You can also print a copy of this information in a report format or store the report in a file on disk for future reference. DOS 5.0 does not include this utility.

You decide to first test the Microsoft Diagnostic Utility on your computer system. If you are using DOS 5.0, you will not be able to complete this section. You can skip to the end-of-chapter "Summary" or you can review the figures so that you are familiar with the information produced by this utility.

To start the Microsoft Diagnostic Utility:

1. Type **MSD** for "Microsoft Diagnostic Utility" and press **[Enter]**. The first screen that you see explains that this utility is examining your computer system. During this examination, the Microsoft Diagnostic Utility might report discrepancies it finds and ask if you want to continue. For example, if one of your environment variables references a subdirectory that does not exist, MSD will display a dialog box and report that the environment string is invalid. You can press the Enter key to continue or, if you are using the mouse, click the OK button.

   After MSD is loaded, the utility's main screen appears. See Figure 7-33. Below the menu bar, the Microsoft Diagnostic Utility displays a series of buttons that provide technical information about specific hardware components or software in your computer system.

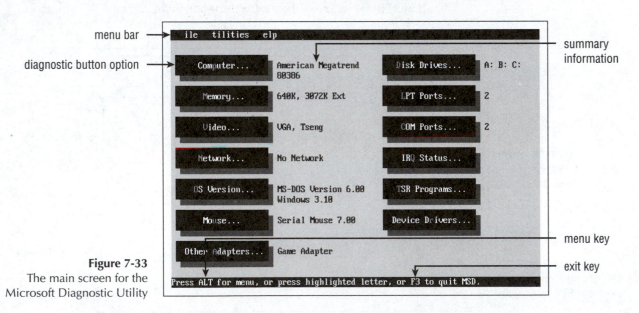

Figure 7-33
The main screen for the Microsoft Diagnostic Utility

Now examine information on the disk drives in your computer system.

2. Type **D** for "Disk Drives."

   If you are using a mouse, click **Disk Drives**.

   The Microsoft Diagnostic Utility then displays a report screen that displays technical information on the diskette drives and hard disk in your computer system. Figure 7-34 shows a report for a computer system with two high-density diskette drives and one hard-disk drive. Your report might be different.

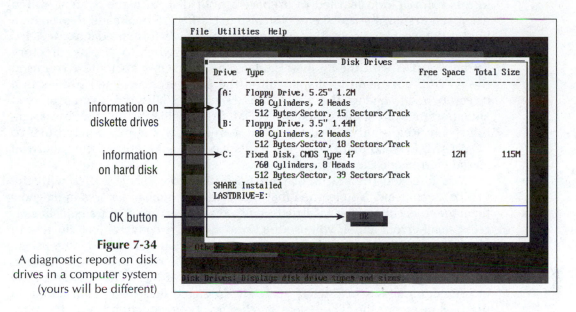

information on diskette drives →

information on hard disk →

OK button →

Figure 7-34
A diagnostic report on disk drives in a computer system (yours will be different)

3. Press **[Enter]** for "OK."

   If you are using the mouse, click **OK**.

   The Microsoft Diagnostic Utility returns to its main screen. Examine any of the other options of interest to you. Some of the information that you see may contain technical information that you do not understand. However, it is important to have a copy of all this information if you or a service person ever needs to troubleshoot a problem or rebuild your hard-disk drive. This report would also be useful if you call Microsoft Corporation about problems you are experiencing with your version of DOS.

You can print a report by selecting the File menu and Print Report. The Print Report screen allows you to select the type of information you want to include in the report and to specify your printer port. You also can print the report to a file on disk under the default filename REPORT.MSD or under another name. The report is approximately 15 to 20 pages long.

You are now ready to exit this utility.

To exit the Microsoft Diagnostic Utility:

1. Press **[F3]** (Quit).

◆

SUMMARY

In this tutorial, you learned to prepare a boot disk with the System switch when you first format a diskette. You also used the SYS command to prepare a boot disk by copying operating system files to a newly formatted diskette.

You used the DIR command and its Attribute switch to display directory listings for files with the System, Hidden, and Read-Only attributes. You used the ATTRIB command to display all of the attributes assigned to files in a directory and to change those attributes. Using DOS 5.0 and 6.0, you protected an important system file, COMMAND.COM, from accidental deletion by assigning it the Read-Only attribute. You assigned the Hidden attribute to COMMAND.COM so that DOS does not display it in a directory listing, and you learned to remove that attribute.

You checked the status of your hard disk and Tutorial Disk with the CHKDSK command. You learned that the CHKDSK command works in diagnostic mode to check the logical structure of a disk for errors. It automatically corrects small errors and, if you use the Fixup switch, it converts lost clusters to files. The CHKDSK command also produces a report on disk and memory usage.

You examined the different techniques and different levels of protection available in DOS 5.0, 6.0, and 6.2 for tracking deleted files. The Standard level of protection allows UNDELETE to recover deleted files using information in the DOS directory file. The Delete Tracker level of protection tracks the location of deleted files with a hidden system file, PCTRACKR.DEL. The Delete Sentry level of protection, available in DOS 6.0 and 6.2, stores deleted files in a hidden directory named SENTRY and improves your chances of recovering a deleted file.

You used the UNFORMAT command to reinstate an accidentally formatted diskette and to rebuild its system area.

You used the Microsoft Diagnostic Utility to examine technical information about your computer system.

Command Reference

DOS Commands

ATTRIB [*drive:*][*path*][*filename*]	An external command that displays file attributes
ATTRIB [*filename*] ±[*attribute*]	An external command that changes file attributes; common switches include: +A To assign the Archive attribute –A To remove the Archive attribute +H To assign the Hidden attribute –H To remove the Hidden attribute +R To assign the Read-Only attribute –R To remove the Read-Only attribute
CHKDSK [*drive:*]	An external command that examines the status of a hard disk or diskette, checks for the presence of errors, and produces a report on disk and memory usage; when used with the Fixup switch (/F), this command converts lost clusters to files
DIR /A[*attribute*]	An internal command that displays a directory of files with a specific attribute when used with the Attribute switch; attribute codes include: A For the Archive attribute H For the Hidden attribute R For the Read-Only attribute S For the System attribute

FORMAT *drive:*	An external command that unconditionally formats a new diskette or that performs a Safe format when reformatting a diskette. The Safe format saves unformat information in a mirror file and erases the contents of the directory file and File Allocation Tables, but does not erase files from the diskette. Common switches include:
	/Q The Quick switch performs a Quick format of a previously formatted diskette by saving unformat information in a mirror file, by erasing the contents of the directory file and File Allocation Tables, by leaving the contents of the files on the diskette, and by skipping the surface scan of the diskette for defective sectors
	/S The System switch copies the operating system files to a diskette after the diskette is formatted
	/U The Unconditional switch performs an Unconditional format of a previously formatted diskette by erasing the contents of the directory file and File Allocation Tables, by erasing the contents of the file on the diskette, and by scanning the surface of the disk for defective sectors
MIRROR /*T*[*drive*]	An external command in DOS 5.0 that loads a TSR to track the locations of deleted files for a specific drive with the use of a hidden system file named PCTRACKR.DEL
MSD	An external command that loads the Microsoft Diagnostic Utility and provides technical information about the computer system

SYS *drive:*	An external command that copies the operating system files to a specific drive from the current drive
UNDELETE [*drive:*] [*path*] [*filename*]	An external command that loads Delete Sentry and stores deleted files in a hidden directory named SENTRY; that loads Delete Tracker and stores locations on deleted files in PCTRACKR.DEL; or that undeletes files using the Standard, Delete Tracker, or Delete Sentry level of protection; common switches include:

	/S[*drive*]	To load Delete Sentry in DOS 6.0 and 6.2
	/T[*drive*]	To load Delete Tracker in DOS 6.0 and 6.2
	/DS	To restore erased files with Delete Sentry in DOS 6.0 and 6.2
	/DT	To restore erased files with Delete Tracker in DOS 5.0, 6.0, and 6.2
	/DOS	Restores files using the Standard level of protection and the DOS directory

UNFORMAT *drive:*	An external command that rebuilds the system area of a reformatted disk using a mirror file created during a Safe or Quick format.

QUESTIONS

1. What distinguishes a boot disk from a data disk? Why is a boot disk important?
2. How can you prepare a boot disk with the FORMAT command?
3. What version of DOS have you been using, and what are the names of the operating system files found in that version?
4. What is the command interpreter, and what does it do?
5. What happens if you leave a data disk in drive A and reboot your computer system?
6. What process does your computer system follow to locate the drive from which to boot?
7. What does the SYS command do, and how do you use it?
8. When you display a directory of a boot disk, how many and what file-names do you see?

9. What are attributes?

10. What does the System attribute indicate?

11. How do the Hidden and Read-Only attributes affect a file?

12. How can you view the names of hidden files with the DIR command?

13. How do you use the ATTRIBUTE command?

14. How can you assign the Read-Only attribute to a file named RECORDS?

15. How can you remove the Hidden attribute from a file named SYSTEM.LOG?

16. What does the CHKDSK command do, and why is it important?

17. What are lost clusters?

18. How can you fix lost clusters with the CHKDSK command?

19. What happens after you fix lost clusters on a hard disk?

20. What are cross-linked files, and how can you repair this problem?

21. What types of summary information does the CHKDSK command provide?

22. What three levels of protection does DOS provide for deleted files, and how do they differ?

23. How do you enable Delete Sentry for drive C?

24. What information does DOS need to restore deleted files with the Standard level of protection?

25. What happens during a Safe format?

26. How can you restore a reformatted diskette to its original condition?

27. What is the Microsoft Diagnostic Utility, and why is it important?

28. How can you determine the amount of RAM in your computer system?

29. How can you determine the number of sectors in an allocation unit, or cluster, on a hard-disk drive?

30. What is a mirror, or image, file?

TUTORIAL ASSIGNMENTS

1. **Examining File Attributes**: You decide to examine file attributes on your computer system's boot drive—drive C. List the commands that you would use to perform the following operations. Also list the names of any files that you find.
   a. Display a list of all system files in all directories.
   b. Display a list of all hidden files in all directories.
   c. Display a list of all read-only files in all directories.
   d. Print a list of all filenames and attributes in the root directory of drive C.
   Answer the following question:
   e. Did DOS include the names of any directories when you specified system, hidden, or read-only files?

2. **Checking the Status of a Hard-Disk Drive**: You want to examine the status of your hard disk. List the commands you would use to perform the following operations:
   a. Check the status of drive C and print a copy of the summary.
   b. Check the status of your Exercise Disk from drive C and print a copy of the summary.

Answer the following questions:

c. How much memory, or RAM, does DOS report when you examine drive C? How much does it report when you examine drive A?

d. How much memory, or RAM, is available for use?

e. How does the size of allocation units differ on the hard disk in drive C and your Exercise Disk in drive A (or drive B)? How many sectors does each allocation unit contain?

f. How many hidden files does drive C have? What are the total number of files? How many directories does drive C have? What are the average number of files per directory?

3. **Tracking Deleted Files**: *Use your Exercise Disk for this Tutorial Assignment.* As you perform the following operations, list the commands that you use.

a. Enable Delete Sentry (in DOS 6.0 and 6.2) or Delete Tracker (in DOS 5.0) for the diskette drive with your Exercise Disk.

b. Delete all the files in the CASHFLOW directory.

c. Undelete all the files that you deleted from the CASHFLOW directory.

d. Delete all the files in the RESUMES directory.

e. Remove the RESUMES directory.

f. Attempt to undelete the files that you deleted from the RESUMES directory.

g. Create a directory named RESUMES.

h. Attempt to undelete the files that you deleted from the original RESUMES directory.

Answer the following questions:

i. Can you restore deleted files to a directory that no longer exists?

j. Can you restore deleted files to a directory that you recreate?

4. **Unformatting Diskettes**: *Use your Exercise Disk for this Tutorial Assignment. If you are assigned both Tutorial Assignments 3 and 4, do Tutorial Assignment 3 first.* As you perform the following operations, list the commands that you use.

a. Perform a Safe format of the Exercise Disk.

b. Unformat the Exercise Disk, and then verify the operation.

c. Perform a Quick format of the Exercise Disk.

d. Unformat the Exercise Disk, and then verify the operation.

e. Perform an Unconditional format of the Exercise Disk.

f. Attempt to unformat the Exercise Disk.

Answer the following questions:

g. Can you unformat a diskette reformatted using a Safe format and the Quick switch?

h. Can you unformat a diskette reformatted with the Unconditional switch?

5. **Using the Microsoft Diagnostic Utility**: Use the Microsoft Diagnostic Utility to document important information (shown on the following page) about your computer system. You can photocopy this list, and then list your responses on that copy.

Component

Type of Processor (or Microprocessor):

Type of Keyboard:

Type of Video Display Adapter (or Card):

DOS Version:

Boot Drive:

Type of Mouse (if applicable):

Mouse Port (if applicable):

Drive A: Storage Capacity:

Drive B: Storage Capacity (if applicable):

Drive C: Storage Capacity:

Drive C: Number of Sectors/Track:

Drive C: Number of Cylinders (or Tracks):

Drive C: Hard-Disk Drive Type Number:

Drive D: Storage Capacity (if present):

Name(s) of LPT Ports:

Name(s) of COM Ports:

Using Batch Files

OBJECTIVES

In this tutorial you will learn to:

- Understand the importance of batch files
- Create a batch file directory
- Use the MS-DOS Editor to create a batch file
- Execute a batch file
- Check and change the DOS path
- Create a batch file to load an application
- Control the display of batch file commands
- Display messages from a batch file
- Temporarily pause batch file execution
- Document batch file operations
- Use replaceable parameters

After several months on the job, you are finally familiar with the procedures for preparing client documents and meeting clients' deadlines, as well as with the office's recordkeeping requirements. You store the documents that you prepare for each client on separate diskettes. You also keep two backup copies of each diskette; one of which is stored off-site for safety. You want to automate and simplify the procedure for formatting diskettes that you will later use as working copies and as backup copies. Rather than enter the FORMAT command with the appropriate switches each time you format a diskette, you want to be able to enter one short command that instructs DOS to execute the FORMAT command with the switches you use.

You also want to automate the process you go through to load the word processing application that you use to prepare and modify client documents. You have noticed that you use the same DOS commands and steps to change to the directory where you work and to load the word processing software. Rather than enter these commands repeatedly each time you use the word processing application, you want to enter one short command that instructs DOS to execute each of these commands and load the software. Once you automate this process, you can apply the same principles to automate the process for using your electronic spreadsheet to document cash flow, invoices, and income.

In your business, time is money. Anything you can do to "work smart" improves your ability to complete client contracts and to meet deadlines.

◆

THE IMPORTANCE OF BATCH FILES

If you find that you perform the same operation or set of operations repeatedly from the DOS prompt, you can store the command or set of commands in a special type of file called a batch file and execute the batch file as you would a program file. A batch file is an ASCII file that contains one or more commands DOS executes when you enter the name of the batch file at the DOS prompt. In order for DOS to recognize a batch file as a program file, you must add the BAT file extension to the filename for the batch file when you create it. Because you are the one who creates a batch file, you can think of these files as user-defined program files.

Batch files represent one important and valuable way in which you can optimize the performance of your computer system. Not only can you automate routine operations with batch files, you can also create batch files to store more complex commands that are difficult to remember or that you use less frequently. You can even safeguard your computer system from commands, such as the FORMAT command, that might create a problem if you inadvertently enter the command incorrectly.

CREATING A BATCH FILE

Your first batch file will format a diskette in the diskette drive in your computer system. Before you create this batch file, you want to create a new subdirectory to store your batch files. Most users create a subdirectory called BAT or BATCH on drive C to store their batch files. When they need to examine or change a batch file, they know exactly where to locate the file.

Because this is the first time you have worked with batch files, you want to create this subdirectory for batch files on your Tutorial Disk. This allows you to create and test your new batch files without affecting the batch files already stored on your hard disk. Later, once you know these batch files are working properly, you can add them to the batch file directory on your hard disk.

Let's start by setting up your system.

To get started:

5.0 *6.0*

6.2

1. After you power on your computer system, access the DOS prompt for drive C.

2. Type **DOSKEY** and press **[Enter]**. If you are using DOS 5.0 or 6.0, DOS will display the message "DOSKey installed" if DOS is not already installed on your computer. If you do not see a message with DOS 5.0 or 6.0, DOSKEY is already installed. DOS 6.2 will not display a message.

3. Type **SET DIRCMD=/P /O** and press **[Enter]**. DOS will display your files and subdirectories in alphabetical order and pause after each screen.

4. Type **SET** and press **[Enter]** to verify that you correctly entered the switches for the DIRCMD environment variable. If not, repeat Step 3.

Creating a Batch File Subdirectory

Now you are ready to create your batch file directory.

To create a subdirectory for batch files:

1. Insert your Tutorial Disk into drive A (or drive B).

2. Type **A:** (or **B:**) to change to drive A (or drive B).

3. Be sure you are at the root directory of drive A (or drive B). If not, type **CD ** and press **[Enter]**. You want to be sure that the batch file directory you create is positioned below the root directory.

4. Type **MD BAT** and press **[Enter]**.

5. Type **DIR** and press **[Enter]**. DOS displays the directory structure of the Tutorial Disk. See Figure 8-1. This directory structure includes the new batch file directory.

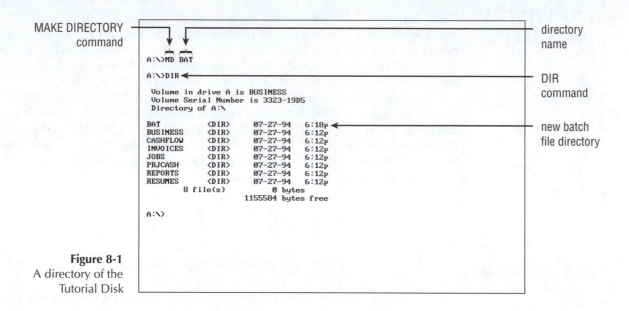

MAKE DIRECTORY command

directory name

DIR command

new batch file directory

Figure 8-1
A directory of the
Tutorial Disk

6. Type **CD BAT** and press **[Enter]**. DOS changes to the batch file directory.

USING THE MS-DOS EDITOR

You are ready to create your first batch file. DOS requires that batch files be ASCII, or text, files. You can use the MS-DOS Editor to create and edit a batch file. The MS-DOS Editor is a text editor—a program for creating and editing any type of ASCII file. The MS-DOS Editor, which was introduced in DOS 5.0, simplifies the process for creating and editing batch files and other types of files used to configure your computer system.

The EDIT command loads the MS-DOS Editor. This command is an external command with the following syntax:

EDIT   [[*drive:*][*path*]*filename*]

If you type EDIT without any parameters, you load the MS-DOS Editor from the current directory and drive. If you specify a filename, the MS-DOS Editor retrieves that file after DOS loads the MS-DOS Editor into memory. If the file is stored on another drive or in another directory, you specify the drive name and path of the file.

EDIT works in conjunction with two other programs: QBASIC.EXE, the text editor, and EDIT.HLP, which contains the help information for the MS-DOS Editor. If DOS cannot find QBASIC.EXE, it cannot load the MS-DOS Editor. If DOS cannot find EDIT.HLP, then the Help feature is not available while you use the MS-DOS Editor.

Let's start the MS-DOS Editor and examine some of its features.

To start the MS-DOS Editor:

1. Type **EDIT** and press **[Enter]**. After the MS-DOS Editor is loaded into memory, you see its Welcome screen. See Figure 8-2. The figures of the MS-DOS Editor in this tutorial show how it appears in text mode. Your

view of the MS-DOS Editor will be different if you are using graphics mode. If you experience difficulties when you attempt to start or use the MS-DOS Editor, ask your instructor or technical support person for assistance. DOS might not be able to locate the program and help files for the MS-DOS Editor.

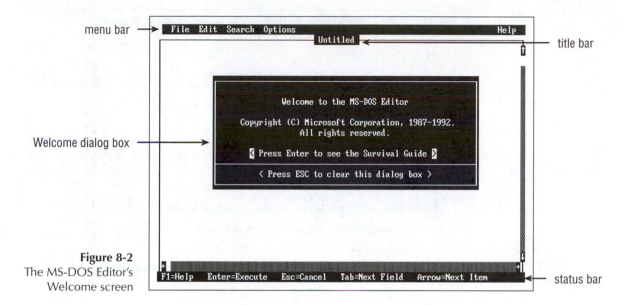

menu bar → | File Edit Search Options   Help |
Untitled → title bar

Welcome dialog box →

Welcome to the MS-DOS Editor

Copyright (C) Microsoft Corporation, 1987-1992.
All rights reserved.

‹ Press Enter to see the Survival Guide ›

‹ Press ESC to clear this dialog box ›

F1=Help   Enter=Execute   Esc=Cancel   Tab=Next Field   Arrow=Next Item ← status bar

Figure 8-2
The MS-DOS Editor's
Welcome screen

The opening screen welcomes you to the MS-DOS Editor, displays copyright information, and gives you two options. One option tells you to press the Enter key to see the Survival Guide. The Survival Guide contains help information on the use of the MS-DOS Editor. The second option tells you to press the Escape key (Esc) to remove the dialog box from your screen. The MS-DOS Editor uses dialog boxes to prompt for information, to list options, and to let you verify the operation. At the top of the screen is a menu bar with a list of menus. The title bar identifies the name of the current screen or shows the filename (if there is one). The status bar at the bottom of the screen contains shortcut keys for performing specific operations.

You will find that the MS-DOS Editor is similar to the DOS Shell. Also, you can use the keyboard and the mouse in the MS-DOS Editor.

EXPLORING THE SURVIVAL GUIDE

You want to examine the Survival Guide so that you know how to find help information on the MS-DOS Editor. That way, if you have a problem while creating or editing an ASCII file, you will know how to navigate around the MS-DOS Editor Help system to find the information you need.

To view the contents of the Survival Guide:

1. With the cursor positioned on the first option, press **[Enter]**. (If you have moved the cursor, press **[Tab]** until you return to the first option; then, press **[Enter]**.)

If you are using the mouse, click the **first option**.

The MS-DOS Editor displays the Survival Guide screen. See Figure 8-3. The Survival Guide provides a brief overview on using the MS-DOS Editor and explains how to navigate around the MS-DOS Editor Help system.

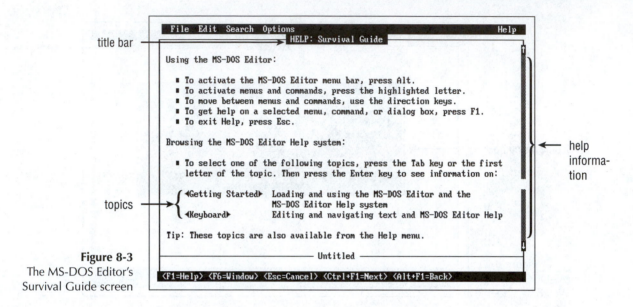

title bar

topics

help informa- tion

Figure 8-3
The MS-DOS Editor's
Survival Guide screen

2. Be sure the cursor is on the option, or topic, entitled "Getting Started." Then press **[Enter]**. (If the cursor is on the topic "Keyboard," which explains how to use different types of keys, press **[Tab]** to return to the first topic, then press **[Enter]**.) You can also select a topic by typing the first character of the topic and pressing the Enter key.

    If you are using the mouse, double-click **Getting Started**.

    The MS-DOS Editor displays the "Getting Started" screen. See Figure 8-4. There are three topics at the top of the screen and a set of more specific topics listed in the next window.

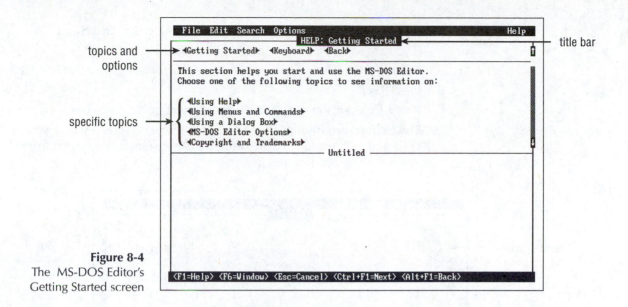

topics and options

specific topics

title bar

Figure 8-4
The MS-DOS Editor's Getting Started screen

3. Press **[Tab]** *twice* to move the cursor to the specific topic "Using Help," then press **[Enter]**.

   If you are using the mouse, double-click **Using Help**.

   The MS-DOS Editor displays the Using Help screen with general tips on how to use the Help feature in the MS-DOS Editor. See Figure 8-5. For example, you can use [F1] (Help) to obtain assistance with menus, commands, and dialog boxes. To adjust the view of the help screen, you could press [PgDn] (Page Down) or [PgUp] (Page Up).

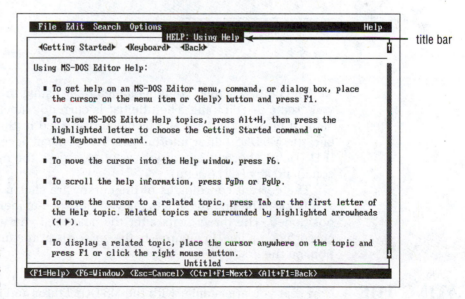

title bar

Figure 8-5
The MS-DOS Editor's Using Help screen

4. Press **[Tab]** *twice* to move the cursor to "Back," then press **[Enter]**.

   If you are using the mouse, double-click **Back**.

   The MS-DOS Editor displays the previous screen.

5. Press **[Tab]** to move the cursor to "Back," then press **[Enter]**.

If you are using the mouse, double-click **Back**.

The MS-DOS Editor returns to the original screen.

6. Press **[Esc]**.

If you are using the mouse, click **Esc=Cancel** in the status bar.

The Help screen disappears, and you see the main screen where you enter and edit text. See Figure 8-6. *You can exit the Help system from any screen by pressing [Esc].*

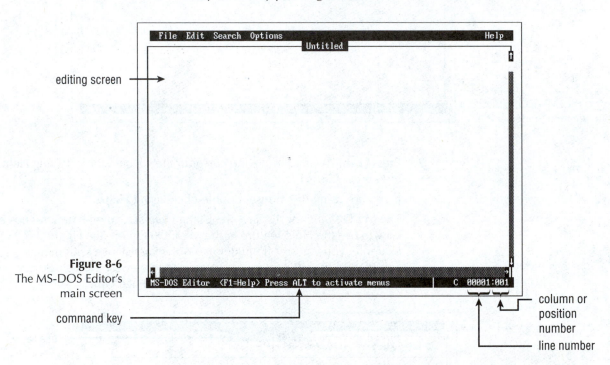

editing screen →

Figure 8-6
The MS-DOS Editor's
main screen

command key →

→ column or position number

→ line number

The editing screen contains a menu bar listing the menus you can use as you create or edit a file. The title bar is currently labeled "Untitled." After you name a file, you will see the filename displayed in the title bar. In the status bar, the MS-DOS Editor informs you that you can access Help by pressing the [F1] (Help) shortcut key. If you want to access the menu bar, you press the command key [Alt] (Menu).

The current coordinates of the cursor are shown on the right side of the status bar. The first five digits tell you the line number on which the cursor is positioned. The three digits after the colon tell you what the position of the cursor is on a line. In Figure 8-6, the cursor is at the first column, or first position, on the first line.

CREATING THE BATCH FILE

Now that you are familiar with the MS-DOS Editor and its Help system, you are ready to create your first batch file. To enter text, you just start typing. Once you enter a line of text, you press the Enter key to advance the cursor to the beginning of the next line.

This batch file needs one line of text—the command for formatting a diskette. You want to use the Unconditional switch in the event you reformat a diskette. The Unconditional switch will erase any information stored on the diskette.

To enter the FORMAT command:

1. Press **[Caps Lock]**. If this feature is activated, you should see the indicator "C" on the status bar to the left of the cursor coordinates. You can enter commands in a batch file in uppercase, lowercase, or mixed case. The figures in this tutorial use uppercase.

2. Type **FORMAT A: /U** (or **FORMAT B: /U**) and press **[Enter]**. If you make a typing mistake, you can stop and use the Backspace key to erase what you have typed.

If you are using a double-density diskette in a high-density or extra-high-density drive, or a high-density diskette in an extra-high-density drive, you will need to include the Format Capacity switch. If you are using a double-density diskette in a double-density drive, a high-density diskette in a high-density drive, or an extra-high-density diskette in an extra-high-density drive, you do not need to use the Format Capacity switch. If you do, however, the FORMAT command will still work.

To specify a Format Capacity switch, if necessary:

1. Press **[↑]** (Up Arrow) to position the cursor at the beginning of the first line. Then press **[→]** (Right Arrow) until the cursor is positioned on the / (Slash) of the Unconditional switch.

   If you are using the mouse, click the **/ (Slash)** of the Unconditional switch.

2. Enter the appropriate setting for the Format Capacity switch:

   ◆ If you are using a 3½-inch double-density diskette in a high-density or extra-high-density drive, type **/F:720** and press **[Spacebar]**.

   ◆ If you are using a 3½-inch high-density diskette in an extra-high-density drive, type **/F:1.44** and press **[Spacebar]**.

   ◆ If you are using a 5¼-inch double-density diskette in a high-density drive, type **/F:360** and press **[Spacebar]**.

By default, the MS-DOS Editor works in **insert mode** and automatically inserts these characters at the position of the cursor. Figure 8-7 shows the contents of the batch file. Your batch file will be different if you used the Format Capacity switch.

batch file
command →

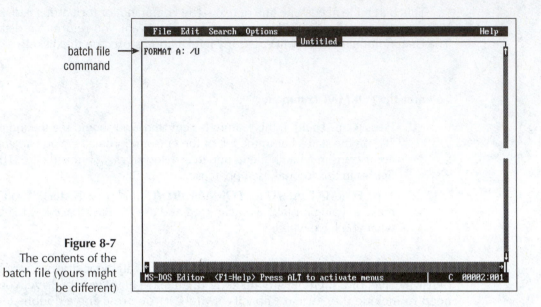

Figure 8-7
The contents of the
batch file (yours might
be different)

SAVING A BATCH FILE WITH THE MS-DOS EDITOR

Now that you have created your first batch file, you want to save it in the current directory on your Tutorial Disk. You can use the File menu to save a file and to exit the MS-DOS Editor.

To save your batch file:

1. Press **[Alt]** (Menu) to access the menu bar. The first menu—the File menu—is highlighted. One letter in each menu is highlighted. To select a menu, you can press an arrow key to highlight the menu name and then press the Enter key, you can type the highlighted letter in the menu name, or you can click the menu name if you are using the mouse. If you want to select the currently highlighted menu, you just press the Enter key.

2. Press **[Enter]** or type **F** to select the File menu.

   If you are using the mouse, click the **File** menu.

   The MS-DOS Editor displays the File menu. See Figure 8-8. This *drop-down menu* has two options for saving a file. The "Save" option saves the file under its currently assigned filename. The "Save As" option allows you to name the file before the MS-DOS Editor saves it. This latter option is also useful if you want to assign a new name to an existing file.

currently selected
menu

drop-down
File menu

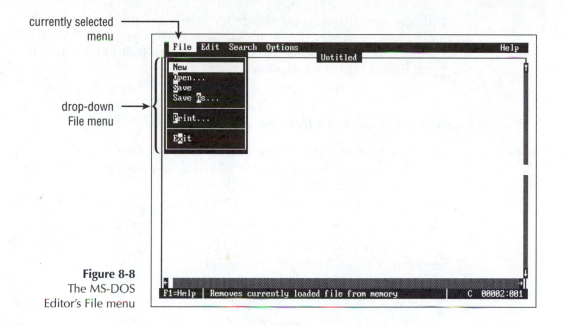

Figure 8-8
The MS-DOS
Editor's File menu

3. Press [↓] (Down Arrow) three times to highlight "Save As." Then press **[Enter]**.

If you are using the mouse, click the **Save As** command.

The Save As dialog box appears. See Figure 8-9.

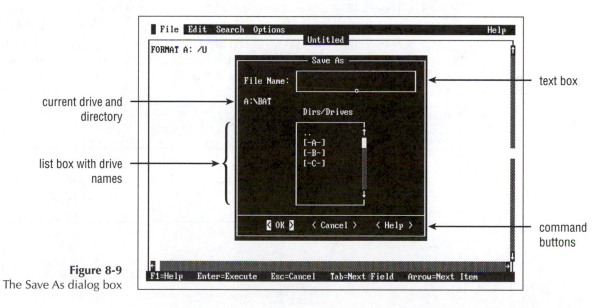

text box

current drive and
directory

list box with drive
names

command
buttons

Figure 8-9
The Save As dialog box

The cursor is positioned in the first text box, next to the "File Name" prompt. Below this box, the MS-DOS Editor shows the current drive and directory (in this case, A:\BAT). In the box labeled "Dirs/Drives," the MS-DOS Editor displays the disk drives available on your computer system. At the bottom of the dialog box are the OK, Cancel, and Help command buttons.

You now have to decide on a name for your batch file. Batch filenames are generally short, to save typing. You choose to name this file FD.BAT. The "FD" is an abbreviation for "Format Disk." DOS requires that you include the file extension BAT as part of a batch file's name.

To assign a filename to this batch file and save it to disk:

1. Type **FD.BAT** and press **[Enter]**. The MS-DOS Editor saves the batch file. The dialog box disappears, and you return to the editing window. The new filename is now shown in the title bar.

Next you want to exit the MS-DOS Editor so that you can test this batch file.

2. Press **[Alt]** (Menu), then press **[Enter]** to select the File menu.

   If you are using the mouse, click **File**.

3. Type **X** to select the "Exit" command.

   If you are using the mouse, click **Exit**.

   You exit the MS-DOS Editor and return to the DOS prompt. (If a dialog box appears asking if you want to save your changes, the MS-DOS Editor assumes you made some further change to the batch file, or simply pressed a key. For example, you might have pressed [Spacebar]. If this occurs, press **[Tab]** to select No and press **[Enter]**. If you are using the mouse, click **No**.)

Now let's examine this new file.

4. Type **DIR** and press **[Enter]**. As is typical of most batch files, this batch file is very small in size (in this example, 16 bytes). Your file size might differ.

5. Type **TYPE FD.BAT** and press **[Enter]**. DOS displays the contents of this text file. See Figure 8-10. The batch file might contain blank lines after the one with the FORMAT command; however, the batch file will still work properly.

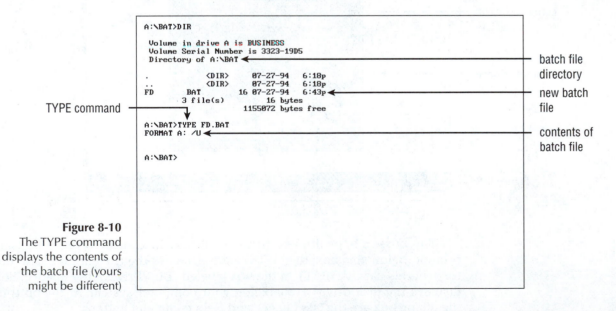

Figure 8-10
The TYPE command displays the contents of the batch file (yours might be different)

EXECUTING A BATCH FILE

You can now test this batch file. To execute the contents of the batch file, you type the filename of the batch file at the DOS prompt. You do not need to specify the file extension, although if you do, the batch file will still work. As with any other command, after you enter the name of the batch file, DOS checks memory to determine if the command that you entered is an internal command. If the command that you enter is not an internal command, DOS checks the current directory for a program file with the filename that you entered and with one of three file extensions: COM, EXE, and BAT. In this instance, DOS looks in the current directory first for a file by the name of FD.COM, then for one by the name of FD.EXE, and, finally, for one by the name of FD.BAT. When it locates FD.BAT, it executes the commands stored in the batch file.

If the batch file is not stored in the current directory, DOS uses the DOS path in an attempt to locate the program file. The **DOS path** is a sequence of directories specified by the PATH command. DOS examines each directory in the DOS path for program files.

Since you are working in the directory where the batch file is stored, you can execute it from this directory. Because this batch file formats a diskette unconditionally, you decide to write-protect your Tutorial Disk.

To write-protect your Tutorial Disk:

1. Remove your Tutorial Disk from drive A (or drive B). If you are using a 3½-inch diskette, turn the diskette over and move the tab on the right side of the diskette down so that you can see through a square hole in the diskette. If you are using a 5¼-inch diskette, place a write-protect tape over the write-protect notch. After you write-protect the Tutorial Disk, insert it into drive A (or drive B).

Next, execute the batch file.

2. Type **FD** and press **[Enter]**. Next to the DOS prompt, DOS displays, or **echoes**, the command stored in the batch file. See Figure 8-11. FORMAT then prompts you to insert a diskette into the drive.

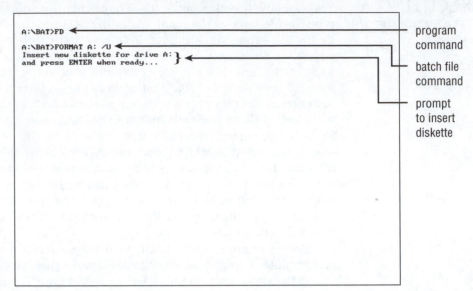

```
A:\BAT>FD
A:\BAT>FORMAT A: /U
Insert new diskette for drive A:
and press ENTER when ready...
```

program command

batch file command

prompt to insert diskette

Figure 8-11
Executing a batch file

3. Remove your Tutorial Disk from the drive, insert the Exercise Disk, and press **[Enter]**. When FORMAT prompts for a volume name, type **BUSINESS** and press **[Enter]**. When FORMAT asks you if you want to format another diskette, type **N** and press **[Enter]**. DOS then prompts you to insert the disk with the batch file. See Figure 8-12. DOS must return to the batch file to determine if there are any more commands in the batch file to execute.

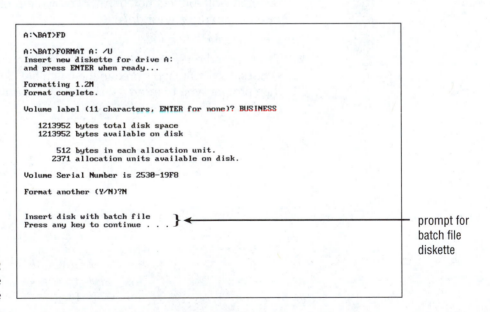

```
A:\BAT>FD

A:\BAT>FORMAT A: /U
Insert new diskette for drive A:
and press ENTER when ready...

Formatting 1.2M
Format complete.

Volume label (11 characters, ENTER for none)? BUSINESS

    1213952 bytes total disk space
    1213952 bytes available on disk

       512 bytes in each allocation unit.
      2371 allocation units available on disk.

Volume Serial Number is 2530-19F8

Format another (Y/N)?N


Insert disk with batch file
Press any key to continue . . .
```

prompt for batch file diskette

Figure 8-12
DOS prompts for the diskette with the batch file

4. Remove the Exercise Disk, insert the Tutorial Disk, and press **[Enter]**. DOS displays the DOS prompt for the root directory. DOS has executed all the commands in the batch file. Any multiple DOS prompts you see are produced by blank lines at the end of the batch file.

Testing the Batch File from Another Directory

It is a good idea to test batch files from different directories and under different conditions. Because you usually start from the root directory, let's test the batch file from that directory.

To execute the batch file from the root directory:

1. If necessary, type **CD ** and press **[Enter]** to return to the root directory.
2. Type **FD** and press **[Enter]**. DOS displays the message "Bad command or file name." See Figure 8-13. If you inadvertently execute another program, ask your instructor or technical support person for assistance.

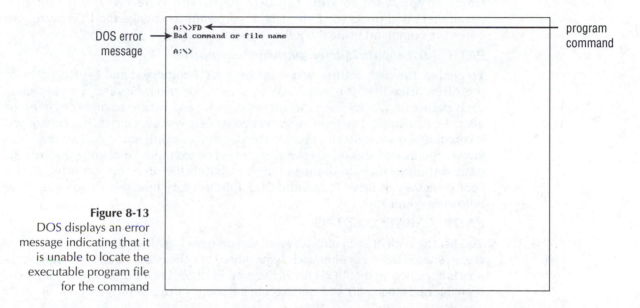

DOS error message →

```
A:\>FD ◄
Bad command or file name
A:\>
```

→ program command

Figure 8-13
DOS displays an error message indicating that it is unable to locate the executable program file for the command

Why does the batch file work in one instance and not the other? In the first instance, you executed the batch file from the directory where you stored it. DOS was able to locate the batch file because it checked the current directory after it checked memory for the command. In the second instance, you attempted to execute the batch file from the root directory. DOS checked the root directory for program files with the names FD.COM, FD.EXE, or FD.BAT. Because there are no program files in the root directory of the current drive, DOS then checks the DOS path. The current path on your computer system probably includes the root directory and a set of subdirectories on your hard disk drive (or on a computer network). If there are no program files with any of these three names in any of those directories, DOS informs you that you issued a bad command or filename. DOS does not check the batch file directory on your Tutorial Disk because it is not included in the DOS path.

THE IMPORTANCE OF THE DOS PATH

Before DOS can execute an external command, it must first locate the program file before it can load the program into memory. By default, DOS automatically searches the current directory on the current drive for executable files—program files with the file extensions COM, EXE, or BAT. If the program file is not located in the current directory on the current drive, DOS searches through each directory listed in the DOS path. If DOS cannot locate a program file after examining all of the directories in the DOS path, it informs you that you used a bad command or filename. If you want DOS to locate and execute your batch files, you must include the name of the batch file directory in the DOS path or you must execute the batch files from the directory where they are located.

The PATH command displays or changes the DOS path. The current setting for the DOS path is stored in the DOS environment along with other settings. If you want to view the DOS path, you type PATH without any parameters and press the Enter key. If you want to change the DOS path, you enter the command using the following syntax:

PATH   [*drive:*]*path1*;[*drive:*]*path2*;[*drive:*]*path3*;...

To change the path setting, you enter the PATH command and list the paths of the directories that you want DOS to search for program files. You separate each path with a semicolon. *No spaces are allowed between paths, or before or after the semicolon. You must use a semicolon between directories; you cannot use a colon.* It is a good idea to include the drive name with each path so that DOS knows the exact location of each directory. For example, to change the current path setting to include the name of your batch file directory on drive A, the root directory of drive C, and the DOS subdirectory on drive C, you enter the following command:

PATH   A:\BAT;C:\;C:\DOS

You list the path of each directory and separate each path with a semicolon. There are no spaces before or after each semicolon. Also, the exact location of each directory is specified so that DOS checks the correct drive. Because the PATH command is an internal command, you can execute it from any drive or directory.

Viewing the DOS Path

You want to examine the DOS path on your system and update it to include the name of your batch file directory so that you can test your batch files from the root directory of the Tutorial Disk.

To view the DOS path:

1. Type **PATH** and press **[Enter]**. DOS displays the current path. See Figure 8-14. The path on your computer system will be different.

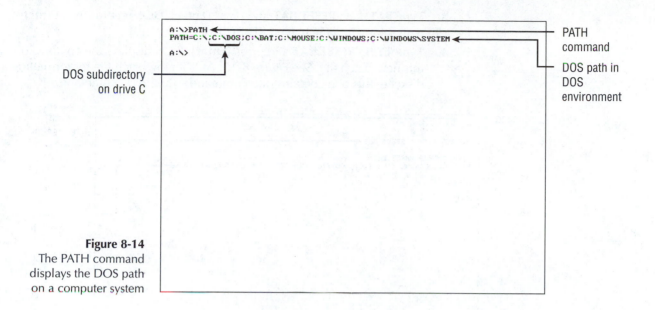

```
A:\>PATH
PATH=C:\;C:\DOS;C:\BAT;C:\MOUSE;C:\WINDOWS;C:\WINDOWS\SYSTEM
A:\>
```

PATH command

DOS path in DOS environment

DOS subdirectory on drive C

Figure 8-14
The PATH command displays the DOS path on a computer system

The DOS path lists a series of directories for DOS to search in order to locate a program file not stored in the current directory where you are working. The path is likely to include a reference to the root directory of your hard disk drive. If you are using a computer network, you will see the names of network drives, such as G:, H:, U:, X:, Y:, and Z:. The names of subdirectories with program files are usually included in the DOS path. These subdirectories contain software applications or utilities. You will also see a reference to the directory on your hard disk drive where the DOS system utilities are stored. This directory is probably named DOS. In the example in Figure 8-14, the path also references a batch file directory on drive C.

Storing the DOS Path in a Batch File

You want to update the path to include a reference to your batch file directory. Before you make this change, you decide to create another batch file with the current path so that you can reset your system after you finish working. As with any other DOS command, you can redirect the output of the PATH command to a batch file. First, however, you must remove the write-protection from your Tutorial Disk.

To remove the write-protection:

1. Remove your Tutorial Disk from the diskette drive. If you are using a 3½-inch diskette, turn the diskette over and move the tab on the right side of the diskette up so that you cover the square hole in the diskette. If you are using a 5¼-inch diskette, remove the write-protect tape over the write-protect notch. Then insert your Tutorial Disk into the diskette drive.

Now create a batch file with the current path setting.

2. Type **CD BAT** and press **[Enter]**. DOS changes to the batch file directory.

3. Type **PATH > RESET.BAT** and press **[Enter]**. DOS records the current path setting in a file named RESET.BAT.

4. Type **TYPE RESET.BAT** and press **[Enter]**. DOS displays the contents of this new batch file. See Figure 8-15. As with the batch file for formatting a diskette, this one contains one command—the PATH command.

PATH command

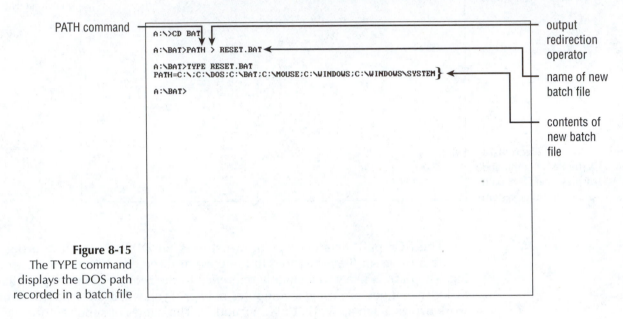

```
A:\>CD BAT
A:\BAT>PATH > RESET.BAT
A:\BAT>TYPE RESET.BAT
PATH=C:\;C:\DOS;C:\BAT;C:\MOUSE;C:\WINDOWS;C:\WINDOWS\SYSTEM
A:\BAT>
```

output redirection operator

name of new batch file

contents of new batch file

Figure 8-15
The TYPE command displays the DOS path recorded in a batch file

5. Type **CD ** and press **[Enter]**. DOS returns to the root directory.

6. Type **CLS** and press **[Enter]**. DOS clears the screen.

Changing the DOS Path

Now you are ready to change the path so that you can test your batch file from another directory. You want the new path to include the name of the batch file directory on drive A (or drive B) so that DOS can locate the batch files you create and store in that subdirectory. You also want the path to include the name of the root directory of drive C and the name of the DOS subdirectory on drive C, because DOS might need to search these directories for program files as it executes your batch files.

To view and change the path setting:

1. Type **PATH** and press **[Enter]**. DOS displays the current path. You might need to reference this path in the next step.

2. If you are working on a computer system with a hard disk drive *and* if your Tutorial Disk is in drive A, type **PATH A:\BAT;C:\;C:\DOS** and press **[Enter]**. If you are working on a computer system with a hard disk drive *and* if your Tutorial Disk is in drive B, type **PATH B:\BAT;C:\;C:\DOS** and press **[Enter]**. *If your DOS subdirectory has another name, use that name instead of DOS in the path.* If you are working on a computer

network, ask your instructor or technical support person for permission to change the path so that it includes the name of your batch file directory, and for the names of any network drives that must be included in the path.

Now verify the path setting.

3. Type **PATH** and press **[Enter]**. See Figure 8-16. Check your new path setting. Be sure your batch file directory is listed first, and be sure there is a reference to the DOS directory on drive C. If you need to make a change, repeat Step 2.

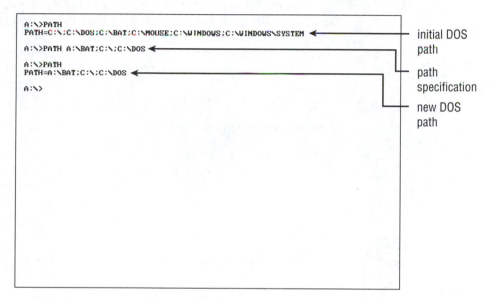

```
A:\>PATH
PATH=C:\;C:\DOS;C:\BAT;C:\MOUSE;C:\WINDOWS;C:\WINDOWS\SYSTEM  ◄────── initial DOS
                                                                      path
A:\>PATH A:\BAT;C:\;C:\DOS ◄──────

A:\>PATH
PATH=A:\BAT;C:\;C:\DOS ◄──────                                         path
                                                                      specification
A:\>
                                                                      new DOS
                                                                      path
```

Figure 8-16
Changing and verifying
the DOS path

Testing the Batch File

Now that you have changed the path setting, you are ready to test your batch file from the root directory. As before, you want to write-protect your Tutorial Disk before you execute the batch file.

To write-protect your Tutorial Disk:

1. Remove your Tutorial Disk from the diskette drive. If you are using a 3½-inch diskette, turn the diskette over and move the tab on the right side of the diskette down so that you can see through a square hole in the diskette. If you are using a 5¼-inch diskette, place a write-protect tape over the write-protect notch. After you write-protect the Tutorial Disk, insert it into drive A (or drive B).

Next test the batch file.

2. Type **FD** and press **[Enter]**. Next to the DOS prompt, DOS displays the command stored in the batch file. FORMAT then prompts you to insert a diskette into the drive.

3. Insert the Exercise Disk into drive A (or drive B), and press **[Enter]**. When FORMAT prompts for a volume name, type **BUSINESS** and press **[Enter]**. When FORMAT asks you if you want to format another diskette, type **N** and press **[Enter]**. DOS prompts you to insert the diskette with the batch file.

4. Remove the Exercise Disk, insert the Tutorial Disk, and press **[Enter]** or any other key to continue. DOS displays the DOS prompt for the root directory. DOS has executed all the commands in the batch file.

You can now see the importance of the DOS path, and you now know how to change the path setting. If you include the names of all directories on your computer that contain program files in the DOS path, DOS can locate any program file from any directory on the hard disk drive or from any other drive.

Before you continue, you want to remove the write-protection.

To remove the write-protection:

1. Remove your Tutorial Disk from the diskette drive. If you are using a 3½-inch diskette, turn the diskette over and move the tab on the right side of the diskette up so that you cover the square hole in the diskette. If you are using a 5¼-inch diskette, remove the write-protect tape over the write-protect notch. Then insert your Tutorial Disk into the diskette drive.

This is a good opportunity to take a short break.

CREATING A BATCH FILE TO START AN APPLICATION

As you prepare résumés and accompanying letters for clients, you work from files that contain a generic format for a résumé or form letter. You store these files as ASCII, or text, files so that you can easily import them into different word processing applications. When you import a file, you are retrieving and using a file that you produced with another program.

Periodically, you need to make changes to the information stored in these files. Now that you are familiar with the MS-DOS Editor, you can make changes with this text editor. When you save the files, they are stored in their original ASCII format. To automate this process, you decide to create a batch file that changes to the subdirectory where these files are stored and then loads the MS-DOS Editor so that you are ready to work.

Defining the Steps for a Batch File

Because this batch file must perform more than one operation, you decide to go through the operations manually.

To get started:

1. Be sure the current drive is the one that contains the Tutorial Disk, and be sure you are at the root directory of drive A (or drive B).

Next, define the steps required for this batch file.

2. Type **CD RESUMES** and press **[Enter]**. DOS changes to the RESUMES directory, where you store these template files. The batch file must perform this step first.

3. Type **EDIT** and press **[Enter]**. DOS loads the MS-DOS Editor, which is the second step required of the batch file.

4. Press **[Esc]**. The MS-DOS Editor removes the Welcome dialog box and displays its editing screen. You could now retrieve and modify a file. Because you are just testing the batch file and do not need to work with a file just yet, you can exit the MS-DOS Editor and complete the testing of the batch file.

5. Press **[Alt]** (Menu). Press **[Enter]** to select the File menu. Type **X** to exit the MS-DOS Editor.

   If you are using the mouse, click **File**, then click **Exit**.

   DOS displays the DOS prompt. Because you performed the last two steps in the MS-DOS Editor (clearing the Welcome dialog box and exiting the MS-DOS Editor), you do not want to include these steps in your batch file.

6. Type **CD ** and press **[Enter]**. You want the batch file to perform this last step and return to the root directory after you use the MS-DOS Editor.

By stepping through the operations manually, you know which steps you need to include in the batch file and the correct order of the steps. Figure 8-17 shows the steps required of this batch file: It changes to the RESUMES subdirectory, loads the MS-DOS Editor, and, after you exit the MS-DOS Editor, returns to the root directory.

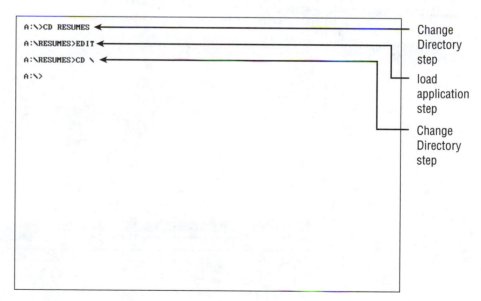

Figure 8-17
Simulating the steps for a batch file that loads the MS-DOS Editor

Creating the Batch File with the MS-DOS Editor

You can also use the MS-DOS Editor to create this batch file.

To create this next batch file:

1. Type **CD BAT** and press **[Enter]**. DOS changes to the batch file directory.
2. Type **EDIT** and press **[Enter]**. DOS loads the MS-DOS Editor.
3. Press **[Esc]**. The MS-DOS Editor clears the Welcome dialog box.

Now you can enter the steps required of this batch file. The steps include the commands that you executed manually from the DOS prompt. When you create a batch file that performs more than one operation, you list each command on a separate line in the batch file. When you test the batch file, DOS executes each command on a line-by-line basis.

To enter the contents of this batch file:

1. Type **CD RESUMES** and press **[Enter]**. You have entered the command for the first operation this batch file must perform.
2. Type **EDIT** and press **[Enter]**. You have entered the command for the second operation this batch file must perform.
3. Type **CD ** and press **[Enter]**. You have entered the command for the third, and last, operation this batch file must perform. Figure 8-18 shows the contents of the batch file. Check your batch file against this figure.

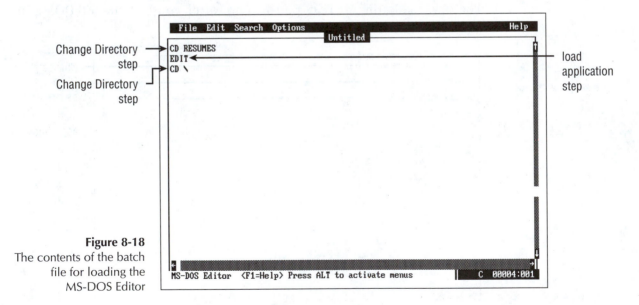

Change Directory step

Change Directory step

load application step

Figure 8-18
The contents of the batch file for loading the MS-DOS Editor

Next you must save your work.

4. Press **[Alt]** (Menu). Type **[Enter]** to select the File menu. Type **A** to select the "Save As" command.

   If you are using the mouse, click **File**, then click **Save As**.

   The MS-DOS Editor displays the Save As dialog box.

5. Type **REVISE.BAT** and press **[Enter]**.

   If you are using the mouse, type **REVISE.BAT**, then click **OK**.

   The MS-DOS Editor saves this batch file as REVISE.BAT in the batch file directory.

   Now exit the MS-DOS Editor and return to the root directory.

6. Press **[Alt]** (Menu). Press **[Enter]** to select the File menu. Type **X**.

   If you are using the mouse, click **File**, then click **Exit**.

   DOS displays the DOS prompt.

7. Type **CD** \ and press **[Enter]**. DOS returns to the root directory.

Testing the Batch File

You are ready to test this batch file under conditions different from those that you will probably encounter when you prepare client documents. First, you will execute this batch file from the root directory.

To execute this batch file:

1. Type **REVISE** and press **[Enter]**. DOS displays and executes the first command—it moves you to the RESUMES directory. DOS then displays and executes the second command—it loads the MS-DOS Editor.

2. Press **[Esc]**. The MS-DOS Editor clears the Welcome dialog box. Now that you have successfully tested the first two steps in the batch file, you can exit the MS-DOS Editor.

3. Press **[Alt]** (Menu). Press **[Enter]** to select the File menu. Type **X** to exit the MS-DOS Editor.

   If you are using the mouse, click **File**, then click **Exit**.

   DOS returns to the batch file, displays and executes the last command—it returns you to the root directory. Figure 8-19 shows the commands that the batch file executed.

```
A:\>REVISE
A:\>CD RESUMES
A:\RESUMES>EDIT
A:\RESUMES>CD \
A:\>
A:\>
A:\>
```

Change Directory step ──────▶ A:\>CD RESUMES

Change Directory step ──────▶ A:\RESUMES>CD \

program command

load application step

Figure 8-19
DOS executes the
batch file for loading
the MS-DOS Editor

Your next step is to test the batch file from another directory, a directory
that you commonly use each workday.

To test the batch file from another directory:

1. Type **CD BUSINESS** and press **[Enter]**.

2. Type **REVISE** and press **[Enter]**. DOS executes the Change Directory
    command and displays an "Invalid directory" message. It then executes
    the EDIT command and loads the MS-DOS Editor.

3. Press **[Esc]**. The MS-DOS Editor clears the Welcome dialog box.

Now exit and finish testing the batch file.

4. Press **[Alt]** (Menu). Press **[Enter]** to select the File menu. Type **X** to exit the
    MS-DOS Editor.

    If you are using the mouse, click **File**, then click **Exit**.

    DOS returns to the batch file, displays and executes the last command,
    and returns to the root directory. Figure 8-20 shows the commands that
    the batch file executed.

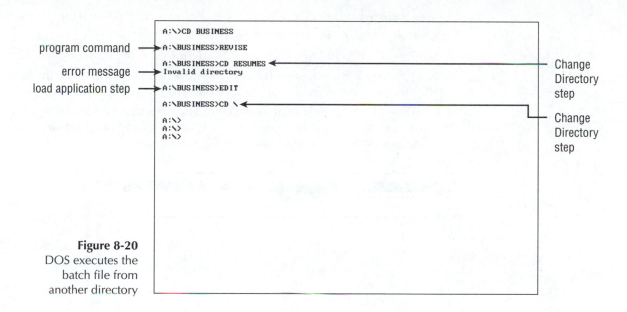

program command

error message

load application step

Change
Directory
step

Change
Directory
step

```
A:\>CD BUSINESS
A:\BUSINESS>REVISE
A:\BUSINESS>CD RESUMES
Invalid directory
A:\BUSINESS>EDIT
A:\BUSINESS>CD \
A:\>
A:\>
A:\>
```

Figure 8-20
DOS executes the
batch file from
another directory

This batch file correctly loaded the MS-DOS Editor and returned you to the root directory after you exited the MS-DOS Editor. However, it did not move you to the RESUMES directory as you might have expected. Instead, DOS remained in the BUSINESS subdirectory. Why? The first command in the batch file is CD RESUMES. When DOS executes this command, it assumes that you want to change to a directory named RESUMES that is positioned *below the current directory*. When you changed to the BUSINESS directory and executed the batch file, DOS displayed an invalid directory message because there is no RESUMES directory located below the BUSINESS directory. DOS then executed the remaining commands in the batch file. Although the batch file was able to complete the remainder of the operations, you were not working in the directory you wanted. The same problem will occur if you switch to another drive.

When creating batch files like this one, you should have the batch file perform two operations: (1) switch to the drive where the directory is stored, and (2) change to the root directory before it changes to the directory where you want to work. Or, after the batch file changes to a drive, you can specify the full path of the subdirectory to guarantee that it switches to the correct directory.

Revising the Batch File

Let's modify the batch file so that it specifies a drive and directory before it loads your application. Then let's test the modifications to the batch file.

To revise the batch file:

1. Type **CD BAT** and press **[Enter]**. DOS changes to the batch file directory.
2. Type **EDIT REVISE.BAT** and press **[Enter]**. If you specify a filename after the EDIT command, DOS loads the MS-DOS Editor, which automatically loads the file.

Now include two additional steps at the beginning of the batch file.

3. Press [**Enter**]. The MS-DOS Editor inserts a blank line.

4. Press [↑] (Up Arrow). The MS-DOS Editor moves the cursor up one line.

5. Type **A:** (or **B:**) and press [**Enter**]. This new step guarantees that the batch file uses drive A (or drive B), where your Tutorial Disk is located.

6. Type **CD** \ but do *not* press the Enter key. This step guarantees that DOS returns to the root directory before it changes to another directory. See Figure 8-21. Check your batch file against this figure.

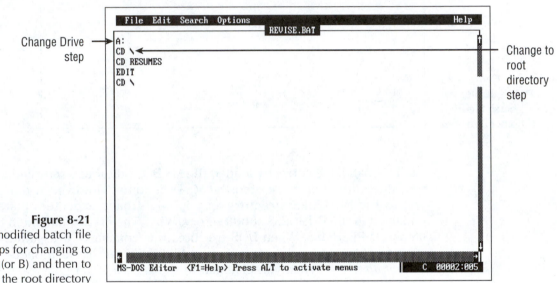

Change Drive step

Change to root directory step

Figure 8-21
The modified batch file with steps for changing to drive A (or B) and then to the root directory

Now save your changes and exit the MS-DOS Editor.

7. Press [**Alt**] (Menu). Type [**Enter**] to select the File menu. Type **S** to select the Save command.

    If you are using the mouse, click **File**, then click **Save**.

   The MS-DOS Editor saves the changes under the current filename.

8. Press [**Alt**] (Menu). Press [**Enter**] to select the File menu. Type **X** to exit the MS-DOS Editor.

   If you are using the mouse, click **File**, then click **Exit**.

   DOS displays the DOS prompt.

9. Type **CD** \ and press [**Enter**]. DOS returns to the root directory.

Testing the Revised Batch File

You are now ready to test the modified batch file. Let's try running the batch file from the BUSINESS directory again.

To test the batch file:

1. Type **CD BUSINESS** and press [**Enter**].

2. Type **REVISE** and press [**Enter**]. After DOS executes the Change Drive command and the first Change Directory command, it executes the second Change Directory command and switches to the RESUMES directory. Then DOS executes the EDIT command in the batch file and loads the MS-DOS Editor.

3. Press [**Esc**]. The MS-DOS Editor clears the Welcome dialog box.

4. Press [**Alt**] (Menu). Press [**Enter**] to select the File menu. Type **X** to exit the MS-DOS Editor.

   If you are using the mouse, click **File**, then click **Exit**.

   DOS returns to the batch file, displays and executes the last command, and returns to the root directory. See Figure 8-22. The batch file changed to the root directory before changing to the RESUMES directory.

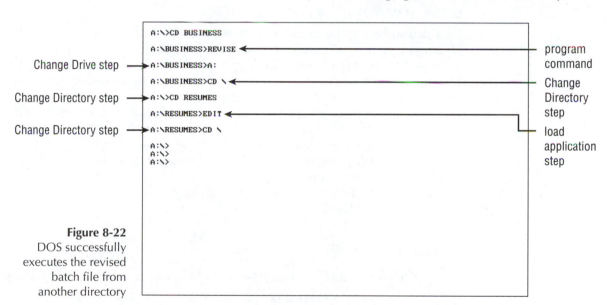

```
A:\>CD BUSINESS
A:\BUSINESS>REVISE          ◄─────────────────   program
Change Drive step    ──►  A:\BUSINESS>A:                              command
A:\BUSINESS>CD \            ◄─────────────────   Change
Change Directory step ──► A:\>CD RESUMES                              Directory
A:\RESUMES>EDIT     ◄─────────────────           step
Change Directory step ──► A:\RESUMES>CD \                             load
A:\>                                             application
A:\>                                             step
A:\>
```

Figure 8-22
DOS successfully executes the revised batch file from another directory

When constructing batch files, you should always consider whether the batch file should start from a specific drive or directory before the batch file changes to another drive or directory. If you include a step to change to a specific drive and you execute the batch file from that drive, no harm is done and no error messages result. However, these types of precautionary steps improve the chances that your batch files will work under different circumstances.

CONTROLLING THE DISPLAY OF BATCH FILE COMMANDS

When DOS executes the commands in a batch file, it displays each command next to a DOS prompt. If the batch file contains any blank lines at the end of the file, you also see several DOS prompts displayed after DOS executes the batch file. After you test and verify that a batch file is working properly, you can use the ECHO command to turn off the display of the batch file commands that DOS executes and the blank lines.

The ECHO command controls what DOS echoes, or displays, on the monitor during batch file execution. By default, DOS sets ECHO to ON and displays each batch file command as it executes the command. To turn this echo off, you place an ECHO OFF command at the beginning of the batch file. When DOS executes the batch file, it does not display any commands that come after the ECHO OFF command. However, it does display the ECHO OFF command itself. To turn off the display of this command as well, you place an @ ("at" symbol) before the ECHO OFF command. Thus, @ECHO OFF included at the beginning of a batch file turns off the display of all commands, including ECHO OFF.

ECHO OFF does not suppress the display of prompts produced by a command, such as the FORMAT command. You still see the prompt, but you do not see the command that produces the prompt. Also, ECHO OFF does not suppress the display of error messages. If you inadvertently enter an incorrect command in a batch file and then execute the batch file, DOS will display an error message when it attempts to execute the incorrect command.

The syntax for ECHO, an internal command, is

ECHO   [*ON | OFF*]

This notation for the ECHO command indicates that you can use the ON parameter or the OFF parameter with the command, but not both. ECHO ON turns on the display of commands, whereas ECHO OFF suppresses the display of commands. If you type ECHO without either of these parameters, the current setting for ECHO (ON or OFF) is displayed.

It is also common practice to include a CLS command after @ECHO OFF (or ECHO OFF). The CLS command clears the screen before DOS executes the remainder of the commands in the batch file. Therefore, any commands or messages already present on the screen are cleared from the screen before the batch file performs its operations.

Let's modify the batch file to include these two steps.

To revise the batch file:

1. Type **CD BAT** and press **[Enter]**. DOS changes to the batch file directory.
2. Type **EDIT REVISE.BAT** and press **[Enter]**. DOS loads the MS-DOS Editor, which automatically retrieves the batch file.
3. Press **[Ctrl][N]**. The MS-DOS Editor inserts a blank line at the beginning of the file—at the current cursor position.
4. Type **@ECHO OFF** and press **[Enter]**.
5. Type **CLS** but do *not* press the Enter key. Figure 8-23 shows these additions to your batch file. Check your batch file against this figure.

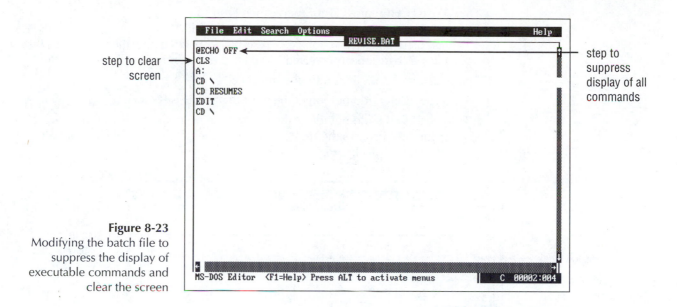

step to clear screen

step to suppress display of all commands

```
 File  Edit  Search  Options                              Help
                          REVISE.BAT
@ECHO OFF
CLS
A:
CD \
CD RESUMES
EDIT
CD \




MS-DOS Editor  <F1=Help> Press ALT to activate menus       C  00002:004
```

Figure 8-23
Modifying the batch file to suppress the display of executable commands and clear the screen

DISPLAYING MESSAGES FROM A BATCH FILE

While you are making changes to the batch file, you realize that you want to add some additional steps. Whenever you revise one of the résumé template or form letter files, you print a copy for your records. You want the batch file to display a message that reminds you to turn on your printer before it loads the MS-DOS Editor.

You can use the ECHO command to display such messages. If you type ECHO followed by a space and then the text of a message, DOS displays the message on the monitor during batch file execution, *even if ECHO is OFF*. The general syntax is

ECHO [*message*]

If you want blank lines before and after a message that DOS displays on the screen, you can use a special variation of the ECHO command. If you type ECHO followed *immediately* by a period, DOS produces a blank line on the monitor when it executes the ECHO command from the batch file.

Let's add these features in your batch file.

To include steps for displaying blank lines before a message:

1. Position the cursor at the beginning of the line with the command for changing to drive A (or B). You can use the Home key to move the cursor to the beginning of a line.

2. Press **[Ctrl][N]** to insert a blank line.

3. Type **ECHO.** (do not forget the period) and press **[Enter]**. *Do not leave a blank space between ECHO and the period; if you do, DOS will display a period on the screen rather than a blank line.*

4. Type **ECHO.** (do not forget the period) again and press **[Enter]**.

Next, specify the message you want to display on the screen during batch file execution.

5. Type **ECHO**, press **[Tab]** *twice*, then type
    *** Be sure the printer is on and operational ***
    and press **[Enter]**. The Tab key inserts blank spaces before the message so that
    the message appears centered when DOS executes this batch file command.

Now display blank lines after the message.

6. Type **ECHO.** (do not forget the period) and press **[Enter]**.

7. Type **ECHO.** (do not forget the period) but do *not* press the Enter key.
    Figure 8-24 shows the message block in the batch file. Check your batch
    file against this figure.

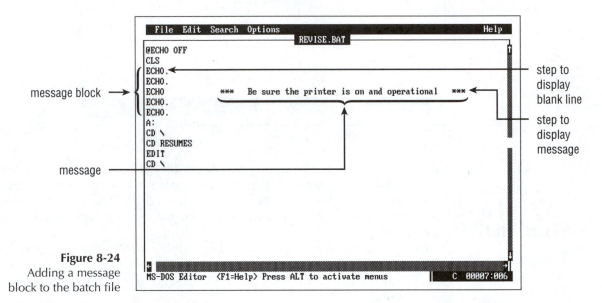

Figure 8-24
Adding a message
block to the batch file

Now you need to include some provision to ensure you see this message.

PAUSING BATCH FILE EXECUTION

Whenever you display a message from a batch file, you should temporarily
stop batch file execution so that you can not only see the message but also
have the chance to act on the message. For example, before a batch file
changes to another drive, you might want to display a message to remind you
to insert a diskette into that drive. You want the batch file to wait until you
check the drive and, if necessary, insert a diskette.

You can use the PAUSE command to temporarily stop a batch file. The
PAUSE command displays a message that tells you to press a key when ready
to continue. When you press a key, DOS executes the remaining steps in the
batch file. The syntax for PAUSE is

PAUSE

After a PAUSE command, you can use a CLS command to erase the message
displayed by the ECHO command and the prompt displayed by the PAUSE
command.

Let's add these additional steps to the batch file.

To insert an option for pausing batch file execution and then clearing the screen:

1. Press **[Enter]**. The MS-DOS Editor moves the cursor to the beginning of the next line.

2. Type **PAUSE** and press **[Enter]**. Be sure the PAUSE command is positioned on the line immediately after the last ECHO command.

3. Type **CLS** but do *not* press the Enter key. Figure 8-25 shows these modifications to the batch file. Check your batch file against this figure.

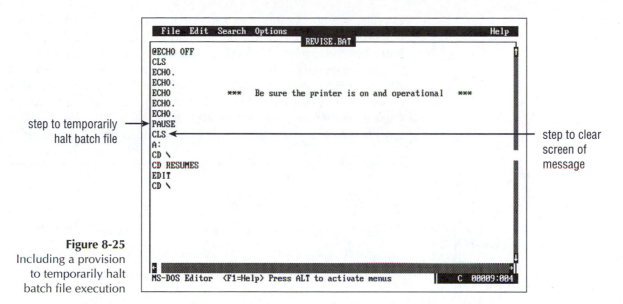

step to temporarily halt batch file

step to clear screen of message

Figure 8-25
Including a provision to temporarily halt batch file execution

DOCUMENTING BATCH FILE OPERATIONS

The batch file now has a number of steps, each of which serves a different purpose. So that you and others can understand and follow the file's logic when you examine it at a later date, you want to document it.

You can use the REM (an abbreviation for "Remark") command to document batch file operations, as follows:

REM [*comments*]

When DOS executes a batch file, it ignores any lines that start with the REM command and any text or comments that follow REM. You can also use REM by itself to create blank space in the batch file and make the batch file easier to read.

In the next step, you will add documentation to the batch file, using Figure 8-26 as a model. Here's some guidelines for moving the cursor and making changes to the batch file as you work in the MS-DOS Editor:

◆ To move to the beginning of a line, position the cursor anywhere on that line and press the Home key.

◆ To move to the end of a line, position the cursor anywhere on that line and press the End key.

◆ To insert a blank line, move the cursor to the beginning of the line and press [Ctrl][N].

◆ To delete a line, position the cursor on that line and press [Ctrl][Y].

◆ To indent lines containing executable commands, move the cursor to the beginning of the line and press the Tab key.

◆ If you indent a line, type text, and press the Enter key, the MS-DOS Editor will automatically indent the next line (a feature called auto-indent). If you need to delete the auto-indent, press the Backspace key.

To document batch file operations:

1. Use Figure 8-26 as a model to add documentation to your batch file, to adjust the spacing in your batch file, and to check the accuracy of your batch file commands. Use REM commands to include lines with a title for the batch file, the batch file's filename, your name, and the current date. Also use REM commands with brief comments to describe the next step or set of steps in the batch file. To improve the spacing in a batch file, you can leave blank lines. When DOS executes a batch file, it ignores any blank lines and any blank spaces before (and after) commands.

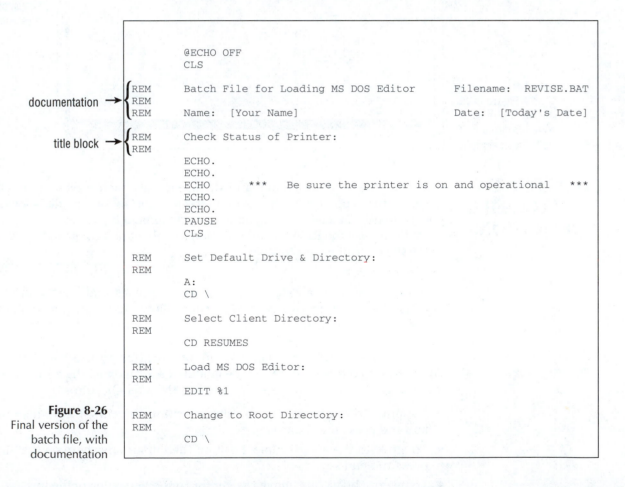

```
                    @ECHO OFF
                    CLS
                  ⎧ REM     Batch File for Loading MS DOS Editor      Filename:  REVISE.BAT
documentation →   ⎨ REM
                  ⎩ REM     Name:  [Your Name]                        Date:  [Today's Date]
                  ⎧ REM     Check Status of Printer:
title block →     ⎨ REM
                  ⎩
                    ECHO.
                    ECHO.
                    ECHO        ***    Be sure the printer is on and operational    ***
                    ECHO.
                    ECHO.
                    PAUSE
                    CLS

                    REM     Set Default Drive & Directory:
                    REM
                    A:
                    CD \

                    REM     Select Client Directory:
                    REM
                    CD RESUMES

                    REM     Load MS DOS Editor:
                    REM
                    EDIT %1

                    REM     Change to Root Directory:
                    REM
                    CD \
```

Figure 8-26
Final version of the batch file, with documentation

After making these changes, you are ready to save your work and test the revised batch file. In the next set of steps, you will save your work as you exit the MS-DOS Editor.

To save these changes:

1. Press **[Alt]** (Menu). Press **[Enter]** to select the File menu. Type **X** to exit the MS-DOS Editor.

   If you are using the mouse, click **File**, then click **Exit**.

   The MS-DOS Editor asks if you want to save your changes.

2. Press **[Enter]** for "Yes."

   If you are using the mouse, click **Yes**.

   DOS displays the DOS prompt.

3. Type **CD** \ and press **[Enter]**. DOS returns to the root directory.

Next, test the batch file.

4. Type **REVISE** and press **[Enter]**. DOS clears the screen, displays a message prompting you to check the printer's status, temporarily pauses batch file execution, and displays another message that informs you how to continue. See Figure 8-27. If DOS displays any error messages, or if your batch file does not work at all, check the contents of your batch file with that shown in Figure 8-26. Make any needed changes and try this step again.

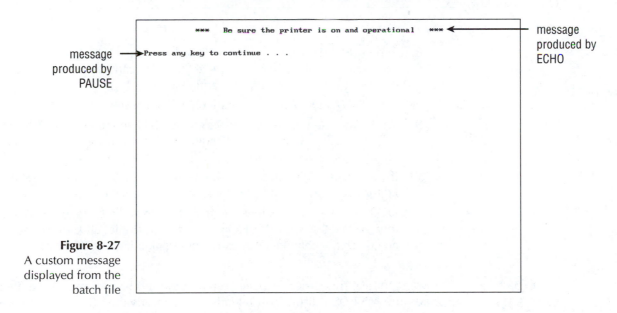

message produced by PAUSE

message produced by ECHO

Figure 8-27
A custom message displayed from the batch file

5. Press **[Enter]** to continue. DOS continues batch file execution and loads the MS-DOS Editor.

6. Press **[Esc]** to clear the Welcome dialog box.

Next, open a resume template file.

7. Press **[Alt]** (Menu). Press **[Enter]** to select the File menu. Type **O** to select the Open command.

   If you are using the mouse, click **File**, then click **Open**.

   The MS-DOS Editor displays the Open dialog box. See Figure 8-28. The MS-DOS Editor assumes files will have the file extension TXT (for Text). If you know the name of the file you want to use, you type it in the File Name box.

currently
selected menu

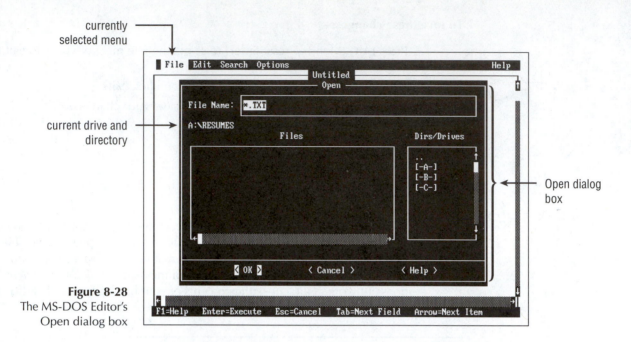

current drive and
directory

Open dialog
box

Figure 8-28
The MS-DOS Editor's
Open dialog box

8. Type **RESUME5.DOC** and press **[Enter]**. The MS-DOS Editor retrieves a copy of one of the résumé template files. You can now either make changes to this file or simply examine it.

Now exit the MS-DOS Editor without changing the file.

9. Press **[Alt]** (Menu). Press **[Enter]** to select the File menu. Type **X** to exit the MS-DOS Editor. If the MS-DOS Editor asks if you want to save your changes, press **[Enter]** for "No."

If you are using the mouse, click **File**, then click **Exit**. If the MS-DOS Editor asks if you want to save your changes, click **No**.

DOS executes the remainder of the batch file and returns to the root directory. Notice that with @ECHO OFF in the batch file, DOS does not display any batch file commands or extra lines containing the DOS prompt.

USING REPLACEABLE PARAMETERS

You want to take this batch file one step further and have it retrieve a file after it loads the MS-DOS Editor. You usually know in advance the name of the file you want to use, and you know that MS-DOS Editor can automatically retrieve a file if you provide its filename after the EDIT command.

DOS allows you to pass this information to the batch file for use with the EDIT command in the batch file. To pass an item of information to the batch file (such as a filename), you include a replaceable parameter after the EDIT command in the batch file. A replaceable parameter is a placeholder in the batch file for an item of information. If you want to reserve a place for one item of information in the batch file, you mark the place for inserting that item by typing %1 (a percent symbol followed by the number 1). When you type the name of the batch file at the command prompt, you type the item of information after the batch file's name. The parameter is used in the batch file *wherever* you have the %1 replaceable parameter.

For example, in this batch file, you can modify the line with the EDIT command to read as follows:

EDIT %1

When you enter the command REVISE RESUME5.DOC at the DOS prompt, DOS assigns %1 as the replaceable parameter for the first item of information after the command. In this example, DOS uses the filename RESUME5.DOC wherever the %1 replaceable parameter occurs in the batch file. The EDIT %1 command in the batch file is then executed as EDIT RESUME5.DOC.

One advantage of using this replaceable parameter is that you can change the name of the file that you provide to the batch file. If you want to edit another file, you type the batch file name and the new filename. That filename is then inserted in the batch file where %1 is used.

If you type only the batch file name and do not provide a filename, DOS substitutes "nothing" for the replaceable parameter. This batch file would still work; DOS will load the MS-DOS Editor, but the MS-DOS Editor will not retrieve a file.

You can also provide a batch file with more than one item of information by using the replaceable parameters %1 through %9. DOS uses the position of the item of information on the command line to assign the parameter to the appropriate replaceable parameter in the batch file. The general syntax is as follows:

%0   %1   %2   %3   ...

COMMAND **PARAMETER 1** **PARAMETER 2** **PARAMETER 3** ...

Each part of a DOS command is assigned a replaceable parameter, even if that part of the command is not used in the batch file. This is also true for the command itself. DOS automatically assigns %0 as the replaceable parameter for the command, the name of the batch file. The first item of information following the command is %1, the second item %2, and so on. You can use any of these replaceable parameters in the batch file, even the 0% replaceable parameter for the batch file command itself.

You want to modify the EDIT command in the batch file so that it uses a replaceable parameter. Let's make that change, and then test the use of the replaceable parameter.

To revise the batch file:

1. Type **CD BAT** and press **[Enter]**. DOS changes to the batch file directory.

2. Type **EDIT REVISE.BAT** and press **[Enter]**. DOS loads the MS-DOS Editor, which automatically retrieves the batch file.

3. Move the cursor to the line with the EDIT command. Then, press **[End]** to move to the end of this line.

4. Press **[Spacebar]** and type **%1** to insert the replaceable parameter. Figure 8-29 shows this modification to the batch file.

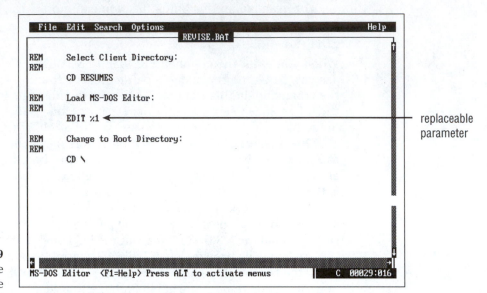

replaceable
parameter

Figure 8-29
Inserting a replaceable
parameter in the batch file

Next save this change.

5. Press **[Alt]** (Menu). Press **[Enter]** to select the File menu. Type **X** to exit the MS-DOS Editor (and save your changes).

    If you are using the mouse, click **File**, then click **Exit**.

    The MS-DOS Editor asks if you want to save your changes.

6. Press **[Enter]** for "Yes."

    If you are using the mouse, click **Yes**.

7. Type **CD ** and press **[Enter]**. DOS returns to the root directory.

Now test the batch file.

8. Type **REVISE RESUME3.DOC** and press **[Enter]**. DOS clears the screen, displays the prompt for checking the status of the printer, and temporarily halts batch file execution.

9. Press **[Enter]** to continue. DOS clears the message from the screen and loads the MS-DOS Editor, which then retrieves the file RESUME3.DOC. You can see the filename in the title bar. You can now examine and change this file, or you can exit.

10. Press **[Alt]** (Menu). Press **[Enter]** to select the File menu. Type **X** to exit the MS-DOS Editor.

    If you are using the mouse, click **File**, then click **Exit**.

    If the MS-DOS Editor asks if you want to save your changes, press **[Tab]** to select "No" and press **[Enter]**, or if you are using the mouse, click **No**. DOS returns you to the root directory after executing the remainder of the batch file.

PRINTING THE CONTENTS OF A BATCH FILE

Next you want to print a copy of your batch file. Not only will this provide you with a record of the contents of the batch file, but you and your coworkers can use it to design other batch files. You want to eventually adapt this batch file to other uses, including loading word processing and spreadsheet applications.

To print your batch file:

1. Be sure the printer is on and on-line, and that the paper is properly aligned in the printer.
2. Type **PRINT \BAT\REVISE.BAT** and press **[Enter]**. If the print utility asks for the printer port, press **[Enter]** to accept the default port or specify another printer port. Then remove the printed copy from the printer.

RESETTING THE DOS PATH WITH A BATCH FILE

Before you can finish, you must reset the path on your computer system. Earlier, you created a batch file named RESET.BAT, which contains the original path setting stored in the DOS environment. If you execute this batch file, DOS replaces the current path setting you specified with the original one stored in this file.

To check, reset, and verify the path:

1. Type **PATH** and press **[Enter]**. DOS shows the current path.
2. Type **RESET** and press **[Enter]**. DOS displays and executes the command in the batch file named RESET.BAT. You see the command because this batch file does not have an @ECHO OFF command.
3. Type **PATH** and press **[Enter]**. DOS shows the change this batch file made to the DOS path. See Figure 8-30.

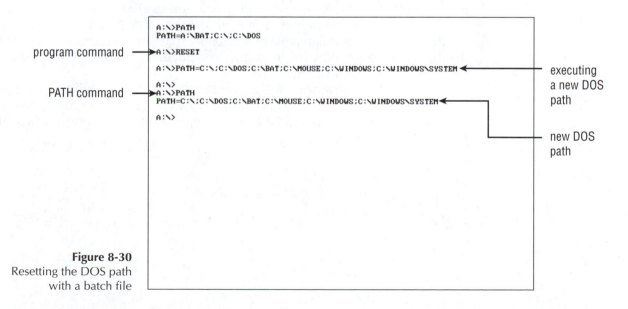

program command →

PATH command →

→ executing a new DOS path

→ new DOS path

Figure 8-30
Resetting the DOS path
with a batch file

MAKING A DUPLICATE COPY OF THE TUTORIAL DISK

During this tutorial, you formatted your Exercise Disk when you tested the first batch file you created. Now you want to copy the contents of your Tutorial Disk onto the Exercise Disk. *You must complete this step because you will use the Exercise Disk in the Tutorial Assignments to create additional batch files.*

To make a copy of the Tutorial Disk:

1. Follow the instructions in Tutorial 1 for using the DISKCOPY command to make a copy of a diskette. During this disk copy operation, your source diskette is the Tutorial Disk and your destination diskette is the Exercise Disk.

◆

SUMMARY

In this tutorial, you learned the importance of batch files in automating routine DOS command operations. You used the MS-DOS Editor to create a simple batch file that formatted a double-density diskette in a high-density drive. You also constructed a more complex batch file that changed directories, loaded the MS-DOS Editor, and returned to the root directory after you exited the MS-DOS Editor. You tested both batch files under different conditions to guarantee their effectiveness.

You learned about the importance of the DOS path. You viewed the DOS path with the PATH command. You redirected the output of this command to a batch file so that you could later reset the path. You modified the path setting with the PATH command.

You included the ECHO command in a batch file to suppress the display of batch file commands during batch file execution. You also used this command to produce blank lines and to display a message that reminds the user to check the status of the printer. You included the PAUSE command in a batch file to temporarily halt batch file execution so that you could check and act on the message displayed by the batch file. You documented batch file operations with the REM (Remark) command.

You modified a batch file to use a replaceable parameter so that you could pass a filename to the batch file for use with the EDIT command. After the batch file loaded the MS-DOS Editor, this replaceable parameter enabled the MS-DOS Editor to load a specific file.

Command Reference

DOS Commands

[*batch filename*]	A user-defined external command that executes the contents of a batch file
[*batch filename*] [*parameter*]	A user-defined external command that passes a parameter, or item of information, to a batch file so that DOS can substitute the item of information in the appropriate replaceable parameter as it executes the contents of the batch file
ECHO [*ON* ⎪ *OFF*]	An internal command that controls the display of batch file commands, as follows: ECHO OFF — Turns off the display of all batch file commands after this command @ECHO OFF — Turns off the display of all batch file commands, including this command ECHO ON — Turns on the display of all batch file commands after this command
ECHO.	An internal command that displays a blank line on the monitor
ECHO [*message*]	An internal command that displays a message on the monitor, even with ECHO OFF
EDIT [[*drive:*] [*path*]*filename*]	An external command that loads the MS-DOS Editor, a text editor program for creating and editing ASCII or text files
PATH	An internal command that displays the DOS path
PATH [*drive:*]*path1;* [*drive:*]*path2;*[*drive:*]*path3;...*	An internal command that changes the DOS path to include the paths of directories and subdirectories

PAUSE	An internal command that temporarily pauses the execution of a batch file and displays a message to press any key to continue
REM [*comments*]	An internal command that documents batch file operations

QUESTIONS

1. What is a batch file? What two characteristics are required of a batch file?
2. How do you enter commands in a batch file? What types of commands can you use?
3. What command can you use from the DOS prompt to display the contents of a batch file?
4. How do you execute a batch file?
5. If you execute a batch file from a diskette and then remove the diskette from the diskette drive, what does DOS do after it executes a command in the batch file?
6. What is the DOS path, and how does DOS use this path?
7. When DOS searches for a program file, what three types of files does it look for? How do these files differ?
8. If DOS is unable to execute a batch file stored in another directory, what is the likely source of the problem?
9. What factors must you consider when testing a batch file?
10. How can you check the path setting?
11. How do you change the path setting?
12. If DOS displays an invalid directory message when you execute a batch file, what two types of problems would you immediately suspect?
13. What provision can you include in a batch file to suppress the display of batch file commands during batch file execution?
14. How do you display a message from a batch file?
15. If you include the ECHO. command in a batch file, what does DOS do when you execute the batch file?
16. How can you pause batch file execution to display a message?
17. How do you document batch file operations?
18. What is the MS-DOS Editor? What type of files does the MS-DOS Editor use?
19. What is the MS-DOS Editor's Survival Guide?
20. What is the difference between the Save and Save As commands on the File menu?
21. What menu and command can you use in the MS-DOS Editor to open a file?
22. What is a replaceable parameter?

23. What is the advantage of using replaceable parameters in a batch file?

24. How do you specify one replaceable parameter in a batch file?

25. How does DOS know where to insert the optional information provided for a replaceable parameter.

26. What does DOS do if you include a replaceable parameter in a batch file but do not provide an item of information for that parameter?

27. Name one way you can use a replaceable parameter in a batch file?

28. How can you print a batch file from the DOS prompt?

29. Name three ways you can use batch files on your computer system to automate routine operations.

30. How are batch files similar to program files?

TUTORIAL ASSIGNMENTS

1. **Creating a Batch File to Print a Directory Tree:** In the batch file directory on the Exercise Disk, create a batch file that prints a directory tree of the Exercise Disk. Use the MS-DOS Editor to construct the batch file so that the batch file performs the following operations in the following order:
   a. Turns off the echo of all commands in the batch file.
   b. Clears the screen.
   c. Produces three blank lines and then displays the following message near the center of the screen:

   *** Be sure the printer is operational ***

   d. Produces three more blank lines.
   e. Temporarily halts batch file processing.
   f. Clears the screen after resuming batch file execution.
   g. Changes to the drive with the Exercise Disk.
   h. Changes to the root directory.
   i. Produces a directory tree of the Exercise Disk, and redirects the output to the printer. *Be sure you specify the correct printer port; if necessary, ask your instructor or technical support person for the name of the printer port.*

   Save your batch file. Before you test the batch file, be sure you store the current path in a batch file and then change the DOS path so that the name of your batch file directory is listed first in the path. Be sure the DOS directory is in the path. Test the batch file from different directories on drive A (or drive B) and drive C. Once you are satisfied that the batch file is operating properly, document batch file operations within the batch file. Also include documentation in the batch file that identifies the purpose, filename, author, and date of the batch file. Finally, print a copy of your batch file, and then reset the path on your computer system.

2. **Creating a Batch File to Display the Contents of an ASCII File:** In the batch file directory on the Exercise Disk, create a batch file to display the contents of a text file on the Exercise Disk. This batch file will make one assumption—that you will first change to a directory before you use the batch file. Use the MS-DOS Editor to construct the batch file so that the

batch file performs the following operations in the following order:

a. Turns off the echo of all commands in the batch file.

b. Clears the screen.

c. Produces three blank lines and then displays the following message near the center of the screen:

   *** Be sure the Exercise Disk is in drive A (or drive B) ***

d. Produces three more blank lines.

e. Temporarily halts batch file processing.

f. Clears the screen after resuming batch file execution.

g. Uses the TYPE command to display the contents of a text file one screen at a time. Use a replaceable parameter for the filename.

Save your batch file. Before you test the batch file, be sure you store the current path in a batch file and then change the DOS path so that the name of your batch file directory is listed first in the path. Be sure the DOS directory is in the path. Use the batch file to display the contents of RESUME1.DOC in the RESUMES directory and BUSINESS.PLN in the BUSINESS directory. You will have to manually change to each of these subdirectories before you test the batch file.

Once you are satisfied that the batch file is operating properly, document batch file operations within the batch file. Also include documentation in the batch file that identifies the purpose, filename, author, and date of the batch file. Finally, print a copy of your batch file, and then reset the path on your computer system.

3. **Creating a Batch File to Document the Status of a Hard Disk:** In the batch file directory on the Exercise Disk, create a batch file to check and document the status of a hard disk. Use the MS-DOS Editor to construct the batch file so that the batch file performs the following operations in the following order:

a. Turns off the echo of all commands in the batch file.

b. Clears the screen.

c. Checks the status of the hard disk on your computer system, and redirects its report to the printer.

Save your batch file. Before you test the batch file, be sure you store the current path in a batch file, and then change the DOS path so that the name of your batch file directory is listed first in the path. Be sure the DOS directory is in the path. *Before you test this batch file, manually use the CHKDSK command to verify that the hard disk does not have any errors. If the CHKDSK reports errors on the hard disk, ask your instructor or technical support person to remove those hard disk errors.* Then test your batch file.

Once you are satisfied that the batch file is operating properly, document batch file operations within the batch file. Also include documentation in the batch file that identifies the purpose, filename, author, and date of the batch file. Finally, print a copy of your batch file, and then reset the path on your computer system.

4. **Creating a Batch File to Specify System Settings:** In the batch file directory on your Exercise Disk, create a batch file that specifies initial settings for you to use after you power on your computer system. Use the MS-DOS

Editor to construct the batch file so that the batch file performs the following operations in the following order:

a. Turns off the echo of all commands in the batch file.

b. Clears the screen.

c. Specifies default switches for the environmental variable (DIRCMD) for the Directory command. Include switches for displaying files in file-name order, one screen at a time, and in lowercase.

d. Loads DOSKEY.

e. Clears the screen.

f. Displays the new settings in the DOS environment.

g. Temporarily halts batch file execution.

h. Clears the screen.

Save your batch file. Before you test the batch file, reboot your computer system to clear the DOS environment of its current settings. Be sure you store the current path in a batch file, and then change the DOS path so that the name of your batch file directory is listed first in the path. Be sure the DOS directory is in the path. Then test the batch file. Once you are satisfied that the batch file is operating properly, document batch file operations within the batch file. Also include documentation in the batch file that identifies the purpose, filename, author, and date of the batch file. Finally, print a copy of your batch file, and reset the path on your computer system.

5. **Creating a Batch File to Start a System Utility:** In the batch file directory on your Exercise Disk, create a batch file that loads the MS-DOS Defragmenter in DOS 6.0 or 6.2. Remember, DOS 5.0 does not have this utility. Use the MS-DOS Editor to construct the batch file so that the batch file performs the following operations in the following order:

a. Turns off the echo of all commands in the batch file.

b. Clears the screen.

c. Changes to drive A (or drive B).

d. Changes to the root directory of drive A (or drive B).

e. Loads the MS-DOS Defragmenter.

Save your batch file. Before you test the batch file, be sure you store the current path in a batch file and then change the DOS path so that the name of your batch file directory is listed first in the path. Be sure the DOS directory is in the path. Test the batch file from different directories on drive A (or drive B) and from drive C. During one of these tests, use the MS-DOS Defragmenter to optimize the diskette and arrange directories and files in alphabetical order by name. Once you are satisfied that the batch file is operating properly, document batch file operations within the batch file. Also include documentation in the batch file that identifies the purpose, filename, author, and date of the batch file. Finally, print a copy of your batch file, and reset the DOS path on your computer system.

Customizing Your System

OBJECTIVES

In this tutorial you will learn to:

- ◆ Understand the importance of the AUTOEXEC.BAT file
- ◆ Create and execute an AUTOEXEC.BAT file
- ◆ Simulate booting
- ◆ Specify the DOS path and prompt in the AUTOEXEC.BAT file
- ◆ Specify settings for the DOS environment in the AUTOEXEC.BAT file
- ◆ Define the characteristics of ports and devices in the AUTOEXEC.BAT file
- ◆ Load TSRs from the AUTOEXEC.BAT file
- ◆ Use the VSAFE anti-viral utility in DOS 6.0 and 6.2
- ◆ Execute DOS utilities from the AUTOEXEC.BAT file
- ◆ Change directories and load an application from the AUTOEXEC.BAT file
- ◆ Print a copy of the AUTOEXEC.BAT file

After you power on your computer system each day, you find that you use the same DOS commands to customize your system and check its status. For example, you specify default switches for the Directory command in the DOS environment, load DOSKEY, load Delete Sentry (or Delete Tracker), change to a specific directory on your client diskette, and load the same software application. You could save valuable time and effort if DOS performed these basic operations for you.

Periodically, you also check the status of your hard disk and client diskette, and you scan both disks for computer viruses. You now want to check the hard disk daily so that you can extend its life and protect it from damage. You want your anti-viral software to continually monitor your computer system and check diskettes inserted into the drives for computer viruses. These additional safeguards will protect your system and your work.

◆

THE IMPORTANCE OF THE AUTOEXEC.BAT FILE

To customize your computer system and automate routine operations, you decide to create a special batch file that DOS automatically executes when you power on your computer system. DOS requires that you name this batch file AUTOEXEC.BAT (for Automatically Execute Batch File), and you must store it in the root directory of your boot disk—usually your hard disk, drive C. In this file, you store any commands that you want DOS to execute automatically after your computer system loads DOS into memory.

Your hard disk already has an AUTOEXEC.BAT file that your predecessor created. But before you make changes to this file on your hard disk, you want to prepare a boot disk and create an AUTOEXEC.BAT file on it. You can then use this AUTOEXEC.BAT file to test different start-up settings. Only after you successfully test these settings should you update the AUTOEXEC.BAT file on your hard disk. You should also always be sure that you have a duplicate copy of this file before you change it. If you make changes to the AUTOEXEC.BAT file and find that they do not work as you initially expected, you can return to the original copy of this file and use it.

PREPARING A BOOT DISK

Your first step is to prepare a boot disk in drive A. This boot disk will initially contain the operating system files. You will then add an AUTOEXEC.BAT file containing the preliminary start-up settings.

Because you will need to boot from drive A with this boot disk, you must format a diskette of the proper size and storage capacity for drive A. It is important to know how to prepare a boot disk with an executable AUTOEXEC.BAT file so that you can boot from drive A if you should ever encounter problems accessing drive C.

To prepare a boot disk:

1. After you power on your computer system and access the DOS prompt, insert the Tutorial Disk, or a new or used diskette, into drive A. You can use the diskette that you formatted as a boot disk in Tutorial 7.

2. Format the diskette with the appropriate formatting option:

   ◆ To format a high-density diskette in a high-density drive, a double-density diskette in a double-density drive, or an extra-high-density diskette in an extra-high-density drive, type **FORMAT A: /U /S** and press **[Enter]**.

   ◆ To format a 3½-inch double-density diskette in a high-density or extra-high-density drive, type **FORMAT A: /F:720 /U /S** and press **[Enter]**.

   ◆ To format a 5¼-inch double-density diskette in a high-density drive, type **FORMAT A: /F:360 /U /S** and press **[Enter]**.

   If you are using your Tutorial Disk or reformatting another diskette, the *Unconditional switch* (/U) will erase any information already on the diskette. If you are using a new diskette, DOS automatically performs an *Unconditional format* on the diskette. The *System switch* (/S) copies the operating system files to the diskette after DOS formats it.

   FORMAT prompts you to insert a diskette into drive A. If you have not inserted a diskette yet, do so now.

3. Press **[Enter]**. After the formatting process is complete, DOS copies the operating system files to the diskette and prompts for a volume label.

4. Type **BOOT DISK** and press **[Enter]**. DOS displays information on the total disk space, the amount of storage space used by the operating system, the remaining available disk space, the size of each allocation unit, and the number of allocation units.

5. When FORMAT asks if you to want to format another diskette, type **N** and press **[Enter]**. DOS then displays the DOS prompt.

Next you will check the contents of the boot disk and protect the Command Processor.

To check the boot disk:

1. Type **A:** to change to drive A. Be sure the DOS prompt changes to A:\>.

2. Type **DIR** and press **[Enter]**. DOS displays a directory listing of the boot disk. The only file shown in the directory is COMMAND.COM.

3. Type **ATTRIB COMMAND.COM +R +H** and press **[Enter]**. DOS assigns the Read-Only and Hidden attributes to the Command Processor. You have added two levels of protection to this file. The file cannot be deleted, and it will not be displayed in directory listings.

4. Type **DIR** and press **[Enter]**. DOS reports that it found no file.

5. Type **ATTRIB** and press **[Enter]**. DOS lists the System and Hidden files on this disk. ATTRIB shows that COMMAND.COM has the Hidden and Read-Only attributes.

CREATING A BATCH FILE DIRECTORY

Before you create the AUTOEXEC.BAT file, you want to create a batch file directory on this boot disk and store the current path in a batch file in the event you need to reset the path.

To create the batch file directory:

1. Type **MD BAT** and press **[Enter]**. DOS creates the batch file directory.
2. Type **CD BAT** and press **[Enter]**. DOS changes to the batch file directory.

   Now store the current path in a batch file.

3. Type **PATH > RESET.BAT** and press **[Enter]**.
4. Type **TYPE RESET.BAT** and press **[Enter]**. DOS displays the contents of the batch file. If you do not see the PATH command and the DOS path in your batch file, ask your instructor or technical support person for assistance.
5. Type **CD ** and press **[Enter]**. DOS returns to the root directory.

CREATING AN AUTOEXEC.BAT FILE

You are now ready to create a copy of an AUTOEXEC.BAT file for your boot disk. You can use the MS-DOS Editor because the AUTOEXEC.BAT is an ASCII, or text, file.

As you've done with other batch files, you want to first include options to suppress the display of commands stored in AUTOEXEC.BAT and to clear the screen. Then you want to add a title to identify the purpose of the file. Finally, you want to add the PATH command to specify a new DOS path and the PROMPT command to guarantee that the DOS prompt shows the full path.

This is a good time to emphasize the importance of entering commands and their settings *exactly as described in the tutorial steps and illustrated in the figures*. Otherwise, these features will not work properly or at all when you test them later, and you might waste valuable time attempting to locate the source of a problem.

To create a copy of an AUTOEXEC.BAT file on your boot disk:

1. Be sure you are at the root directory of drive A.
2. Type **EDIT AUTOEXEC.BAT** and press **[Enter]**. DOS loads the MS-DOS Editor and displays AUTOEXEC.BAT for the filename in the title bar.
3. Press **[Tab]** to indent the cursor on the first line. The cursor moves to the first tab stop and the MS-DOS Editor inserts blank spaces.
4. Press **[Caps Lock]** to turn caps on. Although you can use uppercase or lowercase, or both, the figures in this tutorial show commands entered in uppercase.
5. Type **@ECHO OFF** and press **[Enter]**. The MS-DOS Editor automatically indents the cursor on the next line. This *auto-indent feature* saves you time and effort when you need to indent lines.

   The @ECHO OFF command will suppress the display of all commands executed from the AUTOEXEC.BAT file when you boot from this diskette.

6. Type **CLS** and press **[Enter]**. This command will clear the screen of any information displayed on the monitor as your computer system powers on and loads DOS.

Adding a Title Block in AUTOEXEC.BAT

You next want to add a title to identify this file's purpose.

To add a title:

1. Press [**Enter**] again. The MS-DOS Editor inserts a blank line. DOS ignores blank lines in a batch file when it executes its contents.

2. Press [**Backspace**]. The MS-DOS Editor deletes the tab indent, and the cursor moves back to the beginning of the line.

3. Type **REM** and press [**Tab**]. Press and hold * until you fill the entire row with asterisks—up to position 78. The cursor position is shown on the right side of the status line at the bottom of the screen. Then press [**Enter**].

4. Type **REM** and press [**Enter**].

5. Type **REM** and press [**Tab**] *four times*. Type **Auto-Execute File** and press [**Enter**].

6. Type **REM** and press [**Enter**].

7. Type **REM** and press [**Tab**]. Press and hold * until you fill the entire row with asterisks—up to position 78. Then press [**Enter**].

8. Press [**Enter**] to insert a blank line between the title block and the next set of commands.

Specifying the Path and Prompt

You are now ready to enter the PATH command, to specify the DOS path, and execute the PROMPT command. The PATH command specifies a set of directories for DOS to search in order to locate program files with the file extension COM, EXE, or BAT. The PROMPT command instructs DOS to show the current directory in the DOS prompt.

To include documentation for the path and prompt:

1. Type **REM**, press [**Tab**], type **Specify Path & Prompt** and press [**Enter**].

2. Type **REM** and press [**Enter**].

Now specify the path and prompt.

3. Press [**Tab**], type **PATH A:\;A:\BAT;C:\DOS** and press [**Enter**]. This path includes the root directory of drive A, the batch file directory on drive A, and the DOS directory on drive C. If your DOS directory has another name, use that name in the path. If you are working on a computer network, ask your instructor or technical support person for the drives and directories to include in the path.

Additional subdirectories are usually included in the DOS path; however, the names of these directories depend on the types of software and utilities installed on the computer system. If the AUTOEXEC.BAT does not include a PATH command, DOS will not be able to locate program files stored in directories other than the current directory.

Now you can specify the appearance of the DOS prompt.

To set the characteristics of the DOS prompt:

1. Type **PROMPT PG** and press **[Enter]**. The code $P instructs DOS to include the drive name and full path in the DOS prompt. The code $G instructs DOS to include the greater-than symbol (>) after the path. Figure 9-1 shows your first version of the AUTOEXEC.BAT file.

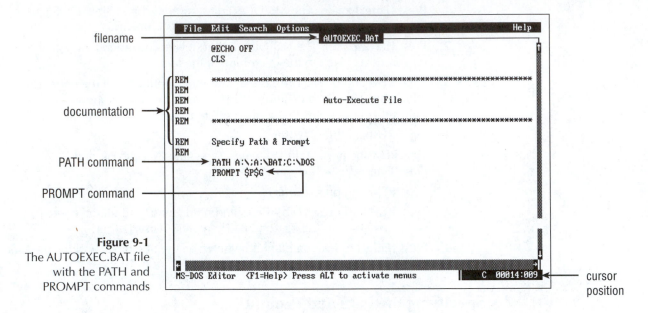

Figure 9-1
The AUTOEXEC.BAT file with the PATH and PROMPT commands

If the AUTOEXEC.BAT file does not include a PROMPT command, DOS defaults to a prompt that shows only the drive name—for example, C> or A>. This default is not useful because DOS does not display subdirectory names as you change from one directory to another, and you will not have a frame of reference while working at the DOS prompt.

As shown in Figure 9-1, you use REM (Remark) commands at the beginning of each line where you want to include a title, documentation, or comments. DOS ignores any REM commands when it executes a batch file. You might want to indent all executable commands, such as PATH and PROMPT, so that you can more readily locate these commands.

Saving the AUTOEXEC.BAT File

Next, save this file and then exit the MS-DOS Editor.

To save and exit:

1. Press **[Alt]** (Menu) to access the menu bar, press **[Enter]** for the File menu, and type **S** for the Save command.

    If you are using the mouse, click **File**, then click **Save**.

    The MS-DOS Editor saves your file under the name you originally provided.

2. Press **[Alt]** (Menu) to access the menu bar, press **[Enter]** for the File menu, and type **X** for the Exit command.

If you are using the mouse, click **File**, then click **Exit**.

You exit the MS-DOS Editor, and DOS displays the DOS prompt.

TESTING THE AUTOEXEC.BAT FILE

You are ready to test your first version of the AUTOEXEC.BAT file. To verify that DOS executes the PATH and PROMPT commands in the AUTOEXEC.BAT file, you first decide to check the DOS path and to change the DOS prompt. Then you can reboot your system and test the AUTOEXEC.BAT file.

Although you usually perform a warm boot after you make changes to the AUTOEXEC.BAT file, you can also simulate this process. If you type the name of this batch file at the DOS prompt, DOS executes it as it would any other batch file. The obvious advantage of using this approach is that all other settings stored on your computer system remain in effect.

Let's check the DOS path, change the DOS prompt, and simulate rebooting.

To check the DOS path:

1. Type **PATH** and press **[Enter]**. DOS displays the current path.

Now change the DOS prompt.

2. Type **PROMPT** and press **[Enter]**. DOS changes the DOS prompt so that it shows only the name of the drive. See Figure 9-2. The prompt does not reference the root directory.

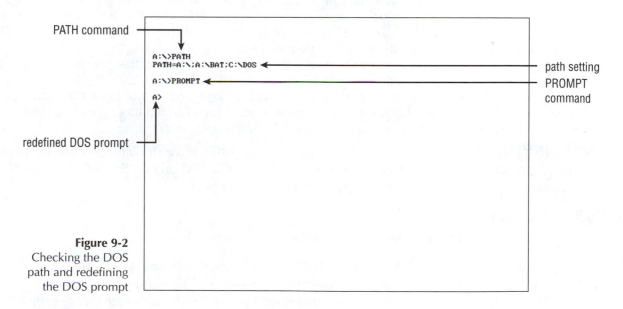

PATH command

A:\>PATH
PATH=A:\;A:\BAT;C:\DOS — path setting
A:\>PROMPT — PROMPT command
A> — redefined DOS prompt

Figure 9-2
Checking the DOS path and redefining the DOS prompt

Next, simulate rebooting.

3. Type **AUTOEXEC** and press **[Enter]**. DOS executes this batch file and displays the DOS prompt. The DOS prompt now shows the current path.

4. Type **PATH** and press [**Enter**]. The DOS path is identical to the one stored in the AUTOEXEC.BAT file. See Figure 9-3.

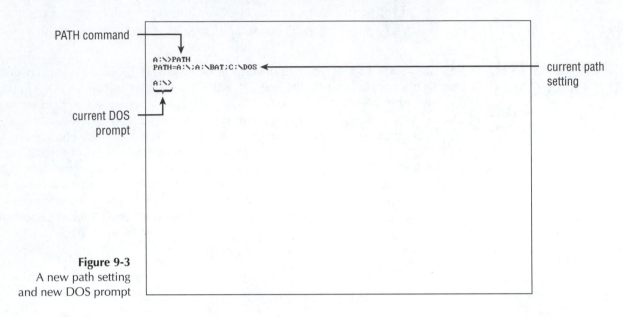

PATH command

current path
setting

current DOS
prompt

Figure 9-3
A new path setting
and new DOS prompt

This path remains in effect until you change it. You can change it by using the PATH command at the DOS prompt, by executing a batch file that contains a PATH command, or by modifying the PATH command in the AUTOEXEC.BAT file and rebooting your computer system. When you install new software on your computer system, you can modify the PATH command in the AUTOEXEC.BAT file to include the names of the subdirectories so that DOS can locate the software program files.

If you modify the directory structure of the hard disk, you must change the directories listed in the PATH command in the AUTOEXEC.BAT file and reboot the system. If you do not make this change and do not reset the system, DOS may not be able to locate some or all of the program files on the hard disk.

SPECIFYING SETTINGS FOR THE DOS ENVIRONMENT

Instead of manually entering default switches for the Directory command each day, you want to modify the AUTOEXEC.BAT file so that DOS automatically stores these settings in the DOS environment.

To specify switches for the Directory command:

1. Type **EDIT AUTOEXEC.BAT** and press [**Enter**]. DOS loads the MS-DOS Editor, which loads the AUTOEXEC.BAT file.

2. Press [**Ctrl**][**End**] to move the cursor to the end of the file. If necessary, position the cursor two lines below the last line of text and be sure the cursor is not indented.

3. Type **REM**, press [**Tab**], type **Specify Settings** and press [**Enter**].

4. Type **REM** and press [**Enter**].

5. Press [**Tab**], type **SET DIRCMD=/O /P** and press [**Enter**].

SPECIFYING A DIRECTORY FOR TEMPORARY FILES

While you are editing this file, you decide to specify one other common setting for the DOS environment. Many programs, including DOS, create temporary files as they process data. After the operation is complete, these programs delete the temporary files. However, if the power fails or if you reboot while a program is still operating, these temporary files remain on disk.

You can specify a default directory for these temporary files so that they do not clutter the root directory or other subdirectories, and so that it is easy to locate and erase any that remain on disk after a power failure or a reboot. As an example, if the name of the directory for temporary files were C:\TEMP, you would enter the following commands in the AUTOEXEC.BAT file:

SET   TEMP=C:\TEMP

SET   TMP=C:\TEMP

Programs that you use will look for either the TEMP or the TMP variable in the DOS environment in order to locate the directory to use for temporary files. In addition, you *must* create the subdirectory for the temporary files.

Let's add these two commands to the AUTOEXEC.BAT file, save the changes, exit the MS-DOS Editor, and create the TEMP directory on your boot disk in drive A.

To specify a default directory for temporary files:

1. Type **SET   TEMP=A:\TEMP** and press [**Enter**].
2. Type **SET   TMP=A:\TEMP** and press [**Enter**]. See Figure 9-4.

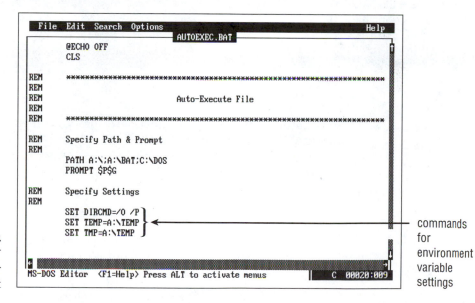

Figure 9-4
The AUTOEXEC.BAT file with settings for the DOS environment

commands for environment variable settings

3. Press [**Alt**] (Menu) to access the menu bar, press [**Enter**] for the File menu, and type **X** for the Exit command.

   If you are using the mouse, click **File**, then click **Exit**.

The MS-DOS Editor displays a dialog box that prompts you about saving the changes.

4. Press **[Enter]** to select Yes.

    If you are using the mouse, click **Yes**.

    The MS-DOS Editor saves your changes, you exit the MS-DOS Editor, and DOS displays the DOS prompt.

5. Be sure you are at the root directory of drive A. Then type **MD TEMP** and press **[Enter]**. DOS creates a TEMP subdirectory.

6. Type **SET DIRCMD=/O** and press **[Enter]**.

7. Type **DIR** and press **[Enter]**. The directory includes the BAT and TEMP subdirectories, as well as the AUTOEXEC.BAT file. See Figure 9-5.

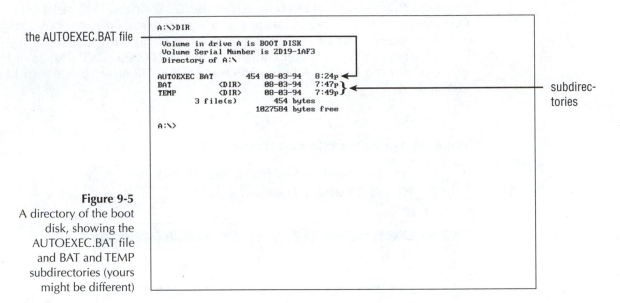

the AUTOEXEC.BAT file

subdirectories

```
A:\>DIR

 Volume in drive A is BOOT DISK
 Volume Serial Number is 2D19-1AF3
 Directory of A:\

AUTOEXEC BAT         454 08-03-94    8:24p
BAT          <DIR>       08-03-94    7:47p
TEMP         <DIR>       08-03-94    7:49p
         3 file(s)          454 bytes
                       1027584 bytes free

A:\>
```

Figure 9-5
A directory of the boot disk, showing the AUTOEXEC.BAT file and BAT and TEMP subdirectories (yours might be different)

Before you test these new settings, you need to remove any settings assigned to the variables DIRCMD, TEMP, and TMP in the DOS environment. Then you can simulate rebooting.

To remove settings from the DOS environment:

1. Type **SET DIRCMD=** and press **[Enter]**. If you do not specify any setting for the environment variable DIRCMD, DOS removes the current settings from the DOS environment.

2. Type **SET TEMP=** and press **[Enter]**. Then type **SET TMP=** and press **[Enter]**. You have now removed any settings that might be associated with these variables.

3. Type **SET** and press **[Enter]**. DOS displays the current settings in the DOS environment. See Figure 9-6.

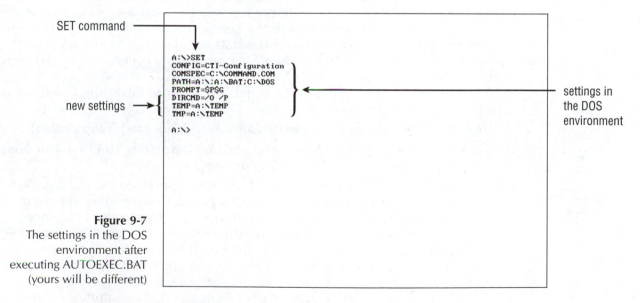

SET command →

```
A:\>SET DIRCMD=
A:\>SET TEMP=
A:\>SET TMP=
A:\>SET
CONFIG=CTI-Configuration
COMSPEC=C:\COMMAND.COM
PATH=A:\;A:\BAT;C:\DOS
PROMPT=$P$G
A:\>
```

removing settings from the DOS environment

current settings in the DOS environment

Figure 9-6
The current environment variable settings in the DOS environment (yours will be different)

Now simulate rebooting.

4. Type **AUTOEXEC** and press **[Enter]**. DOS executes this batch file and displays the DOS prompt.

5. Type **SET** and press **[Enter]**. DOS shows the new settings in the DOS environment. See Figure 9-7.

SET command

```
A:\>SET
CONFIG=CTI-Configuration
COMSPEC=C:\COMMAND.COM
PATH=A:\;A:\BAT;C:\DOS
PROMPT=$P$G
DIRCMD=/O /P
TEMP=A:\TEMP
TMP=A:\TEMP
A:\>
```

new settings →

settings in the DOS environment

Figure 9-7
The settings in the DOS environment after executing AUTOEXEC.BAT (yours will be different)

This is a good opportunity to take a break.

SPECIFYING THE CHARACTERISTICS OF DEVICES

Because your printer is connected to the serial port on your computer, your AUTOEXEC.BAT file must configure your computer for that printer port. Before you can print using your first serial port, which is called COM1, DOS must know the port's characteristics and how to locate the port.

You can use the MODE command to configure system devices from the AUTOEXEC.BAT file. The MODE command is a multi-purpose command that performs the following functions:

◆ Configures parallel and serial communications ports

◆ Redirects output from a parallel port to a serial port

◆ Changes the display mode or characteristics of the monitor

◆ Controls the **typematic rate**, the rate at which a key repeats when you hold down that key

◆ Displays the status of system devices

By default, DOS assumes that a printer is connected to the first parallel port, LPT1, and will automatically route print requests to that port. However, if your printer is connected to a serial port, you must use the MODE command to specify the characteristics of the serial port and to redirect output from a parallel port to the serial port.

As you learned earlier, the two types of ports—parallel and serial—differ in how DOS transmits data through them. In the case of a **parallel printer port**, DOS simultaneously transmits each of the eight bits that constitute a byte (or one character) down eight separate lines in the printer cable. For a **serial printer port**, DOS transmits one bit at a time down one line in the printer cable. Parallel transmission is faster than serial transmission because more bits are transmitted at a time. However, parallel transmission requires that the printer be in close proximity to the computer—usually 10 to 15 feet—to reduce problems associated with **crosstalk**, or electrical interference, in the cable. If you use serial transmission, you can place a computer up to 500 feet away from the printer.

To specify characteristics of a serial port, you use the MODE command in one of the following two ways:

MODE COM*n*:[*baud rate*],[*parity*],[*data bits*],[*stop bits*],[*retry option*]

MODE COM*n*: [*BAUD=baud rate*] [*PARITY=parity*] [*DATA=[data bits*] [*STOP=[stop bits*] [*RETRY=[retry option*]

The number used for *n* is 1, 2, 3, or 4 and corresponds to the number of the serial port. You can find the recommended settings for the other options from the documentation for your hardware device. The **baud rate** is the speed of data transmission. You can set the baud rate to 110, 150, 300, 600, 1200, 2400, 4800, 9600, or 19200. You should use the rate recommended for the hardware device in its reference manual. For example, you might find that the manual for a Hewlett-Packard LaserJet printer recommends a baud rate of 9600.

The number of **data bits** is the number of bits that constitute a character. The value for data bits is usually 8 (for eight bits in each byte), but it may be 7 in certain cases. The **parity bit** is an extra bit that is sometimes included to check for transmission errors. The parity bit is usually E for "Even" (the default), O for "Odd," or N for "None." If the parity is even or odd, the data bits and the parity bit are summed, or added together, to check for a transmission error. If the parity is even and the sum is odd, or if the parity is odd and the sum is even, a transmission error occurred and the data is sent again.

DOS uses one or more additional bits, called **stop bits**, to indicate that the transmission of a character is complete. The default is 1 for baud rates other than 110. The **retry option** specifies the action to take if DOS receives a busy signal from the serial printer port. Although the default is N for "No Action," P for "Continue Retrying" (or automatic retry) is commonly used. In the latter case, transmission continues until the printer accepts the output.

To illustrate the use of this command, let's say the printer at your office is attached to COM1 and requires the following parameters: a baud rate of 9600, no parity checking, 8 bits per character, and 1 stop bit. You want to use the automatic retry option. You can enter one of the following MODE commands:

MODE   COM1:9600,N,8,1,P

MODE   COM1: BAUD=9600 PARITY=N DATA=8 STOP=1 RETRY=P

After you specify the characteristics of the serial port, you must use another MODE command to redirect the output from a parallel port to the serial port. The syntax is as follows:

MODE   LPT*m*:=COM*n*:

The number used for *m* is 1, 2, or 3 and corresponds to the number of the parallel port. As noted previously, the number used for *n* is 1, 2, 3, or 4 and corresponds to the number of the serial port.

Let's assume you do not use the first parallel port, LPT1, on your computer system at work. To redirect output to the first serial port, COM1, from LPT1, you would enter the following MODE command:

MODE   LPT1:=COM1:

In a real-life situation, if another printer is connected to LPT1, as is commonly the case, and if you need to redirect output to a serial port, such as COM1, you would use the name of the next parallel port, LPT2 (assuming it is unused), as follows:

MODE   LPT2:=COM1:

You are now ready to specify the characteristics of your printer port in the AUTOEXEC.BAT file.

To specify the characteristics of your serial printer port:

1. If necessary, insert the Tutorial Disk in drive A, and make drive A the current drive.

2. Type **EDIT AUTOEXEC.BAT** and press **[Enter]**. DOS loads the MS-DOS Editor, which loads the AUTOEXEC.BAT file.

3. Press **[Ctrl][End]** to move the cursor to the end of the file. If necessary, position the cursor two lines below the last line with text and be sure the cursor is not indented.

4. Type **REM**, press **[Tab]**, type **Configure Printer Port** and press **[Enter]**.

5. Type **REM** and press **[Enter]**.

6. Press **[Tab]**, type **MODE COM1:9600,N,8,1,P** and press **[Enter]**.

7. Type **MODE LPT1:=COM1:** and press **[Enter]**. See Figure 9-8.

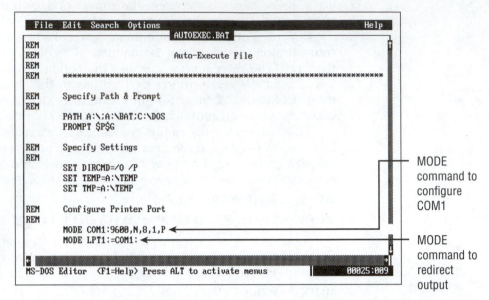

```
 File  Edit  Search  Options                                    Help
                           ┌─ AUTOEXEC.BAT ─┐
REM
REM                            Auto-Execute File
REM
REM        ******************************************************************

REM        Specify Path & Prompt
REM
           PATH A:\;A:\BAT;C:\DOS
           PROMPT $P$G

REM        Specify Settings
REM
           SET DIRCMD=/O /P
           SET TEMP=A:\TEMP
           SET TMP=A:\TEMP

REM        Configure Printer Port
REM
           MODE COM1:9600,N,8,1,P  ◀
           MODE LPT1:=COM1:  ◀

 MS-DOS Editor  <F1=Help> Press ALT to activate menus            00025:009
```

MODE command to configure COM1

MODE command to redirect output

Figure 9-8
The specifications for configuring a serial port in AUTOEXEC.BAT

8. Press [**Alt**] (Menu) to access the menu bar, press [**Enter**] for the File menu, and type **X** for the Exit command.

    If you are using the mouse, click **File**, then click **Exit**.

    The MS-DOS Editor displays a dialog box that prompts you about saving the changes.

9. Press [**Enter**] to select Yes.

    If you are using the mouse, click **Yes**.

    The MS-DOS Editor saves your changes, you exit the MS-DOS Editor, and DOS displays the DOS prompt.

Viewing the Status of Parallel and Serial Ports

Before you test this change, you want to view the current status of the LPT1 and COM1 ports on your computer. You use the MODE command, specify the port name, and add the **Status switch** (/STATUS). Let's check these two ports.

To check the status of LPT1 and COM1:

1. Type **MODE LPT1: /STATUS** and press [**Enter**]. DOS displays the status of LPT1. See Figure 9-9. In this example, DOS indicates that output to this port is not rerouted to another port, and the retry option is set to the default (None). The message about code page operation means that DOS is not configured to support alternate character sets. The MODE command might report different results for LPT1 on your computer.

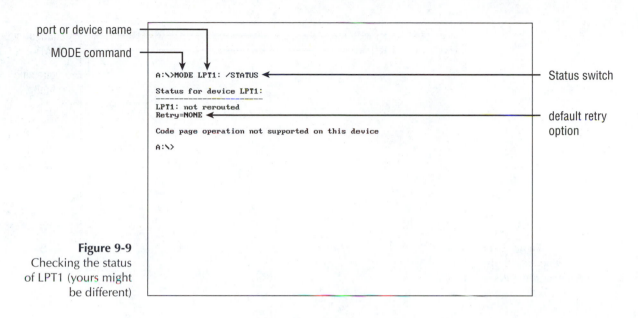

port or device name

MODE command

```
A:\>MODE LPT1: /STATUS

Status for device LPT1:
-----------------------
LPT1: not rerouted
Retry=NONE

Code page operation not supported on this device

A:\>
```

Status switch

default retry option

Figure 9-9
Checking the status of LPT1 (yours might be different)

2. Type **MODE COM1: /STATUS** and press **[Enter]**. DOS displays the status of COM1. See Figure 9-10. In this example, DOS indicates that the default retry option (B for Busy) is currently in effect for this port. The MODE command might report different results for COM1 on your computer.

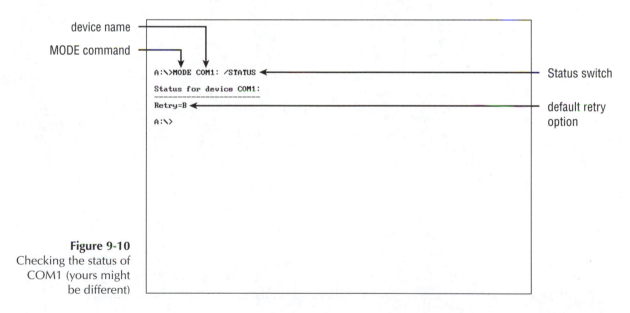

device name

MODE command

```
A:\>MODE COM1: /STATUS

Status for device COM1:
-----------------------
Retry=B

A:\>
```

Status switch

default retry option

Figure 9-10
Checking the status of COM1 (yours might be different)

Now simulate rebooting.

3. Type **AUTOEXEC** and press **[Enter]**. DOS executes the MODE command, displays the characteristics of the COM1 port, and indicates that output is rerouted from LPT1 to COM1. See Figure 9-11. DOS loads a portion of the MODE program into memory as a TSR program to intercept output sent to LPT1 and redirect it to COM1.

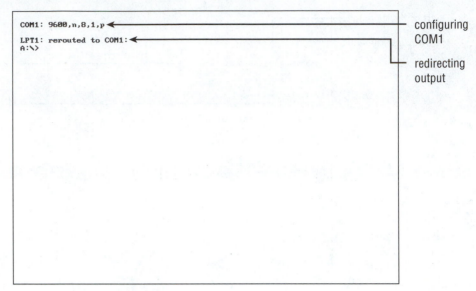

configuring
COM1

redirecting
output

Figure 9-11
DOS executes the
MODE commands in
AUTOEXEC.BAT

Next check the status of LPT1 and COM1.

4. Type **MODE LPT1: /STATUS** and press **[Enter]**. DOS displays the status of LPT1. See Figure 9-12. DOS indicates that output to this port is now rerouted to COM1.

device name

MODE command

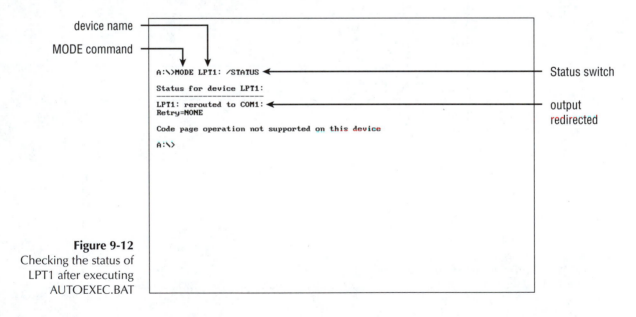

Status switch

output
redirected

Figure 9-12
Checking the status of
LPT1 after executing
AUTOEXEC.BAT

5. Type **MODE COM1: /STATUS** and press **[Enter]**. DOS displays the status of COM1. DOS indicates that the retry option is B (for Busy). This option has the same effect as the P parameter you specified.

You can also use the MODE command for other devices connected to your computer system. For example, you might have a mouse connected to your second serial port, COM2. You would go through the same process to configure it for COM2 and redirect output from the next available parallel port to COM2.

LOADING A TSR

Each time you start your computer system, you load DOSKEY so that you can recall and edit commands at the DOS prompt. You can include this step in the AUTOEXEC.BAT file so that DOS automatically executes and loads DOSKEY during startup. The DOSKEY program is a TSR program that intercepts commands you enter at the DOS prompt and records these commands in its command stack before DOS executes the commands.

You also want to load the TSR that enables Delete Sentry (or Delete Tracker in DOS 5.0) so that you can recover a recently deleted file in the event you deleted it by mistake.

To load a TSR from AUTOEXEC.BAT, you include the command for the program on a separate line in the AUTOEXEC.BAT file.

To include an option for loading DOSKEY in the AUTOEXEC.BAT file:

1. Type **EDIT AUTOEXEC.BAT** and press **[Enter]**. DOS loads the MS-DOS Editor, which loads the AUTOEXEC.BAT file.

2. Press **[Ctrl][End]** to move the cursor to the end of the file. If necessary, position the cursor two lines below the last line of text and be sure the cursor is not indented.

3. Type **REM**, press **[Tab]**, type **Load TSRs** and press **[Enter]**.

4. Type **REM** and press **[Enter]**.

5. Press **[Tab]**, type **DOSKEY** and press **[Enter]**.

Now you will include an option for loading Delete Sentry if you are using DOS 6.0 or 6.2, or Delete Tracker if you are using DOS 5.0.

To enable Delete Sentry *if you are using DOS 6.0 or 6.2* or Delete Tracker *if you are using DOS 5.0*:

6.0 6.2

5.0

1. If you are using DOS 6.0 or 6.2, type **UNDELETE /SA** and press **[Enter]** to enable Delete Sentry for drive A. Figure 9-13 shows the modifications to AUTOEXEC.BAT file for DOS 6.0 and 6.2. If you are using DOS 5.0, type **MIRROR /TA** and press **[Enter]** to enable Delete Tracker for drive A.

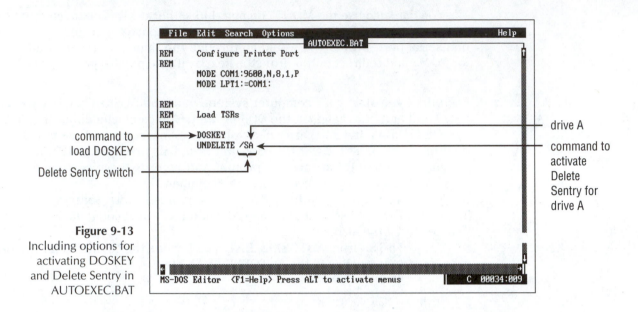

command to
load DOSKEY

Delete Sentry switch

drive A

command to
activate
Delete
Sentry for
drive A

Figure 9-13
Including options for
activating DOSKEY
and Delete Sentry in
AUTOEXEC.BAT

2. Press **[Alt]** (Menu) to access the menu bar, press **[Enter]** for the File menu, and type **X** for the Exit command.

If you are using the mouse, click **File**, then click **Exit**.

The MS-DOS Editor displays a dialog box that prompts you about saving the changes.

3. Press **[Enter]** to select Yes.

If you are using the mouse, click **Yes**.

The MS-DOS Editor saves your changes, you exit the MS-DOS Editor, and DOS displays the DOS prompt.

You are now ready to test these two new changes to the AUTOEXEC.BAT file. This time you will reboot your system. If you are using a network without a hard disk, ask your instructor or technical support person for instructions on how to complete these steps. DOS must be able to access the network and locate the DOS system files.

To reboot your system:

1. Press **[Ctrl][Alt][Del]** or press the **Reset button** on your computer system. During the booting process, DOS locates the AUTOEXEC.BAT file on your boot disk, executes the MODE commands, loads DOSKEY, and then loads Delete Sentry or Delete Tracker. DOS might also activate Delete Sentry or Delete Tracker for other drives. See Figure 9-14.

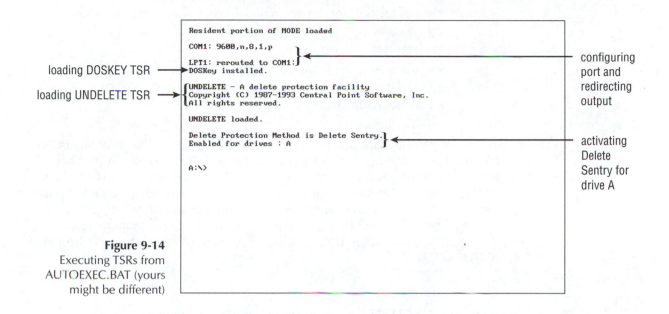

```
Resident portion of MODE loaded

COM1: 9600,n,8,1,p

LPT1: rerouted to COM1:
DOSKey installed.

UNDELETE - A delete protection facility
Copyright (C) 1987-1993 Central Point Software, Inc.
All rights reserved.

UNDELETE loaded.

Delete Protection Method is Delete Sentry.
Enabled for drives : A


A:\>
```

loading DOSKEY TSR ⟶

loading UNDELETE TSR ⟶

configuring port and redirecting output

activating Delete Sentry for drive A

Figure 9-14
Executing TSRs from AUTOEXEC.BAT (yours might be different)

If you use a mouse on your computer system, you can load the software for the mouse from the AUTOEXEC.BAT file just as you do other TSRs.

MONITORING FOR COMPUTER VIRUSES

You check your computer system every few days for computer viruses. However, because of the widespread occurrence of computer viruses, you want to provide your computer system with an additional level of protection.

The VSAFE utility in DOS 6.0 and 6.2 continually monitors your computer system and checks diskettes inserted into drives for the presence of computer viruses. It is another useful TSR that you can load from the AUTOEXEC.BAT file. Its syntax is:

VSAFE

Let's add this TSR to the AUTOEXEC.BAT file. If you are using DOS 5.0, you will not be able to complete this section because DOS 5.0 does not have a VSAFE utility. If you are using DOS 5.0, skip to the section entitled "Executing DOS Utilities from AUTOEXEC.BAT" or read through the following steps to familiarize yourself with loading VSAFE.

_5.0_

_6.0_ _6.2_ **To include the VSAFE TSR in your AUTOEXEC.BAT file** *in DOS 6.0 or 6.2*:

1. Type **EDIT AUTOEXEC.BAT** and press **[Enter]**. DOS loads the MS-DOS Editor, which loads the AUTOEXEC.BAT file.

2. Press **[Ctrl][End]** to move the cursor to the end of the file. Then move the cursor to the blank line below the last line of text.

3. Press **[Tab]**, type **VSAFE** and press **[Enter]**.

4. Press **[Alt]** (Menu) to access the menu bar, press **[Enter]** for the File menu, and type **X** for the Exit command.

   If you are using the mouse, click **File**, then click **Exit**.

The MS-DOS Editor displays a dialog box that prompts you about saving the changes.

5. Press **[Enter]** to select Yes.

If you are using the mouse, click **Yes**.

The MS-DOS Editor saves your changes, you exit the MS-DOS Editor, and DOS displays the DOS prompt.

When you simulate rebooting by executing the AUTOEXEC.BAT file, DOS will attempt to load UNDELETE again. Because this TSR is already in memory, DOS will display a message that it cannot unload UNDELETE because it is already resident in memory. Therefore, before you can simulate rebooting, you must remove the UNDELETE TSR from memory with its **Unload switch** (/U). Although DOSKEY is also a TSR, it does not have a switch for removing itself from memory.

Let's remove the UNDELETE TSR and then test the change to AUTOEXEC.BAT.

To remove UNDELETE from memory and simulate rebooting:

1. Type **UNDELETE /U** and press **[Enter]**. DOS displays a message that it has removed or unloaded this TSR from memory.

2. Type **AUTOEXEC** and press **[Enter]**. DOS executes this batch file, repeats the batch file operations, and loads the VSAFE utility. See Figure 9-15. The utility reports that its hot key is [Alt][V]. A *hot key* is a key combination for accessing a particular computer function, in this case, a TSR. Your report on memory usage by VSAFE might be different.

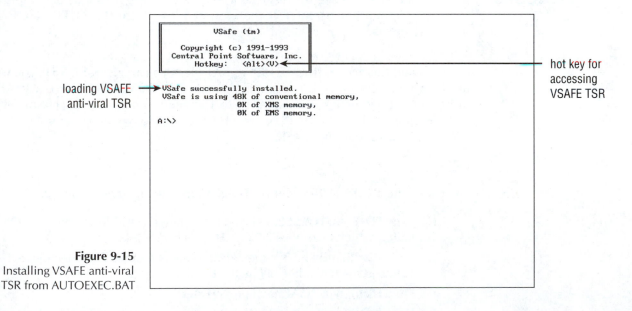

loading VSAFE anti-viral TSR

hot key for accessing VSAFE TSR

Figure 9-15
Installing VSAFE anti-viral TSR from AUTOEXEC.BAT

3. Press [**Alt**][**V**]. DOS displays the VSAFE Warnings Options dialog box. This dialog box allows you to change the types of protection and monitoring provided by VSAFE.

   By default, VSAFE warns of attempts to format and erase the hard drive (HD), checks executable files, checks all disk drives for boot sector viruses, and warns of attempts to write to the hard disk (HD) boot sector or partition table and a diskette boot sector. The options for checking programs that attempt to stay or remain resident in memory, preventing writing to disks, and preventing changes to executable files are by default set to *OFF*. You can toggle these options on or off to meet your needs.

4. Press [**Esc**]. You exit this menu and return to the DOS prompt.

EXECUTING DOS UTILITIES FROM AUTOEXEC.BAT

Another important operation that you frequently perform is to check the status of your hard disk with the CHKDSK command. Because this command can remove minor errors before they become more serious and because it is important to execute this utility frequently, it is a good candidate for inclusion in AUTOEXEC.BAT.

Let's use DOSKEY to search for the last EDIT command that you entered, then add the CHKDSK command to your AUTOEXEC.BAT file.

To locate the last EDIT command:

1. Type **E**, press [**F8**] (Search), then press [**Enter**]. The command line should read "EDIT AUTOEXEC.BAT." When you press [F8] (Search), DOSKEY locates and displays the last command in its command stack that starts with the letter "E." If this command that DOSKEY finds is not the one you want, you can press [F8] (Search) again to locate the previous command that starts with the same first character, and so on until you find the desired command. Press [**Enter**]. After DOS executes the EDIT command you found with DOSKEY, it loads the MS-DOS Editor, which then loads the AUTOEXEC.BAT file.

2. Press [**Ctrl**][**End**] to move the cursor to the end of the file. If necessary, position the cursor two lines below the last line of text and be sure the cursor is not indented.

3. Type **REM**, press [**Tab**], type **Execute DOS Utilities** and press [**Enter**].

4. Type **REM** and press [**Enter**].

5. Press [**Tab**], type **CLS** and press [**Enter**]. After DOS loads VSAFE from AUTOEXEC.BAT, the Clear Screen (CLS) command clears the screen so that you see only the output of the next command, CHKDSK.

6. Type **CHKDSK** and press [**Enter**].

7. Press [**Alt**] (Menu) to access the menu bar, press [**Enter**] for the File menu, and type **X** for the Exit command.

   If you are using the mouse, click **File**, then click **Exit**.

   The MS-DOS Editor displays a dialog box that prompts you about saving the changes.

8. Press **[Enter]** to select Yes.

    If you are using the mouse, click **Yes**.

    The MS-DOS Editor saves your changes, you exit the MS-DOS Editor, and DOS displays the DOS prompt.

If you are using DOS 6.0 or 6.2, you want to remove the VSAFE and UNDELETE TSRs from memory with their Unload switches. You must remove them in reverse order. The last loaded must be the first removed. If you are using DOS 5.0, you do not need to remove the VSAFE and UNDELETE TSRs from memory.

6.0 *6.2*   **To remove these TSRs from memory and test AUTOEXEC.BAT:**

6.0 *6.2*   1. If you are using DOS 6.0 or 6.2, type **VSAFE /U** and press **[Enter]**. DOS removes this utility from memory.

               2. If you are using DOS 6.0 or 6.2, type **UNDELETE /U** and press **[Enter]**. DOS unloads this utility from memory.

5.0 *6.0* *6.2*   Now test AUTOEXEC.BAT using DOS 5.0, 6.0, or 6.2.

               3. Type **AUTOEXEC** and press **[Enter]**. DOS executes this batch file. This
6.2   time, DOS executes CHKDSK and provides a status report on the boot disk because it is the current drive. See Figure 9-16. Your status report will be different from the one in this figure. DOS 6.2 will also recommend that you use ScanDisk.

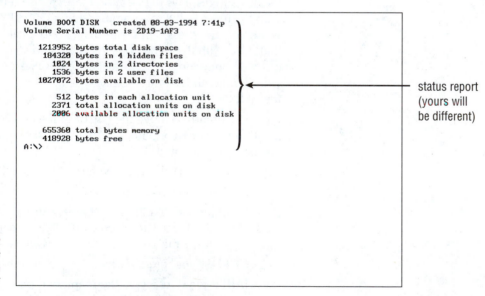

```
Volume BOOT DISK   created 08-03-1994 7:41p
Volume Serial Number is 2D19-1AF3

 1213952 bytes total disk space
  184320 bytes in 4 hidden files
    1024 bytes in 2 directories
    1536 bytes in 2 user files
 1027072 bytes available on disk

     512 bytes in each allocation unit
    2371 total allocation units on disk
    2006 available allocation units on disk

  655360 total bytes memory
  418928 bytes free
A:\>
```

status report
(yours will
be different)

Figure 9-16
Executing the
CHKDSK utility from
AUTOEXEC.BAT

You can add any other DOS utilities that you frequently use to the AUTOEXEC.BAT file so that DOS automatically executes these utilities at startup.

CHANGING DIRECTORIES AND LOADING AN APPLICATION

Suppose that in your job, you always change to a specific subdirectory on your client diskette and load the same word processing application. Rather than manually repeat the commands for these operations at the DOS prompt, you can include them at the end of your AUTOEXEC.BAT file. To mimic the process you use at work, you decide to modify the AUTOEXEC.BAT file so that it changes to the batch file directory and loads the MS-DOS Editor. After you exit the MS-DOS Editor, you want the batch file to return to the root directory.

To specify a start-up directory and application in AUTOEXEC.BAT:

1. Type **E**, press **[F8]** (Search), and press **[Enter]**. The command line should read "EDIT AUTOEXEC.BAT." If not, press **[F8]** (Search) until you locate this command, then press **[Enter]**. DOS loads the MS-DOS Editor, which loads the AUTOEXEC.BAT file.

2. Press **[Ctrl][End]** to move the cursor to the end of the file. Position the cursor on the blank line after the line containing the CHKDSK command. If necessary, press **[Tab]** to indent the line. Then type **PAUSE** and press **[Enter]** *twice*. The PAUSE command will allow you to view the check-disk report before DOS changes directories and loads the MS-DOS Editor.

3. Press **[Backspace]**, type **REM** and press **[Tab]**, type **Change Directory & Load Application** and press **[Enter]**.

4. Type **REM** and press **[Enter]**.

5. Press **[Tab]**, type **A:** and press **[Enter]**. This step guarantees that DOS accesses the correct drive in which the subdirectory is located.

6. Type **CD ** and press **[Enter]**. This step guarantees that DOS starts at the root directory.

7. Type **CD BAT** and press **[Enter]**.

8. Type **EDIT** and press **[Enter]**.

9. Type **CD ** and press **[Enter]**. Figure 9-17 shows the final changes to your AUTOEXEC.BAT file.

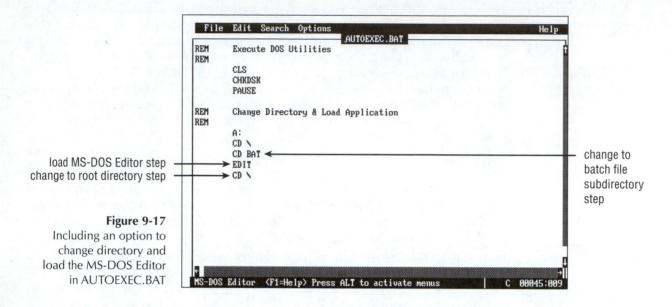

load MS-DOS Editor step →
change to root directory step →

change to
batch file
subdirectory
step

Figure 9-17
Including an option to
change directory and
load the MS-DOS Editor
in AUTOEXEC.BAT

10. Press **[Alt]** (Menu) to access the menu bar, press **[Enter]** for the File
menu, and type **X** for the Exit command.

If you are using the mouse, click **File**, then click **Exit**.

The MS-DOS Editor displays a dialog box that prompts you about saving
the changes.

11. Press **[Enter]** to select Yes.

If you are using the mouse, click **Yes**.

The MS-DOS Editor saves your changes, you exit the MS-DOS Editor,
and DOS displays the DOS prompt.

If you are using a computer network, you will continue to simulate rebooting to maintain your connection to the network. If you are using a computer
with a hard drive, you will perform a warm boot instead of simulating the
rebooting process.

Now you are ready to test the final modifications to the AUTOEXEC.BAT file.

To reboot your computer:

6.0 6.2

1. If you *are not* connected to a network, press **[Ctrl][Alt][Del]** or press
your computer system's **Reset button**. If you *are* connected to a network
and are using DOS 6.0 or 6.2, type **VSAFE/U** and press **[Enter]**. Then type
UNDELETE /U and press **[Enter]**. Type **AUTOEXEC** and press **[Enter]**.
DOS executes commands in the AUTOEXEC.BAT file and pauses after
CHKDSK displays a status report.

2. Press **[Spacebar]** or any other key to continue. DOS changes directories
and loads the MS-DOS Editor.

3. Press **[Esc]** to clear the MS-DOS Editor's Welcome screen.

4. Press **[Alt]** (Menu) to access the menu bar, press **[Enter]** for the File menu, and type **X** for the Exit command.

If you are using the mouse, click **File**, then click **Exit**.

If the MS-DOS Editor displays a dialog box that prompts you about saving changes, type **N** and press **[Enter]**. DOS displays the DOS prompt.

The DOS prompt shows that DOS returned to the root directory after you exited the MS-DOS Editor.

LOADING A MENU FROM AUTOEXEC.BAT

If you use a menu utility to display a list of the software applications on your computer system, you can include the command that starts that utility at the end of the AUTOEXEC.BAT file. After DOS executes the start-up operations that you specify in AUTOEXEC.BAT, it executes the menu utility and displays a menu that provides you with access to the other software applications. Likewise, if you design your own menu system with batch files, you can start your menu system from the AUTOEXEC.BAT file by including the name of the batch file that displays the main menu.

The AUTOEXEC.BAT file optimizes the performance of your computer system by executing commands required to configure your computer system and by executing frequently used utilities and applications.

PRINTING A COPY OF AUTOEXEC.BAT

You want to print a copy of the AUTOEXEC.BAT so that you have a permanent record of your work. You can use this information later to modify the AUTOEXEC.BAT file on your hard disk.

First, you want to reboot your computer system from the hard disk or its network drive so that you can print using the settings on your system.

To print a copy of AUTOEXEC.BAT:

1. Remove your boot disk from drive A.
2. Press **[Ctrl][Alt][Del]** or press the **Reset button**.
3. Insert your boot disk into drive A.
4. Change to drive A.
5. Type **PRINT AUTOEXEC.BAT** and press **[Enter]**. When prompted for the list device, press **[Enter]** to accept the default printer port or enter the name of your printer port. Figure 9-18 shows a printed copy of the AUTOEXEC.BAT file.

In Tutorial 11 you will modify the AUTOEXEC.BAT file and learn how to create a configuration file for use with AUTOEXEC.BAT. Please save the diskette that contains your files and the work you did in this tutorial.

```
        @ECHO OFF
        CLS

REM     **************************************************************
REM
REM                    Auto-Execute File
REM
REM     **************************************************************

REM     Specify Path & Prompt
REM
        PATH A:\;A:\BAT;C:\DOS
        PROMPT $P$G

REM     Specify Settings
REM
        SET DIRCMD=/O /P
        SET TEMP=A:\TEMP
        SET TMP=A:\TEMP

REM     Configure Printer Port
REM
        MODE COM1:9600,N,8,1,P
        MODE LPT1:=COM1:

REM     Load TSRs
REM
        DOSKEY
        UNDELETE /SA
        VSAFE

REM     Execute DOS Utilities
REM
        CLS
        CHKDSK
        PAUSE

REM     Change Directory & Load Application
REM
        A:
        CD \
        CD BAT
        EDIT
        CD \
```

Figure 9-18
A printed copy of
AUTOEXEC.BAT

◆

SUMMARY

In this tutorial, you created an AUTOEXEC.BAT file with the MS-DOS Editor. You specified the DOS path and defined the DOS prompt, specified settings for the DOS environment, specified characteristics of a serial port, redirected output from a parallel to a serial port, loaded TSRs, executed DOS utilities, and specified a default directory and application in this file. After you added each of these features, you tested the AUTOEXEC.BAT file by simulating rebooting. You examined the use and value of loading the MODE, DOSKEY, and UNDELETE TSRs from AUTOEXEC.BAT. DOS 6.0 and 6.2 users examined the use and value of loading the VSAFE TSR from AUTOEXEC.BAT.

Command Reference	
DOS Commands	
MODE COM*n*:[*baud rate*],[*parity*], [*data bits*],[*stop bits*],[*retry option*] MODE COM*n*: [*BAUD=baud rate*] [*PARITY=parity*] [*DATA=*[*data bits*] [*STOP=*[*stop bits*] [*RETRY=*[*retry option*]	An external command that specifies the characteristics of a serial port
MODE LPT*m*:=COM*n*:	An external command that redirects output from a parallel port to a serial port
UNDELETE /U	*DOS 6.0 and 6.2:* An external command that unloads the UNDELETE TSR from memory
VSAFE	*DOS 6.0 and 6.2:* An external command that loads a TSR that continually monitors your computer system for the presence of computer viruses
VSAFE /U	*DOS 6.0 and 6.2:* An external command that unloads the VSAFE utility from memory

QUESTIONS

1. What is the role of the AUTOEXEC.BAT file?
2. Where must you store the AUTOEXEC.BAT file?
3. What type of file is the AUTOEXEC.BAT file?
4. Why is it important to place the PATH command in AUTOEXEC.BAT?
5. Where is the best place for the PATH command in AUTOEXEC.BAT?
6. Why is it important to place a PROMPT command in AUTOEXEC.BAT?
7. Name three ways you can change the DOS path?
8. Why is it important to modify the path in AUTOEXEC.BAT when you install new software or modify the directory structure of a hard disk?
9. What is the purpose of specifying a directory for the TEMP and TMP environment variables in AUTOEXEC.BAT?
10. How can you remove settings for environment variables stored in the DOS environment?
11. Why is the MODE command used in AUTOEXEC.BAT?
12. Name three uses of the MODE command.
13. What port does DOS automatically direct printer output to?

14. What is the difference between serial and parallel transmission?

15. What is the advantage of using serial over parallel transmission, and vice versa?

16. What is the purpose of a baud rate?

17. What does the number of data bits refer to?

18. What is the purpose of a parity bit?

19. What is a stop bit?

20. What does the MODE command's retry option do?

21. You have a printer connected to COM1. Your manual tells you to use a baud rate of 2400, no parity, 8 data bits, and 1 stop bit. How would you configure this port with the MODE command so that DOS can communicate with it? Assume you also want an automatic retry option.

22. You have a printer connected to LPT1 and COM1. After configuring your printer for the COM1 port, you want to redirect output to COM1. How would you redirect output with the MODE command?

23. How would you use the MODE command to determine the status of LPT2?

24. How can you unload, or remove, the UNDELETE and VSAFE TSRs from memory with DOS 6.0 and 6.2?

25. What does the VSAFE utility do? How do you change its warning options?

26. What important DOS utility should you include in AUTOEXEC.BAT to check for potential errors on the hard disk?

27. How can you search for a command in the DOSKEY command stack?

28. If you want to load a menu or an application from AUTOEXEC.BAT, where is the best place to list the command?

29. What is the difference between performing a warm boot and simulating rebooting by typing AUTOEXEC?

30. How would you start the DOS Shell from AUTOEXEC.BAT?

TUTORIAL ASSIGNMENTS

1. **Loading the DOS Shell from AUTOEXEC.BAT**: In this assignment, you will include a provision in the AUTOEXEC.BAT for loading the DOS Shell after you computer boots. Use the DISKCOPY command to make a duplicate copy of the boot disk that you used in this tutorial. Then perform the following operations on the duplicate copy of the boot disk.
   a. Modify the AUTOEXEC.BAT file so that DOS:
      (1) Remains at the root directory after the computer boots
      (2) Loads the DOS Shell as its last operation
   b. Delete the section for changing to the batch file directory and loading the MS-DOS Editor.

   6.0 6.2
   c. If you are using DOS 6.0 or 6.2, remove the UNDELETE and VSAFE TSRs from memory.
   d. Test your AUTOEXEC.BAT file by rebooting or by simulating rebooting. If you encounter any difficulties, correct the problems and reboot.

After you verify that AUTOEXEC.BAT is working properly, remove the duplicate copy of the boot disk from drive A, reboot your computer system from drive C to restore its settings, and print a copy of this file.

2. **Restructuring AUTOEXEC.BAT**: In this assignment, you will reorganize the AUTOEXEC.BAT that you created in the tutorial so that DOS executes commands in a different sequence, so that you are familiar with the process for restructuring an AUTOEXEC.BAT file. Use the DISKCOPY command to make a duplicate copy of the boot disk that you used in this tutorial. Then perform the following operations on the duplicate copy of the boot disk. Remember to include documentation in the AUTOEXEC.BAT file.

    a. Delete the lines with the commands for specifying the location of the temporary directory with the SET command, for configuring a serial port, for loading the UNDELETE (or MIRROR) utility, for pausing after the check-disk operation, and for changing directories and loading the MS-DOS Editor.

    b. Modify the AUTOEXEC.BAT file so that it performs the following operations in the following order:

        (1) Specifies the DOS path and prompt

        6.0 6.2 (2) Loads VSAFE if you are using DOS 6.0 or 6.2

        (3) Loads DOSKEY

        (4) Stores the Order, and Lowercase switches for the Directory command in the DOS environment

        (5) Performs a check disk operation on drive C (or A)

    6.0 6.2 c. If you are using DOS 6.0 or 6.2, remove the UNDELETE and VSAFE TSRs from memory.

    d. Test your AUTOEXEC.BAT file by rebooting or by simulating rebooting. If you encounter any difficulties, correct the problems and test it again.

    After you verify that AUTOEXEC.BAT is working properly, remove the duplicate copy of the boot disk from drive A, reboot your computer system from drive C to restore the settings for your computer system, and print a copy of this file.

    6.0 6.2 If you use DOS 6.0 or 6.2, what advantage is there to including the VSAFE utility at the beginning of AUTOEXEC.BAT?

3. **Protecting AUTOEXEC.BAT**: Use the DISKCOPY command to make a duplicate copy of the boot disk that you used in this tutorial. Then perform the following operations on the duplicate copy of the boot disk and list the commands that you use.

    a. Assign the Read-Only attribute to AUTOEXEC.BAT.

    b. Make a directory named RECORDS, and copy AUTOEXEC.BAT to that directory.

    c. Assign the Hidden attribute to AUTOEXEC.BAT.

    6.0 6.2 d. If you are using DOS 6.0 or 6.2, remove the UNDELETE and VSAFE TSRs from memory.

    e. Test your AUTOEXEC.BAT file by rebooting or by simulating rebooting.

    List the three types of protection you have provided for the AUTOEXEC.BAT file, and explain the advantage of each.

4. **Examining AUTOEXEC.BAT on Drive C**: Use the DISKCOPY command to make a duplicate copy of the boot disk that you used in this tutorial. Then perform the following operations:

    a. Print a copy of the AUTOEXEC.BAT file on your hard disk.

b. Load the MS-DOS Editor and prepare an outline (on the duplicate copy of the boot disk) that:
   (1) Lists and briefly describes each of the operations included in the AUTOEXEC.BAT file. If there are commands or operations not covered thus far in your course, include a notation to this effect.
   (2) Lists commands and operations that might be useful to include in this file.
c. Print a copy of the outline that you prepared in Step b.
Then answer the following questions:
d. Does this file include any documentation to assist you in interpreting its contents?
e. What serial ports, if any, are configured by AUTOEXEC.BAT during startup?
f. Does the AUTOEXEC.BAT file include any provisions for redirecting output from a parallel to a serial port? If so, how does the redirection occur?

5. **Documenting System Specifications with AUTOEXEC.BAT**: In this assignment, you will use AUTOEXEC.BAT to automatically document important system settings and information after you power on your computer. Use the DISKCOPY command to make a duplicate copy of the boot disk that you used in this tutorial. Then perform the following operations:
   a. Create a directory named RECORDS.
   b. Modify the AUTOEXEC.BAT file as follows:
      (1) After the section for specifying settings for environment variables, create a new section, entitled "Document DOS Environment." In this section, use the SET command and the output redirection operator to store a copy of the settings in the DOS environment in a file named ENVIRONS.DOC in the RECORDS subdirectory, as follows:

      SET > A:\RECORDS\ENVIRONS.DOC

      (2) In the section labeled "Execute DOS Utilities," add a TREE command before the CHKDSK command and redirect the output so that DOS stores a copy of the directory tree of drive C (or drive A) in a file named SYSTREE.DOC in the RECORDS subdirectory.
      (3) In the same section, modify the CHKDSK command so that its output (for either drive C or A) is redirected to a file named DSKSTATS.DOC in the RECORDS subdirectory. Use the CHKDSK command to first check the status of drive C (or drive A) for errors before you perform this same operation from the batch file. You must fix any errors before you use the batch file. Also, delete the line with the PAUSE command.

   6.0 6.2
   c. If you are using DOS 6.0 or 6.2, remove the UNDELETE and VSAFE TSRs from memory.
   d. Test your AUTOEXEC.BAT file by rebooting or by simulating rebooting. If you encounter any difficulties, correct the problems and test it again.
   e. After you verify that AUTOEXEC.BAT is working properly, remove the duplicate copy of the boot disk from drive A, reboot your computer system from drive C to restore its settings, and print a copy of this file. Then print a copy of the contents of the files named ENVIRONS.DOC, SYSTREE.DOC, and DSKSTATS.DOC.

Configuring Your System

OBJECTIVES

In this tutorial you will learn to:

- ◆ Understand the importance of the CONFIG.SYS file
- ◆ Create a CONFIG.SYS file
- ◆ Specify the number of disk buffers in the CONFIG.SYS file
- ◆ Set the number of file handles in the CONFIG.SYS file
- ◆ Establish the size of the DOS environment from the CONFIG.SYS file
- ◆ Install device drivers from CONFIG.SYS
- ◆ Use MODE to change the video display mode
- ◆ Load TSRs from CONFIG.SYS
- ◆ Use the FASTOPEN utility
- ◆ Specify multiple startup configurations from CONFIG.SYS
- ◆ Use multiple configurations from AUTOEXEC.BAT
- ◆ Print a copy of CONFIG.SYS

Imagine you now have a job as the supervisor of a Quality Assurance (QA) Division for a large software manufacturer. You must guarantee that newly developed software operates properly under different types of configurations that businesses and individuals use on their computer systems. To achieve this goal, you want to customize and standardize the test systems in your office in order to provide a consistent approach to testing and evaluating new software.

Before you make important changes to the computer systems that your staff uses for testing software, you decide to create a boot disk and experiment with various settings and configuration options. Later, you can apply the results of your findings to all the systems in your office.

◆

THE IMPORTANCE OF THE CONFIG.SYS FILE

DOS uses default settings for configuring your computer system when you power on your computer or perform a warm boot. However, you can create a special file named CONFIG.SYS that contains a set of commands (also called **directives**) that configure and customize DOS to meet your specific needs and to work with special hardware included in your computer system. You cannot execute these commands from the DOS prompt because the commands are specific to CONFIG.SYS.

Like the AUTOEXEC.BAT file, the CONFIG.SYS file is an ASCII file that you must place in the root directory of the hard disk from which your computer system boots. When you perform a cold or warm boot, DOS automatically looks for a file by this name in the root directory of the boot disk and executes the commands in this file to configure the operating system in memory.

During a cold or warm boot, the microprocessor executes self-diagnostic **routines**, or programs, in the BIOS—the Basic Input/Output System stored in ROM. After the Power-On Self Test (POST), the BIOS instructs the microprocessor to check drive A and then drive C for a boot disk containing the operating system files. Once the microprocessor locates the boot disk, it loads IO.SYS (or IBMBIO.COM in PC-DOS), the operating system file that handles input and output operations, into memory. Then, MSDOS.SYS (or IBMDOS.COM in PC-DOS), which provides support functions for applications, loads into memory. If there is a CONFIG.SYS file in the root directory of the boot disk, DOS executes the commands in CONFIG.SYS to further configure itself. Otherwise, it uses its own default settings. Finally, the command interpreter or command processor, COMMAND.COM, loads into memory. COMMAND.COM, which is also responsible for executing batch files, executes the commands in AUTOEXEC.BAT to customize your system before it displays the DOS prompt.

PREPARING A BOOT DISK

Because you will test different configuration settings in CONFIG.SYS, you decide to use a boot disk in drive A rather than change the CONFIG.SYS file on your hard disk. You cannot simulate rebooting as you did with the AUTOEXEC.BAT file. You must perform a warm boot and start the computer system from a boot disk in drive A to execute the commands in CONFIG.SYS. You can use the same boot disk that you used in Tutorial 9.

To simplify the process of testing configuration settings in the CONFIG.SYS file, you decide to remove some of the commands from AUTOEXEC.BAT so that you will have fewer overall operations to perform. You can remove the commands for loading TSRs, executing DOS utilities, changing directories, and loading the MS-DOS Editor. You already know how DOS executes these commands from AUTOEXEC.BAT.

Before you change AUTOEXEC.BAT, you want to make a copy of this file and its current settings.

To copy the AUTOEXEC.BAT file:

1. After you power on your computer system and access the DOS prompt, insert the boot disk that you prepared in Tutorial 9 in drive A. You must use drive A because you will perform test boots from this drive.

2. Type **A:** to change to drive A. *Be sure the DOS prompt changes to A:\>.*

3. Type **COPY AUTOEXEC.BAT AUTOEXEC.01** and press **[Enter]**. DOS copies the original AUTOEXEC.BAT file and produces a new file with the same name but a different file extension. DOS will not execute the contents in AUTOEXEC.01 because it is not a batch file. A batch file must have the file extension BAT. However, you now have a copy of the AUTOEXEC.BAT that you prepared in Tutorial 9.

Modifying AUTOEXEC.BAT

You are now ready to modify the AUTOEXEC.BAT file with the MS-DOS Editor. After you retrieve this file, you will remove the commands that load the TSRs, execute the DOS utilities, change directories, and load the MS-DOS Editor.

To edit the AUTOEXEC.BAT file:

1. Type **EDIT AUTOEXEC.BAT** and press **[Enter]**. DOS loads the MS-DOS Editor, which retrieves the AUTOEXEC.BAT file. See Figure 10-1. You want to move the cursor to the line that contains the command for loading the first TSR.

PROMPT
command

PATH
command

assignments
for
environment
variables

Figure 10-1
A partial view of the
contents of the
AUTOEXEC.BAT file

2. Press **[Caps Lock]** to turn on caps. Although you can use lowercase, uppercase, or mixed case to enter commands in AUTOEXEC.BAT and CONFIG.SYS, the figures in this tutorial show commands entered in uppercase.

Now search for a command.

3. Press **[Alt]** (Menu) to access the menu bar, type **S** for the Search menu, and press **[Enter]** for the Find option.

   If you are using the mouse, click **Search**, then click **Find**.

   The MS-DOS Editor displays the Find dialog box. See Figure 10-2. If you check "Match Upper/Lowercase," you can perform a case-sensitive search. If you check "Whole Word," you can exclude matches that fall within words.

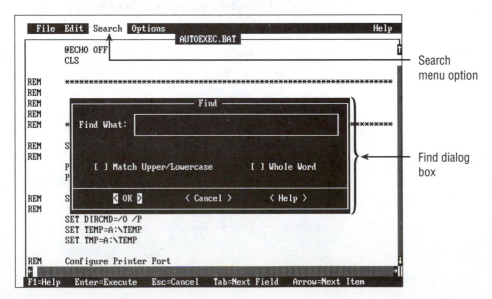

Search
menu option

Find dialog
box

Figure 10-2
The MS-DOS Editor's Find
dialog box

_5.0 6.0 6.2_

_5.0 6.0 6.2_

_5.0_

4. If you are using DOS 6.0 or 6.2, type **UNDELETE** and press **[Enter]**. If you are using DOS 5.0, type **MIRROR** and press **[Enter]**.

   If you are using the mouse with DOS 6.0 or 6.2, type **UNDELETE** and click **OK**. If you are using the mouse with DOS 5.0, type **MIRROR** and click **OK**.

   The MS-DOS Editor moves the cursor to the first occurrence of this word and highlights the word. See Figure 10-3. If you are using DOS 5.0, the MS-DOS Editor will highlight MIRROR instead of UNDELETE.

command found by MS-DOS Editor ⟶

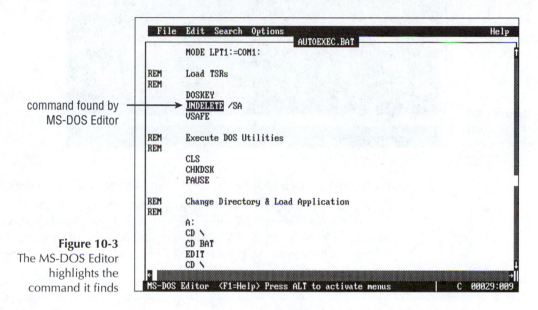

Figure 10-3
The MS-DOS Editor highlights the command it finds

5. Press **[Esc]**. The MS-DOS Editor removes the highlighting.

   You now want to select and delete the remainder of the file.

6. Press **[Shift][Ctrl][End]** by first pressing and holding [Shift] and [Ctrl], and then pressing [End]. Then release all three keys. The MS-DOS Editor selects everything from the current position of the cursor to the end of the file. See Figure 10-4.

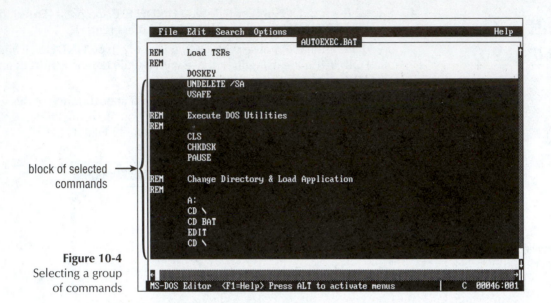

Figure 10-4
Selecting a group
of commands

7. Press **[Del]** or **[Delete]**. The MS-DOS Editor deletes the selected block.

8. Press **[Ctrl][Home]**. The MS-DOS Editor moves the cursor to the beginning of the file. Figure 10-5 shows the remaining commands and documentation in AUTOEXEC.BAT. Your indentation and spacing might be different. Check your AUTOEXEC.BAT file against this figure before you save your changes.

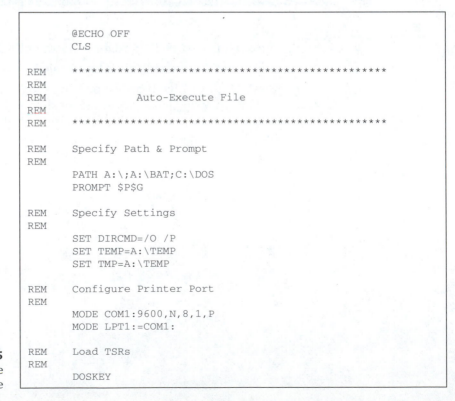

Figure 10-5
The contents of the
AUTOEXEC.BAT file

Now you are ready to save your changes and clear the screen.

9. Press **[Alt]** (Menu) to access the menu bar, press **[Enter]** for the File menu, and type **S** for the Save option.

If you are using the mouse, click **File**, then click **Save**.

The MS-DOS Editor saves your file.

10. Press **[Alt]** (Menu) to access the menu bar, press **[Enter]** for the File menu, and press **[Enter]** for the New option.

If you are using the mouse, click **File**, then click **New**.

The MS-DOS Editor clears the screen. If the MS-DOS Editor asks you if you want to save your changes, press **[Tab]** to select No and then press **[Enter]**, or click **No** with the mouse.

SPECIFYING DISK BUFFERS

You want to configure your computer systems to meet the demands of the software applications that you test on the computers in the QA Division. These software applications frequently access data stored on disk, and you have observed that these frequent disk accesses for data are slow and require an excessive amount of waiting.

The BUFFERS command, when used in CONFIG.SYS, limits disk accesses and speeds up the performance of your computer system. The BUFFERS command instructs DOS to reserve small areas of memory, called **buffers** or **disk buffers**, for storing data retrieved from disk and for storing data prior to being written to disk. These disk buffers are collectively called a **cache** (pronounced "cash"). Each disk buffer is 532 bytes in size and can store a sector of data, which contains 512 bytes. DOS uses the additional 20 bytes in a disk buffer as overhead to manage the disk buffer.

When a program requires data stored on disk, DOS locates and reads this data into a disk buffer. The next time the program needs data, DOS first checks the disk buffers for this data. If DOS locates the data the program needs in the disk buffers, it does not have to read the data from disk. Accessing data stored in memory, or RAM, is significantly faster than reading data from a disk, so your programs function more efficiently and the overall speed and performance of your computer system improves. Periodically, when DOS cannot locate the necessary data in the disk buffers, it will read data from the disk.

The use of disk buffers by DOS also improves the efficiency of recording data on disk. DOS accumulates a sector of data in a disk buffer before it records the sector to disk. Again, this process limits disk accesses and improves the speed and performance of your computer system. When you have finished using a program, you should properly exit the program so that DOS can empty, or **flush**, the buffers and write any remaining data to disk. If you reboot before you save this information and before you exit the program, you will lose this remaining data. Likewise if the computer locks up or if the power fails, you have no choice but to reboot and you will lose everything still stored in the DOS buffers in memory.

If your CONFIG.SYS file does not specify the number of disk buffers for DOS to use, DOS checks the amount of memory and the types of drives in your computer system and uses a value from 2 to 15. For example, if your computer system has the standard 640K of memory and a hard disk drive, the default setting for the number of disk buffers is 15. Because most software applications operate more efficiently with settings in the range of 20 to 50, the default setting selected by DOS is usually insufficient. You can use the BUFFERS command to set the number of disk buffers as follows:

BUFFERS=*n*

N is a value from 1 to 99. If you increase the number of disk buffers available to DOS, DOS can store more sectors of data in memory, increasing the chances that DOS will find the data you need in memory. However, there is a point of diminishing return. If you specify a large number of disk buffers, DOS might spend more time looking for data in the disk buffers than it would take to locate and read the data from disk.

What is the optimum value to use? The manual provided with your software package might recommend a specific value for the BUFFERS command. If the manual does not provide any suggestions, start with 20 buffers for a hard disk with less than 40MB. For each additional 40MB, add 10 to the number of buffers. However, do not use an initial setting higher than 50. For example, for a hard disk with 100MB, use a setting of 40; for a hard disk over 120MB, use a setting of 50.

After you specify a setting for BUFFERS, monitor the performance of your computer system. If the setting is too low, you will notice that the drive light for your hard drive or diskette drives flashes on repeatedly as DOS keeps reading data from the disk. If the setting is too high, you will find yourself waiting for DOS to search the disk buffers before it reads the disk for the necessary data. Also, you do not want to use too high a value for the BUFFERS command because you use more of the memory in your computer system. You then have less memory available for your software applications and the document files that you create with those applications.

After you monitor your computer system for a few days, increase or decrease the setting for buffers by a small amount and notice whether it increases or decreases the performance of your computer system. Continue to make small adjustments to the setting for disk buffers and evaluate your computer's performance until you find the optimal value.

Now you can apply this information to the computers you use in your job in the QA Division. These computer systems have a 110MB hard disk drive, so you decide to set the BUFFERS command to a value of 40.

Creating CONFIG.SYS

Because you are already in the MS-DOS Editor, you can create a CONFIG.SYS file, document its purpose with the REM command, and add a BUFFERS command with a setting of 40.

This is a good time to emphasize the importance of entering commands and their settings in CONFIG.SYS *exactly as described in the tutorial steps and illustrated in the figures*. Otherwise, these features will not work properly or at all when you test them later, and you might waste valuable time attempting to locate the source of a problem.

To document the purpose of the system configuration file:

1. Type **REM** and press **[Tab]**. Press and hold * until you fill the entire row with asterisks—up to position 78. Then press **[Enter]**.

2. Type **REM** and press **[Enter]**.

3. Type **REM** and press **[Tab]** three times. Then type **System Configuration File** and press **[Enter]**.

4. Type **REM** and press **[Enter]**.

5. Type **REM** and press **[Tab]**. Press and hold * until you fill the entire row with asterisks—up to position 78. Then press **[Enter]** *twice*. Figure 10-6 shows the initial documentation.

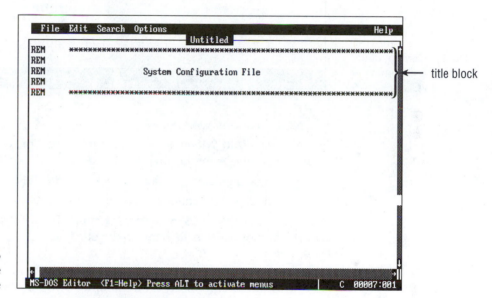

← title block

Figure 10-6
The title block for the
system configuration file

Entering a BUFFERS Setting

Below the title block, you will enter documentation for the BUFFERS command and specify the setting for disk buffers.

To include documentation for the BUFFERS command:

1. Type **REM**, press **[Tab]**, type **Set Disk Buffers** and press **[Enter]**.

2. Type **REM** and press **[Enter]**.

Now specify the number of disk buffers.

3. Press **[Tab]**, type **BUFFERS=40** and press **[Enter]** twice. Figure 10-7 shows the placement of the BUFFERS command.

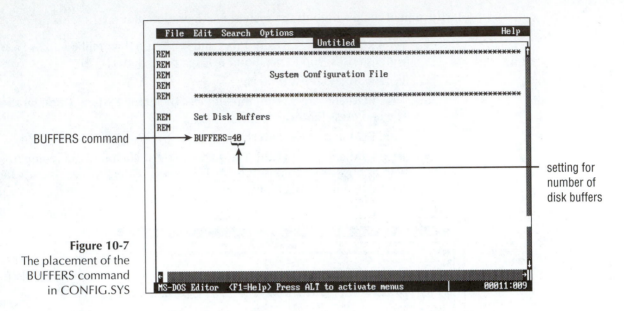

BUFFERS command →

setting for
number of
disk buffers

Figure 10-7
The placement of the
BUFFERS command
in CONFIG.SYS

Next, save your work.

4.   Press **[Alt]** (Menu) to access the menu bar, press **[Enter]** for the File menu,
     and type **A** for the Save As option.

     If you are using the mouse, click **File**, then click **Save As**.

     The MS-DOS Editor displays the Save As dialog box.

5.   Type **CONFIG.SYS** and press **[Enter]**. The MS-DOS Editor saves your file
     and displays its filename in the title bar.

SPECIFYING THE NUMBER OF FILE HANDLES

Software applications must open a variety of program and data files in order to
start or to operate properly. For example, if you use WordPerfect 6.0, you can
open nine document files at the same time and work with each file.
WordPerfect itself opens multiple program files as you perform various operations on these document files.

When you issue certain commands to DOS, it must also be able to open
more than one file to complete the operation. For example, when you use the
TYPE command with the MORE filter to display the contents of a text file, DOS
must open the text file you want to view and it must also open a temporary file
to store the redirected output of the text file.

You can use a FILES command in CONFIG.SYS to specify the maximum
number of open files:

FILES=*n*

N is a value from 8 to 255. If your CONFIG.SYS file does not include a FILES
command, DOS automatically sets this value to 8.

Whether DOS uses the default setting or a setting you specify with the FILES
command, DOS reserves a certain amount of memory for keeping track of open
files. As DOS opens a file, it assigns a number, or a **file handle**, to that file. The
file handle identifies the file and the information DOS keeps on that open file.

DOS also assigns file handles to keep track of devices. DOS automatically
uses one file handle each to keep track of the **standard input device** (the
console's keyboard), the **standard output device** (the console's monitor), the
standard error device for displaying error messages (the console's monitor),

the **standard printer port** (PRN or LPT1), and the **standard communications port** (COM1 or AUX). After you subtract these five file handles from the default setting or the setting you specify for the FILES command, the remaining file handles are available for use by DOS and other programs.

What is the optimal value to use? Again, the manual provided with your software package might recommend a specific value for the FILES command. If you use several types of applications and if each application requires a different number of open files, use the highest value to accommodate the most demanding program.

If your software documentation does not provide a recommended value, start with a value of 20. If you attempt to load a program and see a message that tells you there are an insufficient number of file handles, you should increase the value for the FILES command in the CONFIG.SYS file and then reboot so that DOS uses the new setting.

You do not want to use too high a value for the FILES command because you will use more of the memory in your computer system and will have less memory available for your software applications and the document files that you create with those applications.

You decide to start with a value of 20 in your CONFIG.SYS file.

To include documentation for the FILES command:

1. If necessary, press **[Ctrl][End]** to move the cursor to the end of the file and, if necessary, press **[Backspace]** to delete the tab space and return to the left margin.

2. Type **REM**, press **[Tab]**, type **Set File Handles** and press **[Enter]**.

3. Type **REM** and press **[Enter]**.

Next, specify the number of file handles.

4. Press **[Tab]**, type **FILES=20** and press **[Enter]** twice. Figure 10-8 shows the placement of this command in your CONFIG.SYS file.

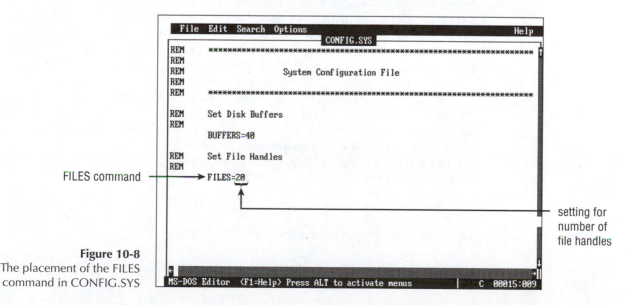

Figure 10-8
The placement of the FILES command in CONFIG.SYS

FILES command

setting for number of file handles

Now save your work.

5. Press **[Alt]** (Menu) to access the menu bar, press **[Enter]** for the File menu, and type **S** for the Save option.

If you are using the mouse, click **File**, then click **Save**.

The MS-DOS Editor saves your file.

SETTING THE SIZE OF THE DOS ENVIRONMENT

Increasingly, you store settings in the DOS environment to automate and customize the use of the computers in the QA Division. You want to ensure that the DOS environment has enough space for the current settings, as well as new ones you might add in the future.

DOS sets the size of the DOS environment to 256 bytes. If you want to increase the size of the DOS environment, you use the SHELL command as follows:

SHELL=[*drive:*][*path*]*filename*   /E:*size*   /P

The full name and location of the command interpreter, including the file extension, is a required parameter. The **Environment switch** (/E) sets the size of the DOS environment. The size can range from 160 (for 160 bytes) through 32768 (for 32,768 bytes). If you use a value that is not divisible by 16, DOS rounds the number up to a multiple of 16 bytes. The **Permanent switch** (/P) indicates that the copy of the command interpreter is to remain in memory.

For example, if you are using COMMAND.COM as the command interpreter and want to set the size of the DOS environment to 1,024 bytes, you enter the command as follows:

SHELL=C:\COMMAND.COM   /E:1024   /P

You can also use the SHELL command in two other ways. If you want to store COMMAND.COM in another directory to protect the file from inadvertent deletion or from harm by computer viruses, you can specify its new location with the SHELL command. Otherwise, DOS assumes COMMAND.COM is stored in the root directory.

As you have discovered, the command interpreter is important because it displays the DOS prompt, interprets commands that you enter at the DOS prompt, loads applications and utilities, executes internal DOS commands, and executes batch files. However, you are not limited to using COMMAND.COM, the command interpreter provided with DOS. You can purchase another command interpreter with more features from another software manufacturer and use it instead of COMMAND.COM. The SHELL command permits you to specify the name of the command interpreter you want to use.

On the computers in the QA Division, you want to set the size of the DOS environment to an initial value of 1,024 bytes so that you have plenty of room for the various settings these systems store. Later, if you need more size, you can increase the value for this setting.

Let's add the SHELL command to CONFIG.SYS and set the size of the DOS environment.

To include documentation for the SHELL command:

1. If necessary, press **[Ctrl][End]** to move the cursor to the end of the file, and press **[Backspace]** to return to the left margin.

2. Type **REM**, press **[Tab]**, type **Set Size of DOS Environment** and press **[Enter]**.

3. Type **REM** and press **[Enter]**.

Now set the size of the DOS environment.

4. Press **[Tab]**, type **SHELL=C:\COMMAND.COM /E:1024 /P** and press **[Enter]** twice. Figure 10-9 shows the SHELL command in your CONFIG.SYS file.

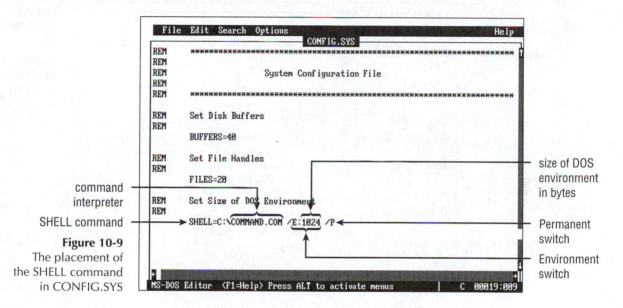

command interpreter →

SHELL command →

Figure 10-9
The placement of the SHELL command in CONFIG.SYS

size of DOS environment in bytes

Permanent switch

Environment switch

Next, save your work and exit.

5. Press **[Alt]** (Menu) to access the menu bar, press **[Enter]** for the File menu, and type **X** for the Exit option.

If you are using the mouse, click **File**, then click **Exit**.

The MS-DOS Editor prompts you about saving your changes.

6. Press **[Enter]** for Yes.

If you are using the mouse, click **Yes**.

The MS-DOS Editor saves your CONFIG.SYS file, and DOS displays the DOS prompt.

TESTING YOUR CONFIGURA-TION FILE

You are now ready to reboot your system and test your CONFIG.SYS file. DOS does not use any new settings you enter in CONFIG.SYS until you reboot. If there are any problems with your CONFIG.SYS file, DOS will display error messages to warn you of the problems. These messages might identify a specific line and command in your CONFIG.SYS file where a problem occurred.

If you are working on a network without a hard disk drive C, ask your instructor or technical support person for directions on how to complete the remainder of the tutorial. DOS must be able to locate files that contain device drivers, TSRs, and utilities whenever you reboot your computer.

To boot your computer system:

1. Press **[Ctrl][Alt][Del]**, or press the **Reset button** on your computer system. During the booting process, DOS executes the commands in CONFIG.SYS to configure itself. DOS then executes the commands in the AUTOEXEC.BAT file, and you should see a message that it configured COM1, redirected output from LPT1 to COM1, and installed DOSKEY. See Figure 10-10.

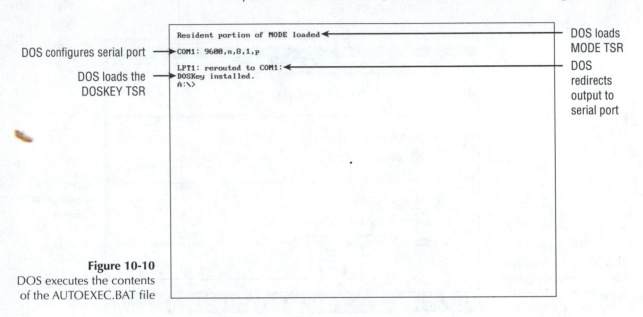

DOS configures serial port

DOS loads the
DOSKEY TSR

```
Resident portion of MODE loaded
COM1: 9600,n,8,1,p

LPT1: rerouted to COM1:
DOSKey installed.
A:\>
```

DOS loads
MODE TSR

DOS
redirects
output to
serial port

Figure 10-10
DOS executes the contents
of the AUTOEXEC.BAT file

2. If DOS reports a problem, notice the source of the error from the message DOS displays, load the MS-DOS Editor, and correct the error. Then repeat Step 1 and reboot.

INSTALLING THE ANSI.SYS DEVICE DRIVER

Each of the computer systems in the QA Division has a video graphics array (VGA) adapter that supports a wide variety of display options. You want to configure DOS to use a device driver that allows you to take full advantage of the features inherent in these systems. Also, you recently purchased a mouse for each system, and you want to install the device driver for operating that hardware component.

A **device driver** is a file with program code that enables DOS to communicate with a specific type of hardware component. DOS itself contains device drivers for communicating with the keyboard, video display, disk drives, and ports. For example, the device driver that communicates with the console unit (keyboard and video display) is named CON (short for console). These device drivers are called **system device drivers** because they are provided with the operating system software. The system device drivers are part of IO.SYS (or IBMBIO.COM in PC-DOS) and are installed when IO.SYS is loaded into memory.

Included with DOS are additional device drivers that you have the option of using. One is ANSI.SYS, a device driver that has extended capabilities for communicating with and controlling the console unit. If you have a VGA or enhanced graphics adapter (EGA), this device driver can set screen colors, display more than 25 lines of text on the monitor, and control the position of the cursor on the monitor. You can also assign commands to function keys. For example, you can assign the command DIR, followed by a code for the Enter key, to [F10] (or any other function key). When you press [F10], DOS will display a directory. This device driver is also important because some applications require you to install ANSI.SYS as the device driver for the console.

Most, but not all, device drivers provided with software have the SYS file extension so that you can easily recognize these files. To install a device driver for use with DOS, you use a DEVICE command in CONFIG.SYS, as follows:

DEVICE=[*drive:*][*path*]*filename* [*parameters*]

The filename is the full name of the device driver, including the file extension. You might also need to specify the drive and path for the device driver. Some device drivers use required or optional parameters, such as switches, and you list these parameters after the filename. You use a different DEVICE command for each device driver you install from CONFIG.SYS.

For example, to install ANSI.SYS as the device driver for the console from the DOS subdirectory, you enter:

DEVICE=C:\DOS\ANSI.SYS

If you have a VGA or EGA adapter and install the ANSI.SYS device driver, you can configure your video display for 43 lines by using the following command:

MODE CON: LINES=43

After MODE, you specify the name of the device. In this case, CON: is the device name for the console unit. Then you specify the number of lines per screen.

However, DOS cannot execute this command without the ANSI.SYS device driver, so you have a way to test the use of ANSI.SYS. If ANSI.SYS is not installed as a device driver and if you enter the MODE command shown above, DOS will either report an error message indicating that you must install ANSI.SYS or that this function is not supported on the video display adapter that you use.

To determine whether ANSI.SYS is installed:

1. Be sure you are at the DOS prompt.
2. Type **MODE CON: LINES=43** and press **[Enter]**. On a computer system with a VGA adapter, DOS displays the error message shown in Figure 10-11.

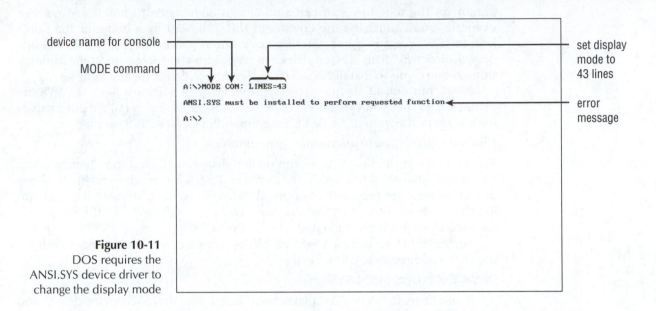

device name for console

MODE command

set display mode to 43 lines

error message

```
A:\>MODE CON: LINES=43

ANSI.SYS must be installed to perform requested function

A:\>
```

Figure 10-11
DOS requires the ANSI.SYS device driver to change the display mode

Including a DEVICE Command for ANSI.SYS in CONFIG.SYS

Because the CONFIG.SYS file does not have a DEVICE command that installs ANSI.SYS, DOS is unable to execute the MODE command. Therefore, let's modify CONFIG.SYS to install the ANSI.SYS device driver, then reboot the system and repeat the MODE command. DOS should execute the MODE command and change the characteristics of the monitor.

To edit CONFIG.SYS:

1. Type **EDIT CONFIG.SYS** and press **[Enter]**. DOS loads the MS-DOS Editor, which loads CONFIG.SYS.

2. Press **[Ctrl][End]** to move the cursor to the end of the file. If necessary, position the cursor on the second line below the last line of text and be sure the cursor is not indented.

3. Type **REM**, press **[Tab]**, type **Install Device Driver** and press **[Enter]**.

4. Type **REM** and press **[Enter]**.

5. Press **[Tab]**, type **DEVICE=C:\DOS\ANSI.SYS** and press **[Enter]** *twice*. If ANSI.SYS is stored in another directory on drive C or if the DOS directory has another name, use that directory's name in the path. Figure 10-12 shows this addition to CONFIG.SYS.

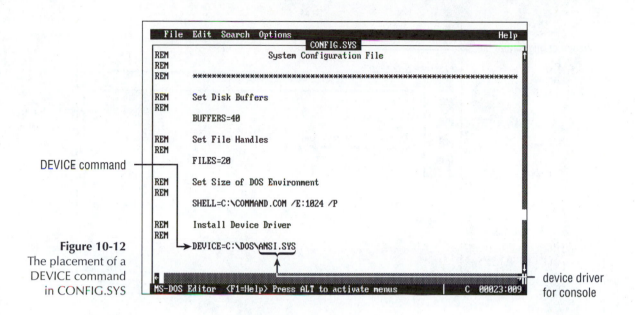

Figure 10-12
The placement of a
DEVICE command
in CONFIG.SYS

6. Press **[Alt]** (Menu) to access the menu bar, press **[Enter]** for the File menu, and type **X** for the Exit option.

   If you are using the mouse, click **File**, then click **Exit**.

   The MS-DOS Editor displays a dialog box that prompts you about saving your changes.

7. Press **[Enter]** to select Yes.

   If you are using the mouse, click **Yes**.

   The MS-DOS Editor saves your changes, you exit the MS-DOS Editor, and DOS displays the DOS prompt.

Testing the Device Driver ANSI.SYS

Next, you must reboot so that DOS can install the device driver ANSI.SYS from the CONFIG.SYS file.

To test the capability of ANSI.SYS:

1. Press **[Ctrl][Alt][Del]**, or press the **Reset button** on your computer system. During the booting process, DOS executes the commands in CONFIG.SYS and in AUTOEXEC.BAT.

2. If DOS reports a problem, load the MS-DOS Editor and correct the source of the error. Then repeat Step 1 and reboot.

3. Type **MODE CON: LINES=43** and press **[Enter]**. DOS displays the DOS prompt again, only smaller.

4. Type **TYPE CONFIG.SYS** and press **[Enter]**. DOS displays the contents of this file using 43 lines per screen. See Figure 10-13.

system configuration file ——

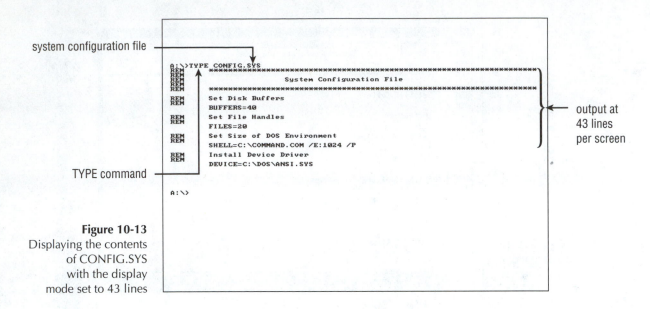

```
A:\>TYPE CONFIG.SYS
REM
REM  *************************************************************
REM
REM                    System Configuration File
REM
REM  *************************************************************
REM
REM  Set Disk Buffers
REM  BUFFERS=40
REM  Set File Handles
REM  FILES=20
REM  Set Size of DOS Environment
REM  SHELL=C:\COMMAND.COM /E:1024 /P
REM  Install Device Driver
REM  DEVICE=C:\DOS\ANSI.SYS
REM

A:\>
```

output at
43 lines
per screen

TYPE command ——

Figure 10-13
Displaying the contents
of CONFIG.SYS
with the display
mode set to 43 lines

Now switch back to the standard display mode.

5.   Type **MODE CON: LINES=25** and press **[Enter]**. The prompt changes to its normal size. If you experience difficulty resetting the display mode to 25 lines, reboot your system or ask your instructor or technical support person for help.

When you purchase a mouse, the manufacturer provides you with software for operating that mouse. That software might be stored in an executable file, such as MOUSE.COM, or it might be included as a device driver stored in a file by the name of MOUSE.SYS. If the mouse software includes the executable file, you can load the mouse software by including a command in AUTOEXEC.BAT similar to the following one:

MOUSE

The DOS path must include the name of the subdirectory with the mouse software, and the path must precede the command to load the mouse software. Otherwise, you must spell out the exact location of the mouse software, as in this example:

C:\MOUSE\MOUSE.COM

If the mouse software includes a device driver, you can load the device driver from CONFIG.SYS with a command similar to the following one:

DEVICE=C:\MOUSE\MOUSE.SYS

The last two examples assume the mouse software is stored in a directory named MOUSE on drive C.

LOADING A TSR

The office computer systems contain an extensive directory structure, and you and others on your staff frequently work with the same files. Every time you issue a command to retrieve a file from disk, you have to wait while DOS searches the directory structure and hard disk to locate the file.

You can further enhance the performance of your computer systems by installing a TSR utility that speeds up the process for locating files. This utility is called FASTOPEN. It creates a **name cache** in memory, where it keeps track of the locations of frequently used files on disk. When you open a file, its name and location are stored in one of the buffers that constitute the name cache. When you need to use that file again, DOS checks the name cache for the location of the file and then immediately locates it on disk. DOS does not have to search through the disk's directory structure to locate the file, and the performance and speed of your computer system improve.

The FASTOPEN utility works only on hard disk drives because it is primarily designed to optimize the performance of a disk with an extensive directory structure. It does not work on network drives or on diskette drives. You cannot execute FASTOPEN from the DOS Shell or from Windows; if you do, you might lock up your computer system. Also, do not run the DOS 6.0 and 6.2 defragmenting utility while FASTOPEN is tracking filenames and locations, because you might lose data.

To install this utility from CONFIG.SYS, you use the INSTALL command, as follows:

INSTALL=[*drive:*][*path*]*filename* [*parameters*]

The filename is the full name of the TSR, including the file extension. You might also need to specify the drive and path for the TSR. Some TSRs might use parameters, such as switches, and you list these parameters after the filename. You use a different INSTALL command for each TSR you install from CONFIG.SYS.

For example, the following command loads the FASTOPEN TSR, creates a name cache for drive C, and instructs FASTOPEN to keep track of the last 100 files opened:

INSTALL=C:\DOS\FASTOPEN.EXE C:=100

After the INSTALL command, you specify the name and location of the FASTOPEN utility. Then you specify each hard drive for which you want FASTOPEN to keep track of files. As in this example, you can also specify the total number of files. The number of files can range from 10 to 999. The generally recommended value is 1 file for each megabyte of hard-disk space. For example, if you have a 120MB hard disk, you would use 120 for the number of files to track. If you do not specify the number of files, FASTOPEN defaults to 48 files.

Let's modify the CONFIG.SYS file again to include a provision for loading FASTOPEN. Before you start, you might want to verify the name of the directory on the hard disk where FASTOPEN.EXE is stored. If you are using a network, skip this section and continue with the next section, "Specifying Multiple Configurations."

To edit CONFIG.SYS:

1. Type **EDIT CONFIG.SYS** and press **[Enter]**. DOS loads the MS-DOS Editor, which loads CONFIG.SYS.

2. Press **[Ctrl][End]** to move the cursor to the end of the file. If necessary, position the cursor on the second line below the last line of text and be sure the cursor is not indented.

3. Type **REM**, press **[Tab]**, type **Install TSR** and press **[Enter]**.

4. Type **REM** and press **[Enter]**.

5. Press **[Tab]**, type **INSTALL=C:\DOS\FASTOPEN.EXE C:=100** and press **[Enter]** *twice*. If FASTOPEN.EXE is stored in another directory, use that directory's name for the path. The value of 100 assumes a hard-disk capacity of 100MB. If you prefer, you can specify another value that is appropriate to your computer system's hard-disk storage capacity. Figure 10-14 shows the placement of this command in CONFIG.SYS.

INSTALL command

Figure 10-14
The placement of an
INSTALL command
in CONFIG.SYS

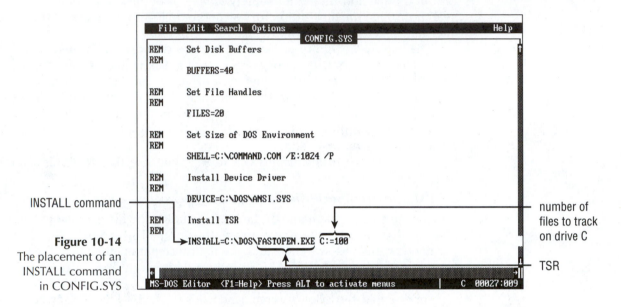

number of
files to track
on drive C

TSR

6. Press **[Alt]** (Menu) to access the menu bar, press **[Enter]** for the File menu, and type **X** for the Exit option.

If you are using the mouse, click **File**, then click **Exit**.

The MS-DOS Editor displays a dialog box that prompts you about saving the changes.

7. Press **[Enter]** to select Yes.

If you are using the mouse, click **Yes**.

The MS-DOS Editor saves your changes, you exit the MS-DOS Editor, and DOS displays the DOS prompt.

Loading a TSR from CONFIG.SYS

Now you can test the process for installing the FASTOPEN TSR from CONFIG.SYS.

To install the FASTOPEN TSR:

1. Press **[Ctrl][Alt][Del]**, or press the **Reset button** on your computer system. During the booting process, DOS executes the commands in CONFIG.SYS to configure itself. During the booting process, DOS displays the message "FASTOPEN installed." Then DOS executes the commands in the AUTOEXEC.BAT file.

You can also load FASTOPEN from the AUTOEXEC.BAT file or from the DOS prompt; however, the syntax is different:

FASTOPEN C:=100

One advantage of installing this TSR from CONFIG.SYS is that you save a small amount of memory.

This is a good opportunity for a short break.

SPECIFYING MULTIPLE CONFIGURATIONS

5.0

You and your staff work on your computer systems either from the DOS prompt or from the DOS Shell. In the past, these two approaches required you and your staff to use different CONFIG.SYS files on different computer systems. To streamline the operation of your computer systems and provide the same configuration options on all the computer systems, you decide it is time to specify multiple configurations from the CONFIG.SYS file.

DOS 5.0 does not permit you to specify multiple configurations from CONFIG.SYS. If you are using DOS 5.0, you can skip to the section entitled "Printing a Copy of CONFIG.SYS and AUTOEXEC.BAT" or, if you prefer, you can read this section so that you are familiar with the process for specifying multiple configurations using DOS 6.0 and 6.2. However, you will not be able to complete the tutorial steps with DOS 5.0.

Specifying a Startup Menu

To specify multiple configurations, you begin by defining a Startup menu in CONFIG.SYS. The **Startup menu** lists menu options for the types of configurations you want to make available from the CONFIG.SYS file. When you boot your computer system, DOS displays a Startup menu from which you can choose the menu option that you want to use.

To define this Startup menu, you create a **menu block**, or menu section, at the beginning of CONFIG.SYS. Figure 10-15 shows a sample menu block.

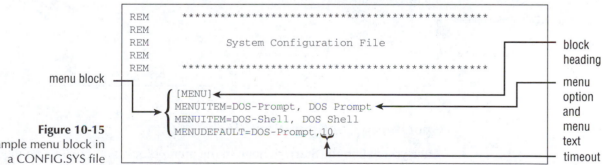

menu block

Figure 10-15
A sample menu block in a CONFIG.SYS file

block heading

menu option and menu text

timeout

You place the **block heading** [MENU] at the beginning of the menu block. Then you use a MENUITEM command for each menu item that you want DOS to display on the Startup menu. The syntax for MENUITEM is as follows:

MENUITEM=*blockname*[,*menu text*]

The **blockname** is the name you assign to the **configuration block** in CONFIG.SYS that contains the set of commands you want DOS to execute if you select this menu option. For example, in Figure 10-15, the MENUITEM commands identify "DOS-Prompt" and "DOS-Shell" as the names of configuration blocks in CONFIG.SYS. Because the blockname must not contain any spaces, you can use hyphens to separate parts of a blockname, such as "DOS-Prompt," as shown in Figure 10-15. The **menu text** is the text that DOS displays for the menu option. If you do not specify menu text, DOS displays the name of the configuration block in CONFIG.SYS. If you include menu text, you separate it from the blockname by a comma. For example, in Figure 10-15, the menu text for the DOS-Prompt menu item is "DOS Prompt" (without the hyphen). After you boot, DOS displays "DOS Prompt" as the menu option on the Startup menu.

You can include up to nine menu options in the menu block, and each menu option is associated with a **block**, or group, of commands in CONFIG.SYS.

The MENUDEFAULT command specifies the configuration to use if you do not select one of the menu items listed on the Startup menu. Its syntax is:

MENUDEFAULT=*blockname***[,***timeout***]**

The **blockname** is the name of the configuration block you want DOS to execute if you do not select another option on the Startup menu. The **timeout** is the number of seconds that DOS will wait for you to select an option from the Startup menu before it uses the default configuration block. The timeout can range from 0 to 90 (seconds). If you enter a timeout, you separate it from the blockname with a comma. In Figure 10-15, the timeout instructs DOS to wait 10 seconds before selecting the default option, DOS-Prompt.

After you perform a cold or warm boot, the Startup menu appears after DOS displays the message "Starting MS-DOS...". Figure 10-16 shows what the Startup menu would look like for the menu block shown in Figure 10-15.

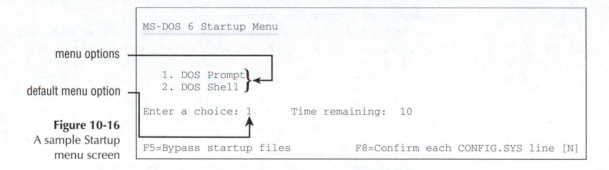

menu options

default menu option

Figure 10-16
A sample Startup
menu screen

```
MS-DOS 6 Startup Menu


    1. DOS Prompt
    2. DOS Shell

Enter a choice: 1       Time remaining:  10

F5=Bypass startup files          F8=Confirm each CONFIG.SYS line [N]
```

Specifying Configuration Blocks

After you define the Startup menu in the menu block, you create a configuration block for each menu item. As noted earlier, the configuration block contains a list of commands for a specific menu option listed on the Startup menu. Each configuration block starts with a **block header**, or blockname, within square brackets. The block header is the same as the configuration blockname listed in the menu block. Figure 10-17 shows configuration blocks for the menu block.

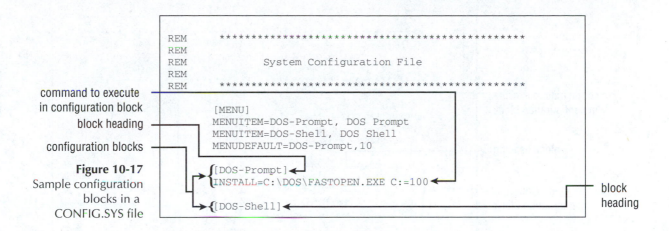

command to execute in configuration block

block heading

configuration blocks

Figure 10-17
Sample configuration blocks in a CONFIG.SYS file

block heading

```
REM     ********************************************
REM
REM              System Configuration File
REM
REM     ********************************************

[MENU]
MENUITEM=DOS-Prompt, DOS Prompt
MENUITEM=DOS-Shell, DOS Shell
MENUDEFAULT=DOS-Prompt,10

[DOS-Prompt]
INSTALL=C:\DOS\FASTOPEN.EXE C:=100

[DOS-Shell]
```

In Figure 10-17, [DOS-Prompt] is the block header for the configuration block for the first menu item. If you select "DOS Prompt" from the Startup menu, DOS executes any commands that follow the DOS-Prompt block header. In this example, DOS installs the FASTOPEN TSR. If you select "DOS Shell" from the Startup menu, DOS executes any commands that follow the DOS-Shell block header. In this example, there are no commands for DOS to execute. If you select "DOS Shell" from the Startup menu, DOS does not install FASTOPEN. However, this setting is stored in the DOS environment and, as you will see later, you can use the setting to execute a specific group of commands from AUTOEXEC.BAT. The use of a Startup menu and multiple configuration blocks permit you to selectively execute commands from CONFIG.SYS.

Specifying a Common Configuration Block

After you select a menu option from the Startup menu, DOS executes the commands in a specific configuration block and does not execute commands in any other block except one. You can create a **Common configuration block** that contains commands that you want DOS to execute, no matter which menu item you select from the Startup menu. You might have more than one Common configuration block. Figure 10-18 shows a Common configuration block before the DOS-Prompt configuration block.

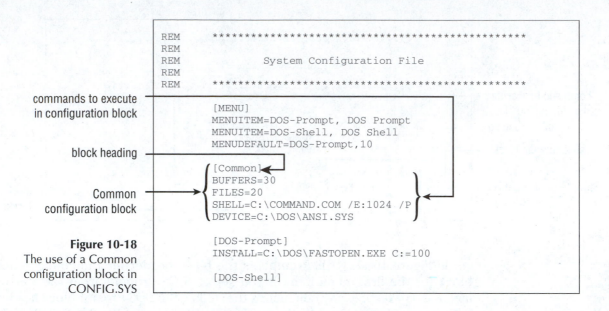

commands to execute
in configuration block

block heading

Common
configuration block

Figure 10-18
The use of a Common
configuration block in
CONFIG.SYS

The Common configuration block in Figure 10-18 contains BUFFERS, FILES, SHELL, and DEVICE commands. DOS executes all of the commands in the Common configuration block, no matter which menu item you select from the Startup menu. Then DOS executes the commands in the configuration block associated with the menu option you selected from the Startup menu.

Modifying CONFIG.SYS to Use Multiple Configurations

You next want to modify your CONFIG.SYS file to include multiple configurations. If you are using a network without a hard disk drive C, ask your instructor or technical support person for instructions on how to complete these steps. DOS must be able to locate the DOSKEY program file and the files used to load DOSSHELL.

5.0   Again, because this feature is not available in DOS 5.0, skip this part of the tutorial if you are using DOS 5.0 and continue with the section entitled "Printing a Copy of CONFIG.SYS and AUTOEXEC.BAT."

6.0 *6.2*   **To modify CONFIG.SYS so that it contains multiple configurations** *using DOS 6.0 or 6.2***:**

1. Type **EDIT CONFIG.SYS** and press **[Enter]**. DOS loads the MS-DOS Editor, which loads CONFIG.SYS.

2. Position the cursor at the beginning of the line that contains the heading "Set Disk Buffers." Then press **[Ctrl][N]** *twice* to insert two blank lines.

3. Press **[Tab]** to indent the line.

Next, specify a menu block with menu items.

4. Enter each line of the following menu block:

[MENU]

MENUITEM=DOS-Prompt, DOS Prompt

MENUITEM=DOS-Shell, DOS Shell

MENUDEFAULT=DOS-Prompt,10

5. Press **[Enter]** *twice.* Figure 10-19 shows the placement of the menu block in your CONFIG.SYS file.

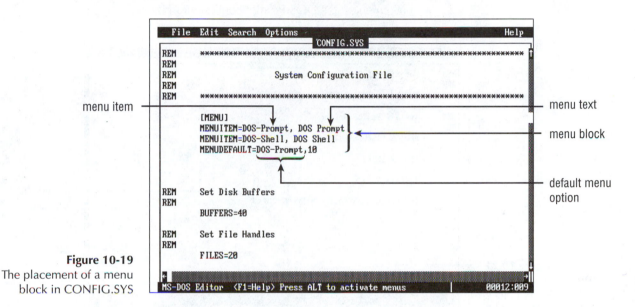

Figure 10-19
The placement of a menu block in CONFIG.SYS

Now you are ready to create the Common configuration block.

6. Type **[COMMON]** but do not press the Enter key. Figure 10-20 shows the placement of the Common block header.

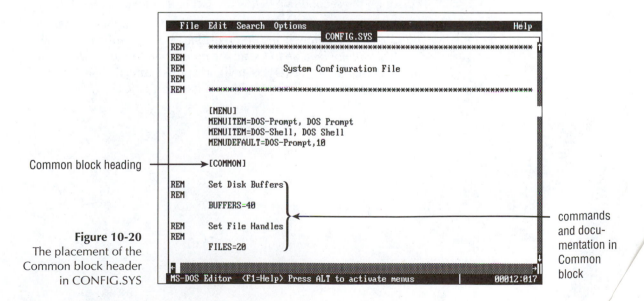

Figure 10-20
The placement of the Common block header in CONFIG.SYS

Now create the DOS-Prompt configuration block.

7. Press **[PgDn]** (Page Down). Next, position the cursor at the beginning of the line that contains the heading "Install TSR." Then press **[Ctrl][N]** *twice* to insert two blank lines.

8. Press **[Tab]** and type **[DOS-Prompt]** but do not press the Enter key. *You must enter the name of the configuration block exactly as shown, and you must include the hyphen in "DOS-Prompt," or DOS will not be able to locate the configuration block when you test this feature later.* Figure 10-21 shows the placement of the DOS-Prompt configuration block.

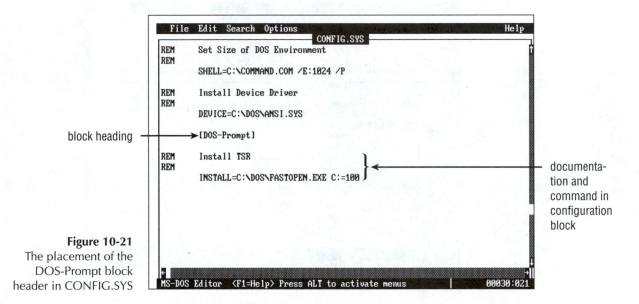

block heading ——→

documenta-
tion and
command in
configuration
block

Figure 10-21
The placement of the
DOS-Prompt block
header in CONFIG.SYS

Next create the DOS-Shell configuration block.

9. Press **[Ctrl][End]** to move the cursor to the end of the file. Position the cursor on the second line below the last line of text.

10. If necessary, press **[Tab]**. *You must enter the name of the configuration block exactly as shown, and you must include the hyphen in "DOS-Shell," or DOS will not be able to locate the configuration block when you test this feature later.* Type **[DOS-Shell]** and press **[Enter]**. Figure 10-22 shows the placement of the [DOS-Shell] configuration block.

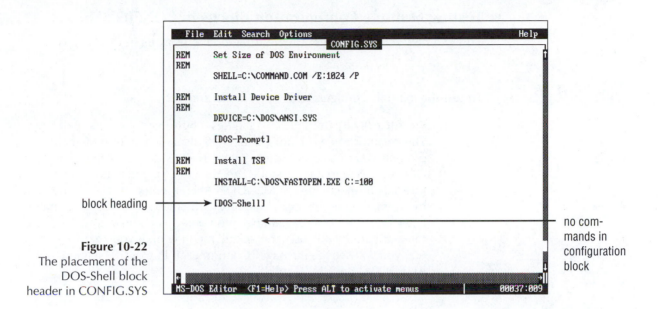

```
    File  Edit  Search  Options                              Help
                                    CONFIG.SYS
    REM      Set Size of DOS Environment                            ↑
    REM
             SHELL=C:\COMMAND.COM /E:1024 /P

    REM      Install Device Driver
    REM
             DEVICE=C:\DOS\ANSI.SYS

             [DOS-Prompt]

    REM      Install TSR
    REM
             INSTALL=C:\DOS\FASTOPEN.EXE C:=100

             [DOS-Shell]

                           ←─────────────────────────────

    MS-DOS Editor   <F1=Help> Press ALT to activate menus  │   00037:009
```

block heading ──────→ [DOS-Shell]

no commands in configuration block

Figure 10-22
The placement of the
DOS-Shell block
header in CONFIG.SYS

The DOS-Shell configuration block is empty because you do not need to execute any commands from CONFIG.SYS for the DOS Shell. However, by including the DOS-Shell menu option and the DOS-Shell configuration block, you can now store this configuration option in the DOS environment so that you can automatically load the DOS Shell from AUTOEXEC.BAT.

Next you want to save your work and exit the MS-DOS Editor so that you can test the multiple configuration blocks in CONFIG.SYS.

6.0 6.2   **To save and exit the MS-DOS Editor** *in DOS 6.0 and 6.2:*

  1. Press **[Alt]** (Menu) to access the menu bar, press **[Enter]** for the File menu, and type **X** for the Exit option.

      If you are using the mouse, click **File**, then click **Exit**.

      The MS-DOS Editor displays a dialog box that prompts you about saving the changes.

  2. Press **[Enter]** to select Yes.

      If you are using the mouse, click **Yes**.

      The MS-DOS Editor saves your changes, you exit the MS-DOS Editor, and DOS displays the DOS prompt.

Testing Multiple Configuration Blocks in CONFIG.SYS

You can now reboot and test the multiple configurations in CONFIG.SYS.

6.0 **6.2**

To test the multiple configurations *in DOS 6.0 and 6.2*:

6.2

1. Press **[Ctrl][Alt][Del]**, or press the **Reset button** on your computer system. The default choice is highlighted. DOS displays a Startup menu and prompts you to enter a choice. Figure 10-23 shows the Startup menu in DOS 6.0. Next to the prompt is the number of the first menu item (the default specified with MENUDEFAULT). You can select a menu item by typing the number or by pointing to the menu item and pressing the Enter key. The "Time remaining" prompt lets you know how much time remains before DOS uses the default menu item. If you are using DOS 6.2, you will see the message "Confirm each line of CONFIG.SYS and AUTOEXEC.BAT [N]" for [F8].

```
MS-DOS 6 Startup Menu


  1. DOS Prompt
  2. DOS Shell

Enter a choice: 1          Time remaining:   10


F5=Bypass startup files              F8=Confirm each CONFIG.SYS line [N]
```

Figure 10-23
The MS-DOS 6
Startup Menu

2. Press **[Enter]** to select the first menu item. DOS executes the commands in the Common configuration block, installs the FASTOPEN utility in the DOS-Prompt configuration block, executes the commands in AUTOEXEC.BAT, and displays the DOS prompt.

Now test the second menu item.

3. Press **[Ctrl][Alt][Del]**, or press the **Reset button** on your computer system. DOS displays a Startup menu and prompts you to enter a choice.

4. Press **[↓]** (Down Arrow). DOS highlights the second menu item.

5. Press **[Enter]**. DOS executes the commands in the Common configuration block, then executes the commands in AUTOEXEC.BAT, and displays the DOS prompt. DOS does not install FASTOPEN.

Now test the menu default item.

6. Press **[Ctrl][Alt][Del]**, or press the **Reset button** on your computer system. DOS displays a Startup menu and prompts you to enter a choice.

7. Wait for at least 10 seconds. After 10 seconds, DOS automatically selects the default menu item, "DOS-Prompt." DOS executes the commands in the Common configuration block, installs the FASTOPEN utility in the DOS-Prompt configuration block, executes the commands in AUTOEXEC.BAT, and displays the DOS prompt.

Bypassing CONFIG.SYS and AUTOEXEC.BAT

When the Startup menu appears, DOS displays information on the use of two function keys at the bottom of the screen. If you press [F5] when the Startup menu appears, DOS will bypass both the CONFIG.SYS and AUTOEXEC.BAT files and will not execute the commands in these files. DOS uses its own default settings. This feature is useful if you are experiencing difficulty in starting your system or if your system locks up when DOS attempts to execute a command.

Selectively Executing Commands in CONFIG.SYS

If you press [F8] when the Startup menu appears and then select an option from the menu, DOS will display each line in CONFIG.SYS and ask if you want to execute the command on that line. DOS displays the command and a Y/N prompt. After DOS processes CONFIG.SYS, DOS asks if you want to process the AUTOEXEC.BAT file (without prompting for each command). You can use this feature to test various combinations of commands, to omit specific commands, and to troubleshoot problems in CONFIG.SYS. In DOS 6.2, you are prompted as to whether you want to execute each command in AUTOEXEC.BAT.

SPECIFYING MULTIPLE CONFIGURATIONS IN AUTOEXEC.BAT

You want to carry this process a few steps further. If you select the "DOS Prompt" menu item from the Startup menu, you want DOS to execute the DOSKEY command from AUTOEXEC.BAT. If you select the "DOS Shell" menu item from the Startup menu, you want DOS to load the DOS Shell from AUTOEXEC.BAT. Because there is no need to use DOSKEY in the DOS Shell, you want DOS to execute DOSKEY only for the "DOS Prompt" menu item.

When you select a menu item from the Startup menu, DOS assigns the block heading, or blockname, to an environment variable named CONFIG. Like other environment variables, this variable is stored in the DOS environment. You can use this setting to select a set of commands in AUTOEXEC.BAT. To use this feature, you group each set of commands as you do in CONFIG.SYS. The first group of commands in the AUTOEXEC.BAT file contains all the commands that you want DOS to execute no matter which menu item you select from the Startup menu. This group of commands contains such commands as PATH and PROMPT, which must always be executed, and is similar to the use of the Common configuration block in CONFIG.SYS.

You then group the commands you want DOS to execute based on the menu item you select from the Startup menu. For example, if you select the "DOS Prompt" from the Startup menu, you want DOS to execute DOSKEY, but not load the DOS Shell. If you select "DOS Shell" from the Startup menu, you want DOS to load the DOS Shell, but not execute DOSKEY.

After you group commands in AUTOEXEC.BAT, you identify each block with a label that begins with a colon. The **label** is a name that identifies the beginning of a block of commands. For example, you might use the label :DOS-Prompt for the group of commands that you want DOS to execute if you select "DOS Prompt" from the Startup menu. In Figure 10-24, the labels :DOS-Prompt and :DOS-Shell identify the beginning of two **label blocks** in AUTOEXEC.BAT. It is important to remember that the names of these two label blocks must be identical to the names used in CONFIG.SYS for the configuration blocks.

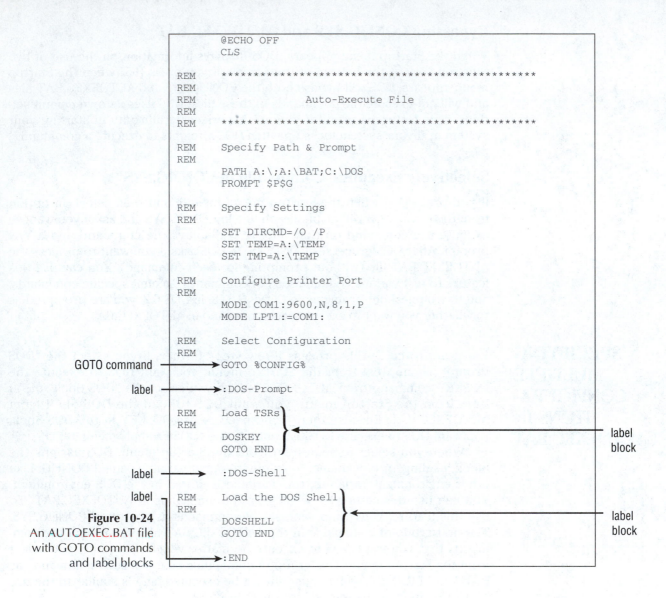

GOTO command →

label →

label →

label →

label →

Figure 10-24
An AUTOEXEC.BAT file
with GOTO commands
and label blocks

```
        @ECHO OFF
        CLS

REM     ****************************************************
REM
REM                      Auto-Execute File
REM
REM     ****************************************************

REM     Specify Path & Prompt
REM
        PATH A:\;A:\BAT;C:\DOS
        PROMPT $P$G

REM     Specify Settings
REM
        SET DIRCMD=/O /P
        SET TEMP=A:\TEMP
        SET TMP=A:\TEMP

REM     Configure Printer Port
REM
        MODE COM1:9600,N,8,1,P
        MODE LPT1:=COM1:

REM     Select Configuration
REM
        GOTO %CONFIG%
        :DOS-Prompt

REM     Load TSRs
REM
        DOSKEY
        GOTO END

        :DOS-Shell

REM     Load the DOS Shell
REM
        DOSSHELL
        GOTO END
        :END
```

label
block

label
block

To direct DOS to a specific group of commands in AUTOEXEC.BAT, you use the GOTO command as follows:

GOTO *label*

As just noted, the **label** is a name that identifies a specific line in AUTOEXEC.BAT. DOS does not execute the label but treats it as a comment. Instead, it executes the command on the next available line after the label. The use of the colon at the beginning of a line in AUTOEXEC.BAT is therefore similar to the use of the REM command.

For example, in Figure 10-24, if you want DOS to execute the commands in the label block that follows the :DOS-Prompt label, you could enter the command:

GOTO DOS-Prompt

However, as noted earlier, either this configuration setting or the one for DOS-Shell are assigned to the environment variable CONFIG and are stored in the DOS environment. To reference this setting for CONFIG in the DOS environment, you use the GOTO command as follows:

GOTO   %CONFIG%

DOS interprets %CONFIG% as an instruction to use the current setting for the CONFIG environment variable in the DOS environment. If the DOS environment contains CONFIG=DOS-Prompt, DOS translates GOTO %CONFIG% to GOTO DOS-Prompt. If this is the case, DOS goes to the line with the label :DOS-Prompt and starts executing commands. If the DOS environment contains CONFIG=DOS-Shell, DOS translates GOTO %CONFIG% to GOTO DOS-Shell. If this is the case, DOS goes to the line with the label :DOS-Shell and starts executing commands. After DOS moves to a specific label, it does not execute any commands between the one with the GOTO command and the line with the label. Figure 10-24 shows how to place the GOTO %CONFIG% command in AUTOEXEC.BAT.

DOS, by default, executes on a line-by-line basis unless directed to a specific line. In your AUTOEXEC.BAT file, you must also place a GOTO command after each label block so that DOS does not execute the commands in other label blocks that follow the one for a specific menu option. For example, at the end of each label block, you could direct DOS to a line with the label :END. This label is placed at the end of the AUTOEXEC.BAT file (Figure 10-24).

Therefore, the use of GOTO %CONFIG%, labels for specific label blocks, and GOTO :END allows DOS to selectively execute a group of commands in the AUTOEXEC.BAT file.

Modifying AUTOEXEC.BAT for Multiple Configurations

Let's modify the AUTOEXEC.BAT file so that you can specify multiple configurations in it—configurations similar to the ones in Figure 10-24.

6.0 6.2

To edit the AUTOEXEC.BAT file *in DOS 6.0 and 6.2*:

1. Type **EDIT AUTOEXEC.BAT** and press **[Enter]**. DOS loads the MS-DOS Editor, which retrieves the AUTOEXEC.BAT file.

2. Press **[Alt]** (Menu) to access the menu bar, type **S** for the Search menu, and press **[Enter]** for the Find option. The MS-DOS Editor displays the Find dialog box.

You want to find the line that contains the heading "Load TSRs."

3. Type **Load TSRs** and press **[Enter]**. The MS-DOS Editor moves the cursor to the first occurrence of this phrase.

4. Press **[Home]** to move to the beginning of this line. Then press **[Ctrl][N]** *twice* to insert two blank lines.

Next, enter documentation for the GOTO command.

5. Type **REM**, press **[Tab]**, type **Select Customization** and press **[Enter]**.

6. Type **REM** and press **[Enter]**.

7. Press **[Tab]**, type **GOTO %CONFIG%** and press **[Enter]** *twice*. Figure 10-25 shows this change to the AUTOEXEC.BAT file.

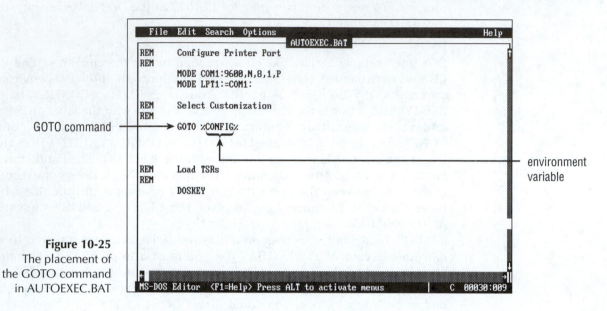

GOTO command →

environment variable

Figure 10-25
The placement of the GOTO command in AUTOEXEC.BAT

Specifying the Label

You are now ready to add the two label blocks that correspond to the two configuration blocks in CONFIG.SYS.

6.0 *6.2*   **To specify the first label block** *in DOS 6.0 and 6.2*:

1. Type **:DOS-Prompt** but do not press [Enter]. *You must enter the name of the label block exactly as shown, and you must include the colon and hyphen in ":DOS-Prompt" or DOS will not be able to locate the label block when you test this feature later.* This label precedes the documentation for loading TSRs and the DOSKEY command.

2. Press **[Ctrl][End]**. After the cursor moves to the end of the file, position the cursor at the beginning of the line after the DOSKEY command.

3. If necessary, press **[Tab]**. Then type **GOTO END** and press **[Enter]** twice.

Now specify the second label block.

4. If necessary, press **[Tab]**, type **:DOS-Shell**, and press **[Enter]** *twice. You must enter the name of the label block exactly as shown, and you must include the colon and hyphen in ":DOS-Shell" or DOS will not be able to locate the label block when you test this feature later.*

5. Press **[Backspace]**, type **REM**, and press **[Tab]**. Type **Load the DOS Shell** and press **[Enter]**.

6. Type **REM** and press **[Enter]**.

7. Press **[Tab]**, type **DOSSHELL**, and press **[Enter]**.

8. Type **GOTO END** and press **[Enter]** *twice.*

Now enter the last label block.

9. Type **:END** and press **[Enter]**. Figure 10-26 shows the two label blocks for the two configurations, DOS-Prompt and DOS-Shell, as well as the label :END.

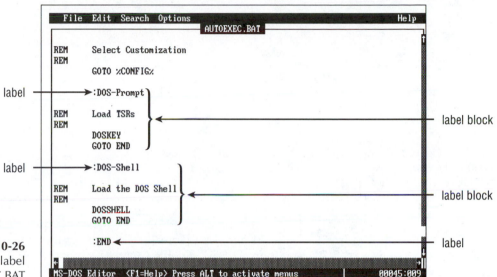

Figure 10-26
The placement of two label blocks in AUTOEXEC.BAT

You are ready to save your changes. Then you can exit the MS-DOS Editor, check the DOS environment, and test these changes to AUTOEXEC.BAT.

6.0 *6.2*

To save your work *in DOS 6.0 and 6.2:*

1. Press **[Alt]** (Menu) to access the menu bar, press **[Enter]** for the File menu, and type **X** for the Exit option.

   If you are using the mouse, click **File**, then click **Exit**.

   The MS-DOS Editor asks if you want to save your changes.

2. Press **[Enter]** to select Yes.

   If you are using the mouse, click **Yes**.

   The MS-DOS Editor saves the changes you made to AUTOEXEC.BAT and, after you exit the MS-DOS Editor, DOS displays the DOS prompt.

   Now test the multiple configurations in AUTOEXEC.BAT.

3. Press **[Ctrl][Alt][Del]**, or press the **Reset button** on your computer system. DOS displays a Startup menu and prompts you to enter a choice.

6.2

4. Press **[Enter]** to select the first menu item. DOS executes the commands in the Common configuration block, installs the FASTOPEN utility in the DOS-Prompt configuration block, executes the initial commands in AUTOEXEC.BAT, executes the DOSKEY command, and displays the DOS prompt. DOS does not load the DOS Shell. See Figure 10-27. DOS 6.2 does not display the message "DOSKey installed."

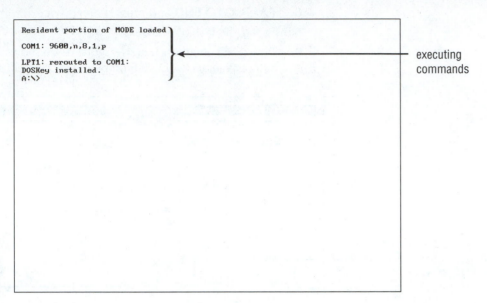

Figure 10-27
Executing the commands
in AUTOEXEC.BAT for the
DOS-Prompt configuration

5. Type **SET** and press **[Enter]**. DOS displays the settings in the DOS environment. The variable CONFIG stores the configuration that you selected—DOS-Prompt. See Figure 10-28.

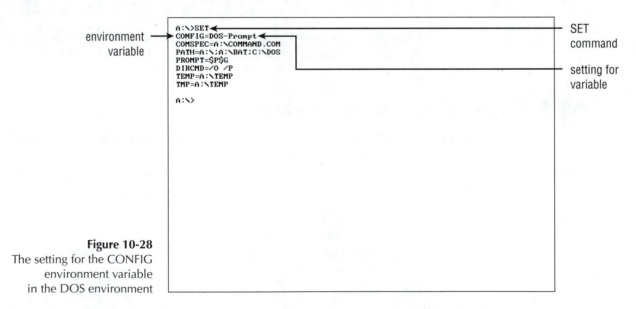

Figure 10-28
The setting for the CONFIG
environment variable
in the DOS environment

Next test the second menu item.

6. Press **[Ctrl][Alt][Del]**, or press the **Reset button** on your computer system. DOS displays a Startup menu and prompts you to enter a choice.

7. Press **[↓]** (Down Arrow) and then press **[Enter]** to select the second menu item. DOS executes the commands in the Common configuration block, then executes the first set of commands in AUTOEXEC.BAT, executes the DOSSHELL command, and loads the DOS Shell. DOS does not execute DOSKEY. See Figure 10-29.

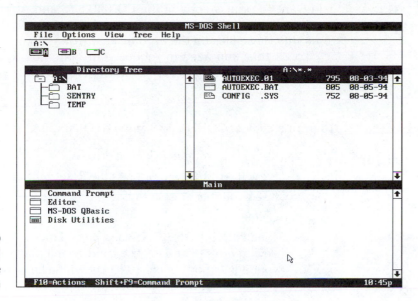

Figure 10-29
DOS loads the DOS Shell after executing the DOS-Shell configuration

Now exit the DOS Shell.

8. Press **[F3]** (Exit). DOS displays the DOS prompt.

9. Type **SET** and press **[Enter]**. See Figure 10-30. DOS displays the settings in the DOS environment. The variable CONFIG stores the configuration that you last selected—DOS-Shell.

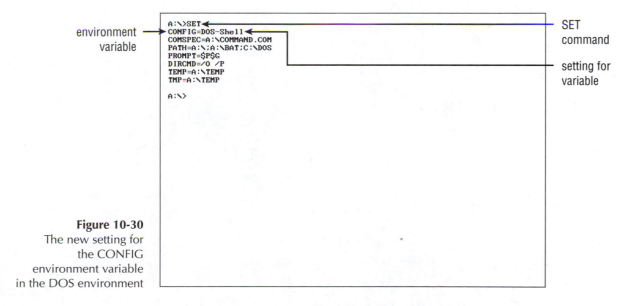

Figure 10-30
The new setting for the CONFIG environment variable in the DOS environment

The use of multiple configurations in your CONFIG.SYS and AUTOEXEC.BAT file provides you with a powerful tool for automating and customizing your use of DOS and your computer system. You can use this feature to design menus that access the major applications that you use on your computer system or to customize your computer system for different client needs.

PRINTING A COPY OF CONFIG.SYS AND AUTOEXEC.BAT

5.0 6.0 6.2

You want to print a copy of the CONFIG.SYS and AUTOEXEC.BAT files so that you have a permanent record of your work. You can then use this information to modify these files on the hard disks in your office.

To do this, you need to reboot your computer system from drive C or its network drive so that you can print using the settings on your system.

To print a copy of CONFIG.SYS and AUTOEXEC.BAT *in DOS 5.0, 6.0, and 6.2*:

1. Remove your boot disk from drive A.
2. Press **[Ctrl][Alt][Del]** or press the **Reset button**.
3. Insert your boot disk into drive A.
4. Change to drive A.
5. Type **PRINT CONFIG.SYS** and press **[Enter]**. When prompted for the list device, press **[Enter]** to accept the default printer port or enter the name of your printer port. Figure 10-31 shows the final contents of CONFIG.SYS. If you are using DOS 5.0, your CONFIG.SYS file will be different from the one shown in Figure 10-31.

5.0

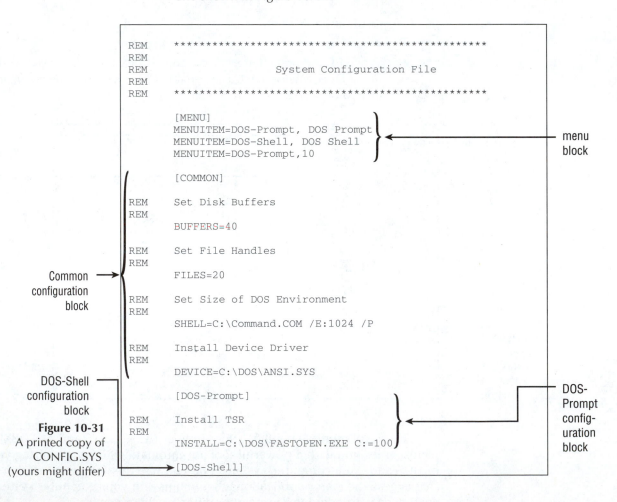

```
REM     ************************************************
REM
REM                   System Configuration File
REM
REM     ************************************************

        [MENU]
        MENUITEM=DOS-Prompt, DOS Prompt
        MENUITEM=DOS-Shell, DOS Shell
        MENUITEM=DOS-Prompt,10

        [COMMON]
REM     Set Disk Buffers
REM
        BUFFERS=40

REM     Set File Handles
REM
        FILES=20

REM     Set Size of DOS Environment
REM
        SHELL=C:\Command.COM /E:1024 /P

REM     Install Device Driver
REM
        DEVICE=C:\DOS\ANSI.SYS

        [DOS-Prompt]

REM     Install TSR
REM
        INSTALL=C:\DOS\FASTOPEN.EXE C:=100

        [DOS-Shell]
```

menu block

Common configuration block

DOS-Shell configuration block

DOS-Prompt configuration block

Figure 10-31
A printed copy of CONFIG.SYS (yours might differ)

5.0

6. Type **PRINT AUTOEXEC.BAT** and press **[Enter]**. Figure 10-32 shows the final contents of AUTOEXEC.BAT. If you are using DOS 5.0, your AUTOEXEC.BAT file will be different from the one shown in Figure 10-32.

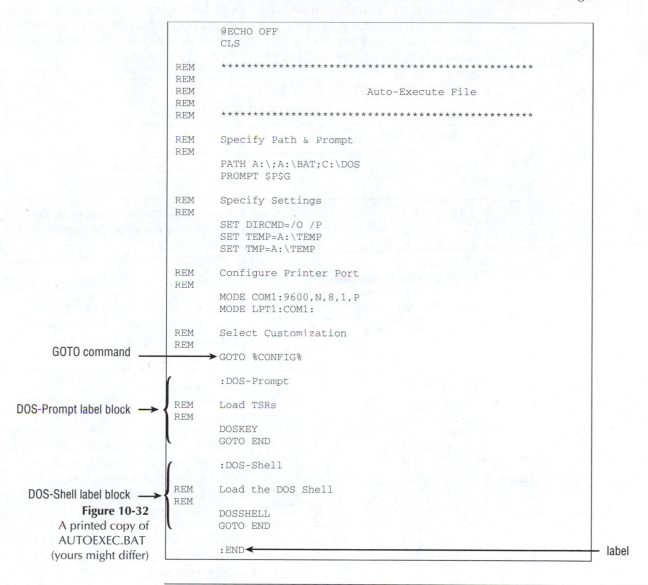

GOTO command →

DOS-Prompt label block →

DOS-Shell label block →

Figure 10-32
A printed copy of
AUTOEXEC.BAT
(yours might differ)

```
          @ECHO OFF
          CLS
REM       **************************************************
REM
REM                       Auto-Execute File
REM
REM       **************************************************

REM       Specify Path & Prompt
REM
          PATH A:\;A:\BAT;C:\DOS
          PROMPT $P$G

REM       Specify Settings
REM
          SET DIRCMD=/O /P
          SET TEMP=A:\TEMP
          SET TMP=A:\TEMP

REM       Configure Printer Port
REM
          MODE COM1:9600,N,8,1,P
          MODE LPT1:COM1:

REM       Select Customization
REM
          GOTO %CONFIG%

          :DOS-Prompt
REM       Load TSRs
REM
          DOSKEY
          GOTO END

          :DOS-Shell
REM       Load the DOS Shell
REM
          DOSSHELL
          GOTO END

          :END
```

← label

◆

SUMMARY

In this tutorial, you created a CONFIG.SYS file with the MS-DOS Editor. You entered a BUFFERS command to create a cache of disk buffers for storing sectors being read from or written to disk. You also entered a FILES command to establish the number of file handles and thereby set a limit on the maximum number of open files. You used the SHELL command to set the size of the DOS environment. You used the DEVICE command to load the ANSI.SYS device driver and the INSTALL command to load the FASTOPEN TSR.

You modified the CONFIG.SYS and AUTOEXEC.BAT files to use multiple configurations with DOS 6.0 and 6.2. In CONFIG.SYS, you created a menu block with a startup menu, a Common configuration block for commands to execute during each boot, and configuration blocks for the menu items in the menu block. In AUTOEXEC.BAT, you used the GOTO command and the setting stored in the CONFIG environment variable to direct DOS to a specific set of commands in the AUTOEXEC.BAT file.

Command Reference	
AUTOEXEC.BAT Commands	
GOTO *label*	A command that directs DOS to a specific label and line in a batch file
:LABEL	A name associated with a specific line and a specific group of commands in AUTOEXEC.BAT
CONFIG.SYS Commands	
[*BLOCKNAME*]	*DOS 6.0 and 6.2:* The name of a configuration block that is used as a block heading for a specific group of commands in CONFIG.SYS
BUFFERS=*n* where [*n* = 1 to 99]	Specifies the number of disk buffers used for storing sectors being read from or written to disk
[COMMON]	*DOS 6.0 and 6.2:* A block heading that identifies a group of commands in CONFIG.SYS that are executed no matter which menu option you select from the Startup menu
DEVICE=[*drive:*][*path*]filename [*parameters*]	Installs a device driver to enable DOS to communicate with a specific hardware component
FILES=*n* where [*n* = 8 to 255]	Specifies the maximum number of open files
INSTALL=[*drive:*][*path*]filename [*parameters*]	Installs a TSR from CONFIG.SYS
[MENU]	*DOS 6.0 and 6.2:* A block heading that identifies the beginning of the Startup menu block in CONFIG.SYS

MENUDEFAULT=*blockname* [,*timeout*]	*DOS 6.0 and 6.2:* Specifies the name of a default configuration block to use and an optional timeout to wait before executing the commands in a default configuration block if you do not select a menu option from the Startup menu
MENUITEM=*blockname* [,*menu text*]	*DOS 6.0 and 6.2:* Specifies the name of a configuration block and optional menu text for a menu item on the Startup menu
REM	Documents operations in CONFIG.SYS
SHELL=[*drive:*][*path*] filename /E:*size* /P	Specifies the name and path of the Command Interpreter, sets the size of the DOS environment with the /E switch, and makes the Command Interpreter permanent
Device Drivers	
ANSI.SYS	An optional device driver that provides extended capabilities for communicating with and controlling the console unit (keyboard and monitor)
CON	The device driver built into DOS for communicating with the console unit (keyboard and monitor)
DOS Commands	
FASTOPEN [*drive*]:=[*files*] where [*files* = 10 to 999]	A TSR that keeps track of previously opened files
MODE CON: LINES=*n* *n* = 25, 43 or 50, depending on capabilities of video card and monitor	Sets the number of lines displayed on the monitor

QUESTIONS

1. What is the purpose of a CONFIG.SYS file? Why is it valuable?
2. What does the BUFFERS command do?
3. What is a disk buffer? How large is a disk buffer? How much data does a disk buffer store?
4. What is a cache?
5. How does DOS use disk buffers when reading data from disk?

6. How does DOS use disk buffers when writing data to disk?

7. What is the advantage of specifying disk buffers with the BUFFERS command?

8. What does the FILES command do?

9. What is a file handle?

10. For what types of devices does DOS use file handles?

11. What is the advantage of specifying a value for the FILES command?

12. What does the SHELL command do?

13. What is the syntax of the SHELL command?

14. How can you change the size of the DOS environment?

15. Name three uses for the SHELL command?

16. What is a device driver?

17. What is the default device driver for the console unit?

18. What is ANSI.SYS, and what features does it offer?

19. How do you load a device driver from CONFIG.SYS?

20. How do you load a TSR from CONFIG.SYS?

21. What is FASTOPEN, and what advantages does it offer?

22. What is a name cache?

23. What is the syntax of the FASTOPEN utility?

24. How do you define a Startup menu in CONFIG.SYS?

25. How do you define configuration blocks in CONFIG.SYS?

26. What is the value of a Common configuration block?

27. Explain how DOS processes multiple configurations in CONFIG.SYS.

28. How do you define label blocks in AUTOEXEC.BAT?

29. How do you direct DOS to a specific label block in AUTOEXEC.BAT?

30. Explain how DOS processes multiple configurations in AUTOEXEC.BAT?

TUTORIAL ASSIGNMENTS

If you are working on a network without a hard disk drive C, ask your instructor or technical support person for directions on how to complete these tutorial assignments. DOS must be able to locate files that contain device drivers, TSRs, and utilities whenever you reboot your computer.

1. **Processing Commands in CONFIG.SYS**: Perform the following operations with the boot disk and the AUTOEXEC.BAT and CONFIG.SYS files that you prepared in this tutorial, and answer the questions.
   a. Boot your computer system with the boot disk in drive A.
   b. Reboot your computer system and select the DOS Prompt option.
   c. Boot your computer system again from drive A.
   d. When DOS displays the Startup menu, press [F8] and select the first menu item. List the prompts that DOS displays.
   e. Explain the advantages of using [F8].

2. **Using the FILES Command**: Make a duplicate copy of the boot disk used in this chapter's tutorial. Then perform the following operations and answer the questions:
   a. Set the FILES command in CONFIG.SYS to 8.

b. Reboot your computer system.

c. Load the MS-DOS Editor, open the CONFIG.SYS file, and access the MS-DOS Editor's Help system. Is DOS able to open enough files to perform all these operations?

d. After you exit the MS-DOS Editor, load a software application (such as WordPerfect or Lotus 1-2-3). Is DOS able to load the application? If not, increase the value for the FILES command by 10, reboot, and load the same application. If necessary, repeat this process until you are able to load the application.

e. Identify the software application, and list the value that you tested for the FILES command that enables you to load that application. If you have a user's or reference manual for that application, what does the manual recommend for the FILES command?

3. **Examining CONFIG.SYS on Drive C:** Perform the following operations:

a. Print a copy of the CONFIG.SYS file on your hard disk drive.

b. Use the MS-DOS Editor to compile an outline that:

(1) Lists and briefly describes each of the commands included in the CONFIG.SYS file. If there are commands not covered thus far in your course, include a notation to this effect.

(2) Lists commands that might be useful to include in this file.

Then answer the following questions:

c. Does this file include any documentation to assist you in interpreting its contents?

d. What are the names of the device drivers, if any, that DOS installs from CONFIG.SYS?

e. What are the names of the TSRs, if any, that DOS installs from CONFIG.SYS?

6.0 6.2

4. **Modifying the Startup Menu in CONFIG.SYS (DOS 6.0 and 6.2):** Make a copy of the boot disk used in this chapter's tutorial. Then perform the following operations:

a. Modify CONFIG.SYS so that the Startup menu includes these additional options: Format-Disk and Copy-Disk

b. Create configuration blocks for these two menu items, but do not include any commands in these configuration blocks.

c. Modify the AUTOEXEC.BAT file so that it includes two label blocks to correspond to the two additional menu items in CONFIG.SYS.

d. In these label blocks, include the appropriate commands for formatting drive A to its maximum storage capacity and for making a duplicate copy of a diskette in drive A.

e. After making these changes, reboot with this boot disk and test these two new menu options.

f. After you verify that the Startup menu works properly, print a copy of the AUTOEXEC.BAT and CONFIG.SYS files.

6.0 6.2

5. **Creating a Startup Utility Menu (DOS 6.0 and 6.2):** Make a duplicate copy of your boot disk. Then perform the following operations:

a. Modify the CONFIG.SYS file so that DOS displays a Startup menu with the following menu items: Anti-Virus, Defragmenter, DOS-Shell, Editor, and MS-Backup.

b. Create configuration blocks for each menu item, but do not include any commands.

c. Remove the INSTALL command that loads FASTOPEN.

d. Modify the AUTOEXEC.BAT file to include label blocks for Anti-Virus, Defragmenter, DOS-Shell, Editor, and MS-Backup.

e. In each of these label blocks, include commands for loading the appropriate utility. Include a provision for bypassing other label blocks.

f. Remove the DOSKEY command from AUTOEXEC.BAT.

g. Boot your computer system and test one of the menu items. Repeat this process until you have tested all the menu items.

h. After you verify that each of the menu items works properly from the Startup menu, print a copy of the AUTOEXEC.BAT and CONFIG.SYS files.

Managing Memory

OBJECTIVES

In this tutorial you will learn to:

- ◆ Identify and understand types of memory
- ◆ View the contents of memory
- ◆ Use memory managers
- ◆ Load DOS into high memory
- ◆ Create upper memory blocks
- ◆ Load TSRs and device drivers into upper memory
- ◆ Use a SmartDrive disk cache
- ◆ Optimize memory with MemMaker

Before you purchased your computer several months ago, you asked the dealer to install 8MB of RAM and a 240MB hard disk to meet the demands of the newer and more sophisticated types of software that you intended to use on your system. After you installed the software, you installed additional device drivers to customize the computer for specific types of hardware. You also purchased and installed Terminate-and-Stay-Resident (TSR) utilities, including a screen saver to extend the useful life of your monitor.

Now, however, when you work on income projections with your favorite electronic spreadsheet application, the program displays an indicator informing you that the computer is low on memory. All of the available memory has been consumed by the applications, device drivers, and TSRs you installed. To resolve this problem and enhance the overall performance of your computer system, you will have to reconfigure your memory so that it is used more efficiently and effectively.

◆

UNDERSTANDING MEMORY

As you learned in the "Essential Computer Concepts" chapter at the beginning of this book, your computer system uses two types of memory—Read-Only Memory (ROM) and Random-Access Memory (RAM). The memory that constitutes RAM and ROM is different from the storage space available on a hard disk. The permanent storage space on a peripheral device such as a hard disk is referred to as *secondary storage*. The term *memory* is more commonly used to refer to RAM because RAM is the predominant type of memory in a computer system.

ROM chips contain prerecorded program instructions and data for starting your computer system, managing the operation of its hardware, and interfacing between the operating system and hardware components. Your computer system can read information from ROM but cannot write over that information.

In contrast, your computer system uses RAM chips to temporarily store the program code for software applications, utilities, TSRs, and device drivers as well as the data contained in documents that you produce with programs. This memory constitutes your **working memory**, or **workspace**. After you load device drivers, TSRs, and a software application into this memory, less memory is available for your document files. As you fill more and more of working memory with programs and data, the performance of your computer system deteriorates. You might even find that programs might not be able to load program modules for optional features, such as a spelling checker, or large document files.

RAM consists of five types of memory, as listed below and illustrated in Figure 11-1:

◆ Conventional memory

◆ Upper memory

◆ Extended memory

◆ High memory

◆ Expanded memory

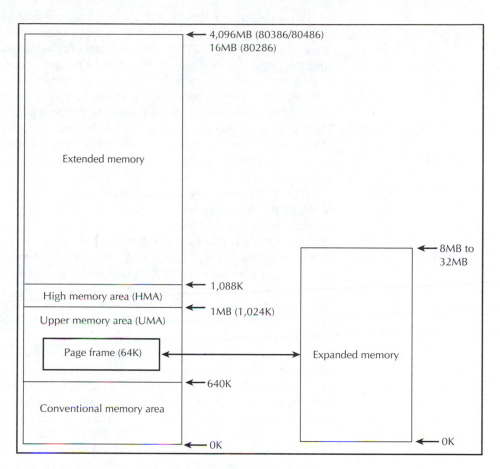

Figure 11-1
The types of RAM in an IBM or IBM-compatible computer system

Conventional memory is the memory that extends from 0K (zero K) to 640K. Most computer systems today have the complete 640K of conventional memory. Older computer systems, however, might have only 512K or 256K. DOS manages this memory and loads device drivers, TSRs, software applications, and utilities into it. DOS also reserves part of conventional memory for the DOS environment, for the data structure that keeps track of open files, and for disk buffers and disk caches. Many people experience what is called "RAM cram" as they attempt to load more and more device drivers and TSRs into this memory. The availability of conventional memory has become the primary limiting factor in the performance of computer systems today.

Upper memory is the memory that extends from 640K to 1MB. Computer systems use part of this memory as address space for program code stored on ROM chips. Memory, as you learned earlier, consists of a series of consecutive memory locations, each of which is assigned an address. DOS uses these addresses to locate program code and data. Upper memory is also called **reserved memory**, or **adapter memory**, because specific segments of upper memory are reserved for system-related operations, such as for video display adapters, network adapters, and the ROM-BIOS (ROM Basic Input/Output System).

What is important to know about upper memory is that part of this memory is not used. For example, the address space reserved for video memory extends from 640K to 728K; however, an adapter might not use all of the available memory space reserved for it. If DOS can access these unused memory spaces in reserved memory, DOS can use that memory. The unused space available in upper memory might range in size from 64K to 200K. If your computer system has an 80386 or 80486 microprocessor chip and if you use DOS 5.0, 6.0, or 6.2, you can move device drivers and memory-resident programs (TSRs) from conventional memory to the upper memory area (UMA) with the use of a **memory manager**, a device driver that manages the use of memory, thereby freeing more conventional memory for your software applications.

Extended memory is the memory above 1MB. When you purchase an 80386 or 80486 computer, that computer might automatically include a certain amount of extended memory, and you have the option of adding more extended memory before or after the purchase. A computer system with an 80386 or 80486 microprocessor can have up to 4 gigabytes (4GB) of extended memory. (A **gigabyte** is 1,024 megabytes, so 4GB is the same as 4,096MB.) A computer system with an 80286 microprocessor can have a maximum of only 16MB of extended memory. Older types of computer systems, such as the IBM PC and XT, do not have extended memory at all because the 8088 and 8086 microprocessors that they use cannot address, or access, memory above 1MB. Although DOS is designed to operate in the first 640K of memory (conventional memory), more and more applications and utilities can use memory locations in extended memory to store program code or data or both. DOS must also use a memory manager to access and manage extended memory so that software applications and utilities can use this memory. The Windows operating environment and operating system can also operate in extended memory and can manage that memory with a memory manager.

High memory is the first 64K of extended memory from 1,024K (1MB) to 1,088K. If you use DOS 5.0, 6.0, or 6.2 on your computer system, you can move most of DOS and the memory it uses for disk buffers from conventional memory to the high memory area (HMA) with the use of a memory manager. By loading DOS **high**, you leave more conventional memory available for software applications and document files. However, you can load only one program into the high memory area at a time.

Expanded memory is an additional type of memory that is separate from conventional and extended memory. In 1985 Intel, Lotus Corporation, and Microsoft developed and released specifications for using expanded memory to resolve memory constraints that spreadsheet and database users frequently encountered. Many software applications, such as Lotus 1-2-3, WordPerfect, and dBASE, use expanded memory. Today, however, the use of extended memory is replacing the use of expanded memory because extended memory is faster and easier to access. Expanded memory provided a means for applications to circumvent the fact that earlier microprocessors, such as the 8088 and 8086, could not address more than 1MB of memory and therefore could not use extended memory.

You commonly add expanded memory to a computer system in one of two ways. You can add an adapter or card with expanded memory chips, or you can convert part of extended memory to expanded memory with the use of a memory manager. Expanded memory can range in size from 8MB to 32MB, and you can use expanded memory in computer systems with 8086, 8088, 80286, 80386, and 80486 microprocessors. To access expanded memory, however, you must use a memory manager. If you purchase an expanded memory board, the manufacturer provides the memory manager with the board.

In conjunction with an expanded memory manager, DOS accesses data stored in expanded memory via a page frame located either in conventional memory or the upper memory area. A **page frame** is a 64K region of memory through which a memory manager swaps data from expanded memory into conventional memory, or vice versa. The memory manager divides each page frame into four pages of equal size. Each **page** is therefore 16K of memory within the page frame. Although expanded memory is slower than extended memory because the memory manager must transfer small blocks of data between expanded and conventional memory, more software applications use expanded memory than extended memory.

USING MEMORY MANAGERS

DOS is a memory manager, because it manages the use of conventional memory by allocating memory space for programs. DOS 5.0, DOS 6.0, DOS 6.2, and Windows 3.1 use two other memory managers, which are also device drivers, to manage extended memory, the high memory area, the upper memory area, and extended memory used as expanded memory. These memory managers are called HIMEM.SYS and EMM386.EXE.

HIMEM.SYS manages extended memory, the high memory area, and the upper memory area. HIMEM.SYS allocates extended memory to applications that can use this type of memory. It also allocates memory in the high memory area to DOS and to applications. DOS can then load itself and its buffers into this part of extended memory. In addition, HIMEM.SYS controls access to the upper memory area and guarantees that no two programs claim the same part of memory. Without a memory manager, if a program attempts to use part of the memory used by another program, your computer system "locks up" and does not respond to commands.

EMM386.EXE carves the upper memory area into upper memory blocks (UMBs) so that DOS can load device drivers and TSRs into the upper memory area. EMM386.EXE can also convert all or part of extended memory into expanded memory for those applications that use expanded memory but not extended memory. This feature is useful if your computer system does not have expanded memory.

HIMEM.SYS and EMM386.EXE work cooperatively with DOS to manage the use of memory within your computer system. Microsoft Corporation provides the same two device drivers with Windows so that it too can manage memory.

EXAMINING MEMORY

You want to test the use of these memory managers on your computer system and determine whether they increase the amount of available memory for use by your software applications and whether they improve the performance of your computer. However, you do not want to change the configuration of your computer system until you are sure that these memory managers are operating properly. To protect your computer system, you decide to configure it using a boot disk in drive A. After you test various configurations from the boot disk, you can modify the CONFIG.SYS and AUTOEXEC.BAT files on your hard disk to include those features that are useful and that work well with your computer system.

As you test configurations with these memory managers, you want to examine the contents of memory so that you can check the efficiency of memory usage and the total available memory. You can use the MEM command to display summary information on the organization and use of memory. This command has two switches that are useful. The **Classify switch** (/C) displays a list of the modules in the first megabyte of memory and a memory summary. A **module** consists of all the memory used by a particular program or device driver. This memory includes the actual program code, a program's environment where it stores settings for its own use, and an area where it stores data for its own use. In DOS 6.0 and 6.2, the **Pause switch** (/P) displays the memory usage report one screen at a time. If you are using DOS 5.0, you must use the pipe operator and the MORE filter to display a memory usage report one screen at a time.

Because the reports that the MEM command produces in DOS 5.0 differ substantially from those in DOS 6.0 and 6.2, the tutorial will show screens for both DOS 5.0 and for DOS 6.0. If you are using DOS 6.2, you will find that your screen views are very similar to those produced by DOS 6.0.

You are now ready to reboot your computer system and examine its memory. If you are using a network without a hard disk drive C, ask your instructor for instructions on how to complete this tutorial. DOS must be able to locate the directory that contains the DOS utilities.

To boot your computer system:

1. Insert the boot disk that you prepared in Tutorial 10 in drive A.
2. Press **[Ctrl][Alt][Del]**, or press the **Reset button** on your computer system.

6.0 6.2

If you are using DOS 6.0 or 6.2, DOS displays the Startup menu that you created in Tutorial 10 and highlights the first option, DOS-Prompt. Press **[Enter]** to select DOS Prompt. DOS selects the first menu item, executes the appropriate commands in CONFIG.SYS and AUTOEXEC.BAT, and displays the DOS prompt.

5.0

If you are using DOS 5.0, DOS executes the commands in CONFIG.SYS and the commands in AUTOEXEC.BAT, then displays the DOS prompt.

3. Type **CLS** and press **[Enter]**. DOS clears the screen.

Now view the contents of memory.

4. Type **MEM** and press **[Enter]**. DOS displays a short report on memory usage. See Figure 11-2 (for DOS 6.0 and 6.2) or Figure 11-3 (for DOS 5.0). DOS 6.2 refers to "Adapter RAM/ROM" as "Reserved memory."

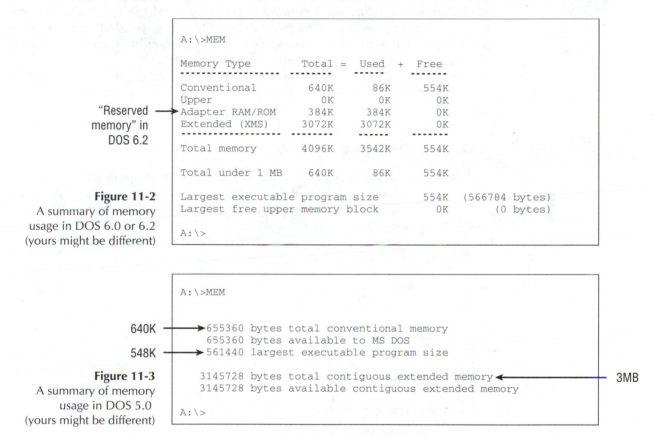

"Reserved memory" in DOS 6.2

```
A:\>MEM

Memory Type          Total =   Used +   Free
-------------------  --------  ------  -------
Conventional            640K     86K     554K
Upper                     0K      0K       0K
Adapter RAM/ROM         384K    384K       0K
Extended (XMS)         3072K   3072K       0K
-------------------  --------  ------  -------
Total memory           4096K   3542K     554K

Total under 1 MB        640K     86K     554K

Largest executable program size          554K   (566784 bytes)
Largest free upper memory block            0K       (0 bytes)

A:\>
```

Figure 11-2
A summary of memory usage in DOS 6.0 or 6.2 (yours might be different)

```
A:\>MEM

  655360 bytes total conventional memory
  655360 bytes available to MS DOS
  561440 largest executable program size

 3145728 bytes total contiguous extended memory
 3145728 bytes available contiguous extended memory

A:\>
```

640K
548K

3MB

Figure 11-3
A summary of memory usage in DOS 5.0 (yours might be different)

In Figure 11-2, DOS 6.0 and 6.2 show the types of memory available on a specific computer system. DOS 6.2 requires more memory than DOS 6.0. The report for your system will probably be different. In the summary shown in Figure 11-2, the total amount of conventional memory is 640K. Of that 640K, 86K of conventional memory is currently used by programs, and 554K (or 87 percent) is free and available for use by programs and files. The last line of the report shows that none of the upper memory area is currently available for use. The "Adapter RAM/ROM" in DOS 6.0 (or "Reserved memory" in DOS 6.2) is the amount of memory (384K) between 640K and 1MB reserved for use as address space for ROM. This computer system also has 3MB of extended memory. The total amount of memory available is therefore 4MB. This computer can then be said to have 4MB of RAM.

The DOS 5.0 summary for this same computer system (Figure 11-3) shows the total amount of conventional memory (655,360 bytes, or 640K) and the maximum available conventional memory (655,360 bytes, or 640K). The amount for largest program size (561,440 bytes, or approximately 548K) reflects the amount of memory left for use by software applications or utilities after DOS, device drivers, and TSRs are loaded. (Remember, to convert bytes to kilobytes, divide the total number of bytes by 1,024.) DOS 5.0 also reports on the amount of extended memory (3,145,728 bytes, or 3MB) for the computer illustrated in this figure. Under DOS 5.0, 86 percent of conventional memory is available for use by applications on this system.

Let's produce a more detailed memory usage report by using the Classify switch.

_6.0_ _6.2_   **To view a detailed report of memory usage:**

     1.   If you are using DOS 6.0 or 6.2, type **MEM /C /P** and press **[Enter]**. DOS displays the first screen of this memory usage report and pauses, telling you to press any key to continue. Press **[Spacebar]** or any other key to display the next part of the report. See Figures 11-4a and 11-4b. Note that the DOS 6.2 Memory Summary section of a memory usage report does not include the values shown in parentheses for Total, Used, and Free memory.

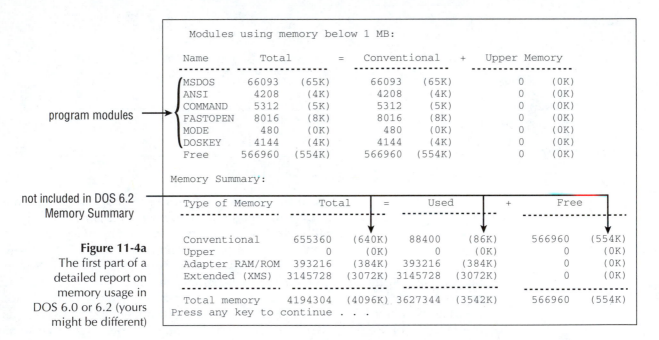

program modules →

not included in DOS 6.2 Memory Summary

Figure 11-4a
The first part of a detailed report on memory usage in DOS 6.0 or 6.2 (yours might be different)

```
    Modules using memory below 1 MB:

    Name         Total      =   Conventional  +  Upper Memory
    ---------  --------------      ------------      ------------
    MSDOS      66093   (65K)       66093   (65K)          0   (0K)
    ANSI        4208    (4K)        4208    (4K)          0   (0K)
    COMMAND     5312    (5K)        5312    (5K)          0   (0K)
    FASTOPEN    8016    (8K)        8016    (8K)          0   (0K)
    MODE         480    (0K)         480    (0K)          0   (0K)
    DOSKEY      4144    (4K)        4144    (4K)          0   (0K)
    Free      566960  (554K)      566960  (554K)          0   (0K)

Memory Summary:

    Type of Memory        Total      =      Used       +      Free
    --------------     ------------      ------------      ------------

    Conventional        655360  (640K)     88400   (86K)   566960  (554K)
    Upper                    0   (0K)          0   (0K)         0   (0K)
    Adapter RAM/ROM     393216 (384K)     393216 (384K)         0   (0K)
    Extended (XMS)     3145728 (3072K)   3145728 (3072K)        0   (0K)
    --------------     ------------      ------------      ------------
    Total memory       4194304 (4096K)   3627344 (3542K)   566960  (554K)
Press any key to continue . . .
```

```
Press any key to continue . . . .

   Total under 1 MB      655,360       88,400       566,960

   Largest executable program size        566,784    (554K)
   Largest free upper memory block             0      (0K)

A:\>
```

Figure 11-4b
The last part of a detailed
report on memory usage
in DOS 6.0 or 6.2
(yours might be different)

5.0

If you are using DOS 5.0, type **MEM /C | MORE** and press **[Enter]**. DOS
displays a memory usage report and will either pause or display the DOS
prompt. If necessary, press **[Spacebar]** or any other key to display the next
part of the report. See Figure 11-5.

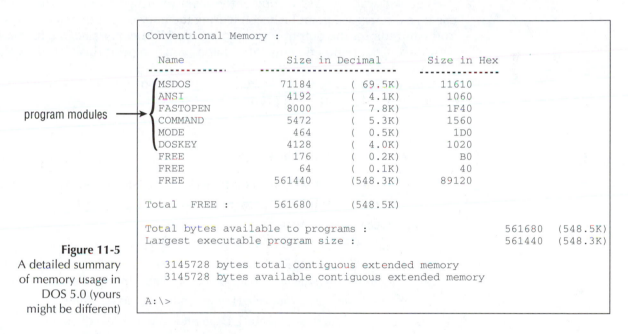

```
Conventional Memory :

    Name              Size in Decimal        Size in Hex
    -----------       -------------------    ---------------
    MSDOS                71184      ( 69.5K)     11610
    ANSI                  4192      (  4.1K)      1060
    FASTOPEN              8000      (  7.8K)      1F40
    COMMAND               5472      (  5.3K)      1560
    MODE                   464      (  0.5K)       1D0
    DOSKEY                4128      (  4.0K)      1020
    FREE                   176      (  0.2K)        B0
    FREE                    64      (  0.1K)        40
    FREE                561440      (548.3K)     89120

  Total   FREE :      561680      (548.5K)

  Total bytes available to programs :            561680    (548.5K)
  Largest executable program size :              561440    (548.3K)

    3145728 bytes total contiguous extended memory
    3145728 bytes available contiguous extended memory

A:\>
```

program modules

Figure 11-5
A detailed summary
of memory usage in
DOS 5.0 (yours
might be different)

The DOS 6.0 and 6.2 report (Figures 11-4a and 11-4b) shows the program
modules below 1MB and the amount of memory used by each program module. It also shows whether a program module uses conventional memory or
upper memory. The modules include MSDOS (for the operating system files
IO.SYS and MSDOS.SYS), ANSI (for the device driver ANSI.SYS), COMMAND (for
the Command Interpreter COMMAND.COM), FASTOPEN (for the FASTOPEN.EXE
TSR), MODE (for the MODE.COM TSR), and DOSKEY (for the DOSKEY.COM TSR).
In this figure, the size of programs and free areas of memory are shown using the
decimal and hexidecimal ("hex") numbering systems.

The Memory Summary section shows total memory usage by type of memory. Note that in this computer, only conventional memory is used currently. This report is similar to the more concise report produced without using the Classify switch.

The DOS 5.0 report (Figure 11-5) lists each program module in conventional memory and the program's size, in bytes and kilobytes. The program modules include those for MSDOS (for the operating system files IO.SYS and MSDOS.SYS), ANSI (for the device driver ANSI.SYS), FASTOPEN (for the FASTOPEN.EXE TSR), COMMAND (for the Command Interpreter COMMAND.COM), MODE (for the MODE.COM TSR), and DOSKEY (for the DOSKEY.COM TSR). The report also shows the amount of free conventional memory (561,680 bytes, or 548.5K), the total memory available for programs (561,680 bytes, or 548.5K), and the amount of extended memory (3,145,728 bytes, or 3MB). The reported memory usage figures may be different on your system.

You will want to save a copy of the memory usage report so that you can use it as a reference point for reconfiguring memory on your computer system. You can redirect the output produced by the MEM command to a file on disk with the output redirection operator. Later, you can print this text file with the PRINT utility.

You decide to create a directory on your boot disk for storing this and other reports that you might produce.

To create a directory for reports:

1. Type **MD REPORTS** and press **[Enter]**. DOS creates the REPORTS directory.
2. Type **CD REPORTS** and press **[Enter]**. DOS changes to the REPORTS directory.

Now create a copy of this memory usage report.

3. Type **MEM /C > REPORT1** and press **[Enter]**.
4. Type **TYPE REPORT1 ⎮ MORE** and press **[Enter]**. DOS displays the contents of this file—the memory usage report produced by the MEM command.
5. If necessary, press **[Spacebar]** or any other key to continue.
6. Type **CD ** and press **[Enter]**. DOS returns to the root directory.

LOADING DOS HIGH

You want to start by loading the majority of DOS and its disk buffers into the high memory area (HMA). Before you can perform this operation, you must install the HIMEM.SYS device driver from CONFIG.SYS with a DEVICE command, as in the following example:

DEVICE=C:\DOS\HIMEM.SYS

You must include the drive name, full path, and full filename of HIMEM.SYS. Although it is common practice to store HIMEM.SYS in the root directory of drive C, you should first verify where it is stored before you add this command to CONFIG.SYS.

You must place this DEVICE command in your CONFIG.SYS file *before* any other DEVICE commands that load device drivers and any INSTALL commands that load TSRs. Although this device driver has a variety of switches, the default values work with most hardware. If DOS reports memory problems when you boot, if you receive out-of-memory error messages while using applications, or if your computer does not operate properly, verify the documentation for HIMEM.SYS and its switches in your DOS reference manual or user's guide.

To load DOS high, you use the DOS command, as follows:

DOS=HIGH

You place this command *after* the DEVICE command that installs HIMEM.SYS.

Before you can use the extended memory manager and load DOS high, your computer must have extended memory. If you are using a computer with an 80286, 80386, or 80486 microprocessor, if your computer has extended memory, and if you are using DOS 5.0, 6.0, or 6.2, you can modify the CONFIG.SYS file to install the DOS memory manager for extended memory and then load DOS high. If you are using an older computer system with an 8086 or 8088 microprocessor, you will not be able to complete the remainder of this chapter's tutorial.

Adding the HIMEM.SYS Memory Manager to CONFIG.SYS

You are now ready to add the DOS extended memory manager, HIMEM.SYS, to CONFIG.SYS.

To modify CONFIG.SYS to include a memory manager:

1. Check the DOS prompt, and be sure the current drive is drive A. You do not want to inadvertently edit CONFIG.SYS on your hard disk.

2. Type **DIR C:\HIMEM.SYS /S** and press **[Enter]**. DOS checks all the directories on drive C with the Subdirectory switch (/S) for the location of HIMEM.SYS. More than likely, it will be in the DOS subdirectory, the root directory, or the Windows subdirectory. If you locate a copy of HIMEM.SYS in the Windows subdirectory *and* one in the root directory or the DOS subdirectory, use the one in the DOS subdirectory. Both DOS and Windows come with a copy of HIMEM.SYS.

3. Type **EDIT CONFIG.SYS** and press **[Enter]**. DOS loads the MS-DOS Editor, and the MS-DOS Editor then loads CONFIG.SYS.

4. Position the cursor at the beginning of the line that contains the REM command followed by the title "Set Disk Buffers." Then press **[Ctrl][N]** to insert a blank line.

5. Type **REM**, press **[Tab]**, type **Install Memory Managers** and press **[Enter]**. Then type **REM** and press **[Enter]**.

6. Press **[Tab]**, type **DEVICE=C:\DOS\HIMEM.SYS** and press **[Enter]** *twice. If HIMEM.SYS is stored in another directory on drive C, use that directory's name in the path.* For example, if HIMEM.SYS is stored in the root directory, your DEVICE command should read DEVICE=C:\HIMEM.SYS.

Adding the DOS Command to CONFIG.SYS to Load DOS High

Now you can add the command to load DOS high to CONFIG.SYS.

To modify CONFIG.SYS to load DOS high:

1. Press **[Backspace]** to delete the indent. Type **REM**, press **[Tab]**, type **Load DOS High** and press **[Enter]**. Then type **REM** and press **[Enter]**.
2. Press **[Tab]**, type **DOS=HIGH** and press **[Enter]**. Figure 11-6 shows the placement of the DEVICE command for installing HIMEM.SYS and the DOS command for loading DOS high.

command to load
extended
memory manager

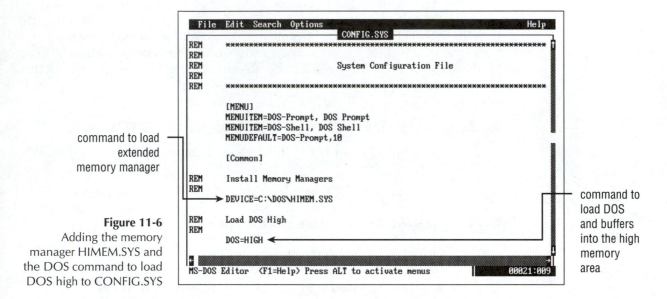

command to
load DOS
and buffers
into the high
memory
area

Figure 11-6
Adding the memory
manager HIMEM.SYS and
the DOS command to load
DOS high to CONFIG.SYS

Saving Modifications to CONFIG.SYS

You can now save your work and test the memory manager.

To save your work:

1. Press **[Alt]** (Menu) to access the menu bar, press **[Enter]** for the File menu, and type **X** for the Exit command.

   If you are using the mouse, click **File**, then click **Exit**.

   The MS-DOS Editor displays a dialog box that prompts you about saving the changes.

2. Press **[Enter]** to select Yes.

   If you are using the mouse, click **Yes**.

   The MS-DOS Editor saves your changes, you exit the MS-DOS Editor, and DOS displays the DOS prompt.

Testing Changes to CONFIG.SYS

Now you must reboot your computer system so that the new settings in CONFIG.SYS can take effect. During the rebooting process, DOS will install or load the HIMEM.SYS memory manager into conventional memory, and HIMEM.SYS will allow DOS to install or load itself into the high memory area.

To reboot your computer system:

_6.0_ _6.2_

_5.0_

1. Press **[Ctrl][Alt][Del]**, or press the **Reset button** on your computer system.

   If you are using DOS 6.0 or 6.2, select DOS-Prompt when DOS displays the Startup menu, then press **[Enter]**. DOS displays the DOS prompt.

   If you are using DOS 5.0, DOS executes the commands in CONFIG.SYS, informs you that the high memory area is available, executes the commands in AUTOEXEC.BAT, and displays the DOS prompt.

2. Type **MEM** and press **[Enter]**. MEM displays a memory usage report that informs you DOS is resident in the high memory area (that is, it is loaded high) and that it is using 64K. See Figure 11-7 (for DOS 6.0 and 6.2) or Figure 11-8 (for DOS 5.0). If, for some reason, DOS cannot load itself high, DOS will display a message that the HMA is unavailable and that DOS is loading itself low. When DOS loads a program *low*, it loads the program in conventional memory. If DOS loads low, compare your CONFIG.SYS file with Figure 11-4, correct any errors, and repeat these two steps.

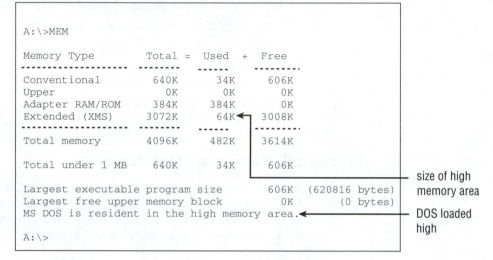

Figure 11-7
A memory usage report for DOS 6.0 and 6.2 showing DOS in the high memory area (yours might be different)

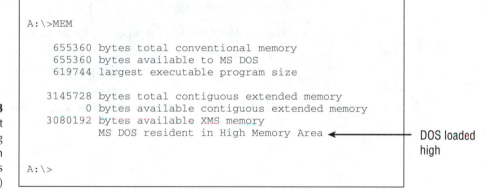

Figure 11-8
A memory usage report for DOS 5.0 showing DOS in the high memory area (yours might be different)

The DOS 6.0 and 6.2 report in Figure 11-7 shows that programs, device drivers, and TSRs are using only 34K of conventional memory on the computer system illustrated in this figure. Your report might show slightly different results. However, by loading DOS and its buffers high, the computer system illustrated in Figure 11-7 gained 52K of conventional memory over the report shown in Figures 11-4a and 11-4b. This one change to the memory configuration of this system increased available conventional memory from 554K to 606K—a 9.4 percent increase. The report in Figure 11-7 also shows that 64K of extended memory is currently in use—the size of the high memory area.

If you compare the DOS 5.0 report in Figure 11-8 with that shown in Figure 11-5, you will find that this one change to the memory configuration of this system increased available conventional memory from 561,440 bytes to 619,744 bytes—a 10 percent increase. The difference between the total amount of extended memory and the amount of XMS (extended) memory is 65,536 bytes, or 64K. This is the size of the high memory area.

CREATING UPPER MEMORY BLOCKS

You want to claim the unused space in the upper memory area so that you can load device drivers into this part of memory. To access memory blocks in the upper memory area, you must install another memory manager, EMM386.EXE, from CONFIG.SYS. This memory manager creates upper memory blocks, or UMBs, for use by device drivers and TSRs.

When you install this memory manager, you must also specify one of two switches to determine how EMM386 manages and uses the UMBs. The **No Expanded Memory Specification switch**, or NOEMS, is a switch without a slash preceding it; it informs EMM386.EXE that you do not have expanded memory and that you do not want to convert extended memory to expanded memory. With this switch, EMM386.EXE reserves all the upper memory blocks for use by DOS, so that you can load device drivers and TSRs into upper memory rather than into conventional memory. If the programs you use do not require expanded memory but might use extended memory, this switch guarantees that all of extended memory is designated solely as extended memory.

To install EMM386.EXE on a computer system in which you are not using extended memory for expanded memory, you enter a DEVICE command similar to the following example:

DEVICE=C:\DOS\EMM386.EXE   NOEMS

You specify the drive name, full path, and full filename of EMM386.EXE. You must also specify the NOEMS switch; otherwise, you cannot load device drivers and TSRS into upper memory.

The **RAM switch**, RAM, instructs EMM386.EXE to use part of extended memory as expanded memory. EMM386.EXE creates a 64K page frame in the upper memory area for transferring data from expanded memory to conventional memory, and vice versa. When you use the RAM switch, you can also specify the amount of extended memory that the memory manager should designate as expanded memory. The value can range from 64K to 32,768K. The default is the amount of free extended memory. If you use the RAM switch, therefore, less of the upper memory area is available for loading device drivers and TSRs. If you have programs such as Lotus 1-2-3 or WordPerfect, which use expanded memory, you might want to allocate part of extended memory as expanded memory with this switch so that those programs can store program code and documents in expanded memory. With access to expanded memory, these programs can operate more effectively and will allow you to work with larger documents.

To install EMM386.EXE on a computer system in which all or part of extended memory is used as expanded memory, you enter a DEVICE command similar to the following example:

DEVICE=C:\DOS\EMM386.EXE RAM [*memory*]

You specify the drive name, full path, and full filename of EMM386.EXE. You must also specify the RAM switch; otherwise, EMM386.EXE will not convert extended memory to expanded memory. If you use the RAM switch, you can also specify in kilobytes the amount of extended memory that EMM386.EXE will use as expanded memory.

You can use either the NOEMS switch or the RAM switch with EMM386.EXE. *You cannot use both switches at the same time.*

After you instruct EMM386.EXE to carve out the upper memory blocks, you must include a DOS command so that DOS can use the upper memory blocks:

DOS=UMB

This command is required; otherwise, DOS cannot load device drivers or TSRs into the upper memory area. You can also combine this command with the one that loads DOS high, as follows:

DOS=HIGH,UMB

Because you do not want to set aside any of the extended memory on your computer system as expanded memory, you decide to use the NOEMS switch. Let's edit CONFIG.SYS, specify this memory manager, and reboot. Once you reboot, the MEM command will report on the amount of memory claimed as upper memory blocks in the upper memory area.

To continue with this tutorial, you must be working on a 80386 or 80486 computer system with extended memory. If you are using a computer with an 80286, 8088, or 8086 microprocessor, you will not be able to complete most of the remainder of this chapter's tutorial because you cannot access the upper memory area on these systems. If you are using a computer with an 80286, 8088, or 8086 microprocessor, you *can* continue with the section entitled, "Printing Copies of Your Documentation," the last section before the Command Summary at the end of the tutorial. If necessary, check with your instructor or technical support person to find out whether you can continue.

Adding the EMM386.EXE Memory Manager to CONFIG.SYS

Now you are ready to add the DOS memory manager EMM386.EXE to CONFIG.SYS so that it can manage the upper memory area.

To modify CONFIG.SYS to use EMM386.EXE:

1. Check the DOS prompt and be sure the current drive is drive A. You do not want to inadvertently edit CONFIG.SYS on your hard disk.

2. Type **DIR C:\EMM386.EXE /S** and press **[Enter]**. DOS checks all the directories on drive C with the Subdirectory switch (/S) for the location of EMM386.EXE. More than likely, it will be in the DOS subdirectory, the root directory, or the Windows subdirectory. If you locate a copy of EMM386.EXE in the Windows subdirectory *and* one in the root directory or DOS subdirectory, use the one in the DOS subdirectory. Both DOS and Windows come with a copy of EMM386.EXE.

3. Type **EDIT CONFIG.SYS** and press **[Enter]**. DOS loads the MS-DOS Editor, which loads CONFIG.SYS.

4. Position the cursor at the beginning of the blank line that follows the one with the DEVICE command for HIMEM.SYS.

5. Press **[Tab]**, type **DEVICE=C:\DOS\EMM386.EXE NOEMS** and press **[Enter]**. *If EMM386.EXE is stored in another directory on drive C, use that directory's name in the path.* For example, if EMM386.EXE is stored in the root directory, your command should read DEVICE=C:\EMM386.EXE NOEMS.

Modifying the DOS Command to Access the Upper Memory Blocks

Next, you must add the command that grants DOS access to the upper memory blocks.

To allow DOS access to the upper memory blocks:

1. Position the cursor on the line that contains the DOS=HIGH command. Then press **[End]** to move the cursor to the end of this line.

2. Type **,UMB** so that the command reads DOS=HIGH,UMB. *Be sure you type a comma before UMB.* Figure 11-9 shows the placement of the DEVICE command for installing EMM386.EXE and the DOS command for accessing upper memory blocks.

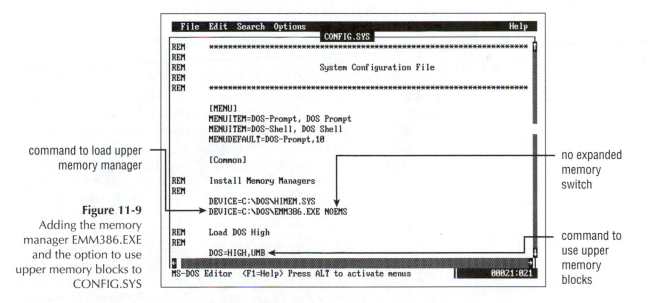

command to load upper memory manager

no expanded memory switch

command to use upper memory blocks

Figure 11-9
Adding the memory manager EMM386.EXE and the option to use upper memory blocks to CONFIG.SYS

Saving Changes to CONFIG.SYS

You can now save your work and test these changes to CONFIG.SYS.

To save your work:

1. Press **[Alt]** (Menu) to access the menu bar, press **[Enter]** for the File menu, and type **X** for the Exit command. Press **[Enter]** to select Yes in the dialog box to save your changes and exit the MS-DOS Editor.

   If you are using the mouse, click **File**, then click **Exit**, then click **Yes** in the dialog box to save your changes and exit the MS-DOS Editor.

   The MS-DOS Editor saves your changes, you exit the MS-DOS Editor, and DOS displays the DOS prompt.

Testing the Modifications to CONFIG.SYS

Now you must reboot your computer system so that the new settings in CONFIG.SYS can take effect. During the rebooting process, DOS will install HIMEM.SYS and EMM386.EXE into conventional memory and load itself high. EMM386.EXE will locate upper memory blocks, and the DOS command will allow DOS to use the upper memory blocks.

To reboot your computer system:

__6.0__ *__6.2__*

__5.0__

1. Press **[Ctrl][Alt][Del]**, or press the **Reset button** on your computer system.

   If you are using DOS 6.0 or 6.2, select DOS-Prompt when DOS displays the Startup menu, then press **[Enter]**. DOS displays the DOS prompt.

   If you are using DOS 5.0, DOS executes the commands in CONFIG.SYS, informs you that EMM386 was successfully installed and is active, executes the commands in AUTOEXEC.BAT, and displays the DOS prompt.

__6.0__ *__6.2__*

2. If you are using DOS 6.0 or 6.2, type **MEM** and press **[Enter]**. See Figure 11-10. The memory usage report for the computer system used in Figure 11-10 shows that EMM386.EXE found 155K of unused space in the upper memory area for use by DOS. The total amount of memory available for DOS to use is now 795K, instead of 640K—an impressive memory gain of 24 percent. Your results might be different.

__5.0__

   If you are using DOS 5.0, type **MEM /C** and press [Enter]. See Figure 11-11. The latter part of the memory usage report for the computer system used in Figure 11-11 shows that EMM386.EXE found 96K of unused space in the upper memory area for use by DOS. The total amount of memory available for use by DOS is approximately 693K instead of 640K—a memory gain of eight percent. Your results might be different.

upper memory blocks

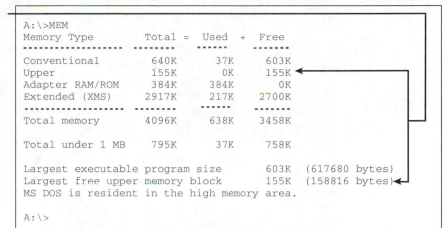

```
A:\>MEM
Memory Type       Total =  Used  +  Free
----------------  -------- ------- -------
Conventional        640K      37K     603K
Upper               155K       0K     155K
Adapter RAM/ROM     384K     384K       0K
Extended (XMS)     2917K     217K    2700K
----------------  -------- ------- -------
Total memory       4096K     638K    3458K

Total under 1 MB    795K      37K     758K

Largest executable program size         603K   (617680 bytes)
Largest free upper memory block         155K   (158816 bytes)
MS DOS is resident in the high memory area.

A:\>
```

Figure 11-10
A memory usage report for DOS 6.0 and 6.2 showing available upper memory blocks (yours might be different)

```
      FREE               112    (  0.1K)         70
      FREE               128    (  0.1K)         80
      FREE            611312    (597.0K)      953F0

Total  FREE :         611712    (597.4K)

Upper Memory :

  Name              Size in Decimal      Size in Hex
  ---------------   -------------------  ----------------
   SYSTEM            163840    (160.0K)         28000
   FREE               98272    ( 96.0K)         17FE0

Total  FREE :          98272    ( 96.0K)

Total bytes available to programs (Conventional+Upper) : 709984 (693.3K)
Largest executable program size :                         611312 (597.0K)
Largest available upper memory block :                     98272 ( 96.0K)

   3145728 bytes total contiguous extended memory
         0 bytes available contiguous extended memory
   2894848 bytes available XMS memory
         MS DOS resident in High Memory Area

A:\>
```

upper memory blocks

Figure 11-11
A memory usage report for DOS 5.0 showing available upper memory blocks (yours might be different)

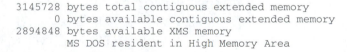

This is a good opportunity for a break.

LOADING DEVICE DRIVERS AND TSRs INTO UPPER MEMORY

You can take advantage of the additional memory in the upper memory area by loading device drivers and TSRs into that part of memory.

To load a device driver from CONFIG.SYS into the upper memory area, use the DEVICEHIGH command instead of the DEVICE command. If DOS is unable to load a device driver into the upper memory area for lack of available space, it automatically loads low into conventional memory. *You cannot load HIMEM.SYS and EMM386.EXE into the upper memory area. You must load them into conventional memory.* HIMEM.SYS and EMM386.EXE use a small amount of conventional memory (approximately 4K) but give you access to far more memory in the upper memory area and in extended memory.

To load a TSR into the upper memory area, you must use a LOADHIGH or LH (Load High) command in the AUTOEXEC.BAT file. You cannot load a TSR into the upper memory area from CONFIG.SYS. Again, if DOS is unable to load the TSR into the upper memory area for lack of available space, it automatically loads the TSR low into conventional memory.

Currently, the console device driver ANSI.SYS is loaded in conventional memory. We can modify CONFIG.SYS to load it into upper memory. We can also remove the INSTALL command that loads FASTOPEN from CONFIG.SYS, then load this TSR into upper memory from the AUTOEXEC.BAT file.

Modifying CONFIG.SYS to Load Device Drivers into Upper Memory

You are ready to modify CONFIG.SYS so that DOS can load device drivers into upper memory when you reboot.

To modify CONFIG.SYS for loading device drivers high:

1. If necessary, insert your boot disk into drive A. Check the DOS prompt and be sure the current drive is drive A. You do not want to inadvertently edit CONFIG.SYS on your hard disk.
2. Type **EDIT CONFIG.SYS** and press **[Enter]**. DOS loads the MS-DOS Editor, which loads CONFIG.SYS.
3. If necessary, press **[PgDn]** (Page Down). Next, position the cursor on the line that contains the DEVICE command for ANSI.SYS. Then position the cursor on the equal sign after the word DEVICE.
4. Type **HIGH** so that the command reads DEVICEHIGH= followed by the drive, path, and name of the device driver ANSI.SYS.

While in CONFIG.SYS, you want to remove the section that loads the FASTOPEN TSR so that you can load it into upper memory from the AUTOEXEC.BAT file. DOS does not load TSRs into upper memory from CONFIG.SYS.

To remove the section for loading FASTOPEN:

1. Position the cursor at the beginning of the line that contains the REM command followed by the title "Install TSRs."

2. If you are using DOS 6.0 or 6.2, press and hold **[Shift]** and press **[↓]** (Down Arrow) until you highlight the blank line before the one that contains the DOS-Shell configuration block header, "[DOS-Shell]." *Do not include the line with the DOS-Shell configuration block header in the highlighted block.*

If you are using DOS 5.0, press and hold **[Shift]** and press **[↓]** (Down Arrow) until you reach the end of the file.

This step selects the block for documenting and installing TSRs.

3. Press **[Alt]** (Menu) to access the menu bar, type **E** for the Edit menu, and type **T** for the Cut command.

If you are using the mouse, click **Edit**, then click **Cut**.

The MS-DOS Editor removes this highlighted block of text from CONFIG.SYS. Figure 11-12 shows these revisions to CONFIG.SYS.

command to load device driver in upper memory

Figure 11-12
The use of the DEVICEHIGH command in CONFIG.SYS

Saving Changes to CONFIG.SYS

You must save these changes to CONFIG.SYS before you modify AUTOEXEC.BAT.

To save your changes to CONFIG.SYS:

1. Press **[Alt]** (Menu) to access the menu bar, press **[Enter]** for the File menu, and type **S** for the Save command.

If you are using the mouse, click **File**, then click **Save**.

The MS-DOS Editor saves this file.

Modifying AUTOEXEC.BAT to Load TSRs High

Now you are ready to modify AUTOEXEC.BAT to include LOADHIGH commands, which allow DOS to load TSRs into upper memory.

To retrieve AUTOEXEC.BAT:

1. Press **[Alt]** (Menu) to access the menu bar, press **[Enter]** for the File menu, and type **O** for the Open command.

   If you are using the mouse, click **File**, then click **Open**.

   The MS-DOS Editor displays the Open dialog box.

2. Type **AUTOEXEC.BAT** and press **[Enter]**. The MS-DOS Editor retrieves this file. If the MS-DOS Editor prompts you about saving changes to CONFIG.SYS, press **[Enter]** for Yes.

   If you are using the mouse and the MS-DOS Editor prompts you about saving changes to CONFIG.SYS, click **Yes**.

You can now add LOADHIGH commands for the MODE TSRs.

To load the MODE TSRs into upper memory:

1. Press **[PgDn]** (Page Down). Position the cursor on the line that contains the first MODE command, which specifies the characteristics of the serial communications port. Then position the cursor on the "M" in MODE.

2. Type **LOADHIGH** and press **[Spacebar]**. The command should read LOADHIGH MODE COM1:9600,N,8,1,P.

3. Position the cursor on the line that contains the second MODE command, which redirects output from LPT1 to COM1. Then position the cursor on the "M" in MODE.

4. Type **LOADHIGH** and press **[Spacebar]**. The command should read LOADHIGH MODE LPT1:=COM1:.

Next you want to add the FASTOPEN utility to AUTOEXEC.BAT, using a LOADHIGH command to load it into upper memory. You also want to load DOSKEY into upper memory.

To add these changes:

1. Position the cursor on the line with the DOSKEY command. Then position the cursor on the "D" in DOSKEY.

2. Press **[Ctrl][N]** to insert a blank line.

3. Type **LOADHIGH FASTOPEN C:=100** and move the cursor to the next line with the DOSKEY command.

4. Position the cursor on the "D" in DOSKEY.

5. Type **LOADHIGH** and press **[Spacebar]**. Figure 11-13 shows the changes that you have made to the AUTOEXEC.BAT file.

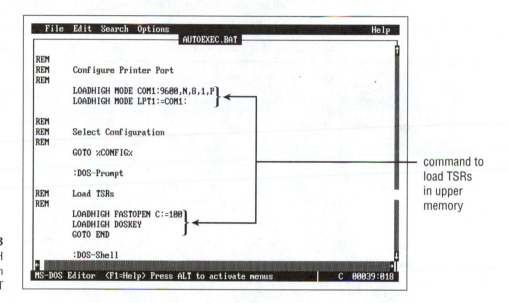

Figure 11-13
The use of LOADHIGH
command in
AUTOEXEC.BAT

Now save these changes.

6. Press **[Alt]** (Menu) to access the menu bar, press **[Enter]** to select the File menu, and type **X** for the Exit command.

If you are using the mouse, click **File**, then click **Exit**.

The MS-DOS Editor asks you if you want to save these changes.
Press **[Enter]** to select Yes.

If you are using the mouse, click **Yes**.

The MS-DOS Editor saves your changes, you exit the MS-DOS Editor, and DOS displays the DOS prompt.

Examining Current Memory Usage

Before you reboot your computer system, you want to examine the current status of memory usage in detail.

To display current memory usage:

_6.0_ _6.2_

1. If you are using DOS 6.0 or 6.2, type **MEM /C /P** and press **[Enter]**. See Figure 11-14. The first part of the memory usage report in Figure 11-14 shows that the device driver ANSI.SYS is loaded in conventional memory along with the FASTOPEN, MODE, and DOSKEY TSRs. Nothing is loaded in upper memory.

available upper memory

programs in
conventional memory

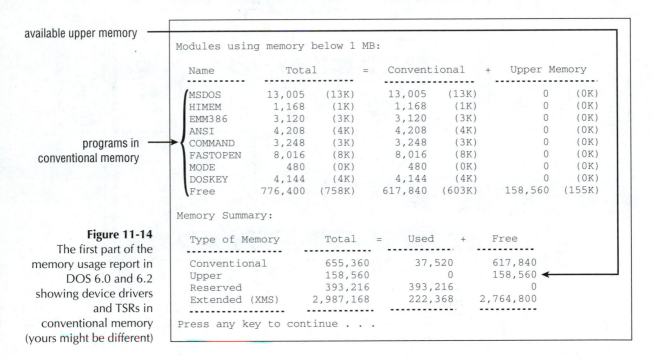

```
Modules using memory below 1 MB:

  Name          Total        =   Conventional   +   Upper Memory
  --------    ------------      --------------      --------------
  MSDOS        13,005  (13K)     13,005  (13K)            0   (0K)
  HIMEM         1,168   (1K)      1,168   (1K)            0   (0K)
  EMM386        3,120   (3K)      3,120   (3K)            0   (0K)
  ANSI          4,208   (4K)      4,208   (4K)            0   (0K)
  COMMAND       3,248   (3K)      3,248   (3K)            0   (0K)
  FASTOPEN      8,016   (8K)      8,016   (8K)            0   (0K)
  MODE            480   (0K)        480   (0K)            0   (0K)
  DOSKEY        4,144   (4K)      4,144   (4K)            0   (0K)
  Free        776,400 (758K)    617,840 (603K)      158,560 (155K)

Memory Summary:

  Type of Memory      Total     =     Used     +     Free
  --------------    ----------      ----------      ----------
  Conventional        655,360          37,520         617,840
  Upper               158,560               0         158,560
  Reserved            393,216         393,216               0
  Extended (XMS)    2,987,168         222,368       2,764,800
  --------------    ----------      ----------      ----------
Press any key to continue . . .
```

Figure 11-14
The first part of the memory usage report in DOS 6.0 and 6.2 showing device drivers and TSRs in conventional memory (yours might be different)

5.0

If you are using DOS 5.0, type **MEM /C | MORE** and press **[Enter]**. See Figure 11-15a. The first part of the memory usage report in Figure 11-15a shows that the device driver ANSI.SYS is loaded in conventional memory along with the FASTOPEN, MODE, and DOSKEY TSRs.

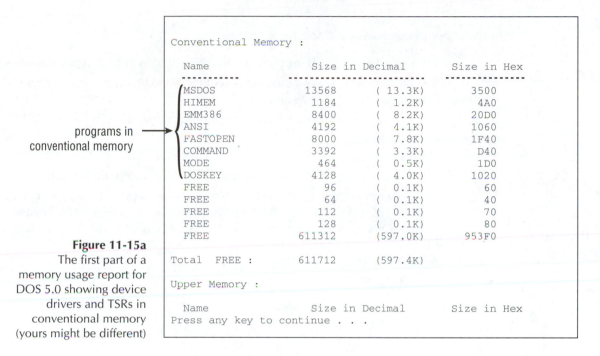

```
Conventional Memory :

   Name                     Size in Decimal        Size in Hex
   ----------               -------------------    ---------------
   MSDOS                    13568    ( 13.3K)      3500
   HIMEM                     1184    (  1.2K)       4A0
   EMM386                    8400    (  8.2K)      20D0
   ANSI                      4192    (  4.1K)      1060
   FASTOPEN                  8000    (  7.8K)      1F40
   COMMAND                   3392    (  3.3K)       D40
   MODE                       464    (  0.5K)       1D0
   DOSKEY                    4128    (  4.0K)      1020
   FREE                        96    (  0.1K)        60
   FREE                        64    (  0.1K)        40
   FREE                       112    (  0.1K)        70
   FREE                       128    (  0.1K)        80
   FREE                    611312    (597.0K)     953F0

Total  FREE :             611712    (597.4K)

Upper Memory :

   Name                     Size in Decimal        Size in Hex
Press any key to continue . . .
```

programs in conventional memory

Figure 11-15a
The first part of a memory usage report for DOS 5.0 showing device drivers and TSRs in conventional memory (yours might be different)

5.0

2. If necessary, press **[Spacebar]** or any other key to continue.

If you are using DOS 5.0, the latter part of the memory usage report shows that nothing is loaded in upper memory. See Figure 11-15b.

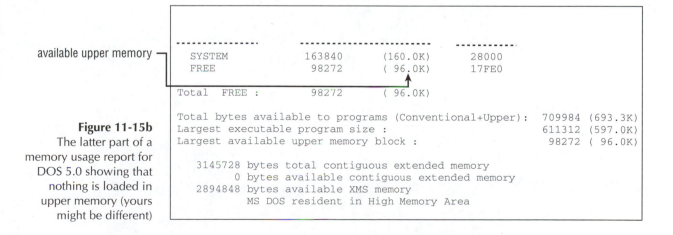

```
   ---------------          -------------------    -----------
   SYSTEM                   163840   (160.0K)      28000
   FREE                      98272   ( 96.0K)      17FE0

Total  FREE :               98272   ( 96.0K)

Total bytes available to programs (Conventional+Upper):  709984 (693.3K)
Largest executable program size :                        611312 (597.0K)
Largest available upper memory block :                    98272 ( 96.0K)

   3145728 bytes total contiguous extended memory
         0 bytes available contiguous extended memory
   2894848 bytes available XMS memory
         MS DOS resident in High Memory Area
```

available upper memory

Figure 11-15b
The latter part of a memory usage report for DOS 5.0 showing that nothing is loaded in upper memory (yours might be different)

Testing the Modifications to CONFIG.SYS and AUTOEXEC.BAT

Now you are ready to test the commands in CONFIG.SYS and AUTOEXEC.BAT for loading device drivers and TSRs into the upper memory area.

Now boot your system and test these changes:

6.0 6.2

5.0

1. Press **[Ctrl][Alt][Del]**, or press the **Reset button** on your computer system.

   If you are using DOS 6.0 or 6.2, select DOS-Prompt and press **[Enter]**. DOS displays the DOS prompt.

   If you are using DOS 5.0, DOS executes the commands in CONFIG.SYS, the commands in AUTOEXEC.BAT, and displays the DOS prompt.

6.0 6.2

5.0

2. If you are using DOS 6.0 or 6.2, type **MEM /C /P** and press **[Enter]**.

   If you are using DOS 5.0, type **MEM /C | MORE** and press **[Enter]**.

   The memory usage reports for DOS 6.0 and 6.2 in Figure 11-16 and for DOS 5.0 in Figure 11-17a show that DOS loaded the device driver ANSI.SYS and the MODE, FASTOPEN, and DOSKEY TSRs into upper memory.

```
Modules using memory below 1 MB:

   Name          Total      =   Conventional   +   Upper Memory
   ----------    --------       ------------       ------------
   MSDOS         12989  (13K)    12989  (13K)           0   (0K)
   HIMEM          1168   (1K)     1168   (1K)           0   (0K)
   EMM386         3120   (3K)     3120   (3K)           0   (0K)
   COMMAND        3232   (3K)     3232   (3K)           0   (0K)
   ANSI           4240   (4K)        0   (0K)        4240   (4K)
   MODE            480   (0K)        0   (0K)         480   (0K)
   FASTOPEN       8016   (8K)        0   (0K)        8016   (8K)
   DOSKEY         4144   (4K)        0   (0K)        4144   (4K)
   Free         776656 (758K)   634704 (620K)      141952 (139K)

Memory Summary:

   Type of Memory        Total       =      Used       +       Free
   --------------        --------           --------           --------
   Conventional      655360  (640K)     20656   (20K)     634704  (620K)
   Upper             158832  (155K)     16880   (16K)     141952  (139K)
   Adapter RAM/ROM   393216  (384K)    393216  (384K)          0    (0K)
   Extended (XMS)   2986896 (2917K)    222096  (217K)    2764800 (2700K)
Press any key to continue . . .
```

device driver and TSRs loaded in upper memory

Figure 11-16
This first part of a memory usage report for DOS 6.0 and 6.2 showing device drivers and TSRs loaded in upper memory (yours might be different)

```
Conventional Memory :

   Name                 Size in Decimal          Size in Hex
   -----------          ---------------------    ----------------
   MSDOS                13568        ( 13.3K)    3500
   HIMEM                 1184        (  1.2K)    4A0
   EMM386                8400        (  8.2K)    20D0
   COMMAND               3392        (  3.3K)    D40
   FREE                    64        (  0.1K)    40
   FREE                628544        (613.8K)    99740

Total   FREE :          628608        (613.9K)

Upper Memory :

   Name                 Size in Decimal          Size in Hex
   -----------          ---------------------    ----------------
   SYSTEM              163840        (160.0K)    28000
   ANSI                  4192        (  4.1K)    1060
   MODE                   464        (  0.5K)    1D0
   FASTOPEN              8000        (  7.8K)    1F40
   DOSKEY                4128        (  4.0K)    1020
   FREE                   112        (  0.1K)    70
Press any key to continue . . .
```

device driver and TSRs loaded in upper memory

Figure 11-17a
The first part of a memory usage report for DOS 5.0 showing device drivers and TSRs loaded in upper memory (yours might be different)

5.0

3. If necessary, press **[Spacebar]** or any other key to continue.

    If you are using DOS 5.0, you will see a second part of the report, similar to Figure 11-17b, which shows that part of upper memory (79.5K) is still available.

available upper memory

```
   FREE                   128        (  0.1K)    80
   FREE                 81136        ( 79.2K)    13CF0

Total   FREE :           81376        ( 79.5K)

Total bytes available to programs (Conventional+Upper):709984 (693.3K)
Largest executable program size :                       628416 (613.7K)
Largest available upper memory block :                   81136 ( 79.2K)

   3145728 bytes total contiguous extended memory
         0 bytes available contiguous extended memory
   2894848 bytes available XMS memory
           MS DOS resident in High Memory Area
```

Figure 11-17b
The latter part of a memory usage report for DOS 5.0 showing the status of upper memory (yours might be different)

As shown in Figures 11-16, 11-17a, and 11-17b, DOS 6.0 and 6.2 gained an additional 16K of conventional memory and DOS 5.0 gained an additional 16.7K of conventional memory on these computer systems by loading device drivers and TSRs into upper memory. This computer still has additional space available in upper memory for loading other device drivers and TSRs. In addition, conventional memory on these systems now has approximately 620K (for DOS 6.0 and 6.2) or approximately 614K (for DOS 5.0) out of 640K available for software applications, such as WordPerfect, Lotus 1-2-3, and dBASE. When you first started this process, 86 to 87 percent of conventional memory was available for software applications on this system. Now, after reconfiguring memory, 96 to 97 percent of conventional memory is available for software applications. Therefore, you successfully increased conventional memory by approximately 10 percent. If you use additional device drivers and TSRs on your computer system, you can load them into upper memory and show even more impressive gains in available conventional memory by using these techniques for reconfiguring memory.

USING A SMARTDRIVE DISK CACHE

Although these new techniques for reconfiguring memory will improve the performance of a computer system, the computers illustrated in these examples are using only the first 64K of the 3MB of extended memory. You want to find a good use for this additional memory on your computer system.

One of the best ways to use your extended memory is to create a disk cache in extended memory with the use of SmartDrive. A **disk cache** is an area of memory used to store data read from disk or in the process of being written to disk. Although the BUFFERS command creates a disk cache for DOS, SmartDrive stores and locates data faster than DOS in a disk cache, and SmartDrive also uses extended memory rather than conventional memory for the disk cache. In DOS 5.0, SmartDrive is a device driver loaded from CONFIG.SYS, while in DOS 6.0 or 6.2, SmartDrive is a TSR loaded from AUTOEXEC.BAT. If you use SmartDrive, you can reduce the value for BUFFERS to a minimal value, such as 10 or less.

In DOS 6.0 and 6.2, you use the following general syntax in your AUTOEXEC.BAT file:

SMARTDRV [*drive*] [*memory*]

You can specify one or more drives, and you can specify the size of extended memory used for the disk cache. If you do not specify the amount of memory, SmartDrive uses all of extended memory if your computer has 1MB of extended memory; it uses 1MB of extended memory if your computer has from 1MB to 4MB of extended memory; and it uses 2MB of extended memory if your computer has 4MB or more of extended memory. You do not need to use the LOADHIGH command because DOS 6.0 and 6.2 automatically load SmartDrive into upper memory.

In DOS 5.0, you can load the SMARTDRV.SYS device driver from your CONFIG.SYS file with a DEVICEHIGH command, as follows:

DEVICEHIGH=[*drive name:*][*path*]SMARTDRV.SYS [*memory*]

You must specify the drive name, path, and full filename of SmartDrive. The value for memory can range from 128K to 8,192K. If you do not specify a value, SmartDrive uses 256K.

SmartDrive improves the performance of your computer system by locating data stored in the disk cache and minimizing the number of times that DOS must access a physical disk drive for data.

Specifying SmartDrive in CONFIG.SYS or AUTOEXEC.BAT

Let's specify an option for using SmartDrive and test its effect on memory. First, let's locate where SMARTDRV.EXE or SMARTDRV.SYS is stored on your hard disk. You can also change the value of the BUFFERS command at the same time.

To locate SmartDrive:

1. Check the DOS prompt and be sure the current drive is drive A. You do not want to inadvertently edit CONFIG.SYS or AUTOEXEC.BAT on your hard disk.

6.0 6.2

2. If you are using DOS 6.0 or 6.2, type **DIR C:\SMARTDRV.EXE /S** and press **[Enter]**. DOS checks all the directories on drive C with the Subdirectory switch (/S) for the location of SMARTDRV.EXE. More than likely, it will be in the DOS subdirectory, the root directory, or the Windows subdirectory. If you locate a copy of SMARTDRV.EXE in the Windows subdirectory *and* one in the DOS subdirectory or root directory, use the one in the DOS subdirectory or root directory. Both DOS and Windows come with a copy of SMARTDRV.EXE.

5.0

If you are using DOS 5.0, type **DIR C:\SMARTDRV.SYS /S** and press **[Enter]**. DOS checks all the directories on drive C with the Subdirectory switch (/S) for the location of SMARTDRV.SYS. More than likely, it will be in the DOS subdirectory, the root directory, or the Windows subdirectory. If you locate a copy of SMARTDRV.SYS in the Windows subdirectory *and* one in the DOS subdirectory or root directory, use the one in the DOS subdirectory or root directory. Both DOS and Windows come with a copy of SMARTDRV.SYS.

Now change the BUFFERS command in CONFIG.SYS.

3. Type **EDIT CONFIG.SYS** and press **[Enter]**. DOS loads the MS-DOS Editor, which loads CONFIG.SYS.

4. Position the cursor on the value for the BUFFERS command. Then press **[Ins]** (Insert) to access typeover or overtype mode, and type **1** to replace the 4 in 40. The command should read BUFFERS=10.

5. Press **[Ins]** (Insert) to return to insert mode.

If you are using DOS 5.0, you can add a DEVICEHIGH command to install SmartDrive from CONFIG.SYS. If you are using DOS 6.0 or 6.2, skip the next set of steps and proceed with the instructions for saving your changes to CONFIG.SYS.

5.0

To add SmartDrive to CONFIG.SYS _for DOS 5.0 users only_:

1. Position the cursor on the line with the DEVICEHIGH command that installs ANSI.SYS. Then press **[Ctrl][N]** to insert a blank line.

2. Type **DEVICEHIGH=C:\DOS\SMARTDRV.SYS** but do not press **[Enter]**. If SMARTDRV.SYS is stored in another directory on drive C (such as the root directory), use that directory's name in the path.

Now you can save your changes to CONFIG.SYS. If you are using DOS 5.0, you have completed all the changes you need to make before saving. If you are using DOS 6.0 or 6.2, you will need to edit AUTOEXEC.BAT.

To save the changes to CONFIG.SYS:

6.0 6.2

5.0

1. If you are using DOS 6.0 or 6.2, press **[Alt]** (Menu) to access the menu bar, press **[Enter]** for the File menu, and type **S** for the Save command.

   If you are using the mouse, click **File**, then click **Save**.

   If you are using DOS 5.0, press **[Alt]** (Menu) to access the menu bar, press **[Enter]** for the File menu, and type **X** for the Exit command.

   If you are using the mouse, click **File**, then click **Exit**.

   The MS-DOS Editor displays a dialog box that prompts you about saving the changes. Press **[Enter]** to select Yes.

   If you are using the mouse, click **Yes**.

   The MS-DOS Editor saves your changes, you exit the MS-DOS Editor, and DOS displays the DOS prompt.

If you are using DOS 5.0, skip the next set of steps and proceed to the section entitled, "Testing the Use of SmartDrive." If you are using DOS 6.0 or 6.2, continue with the next set of steps.

To specify SmartDrive for AUTOEXEC.BAT _for DOS 6.0 and 6.2 users only_:

1. Press **[Alt]** (Menu) to access the menu bar, press **[Enter]** for the File menu, and type **O** for the Open command.

   If you are using the mouse, click **File**, then click **Open**.

   The MS-DOS Editor displays the Open dialog box.

2. Type **AUTOEXEC.BAT** and press **[Enter]**. The MS-DOS Editor retrieves this file. If the MS-DOS Editor prompts you about saving changes to CONFIG.SYS, press **[Enter]** for Yes, or click **Yes**.

3. Position the cursor at the beginning of the line with the title "Configure Printer Port." Then press **[Ctrl][N]** to insert a blank line.

4. Type **REM**, press **[Tab]**, type **Create Disk Cache**, and press **[Enter]**. Then type **REM** and press **[Enter]**.

5. Press **[Tab]**, type **SMARTDRV A** and press **[Enter]**. The "A" instructs SMARTDRV to enable disk caching for drive A. You do not need to specify its full name and path because DOS can locate this information by examining the DOS path specified with the PATH command.

6. Press **[Alt]** (Menu) to access the menu bar, press **[Enter]** for the File menu, and type **X** for the Exit command.

   If you are using the mouse, click **File**, then click **Exit**.

   The MS-DOS Editor displays a dialog box that prompts you about saving the changes. Press **[Enter]** to select Yes or, if you are using the mouse, click **Yes**. The MS-DOS Editor saves your changes, you exit the MS-DOS Editor, and DOS displays the DOS prompt.

Testing the Use of SmartDrive

Regardless of whether you are using DOS 5.0, 6.0, or 6.2, you must reboot your computer system to create this disk cache in extended memory.

To boot your computer system:

1. Press **[Ctrl][Alt][Del]**, or press the **Reset button** on your computer system.

   6.0 6.2 If you are using DOS 6.0 or 6.2, select DOS-Prompt when DOS displays the Startup menu, and press **[Enter]**. DOS displays the DOS prompt.

   5.0 If you are using DOS 5.0, DOS executes the commands in CONFIG.SYS, displays information on the installation of SmartDrive, executes the commands in AUTOEXEC.BAT, and displays the DOS prompt.

2. *6.0 6.2* If you are using DOS 6.0 or 6.2, type **MEM /C /P** and press **[Enter]**. MEM displays the first part of a memory usage report. See Figure 11-18.

   5.0 If you are using DOS 5.0, type **MEM /C | MORE** and press [Enter]. MEM displays the first part of a memory usage report. See Figure 11-19a.

   The memory usage reports for DOS 6.0 and 6.2 in Figure 11-18 and that for DOS 5.0 in Figure 11-19a show that the SMARTDRV module is loaded in the upper memory area.

disk cache and DOS
in extended memory

SmartDrive

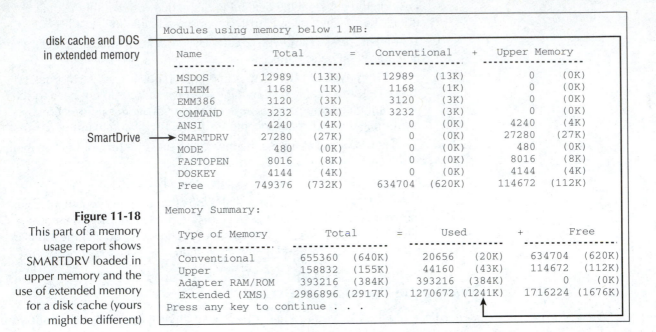

```
Modules using memory below 1 MB:

    Name          Total      =    Conventional   +    Upper Memory
    ----------    ----------      ----------------      ----------------
    MSDOS         12989   (13K)     12989   (13K)          0    (0K)
    HIMEM          1168    (1K)      1168    (1K)          0    (0K)
    EMM386         3120    (3K)      3120    (3K)          0    (0K)
    COMMAND        3232    (3K)      3232    (3K)          0    (0K)
    ANSI           4240    (4K)         0    (0K)       4240    (4K)
    SMARTDRV      27280   (27K)         0    (0K)      27280   (27K)
    MODE            480    (0K)         0    (0K)        480    (0K)
    FASTOPEN       8016    (8K)         0    (0K)       8016    (8K)
    DOSKEY         4144    (4K)         0    (0K)       4144    (4K)
    Free         749376  (732K)    634704  (620K)     114672  (112K)

Memory Summary:

    Type of Memory       Total       =       Used       +        Free
    ----------------    ----------         ----------          ----------
    Conventional        655360  (640K)      20656   (20K)      634704  (620K)
    Upper               158832  (155K)      44160   (43K)      114672  (112K)
    Adapter RAM/ROM     393216  (384K)     393216  (384K)           0    (0K)
    Extended (XMS)     2986896 (2917K)    1270672 (1241K)     1716224 (1676K)
Press any key to continue . . .
```

Figure 11-18
This part of a memory
usage report shows
SMARTDRV loaded in
upper memory and the
use of extended memory
for a disk cache (yours
might be different)

SmartDrive

```
Conventional Memory :

    Name              Size in Decimal          Size in Hex
    ----------        ----------------          ----------------
    MSDOS             13568   ( 13.3K)            3500
    HIMEM              1184   (  1.2K)             4A0
    EMM386             8400   (  8.2K)            20D0
    COMMAND            3392   (  3.3K)             D40
    FREE                 64   (  0.1K)              40
    FREE             628544   (613.8K)           99740

Total   FREE :       628608   (613.9K)

Upper Memory :

    Name              Size in Decimal          Size in Hex
    ----------        ----------------          ----------------
    SYSTEM           163840   (160.0K)           28000
    SMARTDRV          24336   ( 23.8K)            5F10
    ANSI               4192   (  4.1K)            1060
    MODE                464   (  0.5K)             1D0
    FASTOPEN           8000   (  7.8K)            1F40
    DOSKEY             4128   (  4.0K)            1020
Press any key to continue . . .
```

Figure 11-19a
The first part of a
memory usage report for
DOS 5.0 showing
SMARTDRV loaded in
upper memory (yours
might be different)

_**5.0**_

3. If necessary, press **[Spacebar]** or any other key to continue.

    The latter part of the DOS 5.0 memory usage report (Figure 11-19b) shows that part of extended memory on the computer system used for this figure is now set aside for the disk cache created by SmartDrive. Your memory usage report might be different.

```
  FREE                 112     (  0.1K)          70
  FREE                 128     (  0.1K)          80
  FREE               56784     ( 55.5K)        DDD0

Total  FREE :         57024    ( 55.7K)

Total bytes available to programs (Conventional+Upper): 685632 (669.6K)
Largest executable program size :                       628416 (613.7K)
Largest available upper memory block :                   56784 ( 55.5K)

   3145728 bytes total contiguous extended memory
         0 bytes available contiguous extended memory
   2632704 bytes available XMS memory
           MS DOS resident in High Memory Area

A:\>
```

difference represents disk cache and DOS in extended memory

Figure 11-19b
The latter part of a memory usage report for DOS 5.0 showing the use of extended memory for a disk cache (yours might be different)

Later, when you adapt SmartDrive for use with your hard disk, you will notice that the drive light flashes on less frequently as SmartDrive locates the data you need in its disk cache in extended memory.

OPTIMIZING MEMORY WITH MEMMAKER

The CONFIG.SYS and AUTOEXEC.BAT files on your hard disk are similar to the ones that you are testing on the boot disk in drive A. You want to modify these files on your hard disk and optimize the use of memory in your computer system.

DOS 6.0 and 6.2 contain a utility called MemMaker that automatically optimizes memory on a computer system. MemMaker examines your existing system startup files—CONFIG.SYS and AUTOEXEC.BAT—and determines the optimum configuration by moving device drivers and memory-resident programs (TSRs) to the upper memory area. In order to use MemMaker, you must have DOS 6.0 or 6.2 and a computer system with an 80386 or 80486 microprocessor and extended memory. If you use multiple startup configurations in CONFIG.SYS, you must create a separate set of CONFIG.SYS and AUTOEXEC.BAT files for each configuration on your startup menu, test each configuration with MemMaker, and combine the optimized files into one set of startup configuration files.

Because MemMaker reconfigures your system based on the contents of your hard disk and the amount of memory you have, you decide to test MemMaker using sample system startup files on your hard disk. First, you will rename CONFIG.SYS and AUTOEXEC.BAT files so that they are unaffected by MemMaker. Next, you will write-protect these renamed files so that you do not inadvertently delete or change them. Finally, you will create new CONFIG.SYS and AUTOEXEC.BAT files for use with MemMaker. *If you are working in a computer lab, ask your instructor or technical support person for permission to make changes to these files on the hard disk. Do not modify the configuration of your computer system without permission. After you complete this tutorial, you must restore the original CONFIG.SYS and AUTOEXEC.BAT files to the hard disk.*

5.0

If you are using DOS 5.0, you will not be able to complete the steps in the sections that involve optimizing memory with MemMaker, because DOS 5.0 does not contain this utility. If you are using DOS 5.0, you can skip the remainder of this section and continue with the section entitled "Printing Copies of Your Documentation."

If you are using a computer with an 80286, 8088, or 8086 microprocessor, you also will not be able to complete the remainder of this section. If this is the case, skip to the section entitled "Printing Copies of Your Documentation."

Let's start by protecting your current system startup files.

6.0 6.2   **To rename and write-protect CONFIG.SYS and AUTOEXEC.BAT** *using DOS 6.0 or 6.2:*

1. Change to drive C. If necessary, change to the root directory.
2. Type **ATTRIB CONFIG.SYS** and press **[Enter]**. DOS displays the attributes assigned to this file. If this file is write-protected, type **ATTRIB -R CONFIG.SYS** and press **[Enter]**. If this file is assigned the hidden attribute, type **ATTRIB -H CONFIG.SYS** and press **[Enter]**.
3. Type **REN CONFIG.SYS CF.SYS** and press **[Enter]**. Then type **ATTRIB +R CF.SYS** and press **[Enter]**. You have now renamed and write-protected your original CONFIG.SYS file.
4. Type **ATTRIB AUTOEXEC.BAT** and press **[Enter]**. DOS displays the attributes assigned to this file. If this file is write-protected, type **ATTRIB -R AUTOEXEC.BAT** and press **[Enter]**. If this file is assigned the hidden attribute, type **ATTRIB -H AUTOEXEC.BAT** and press **[Enter]**.
5. Type **REN AUTOEXEC.BAT AE.BAT** and press **[Enter]**. Then type **ATTRIB +R AE.BAT** and press **[Enter]**. You have now renamed and write-protected your original AUTOEXEC.BAT file.

Creating New System Startup Files

You are now ready to create a new CONFIG.SYS and AUTOEXEC.BAT file to test with MemMaker.

6.0 6.2   **To create new system startup files** *using DOS 6.0 or 6.2:*

1. Use the MS-DOS Editor to create the CONFIG.SYS file shown in Figure 11-20. *When you specify the location of memory managers and device drivers, be sure you are using the correct directories on your hard disk.*

```
rem     ************************************************
rem
rem                 Auto-Configure File
rem
rem     ************************************************

rem     Install Memory Managers
rem
        device=c:\dos\himem.sys
        device=c:\dos\emm386.exe noems

rem     Load DOS High & Access UMBs
rem
        dos=high,umb

rem     Set Disk Buffers & Files
rem
        buffers=30
        files=40

rem     Specify Size of DOS Environment
rem
        shell=c:\command.com c:\ /e:512 /p

rem     Install Device Drivers
rem
        device=c:\dos\ansi.sys
```

Figure 11-20
The CONFIG.SYS
file that you will use
with MemMaker

2. Save this CONFIG.SYS file to your hard disk.

3. Create the AUTOEXEC.BAT file shown in Figure 11-21. *When you specify the location of utilities and TSRs, be sure you are using the correct directories on your hard disk.*

```
        @echo off
        cls

rem     ************************************************
rem
rem                 Auto-Execute File
rem
rem     ************************************************

rem     Set Path & Prompt
rem
        path c:\;c:\dos
        prompt $p$g

rem     Specify Environment Variables
rem
        set dircmd=/o /p

rem     Create Disk Cache
rem
        smartdrv c

rem     Load TSRs
rem
        fastopen c:=100
        doskey
```

Figure 11-21
The AUTOEXEC.BAT
file that you will use
with MemMaker

4. Save this AUTOEXEC.BAT file to your hard disk.

Testing the New System Startup Files

You are ready to test these system startup files. First, however, you *must* remove the boot disk in drive A.

6.0 6.2   **To boot your computer system:**

1. *Remove the boot disk from drive A.*
2. Press **[Ctrl][Alt][Del]**, or press the **Reset button** on your computer system. Wait until you see the DOS prompt for drive C. If DOS reports any errors, such as an error for a line in CONFIG.SYS, or reports that it is unable to locate or install a device driver or TSR, check your CONFIG.SYS and AUTOEXEC.BAT files, correct any errors, and repeat these two steps.

Preparing a Memory Usage Report

Before you use MemMaker, you want to create a copy of a memory usage report. After MemMaker reconfigures your system, you can compare the new configuration with the current configuration. You already have a REPORTS directory on your boot disk, so you can store this report in that directory.

6.0 6.2   **To create a memory usage report:**

1. After DOS displays the prompt for drive C, insert the boot disk into drive A.
2. Type **MEM /C > A:\REPORTS\REPORT2** and press **[Enter]**.

Optimizing Your System with MemMaker

You are now ready to use MemMaker. After you start MemMaker, it will display a series of screens with information and options so that you can follow the status of its progress. Before you load MemMaker, be sure you do not have your boot disk in drive A. MemMaker will boot and reconfigure system startup files on drive C.

6.0 6.2   **To optimize your system with MemMaker** *using DOS 6.0 or 6.2:*

1. *Remove your boot disk from drive A.*
2. After removing your boot disk from drive A, type **MEMMAKER** and press **[Enter]**. MemMaker displays a Welcome screen, which explains what MemMaker does and how to use it. See Figure 11-22. At this screen, you have the option to continue or exit. If you wanted to change the default option, Continue, so that you can exit, you would press [Spacebar]. You can access Help at any time by pressing [F1], and you can exit by pressing [F3].

```
Microsoft MemMaker

Welcome to MemMaker.

MemMaker optimizes your system's memory by moving memory-resident
programs and device drivers into the upper memory area. This
frees conventional memory for use by applications.

After you run MemMaker, your computer's memory will remain
optimized until you add or remove memory-resident programs or
device drivers. For an optimum memory configuration, run MemMaker
again after making any such changes.

MemMaker displays options as highlighted text. (For example, you
can change the "Continue" option below.) To cycle through the
available options, press SPACEBAR. When MemMaker displays the
option you want, press ENTER.

For help while you are running MemMaker, press F1.

                Continue or Exit? Continue

ENTER=Accept Selection  SPACEBAR=Change Selection  F1=Help  F3=Exit
```

Figure 11-22
The MemMaker
Welcome screen

3. Press **[Enter]** to continue. MemMaker displays another screen that describes the two ways in which you can run MemMaker. See Figure 11-23. If you select the default option, Express Setup, MemMaker automatically optimizes memory for you. If you select Custom Setup, you can specify details of the optimization process, but you must know enough of the technical specifications of your computer system and your software applications to use this option. In most cases, you will use Express Setup, because MemMaker is designed to optimize memory automatically.

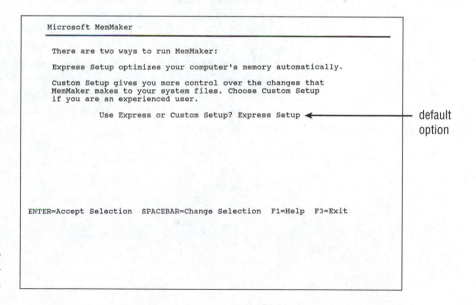

```
Microsoft MemMaker

There are two ways to run MemMaker:

Express Setup optimizes your computer's memory automatically.

Custom Setup gives you more control over the changes that
MemMaker makes to your system files. Choose Custom Setup
if you are an experienced user.

        Use Express or Custom Setup? Express Setup ◄────── default
                                                          option




ENTER=Accept Selection  SPACEBAR=Change Selection  F1=Help  F3=Exit
```

Figure 11-23
Options for MemMaker
Express Setup or
Custom Setup

4. Press **[Enter]** to select Express Setup. MemMaker displays a screen on the use of expanded memory. See Figure 11-24. If you intended to use expanded memory, you would specify it at this point. The default option in DOS 6.0, "No," assumes you do not want to use expanded memory or that you do not know whether any program you use requires it. The default option in DOS 6.2 is "Yes." If you are using DOS 6.2, press **[Spacebar]** to change "Yes" to "No."

6.0

6.2

```
Microsoft MemMaker
_____

    If you use any programs that require expanded memory (EMS), answer
    Yes to the following question.  Answering Yes makes expanded memory
    available, but might not free as much conventional memory.

    If none of your programs need expanded memory, answer No to the
    following question.  Answering No makes expanded memory unavailable,
    but can free more conventional memory.

    If you are not sure whether your programs require expanded memory,
    answer No.  If you later discover that a program needs expanded
    memory, run MemMaker again and answer Yes to this question.

    Do you use any programs that need expanded memory (EMS)? No




ENTER=Accept Selection   SPACEBAR=Change Selection   F1=Help   F3=Exit
```

Figure 11-24
MemMaker asks about the use of expanded memory

5. Press **[Enter]** to accept "No." MemMaker briefly displays a screen that informs you it is checking your hard disk for Windows. See Figure 11-25. If Windows is installed on your hard disk, MemMaker takes this factor into account when reconfiguring your system. MemMaker next displays a screen that informs you it will restart your computer system once you press **[Enter]**. See Figure 11-26. It also informs you what to do in case of problems. If your computer system does not work properly after this step, you would turn it off and then on. MemMaker will automatically recover your original system files.

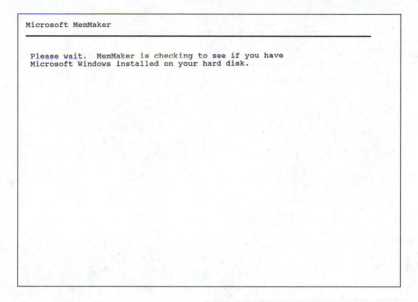

```
Microsoft MemMaker


    Please wait.  MemMaker is checking to see if you have
    Microsoft Windows installed on your hard disk.
```

Figure 11-25
MemMaker checks for
Windows on hard disk

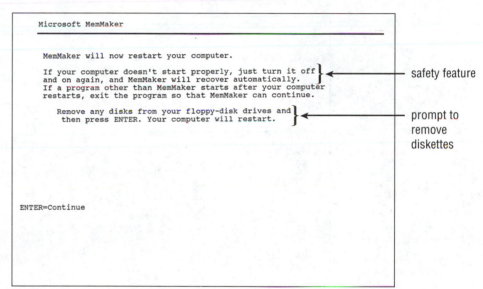

```
Microsoft MemMaker


    MemMaker will now restart your computer.

    If your computer doesn't start properly, just turn it off
    and on again, and MemMaker will recover automatically.
    If a program other than MemMaker starts after your computer
    restarts, exit the program so that MemMaker can continue.

      Remove any disks from your floppy-disk drives and
        then press ENTER. Your computer will restart.




ENTER=Continue
```

safety feature

prompt to
remove
diskettes

Figure 11-26
MemMaker is ready
to reboot computer

6. Press **[Enter]** to continue. After your system reboots, MemMaker briefly
    displays a screen that informs you of the number of memory configurations
    possible for your computer system. See Figure 11-27. After its calculations
    are complete, it displays another screen that informs you that it has selected
    the optimum memory configuration. See Figure 11-28. It then updates your
    system startup files. Next, it displays a screen that informs you that it will
    restart your computer system with the new configuration. See Figure 11-29.
    It also warns you to pay attention to any unusual messages that DOS might
    display or any problems that might occur.

```
Microsoft MemMaker
─────────────────────────────────────────────────────────

Please wait.  MemMaker is determining the optimum memory
configuration for your computer and has considered
        1 configuration(s).

Calculations Complete.
```

Figure 11-27
MemMaker determines
the number of optimum
memory configurations

```
Microsoft MemMaker
─────────────────────────────────────────────────────────

 MemMaker has determined the optimum memory configuration
 for your computer and is now updating your system startup files.
```

Figure 11-28
MemMaker updates
system files for new
memory configuration

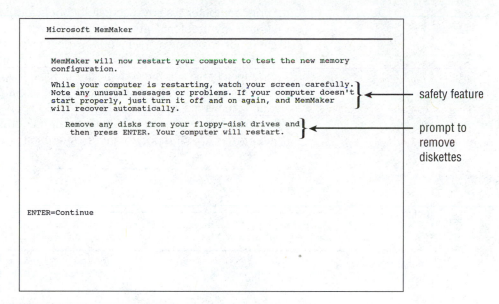

safety feature

prompt to
remove
diskettes

Figure 11-29
MemMaker is ready to test
the new configuration

7. If necessary, remove any diskettes from your diskette drives. Then press
[Enter] to continue. MemMaker reboots your computer system.
MemMaker displays a screen that asks you whether your computer
system is operating properly. See Figure 11-30.

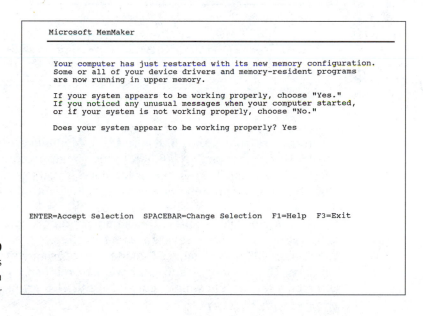

Figure 11-30
MemMaker asks
about the operation
of your computer

8. If your computer system successfully boots and appears to be operating without any problems, press **[Enter]** to select Yes. If your computer system is not operating as you would expect, press **[Spacebar]** to change Yes to No and press **[Enter]**. If you select "No," MemMaker will allow you to undo the changes to the system startup files. If you select "Yes," MemMaker displays a summary table that explains the changes made to your system's memory usage. Figure 11-31 shows a sample report produced by MemMaker in DOS 6.0 after it reconfigured memory on a computer system. Your report might be different.

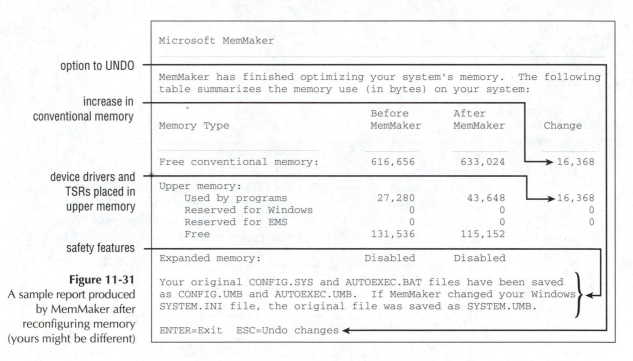

option to UNDO

increase in conventional memory

device drivers and TSRs placed in upper memory

safety features

Figure 11-31
A sample report produced by MemMaker after reconfiguring memory (yours might be different)

```
Microsoft MemMaker


MemMaker has finished optimizing your system's memory.  The following
table summarizes the memory use (in bytes) on your system:

                                 Before         After
Memory Type                      MemMaker       MemMaker      Change


Free conventional memory:        616,656        633,024       16,368

Upper memory:
    Used by programs              27,280         43,648       16,368
    Reserved for Windows               0              0            0
    Reserved for EMS                   0              0            0
    Free                         131,536        115,152

Expanded memory:                 Disabled       Disabled

Your original CONFIG.SYS and AUTOEXEC.BAT files have been saved
as CONFIG.UMB and AUTOEXEC.UMB.  If MemMaker changed your Windows
SYSTEM.INI file, the original file was saved as SYSTEM.UMB.

ENTER=Exit   ESC=Undo changes
```

In the example shown in Figure 11-31, MemMaker increased the amount of conventional memory by 16,368 bytes (or approximately 16K) by moving device drivers and TSRs to upper memory. If you use more device drivers and TSRs on your computer system, you might gain substantially more conventional memory.

After MemMaker displays this summary report, you can exit and retain the changes made to your system startup files, or you can press [Esc] and MemMaker will undo changes it made by restoring your original system files. If you save these changes and later want to restore your original system files, you can enter the following command at the DOS prompt:

MEMMAKER /UNDO

MemMaker then automatically restores your original CONFIG.SYS and AUTOEXEC.BAT files.

You want to save the changes made by MemMaker and create a copy of a memory usage report. Then you want to copy the modified CONFIG.SYS and AUTOEXEC.BAT files to the REPORTS subdirectory on the boot disk in drive A for future reference.

6.0 6.2 **To save your changes:**

1. Press **[Enter]**. DOS displays the DOS prompt.

Now create a memory usage report.

2. Insert your boot disk into drive A, and be sure the current drive is drive C.

3. Type **MEM /C > A:\REPORTS\REPORT3** and press **[Enter]**.

Now copy the system startup files.

4. Type **COPY CONFIG.SYS A:\REPORTS\CONFIG.SYS** and press **[Enter]**.

5. Type **COPY AUTOEXEC.BAT A:\REPORTS\AUTOEXEC.BAT** and press **[Enter]**.

Restoring the Original System Startup Files

You can now delete these files from drive C and restore the original CONFIG.SYS and AUTOEXEC.BAT files.

6.0 6.2 **To restore your hard disk to its original state:**

1. Type **DEL CONFIG.SYS** and press **[Enter]**.

2. Type **DEL AUTOEXEC.BAT** and press **[Enter]**.

3. Type **ATTRIB -R CF.SYS** and press **[Enter]**. DOS removes the Read-Only attribute assigned to this file.

4. Type **REN CF.SYS CONFIG.SYS** and press **[Enter]**. You now have your original CONFIG.SYS file.

5. Type **ATTRIB -R AE.BAT** and press **[Enter]**. DOS removes the Read-Only attribute assigned to this file.

6. Type **REN AE.BAT AUTOEXEC.BAT** and press **[Enter]**. You now have your original AUTOEXEC.BAT file.

7. If necessary, assign any attributes, such as Read-Only and Hidden, to these files. If you do not remember which, if any, to assign, ask your instructor or technical support person for assistance.

PRINTING COPIES OF YOUR DOCU- MENTATION

You want to print copies of your memory usage reports and the contents of the CONFIG.SYS and AUTOEXEC.BAT files modified by MemMaker. You can use this documentation later to update the configuration on your hard disk drive.

You must reboot your computer system from drive C so that you can print using the settings on your system.

5.0 6.0 6.2 **To reset your system:**

1. Remove your boot disk from drive A.

2. Press **[Ctrl][Alt][Del]** or press the **Reset button**.

Next print copies of your configuration files and memory reports.

3. Insert your boot disk into drive A, and change to drive A.

4. Type **CD REPORTS** and press **[Enter]**.

5. Type **PRINT CONFIG.SYS AUTOEXEC.BAT** and press **[Enter]**. If prompted for the list device, press **[Enter]** to accept the default printer port and enter the name of your printer port. DOS prints a copy of the CONFIG.SYS and AUTOEXEC.BAT files.

6.0 6.2

6. If you are using DOS 6.0 or 6.2, type **PRINT REPORT1 REPORT2 REPORT3** and press **[Enter]**. DOS prints copies of the three reports you produced. REPORT1 contains a report showing memory usage before you made any changes to CONFIG.SYS and AUTOEXEC.BAT. REPORT2 contains a report showing memory usage before you used MemMaker, and REPORT3 contains a report showing memory usage after MemMaker optimized memory.

5.0

If you are using DOS 5.0, type **PRINT REPORT1** and press **[Enter]**. DOS prints a copy of REPORT1, which contains a memory usage report before you made any changes to CONFIG.SYS or AUTOEXEC.BAT.

7. Remove your printed copies of these files from the printer.

◆

SUMMARY

In this tutorial, you examined the types of memory used in a computer system and their classifications. You used the MEM command to produce memory usage reports that showed the use of conventional, upper, and extended memory. You also used the Classify switch with this command to produce a detailed report showing the location of programs in conventional and upper memory.

You modified your CONFIG.SYS file and installed the memory managers HIMEM.SYS and EMM386.EXE to manage extended and upper memory. You used the DOS command to load DOS and its buffers into the high memory area and to access the upper memory blocks created by EMM386.EXE. You used the DEVICEHIGH command to load device drivers into upper memory from CONFIG.SYS. You also used the LOADHIGH command in AUTOEXEC.BAT to load TSRs into upper memory. You then created a disk cache in extended memory with SmartDrive.

If you are a DOS 6.0 or 6.2 user, you optimized memory on your hard disk with MemMaker and you documented the results of changes to CONFIG.SYS and AUTOEXEC.BAT by MemMaker.

Command Reference	
CONFIG.SYS Commands	
DEVICEHIGH	Loads device drivers into the upper memory area if space is available
DOS=HIGH,UMB	Loads DOS and its buffers into the high memory area, and allows DOS access to upper memory blocks
Device Drivers	
SMARTDRV.SYS [*memory*]	*DOS 5.0:* Creates a disk cache in extended memory
Memory Managers	
DOS	Manages the use of conventional memory
EMM386.EXE NOEMS EMM386.EXE RAM [*memory*]	A device driver that creates upper memory blocks in upper memory and that converts extended memory to expanded memory
HIMEM.SYS	A device driver that manages the use of extended memory, the high memory area, and upper memory
DOS Commands	
LOADHIGH LH	Loads memory-resident programs (or TSRs) into upper memory if space is available
MEM	Displays a memory usage report on conventional, upper, adapter, and extended memory
MEM /C	Displays a memory usage report that shows program modules in conventional and upper memory
MEM /P	*DOS 6.0 and 6.2:* Displays a memory usage report and pauses after each screen

MEMMAKER	DOS 6.0 and 6.2: Optimizes memory by moving device drivers and TSRs into upper memory and by reconfiguring CONFIG.SYS and AUTOEXEC.BAT
MEMMAKER /UNDO	DOS 6.0 and 6.2: Restores the original CONFIG.SYS and AUTOEXEC.BAT files
SMARTDRV [drive] [memory]	DOS 6.0 and 6.2: Creates a disk cache in extended memory

QUESTIONS

1. Describe the two basic types of memory and their purpose in a computer system.
2. Name the five types of RAM.
3. What is conventional memory?
4. What is a memory manager?
5. What is the memory manager for conventional memory? What types of programs and data does this memory manager manage?
6. What is upper memory?
7. How can DOS use upper memory?
8. What is extended memory?
9. What is high memory?
10. How can DOS use high memory?
11. What is expanded memory?
12. How does DOS access data in expanded memory?
13. What is a page frame? a page?
14. What is the role of HIMEM.SYS in managing memory?
15. What command can you use to examine the contents of memory? Name two switches you can use with this command and describe their purpose.
16. How do you load DOS high?
17. What is the role of EMM386.EXE in managing memory?
18. How do the NOEMS and RAM switches affect how EMM386.EXE manages memory?
19. How do you grant DOS access to upper memory blocks?
20. How do you load device drivers into upper memory?
21. How do you load TSRs into upper memory?
22. Where must you load HIMEM.SYS and EMM386.EXE?
23. What is SmartDrive, and how does it improve the performance of your computer system?

24. What version of DOS do you use, and how do you load SmartDrive in that version?
25. What is MemMaker, and how does it help you manage memory?
26. What types of RAM are available on the 80286 computer system?
27. What types of RAM are available on the 80386 and 80486 computer systems?
28. How does the SmartDrive disk cache compare with that produced by BUFFERS and used by DOS?
29. What is the advantage of loading device drivers and TSRs into upper memory and loading DOS and its buffers into high memory?
30. After you make changes to CONFIG.SYS and AUTOEXEC.BAT, what must you do to install those changes on your computer system?

TUTORIAL ASSIGNMENTS

1. **Testing the Importance of Memory Managers**: Make a duplicate copy of the boot disk used in this tutorial. Then perform the following operations on that new copy of the boot disk:

   6.0 6.2
   a. Boot your computer system with this new boot disk in drive A, and if you are using DOS 6.0 or 6.2, select the DOS Prompt option from the Startup menu.
   b. Redirect a copy of a memory usage report to a disk file as follows:

      MEM/C>REPORTS\MEMRPT1B.TXT

   c. Remove the "Install Memory Managers" block and the commands that load HIMEM.SYS and EMM386.EXE from CONFIG.SYS, and save this change.

   6.0 6.2
   d. Boot your computer system again from drive A, and if you are using DOS 6.0 or 6.2, select the DOS Prompt option from the Startup menu.
   e. Redirect a copy of a memory usage report to a disk file as follows:

      MEM/C>REPORTS\MEMRPT1E.TXT

   f. Remove the boot disk from drive A and reboot your computer system from drive C to reinstate your system's settings.
   g. Insert your boot disk in drive A, change to the REPORTS directory on drive A, and print a copy of MEMRPT1B.TXT and MEMRPT1E.TXT. Then compare the two memory usage reports.

   Answer the following questions:

   h. Did DOS load SmartDrive? If not, why not?
   i. DOS executed the DEVICEHIGH commands in CONFIG.SYS and the LOADHIGH commands in AUTOEXEC.BAT. However, where did DOS load the device drivers and TSRs after you removed the memory managers from CONFIG.SYS?
   j. Is any of extended memory allotted for loading DOS into the high memory area? Where is DOS loaded?

2. **Creating Expanded Memory from Extended Memory**: Make a duplicate copy of the boot disk used in this tutorial. Then perform the following operations on an 80386 or 80486 computer system with extended memory:

   6.0 6.2
   a. Boot your computer system with this new boot disk in drive A, and if you are using DOS 6.0 or 6.2, select the DOS-Prompt option from the Startup menu.

b. Redirect a copy of CONFIG.SYS to a disk file as follows:

TYPE CONFIG.SYS>REPORTS\CFSYS2B.TXT

c. Redirect a copy of a memory usage report to a disk file as follows:

MEM/C>REPORTS\MEMRPT2C.TXT

d. Use MEM/C to determine the amount of unused extended memory in your computer. Modify the DEVICE command for EMM386.EXE in CONFIG.SYS so that EMM386.EXE converts one-half of the available or free extended memory to expanded memory.

_**6.0 6.2**_

e. Reboot your computer system from the boot disk in drive A, and if you are using DOS 6.0 or 6.2, select the DOS Prompt option from the Startup menu. DOS may adjust the size of the expanded memory pool during booting.

f. Document any changes to the use of extended memory. Redirect a copy of a memory usage report to a disk file as follows:

MEM/C>REPORTS\MEMRPT2F.TXT

g. Redirect a copy of the revised CONFIG.SYS to a disk file as follows:

TYPE CONFIG.SYS>REPORTS\CFSYS2G.TXT

h. Remove the boot disk from drive A and reboot your computer system from drive C to reinstate your system's settings.

i. Insert your boot disk in drive A, change to the REPORTS directory on drive A, and print a copy of CFSYS2B.TXT, MEMRPT2C.TXT, CFSYS2G.TXT, and MEMRPT2F.TXT.

3. **Examining CONFIG.SYS and AUTOEXEC.BAT on Drive C**: Perform the following operations:

a. Reboot your computer system from its hard disk. _Do not use the boot disk that you used in this tutorial._

b. Print a copy of the CONFIG.SYS and AUTOEXEC.BAT files on your hard disk.

c. Print a detailed memory usage report with the MEM command's Classify switch.

d. Use the MS-DOS Editor to compile a three-part outline that:

   (1) Lists the device drivers loaded from CONFIG.SYS and that identifies where these device drivers are stored in RAM.

   (2) Lists the TSRs loaded from CONFIG.SYS and AUTOEXEC.BAT and that identifies where these TSRs are stored in RAM.

   (3) Lists improvements that you can make to CONFIG.SYS and AUTOEXEC.BAT to improve memory usage on your computer system.

e. Print a copy of the outline that you prepared in the previous step.

4. **Using SmartDrive**: Make a copy of the boot disk used in this tutorial. Then perform the following operations:

_**6.0 6.2**_

a. Boot your computer system with this new boot disk in drive A, and if you are using DOS 6.0 or 6.2, select the DOS-Prompt option from the Startup menu.

b. Find out how much extended memory you have in your computer system. Redirect a copy of a memory usage report to a disk file as follows:

MEM/C>REPORTS\MEMRPT4B.TXT

c. Use MEM/C to determine the amount of unused extended memory in your computer. Modify SmartDrive so that it creates a disk cache that uses all of your extended memory.

d. Reboot your computer system and test your revised CONFIG.SYS or AUTOEXEC.BAT file.

e. Document the existence of the SmartDrive disk cache. Redirect a copy of a memory usage report to a disk file as follows:

MEM/C>REPORTS\MEMRPT4E.TXT

f. Redirect a copy of CONFIG.SYS and AUTOEXEC.BAT to a disk file as follows:

TYPE CONFIG.SYS>REPORTS\CFSYS4F.TXT

TYPE AUTOEXEC.BAT>REPORTS\AEBAT4F.TXT

g. Remove the boot disk from drive A and reboot your computer system from drive C to reinstate your system's settings.

h. Insert your boot disk in drive A, change to the REPORTS directory on drive A, and print a copy of MEMRPT4B.TXT, MEM4RPT4E.TXT, CFSYS4F.TXT, and AEBAT4F.TXT.

_6.0_ _6.2_

5. **Using MemMaker** (*for DOS 6.0 or 6.2 users only*): Use MemMaker to optimize memory and the CONFIG.SYS and AUTOEXEC.BAT files on your computer system's hard disk. *If you are working in a computer lab, ask your instructor or technical support person for permission to make changes to these files on the hard disk. Do not modify the configuration of the computer system without permission. After you complete this tutorial, you must restore the original CONFIG.SYS and AUTOEXEC.BAT files to the hard disk.*

a. Reboot your computer system from its hard disk. *Do not use the boot disk that you used in this tutorial.*

b. Print a copy of the CONFIG.SYS and AUTOEXEC.BAT files on the hard disk.

c. Make duplicate copies of the CONFIG.SYS and AUTOEXEC.BAT files so that you can restore the original files later.

d. Use MemMaker to optimize memory on your system. Assume that you do not need to use expanded memory. After MemMaker produces a report of the changes that it made, use the Print Screen key to print a copy of that report. Then exit MemMaker and save these configuration changes.

e. Print a copy of the modified CONFIG.SYS and AUTOEXEC.BAT files.

f. Use MemMaker's Undo switch to restore the original CONFIG.SYS and AUTOEXEC.BAT files.

g. Compare the restored files to your printed copies of these original files in order to verify the Undo operation. If the files do not match the printed copies, replace CONFIG.SYS and AUTOEXEC.BAT with the duplicate copies of these files.

Answer the following questions:

h. Did MemMaker increase the amount of conventional memory? If so, by how much did memory increase?

i. Examine the printed copies of the CONFIG.SYS and AUTOEXEC.BAT files modified by MemMaker and explain, where possible, how MemMaker increased the amount of conventional memory.

WINDOWS™ 3.1

Tutorials

◆

Exploring Windows 3.1

OBJECTIVES

In this tutorial you will learn to:

- ◆ Start Windows 3.1
- ◆ Use the Windows graphical interface
- ◆ Identify the elements of a window
- ◆ Adjust the Program Manager window
- ◆ Use the Control-menu box
- ◆ Select menus from the menu bar
- ◆ Obtain help information
- ◆ Open the Main Group
- ◆ Examine applications in the Main Group
- ◆ Set the date and time
- ◆ Use the MS-DOS Prompt icon
- ◆ Move a window and change its size
- ◆ Tile and cascade windows
- ◆ Exit Windows

At a meeting of your workgroup, your supervisor and coworkers discuss the possibility of using Windows on each of the computer systems in the office. Most of your coworkers agree that Windows provides a friendlier and more visual interface than the DOS prompt and the DOS Shell. Several coworkers also emphasize that Windows contains a variety of applications for customizing, managing, and using your computer system and its resources, including files, disks, and software applications. Your supervisor notes that you can switch between applications easily as you work. Everyone agrees that the next logical step is to install Windows on each computer system and to become familiar with the basics of using the program.

◆

THE WINDOWS 3.1 GRAPHICAL USER INTERFACE

When you work from the DOS prompt, you are using a command-line interface that requires you to know how to enter and execute commands. The only real information that this interface provides is the name of the current drive and directory.

In contrast, the DOS Shell, as you have learned, uses a **graphical user interface** (GUI) that provides a more visual and supportive working environment than DOS. For example, you can view the directory tree for a disk drive, and you can easily select a directory and view its files. You can select commands from menus that clearly identify your options, and you can use the mouse to point and select commands and objects on the screen. Many DOS operations, such as renaming, moving, copying, and deleting files, are easier to perform in the DOS Shell than at the DOS prompt.

In contrast to the DOS Shell, Windows 3.1 provides an even richer graphical user interface and many more options for working with drives, directories, applications, and files. You can open more than one application at a time and quickly switch from one application to another. Each application is displayed in its own window so that you can distinguish and work with different applications in different windows. Also, Windows 3.1 includes a variety of additional applications that you will find useful in your daily work.

STARTING WINDOWS

You are ready to examine the basic features of Windows 3.1. The instructions that follow describe how to start Windows 3.1 from the DOS prompt. If your computer setup is different, follow the instructions provided by your instructor or technical support person on how to start Windows.

To start Windows 3.1 from the DOS prompt:

1. Be sure you see the operating system prompt for drive C on your monitor.
2. Type **WIN** and press **[Enter]**. As Windows loads into memory, you see the Windows 3.1 logo. As you work in Windows, you may also see the image of an hourglass when Windows wants you to wait until it has finished performing an operation. If this is the first time you have used Windows, you will next see the Program Manager and Main Group windows. See Figure 12-1. Your initial view might be different from that shown in Figure 12-1; for example, you might see more than one window and different icons.

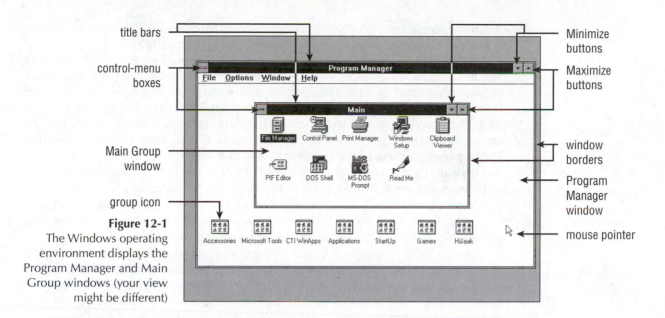

title bars

control-menu boxes

Minimize buttons

Maximize buttons

Main Group window

window borders

Program Manager window

group icon

mouse pointer

Figure 12-1
The Windows operating environment displays the Program Manager and Main Group windows (your view might be different)

THE WINDOWS DESKTOP

You can compare your view of Windows to your desktop on a busy workday. Your desktop contains a variety of tools as well as printed copies of documents. Windows organizes your screen into **windows**, or views, so that you can work with the tools available through Windows. In this sense, you can compare windows on your screen to "in" and "out" boxes as well as desk accessory organizers on your desktop. One of the advantages of using Windows is that you can customize your screen view to meet your needs.

The Program Manager window automatically appears when you load Windows. **Program Manager** is a software application that manages the use of other Windows components. You start other applications from the Program Manager, and use it to organize applications and files into logical groups within Windows for ease of access and use. The Main Group window contains applications specific to Windows. Before you examine these applications, let's look more closely at the organization of a window.

Identifying the Elements of a Window

Each window contains the same basic elements, so that you have a standardized operating environment. Each window contains a **window border**, which appears as a double outline, around the window's contents. Each window has a title that appears on its **title bar**. For example, as you can see in Figure 12-1, the Program Manager title appears on the title bar for the Program Manager window. Each window also contains a set of **icons**, or pictures, that represent software and hardware components that you can use.

The Program Manager window contains a set of icons known as group icons. A **group icon** represents a set of related applications that Windows displays when you select that icon. For example, if you select the Accessories Group icon, Windows displays another window that includes icons for Write, a word-processing program; Paintbrush, a drawing program; Calculator, an on-screen calculator program; Calendar, a calendar and daily appointment book program; Cardfile, a program for organizing addresses and other information, much like a Rolodex; and Clock, an on-screen clock program.

If the Main Group window is open, you will see a variety of icons in this window. Each of the icons in a group window is called a **program-item icon**, and each represents an application for a specific task. When you select one of these program-item icons, Windows opens a window that displays the application. For example, one of the icons in the Main Group window appears as a filing cabinet. This icon is the File Manager icon. **File Manager** is an application for managing the use of drives, directories, and files.

If your copy of DOS 6.0 or 6.2 is installed for use with Windows, you might also see a Microsoft Tools Group in the Program Manager window. If you open the Microsoft Tools Group, you will find an Undelete icon for undeleting files from Windows, a Backup icon for using Microsoft Backup from Windows, and an Anti-Virus icon to check for computer viruses from Windows.

Each window contains a **Control-menu box** in the upper-left corner next to the title bar. This Control-menu box contains a short horizontal bar in a square. If you click the Control-menu box, Windows displays a drop-down Control menu that you can use to adjust windows or to exit the application window. If you double-click the Control-menu box, Windows closes the current application and its window.

Each window also contains a Minimize and Maximize button in the upper-right corner next to the title bar. You can use these buttons to adjust the size of a window. The **Minimize button** appears as a triangle pointing downward, and the **Maximize button** appears as a triangle pointing upward. When you click the Minimize button, Windows reduces the window to an icon and displays the icon at the bottom of the screen. When you click the Maximize button, Windows enlarges the window to fill the entire screen and the Maximize button changes to a **Restore button**, which has one triangle pointing upward and another pointing downward. You use the Restore button to return the window to its original size.

As you work with Windows, you will discover that the mouse is indispensable. Although you can perform most operations in Windows with the keyboard, you will find that the mouse is easier to use than the corresponding key combinations. The **mouse pointer** appears as an arrow in outline; however, its shape may change as you perform specific tasks. *Because it is assumed you will use the mouse rather than the keyboard in these Windows tutorials, the mouse icon you became familiar with in the DOS tutorials does not appear in the text of the two Windows tutorials.*

Now you are ready to explore Windows 3.1. However, you do not want to change any settings until you know more about the use of Windows 3.1. In the steps that follow, you will use a mouse to point and select options.

To get started:

1. If the Main Group window appears in front of the Program Manager window, double-click the **Control-menu box** in the upper-left corner of the Main Group window. The Control-menu box is to the left of the title bar. Windows closes the Main Group window and reduces the window to an icon. See Figure 12-2. If multiple windows are open, you can double-

click each window's Control-menu box until you close all windows *except* the Program Manager window. Your Program Manager window might contain different icons. If you need assistance, ask your instructor or technical support person to adjust your view so that only the Program Manager window is open.

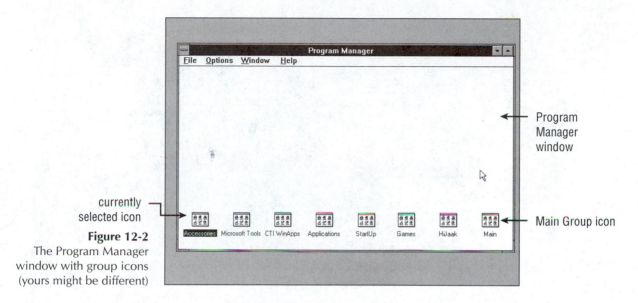

Program Manager window

currently selected icon

Main Group icon

Figure 12-2
The Program Manager window with group icons (yours might be different)

Now adjust the size of the Program Manager window.

2. Click the **Minimize button**. The Minimize button is located to the immediate right of the title bar and contains a triangle that points downward. Windows converts the Program Manager window to an icon that appears at the bottom of the screen. See Figure 12-3.

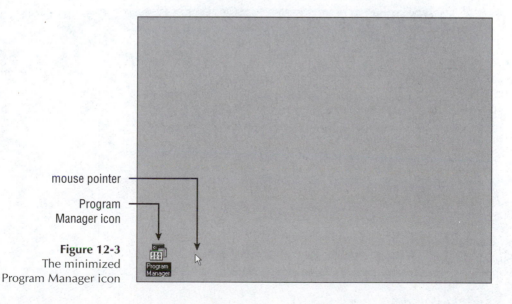

mouse pointer

Program Manager icon

Figure 12-3
The minimized Program Manager icon

3. Double-click the **Program Manager icon**. Windows displays the Program Manager window at its original size. If you click the Program Manager icon once, Windows displays a Control menu. See Figure 12-4. You can click the Restore option on the menu to return the Program Manager window to its original size.

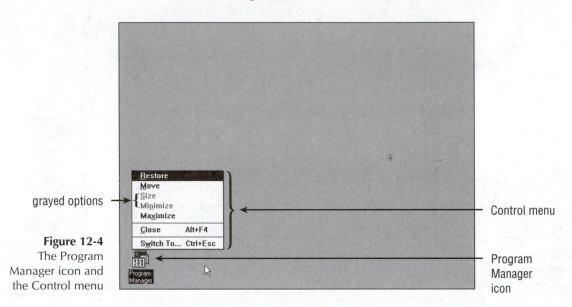

grayed options →

Control menu

Figure 12-4
The Program Manager icon and the Control menu

Program Manager icon

4. Click the **Maximize button**. The Maximize button is located to the far right of the title bar and contains a triangle that points upward. Windows displays a full-screen view of the Program Manager window. See Figure 12-5. It also converts the Maximize button to a Restore button that contains two triangles, one pointing upward and the other pointing downward.

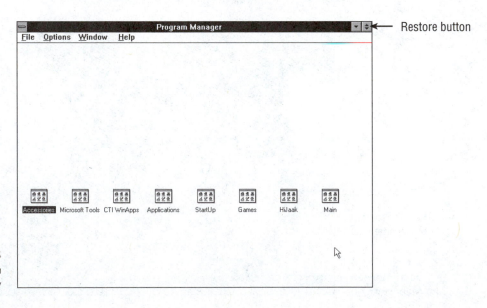

Restore button

Figure 12-5
The maximized Program Manager window

5. Click the **Restore button**. Windows returns the Program Manager window to its original size. It also converts the Restore button to a Maximize button.

Using the Control Menu

You can also adjust the Program Manager Window with the Control-menu box. Let's view the Control menu and try these same operations.

To display the Control menu:

1. Click the **Control-menu box** in the Program Manager window. The Control-menu box is located in the upper-left corner of the window to the left of the title bar, and it contains a bar icon. Windows displays the Control menu. See Figure 12-6. This menu contains commands for minimizing, maximizing, and restoring the size of a window, as well as commands for moving, sizing, and closing a window. (If you inadvertently double-click the Control-menu box, Windows displays an Exit Windows dialog box and asks if you want to exit Windows. If this occurs, click the Cancel button to return to Program Manager and try again.)

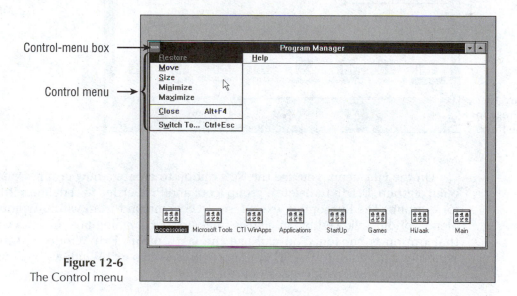

Figure 12-6
The Control menu

2. Click the **Minimize option**. Windows again converts the Program Manager window to an icon that appears at the bottom of the screen.

3. Click the **Program Manager icon**. Windows displays a Control menu instead. Click **Restore** to return the Program Manager window to its original size.

4. Click the **Control-menu box**. Then click **Maximize**. Windows again displays a full-screen view of the Program Manager window.

5. Click the **Control-menu box**. Then click **Restore**. Windows returns the Program Manager window to its original size.

EXAMINING THE PROGRAM MANAGER MENUS

Now that you are familiar with the Control menu and buttons for sizing a window, let's examine the menus on the menu bar.

To display the File menu:

1. Click **File**. Program Manager displays the File menu. See Figure 12-7. Like the DOS Shell menus, the Program Manager menus display a list of commands and, in some cases, shortcut keys for certain commands. Commands that are shown in gray are unavailable for use because they do not apply to the current window.

grayed options

File menu

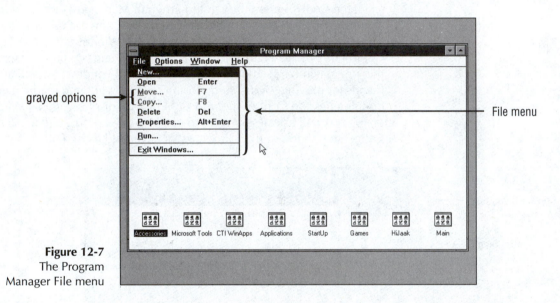

Figure 12-7
The Program
Manager File menu

On the File menu, you use the New option to create a new group, Open to open a group, Delete to delete a group icon, and Properties to redefine settings for a group. The Run option executes a DOS command from within Windows. Menu options followed by an ellipsis indicate that a dialog box appears when that option is chosen. You can use the last option, Exit Windows, to exit Windows and return to the DOS prompt. You can also exit Windows by double-clicking the Program Manager's Control-menu box.

The Options Menu

Next let's look at the Options menu. This menu allows you to select some default settings for the operation of Windows.

To display the Options menu:

1. Click **Options**. Program Manager closes the File menu and displays the Options menu. See Figure 12-8.

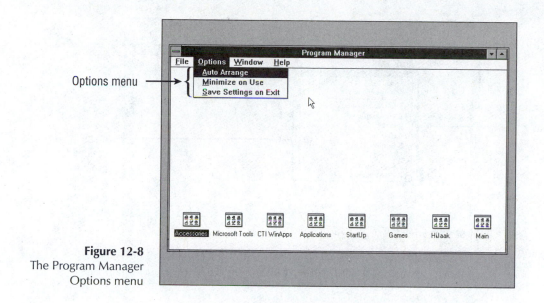

Figure 12-8
The Program Manager
Options menu

Options menu

The options on this menu can be toggled on or off. When an option is activated, a check mark appears next to it. When an option is deactivated, the check mark disappears. If you activate the Auto Arrange option, Windows will automatically adjust the position and arrangement of icons in a window as you change the size of the window. If you activate the Minimize on Use option, the Program Manager will appear as an icon, not an open window, when Windows loads. If you activate the Save Settings on Exit option, any changes you make to Windows are saved when you exit Windows.

The Window Menu

You can use the Window menu to control the arrangement of windows on the screen and to select groups. Let's examine the Window menu.

To display the Window menu and its options:

1. Click **Window**. Program Manager closes the Options menu and displays the Window menu. See Figure 12-9. Your list of group icons will be different.

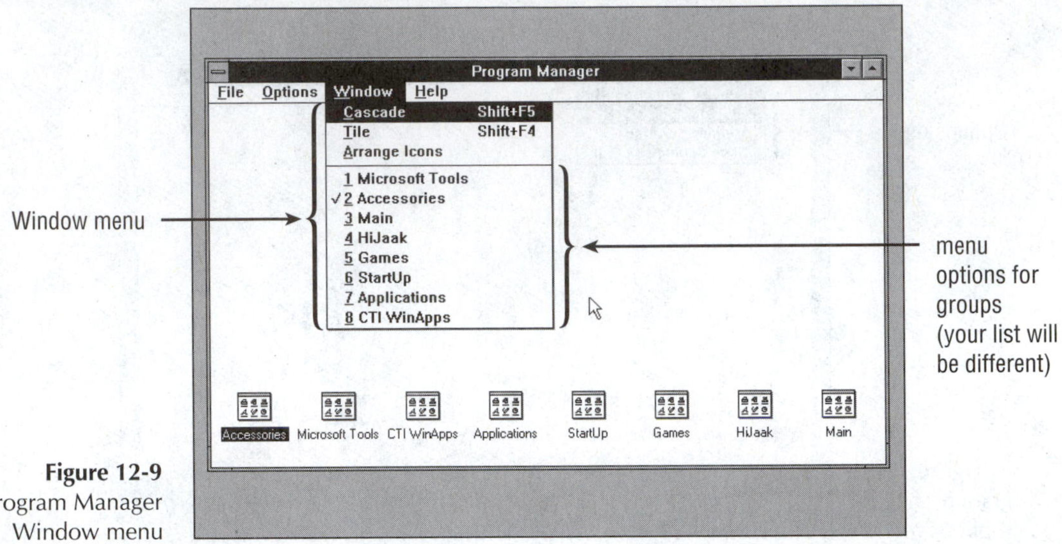

Window menu ⟶

menu
options for
groups
(your list will
be different)

Figure 12-9
The Program Manager
Window menu

The Cascade option overlaps windows so that you can see the title bars of
each window. In contrast, the Tile option arranges windows side by side.
Although the windows are smaller, you can see each window. You can use the
Arrange Icons option to arrange icons in even rows in a window. The second part
of the menu is a numbered list of options; each group icon is assigned a number
so that you can quickly open a group from this menu by typing the number or
clicking the option. Your list of group icons will be different from Figure 12-9.

USING HELP

The last menu, Help, takes you into the Windows Help system, which puts help
information on procedures, commands, and terms at your fingertips to assist
you in the use of Windows. You can also learn more about Windows through a
built-in Windows tutorial. Let's look more closely at the Help menu.

To display the Help menu:

1. Click **Help**. Program Manager closes the Window menu and displays the
   Help menu. See Figure 12-10.

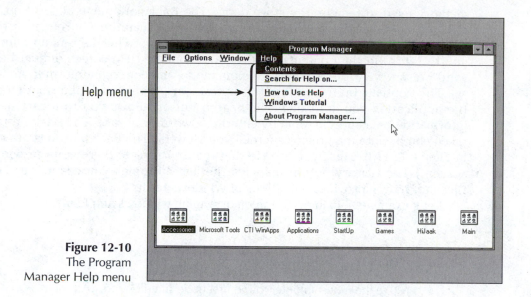

Figure 12-10
The Program
Manager Help menu

2. Click **Contents**. After the Program Manager displays the Program
   Manager Help window, click the Program Manager Help **Maximize
   button**. See Figure 12-11. The text in the Help window explains the
   value of the Program Manager, and it lists procedures under "How To"
   and menu options under "Commands." If you click one of the underlined options, Windows Help displays help information on that option.

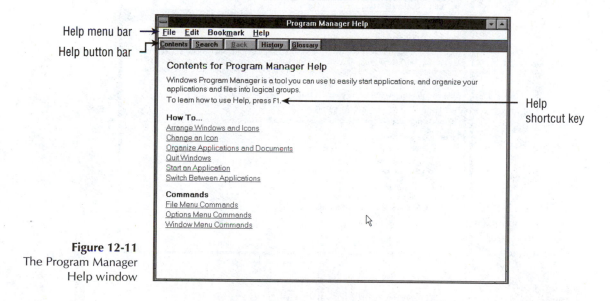

Figure 12-11
The Program Manager
Help window

The Help window contains Help menus, Help buttons, and a list of topics
for which help information is available. The Help File menu allows you to open
a help file on a Windows application, print information displayed on a help
topic, specify printer settings, or exit Help. The Edit menu command allows
you to copy text from a help screen to another application via the Clipboard or
to **annotate**, or add, comments to a help screen. (The **Clipboard** is an area of

memory used to temporarily store data.) The Bookmark menu allows you to assign a name to a certain help screen. Later, you can quickly return to the same help screen by indicating the bookmark name. The Help menu allows you to return to the Contents for Program Manager Help screen, adjust help windows, and view the Windows version, mode, and copyright information.

The Contents button on the Help button bar provides help information on the application you are using. The Search button allows you to locate help information on a specific topic by entering a word or phrase. The Back button takes you back to the previous screen you viewed. (The Back button is grayed in Figure 12-11 because you are viewing the first screen; there is no previous screen.) The History button displays the last 40 topics you examined. The Glossary button provides definitions of Windows terms.

Let's examine help information on arranging windows and icons.

To obtain "How To..." help information:

1. Move the mouse pointer to the first underlined option, "Arrange Windows and Icons." The mouse pointer changes to a hand with a finger pointing to this option.

2. Click **Arrange Windows and Icons**. Windows Help displays help information on arranging windows and icons. See Figure 12-12. Windows Help explains how to use three commands to arrange windows and icons on the screen.

Help text →

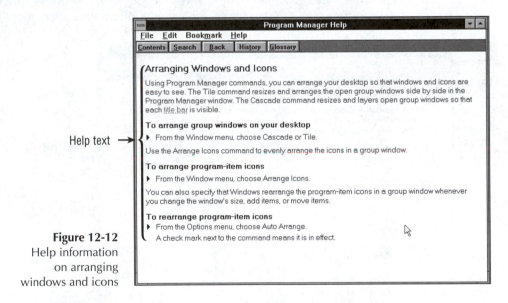

Figure 12-12
Help information
on arranging
windows and icons

Now view the glossary's definition of an icon.

3. Click the **Glossary button** on the Help button bar. Windows Help displays a glossary window. See Figure 12-13. Terms are listed in alphabetical order.

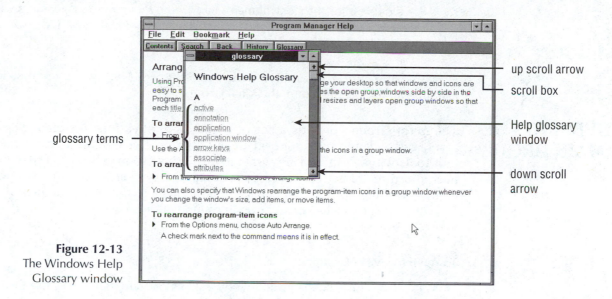

Figure 12-13
The Windows Help
Glossary window

4. Drag the **scroll box** halfway down the scroll bar located on the right side of the glossary window, or click the **down scroll arrow**, until you see terms that start with the letter "I."

5. Click the term **icon**. Windows Help displays a Help window for this term. See Figure 12-14.

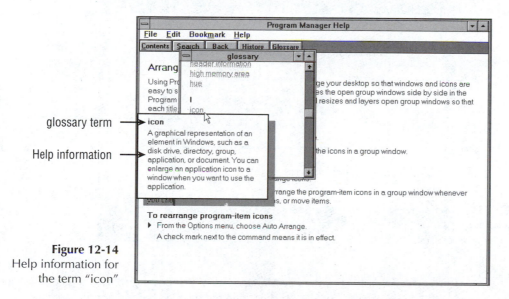

Figure 12-14
Help information for
the term "icon"

6. Click the **right mouse button**. The Help window closes.

7. Double-click the **Control-menu box** for the glossary window. Windows Help closes the glossary window and returns you to the Help window on arranging windows and icons.

8. Double-click the **Control-menu box** for the Program Manager Help window. Windows closes the Program Manager Help window and displays the Program Manager window.

Now that you are familiar with the Program Manager's menus, let's examine an important group, the Main Group.

OPENING THE MAIN GROUP

The **Main Group** contains a set of Windows applications for managing the resources on your computer system and, therefore, is one of the more important tools within Windows. Program items in this group enable you to manage files and directories, configure your computer system, customize Windows, control printing, specify new applications, and exit to the DOS prompt.

Let's open this window and examine some of these uses.

To open the Main Group:

1. If you have opened windows other than Program Manager, close them by double-clicking the **Control-menu box** for each window. Leave the Program Manager window open; do not exit Windows.

2. Double-click the **Main icon**. Windows displays the Main Group window and its program items. See Figure 12-15.

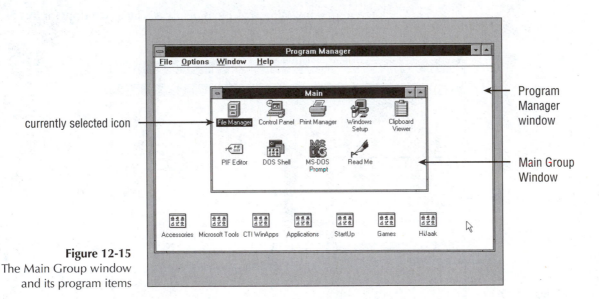

currently selected icon

Program Manager window

Main Group Window

Figure 12-15
The Main Group window and its program items

3. Double-click the **File Manager icon**. Windows displays the File Manager window. The File Manager title bar displays a drive and file specification for the root directory of drive C. See Figure 12-16. If you do not see the specification C:*.* in the title bar, click the **up scroll arrow** until you see the icon for the root directory, then click the **root directory icon**. The File Manager contains drive icons, a directory tree window, and a contents list window, all of which look similar to the equivalent features in the DOS Shell. Using File Manager and its menus, you can perform disk, directory, and file operations from within Windows. (The next tutorial examines the File Manager in detail.)

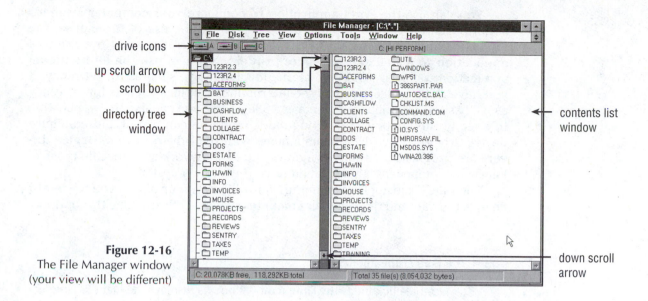

drive icons
up scroll arrow
scroll box
directory tree window
contents list window
down scroll arrow

Figure 12-16
The File Manager window
(your view will be different)

4. Double-click the **Control-menu box**. Windows closes the File Manager window and displays the Main Group window.

5. Double-click the **Control Panel icon**. Windows displays the Control Panel window. See Figure 12-17. The Main Group window is now behind the Control Panel window.

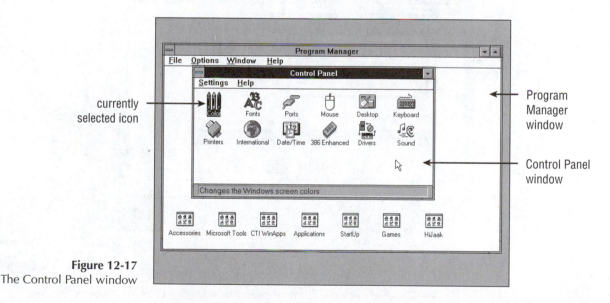

currently selected icon
Program Manager window
Control Panel window

Figure 12-17
The Control Panel window

The Control Panel

The **Control Panel** contains program items for customizing and configuring Windows and your computer system. For example, you can use the Color application to select or design a color scheme for Windows, the Fonts application to specify a font for the Windows screen display, and the Desktop application to further customize the Windows desktop.

You can use the Ports application to configure your computer system's serial ports, the Mouse application to customize the use of the mouse, the Keyboard application to adjust the keyboard's operation, and the Printers application to install and configure printers. You can use the International application to specify and use international settings, such as for currency. If you have a 386 or 486, you will see international settings such as for currency as well as the 386 Enhanced icon. On a 386 or 486, you can use this application to specify the Windows operating mode, and you can install and configure device drivers for hardware components with the Drivers option. **Device drivers** are programs that allow Windows and DOS to work with specific types of hardware components that you add to your computer system.

The Date/Time application in the Control Panel group allows you to view or change the date and time on your computer system. Let's examine this option.

To use the Date/Time application:

   1. Double-click the **Date/Time icon**. Windows displays the Date & Time dialog box. See Figure 12-18. If you want to change the date, you double-click the month, day, or year and then click the up or down triangle to the right of the date to adjust that component in one direction or the other.

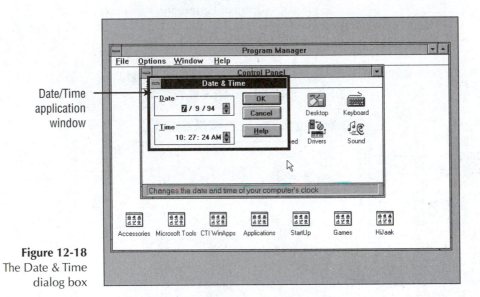

Date/Time application window

Figure 12-18
The Date & Time dialog box

   2. Click **OK**. Windows closes the Date & Time dialog box.
   3. Double-click the **Control-menu box** for the Control Panel. Windows closes the Control Panel window, and you see the Main Group window.

Using the MS-DOS Prompt

Occasionally you might want to work from the DOS prompt. If you select the MS-DOS Prompt icon in the Main Group, you temporarily exit to the DOS prompt so that you can issue a DOS command. Let's try it.

To use the MS-DOS Prompt:

1. Double-click the **MS-DOS Prompt icon**. Windows displays the DOS prompt, the DOS version, and information on how to return to Windows. When you exit Windows from the MS-DOS Prompt, Windows loads a second copy of the Command Interpreter so that you can work from the DOS prompt.

2. Type **TREE C:\ | MORE** and press **[Enter]**. DOS displays the first part of the directory tree of drive C. Continue to press **[Spacebar]** or any other key until you view the entire directory tree.

3. Type **EXIT** and press **[Enter]**. You must return to Windows by entering the EXIT command. Now your screen returns to Windows.

4. Double-click the **Control-menu box** for the Main Group. Windows closes the Main Group window and displays the Program Manager window.

MOVING A WINDOW

If you need to adjust your view of a window or its position on the screen, you can easily move the window using the mouse. You click the window's title bar and drag the window to its new location. You can also move a window by using the Move command on the Control menu. You can use the same techniques to move dialog boxes.

Let's adjust the position of the Program Manager window.

To move a window using the mouse:

1. Click the **Program Manager title bar**, hold down the left mouse button, and drag the window to a new location on the screen. As you move the mouse pointer, you see an outline of the window that you are moving. See Figure 12-19.

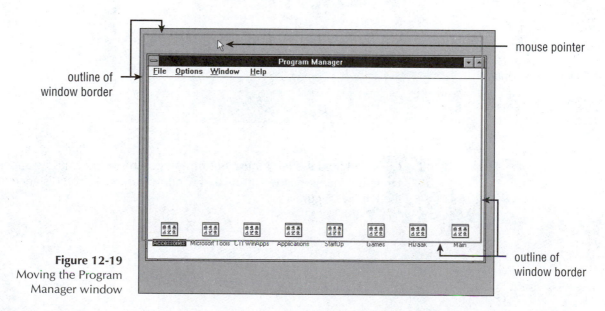

Figure 12-19
Moving the Program Manager window

2. Release the mouse button. The Program Manager window moves to its new location.

Now move the window using the Control menu.

3. Click the **Control-menu box**, then click **Move**. The mouse pointer changes to a four-headed arrow, and the window has an outline around it.

4. Use the keyboard arrow keys to move an outline of the window to a new location. Then press **[Enter]**.

CHANGING THE SIZE OF A WINDOW

You can also change the size of a window. You might need to enlarge a window to see all of the applications available in that window. Or you might want to reduce the size of a window so that you can open and view another window on the same screen.

Let's adjust the size of the Program Manager window.

To change the size of a window:

1. Position the mouse pointer on the right border of the Program Manager window. The mouse pointer changes to a double-headed arrow. See Figure 12-20.

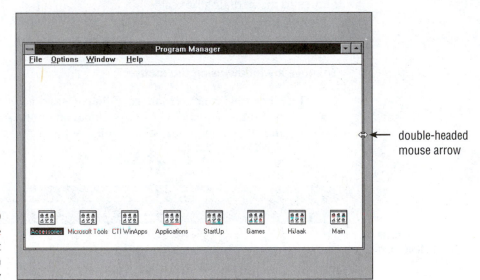

double-headed
mouse arrow

Figure 12-20
Positioning the mouse
pointer on the right
border of the Program
Manager window

2. Click and hold the **left mouse button**. An outline of the window appears. Drag the double-headed arrow and window outline a short distance to the left. See Figure 12-21.

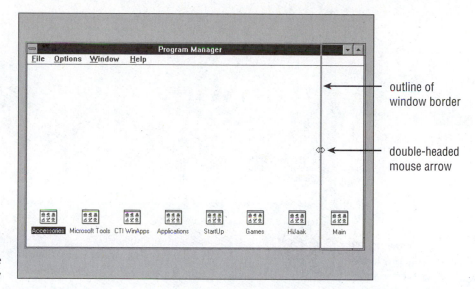

Figure 12-21
Dragging an outline of the
Program Manager window

outline of
window border

double-headed
mouse arrow

3. Release the mouse button. Windows adjusts the size of the window to match the outline that you specified. See Figure 12-22.

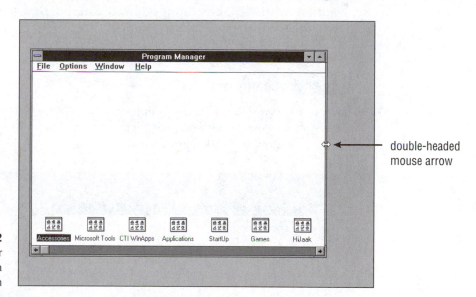

Figure 12-22
The Program Manager
window adjusted for a
new width

double-headed
mouse arrow

4. Position the mouse pointer on the bottom window border. The mouse pointer again changes to a double-headed arrow.

5. Click and hold the **left mouse button**. An outline of the window appears. Drag the double-headed arrow and window outline up a short distance, above the bottom row of icons.

6. Release the mouse button. Windows adjusts the size of the window to match the outline that you specified.

7. Click **Window**, then click **Arrange Icons**. Windows rearranges the icons within the window. See Figure 12-23.

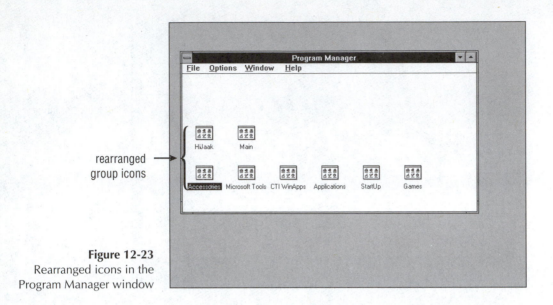

Figure 12-23
Rearranged icons in the
Program Manager window

If you want to enlarge or decrease the width and height of a window at the same time, you position the mouse pointer on a window corner and drag the outline of the window until you redefine its size. Let's use this method to enlarge the Program Manager window.

To enlarge a window:

1. Position the mouse pointer on the bottom-right corner of the Program Manager window. See Figure 12-24. The mouse pointer changes to a double-headed arrow.

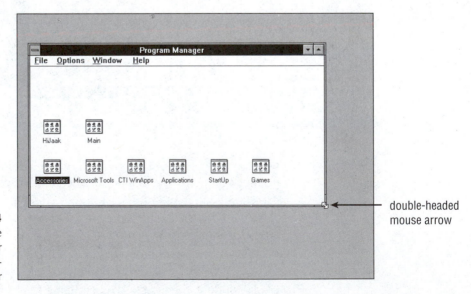

Figure 12-24
Positioning the
mouse pointer
on the lower-
right border

2. Click and hold the **left mouse button**. An outline of the window appears. Drag the double-headed arrow and window outline to the right and down. See Figure 12-25.

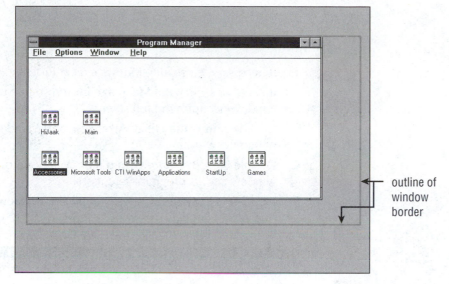

outline of window border

Figure 12-25
Enlarging the Program Manager window

3. Release the mouse button. Windows adjusts the size of the window to match the outline of the window that you specified and rearranges the icons.

4. Click **Window**, then click **Arrange Icons**. Windows rearranges the icons within the window.

CASCADING AND TILING WINDOWS

As you open one window after another, Windows overlaps the windows so that they appear similar to the arrangement of papers on a desktop. The **current window**, or **active window**, is the window with the highlighted title bar. By default, Windows displays only a part of each of the other windows that you previously opened. If you open multiple windows, one window may hide another window.

You can arrange the windows by cascading or tiling them. When you **cascade** windows, Windows places each window to the right and below the previous window. If you want to select a window, you click on that window. The contents of that window then appear above the other windows.

When you **tile** windows, Windows reduces the size of each window and arranges the windows side by side so that you can view each window at the same time. Although the windows are smaller and although you might not be able to view all the icons in a window, you can quickly switch from one window to another by clicking on the window you want to use. If you open new windows, Windows does not automatically cascade or tile the new windows.

You want to first tile and then cascade the Main and Accessories windows.

To open, tile, and then cascade the open windows:

1. If necessary, close all windows except Program Manager.

2. If necessary, click the **Maximize button** so that the Program Manager window occupies the full screen.

3. Click **Window**, then click **Arrange Icons**. Windows rearranges the icons within the window.

4. Double-click the **Main Group icon**. Windows displays the Main Group window and its program-item icons.

5. Double-click the **Accessories Group icon**. Windows opens and overlaps the Accessories Group window over the Main Group window. See Figure 12-26.

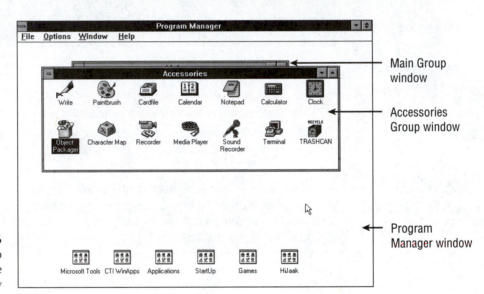

Figure 12-26
The Accessories Group window in front of the Main Group window

(labels pointing to figure:) Main Group window — Accessories Group window — Program Manager window

6. Click **Window**, then click **Tile**. Windows arranges the Main Group and Accessories Group windows side by side. See Figure 12-27. The Accessories Group window is the active, or current, window. Windows will add scroll bars at the bottom of a window or on the right side of a window if it cannot display all the icons in a window.

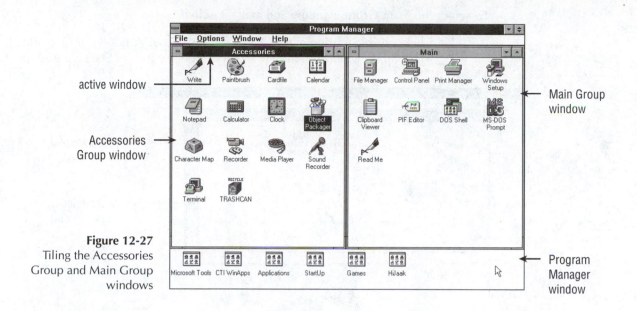

active window

Main Group window

Accessories Group window

Figure 12-27
Tiling the Accessories Group and Main Group windows

Program Manager window

7. Click **Window**, then click **Cascade**. Windows rearranges the windows so that they overlap one another. See Figure 12-28. Again, the Accessories Group window is the current window.

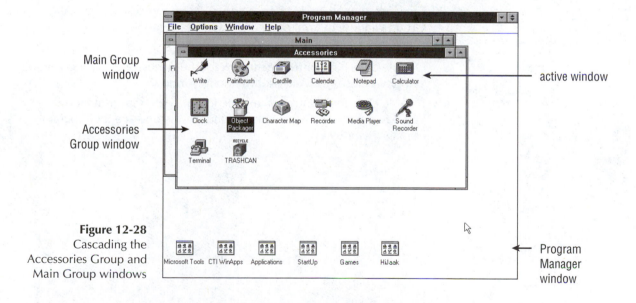

Main Group window

Accessories Group window

active window

Figure 12-28
Cascading the Accessories Group and Main Group windows

Program Manager window

Selecting a Window

You can change windows by clicking on the window you want to use or by using the Window menu to choose a window. Let's make the Main Group window the active window and then return to the Accessories Group window.

To select the Main Group window and make it active:

1. Click a **visible portion** of the Main Group window. Windows displays the Main Group window in front of the Accessories window. See Figure 12-29.

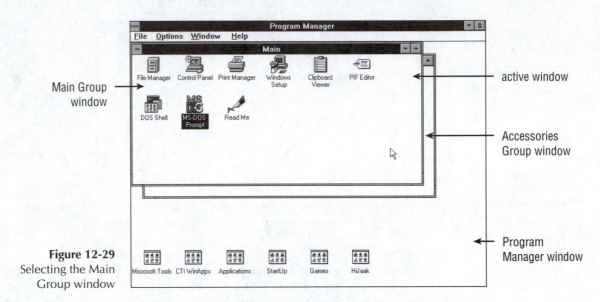

Main Group window

active window

Accessories Group window

Program Manager window

Figure 12-29
Selecting the Main Group window

Now select the Accessories Group window using the Window menu.

2. Click **Window**, then click **Accessories**. Windows displays the Accessories Group window in front of the Main Group window.

Next close both windows.

3. Double-click the **Control-menu box** for the Accessories Group window. Windows closes the Accessories Group window.

4. Double-click the **Control-menu box** for the Main Group window. Windows closes the Main Group window and you see the Program Manager window.

EXITING WINDOWS

You decide to exit Windows before you leave for lunch. You can exit Windows in one of three ways using the mouse. You can double-click the Program Manager Control-menu box. You can click the Program Manager Control-menu box and then select the Close command. Or you can select the Exit Windows command on the Program Manager's File menu.

To exit Windows:

1. If necessary, close all open windows by double-clicking each window's **Control-menu box**.
2. Double-click the Program Manager **Control-menu box**. Windows displays an Exit Windows dialog box and asks you to verify that you want to exit Windows.
3. Click **OK**. You exit Windows and return to the DOS prompt.

◆

SUMMARY

In this tutorial, you learned how to use and identify the components of the Windows 3.1 graphical user interface. You used the Control menu and the Minimize, Maximize, and Restore buttons to adjust the size of a window. You explored the command options available on the Program Manager File, Options, and Window menus. You examined how to use the Windows Help system.

You opened and examined applications in the Main Group, including the File Manager and the Control Panel. In the Control Panel, you examined the Date/Time application for viewing and changing the system date and time. You used the MS-DOS Prompt application to display the DOS prompt from within Windows, you executed a DOS command, and then returned to Windows.

You practiced the techniques for moving, sizing, tiling, cascading, and selecting windows.

Features Reference

Windows Tools and Groups

Accessories	A Program Manager group that contains a variety of Windows applications, such as a word processing application, a text editor, a drawing program, a calculator, a cardfile, a calendar, and a clock
Applications	A Program Manager group for installed software applications, such as word processing, electronic spreadsheets, and database applications
Control Panel	A group in the Main Group that contains applications for changing the configuration of your system
File Manager	An application in the Main Group for managing drives, directories, and files
Main Group	A Program Manager group that contains Windows system applications
MS-DOS Prompt	An application in the Main Group for temporarily exiting to the DOS prompt
Program Manager	A tool for starting applications and for organizing applications and files into groups

Windows Buttons

Control-menu box	Displays the Control menu if you click; closes the open window if you double click
Maximize	Enlarges the window to fill the screen
Minimize	Reduces a window to an icon
Restore	Returns a window to its original size

Windows Commands

File/Exit Windows	Exits Windows after all applications are closed
Help	Access the Windows Help system
Window/Arrange Icons	Arranges icons in even rows near the bottom of the Program Manager window

Window/Cascade	Arranges windows in an overlapping pattern
Window/Tile	Arranges windows side by side

QUESTIONS

1. What is Program Manager, and why is it important?
2. What is a group icon? Give an example.
3. What is File Manager, and why is it important?
4. What is a program-item icon? Give an example.
5. What is the Control-menu box, and how can you use it?
6. What does the Minimize button do?
7. What does the Maximize button do?
8. What does the Restore button do?
9. What does Auto Arrange on Program Manager's Options menu do?
10. How can you locate the definition for a Windows term?
11. How can you locate help information on a specific topic?
12. Name two important options available in the Main Group?
13. What is the Control Panel, and how can you use it? Give an example.
14. How can you set the date and time on your computer system from Windows?
15. What element of a window do you select when you want to move a window? To resize a window?
16. How can you enter commands from the DOS prompt without exiting Windows?
17. How do you move a window with the mouse?
18. How do you move a window with the Control menu?
19. How can you widen a window?
20. How can you adjust the width and height of a window at the same time?
21. What does Windows do when you tile windows?
22. What does Windows do when you cascade windows?
23. How do you reduce a window to an icon?
24. What other DOS graphical user interface is similar to Windows?
25. If you have not enabled Auto Arrange from the Program Manager's Options menu, how can you rearrange icons when you change the size of a window?
26. Name two ways to exit Windows.
27. How do you select a window behind the current window?
28. If you use the MS-DOS Prompt icon to exit Windows temporarily, how do you return to Windows from the MS-DOS Prompt?

29. How can you identify the current or active window?

30. What is the difference between a window and an icon?

TUTORIAL ASSIGNMENTS

1. **Using Windows Help**: Use Windows Help to answer the following questions.
   a. What two steps are required to start an application from a group?
   b. How can you arrange windows in an overlapping pattern?
   c. What is the function of the Control menu?
   d. What is a group?
   e. What is an icon?
   f. What is a program item?
   Close Windows Help and exit Windows.

2. **Sizing Windows**: Perform the following operations and list the steps or commands that you use.
   a. Load Windows.
   Use the mouse to:
   b. Minimize the Program Manager window.
   c. Restore the Program Manager window.
   d. Maximize the Program Manager window.
   e. Restore the Program Manager window to its original size.
   Use the Control menu to:
   f. Minimize the Program Manager window.
   g. Restore the Program Manager window.
   h. Maximize the Program Manager window.
   i. Restore the Program Manager window to its original size.
   Close all open windows and exit Windows.

3. **Adjusting Windows**: Perform the following operations and list the steps and commands that you use.
   a. Load Windows.
   b. Maximize the size of the Program Manager window.
   c. Rearrange the icons in the Program Manager window.
   d. Open the Main Group.
   e. Maximize the size of the Main Group window.
   f. Open the Applications window.
   Close all open windows and exit Windows.

4. **Moving Windows**: Perform the following operations and list the steps or commands that you use.
   a. Load Windows.
   b. Open the Main Group.
   c. Open the Accessories Group.
   d. Reduce the size of the Accessories Group window.
   e. Move the Accessories Group window so that you can see the Main Group window.
   f. Reduce the size of the Main Group window.
   g. Move the Main Group and Accessories Group windows so that they are side by side in the middle of the screen.
   Close all open windows and exit Windows.

5. **Arranging Windows**: Perform the following operations and list the steps and commands you use.
   a.   Open the Main Group.
   b.   Open the Accessories Group.
   c.   Tile the windows.
   d.   Maximize the Program Manager window.
   e.   Open the Applications Group.
   f.   Tile the windows.
   g.   Cascade the windows.
   h.   Select the Main Group.

   Close all open windows and exit Windows.

Using File Manager

OBJECTIVES

In this tutorial you will learn to:

- ◆ Open and use File Manager
- ◆ Format a diskette
- ◆ Copy the contents of a diskette
- ◆ Change drives
- ◆ Expand the directory tree
- ◆ Select a directory
- ◆ Change the details displayed with filenames
- ◆ Modify the directory structure of a disk
- ◆ Rename a directory
- ◆ Create a directory
- ◆ Copy files from one directory to another
- ◆ Move directories

The director of your department informs you that one of your coworkers has resigned so that he can return to school. She asks you if you want to switch from part-time to full-time employment and assume the client responsibilities of the departing coworker. You tell her that you are definitely interested in a full-time position and in increasing your responsibilities and opportunities.

You ask your coworker for his client diskette so that you can make a copy of the diskette and familiarize yourself with his client files before he leaves. Because time is an important factor in completing client jobs, you want to ensure that the directories and files on his client diskette are organized in a manner that is similar to the way you currently organize your own client files.

◆

USING FILE MANAGER

Because you and other staff members have switched to the Windows operating environment, you decide to use File Manager to examine your coworker's client diskette.

File Manager is a Windows tool for viewing and organizing directories and files on a diskette or hard disk. You can use File Manager for the common types of operations that you perform at the DOS prompt and in the DOS Shell, such as creating, renaming, moving, and removing directories; copying and moving files from diskette to diskette or from directory to directory; renaming and deleting files; and viewing and printing documents.

Before you examine your coworker's client files, you want to format a diskette and make a copy of his client diskette using File Manager.

To get started:

1. If you are at the DOS prompt for drive C, type **WIN** and press **[Enter]**. If your computer setup is different, follow the instructions provided by your instructor or technical support person for starting Windows.

2. After you load Windows, close all open windows except Program Manager.

3. Double-click the **Main Group icon**. Windows displays the Main Group window. See Figure 13-1. The group icons in your Program Manager window and the application icons in your Main Group window will probably be different.

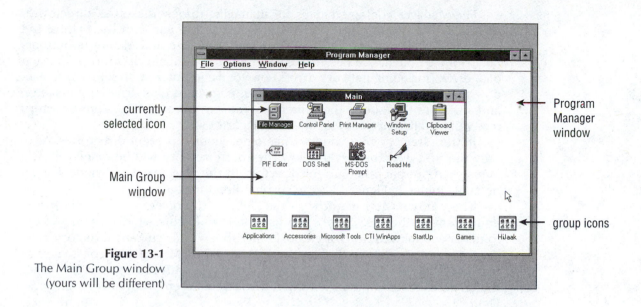

Figure 13-1
The Main Group window
(yours will be different)

4. Double-click the **File Manager icon**. Windows displays the File Manager window and a directory window.

5. If File Manager does not occupy the full window, click the **Maximize button** for the File Manager window. See Figure 13-2.

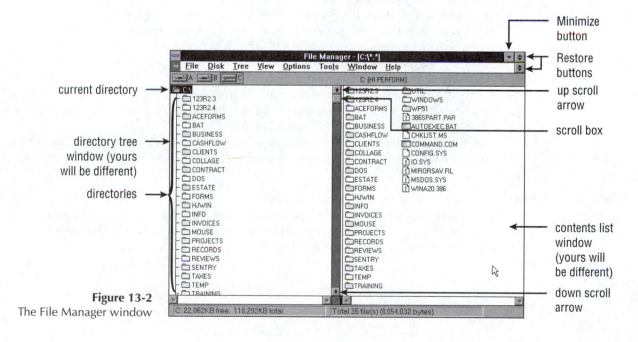

Figure 13-2
The File Manager window

6. If the window for drive C showing the directory structure and filenames does not occupy the full window, click the **Maximize button** for this window.

File Manager contains menus for managing drives, diskettes, directories, and files. The File Manager window contains a title bar with the path of the current directory, a Control-menu box, and Minimize and Maximize buttons. Like the DOS Shell, the File Manager window contains a drive icon for each disk drive (including network drives) on your computer, a directory tree window that shows the directory structure of your hard disk drive or a diskette, and a window that shows the contents of the current directory. Your directory tree will be different from that shown in Figure 13-2.

In the **directory tree window**, file folder icons represent directories. Also, only the first directory level below the root directory will be displayed. File Manager represents the current directory in the directory tree window as an open file folder. In Figure 13-2, the current directory is C:\.

The **contents list window** to the right of the directory tree window is equivalent to the DOS Shell's file list window. In this window, you see file folder icons for subdirectories positioned below the current directory; program file icons, such as the one for COMMAND.COM; and file icons, such as the one for IO.SYS, that appear as sheets of paper with the upper-right corner folded down. Your contents list window will be different from the one shown in Figure 13-2.

Each of these windows has a set of scroll bars for adjusting the screen view onto the window.

As you use File Manager in this tutorial, you will discover that drive, directory, and file operations are performed more easily from Windows than from DOS. However, it is important to understand how to perform these operations from DOS. Windows 3.1 is an operating *environment*, not an operating system. Even with Windows, DOS is required to boot your computer system and to manage its resources. After you load DOS, you can load Windows. Windows then works in conjunction with DOS, and DOS provides underlying support for Windows. The drive, file, and directory organization evident in Windows depends on the ability of DOS to manage drive, files, and directories. Furthermore, Windows does not have menus for all of the DOS commands. If you work on computers that do not have Windows, you must know how to perform drive, directory, and file operations from DOS.

The obvious value of Windows is that it simplifies the task of managing your computer and its resources through a friendly and easy-to-use interface.

FORMATTING A DISKETTE WITH FILE MANAGER

To begin, you must format two diskettes using the File Manager Disk menu. The Disk menu provides a more friendly user interface and lets you select the options that you need for formatting a diskette—including a disk drive, a formatting capacity, and a volume label.

To format a diskette:

1. Insert your Tutorial Disk into a diskette drive.

2. Click **Disk**. File Manager displays the Disk menu. See Figure 13-3. From this menu, in addition to formatting a diskette, you also can copy a diskette, assign a volume label to a diskette, make a system or boot diskette, and select a disk drive. You might even see other options, such as one for network connections.

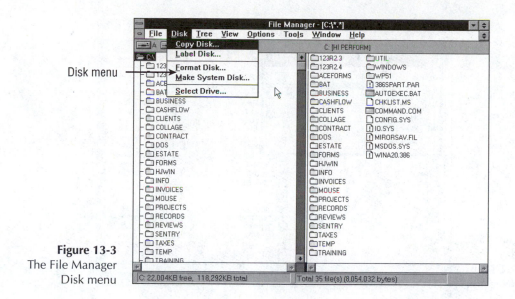

Disk menu

Figure 13-3
The File Manager
Disk menu

3. Click **Format Disk**. File Manager displays the Format Disk dialog box. See Figure 13-4. The Disk In list box shows the default drive for formatting, and the Capacity list box shows the default formatting capacity (yours might be different) for the default drive.

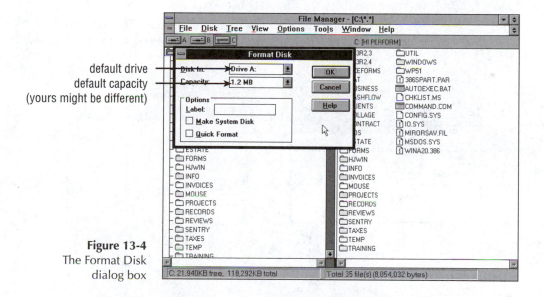

default drive
default capacity
(yours might be different)

Figure 13-4
The Format Disk
dialog box

4. If you need to specify another drive, click the **down arrow** to the right of the Disk In list box. File Manager displays a drop-down list box. See Figure 13-5. Click the **drive** that you want to use. File Manager displays the drive you selected in the Disk In list box.

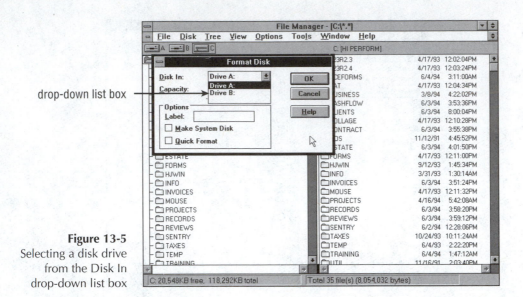

drop-down list box

Figure 13-5
Selecting a disk drive
from the Disk In
drop-down list box

5. If you need to specify another format capacity, such as 720K for a
double-density 3½-inch diskette, click the **down arrow** to the right of the
Capacity list box. File Manager displays a drop-down list box. Click the
storage capacity that you want to use. File Manager displays the new
format capacity in the Capacity list box.

6. Click the **Label text box** to specify a volume label. The *insertion point
cursor* appears as a flashing vertical bar, and the mouse pointer appears
as an *I-bar*. See Figure 13-6.

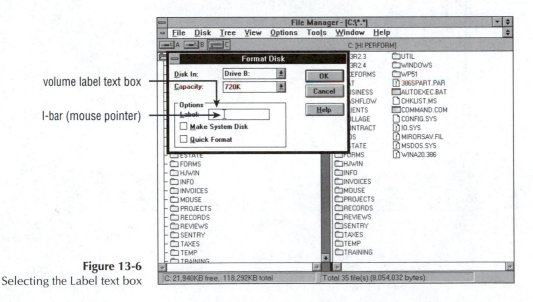

volume label text box

I-bar (mouse pointer)

Figure 13-6
Selecting the Label text box

7. Type **BUSINESS** in the Label text box. Then click **OK**. File Manager displays a Confirm Format Disk dialog box and warns that it will erase all data on the disk.

8. Click **Yes**. File Manager displays a Formatting Disk dialog box. This dialog box shows the percentage of formatting completed. If you want to stop the formatting for any reason, click the **Cancel button**. When the formatting is complete, this dialog box informs you that File Manager is creating the root directory on the formatted diskette. It then displays a Format Complete dialog box with information on the total diskette space and available space, and asks if you want to format another diskette.

You need to format another diskette because you want to make a backup copy.

To format another diskette:

1. Remove the Tutorial Disk from the diskette drive, and insert your Exercise Disk.

2. Click **Yes**. File Manager displays the Format Disk dialog box. File Manager will use the same settings that you specified for the first diskette.

3. Click **OK**. File Manager displays the Confirm Format dialog box.

4. Click **Yes**. File Manager formats the diskette. When the formatting is complete, File Manager displays another Format Complete dialog box and asks if you want to format another diskette.

5. Click **No**. File Manager closes the dialog box and the Disk menu.

COPYING THE CONTENTS OF A DISKETTE WITH FILE MANAGER

Next you want to copy the contents of your coworker's diskette onto your newly formatted diskettes. To do so, you will use the Copy Disk option on the Disk menu. Making a duplicate copy of a diskette is easier with Windows than with DOS. If you use the DISKCOPY command at the DOS prompt in DOS 5.0 or 6.0, you must swap the source and target diskettes several times. In Windows, you insert the source and target diskettes only once. Not only is it easier and faster, but it is also less confusing and there is less chance for error.

Your instructor will prepare a Windows Data Disk (which contains the contents of your coworker's diskette) for you to copy. This Data Disk contains a directory structure similar to the one used in previous tutorials. You will need to borrow this diskette so that you can make duplicate copies of it.

To copy the Windows Data Disk onto your Tutorial Disk:

1. Insert the Windows Data Disk into the appropriate drive.

2. Click **Disk**, then click **Copy Disk**. File Manager displays the Copy Disk dialog box. See Figure 13-7. The default settings for the source and destination diskettes are shown in list boxes. If you need to change the drive for the source diskette, click the **down arrow** to the right of the Source In list box. Then click the **drive** you want to use from the drop-down list. If you need to change the drive for the destination diskette, click the **down arrow** to the right of the Destination In list box. Then click the **drive** you want to use from the drop-down list.

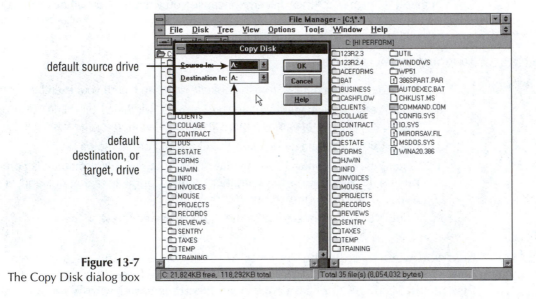

Figure 13-7
The Copy Disk dialog box

3. Click **OK**. If File Manager displays a Confirm Copy dialog box and warns that it will erase all data on the destination diskette, click **YES**. File Manager displays a Copy Disk dialog box that prompts you to insert the source diskette.

4. If necessary, insert your Windows Data Disk into the drive you specified.

5. Click **OK**. File Manager displays a Copying Disk dialog box that shows the percentage of formatting completed. When File Manager shows 49% completed, it has copied the source diskette. File Manager then displays a Copy Disk dialog box that prompts you to insert the destination diskette.

6. Remove the Windows Data Disk from the diskette drive, and insert your Tutorial Disk in the drive. Click **OK**. After the disk copy is complete, File Manager closes the dialog box and the Disk menu.

7. Remove your Tutorial Disk from the diskette drive, and insert the Windows Data Disk in the drive.

8. Repeat the same process to copy the contents of the Windows Data Disk to your Exercise Disk.

9. Remove your Exercise Disk, and insert your Tutorial Disk into the diskette drive.

10. Return the Windows Data Disk that you borrowed.

SELECTING A DRIVE WITH FILE MANAGER

Next you want to examine your copy of your coworker's client diskette. You can select a drive by clicking on the appropriate drive icon or by using the Disk menu and the Select Drive option. The current drive is shown in outline in the drive icon window.

To change drives:

1. Click the **drive icon** for the drive that contains your Tutorial Disk. File Manager updates the directory tree window and the contents list window. See Figure 13-8. The current directory is the root directory of the drive you selected, A:\ or B:\. The contents list window shows the directories in the root directory.

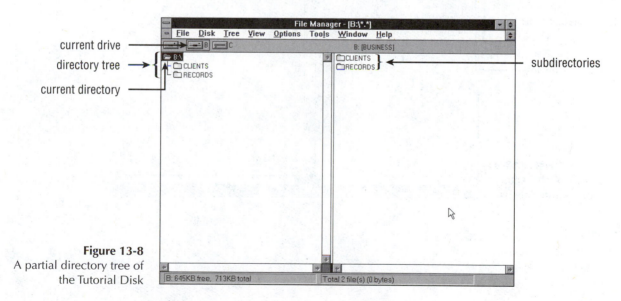

Figure 13-8
A partial directory tree of the Tutorial Disk

EXPANDING THE DIRECTORY TREE

Your coworker has organized his client diskette so that there are two directories positioned below the root directory—one named CLIENTS for client files and the other named RECORDS for business files. You want to expand the directory tree so that you can see the complete directory structure of this diskette. When you select a drive, File Manager shows you only the first level of subdirectories located below the root directory. You can use the Tree menu to expand the directory tree.

To view the entire directory structure:

1. Click **Tree**. File Manager displays the Tree menu. The Tree menu and its options are similar to those in the DOS Shell. You can expand one more level of the directory tree, expand one branch of the directory tree, expand the entire directory tree, or collapse a branch of the directory tree. You also can specify if you want File Manager to indicate branches of the directory tree that could be expanded.

2. Click **Expand All**. File Manager displays the entire directory tree of your Tutorial Disk. See Figure 13-9.

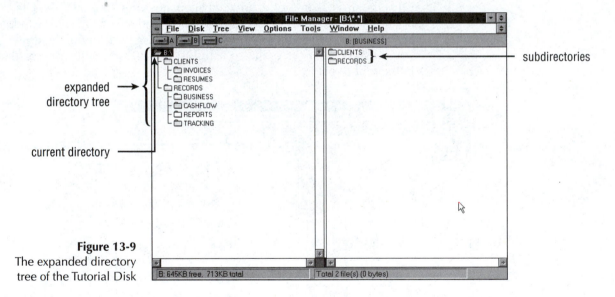

Figure 13-9
The expanded directory tree of the Tutorial Disk

SELECTING A DIRECTORY

You want to examine the files in the two client directories. The process is the same as in the DOS Shell. To select a directory, you click the directory folder icon or the directory name.

To select the INVOICES subdirectory:

1. Click the **INVOICES directory name** in the directory tree window. File Manager highlights the directory name and updates the contents list to show the files in this directory. See Figure 13-10.

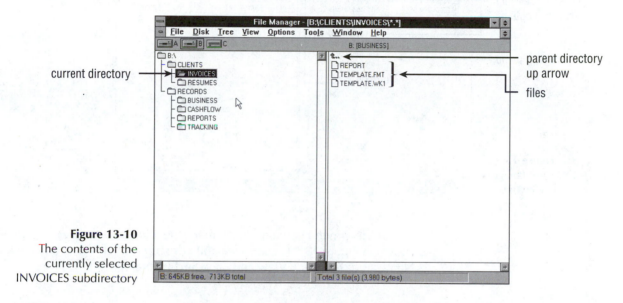

Figure 13-10
The contents of the currently selected INVOICES subdirectory

Now select the RESUMES directory.

2. Click **RESUMES** in the directory tree window. File Manager highlights this directory name and updates the contents list to show the files in this directory.

ORGANIZING THE DISPLAY OF FILENAMES

You want to see more detail on the client files than just the filename—you want to view the sizes, dates, and times of the files. By default, File Manager lists directories and files in alphabetical order in the contents list window. You can change the order of the listing and specify more detail with the View menu.

To change the view in the contents list window:

1. Click **View**. File Manager displays the View menu. See Figure 13-11. Check marks next to specific menu options indicate the current settings for displaying filenames in the contents list window.

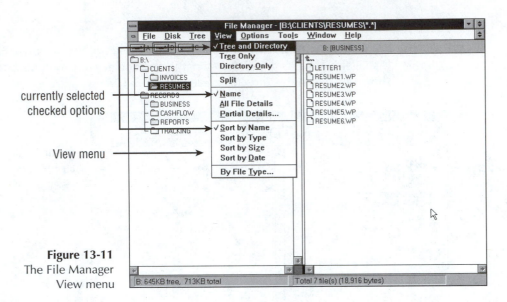

currently selected
checked options

View menu

Figure 13-11
The File Manager
View menu

2. If your View menu contains check marks next to options other than those shown in Figure 13-11, click **Tree and Directory**, click **View**, and click **Name**, and then click **View** and click **Sort by Name**.

The first three options on the View menu determine which window or windows you see. The check mark next to Tree and Directory instructs File Manager to display a directory tree window and a contents list window. You could adjust the display with the next two options to show only the directory tree window (Tree Only) or only the contents list window (Directory Only).

The Split option allows you to adjust the relative sizes of the two windows. The next three options allow you to determine how much information is displayed on files. The check mark next to Name instructs File Manager to display only the names of files. You can also choose to display all file details, or, by selecting Partial Details, choose only the file details you want.

The next four options determine the sort order of the files. The check mark next to Sort by Name instructs File Manager to list filenames in alphabetical order by name and extension. You can also quickly organize files by type (file extension), size (from the largest to the smallest), or date (from the most recent to the oldest).

The last option, By File Type, allows you to limit the display in the contents list window to specific groups of files—directories, programs, documents, and other types of files. You can also specify if you want to see system and hidden files. **System files** include the files that contain the DOS operating system. **Hidden files** are files that DOS does not display in a directory listing, such as the operating system files.

If you instruct File Manager to view all file details, it will display file sizes, dates, times, and attributes. **File attributes** are special characteristics assigned to a file by DOS. Each attribute is represented by a code—S for System file, H for Hidden file, R for Read-Only file, and A for Archive. You can retrieve Read-Only files, but you cannot modify or delete these files. DOS assigns the **Archive attribute** to files that you created or modified since your last backup.

Let's view all the details on these files.

To view all file details:

1. If necessary, click **View** to display the View menu. Click **All File Details**. File Manager displays details next to the filenames. See Figure 13-12. If your screen view does not show five columns of file information, including the filenames, you can adjust the width of this window. In Figure 13-12 only four columns of information are displayed.

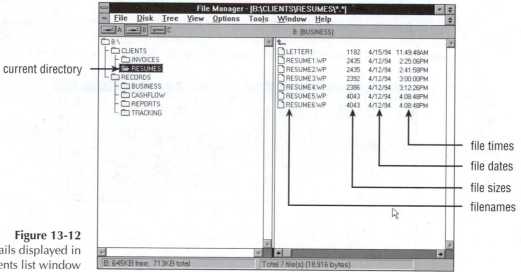

Figure 13-12
The file details displayed in the contents list window

2. If you need to expand the width of the contents list window, position the mouse pointer on the **split bar**—the thin vertical bar to the left of the filenames in the contents list window and to the right of the vertical scroll bar for the directory tree window. See Figure 13-13. The mouse pointer changes to a vertical bar with arrows pointing in both directions.

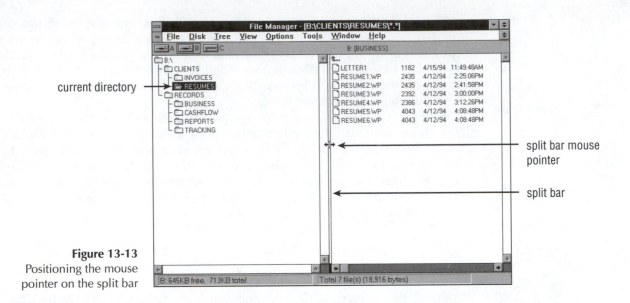

Figure 13-13
Positioning the mouse
pointer on the split bar

3. Press and hold the **left mouse button** as you drag the split bar to the left a short distance. As you move the split bar, it appears as a dark vertical bar. Then release the left mouse button. File Manager adjusts the widths of the two windows, and you should be able to see all five columns of information. See Figure 13-14. If necessary, repeat Steps 2 and 3 to further adjust the width of this window. The last column in the contents list window lists file attributes. The Archive attribute indicates that these files are newly created or modified files that have not been backed up.

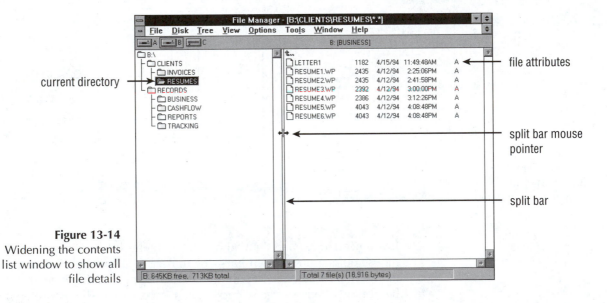

Figure 13-14
Widening the contents
list window to show all
file details

For your daily needs, you do not need to view file attributes. However, you may need to view more complex directory trees with more directory levels. You decide to adjust the display of file details. This time you also want to try the Split option on the View menu to adjust the width of the contents list window, as you did earlier using the split bar.

To view only the file sizes, dates, and times:

1. Click **View**, then click **Partial Details...**. File Manager displays a Partial Details dialog box. Each of the four options—size, date, time, and file attributes—are checked.

2. Click the **check box** next to File Attributes. File Manager removes the "X" from this check box. See Figure 13-15.

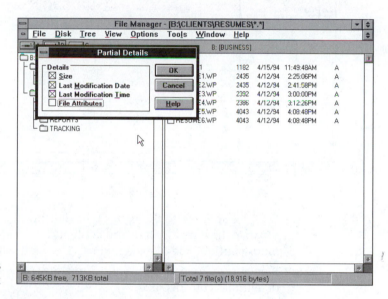

Figure 13-15
The Partial Details
dialog box

3. Click **OK**. File Manager closes this dialog box and updates the display of the contents list window. You no longer see file attributes.

Now adjust the width of the contents list window again.

4. Click **View**, then click **Split**. File Manager displays a dark wide vertical bar with the mouse pointer next to it. See Figure 13-16. This split bar is easier to see and use. As you slide the mouse across the desktop, the split bar moves in the corresponding direction.

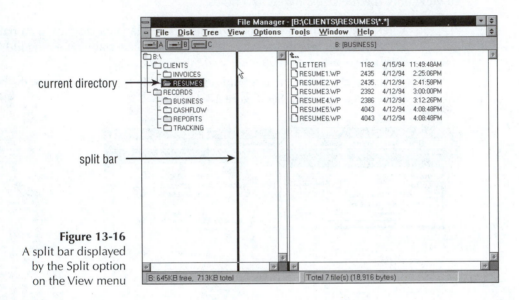

current directory →

split bar →

Figure 13-16
A split bar displayed
by the Split option
on the View menu

5. Drag the **split bar** to the right so that it is positioned where you want to separate the directory tree and contents list windows, then click the **left mouse button**. File Manager adjusts the width of this window.

6. If necessary, repeat Steps 4 and 5 to adjust the view so you see the file details that you specified.

RENAMING AND COPYING FILES

You need to copy the standard cover letter stored in the file named LETTER1 so that later you can produce a variation of this letter for résumés. You decide to rename it to COVER1.LTR with the Rename option on the File menu, and then copy it using the Copy option on the File menu. When you copy files, Windows automatically prompts you if you attempt to copy over an existing file.

To rename a file:

1. Click **LETTER1** in the contents list window. File Manager highlights this filename, and an outline appears around the current directory in the directory tree window. See Figure 13-17.

current directory ➞

currently selected filename

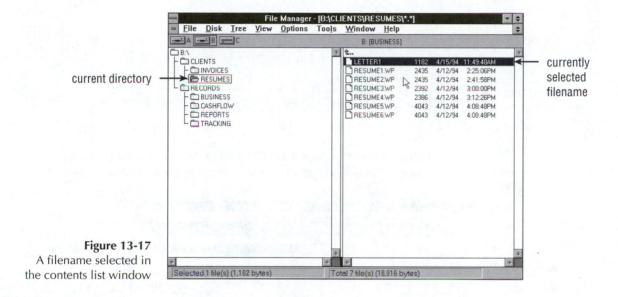

Figure 13-17
A filename selected in the contents list window

2. Click **File**, then click **Rename**. File Manager displays a Rename dialog box. See Figure 13-18.

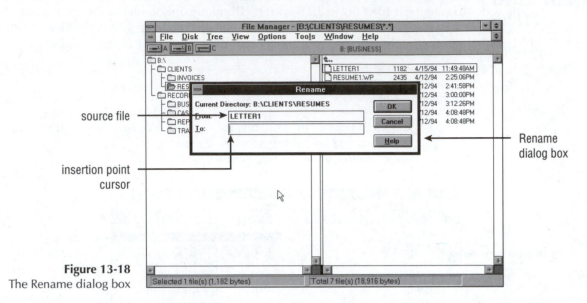

source file

insertion point cursor

Rename dialog box

Figure 13-18
The Rename dialog box

3. In the To text box, type **COVER1.LTR** and click **OK**. File Manager renames the file and updates the contents list window. See Figure 13-19.

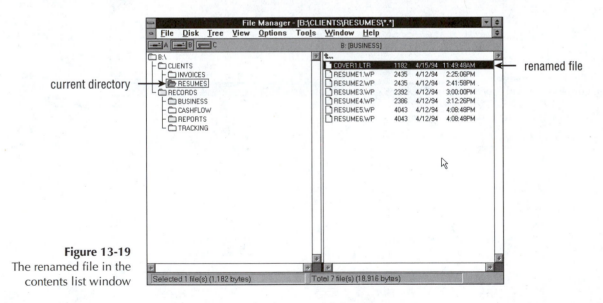

current directory

renamed file

Figure 13-19
The renamed file in the contents list window

Now copy this file.

4. Be sure the file named COVER1.LTR is highlighted in the contents list window.

5. Click **File**, then click **Copy**. File Manager displays a Copy dialog box. See Figure 13-20. The dialog box shows the current directory and the file selected for the copy operation. You are automatically placed in the To text box.

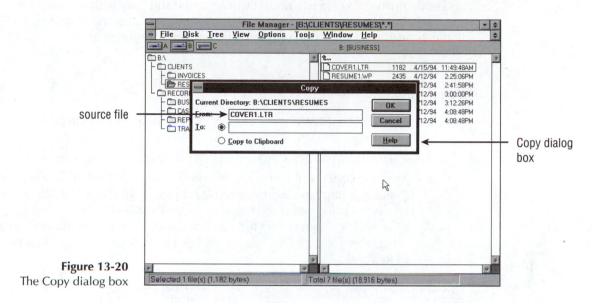

source file

Copy dialog box

Figure 13-20
The Copy dialog box

6. In the To text box, type **COVER2.LTR** and click **OK**. File Manager copies COVER1.LTR, produces a new file named COVER2.LTR, and updates the contents list window. See Figure 13-21.

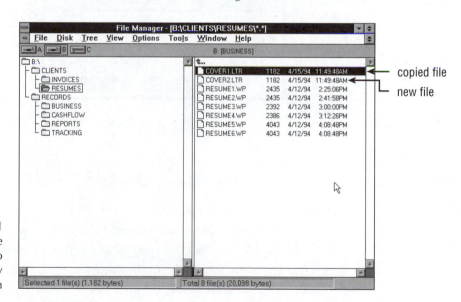

copied file

new file

Figure 13-21
File Manager updates the contents list window to show the file produced by the copy operation

If you want to copy a file to another drive, you specify the drive name with the filename. If you want to copy a file to another subdirectory, you specify the path for that subdirectory with the filename. If you want to copy a file to a subdirectory on another drive, you specify both the drive name and path with the filename.

You also want to make a copy of the second résumé template file, so that you can produce a variation of this résumé for one of your clients.

To copy this file:

1. Click **RESUME2.WP** in the contents list window. File Manager highlights this filename.

2. Click **File**, then click **Copy**. File Manager displays a Copy dialog box.

3. Type **RESUME6.WP** and click **OK**. File Manager displays a Confirm File Replace dialog box. See Figure 13-22. In the dialog box, File Manager shows the drive, path, and filename for an existing file named RESUME6.WP and for the file you want to copy. It asks if you want to replace the existing file. You do *not* want to replace this file with a copy of RESUME2.WP.

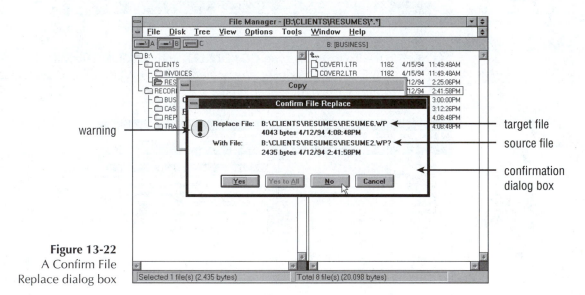

Figure 13-22
A Confirm File
Replace dialog box

4. Click **No**. File Manager closes the dialog boxes and the File menu.

Now specify another filename for this copy operation.

5. Click **File**, then click **Copy**. File Manager displays a Copy dialog box.

6. Type **RESUME7.WP** and click **OK**. File Manager copies RESUME2.WP and produces a new file named RESUME7.WP. It then updates the contents list window.

MODIFYING THE DIRECTORY STRUCTURE

You decide to modify the directory structure so that it more closely resembles that of your own client diskette. You want to move those subdirectories currently positioned below the CLIENTS and RECORDS directories so that they are immediately below the root directory.

To move the INVOICES directory:

1. Click the **INVOICES directory name** in the directory tree window. File Manager updates the contents list window to show the files in this subdirectory.

2. Be sure the mouse pointer points to the INVOICES directory name or to the file folder icon. Then press and hold the **left mouse button** as you drag the mouse pointer, now represented as an arrow pointing to a sheet of paper, to the file folder for the root directory, A:\ or B:\. See Figure 13-23.

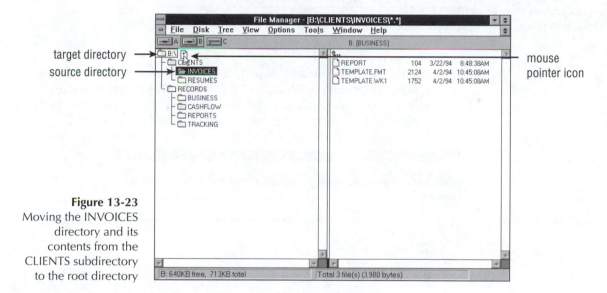

Figure 13-23
Moving the INVOICES directory and its contents from the CLIENTS subdirectory to the root directory

3. Release the left mouse button. File Manager displays a Confirm Mouse Operation dialog box and asks if you want to move the selected files or directories to A:\ or B:\. See Figure 13-24.

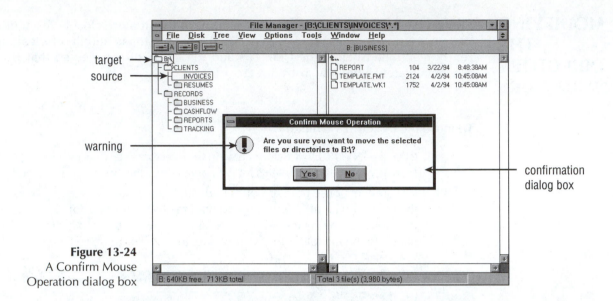

Figure 13-24
A Confirm Mouse
Operation dialog box

4. Click **Yes**. File Manager displays a Moving dialog box and informs you that it is creating A:\INVOICES (or B:\INVOICES). It then moves the files in the original directory to the new directory. Finally, it removes the original directory. Figure 13-25 shows the modified directory tree.

Figure 13-25
The modified directory
tree after moving the
INVOICES subdirectory

5. Click the **INVOICES file folder icon**. File Manager updates the contents list window to show the files in this directory.

6. Move the RESUMES directory using the same approach as you used for the INVOICES directory. Figure 13-26 shows the modified directory tree.

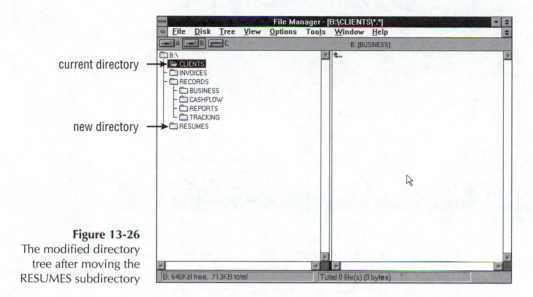

current directory

new directory

Figure 13-26
The modified directory
tree after moving the
RESUMES subdirectory

7. If necessary, click the **CLIENTS file folder icon**. The contents list window shows that this directory is now empty.

REMOVING A DIRECTORY

Now that you have moved the INVOICES and RESUMES subdirectories from the CLIENTS directory, you can remove the CLIENTS directory. As in the DOS Shell, you can remove the directory with one of the Delete keys.

To remove a directory:

1. Be sure the file folder icon for the CLIENTS directory is highlighted.

2. Press **[Delete]** or **[Del]**. (Instead of using this shortcut key, you could also use the Delete option on the File menu.) File Manager displays a Delete dialog box that shows the current directory. See Figure 13-27.

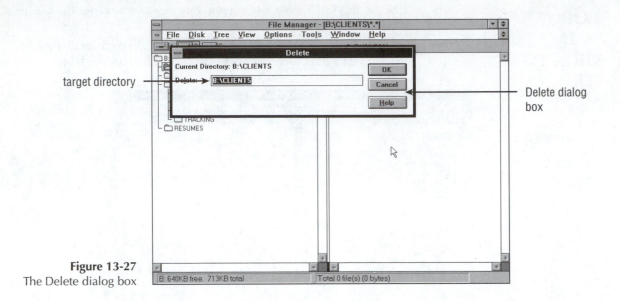

Figure 13-27
The Delete dialog box

3. Click **OK**. File Manager displays a Confirm Directory Delete dialog box.

4. Click **Yes**. File Manager removes the CLIENTS directory and updates the view of the directory tree. See Figure 13-28.

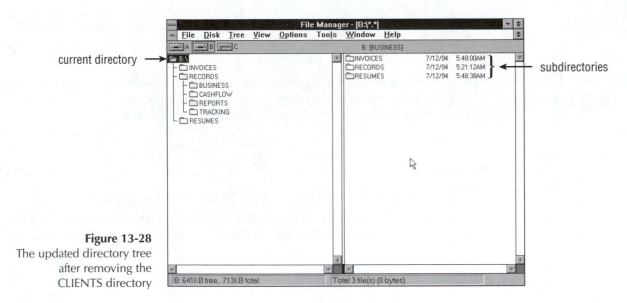

Figure 13-28
The updated directory tree
after removing the
CLIENTS directory

REORGANIZ-ING THE DIRECTORY STRUCTURE

Next you want to move all the directories currently located below RECORDS so that they are immediately below the root directory. Follow the same process that you used to move the directories located below the original CLIENTS directory.

To make the final modifications to the directory structure:

1. Move all the directories below RECORDS and place them below the root directory.

2. Delete the empty directory RECORDS.

3. Click the **file folder icon** for the root directory. Your new directory tree should be identical to that shown in Figure 13-29.

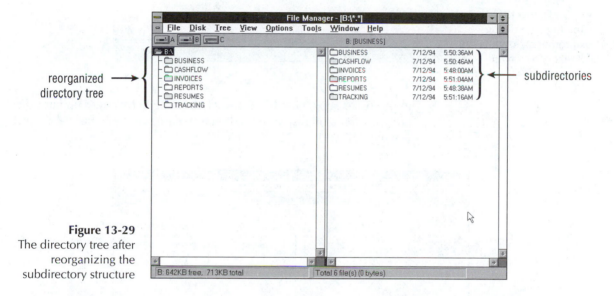

reorganized directory tree

subdirectories

Figure 13-29
The directory tree after reorganizing the subdirectory structure

RENAMING A DIRECTORY

Now that you have reorganized the directory structure, you want to change the name of the TRACKING directory to JOBS so that it is similar to your own client diskette. The process for renaming directories is similar to that in the DOS Shell.

To rename the TRACKING directory:

1. Click the **TRACKING file folder icon**.

2. Click **File**, then click **Rename**. File Manager displays a Rename dialog box with the name of the current directory—the directory name that you want to change. See Figure 13-30.

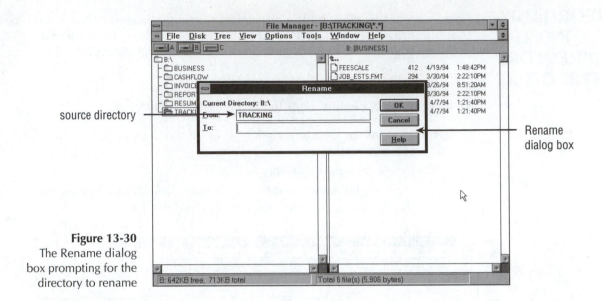

Figure 13-30
The Rename dialog box prompting for the directory to rename

source directory

Rename dialog box

3. In the To text box, type **JOBS** and click **OK**. File Manager updates the directory tree and displays the directory names in alphabetical order. See Figure 13-31.

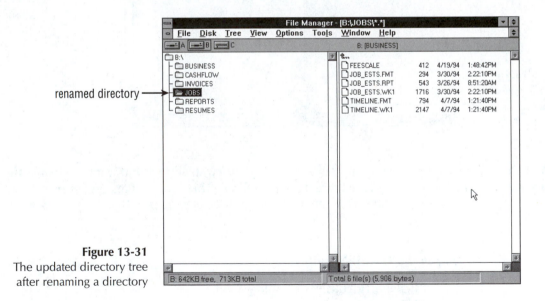

renamed directory

Figure 13-31
The updated directory tree after renaming a directory

CREATING A DIRECTORY

Your client diskette contains a directory named PRJCASH that contains income projection reports for the first five years as well as report formats for quarterly and yearly projected income. You want to modify this copy of your coworker's diskette so that it contains the same directory and the same set of files as the client diskette.

The process for creating a directory and moving files is similar to that used in the DOS Shell. Before you create a directory, you must select the directory that will be the parent directory of the new directory. In this case, you want the new directory to appear below the root directory.

To create a directory:

1. Click the **file folder icon** for the root directory, A:\ or B:\. File Manager highlights the directory name.

2. Click **File**, then click **Create Directory**. File Manager displays a Create Directory dialog box. See Figure 13-32. The current directory is A:\ or B:\. The insertion point cursor is positioned in the Name text box.

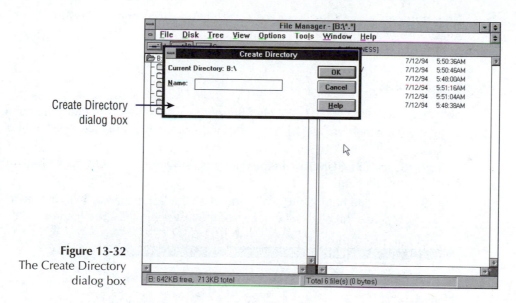

Create Directory dialog box

Figure 13-32
The Create Directory dialog box

3. In the Name text box, type **PRJCASH** and click **OK**. File Manager includes the new directory in the directory tree. See Figure 13-33.

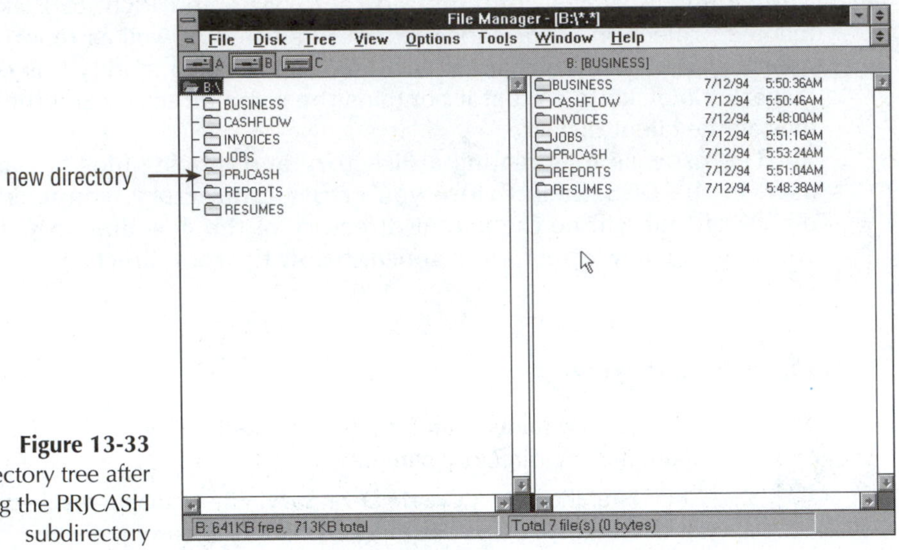

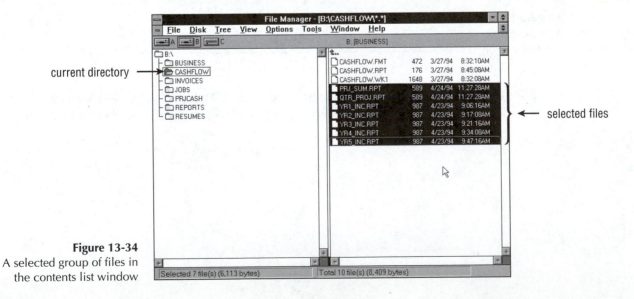

Figure 13-33
The directory tree after
adding the PRJCASH
subdirectory

MOVING FILES

Now you can move files from the CASHFLOW directory to the new directory. Again, the process is similar to that in the DOS Shell.

To move files:

1. Click the **CASHFLOW file folder icon**. File Manager updates the contents list window. The last seven files in this directory are the ones that you want to move.

2. Click **PRJ_SUM.RPT** in the contents list window. File Manager highlights this filename.

3. Press and hold **[Shift]** while you click the last filename, **YR5_INC.RPT**. File Manager highlights the names of the last seven files. See Figure 13-34.

Figure 13-34
A selected group of files in
the contents list window

4. Position the mouse pointer over the selected files. Press and hold the **left mouse button** as you drag the icon of a stack of papers to the PRJCASH directory name in the directory tree window. See Figure 13-35.

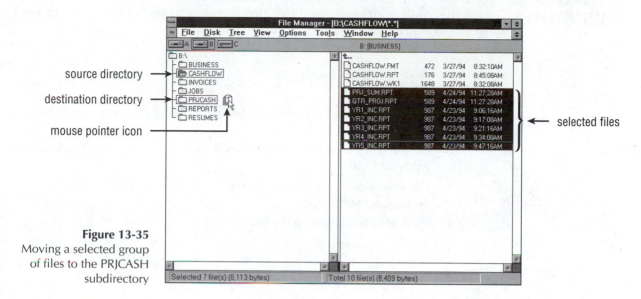

source directory

destination directory

mouse pointer icon

selected files

Figure 13-35
Moving a selected group of files to the PRJCASH subdirectory

5. After you position the icon representing a stack of papers on the PRJCASH directory name, release the left mouse button. File Manager displays a Confirm Mouse Operation dialog box and asks if you want to move the selected files to the PRJCASH directory.

6. Click **Yes**. File Manager displays a Moving dialog box. After it completes this operation, you see the remaining files in the CASHFLOW directory.

7. Click the **PRJCASH file folder icon**. File Manager updates the contents list window and shows you the files moved to this new directory. See Figure 13-36.

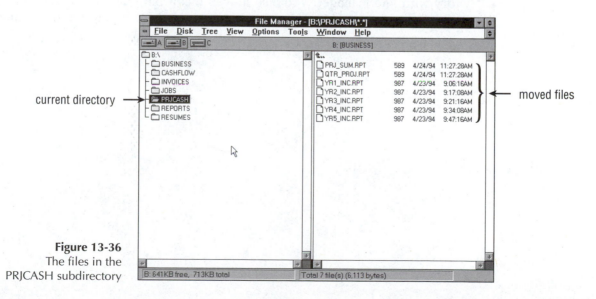

current directory

moved files

Figure 13-36
The files in the PRJCASH subdirectory

8. Click the **root directory icon** in the directory tree window.

EXITING WINDOWS

Now that you have completed your examination of a copy of your coworker's diskette and have reorganized the directories on this diskette, you are ready to exit Windows.

To exit Windows:

1. Double-click the **Control-menu box** for File Manager. Windows closes File Manager.

2. Double-click the **Control-menu box** for the Main Group. Windows closes the Main Group.

3. Double-click the **Control-menu box** for Program Manager. Windows prompts for verification.

4. Click **OK**. You return to the DOS prompt.

◆

SUMMARY

In this tutorial, you learned how to use File Manager and its directory window. You formatted and copied diskettes with File Manager. You changed drives and expanded the directory tree in the directory tree window. You selected a directory to examine the directory's files. You viewed full and partial details on files in the contents list window.

You used File Manager to modify the directory structure of a diskette. You moved directories, and their files, from one level in the directory tree to another level. You removed empty directories, renamed a directory, and created a directory with File Manager. You also moved files from one directory to another. When you completed these operations, you closed File Manager and its window.

Command Reference	
File Manager Commands	
Disk/Copy Disk	Copies the contents of a diskette from a source drive to another diskette in a destination drive
Disk/Format Disk	Formats a diskette in a specific drive to a specific storage capacity
File/Create Directory	Creates a directory below the current directory
File/Rename	Renames a directory or a file
Tree/Expand All	Expands the directory tree to include all subdirectories
View/All File Details	Displays the filename, extension, size, date, time, and attributes of files in the contents list window
View/Name	Displays filenames only in the contents list window
View/Partial Details	Specifies the details displayed on files in the contents list window
View/Sort by Name	Displays filenames in the contents list window in order by filename and file extension
View/Split	Displays a split bar so that you can visually adjust the relative widths of the directory tree window and the contents list window
View/Tree and Directory	Displays a directory tree window and a contents list window

QUESTIONS

1. What windows does File Manager display, and what information is displayed in each window?

2. What formatting options are available when you format a diskette in File Manager?

3. What advantage(s) does File Manager have over DOS when you need to format a diskette?

4. What advantage(s) does File Manager have over DOS 5.0 and 6.0 when you need to copy a diskette?

5. How do you select a drive with File Manager?

6. How can you expand the directory tree in the directory tree window in File Manager?

7. How do you select a directory in File Manager?

8. What three ways can you control the display of the File Manager window?

9. What three options are available for displaying information on files in the contents list window in File Manager?

10. What options are available for determining the sort order in the contents list window in File Manager?

11. If you indicate that you want to view all details on files in the contents list window, what information does File Manager display?

12. Name two ways to adjust the relative widths of the directory tree window and contents list window in File Manager.

13. What is a file attribute? Identify the four file attributes and the code that DOS and Windows use for each attribute.

14. How do you copy a file in File Manager?

15. How do you rename a file in File Manager?

16. How can you move a directory from one level of the directory tree to another with File Manager?

17. What three operations does File Manager perform when you move a directory?

18. How do you rename a directory in File Manager?

19. How do you create a directory in File Manager? What one consideration must you take into account before you create a directory?

20. Describe the steps you would use to move a group of files from one directory to another directory in File Manager?

21. What types of drives does File Manager display in its drive window?

22. Name three ways to identify the current directory in File Manager.

23. What types of icons does File Manager use for directories, program files, and document files?

24. How does the File Type option on the View menu affect the display in the contents list window?

25. What options are available in File Manager for controlling the display of the directory tree?

26. What is a split bar, and how do you use it in File Manager?

27. How do you remove a directory in File Manager?

28. What does File Manager do when you attempt to copy a file over an existing file?

29. What information must you specify if you want to copy a file to another drive in File Manager?

30. What information must you specify if you want to copy a file to another subdirectory in File Manager?

TUTORIAL ASSIGNMENTS

1. **Viewing File Details in File Manager**: *Use your Tutorial Disk for this Tutorial Assignment.* Start Windows, open File Manager, and switch to the drive that contains your Tutorial Disk. Perform the following operations in File Manager, list the commands or steps that you use for each operation, and answer any questions.

   a. Select the JOBS subdirectory.
   b. Display files in the contents list window with only the name and date. What file has the most recent date? The oldest file date?
   c. Display files in the contents list window with only the name and size. What file is the largest? What file is the smallest?
   d. Display files in the contents list window with all file details. Then remove file attributes from the display. If necessary, adjust the size of the contents list window. What information does File Manager display for the filename FEESCALE?
   e. Display files in the contents list window by name. What is the name of the first file? The last file?

   Close File Manager, then exit Windows.

2. **Changing the File Order in File Manager**: *Use your Tutorial Disk for this Tutorial Assignment.* Start Windows, open the Main Group, open File Manager, and switch to the drive that contains your Tutorial Disk. Perform the following operations in File Manager, list the commands or steps that you use for each operation, and answer any questions.

   a. Select the BUSINESS subdirectory.
   b. Display files in order by date. Does File Manager display the most recently created or the oldest file first? What is the name of the first file? The last file?
   c. Display files in order by size. Does File Manager display the largest or the smallest file first? What is the name of the first file? The last file?
   d. Display files in order by type. What part of the filename determines the sort order? What is the name of the first file? The last file?
   e. Display files in order by name. Does File Manager display filenames in alphabetical order by both the filename and file extension? What is the name of the first file? The last file?

   Close File Manager and exit Windows.

3. **Renaming and Copying Files**: *Use your Exercise Disk for this Tutorial Assignment.* Start Windows, open the Main Group, open File Manager, and switch to the drive that contains your Exercise Disk. If necessary, expand the directory tree. Then perform the following operations, list the commands and steps that you use for each operation, and answer any questions.

   a. Select the INVOICES subdirectory.
   b. Change the name of the file REPORT to REPORT.FRM.

c. Copy the file named REPORT.FRM to produce a new file named INTERIM.RPT.

d. Copy the file named REPORT.FRM to produce a new file named FINAL.RPT.

e. Select the REPORTS subdirectory.

f. Copy the file named JUN.RPT to produce a new file named SUMMARY.RPT.

g. Copy the file named JUN.RPT to produce a new file named JUL.RPT.

Exit Windows and, from the DOS prompt, use the TREE command to print the modified directory structure of your diskette with a list of filenames by directory.

4. **Moving Files**: *Use your Exercise Disk for this Tutorial Assignment.* Start Windows, open the Main Group, open File Manager, and switch to the drive that contains your Exercise Disk. If necessary, expand the directory tree. Then perform the following operations, list the commands and steps that you use for each operation, and answer any questions.

a. Select the RECORDS subdirectory.

b. Create a new subdirectory named LISTS positioned below the RECORDS directory.

c. Select the BUSINESS subdirectory.

d. Copy all the files with the file extension LST from this subdirectory to the LISTS subdirectory.

e. Select the RECORDS subdirectory.

f. Create a new subdirectory named SUMMARY positioned below the RECORDS directory.

g. Select the CASHFLOW subdirectory.

h. Copy the file named PRJ_SUM.RPT to the SUMMARY subdirectory. Then select and copy the files with the file specification YR?_INC.RPT to the SUMMARY directory.

Exit Windows and, from the DOS prompt, use the TREE command to print the modified directory structure of your diskette with a list of filenames by directory.

5. **Reorganizing the Directory Structure of a Diskette with File Manager**: *Use your Exercise Disk for this Tutorial Assignment.* Start Windows, open the Main Group, open File Manager, and switch to the drive that contains your Exercise Disk. If necessary, expand the directory tree. Then perform the following operations.

a. Move all the subdirectories currently located below CLIENTS to below the root directory.

b. Move all the subdirectories currently located below RECORDS to below the root directory.

c. Delete the empty subdirectory named RECORDS.

d. Change the name of the subdirectory called TRACKING to JOBCOSTS.

Exit Windows and, from the DOS prompt, print the modified directory structure of your diskette with a list of filenames by directory.

Glossary

Symbols

. The notation used in a directory listing to refer to the current directory

.. The notation used in a directory listing to refer to the directory one level higher than the current directory; the parent directory

? The question-mark wildcard character that substitutes for a single character in the filename or file extension of a file specification

* The asterisk wildcard character that substitutes for any and all characters in a filename or file extension of a file specification

\ A notation that indicates the root directory; a notation that separates two directory names in a path or a directory name and filename in a file specification

8086 An obsolete microprocessor chip introduced in 1983-84, used in XT compatibles, and capable of processing and transmitting 16 bits at a time, accessing 1MB of memory, and operating at a clock speed of 5 to 10MHz

8088 An obsolete microprocessor chip introduced in 1983, used in IBM PCs and PC/XTs, and capable of processing 16 bits at a time, transmitting only 8 bits at a time, accessing 1MB of memory, and operating at a clock speed of 5 to 8MHz

80286 A microprocessor chip introduced in 1984, used in ATs (IBM PC/ATs and 286s), and capable of processing and transmitting 16 bits at a time, accessing 16MB of memory, and operating at a clock speed of 8 to 12 MHz

80386DX A microprocessor chip introduced in 1985, used in 386DXs, and capable of processing and transmitting 32 bits at a time, accessing 4GB of memory, and operating at a clock speed of 16 to 33MHz

80386SX A microprocessor chip introduced in 1988, used in 386SXs, and capable of processing 32 bits at a time, transmitting only 16 bits at a time, accessing 16MB of memory, and operating at a clock speed of 16 to 20MHz

80486DX A microprocessor chip with a math coprocessor introduced in 1989, used in 486DXs, and capable of processing and transmitting 32 bits at a time, accessing 4GB of memory, and operating at a clock speed of 25 to 50MHz

80486SX A microprocessor chip with a disabled math coprocessor introduced in 1991, used in 486SXs, and capable of processing and transmitting 32 bits at a time, accessing 4GB of memory, and operating at a clock speed of 16 to 25MHz

80486DX2 A microprocessor chip with a math coprocessor introduced in 1992, used in 486DX2s, and capable of processing and transmitting 32 bits at a time, accessing 4GB of memory, and operating at a clock speed of 50 to 66MHz

A

A: The drive name assigned to the first diskette drive in a computer system

A prompt The DOS prompt for drive A

access hole The oval-shaped recording window on a 3½-inch diskette

access time The time required to read or write a byte of data to a disk

active window The currently selected window in Windows with a highlighted title bar

adapter card A circuit board that is inserted in the system unit and connected to the motherboard so that the computer system can work with a hardware component

adapter memory The upper memory area that extends from 640K to 1MB and that is reserved for system-related operations, such as for video display adapters, network adapters, and the ROM-BIOS (ROM Basic Input/Output System)

add-in card A circuit board that is inserted in the system unit and connected to the motherboard so that the computer system can work with a hardware component

address bus The combination of address lines that access memory

address lines The electronic circuitry used to access specific storage locations in memory

allocation error An error in the allocation of space to a file on disk

allocation unit One or more sectors used by DOS as the minimum storage space when it allocates storage space on a disk to a file; a cluster

analog Varying continuously over a range, such as the amplitude of a sound wave signal

annotate To add comments to a Windows Help screen

anti-viral software A program that scans a disk for computer viruses and removes computer viruses, or monitors a computer system for the presence of computer viruses

application software Software that allows a user to accomplish a specific task on a computer system, such as word processing, electronic spreadsheet, database, graphics, desktop publishing, or communications software

archive attribute An attribute assigned to a file by DOS to indicate that the file was created or modified since the last backup

archive To store less frequently used files on diskettes

Archive attribute An attribute, represented by the code "A," assigned to a file to indicate that it is a new or modified file and that it has not been backed up

ascending order Arranged in alphabetical order from A to Z, in numerical order from the lowest to the highest value, or in date and time order from the most recent date to the oldest date

ASCII An abbreviation for *American Standard Code for Information Interchange*, a coding scheme for representing characters and symbols

ASCII code The numerical code for an ASCII control code or character

ASCII file A simple file format in which data is stored as text

ASCII value The numerical code for an ASCII control code or character

attribute A special characteristic assigned to a file by DOS, such as the System, Hidden, Read-Only, or Archive attribute

AUTOEXEC.BAT A special, auto-executing batch file that is stored in the root directory of drive C and that contains commands executed by DOS during the initial startup of a computer system when you power on the computer

auto-indent A feature of the MS-DOS Editor in which it automatically indents the next line to match the indentation on the previous line

auto-park A safety feature that automatically moves or parks the read/write heads in a landing zone on the innermost surface of the hard disk when the computer's power is switched off

B

B: The drive name assigned to the second floppy disk drive in a computer system, or to the first disk drive if there is only one drive

B prompt The DOS prompt for drive B

backtab key A key combination, [Shift][Tab], that moves the selection cursor to the previous window in the DOS Shell

backup catalog A file that contains information about files backed up by MSBACKUP

backup copy An extra or duplicate of a diskette, file, or files kept in reserve in the event you need to restore the original diskette, file, or files

backup cycle A periodic cycle used to back up files on a hard disk

backup set A set of diskettes that contain duplicate copies of files stored on a hard disk

bad sector A defective area on a hard disk or diskette that DOS marks as unusable

batch file An ASCII file that contains one or more commands that DOS executes when you enter the name of the batch file at the DOS prompt

baud rate The speed of transmitting data, in bits per second

binary digit The number 1 or 0 in the binary numbering system

BIOS An abbreviation for *Basic Input/Output System*

bit An abbreviation for a binary digit that consists of the number 1 or 0

block header The name of a configuration block enclosed within square brackets and preceding the commands in the configuration block

block heading A heading at the beginning of the menu block or a configuration block in CONFIG.SYS

block name The name assigned to a configuration block in CONFIG.SYS that contains the set of commands DOS executes if you select the corresponding menu option

boot To start a computer system

boot disk A diskette that contains the DOS system files and that is used to start a computer

boot record A hidden file that contains information about the version of DOS used to format a disk and the physical characteristics of the disk, such as the number of bytes per sector, sectors per cluster, maximum number of files per disk, total number of sectors, and sectors per track

boot sector virus A type of virus that replaces the boot sector with its own program code to guarantee that it is automatically loaded into memory when the computer system boots

boot sector A hidden file that contains information about the version of DOS used to format a disk and the physical characteristics of the disk, such as the number of bytes per sector, sectors per cluster, maximum number of files per disk, total number of sectors, and sectors per track

booting The process of powering on a computer system and loading DOS into memory

bootstrap loader program A program that is located in the boot record of a boot disk and that locates and loads DOS from the boot disk

buffers A small area of memory for storing data retrieved from disk and for storing data prior to being written to disk

byte A combination of eight bits used to encode a character, including letters of the alphabet, numbers, and symbols

C

C: The drive name assigned to the first hard disk drive in a computer system

C prompt The DOS prompt for drive C

cache Disk buffers for storing data read from disk or for storing data prior to being written to disk

cascade To arrange each open window in Windows in an overlapping pattern to the right and below the previous window

central processing unit The microprocessor chip that processes data under the direction of instructions in a program

chain A sequence of lost clusters that once belonged to a file

check box A box within a dialog box for selecting or removing an option

checksum A value calculated by Microsoft Anti-Virus for a program file, based on characteristics of the program file, including its size, date, and time

click To quickly press and release a mouse button

Clipboard An area of memory used by Windows to temporarily store data

clock rate The rate, measured in megahertz, at which the microprocessor executes program instructions

clock speed The rate, measured in megahertz, at which the microprocessor executes program instructions

cluster One or more sectors used by DOS as the minimum storage space when it allocates storage space on a disk to a file; an allocation unit

cold boot Starting a computer system by turning on the power switch

column A position on a line on the monitor

COM1: The device name assigned by DOS to the first communications, or serial, port in a computer system

COM2: The device name assigned by DOS to the second communications, or serial, port in a computer system

COM3: The device name assigned by DOS to the third communications, or serial, port in a computer system

COM4: The device name assigned by DOS to the fourth communications, or serial, port in a computer system

command An instruction to perform a task, issued by a user to a program

COMMAND.COM The MS-DOS and PC-DOS operating system file responsible for interpreting commands entered at the DOS prompt; locating and executing internal and external DOS commands; redirecting input and output; locating and loading an application, programming language, or utility; and executing commands stored in batch files

command interpreter The operating system file, usually COMMAND.COM, that interprets commands entered at the DOS prompt; locates and executes internal and external DOS commands; locates and loads an application, programming language, or utility; and executes commands stored in batch files

command line The line to the right of the DOS prompt where you enter commands

command line interface The use of the DOS prompt to interact with the operating system

command processor The operating system file, COMMAND.COM, that interprets commands entered at the DOS prompt; locates and executes internal and external DOS commands; locates and loads an application, programming language, or utility; and executes commands stored in batch files

command stack A small area of memory used by DOSKEY to keep track of commands entered at the DOS prompt

Common configuration block A configuration block that contains commands that DOS executes no matter which menu option you select from a Startup menu

communications software Software that enables you to use your computer system to communicate with other computer systems in the same office or in other offices around the country or world with the use of a modem and a telephone line connection

compatibility test A backup test performed by MSBACKUP to configure a computer for a backup and to test the reliability of the backup process

compressed drive A compressed volume file that appears as a real disk drive to programs

compressed volume A compressed drive

compressed volume file A special, hidden, system file that contains the contents of a compressed drive

compression The process by which DoubleSpace or another disk compression utility examines files for repetitive sequences that can be coded more compactly and then compresses the files

computer virus A program that adversely affects the performance of a computer system

CON The device name assigned by DOS to the console unit—the keyboard and monitor

CONFIG.SYS A special, auto-executing system file that is stored in the root directory of drive C and that contains commands for customizing DOS as DOS is being loaded into memory after powering on a computer

configuration block A group of commands in CONFIG.SYS for configuring a computer system

contents list window The File Manager window that displays information on files in the current directory and on the current drive

contiguous sectors Adjacent sectors of a file on a hard disk or diskette

control code A code for the use of the Ctrl (Control) key with another key

control lines The electronic circuitry used to synchronize operations

Control Panel A group of Windows applications for customizing and configuring Windows and a computer system

Control-menu box A Windows button located to the left of the title bar and used to display a Control menu or to exit Windows

conventional memory The base or standard memory that extends from 0K ("zero K") to 640K and that contains the operating system and installed device drivers as well as TSRs, software applications, and utilities that DOS loads into this memory

coprocessor An additional microprocessor that works in conjunction with the main microprocessor to dramatically increase the speed of mathematical calculations and processing of graphics

cross-linked cluster A cluster that belongs to, or is shared by, two or more files

CPU The abbreviation for *central processing unit*, the microprocessor chip that processes data under the direction of instructions in a program

crosstalk Electrical interference in a cable

CRT The abbreviation for *cathode ray tube*, the main component of a monitor

current directory The directory or subdirectory that is currently in use and whose path is displayed as part of the DOS prompt

current drive The drive DOS uses to locate commands and files if no other drive is specified

current window The currently selected window in Windows with a highlighted title bar

cursor A blinking underscore character (_) or a small solid rectangle that identifies your current working position on the screen and that marks where the next character that you type will appear on the screen

customize To configure a computer system to meet a specific set of needs

CVF An abbreviation for *compressed volume file*

D

data Facts, figures, and images

data bits The number of bits in a byte that constitute a character

data bus The electronic circuitry that connects the CPU with internal and external hardware components

data file A file that contains a document or data

data lines The electronic circuitry used to transmit and receive data from other hardware components

database software Software for storing and managing large quantities of information in a table format

date stamp The date assigned by DOS to a file

DBLSPACE.BIN The operating system file that provides access to compressed drives

DBLSPACE.SYS A device driver that loads DBLSPACE.BIN into memory

default The setting or reference point DOS uses unless you specify another setting or reference point

default directory The directory or subdirectory that is currently in use and whose path is displayed as part of the DOS prompt

default drive The drive DOS uses to locate commands and files if no other drive is specified

defragmenting utility A program that rearranges files on a hard disk or a diskette so that all sectors of each file are stored in consecutive sectors

Delete Sentry level of protection A level of protection for recovering deleted files in which the Undelete utility stores deleted files in a hidden directory named SENTRY on drive C

Delete Tracker level of protection A level of protection for recovering deleted files in which the Undelete utility stores the names and locations of deleted files in a hidden system file named PCTRACKR.DEL in the root directory of drive C

descending order Arranged in reverse alphabetical order from Z to A, in reverse numerical order from the highest to the lowest value, or in reverse date and time order from the oldest date to the most recent date

desktop publishing software Software used to produce high-quality, professional-looking documents for presentation or reproduction

destination file A file that DOS copies to

device A component within a computer system, such as a keyboard, mouse, system unit, monitor (or video display unit), disk drive, or a printer

device driver A file with program code for managing hardware or software

device name A name DOS assigns to a device or hardware component

diagnostic mode An operating mode in which CHKDSK examines a disk for errors, reports the presence of errors, and simulates the process of removing those errors

diagnostic utility A program that checks the status of components and reports technical information about a computer system

dialog box An outlined area of the screen where a program displays options for you to select or useful information, including messages and warnings

differential backup A backup performed during a backup cycle, which includes all files altered since the last full backup

digital Consisting of data stored in discrete units, such as 0s and 1s

directive A command in CONFIG.SYS

directory A list of information on files stored on a diskette or a hard disk produced by the DIR command; the root directory or a subdirectory that tracks information on other files

directory file A special file created by DOS to keep track of information on files, including subdirectories

directory tree A diagrammatic representation of the directory structure of a hard disk or diskette

directory tree window The area of the screen where the DOS Shell and the File Manager displays a graphical representation of the directory structure of a hard disk or diskette

disk A device used to store program and data files

disk buffers A small area of memory for storing data retrieved from disk and for storing data prior to being written to disk

disk cache An area of memory used by SmartDrive, DOS, or another program to store data read from disk or in the process of being written to disk

disk compression The process by which DoubleSpace or another disk compression utility examines files for repetitive sequences that can be coded more compactly and then compresses the files

disk drive A hardware component that records data onto or retrieves data from storage media, such as a diskette or a hard drive

disk jacket A case that encloses and protects the flat, circular plastic disk that constitutes a diskette

disk map A visual representation of the organization of clusters on a hard disk or diskette

disk order The order in which DOS keeps track of files on a diskette or hard disk

diskette A common storage medium that consists of a flat, circular plastic disk with a magnetic coating enclosed in a case for protection

DOS The abbreviation for *Disk Operating System*, the primary operating system software used on IBM and IBM-compatible microcomputers

DOS environment A small area of memory where DOS stores important settings that it and other programs use

DOS file A type of ASCII file

DOS path The sequence of directory and subdirectory names that identify the location of a subdirectory where executable files are stored

DOS prompt The command line interface for interacting with DOS

DOS text file A type of ASCII file

dot The notation used in a directory listing to refer to the current directory

dot dot The notation used in a directory listing to refer to the directory one level higher than the current directory; the parent directory

dot-matrix printer A type of impact printer that uses small pins in the print head to produce a character composed of an array, or matrix, of dots

double-click To quickly press twice and release a mouse button

double-density disk A 5¼-inch diskette with a storage capacity of 360K, or a 3½-inch diskette with a storage capacity of 720K

double-sided disk A type of diskette in which data is recorded on both sides of the disk

draft mode An operating mode in which a printer prints quickly but produces lower quality output

drag To hold down the left mouse button, move the mouse, and then release the mouse button, usually to select a group of filenames or to select and move an object or icon on the screen

drive icon An icon that represents a disk drive in a computer system

drive name A device name that consists of a letter of the alphabet and a colon and that is assigned to a disk drive in a computer system

drive window An area of the screen where a program displays a list of the drives available in a computer system

drop-down menu A menu that drops down from the menu bar when you select a menu name

E

echo To display on the monitor

editing keys A set of keys that allow you to change or modify text

electronic spreadsheet A type of software application for performing calculations on numbers arranged in a table of columns and rows and for building models

ellipsis Three dots (...) next to a menu option that indicate a program will display a dialog box when you select the menu option

EMM386.EXE A device driver that carves the upper memory area into upper memory blocks (UMBs) so that DOS can load device drivers and TSRs into the upper memory area, and that can convert all or part of extended memory into expanded memory for those applications that use expanded memory but not extended memory

end-of-file code A control code, [Ctrl][Z], that marks the end of an ASCII file

environment variable A name that DOS associates with a setting stored in the DOS environment

EOF The abbreviation for *end of file*

executing Carrying out instructions in a program that is already loaded in memory

expansion slot A slot for inserting and attaching an adapter or add-in card to the motherboard

expanded memory Additional memory outside of conventional, upper, and extended memory that is added to a computer system by an expanded memory board or by converting extended memory into expanded memory

extended memory The memory above 1MB

external command A command that is executed by DOS after DOS locates the program file with the program instructions on disk and then loads the program instructions into memory

external modem A modem that consists of a separate hardware unit that connects to one of the serial ports on a computer system

extra-high-density diskette A 3½-inch diskette with a storage capacity of 2.88M

F

FAT An abbreviation for *File Allocation Table*

fax board An adapter inserted in the system unit and mounted on the motherboard for the purpose of sending and receiving facsimiles (faxes)

file A certain amount of storage space on a diskette or hard disk that is set aside for the contents of a program, document, or data file

File Allocation Table A file that contains a list of each allocation unit or cluster on a disk along with information on whether each allocation unit or cluster is available, in use, or defective (i.e., contains a bad sector)

file attribute A special characteristic assigned to a file by DOS

file extension An additional one to three characters included after the main part of a filename, usually to identify the type of data in the file

file folder icon A DOS Shell or Windows icon that represents a directory or subdirectory

file handle A number DOS assigns to an open file to identify the file and track information on that file

file icon A DOS Shell or Windows icon that represents a file

file list window The area on the screen where the DOS Shell displays filenames for a specific directory and drive

File Manager A Windows application for managing the use of drives, directories, and files

file specification The use of a drive name, path, filename, and wild-cards to select one or more files

filename A name assigned to a program, document, or data file to identify its contents

filter A DOS command that can modify the output of another DOS command

fixed disk An internal disk drive unit that consists of two or more unremovable metallic disks or platters with a magnetic coating on both surfaces of the disk

Fixup mode An operating mode in which CHKDSK locates and corrects errors on a disk

floppy disk A common storage medium that consists of a flat, circular plastic disk with a magnetic coating enclosed in a case for protection

flush To empty the contents of disk buffers by writing any remaining data to disk

format To prepare a diskette for use in a computer

formatted diskette A diskette prepared by DOS so that DOS can store data on the diskette

fragmented file A file stored in noncontiguous, or non-adjacent, sectors on a hard disk or diskette

full backup A backup that marks the start of a backup cycle and that includes all or part of the contents of a hard disk

function keys A set of program-specific keys labeled [F1] through [F10] or [F12] used for specific tasks by a program, such as saving or printing

G

G A common abbreviation for *gigabyte*

GB A common abbreviation for *gigabyte*

gigabyte 1,024 megabytes, or approximately one billion bytes, of storage space

graphical user interface An interface that provides a more visual method for interacting with the operating system through the use of icons, menus, and multiple windows

graphics adapter A video display card mounted in an expansion slot on the motherboard to control the display of text and graphics on the monitor

graphics mode A video display mode for displaying graphic images as well as text

graphics software Software used to create illustrations, diagrams, graphics, charts, and freehand drawings

group icon An icon that represents a set of related applications in Windows

GUI The abbreviation for *graphical user interface*, an interface that provides a more visual method for interacting with the operating system through the use of icons, menus, and multiple windows

H

hardcopy The paper copy of computer output

hard disk An internal disk drive unit that consists of two or more unremovable metallic disks or platters with a magnetic coating on both surfaces of a disk, that stores substantially more data than a diskette, and that accesses data substantially faster than a drive unit for a diskette

hard disk partition table A file on a hard disk that contains information that identifies where each hard drive starts and which drive on the hard disk is the boot drive

hardware The physical components of a computer system

head crash A hard disk failure resulting from the read/write heads gouging the surface of a platter in a hard disk

head slot The oval-shaped recording window on a 5¼-inch diskette

help information Information provided by a program to assist you with a program task

Hidden attribute An attribute, represented by the code "H," assigned to a file to indicate that the file should not be displayed in a directory listing

hidden file A file that is not displayed in a directory list

high-density disk A 5¼-inch diskette with a storage capacity of 1.2M, or a 3½-inch diskette with a storage capacity of 1.44M

high memory area The first 64K of extended memory from 1,024K (1MB) to 1,088K where most of DOS and its buffers can be loaded

HIMEM.SYS A device driver that manages extended memory, the high memory area, and the upper memory area

HMA An abbreviation for *high memory area*

hot key A combination of keys that activate a TSR

I

I-bar The mouse pointer used in Windows

IBMBIO.COM The PC-DOS operating system file responsible for assigning device names and handling input and output operations

IBMDOS.COM The PC-DOS operating system file that constitutes the core of DOS and that is responsible for drive, directory, and file management

icon An image or picture displayed on the screen to represent common objects—such as a drive, disk, program, or file—and tasks

image file A special file created on a reformatted disk to store the contents of the directory file and the File Allocation Table so that a disk can be unformatted

impact printer A type of printer that produces a character on paper by striking a metallic element against an inked ribbon

import To retrieve the contents of a file produced with another program

incremental backup A backup performed during a backup cycle which includes only those files that have changed since the last full or last incremental backup

installable device drivers Device drivers that are installed from CONFIG.SYS with the use of DEVICE or DEVICEHIGH commands

initialization file A file that contains initial settings used by a program

ink-jet printer A type of non-impact printer that sprays tiny dots of ink onto paper to form characters or graphics

input The process of providing program instructions, commands, and data to a computer system so that it can accomplish some type of useful task with the data

input device A hardware component, such as the keyboard or mouse, used to provide program instructions, data, and commands to a computer

insert mode A working mode in which what you type is inserted at the position of the cursor and characters to the right of the cursor are shifted to the right

insertion point cursor A flashing vertical bar used as a cursor in Windows

integer A whole number

integrated software A software package that combines two or more applications into one product

interface The means or way in which you interact with a computer system

intermediate file A temporary file created by DOS during the processing of a command and deleted after the operation is complete

internal command A DOS command for which the program instructions are stored in the computer's memory as part of the operating system software

internal modem A modem that is mounted on a card and inserted into one of the expansion slots inside a computer

interrupt command The [Ctrl][Break] key combination, which interrupts a DOS command

I/O The abbreviation for *input/output*

IO.SYS The MS-DOS operating system file responsible for assigning device names and handling input and output operations

K

K A common abbreviation for *kilobyte*

KB A common abbreviation for *kilobyte*

kilobyte 1,024 bytes, or approximately 1,000 bytes, of storage space

L

label A name, preceded with a colon, that identifies the beginning of a block of commands in AUTOEXEC.BAT

LAN The abbreviation for *local area network*, a collection of computers and other peripherals joined by direct cable links and located relatively close to each other, usually in the same building, so that users can share hardware and software resources and files

landing zone The innermost surface of a hard disk where read/write heads rest when the computer's power is switched off

laptop computer A small, lap-size microcomputer

laser printer A type of non-impact printer that uses a laser beam to form an electrostatic, or electrically charged, image on a rotating photosensitive drum, which in turn attracts toner and that uses heat to bond the toner to paper

LCD The abbreviation for *liquid crystal display*, a type of display medium used with laptops and notebooks

list box A box within a dialog box that lists options from which to choose

list device The name of a printer port DOS uses to list output

loading Copying programs or data into a computer's memory

loading high Loading DOS or another program into the high memory area, or loading programs into the upper memory area

loading low Loading DOS or another program into conventional memory

local area network A collection of computers and other peripherals joined by direct cable links and located relatively close to each other, usually in the same building, so that users can share hardware and software resources and files

log file A file in which the BACKUP command stores a record of the path and filename of each file backed up on a hard disk

logical structure of a disk The combination of the File Allocation Tables, the root directory file, and the subdirectory files that track allocation of space and files on a disk

lost cluster A cluster on a hard disk or diskette that no longer belongs to a file

LPT1: The device name assigned by DOS to the first parallel port in a computer system

LPT2: The device name assigned by DOS to the second parallel port in a computer system

LPT3: The device name assigned by DOS to the third parallel port in a computer system

M

M A common abbreviation for *megabyte*

macro A set of stored keystrokes or commands for an operation or set of operations that a program can automatically execute

main directory The first and most important directory created by the FORMAT command on a hard disk or diskette

Main Group A set of Windows applications for managing the resources on a computer system

mainframe computer A computer which has substantially greater capacities for storing and processing data than minicomputers and microcomputers, that operates 10 to 100 times faster than a microcomputer, and which requires a specially controlled environment

major upgrade A major change or major enhancement to a software package

map legend An explanation of the notations used by the Defragmenter to identify cluster usage on a hard disk or diskette

master catalog A file produced by MSBACKUP to keep track of all the backups performed during a backup cycle

Maximize button A Windows button for enlarging a window to fill the entire screen

MB A common abbreviation for *megabyte*

media descriptor byte A byte stored in the boot sector that identifies the disk drive as one that will work with MS-DOS or PC-DOS

megabyte 1,024 kilobytes, or approximately one million bytes, of storage space

megahertz A unit of measurement representing millions of cycles per second

memory A set of storage locations where instructions and data are stored while you use a microcomputer

memory manager A device driver that manages the use of memory

menu A list of command choices presented by a program

menu bar A bar near the top of the screen where programs, such as the MS-DOS Editor, the DOS Shell, Windows, and DOS utilities, display a list of menu names

menu block A menu section at the beginning of CONFIG.SYS where menu options for different startup system configurations are defined

menu text The text that DOS displays as the menu option for a configuration block defined in the menu block in CONFIG.SYS

MHz The abbreviation for *megahertz*

microcomputer A single-user, personal computer system

microprocessor A special computer chip that constitutes the central processing unit of a microcomputer and that processes data using program instructions

minicomputer A larger and more powerful computer that requires more office space than a microcomputer, operates three to 25 times faster, and stores and processes much larger quantities of data

Minimize button A Windows button for reducing a window to an icon

minor upgrade A minor change or enhancement to a software package

mirror file A special file created on a reformatted disk to store the contents of the directory file and the File Allocation Table so that a disk can be unformatted

modem A hardware device that transmits and receives data between computers over telephone lines

modifier key A key that is pressed in conjunction with another key to change the keyboard output

module The memory used by a program, including the actual program code, a program's environment where it stores settings for its own use, and a buffer where it stores data for its own use, or the memory used by a device driver

monitor A TV-like video screen that displays input and output

motherboard The main system board with the microprocessor, supporting electronic circuitry and expansion slots

mounting Using a compressed volume

mouse A hand-held device used to position a pointer on the screen so that you can select options and perform specific operations

mouse pointer A type of cursor in the shape of an arrow or a rectangle that moves in the direction in which the mouse is moved over a desktop

MS-DOS Microsoft Disk Operating System; the brand of DOS used on IBM-compatibles

MS-DOS Prompt icon A Windows application for temporarily exiting to the DOS prompt

MSDOS.SYS The MS-DOS operating system file that constitutes the core of DOS and that is responsible for drive, directory, and file management

multiple configurations A set of system configurations defined in CONFIG.SYS with the use of a menu block and configuration blocks

multitasking The ability to use several different programs at the same time

multiuser system A computer system that supports the use of several people, each with their own keyboard and monitor, at the same time

N

name cache An area of memory where the Fastopen utility keeps track of the names and locations of frequently used files on disk

near-letter-quality mode An operating mode in which a printer produces typewriter-quality output but at a slower rate than when used in draft mode

network A collection of interconnected computers and peripherals that enables users to share software, hardware, and data with other members of the team

network board An adapter inserted into a computer on a network and joined by an electrical cable to the network server

network server A computer with a high capacity drive that provides software and data to the other computers and peripherals on the network

NLQ The abbreviation for *near-letter-quality*

non contiguous sectors Non-adjacent sectors of a file scattered across the surface of a hard disk or diskette

non-impact printer A type of printer that sprays ink or uses heat to fuse ink onto paper to produce an image of a character

notebook computer A small microcomputer that can easily fit into a briefcase

numeric keypad A set of keys on the right side of the keyboard used to enter numbers or to move the cursor

O

open file folder A Windows icon that indicates the current directory or subdirectory

operating environment An interface, such as Windows, between the operating system (DOS) and an application or utility

operating system software The software that manages and coordinates all the activities within a computer, including all the input and output operations to and from the peripherals

operating system The software that manages the operation of the computer system and the use of other software

operating system level Interacting with DOS through the DOS prompt after the operating system is loaded into memory

option button A small round button for selecting an option within a dialog box

output The transmission of the results of computer processing to the user or to a storage site

output device A hardware component used to display, print, or store information that results from processing data

output redirection operator The greater-than symbol (>), used to redirect output

overlay file A file that contains a module of program code (such as a spelling checker) that is only loaded into memory when needed

overtype mode A working mode in which what you type replaces existing text on a character-by-character basis

P

page 16K of memory within a page frame

page frame A 64K region of upper memory (or conventional memory) through which a memory manager swaps data from expanded memory into conventional memory, or vice versa

parallel data transmission The simultaneous transmission of eight bits that constitute a byte down eight separate data lines in a printer cable

parallel port A port or connection for transmitting data between the microprocessor and another component eight bits, or one byte, at a time

parameter An optional or required item of information

parent directory The directory one level higher than the current directory

parity An extra bit added to the data bits for a character to check for data transmission errors

park To position the read/write heads of a hard disk drive in a landing zone on the innermost surface of the disk when the computer's power is switched off

path The sequence of directory and subdirectory names that identify the location of a subdirectory or a file

PC-DOS Personal Computer Disk Operating System, the brand of DOS used on IBM microcomputers

Pentium A microprocessor chip with a math coprocessor introduced in 1993, used in Pentium PCs, and capable of processing 32 bites at a time, transmitting 64 bits at a time, accessing an unlimited amount of memory, and operating at a clock speed of 60 to 100MHz

peripheral An external hardware component, such as a printer or monitor, that is connected to the system unit

personal computer (**PC**) A single-user, personal computer system

pipe operator (|) A vertical-bar symbol that redirects the output of one DOS command operation so that it becomes the input for another DOS command

piping The process of redirecting the output of one DOS command operation so that it becomes the input for another DOS command

pixel An abbreviation for a picture element, the smallest element on a video monitor display that can be illuminated

platter A disk within a hard disk drive unit

point To move the mouse pointer to a specific area of the screen, usually to highlight a menu, command, drive name, filename, icon, or another object displayed on the screen

port An electronic pathway or connection for passing data between the computer's microprocessor and its peripherals

POST An abbreviation for *Power-On Self Test*, a set of diagnostic programs for testing the system components at start-up

preformatted diskette A diskette formatted prior to sale

print file A type of ASCII file

print queue A list of files waiting to be printed

printer A hardware component that produces a paper copy of text or graphics processed by the computer

PRN The device name assigned by DOS to the first printer port in a computer system

processing The ways in which a computer uses input to produce meaningful information, including arithmetic computations, logical comparisons, rearrangement of data, and the production of images or pictures

program A detailed step-by-step set of instructions that tell the computer how to accomplish a task

program file icon A DOS Shell or Windows icon that represents a program

program file A file that contains program instructions for a software application, utility, or programming language

program list window The area on the screen where the DOS Shell displays a list of program groups or program items

Program Manager The primary Windows software application that acts as an interface between DOS and the user, that organizes applications as icons, and that manages other Windows components

program-item icon An icon in a Windows group window that represents an application for a specific task

programming language software Programs that enable you to design and write application software for use on a computer system

prompt A message or request for information displayed on the monitor by a program

Q

Quick format A type of format in which the Format utility skips the surface scan of a previously formatted disk, but stores a copy of the directory file and File Allocation Table in a mirror or image file on the reformatted disk so that the disk can be unformatted

R

RAM The abbreviation for *Random-Access Memory*

Random-Access Memory That part of a computer's memory used to store program instructions, input, processing, and output

read To retrieve instructions or data stored in memory or on disk

read/write head The magnetic mechanism on a read/write arm that reads data from or writes data to a disk

read/write arm The arm that moves across the surface of a hard disk or diskette to locate and read data or to record data onto the surface of the platter or diskette

Read-Only attribute An attribute, represented by the code "R," assigned to a file to indicate that DOS can read from, but not write to, the file

Read-Only file A file that DOS can read from, but not write to

Read-Only Memory The part of a computer's memory which includes instructions for starting the computer system, for testing the system components at startup (the POST, or Power-On Self-Test), for locating drives A and C, and for transferring the operating system software from the disk in drive A or C to Random-Access Memory

record A set of related information, for example, information about employees, clients, schedules, supplies, equipment, inventories, or catalog entries

redirect To change the destination of output or the source of input

replaceable parameter A placeholder (e.g., %1) in a batch file for an item of information that is provided on the command line and inserted at the appropriate places in the batch file

reserved memory The upper memory area that extends from 640K to 1MB and that is reserved for system-related operations, such as for video display adapters, network adapters, and the ROM-BIOS (ROM Basic Input/Output System)

resident Remaining in memory

resolution The sharpness and distinctness of an image

Restore button A Windows button for restoring a window to its original size

retry option The type of action for DOS to take if it receives a busy signal from the serial printer port

ROM The abbreviation for *Read-Only Memory*

root directory The first and most important directory created by the FORMAT command on a hard disk or diskette

routine A startup program for a specific function

S

Safe format A type of format in which the Format utility stores a copy of the directory file and File Allocation Table in a mirror or image file on the reformatted disk so that the disk can be unformatted

scanner A device that you move over an image on paper to copy that image into the computer system and store it so that you can later enhance and print it

scroll arrows Up and down arrows on a scroll bar that indicate the direction in which you can move a window if you click with the mouse on the up or down arrow or scroll bar

scroll bar A bar with scroll arrows placed on the right hand side or bottom of a window so that you can adjust the view within the window with the mouse

scroll box A box in a scroll bar that is used to adjust the view onto a window in larger increments by moving the scroll box with the mouse

scrolling A process by which DOS adjusts the screen view

sector The basic unit of storage space on a diskette or hard drive that holds 512 bytes of data

selection cursor A special type of cursor used in the DOS Shell and in Windows to highlight a drive, directory name, filename, program name, or dialog box option

serial data transmission The transmission of each of the eight bits in a byte, one bit at a time down one data line in a printer cable

serial number A unique ID number produced by DOS from the date and time on a computer and assigned to a disk during formatting

serial port A port or connection for sending information between the microprocessor and another component one bit at a time

server A computer with a high capacity drive that provides software and data to the other computers and peripherals on the network

setup file A file in which MSBACKUP stores settings for a specific type of backup

shutter The metal plate that covers the access hole of a 3½-inch diskette

signature A sequence of program code unique to a specific virus, or a family of viruses that affect a computer system in similar ways

software A collection of computer programs that enable a computer to perform a useful task

sort order parameter A parameter that determines the order in which information on files is listed with the DIR command

source drive The disk drive that contains a diskette you want to copy

source file The file that DOS copies

split bar The vertical bar used in File Manager to adjust the relative widths of the directory tree window and the contents list window

standard communications port COM1 or AUX, the first serial port

standard error device The monitor, the device DOS uses to display error messages

standard input device The keyboard, the device DOS uses for input

Standard level of protection The default level of protection provided by DOS for recovering deleted files by specifying the first character in the deleted file's name

standard output device The monitor, the device DOS uses for output

standard printer port PRN or LPT1, the port that DOS directs printer output to

startup files The CONFIG.SYS and AUTOEXEC.BAT files, used to configure and customize a system

Startup menu A user-defined menu in CONFIG.SYS that displays options for various types of system configurations when a computer is booted

status bar A bar near the bottom of the screen where programs, such as the MS-DOS Editor and the DOS Shell, display command keys, shortcut keys, uses for function keys, help information, cursor coordinates, and settings, such as the time

stop bits An additional bit or bits added to the data bits for a character to indicate that the transmission of a character is complete

storage The process of recording data and information on some type of permanent storage medium, such as a disk or magnetic tape

string A sequence of characters or text used as a setting

subdirectory A directory that is subordinate to the root directory or to another subdirectory

supercomputer The largest and fastest computer that operates 50 to 10,000 times faster than a microcomputer and that handles complex problems such as weather forecasting, earthquake prediction, and petroleum surveying

Survival Guide The on-line Help system for the MS-DOS Editor

SVGA The abbreviation for *SuperVGA*, a type of high-resolution video display adapter and monitor

switch An optional parameter that modifies the way in which a command operates

syntax diagram The notation that describes the proper way to enter a command with required or optional parameters and switches

syntax The keystrokes and order used to enter a command

system area The area of a disk that contains the boot sector, File Allocation Tables, and directory file

System attribute An attribute, represented by the code "S," that identifies a file as a system file

system board The main board, or motherboard, with the microprocessor, supporting electronic circuitry and expansion slots

system bus The network of electronic circuitry (data, address, and control lines) responsible for transmitting data and signals between the microprocessor and various components as well as storing information on the location of instructions and data in memory

system date The current date on a computer system

system device drivers Device drivers provided with the operating system software for communicating with the keyboard, monitor, disk drives, and ports

system disk A diskette that contains the DOS system files and that is used to start a computer

system files The program files that constitute the operating system software

system prompt The DOS prompt that is displayed when you access the operating system level of the computer

system reset Rebooting a computer system by pressing [Ctrl], [Alt], and [Del]

system time The current time on a computer system

system unit The computer case that houses the microprocessor, memory, electronic circuitry, adapters, disk drives, and power supply

system utility software Special programs provided with operating system software to enhance the performance of your computer system, such as optimizing the use of memory, maximizing the use of storage space on a hard disk, correcting errors on a hard disk, obtaining technical or diagnostic information about your computer system, or preparing diskettes for use on a computer system

systems software The programs that manage the fundamental operations within a computer, such as starting the computer, loading or copying programs and data into memory, executing or carrying out the instructions in programs, saving data to a disk, displaying information on the monitor, and sending information through a port to a peripheral

T

target drive The disk drive used for the diskette that DOS copies to

target file A file that results from a copy operation

template A file that contains the general format or layout of a document but little or no data

temporary file A file created by DOS, a utility, or an application to store the intermediate results of processing and deleted after the operation is complete

Terminate-and-Stay-Resident program A program that remains in memory and is active while you use other programs

text box A box within a dialog box for entering a response

text editor A program for creating and editing an ASCII file

text file A type of ASCII file

text mode A simple video display mode for displaying text, including letters, numbers, symbols, and special characters

text user interface The use of the DOS prompt to interact with the operating system

tile To arrange each open window in Windows side by side

timeout The number of seconds that DOS waits after displaying a Startup Menu and before executing the commands in the default configuration block if no menu option is selected

time stamp The time assigned by DOS to a file

title bar A bar near the top of the screen where programs, such as the MS-DOS Editor, the DOS Shell, and Windows, display the name of a program, the name of the current screen, or a filename

toggle key An on/off key that alternates between two uses each time you press the key

toner A black, powdery substance used in laser printers to reproduce an image

track A concentric recording band on a diskette or hard disk for storing data

TSR An abbreviation for *Terminate-and-Stay-Resident*, a program that remains in memory and is active while you use other programs

TUI An abbreviation for *text user interface*, the use of the DOS prompt to interact with the operating system

typematic rate The rate at which a key repeats when you hold down that key

typeover mode A working mode in which what you type replaces existing text on a character-by-character basis

U

Unconditional format A type of format in which the Format utility creates a boot sector, creates new File Allocation Tables and a new directory file, erases the contents of a previously formatted disk, and performs a surface scan for defects

uncompressed drive A drive that contains files, such as the operating system files, that should not be compressed and that acts as the host for the compressed drive

undeleting Using the DOS directory or the Undelete utility to recover a deleted file

unformat information The copy of the directory file and File Allocation Table that is stored in the mirror file during reformatting of a disk

unformatted diskette A blank diskette that has not been prepared for use in a computer

unformatting Restoring the original directories and files to a reformatted diskette

UMA An abbreviation for *upper memory area*

UMB An abbreviation for *upper memory block*

unmounting Disconnecting a compressed volume

upper memory The memory that extends from 640K to 1MB and that is used as address space for program code stored on ROM chips

upper memory area The memory that extends from 640K to 1MB and that is used as address space for program code stored on ROM chips

upper memory blocks The unused memory in the Upper Memory Area

user-defined program file A batch file created by a user

V

variant A functionally similar computer virus

VGA An abbreviation for *video graphics array*, a type of video high-resolution display adapter and monitor

video card A video display card mounted in an expansion slot on the motherboard to control the display of text and graphics on the monitor

volatile Dependent on the availability of power, and therefore temporary

volume label A name assigned to a hard disk or diskette to identify the type of information contained on the disk

W

warm boot Starting a computer system by pressing [Ctrl], [Alt], and [Del]

wildcard An asterisk or question mark that substitutes for all or part of a filename in a file specification

window border The double outline border around a window's contents in Windows

window An outlined area on the screen through which you use programs, view information, and display the contents of files

Windows A graphics-based operating environment designed to make your computer easier to use by acting as an interface between the operating system and an application or utility

word processing software Software for creating, editing, enhancing, and printing documents electronically

working memory RAM

workspace RAM

workstation A single-user microcomputer

write protect To protect a diskette so that a computer cannot record data onto the diskette

write To record instructions or data in memory or on disk

Index